Tensions within the Internal Market

The Functioning of the Internal Market and the Development of Horizontal and Flanking Policies

Sybe Alexander de Vries

Europa Law Publishing is a publishing company specializing in European Union Law.
For further information please contact Europa Law Publishing via email: info@europalawpublishing.com or visit our website at: www.europalawpublishing.com.

Typeset in Scala and Scala Sans, Graphic design by G2K Designers, Groningen/Amsterdam

NUR 828; ISBN 90-76871-53-1

British Library Cataloguing-in-Publication Data
A catalogue record for this book is available from the British Library

To Victor and Harald

Acknowledgements

Without the help and support of many people this book would never have become a reality. I would therefore sincerely like to thank all those who helped and supported me in the process of writing this book. Of all those who supported me I can only mention a few here.

In the first place I would like to thank my *promotor,* professor Mortelmans, and my *copromotor,* Dr. Van de Gronden for having given me the chance to do this research. Kamiel and Johan, you guided me through the process of writing this PhD thesis, on the one hand by giving me the necessary confidence, and on the other by teaching me how to present a critical view on the subject matter. For better and worse, you were always there for me!

I also would like to thank the esteemed members of the reading committee, professors Hessel, Geelhoed, Prechal, Sevenster and Barents for reading, improving and, thankfully, finally approving my PhD thesis.

Many thanks also to Ms. L. Smit for her careful copy-editing of the texts and for making the index of this book. Wies, your work has been invaluable, since after all language is the armoury of the human mind. In addition I would like to thank my former colleague at the Department of Public Economic Law, Sietske van 't Hooft, for her work on behalf of the lay-out of this book, and Alyssa Bos and Ekram Belhadj for their general assistance.

A word of gratitude is due to my colleagues at the department of Public Economic Law for having created an agreeable and most encouraging working environment, for taking over a lot of my work and allowing me the freedom to work on my thesis. In particular, I like to thank Hanneke Luijendijk, my colleague and roommate, who always and with a smile supported me during the process of writing and helped me with a lot of administrative questions relating to the emergence of the PhD thesis.

I also have to thank my friends for listening to me and for at least trying to understand my monologues on my research. Special thanks to Olivier Linden, who is always willing to lend an ear and offer what advice he can. Olivier, I value our friendship very much: C'est dans le besoin qu'on reconnaît ses vrais amis!

And of course I also like to thank my parents for encouraging me to study further and to write this PhD thesis. Mum and Dad, you have not only laid the basis for my academic career, you have always supported it and you were always there when it mattered. This is certainly also true for my two brothers, Gos and Huug. Due to the kindness of my in-laws, Gert and Gunilla, I found another welcoming home, but in Sweden.

Last but definitely not least I would like to address a special word of thanks to my wife Louise for her ceaseless support and for giving me the strength to finish this book. Louise, your role in encouraging me in the process of writing has been essential. You have even been willing to thoroughly correct the texts of this book. You, and our two sons Victor and Harald, were there when it mattered, all day, every day. I will never forget that. Victor and Harald, now that Daddy's book is finished, he is ready to play with you more often. I therefore dedicate this book to you two.

I thank you all.

Sybe de Vries
Castricum, November 2005

CHAPTER I

Introduction

1 The origin of this study: tensions within the internal market

This study focuses on the relationship between the rules on free movement, competition and horizontal and flanking policies in Community law. Books, for example, can be used as illustration of cultural policy, falling within the field of horizontal and flanking policies.

The example of books and Plato's praise for harmony

In Book VI (502d-end) of Plato's *The Republic* Socrates turns to the final stage in the construction of the just city: the question of how to produce philosopher-kings. The most important subject for a philosopher-king is, according to Plato, the study of the Form of the Good.[1] The Form of the Good has been explained as harmony. Throughout *The Republic* Plato praises harmony, order, balance and proportion. Harmony between the three classes of society makes for a healthy, just city and harmony in the soul makes for a healthy, just soul.

Suppose the Belgian publisher *Politeia* would like to let its customers enjoy Plato's praise for harmony, order and balance through the publication and sale of a newly translated edition of *The Republic* on the Belgian and Dutch markets, preferably against a fixed retail price. The purpose of fixed book prices is to protect the sale of the less popular books (high literature), like Plato's *The Republic* vis à vis more profitable books, like the bouquet series, and to promote a wide selection of titles in general. The European Commission, however, would like to protect consumers against price cartels violating the cartel prohibition, one of the core pillars in the EC Treaty and an essential tool for the realisation of the internal market.

This example illustrates that the relationship between culture as a horizontal and flanking policy field and Community law, in particular the EC rules on competition, can not always be regarded as harmonious, balanced and orderly; on the contrary, its relationship is tense and it is unavoidable that conflicts exist within the internal market.

The tension further explained

Whereas horizontal and flanking policies are directed towards the expression of general, public values such as the protection of the environment, the protection of cultural property and cultural diversity, the protection of public health and the protection of consumers, free movement and competition aim at more efficiency, lower prices and the production of material goods. Some argue with respect to the *Trade & Environment* debate, that free trade is a precondition for

1 The Form of the Good is the source of all other Forms – the source of the entire intelligible realm, of intelligibility itself and of our cognitive capacity to know; this explanation and a reference to the text of Plato's *The Republic* can be found at http://www.sparknotes.com/philosophy/republic/, a study guide from Barnes & Noble.

realising such aims as environmental protection and social progress.[2] The free flow of wastes, for example, may lead to more efficiency and economies of scale in disposal techniques, and may entail an obligation for Member States to share natural resources for the common good.

But others bring forward that unlimited trade will damage our environment, and that states should therefore develop adequate waste disposal facilities themselves, rather than relying on installations in other Member States.[3] Plurality of the media, both broadcasting and press, may be promoted through the application of the competition rules. The opening up of the media market guarantees a wider access to other market participants. However, increased channel choice does not necessarily increase the freedom of expression. An open market may lead to media concentration with negative consequences for a pluralist media system.[4]

At the level of the Community the tension between horizontal and flanking policies on the one hand and free movement and competition on the other has obtained an additional dimension. Whereas at national level horizontal and flanking policies have been regarded as a necessary complement for the creation of a socio-economic society,[5] at Community level national horizontal and flanking measures must be compatible with the legal order of the Community and in particular with the requirements of the internal market, which means that Member States or undertakings should in principle refrain from adopting measures with restrictive effects on trade or competition. Particularly in cases where the Community legislature has not been sufficiently empowered to adopt effective and legitimate horizontal and flanking measures, there appears to be a "basic asymmetry between market-creating and market-correcting policies at the European level".[6]

Against this background the following three main sources of tension can be identified.

The four freedoms

The provisions on the four freedoms, i.e. the free movement of goods, persons, services and capital, set limitations to national competence in the field of horizontal and flanking policies. National measures, for example, restricting the free flow of wastes for environmental reasons, the free movement of works of art or books for cultural reasons, the free movement of teachers for educational

2 Van Calster (2000), p. 9.

3 Geradin (1997), pp. 55-59.

4 V. Porter, Public Service Broadcasting and European Regulation, *Mediaforum*, 1995, p. 32.

5 G. Majone, The European Community between social policy and horizontal and flanking policies, *EUI Working Paper*, 1993, No. 92/27, p. 7.

6 F. W. Scharpf, European Governance: Common Concerns vs. the Challenge of Diversity, Jean Monnet Working Paper 2001, No. 01/07, p. 3. To be found at: http://www.jeanmonnetprogram.org/papers/01/010601.html.

or cultural reasons, or the free movement of television services for cultural reasons and reasons of consumer protection may come into conflict with the prohibitive provisions of the EC Treaty.

Objectives of horizontal and flanking policies are – under certain conditions – recognised as justification grounds for the restriction of intra-Community trade, either by the Treaty itself or by the Court of Justice in its case law. Where national measures unjustifiably restrict free movement, they will have to be removed. This process of market integration is referred to as *negative integration*.[7] The case law of the Court of Justice dealing with state measures and the prohibitive provisions on free movement of the EC Treaty is further analysed in Chapter 2 of this book.

The competition rules

If undertakings enter into agreements, are granted subsidies or are entrusted with exclusive rights, the competition provisions of the Treaty may be applicable. The application of the EC rules on competition (Articles 81-89 EC) entails that both Member States and private parties are limited to enact measures with objectives of horizontal and flanking policies, but with economic, anti-competitive, consequences.

The question is whether horizontal and flanking policy interests can play a role at all in exempting restrictive practices from the imperative demands of undistorted competition, and if so, to what extent. Chapter 3 analyses the decision practice of the Commission and the case law of the Community courts in competition matters.

Harmonisation

Harmonisation measures are put in place in areas regulated by the Member State to gradually remove the still existing barriers to trade. This process is referred to as *positive integration* and complements negative integration in the realisation of a Community wide internal market.[8] It may therefore be an important tool in removing the tension between primary Community law and national legislation. At the same time, harmonisation measures must also be in conformity with primary Community law, i.e. the free movement rules. The question is whether the Community legislature is bound by the rules on free movement in the same way as the national legislature is.

The process of harmonisation and the possibilities the Community legislature has in adopting harmonisation measures for the attainment of horizontal and flanking policy objectives will be discussed in Chapter 4.

---

7 Pelkmans (2001), p. 7.

8 Pelkmans (2001), p. 7.

2 The purpose, central question and background of this study

The purpose of this study is firstly to reveal the dilemma of balancing the requirements of the internal market with the need to maintain a high level of protection of horizontal and flanking policy interests and then to assess how, from the perspective of both the Member States and the Community, closer harmony between free movement, competition and horizontal and flanking policies can be attained with a view to control or to ultimately resolve the tension between these policies. The central question is addressed from a purely *legal* perspective and the suggestions for the attainment of closer harmony are also made from a legal viewpoint.

The central question in this study is therefore:

how from the perspective of the bodies involved in the policy and law-making process at national and Community level a coherent legal approach can be developed to the problem of tension between free movement and competition on the one hand and horizontal and flanking policies on the other.

Three important developments have dynamically informed the relationship between horizontal and flanking policies and the internal market. Firstly, from a legal perspective the codification of horizontal and flanking policies in the EC Treaty was probably the main step in the development of horizontal and flanking policies at Community level. However, even before subsequent amendments to the Treaties in 1986 (Single European Act), 1992 (Treaty of Maastricht) and 1997 (Treaty of Amsterdam) had provided for the incorporation of 'non-economic' objectives in the EC Treaty, the objective of economic integration also appeared to be a powerful incentive for the establishment of horizontal and flanking policies, most notably consumer policy and environmental policy.[9] The Treaty of Nice (2002) has not brought about any changes to the EC Treaty which are relevant for the subject matter. Since the legal status of the Treaty establishing a Constitution for Europe has become unclear due to the negative results of the referendums in France and the Netherlands, it will only be briefly referred to in Chapter 6.

The grant of a constitutional status to horizontal and flanking policies entails that the internal market policy of the Community, originally oriented towards economic growth, cannot be justified anymore without taking account of horizontal and flanking policy interests. In other words, the still considerable importance of the principles of free trade and undistorted competition within the common market must not mean that the possibilities for Member States or

9 For environmental policy see: H. Somsen, Dynamics, process and instruments of environmental decision-making in the European Union, in: T. Jewell and J. Steele (Eds), *Law in Environmental Decision-Making* (Clarendon Press, Oxford, 1998), p. 165.

even undertakings to pursue horizontal and flanking policies are eroded. This is also reflected in the general objective of Article 2 EC in which more emphasis is put on the *qualitative aspects* of economic development rather than the *quantitative aspects* of economic growth.

Secondly, tendencies towards privatisation, liberalisation, deregulation and the use of more 'market-based instruments' in the (Member States of the) European Union have drawn the attention to the role and function of the competition rules in areas of horizontal and flanking policies, as in the fields of culture, the environment and public health. If, for example, the state leaves the responsibility for the attainment of certain horizontal and flanking policy objectives up to private companies, which consequently start to co-operate with each other with a view to attain these public policy aims, the cartel prohibition may put a spoke in the state's wheel. The application of the competition rules raises important questions on how horizontal and flanking policy interests at stake can be recognised and how these interests can counterbalance the imperative of undistorted competition.

Thirdly, apart from the legal developments, increasing societal concerns about, for example, safe food, public health – including health care – and developments in the sphere of technology, like information technology or biotechnology,[10] also dynamically inform the relationship between free trade, competition and horizontal and flanking policies. The BSE crisis, for example, has shown the imperfections of the internal market and has called for effective co-ordinated action to guarantee safe food and to restore public confidence in Europe's food policy. The increasingly long waiting lists for hospital treatment in some Member States incite patients to travel to another Member State with a view to receive medical treatment there. This may also call for effective co-ordinated action at European level in order to prevent that the organisation and financing of the national health systems will be undermined by medical tourism.

3 Horizontal and flanking policies and the internal market: defining and delimiting the topic

Before the first source of tension, the Treaty rules on free movement, will be analysed in the next chapter, it is first necessary to provide a definition of the main objects of this study: horizontal and flanking policies and the internal market.

---

[10] See also Communication from the Commission "Towards a strategic vision of life sciences and biotechnology: Consultation Document", COM(2001) 454 final.

3.1 Horizontal and flanking policies

Horizontal and flanking policies are a generic term including policies on *inter alia* the environment, consumer protection, public health, culture, sport and education.

Defining the Janus-like concept of horizontal and flanking policies

Horizontal and flanking policies are the caring, idealistic and spending policy areas, affecting everybody and characterised by the Court of Justice as non-economic, but with economic consequences.[11] They are like Janus, the Roman god represented with a double-faced head, each looking in opposite directions.[12]

In literature different terms are used to define a similar concept. For example, the term social regulation is introduced as a concept comprising rules which attempt to solve certain problems created by market failure.[13] In Dutch literature horizontal and flanking policies have been introduced as 'facettenbeleid', based on the term used in a governmental policy document, that addressed the negative effects of material economic growth on some policy areas.[14] In German literature it is referred to as 'Förderung und Schutz diffuser Interessen', a term relating to policies which do not address clearly defined groups or persons (commonly referred to as special interest groups), but potentially all people. They primarily address quality of life issues and consequently include environmental protection, protection of the economic interests of the consumer, working conditions and more specifically health,[15] but also culture or even sports. More recently, German literature refers to 'Politiken der EG' similar to New Policy Areas in English literature,[16] but this definition is somewhat problematic as it comprises many policy areas, including economic policy.[17]

---

11 K.J.M. Mortelmans, De Interne Markt en het Facettenbeleid: nationaal beleid, vrij verkeer of harmonisatie, *SEW*, 1994, p. 237. Kapteyn & VerLoren van Themaat (edited by L.W. Gormley) (1998), p. 1084.

12 Janus was the Roman god of gates and doors (*ianua*), beginnings and endings, and hence he was represented with a double-faced head. "He was worshipped at the beginning of the harvest time, planting, marriage, birth, and other types of beginnings, especially the beginnings of important events in a person's life. Janus also represents the transition between primitive life and civilization, between the countryside and the city, peace and war, and the growing-up of young people": M. F. Lindemans, at: http://www.pantheon.org/articles/j/janus.html?esc.

13 See with regard to the context of the European Community: Ch. Joerges, The market without the State? States without a market? : two essays on the law of the European Economy, *EUI Working Paper RSC*, 1996, No.96/2; G. Majone, The European Community between social policy and social regulation, *EUI Working Paper*, 1993, No.92/27.

14 Kapteyn & VerLoren van Themaat (2003), p. 927 *et seq.*

15 Reich (1987); see also: Krämer, Micklitz, Tonner (Eds) (1997).

16 R. Lane, New Community competences under the Maastricht Treaty, *CMLRev.*, 1993, p. 942.

17 See also Rengeling (Ed.) (1993).

From an economic perspective, the road from economic interests to non-economic interests is neither long nor paved. Economists regard horizontal and flanking policy interests as sources of prosperity. The broader welfare concept does not only include productive efficiency, but also other benefits relevant to consumer welfare in general.[18] With regard to the environment, nature can be considered as an end product that meets the needs of human beings. Economy and culture are not "watertight compartments, but closely interrelated social spheres".[19]

The *Janus*-like concept of horizontal and flanking policies implies that trade liberalisation may have both positive as well as negative effects on horizontal and flanking policies. The economic dimension cannot conceal the eventually non-economic ends of horizontal and flanking policies. As stated before, the removal of export controls may, for example, facilitate the introduction of new environmentally friendly techniques; yet an increase of trade in dangerous goods and substances may have considerable ecological consequences.[20] Hence, in order to meet these non-economic objectives, governmental intervention will be necessary.

Horizontal and flanking policies which concern the market for goods and services should be distinguished from social policy, concerning the labour market, where trade unions and employers' organisations are involved in collective bargaining. The collective agreement is a co-ordinated attempt to influence the political decision-making and would not appear to distort competition.[21] Horizontal and flanking policies should also be distinguished from sectoral policies, which relate to a specific sector of the economy.

Delimiting the study to environmental, consumer, public health and cultural policies

The point of departure of this study is the relationship between horizontal and flanking policies in general on the one hand and the rules on free movement and competition on the other. Regarding these policies there have been important developments in this relationship. Recently, for example, there have been important developments in the relationship between sport and free movement and competition, and between education and free movement.[22]

---

18 G. Monti, Article 81 EC and public policy, *CMLRev.*, 2002, p. 1065. See also E.E.C. van Damme, Op de Welvaartseconomie gebaseerd Mededingingsbeleid, in: J.W. van de Gronden and K.J.M. Mortelmans (Eds), *Mededinging en niet-economische belangen*, (Kluwer, Deventer, 2001), pp. 55-57.

19 B. De Witte, The Cultural Dimension of Community Law, in: Academy of European Law, *Collected Courses of the Academy of European Law*, Vol. IV, Book 1, (Kluwer Law International, The Hague, 1995), p. 249.

20 OECD-report, The Environmental Effects of Trade (Paris, 1994).

21 Annotation L. Gyselen of Case C-67/96, *Albany*, Joined Cases C-115-117/97, *Brentjens* and Case C-219/97, *Drijvende Bokken*, *CMLRev.*, 2000, pp. 441-442.

22 See with regard to sport, for example, Case T-313/02, *Meca-Medina*; with regard to education, for example, Case C-209/03, *Bidar*. See further Chapters 2 and 3 of this book.

This study will specifically focus on four policies, i.e. environmental policy, consumer policy, public health policy and cultural policy. The assessment of in particular these four areas of horizontal and flanking policies is interesting from both the perspective of the problem of tension as well as from the perspective of the competences to regulate in these areas.

First, from the perspective of the problem of tension, consumer policy appears closest related to the internal market policy, since the economic dimension of consumer policy – the consumer as purchaser of goods and services and as beneficiary of the internal market process – is generally more clear than in respect of the other policies. Cultural policy seems to be the most remote from the internal market; the national state continues to play an active and predominant role in supporting national, regional and cultural policies. Besides, the creation of a Community wide internal market is generally considered to pose serious threats to cultural diversity.[23] Culture is still considered a sensitive non-economic sphere.[24]

Environmental and public health policies take a middle position. The fact that these policies involve values which are common to all European citizens is more clear than in respect of cultural policy, where Article 151 EC merely contains, at least so far, open-ended references to the notions of European identity or common cultural heritage.[25] Environmental and public health policies are certainly not always concerned with the protection of typically national interests. The creation of a Community wide internal market may therefore offer challenges too. Cultural policy primarily remains a national affair, although the concept of common cultural heritage undoubtedly transcends purely national cultural interests, like language.

Second, from the perspective of competences, a study of these four policies is also interesting. The scope of the Community's legislative powers in the areas of environmental and consumer policy is similar; in these areas the Treaty *includes* harmonisation powers for the Community legislature outside the framework of the internal market. The scope of the Community's legislative powers in the areas of public health and culture is also similar: in these areas the Treaty explicitly *excludes* the possibility of harmonisation.[26] These similarities and differences make a comparison of these four policies particularly attractive.

---

[23] See with regard to cultural diversity and the free movement of goods, for example: N. Nic Shiuibhne, Labels, Locals, and the Free Movement of Goods, in: R. Craufurd Smith (Ed.), *Culture and European Union Law* (Oxford University Press, Oxford, 2004), pp. 81-112.

[24] R. Lane, New Community competences under the Maastricht Treaty, *CMLRev.*, 1993, p. 956.

[25] R. Craufurd Smith, Article 151 EC and European Identity, in: R. Craufurd Smith (Ed.), *Culture and European Union Law* (Oxford University Press, Oxford, 2004), p. 294.

[26] As we will see, the public health paragraph in the Treaty only provides specific harmonisation powers in the fields of veterinary diseases and human blood products and organs.

The following scheme shows that a common approach to horizontal and flanking policies can be traced in the Treaty. They are mainly based on the principle of subsidiarity and the Community powers to take action are, to a more or lesser extent, shared with the Member States. All Treaty provisions indicate the objectives the Community is to pursue, the instruments to be used and the decision-making procedure to be followed. The Treaty also contains integration clauses stipulating that horizontal and flanking policy interests must be taken into account in other Community policies. The Treaty of Amsterdam moved the environmental integration clause from the environmental paragraph to part one of the Treaty, the principles of Community law (Article 6 EC). The title on consumer protection did not contain an integration clause until after the adoption of the Treaty of Amsterdam. Irrespective of this common approach differences continue to exist in respect of the scope of Community action, the objectives of the respective policies and the formulation of the integration clauses.

Articles 174-176 EC (Environmental protection)

Objective: preserving, protecting and improving the quality of the environment; protecting human health; prudent and rational utilisation of natural resources; promoting measures at international level to deal with regional or worldwide environmental problems.

Instruments: harmonisation measures, action programmes.

Procedure:

- Qualified majority and co-decision
- Unanimity and co-decision in the following areas:
  - Provisions of a primarily fiscal nature;
  - Measures concerning town and country planning, land use and management of water resources;
  - Measures significantly affecting a Member State's choice between different energy resources and the general structure of its energy supply.

External policy: co-operation with third countries and international organisations, agreements between the Community and third parties.

Integration clause: **Article 6 EC**: environmental protection requirements must be integrated into the definition and implementation of the Community policies and activities referred to in Article 3, in particular with a view to promoting sustainable development.

Article 153 EC (Consumer protection)

Objective: the protection of the health, safety and economic interests of consumers as well as the promotion of their right to information, education and to organise themselves.

Instruments:

- measures based on Article 95 EC;
- measures based on Article 153 EC, to support, supplement and monitor the policy pursued by the Member States.

Procedure: qualified majority and co-decision.

Integration clause: consumer protection requirements shall be taken into account in defining and implementing other Community policies and activities.

Article 152 EC (Public health)

Objective: improving public health, preventing diseases, obviating sources of danger to human health, promoting research, health information and education.

Instruments:

- Incentive measures and recommendations to protect and improve public health, excluding harmonisation;
- Harmonisation in the fields of quality and safety of organs, and substances of human origin, blood and blood derivatives;
- Harmonisation in the veterinary and phytosanitary fields.

Procedure: qualified majority and co-decision.

External policy: co-operation with third countries and international organisations.

Integration: a high level of human health protection shall be ensured in the definition and implementation of all Community policies and activities.

Article 151 EC (Culture)

Objective: contributing to the flowering of the cultures of the Member States, while respecting their national and regional diversity and at the same time bringing the common cultural heritage to the fore.

Instruments: incentive measures and recommendations, excluding harmonisation.

Procedure: Article 251: unanimity and co-decision.

External policy: co-operation with third countries and international organisations.

Integration clause: the Community shall take cultural aspects into account in its action under other provisions of this Treaty in particular in order to respect and to promote the diversity of its cultures.

3.2 The internal market

The establishment of the internal market plays a central role in the attainment of the objectives of the EC Treaty as laid down in Article 2 EC. The adoption of the concept *internal market* in 1987, when the Single European Act came into force, has led to several discussions with regard to its content as compared to the already existing term *common market*.[27] For the purposes of

[27] C.D. Ehlermann considered the internal market a relevant and useful addition to the concept of common market, The Internal Market Following the Single European Act, *CMLRev.*, 1987, pp. 364-366; P. Pescatore, on the other hand, regarded the Single European Act as fundamentally deceptive for the well balanced notion of common market had been replaced by the one-sided notion of an internal market, in: Some Critical Remarks on the "Single European Act", *CMLRev.* 1987, pp. 9-19.

this study the concepts of internal market and common market are used interchangeably. In this study a broad definition of the internal market is therefore used, comprising both the rules on free movement and on competition.[28] These are the core provisions of internal market law, which form the 'backbone' of the Community.

To get the Community 'up off its backside and running' in 1985 the Commission launched it's White Paper on the Internal Market,[29] resulting in the adoption of Article 14 EC. It proposed the complete removal of all physical, technical barriers within the Community: "The internal market shall comprise of an area without internal frontiers in which the free movement of goods, persons, services and capital is ensured in accordance with the provisions of this Treaty".[30] Whereas at first the internal market seemed to be mainly concerned with the abolition of trade barriers – the attainment of the internal market in the economic sense of the term – later a broader conception of the internal market can be found, conceptualised in more holistic terms, including consumer safety and the environment.[31] In its Internal Market Strategy 2003-2006 the Commission now makes clear that within the internal market context it has to address horizontal and flanking policy concerns, like the protection of the environment and public health, as well.[32]

The four freedoms

The four freedoms encompass the free movement of goods (Articles 23-31 EC), persons (workers and establishment) (Articles 39-48 EC), services (Articles 49-55 EC) and capital (including payments, which is also considered to be the 'fifth freedom') (Articles 56-60 EC).[33] Not only measures adopted by Member States, but also Community measures must in principle be in conformity with the provisions on free movement. But the aim of creating an internal market does not explain what role the Court of Justice should play and what tests it should use to attain this objective and ultimately the objectives laid down in Article 2 EC.[34]

---

28 See also Barnard (2004), p. 12.

29 Lord Cockfield, a British member of the Commission, quoted from: Weatherill and Beaumont (1995), p. 24.

30 This programme was a mixture of deregulation and re-regulation: see K. Mortelmans, The common market, the internal market and the single market, what's in a market? *CMLRev.*, 1998, pp. 101-136.

31 This developed across time, see: Paul Craig, The Evolution of the Single Market, in: C. Barnard and J. Scott (Eds), *The Law of the Single European market – Unpacking the Premises* (Hart Publishing, Oxford and Portland, 2002), p. 38.

32 COM(2003) 238 final.

33 Kapteyn & VerLoren van Themaat (2003), p. 488.

34 See also Snell (2002), pp. 1-2.

The cornerstone of the four freedoms is the principle of non-discrimination on grounds of nationality as laid down in Article 12 EC and further elaborated in the specific Treaty provisions on free movement.[35] One reading of the free movement provisions is that these rules aim at preventing the adoption and maintenance of protectionist measures and at preventing discrimination, but no more. In general Member States should not be able to circumvent the free trade rules by protecting their own markets, products or industries.

Another reading departs from the idea that the issue is not protectionism or discrimination, but the prevention of any adverse effects on trade and free movement.[36] This implies that the limits imposed upon Member States, which in principle retain the freedom to regulate, are more stringent. Any national law or Community harmonisation measure restricting free movement should be struck down, unless it can be justified. Such a broad reading of the four freedoms can be explained by the ordoliberal influence on Community law. The ordoliberal school originating in the 1930s in Freiburg believed that the constitution must protect the economic freedoms which "are as integral to the protection of human dignity, and as indicative of a free society, as political freedoms, which are themselves liberal in nature and which therefore underscore individual economic freedoms".[37] Public intervention by the Member States or the Community as well as private intervention by individual undertakings should yield to the protection of the economic freedoms.

One may wonder how far the analogy between the EC Treaty and the 'economic constitution' can be drawn.[38] The Treaty provisions on free movement are a means to attain the objectives laid down in Article 2 EC, which are not primarily economic (anymore). The realisation of an internal market and the liberalisation of trade are not ends in themselves, but important tools to increase welfare and promote sustainable development. Furthermore, as has been mentioned above, the conceptualisation of the internal market in more holistic terms as developed over the years does not seem to correspond to this view.

Competition rules

The competition rules do not only comprise the rules directed at undertakings, i.e. the cartel prohibition (Article 81 EC), the prohibition on abusive behaviour by dominant undertakings (Article 82 EC) and merger control (Regulation 194/2004), but also the rules directed at Member States, i.e. states granting exclusive or special rights to undertakings (Article 86 EC), rules on state aid (Article 87 EC) and the useful effect doctrine (Articles 3g(1), 10, 81 & 82 EC).

---

35 Barnard (2004), p. 18.

36 Snell (2002), p. 2.

37 D. Chalmars, The single market: from prima donna to journeyman, in: J. Shaw and G. More (Eds), *New legal dynamics of European Union* (Clarendon Press, Oxford, 1995), p. 57; Barnard (2004), p. 21.

38 Barnard (2004), p. 21; see also with regard to the Community's economic constitution: Baquero Cruz (2002), pp. 63-84.

Originally EC competition policy was also strongly influenced by the German ordoliberals, whereby the focus was put on economic freedom rather than on freedom of contract.[39] Furthermore, the competition rules are an essential component to the rules on free movement as they prevent private actors from erecting barriers to intra-Community trade. A regime of free and undistorted competition complements the four freedoms and is indispensable for the creation of an internal market.[40] They can be considered as communicating vessels.

According to the Court Articles 81 and 82 EC seek the same aim: "The rules are designed to maintain effective competition, meaning that in each market there must be sufficient competition to ensure the observance of the basic requirements and the attainment of the objectives of the Treaty, in particular the creation of a single market achieving conditions similar to those of a domestic market."[41]

Hence, the aim of EC competition policy is twofold: the protection of the competitive structure of the market, whereby the interest of consumers as direct beneficiaries of the application of competition rules is an important aim, and the attainment and functioning of the internal market. But the competition rules are part of the EC Treaty as well and have to interact with other Community policies.[42] EC competition policy can therefore not be pursued in isolation from other considerations, like horizontal and flanking policy considerations.

4 The relevant general principles of Community law

Several general principles of Community law play an important role in the relationship between the internal market and horizontal and flanking policies and in developing a coherent legal approach to resolving the conflicts in the internal market.

4.1 The principle of proportionality

The principle of proportionality has become an important general principle of Community law, not only in respect of national measures infringing the Treaty provisions on free movement or competition, but also in respect of Community measures, which has been explicitly laid down in Article 5 EC, stipulating that action by the Community shall not go beyond what is necessary to achieve the objectives of the Treaty.[43]

---

39 Drahos (2001), p. 40 and p. 53.

40 Schrauwen (1997), p. 214.

41 Case 6/72, *Continental Can*, paragraph 25; see also Jones & Sufrin (2004), p. 35.

42 Jones and Sufrin (2004), p. 40.

43 See with regard to the principle of proportionality in general, for example, Emiliou (1996).

Under the common name proportionality the following different norms with different addressees can be found:[44]

First, as a ground for review of measures derogating from the basic rules of the internal market; the study focuses on this first norm of proportionality. Whereas in literature the internal market rules are generally referred to as the four freedoms,[45] here the broad definition of the internal market comprises the competition rules as well, meaning that this norm of proportionality could be divided into the following norms or sub-norms:

(i) a ground for review of national measures derogating from the rules on free movement; with regard to national measures, the application of the principle of proportionality has been developed in the case law of the Court of Justice as an important condition for the successful invoking of justification grounds.

(ii) a ground for review of measures taken by private market participants derogating from the competition rules; for example, the fact that agreements restricting competition and trade must, according to Article 81(3), be *indispensable* to the achievement of the benefits resulting from the restrictive agreement to be exempted from the cartel prohibition amounts to a proportionality test.

(iii) a ground for review of measures adopted by the state, or public service undertakings, from the competition rules; Article 86(2) EC includes an exception for the pursuance of services of general economic interest and Article 87(3) EC provides a derogation from the prohibition on state aid.

(iv) a ground for review of Community measures derogating from the rules on free movement; it is commonly said that the Court traditionally employs a stricter degree of scrutiny in the application of the proportionality test where a national measure is concerned than where a Community measure is concerned.[46] This point will be further explored in the following chapters.

The second and third norms of proportionality, which are less relevant to the subject matter, are proportionality as a principle governing the exercise by the Community of its legislative competence (the rule laid down in Article 5(3) EC): proportionality within this institutional meaning has been considered the half-sister of subsidiarity.[47]

And lastly, proportionality as a substantive ground for the review of Community measures: proportionality within this meaning must prevent that disproportionate burdens are imposed on European citizens.

---

[44] Tridimas (1999), p. 90; Vandamme (2004), p. 175.

[45] Tridimas (1999), p. 124.

[46] G.A. Bermann, Proportionality and Subsidiarity, in: C. Barnard and J. Scott (Eds), *The Law of the Single European Market – Unpacking the Premises* (Hart Publishing, Oxford and Portland, 2002), p. 38.

[47] Vandamme (2004), p. 175.

4.2 The principle of Community loyalty

The principle of Community loyalty is "particularly important because the Community, unlike most federations, has no clear or fixed boundary between Community and state powers, and because the Community depends much more than most federations on having its policies carried out by Member States".[48] An example is the area of competition policy, where since the entering into force of Regulation 1/2003, the application of Articles 81 and 82 EC has been decentralised and has to a considerable extent been left in the hands of the national authorities.[49]

The principle of Community loyalty is laid down in Article 10 EC which reads as follows:

"Member States shall take all appropriate measures, whether general or particular, to ensure fulfilment of the obligations arising out of this Treaty or resulting from action taken by the institutions of the Community. They shall facilitate the achievement of the Community's tasks.

They shall abstain from any measure which could jeopardise the attainment of the objectives of this Treaty."

Article 10 EC is in particular addressed to the Member States, including any national authority exercising governmental powers of any kind,[50] hence including the central authorities, the local and regional authorities, regulatory bodies, state companies and the national judiciary.[51]

However, the Community Institutions are also bound by the principle of Community loyalty, which does not derive from the wording from Article 10 EC itself, but from a general principle of mutual co-operation underlying that provision.[52]

---

48 J. Temple Lang, Community Institutional Law: Article 5 EEC Treaty, *CMLRev.*, 1990, p. 647.

49 Regulation 1/2003 on the implementation of the rules on competition laid down in Articles 81 and 82 of the Treaty, OJ 2003, L 1/1.

50 J. Temple Lang, The Duties of National Authorities Under Community Constitutional Law, *ELRev.*, 1998, p. 112.

51 See J. W. de Zwaan, The Netherlands (judiciary and authorities) and Article 10 of the EC Treaty – Report for FIDE 2000, XIX Congress, Helsinki 1-3 June 2000, *SEW*, 2000, p. 133.

52 Kapteyn & VerLoren van Themaat (edited by Gormley) (1998), p. 160. This is also referred to as the 'Zwartveld' doctrine. In Case C-2/88, *Zwartveld*, the Court held that the Commission is under an obligation to give its active assistance to national legal proceedings in which the national court requests information from the Commission.

Article 10 EC contains two general duties and one general prohibition, or two positive obligations and one negative. In literature these obligations have been further subdivided and specified.[53]

In this study the duty of mutual co-operation between the national authorities and the Community Institutions is particularly relevant, for example, to prevent the adoption of conflicting decisions by national authorities and the European Commission in the field of competition policy. The 'practical implementation' of Article 10 EC by means of the establishment of a European Competition Network is an example.

Furthermore, on the basis of Article 10 EC the Member States must prevent conflicts between the Community rules on free movement and competition and the national rules on horizontal and flanking policies. After all, they are under a positive obligation to take appropriate measures to ensure the effective application of Community law, and under a negative obligation to abstain from measures that could jeopardise the attainment of the objectives of the Treaty.[54]

4.3 The integration principle

Under the integration principle is understood the various integration clauses which are laid down in the Treaty and require the Community Institutions to integrate horizontal and flanking policy interests in other Community policies, including internal market and competition policy. It does not have a similarly broad scope of application as the other (general) principles of Community law since it relates to specific horizontal and flanking policy interests. The integration principle reinforces horizontal and flanking policies as an essential and unavoidable dimension of Community law.[55] Furthermore, it emphasises the horizontal character of horizontal and flanking policies, since there are so many linkages between environmental, consumer, public health and cultural policy as well as between these policies and the internal market. They are therefore also referred to as 'horizontal clauses'.

The exact legal consequences of the integration principle are rather unclear, mainly due to the still developing case law. The legal value of the integration-principle is generally presumed to be limited, but its legal status can certainly not be disregarded.[56] In this respect the following general remarks should be made. Firstly, the integration principle delimits the Community's discretionary powers in the sense that the full effect of the internal market must be mitigated

---

53 For a specification of these duties and an analysis of the case law, see J. Temple Lang, Community constitutional law: Article 5 EEC Treaty, *CMLRev.*, 1990, p. 646. See also Kapteyn & VerLoren van Themaat (edited by Gormley) (1998), p. 148.

54 See also Kapteyn & VerLoren van Themaat (edited by Gormley) (1998), pp. 148-163.

55 Commentaire Mégret (1996), p. 12.

56 See with respect to the environmental integration clause: Dhondt (2003), p. 183.

where horizontal and flanking policy interests are at stake.[57] This also appears from the *Preussen Elektra* case,[58] which will be discussed in Chapter 2, where the Court has relied on Article 6 EC in the interpretation of Article 28 EC.[59] The *Concordia* case makes clear that where national authorities choose to use environmental criteria in a tender procedure when assessing the economically most advantageous tender, based on the EC procurement directives, this must be possible, even though the directives themselves do not mention environmental criteria. The Court hereby referred to the integration clause laid down in Article 6 EC.[60] Furthermore, the integration principle requires that in the field of competition policy, where a reference to horizontal and flanking policies is lacking, apart from Article 87(3) sub d EC on state aid for cultural reasons, horizontal and flanking policies should at least be taken into consideration.

Nonetheless, the Community's discretionary powers, although limited, continue to be wide as to how and which horizontal and flanking policy interests should be pursued within the context of other policies. But there rests a strong duty of motivation on the Community. [61]

Secondly, the integration principle reaffirms the view that horizontal and flanking policy interests must be promoted within the context of the internal market. First, the horizontal and flanking policy dimension of the internal market is reinforced by the integration principle: in its proposals concerning health, safety, environmental protection and consumer protection under Article 95 EC the Commission must take as a base a high level of protection, according to Article 95(3) EC. Where cultural interests are at stake, according to Article 151(4) EC the Community must at least take these interests into account. Where other internal market legal bases do not refer to horizontal and flanking policy interests, the integration clauses are particularly relevant.

Furthermore, the integration principle may contribute to a broad regulatory competence under Article 95 EC and other internal market provisions.[62] This is particularly relevant in the areas of public health and culture, where harmonisation of national laws is excluded.

---

[57] B. De Witte, The Cultural Dimension of Community Law, in: Academy of European Law (Ed.), *Collected Courses of the Academy of European Law*, Volume IV, Book 1 (Kluwer Law International, The Hague, 1995), p. 295.

[58] Case C-379/98, *Preussen Elektra*.

[59] H.-W. Micklitz, N. Reich and S. Weatherill, EU Treaty Revision and Consumer Protection, *Journal of Consumer Policy*, 2004, p. 378.

[60] Case C-513/99, *Concordia Bus Finland*. See also Dhondt (2003), p. 163. The Commission published an interpretative communication on the possibilities for integrating environmental considerations into public procurement, OJ 2001, C 333/12.

[61] Within the context of consumer policy, see: Reich (2003), p. 31. J. Stuyck, European consumer law after the Treaty of Amsterdam: consumer policy in or beyond the internal market? *CMLRev.*, 2000, p. 386; see also Cseres (2005), p. 200.

[62] With regard to consumer policy, see: H.-W. Micklitz, N. Reich and S. Weatherill, EU Treaty Revision and Consumer Protection, *Journal of Consumer Policy*, 2004, p. 379.

Finally, the integration clauses appear to address the Community Institutions, and not the Member States. Indirectly, however, the Member State may have to meet the requirements arising from the application of the integration clause when they implement Community legislation.[63] From *Concordia* it appears that the environmental integration clause also provides a possibility for *national* authorities to pursue environmental aims under Community directives laying down merely economic criteria.

As can be seen from the scheme presented in section 3, the integration clauses have been differently formulated, either in stronger terms, like the environmental integration clause contained in Article 6 EC, or in weaker terms, like the cultural integration clause contained in Article 151(4) EC. In the following a few comments in respect of these different clauses will be made.

Environment

Originally, a requirement to integrate environmental protection requirements into other policies had been laid down in the environmental title introduced by the Single European Act. The change of place has turned the integration principle into an instrument to enforce the principle of sustainable development as referred to in Article 2 EC.[64] The upgrading of the integration principle by its inclusion in Article 6 EC also stresses its importance in Community law compared with the other policy integration clauses in the titles on culture, public health and consumer protection.[65] The weight and added value of environmental objectives had become even more apparent in relation to other Community objectives, including the objective of the free movement of goods or undistorted competition.[66]

The current integration principle is "worded forcefully and refers explicitly to implementation of the Community policies".[67] The word 'must' instead of 'shall' as well as its place among the principles of Community law makes it the strongest integration clause in the EC Treaty.[68]

Environmental protection requirements include the environmental policy objectives of Article 174(1) EC and the principles referred to in Article 174(2) EC.[69] This interpretation leads to a general obligation for the Community "to

---

63 Dhondt (2003), pp. 52-53.

64 See also Ch. Callies, Die neue Querschnittsklausel des Art. 6 ex 3c EGV als Instrument zur Umsetzung des Grundsatzes der Nachhaltigen Entwicklung, *DVBL*, 1998, p. 565.

65 Ch. Callies, Die neue Querschnittsklausel des Art. 6 ex 3c EGV als Instrument zur Umsetzung des Grundsatzes der Nachhaltigen Entwicklung, *DVBL*, 1998, p. 564.

66 See M. Wasmeier, The integration of environmental protection as a general rule of interpreting Community law, *CMLRev.*, 2001, p. 161.

67 Jans (2000) , p. 17.

68 Dhondt (2003), pp. 102-103.

69 Jans (2000), p. 18.

reach an integrated and balanced assessment of all the relevant environmental aspects when adopting other policy".[70] The strong interpretation of Article 6 entails that "the other policy area must *pursue* the environmental objectives, *be based* on the environmental principles and *take account of* the environmental criteria".[71] This means that environmental objectives have to be pursued in a systematic manner.[72]

In addition Article 95(3) EC requires the Commission to take as a basis a high level of environmental protection in its proposals for internal market legislation.

Consumer protection

Since the entering into force of the Treaty of Amsterdam the consumer paragraph also contains an integration clause stipulating that consumer protection requirements shall be taken into account in defining and implementing other Community policies and activities.[73] This obligation seems somewhat weaker and less fundamental than the obligation to integrate environmental interests laid down in Article 6 EC.[74]

Consumer protection requirements probably concern the health, safety and economic interests of consumers, as well as their right to information, education and to organise themselves, as mentioned in Article 153(1) EC.

In consumer law literature the integration principle is generally considered to be weak, particularly due to the lack of institutional support.[75] This is mitigated by the fact that Article 95(3) EC includes a high level of consumer protection as a basis for internal market legislation, which is particularly relevant now most consumer measures have been based on Article 95 EC. It should also be noted that the Commission in its communication on a proposal for a programme of Community action in the field of Health and Consumer protection 2007-2013 appoints the integration of health and consumer concerns into other Community policies as one of three key objectives of its policy.[76]

Public health

A rather strongly formulated integration clause can be found in Article 152(1) EC, stipulating that a high level of human health protection *shall* be ensured in the *definition and implementation of all Community policies and activities.*

---

70 Jans (2000), p. 18.

71 Dhondt (2003), p. 105.

72 Dhondt (2003), p. 105.

73 Howells and Weatherill (2005), p. 129.

74 J. Stuyck, European consumer law after the Treaty of Amsterdam: consumer policy in or beyond the internal market? *CMLRev.*, 2000, p. 386.

75 H.-W. Micklitz, N. Reich and S. Weatherill, EU Treaty Revision and Consumer Protection, *Journal of Consumer Policy*, 2004, p. 378.

76 COM(2005) 115 final.

Also here we must presume that 'health protection' includes the objectives mentioned in the second sentence of Article 152(1) EC, i.e. the improvement of public health, preventing human illness and diseases, and obviating sources of danger to human health.

As with the other integration clauses, it can be brought forward that Article 152 EC introduces a kind of 'health impact assessment' for all Community policies and activities. In other words, the Community has become a 'Health Community'.[77] The fact that the Community conducts some form of health impact assessment of how and why health considerations have been addressed also appears from a practical guide published by the Commission and called 'ensuring a high level of health protection'.[78] The latest report of the Commission on the integration of health protection requirements in Community policies, however, dates from no later than 1999.

Lately it can be noticed that more attention has been drawn to the linkages between public health and the protection of the environment; after all the environment is an important determinant for health and there can be no good health in an unhealthy environment.[79] In the Commission's proposal for a Programme of Community action in the field of Health and Consumer protection for the period 2007-2013, however, the emphasis is laid on the coherence between health and consumer policies.[80]

In all these situations health considerations that lay outside the context of health care are involved. Public health *stricto sensu* should also be distinguished from the provision of health care, which regulation, according to Article 152 EC, remains the primary responsibility of the Member State.

In addition, Article 95(3) EC refers to a high level of health protection to be taken as a basis in proposals for internal market legislation.

Culture

Similar to the other integration clauses Article 151(4) EC at least contains a legal and not merely a political obligation for the Community to take account of cultural aspects.[81] However, its formulation is even more vague and prob-

---

77 Berg (1997), p.464.

78 Practical guide of 17 December 2001 published by DG-Health and Consumer Protection. See also Decision 1786/2002 of the Council adopting a programme of Community action in the field of public health (2003-2008), OJ 2002, L 271/1.

79 See in particular Article 7 of the decision laying down the Sixth Community Environmental Action Programme covering the objectives and priority areas for action on environment and health and quality of life: Decision 1600/2002, OJ 2002, L 242/1; see also G. Silberschmidt of the International Society of Doctors for the Environment and the case of integrating health into Article 6 of the EC Treaty, to be found at: http://www/epha.org/a/530.

80 COM(2005) 115 final.

81 G. Ress and J. Ukrow, Auswirkungen von Art. 128 Abs. 4 EGV auf die Wettbewerbsrechtliche beurteilung von Buchpreisbindungssystemen, *ZeuS*, 1999, p. 40.

lematic as compared to the other integration clauses.[82] Firstly, it is not clear what cultural aspects mean. Does this include the notion of common cultural heritage? Cultural aspects probably refers to the objectives of Article 151 EC, including the promotion of the common cultural heritage of the Community. It certainly also includes the protection of national regional cultural diversity,[83] which is reinforced by the last part of the sentence *in particular in order to respect and to promote the diversity of its cultures*, included by the Treaty of Amsterdam (1997).

Secondly, the term 'take into account' imposes a more limited obligation on the Community to integrate than in the case of, for example, Article 6 EC, which is more strongly formulated. Furthermore, Article 95(3) EC does not refer to culture and that a high level of protection of cultural interests would have to be taken as a basis for internal market legislation.[84]

In its first report on the consideration of cultural aspects in European Community action the Commission presents its view on the implications of Article 151(4) EC.[85] In this report the Commission examines the way in which the various Community instruments and policies have taken cultural aspects into account in action relating to the internal market, action under internal policies such as economic and social cohesion, the environment, the information society and education, and action under external policies, such as trade policy and cultural co-operation with non-member countries. With regard to competition policy, for example, the Commission states that the cultural sector, in its economic aspects, is subject to the rules of competition as are the other sectors. According to the Commission, it is therefore necessary for this sector also to guarantee that competition is not distorted. The relationship between cultural policy and other policies is mapped out in this report, but a thorough discussion on the legal implications of Article 151(4) EC is still lacking.[86] In 2002 the

---

82 R. Craufurd Smith, Community Intervention in the Cultural Field: Continuity or Change?, in: R. Craufurd Smith (Ed.), *Culture and European Union Law* (Oxford University Press, Oxford, 2004), p. 54.

83 Schmahl (1996), p. 226.

84 R. Craufurd Smith, Community Intervention in the Cultural Field: Continuity or Change?, in: R. Craufurd Smith (Ed.), *Culture and European Union Law* (Oxford University Press, Oxford, 2004), p. 54.

85 COM(96) 160.

86 S. de Vries, Cultuur en Mededinging: harmonie of dissonantie?, in: J.W. van de Gronden and K.J.M. Mortelmans (Eds), *Mededinging en niet-economische belangen* (Kluwer, Deventer, 2001), p. 98; S. De Vries, Culture and Competition, an ambivalent relationship?, in: U. Bernitz and E. Edwardsson (Eds), *Konkurrens på reglerade marknader – hur långt kan konkurrenslagen tillämpas?* (Juridiska Fakulteten Nr 59 Skriftserien, Stockholm, 1999). Meanwhile the Council had taken action by adopting various resolutions and decisions, such as resolutions on the integration of cultural aspects into Community action (OJ 1997, C 36/4), on the application of the competition rules on fixed book prices in homogeneous cross-border linguistic areas (OJ 1999, C 42/3) and on the application of national fixed book price systems (OJ 2001, C 73/5); see also Chapter 3.

Council acknowledged in a resolution that the implementation of the integration clause definitely needed to be improved.[87]

5 The plan

As stated before, the three sources of tension will be analysed in Chapters 2, 3 and 4. In Chapter 5 a synthesis of the case law of the Court on free movement, the decision practice of the Commission in competition cases and secondary legislation will be presented. The aim is to identify whether a common legal approach in respect of these three sources of tension is possible. The establishment of whether, and if so to what extent, a degree of coherence exists between the free movement rules, the free movement rules and the competition rules[88] and between horizontal and flanking policies is relevant for the solutions presented in Chapter 6. In this chapter suggestions will be made how closer harmony can be achieved between horizontal and flanking policies and the internal market. The example of books as both commercial goods within the meaning of the EC Treaty and cultural products, and the regulation of the book market for cultural purposes, will be used as illustration; from this example it appears that several general principles of Community law, which are introduced in section 4 of this chapter, may play an important role in the attainment of closer harmony.

Of course, throughout this book the present numbering of the EC Treaty provisions is being used (as amended by the Treaty of Amsterdam).

This study was closed on 1 July 2005.

---

87 OJ 2002, C 32/2.

88 K. Mortelmans, Towards convergence in the application of the rules on free movement and on competition, *CMLRev.*, 2001, p. 613.

CHAPTER 2

The Application of the Free Movement Rules

1 Introduction

This chapter will show how the European Court of Justice has acted as arbitrator to settle disputes over competing demands of market integration and objectives of horizontal and flanking policies. The case law reveals that the Court has developed and consolidated a system of trade liberalisation based on prohibitions imposed on the Member States, yet at the same time has acknowledged that national horizontal and flanking measures, even though restricting free movement, may under conditions be upheld.

The problem of tension, therefore, essentially involves two elements:[1]

- The existence of a trade (free movement) restricting measure, whether (in)directly discriminatory or facially neutral and indistinctly applicable.
- The existence of some sort of justification in terms of a recognised non-trade purpose, for instance to implement horizontal and flanking policies.

Before the existence of a trade restricting measure can be established, the scope of the prohibitive provisions on free movement and their applicability to horizontal and flanking measures need to be assessed (section 2). Once it has been established that the free movement rules are applicable, it can be assessed what sort of national horizontal and flanking policy measures are prohibited in the light of the prohibitive rules on free movement (section 3). In section 4 the exceptions to free movement will be discussed and also the extent to which Member States may justify restrictions on free movement for horizontal and flanking policy reasons.

2 The material, personal and territorial scope of the free movement rules

The assessment of the material, personal and territorial scope of application of the free movement rules is essential in that it becomes apparent whether national horizontal and flanking policies will be exposed to Community law in the first place. If it appears that the free movement rules are not applicable, there can be no question of a trade dispute and hence no problem of tension will arise.

---

1 In the context of the GATT, D.E. Farber and R.E. Hudec, Gatt Legal Restraints on Domestic Environmental Regulations, in: J.N. Bhagwati and R.E. Hudec (Eds), *Fair Trade and Harmonization – Prerequisites for Free Trade*, volume II (The MIT Press, Cambridge, 1996), p. 80.

2.1 The material scope

The Treaty provisions on free movement do not offer a definition of the terms goods, services or persons. The scope of the rules on free movement is therefore in the first place dependent on how these terms must be defined. The Court has applied a functional test and has thereby couched non-market values "in the language of economics".[2]

2.1.1 In general

Activities generally fall within the scope of the provisions on free movement in so far as they can be considered to be *economic* activities. With regard to goods, the Court defined goods as products having a commercial value, including products having a negative value but which form the subject of commercial transactions.[3] Hence, depending on their commercial value cultural goods, like paintings or other works of art, or goods such as narcotic drugs[4] or waste products – whether recyclable or not[5] – are considered goods within the meaning of the Treaty. The provisions on the free movement of persons have been interpreted in a similarly broad fashion by the Court. A worker is an individual who performs services for and under the direction of another person for remuneration.[6]

Where certain activities cannot be considered economic, because there is no gainful activity involved, or where certain goods are not subject to commercial transactions, the Treaty provisions on free movement will not be applicable. An example is provided by the *Humbel* ruling involving the payment of a fee (the minerval) charged to nationals of other Member States (than Belgium) for access to a state educational establishment. The question was whether courses taught in a technical institute which form part of the secondary education provided under the national education system are to be regarded as services within the meaning of Article 49 EC. The Court held that the essential characteristic of remuneration is absent in the case of courses provided under the national education system. "First of all, the State, in establishing and maintaining

2 D. Chalmers, The Single Market: From Prima Donna to Journeyman, in: J. Shaw and G. More (Eds), *New Legal Dynamics of European Union* (Clarendon Press, Oxford, 1995), p. 63.

3 Case C-2/90, *Commission v. Belgium (Walloon Waste)*. See more generally about the meaning of goods: Oliver (assisted by Malcolm Jarvis) (2003), pp. 16-23.

4 Case C-324/93, *Evans Medical*, paragraph 20: "According to the Court's case law, goods taken across a frontier for the purposes of commercial transactions are subject to Article 30 of the Treaty, whatever the nature of those transactions. Since they have those characteristics, the drugs covered by the Convention and marketable under it are subject to Article 30."

5 Case C-2/90, *Commission v. Belgium (Walloon Waste)*.

6 Case 66/85, *Lawrie-Blum*; Case C-415/93, *Bosman*.

such a system, is not seeking to engage in gainful activity but is fulfilling its duties towards its own population in the social, cultural and educational fields. Secondly, the system in question is, as a general rule, funded from the public purse and not by pupils or their parents."[7] In *Wirth* the Court took a similar approach, but it made clear that when courses are given in establishments of higher education which are financed essentially out of private funds, in particular by students and their parents, and which seek to make a profit, they become services within the meaning of Article 50 EC.[8] The *Neri* judgment, however, seems to suggest that the free movement rules can in a more general sense be relevant for the organisation of education. The Court held that the organisation for remuneration of university courses is an economic activity falling within the scope of the freedom of establishment, Article 43 EC.[9]

The potentially broad material scope of application of the free movement rules also in areas that are not included in the Treaty has been reinforced in the case law on sport.[10] The application of the free movement rules in the sport sector has not always been regarded as self-evident. The relationship between Community law and sport has *inter alia* been determined by the supposedly "eccentric cultural and economic nature of sport".[11] In the *Bosman* case the Court, having to consider whether professional football players are workers within the meaning of Article 39 EC, 'broke the ice'. The German government argued that in most cases a sport such as football is not an economic activity. It further submitted that sport in general has points of similarity with culture and pointed out that under Article 151 of the Treaty, the Community must respect the national and regional diversity of the cultures of the Member States. The Court rejected this cultural argument and held that activities of professional or semi-professional footballers constitute economic activities within the meaning of Article 2 EC.[12] This was confirmed in the *Deliège* and the *Lehtonen* cases.[13]

---

7 Case 263/86, *Humbel*, paragraph18.

8 Case C-109/92, *Wirth*, paragraph 17.

9 Case C-153/02, *Valentina Neri*, paragraph 39. The developments in the case law on the free movement of persons and education fall beyond the scope of this research. Important cases are, for example, Case C-209/03, *Bidar* (annotation K.J.M. Mortelmans and J. Luijendijk, *AA*, 2005, pp. 488-499) and Case C-147/03, *Commission v. Austria*. See also Chapter 1, section 3.

10 With regard to sport and the concept of economic activity see also: Van den Bogaert (2005), pp. 42-69.

11 S. Weatherill, "Fair Play Please!": Recent developments in the application of EC law to sport, *CMLRev.*, 2003, p. 55.

12 Case C-415/93, *Bosman*. With regard to sporting activities see also: Case 36/74, *Walrave & Koch* and Case 13/76, *Dona*.

13 In these cases the Court also referred to Declaration 29 on Sport annexed to the final act of the Conference which adopted the text of the Amsterdam Treaty, to emphasise that this declaration is consistent with the case law in so far as it relates to situations in which sport constitutes an economic activity. The Declaration on Sport emphasises the social significance of sport and calls on the bodies of the European Union to give special consideration to the particular characteristics of amateur sport: Joined Cases C-51/96 and C-191/97, *Deliège*, paragraph 42; Case C-176/96, *Lehtonen*, paragraph 33.

What nonetheless also becomes clear from *Deliège* and the more recent *Meca-Medina* case is that a distinction must be made between sporting activities that can be considered economic, and activities of which the regulation is characterised as purely sportive, and hence do not fall within the scope *ratione materiae* of the free movement rules.[14]

2.1.2 Horizontal and flanking activities

The specific and sometimes non-economic nature of a certain activity does not necessarily curtail the application of the free movement provisions; nor does the Treaty make a deliberate derogation with the intention to remove certain horizontal and flanking activities from the ambit of the free movement rules. As regards public health, environmental, cultural or consumer policy, there is no provision in the Treaty which explicitly excludes the application of the free movement rules.[15] In fact explicit references to areas of horizontal and flanking policies, such as culture, public health and the protection of animals and plants in Articles 30 EC, 39(3) EC and 46 EC make clear that these areas are not sheltered from the application of Community law. As can be seen from the following examples, the applicability *ratione materiae* of the free movement rules is generally very broad, with few exceptions.

Public health

Medical devices are generally considered to be goods, whereas medical activities are generally considered to be services within the meaning of Article 49 EC.[16] In the *Smits and Peerbooms* judgment the ECJ rejected the argument of hospital services in the context of Dutch legislation not being economic activities within the meaning of Article 50 EC.[17] According to the Court the special nature

---

[14] Vogelaar (2000). See in general with regard to EC law and sports: S. Weatherill, "Fair Play Please!": Recent developments in the application of EC law to sport, *CMLRev.*, 2003, p. 55. Even though the *Meca-Medina* case mainly involved the application of the competition rules, the ECJ in a more general sense held that anti-doping rules set up by the International Swimming Federation – 'FINA' are based on purely sporting considerations, which means that these rules do not come within the scope of *inter alia* Article 49 EC: Case T-313/02, *Meca-Medina*; see also Chapter 3, section 4.1.2.4.

[15] See with regard to the scope of application of the competition rules AG Jacobs in his Joined Opinion in Case C-67/96, *Albany*, Joined Cases C-115/97, C-116/97 and C-117/97, *Brentjens* and Case C-219/97, *Drijvende Bokken*, paragraphs 123 and 124.

[16] In the *Grogan* case the ECJ held that medical termination of pregnancy, performed in accordance with the law of the state in which it is carried out, constitutes a service within the meaning of Article 50 of the Treaty; the provision of information about the identity and location of clinics in Member States providing abortions, though, was not considered an economic activity because it was not distributed on behalf of an economic operator established in another Member State, but by a students' union: see Case C-159/90, *Grogan*.

[17] With regard to the applicability of the freedom of services to public health care: annotation of Case C-385/99, *Müller-Fauré* by M. Flear, *CMLRev.*, 2004, pp. 217-223.

of certain services does not remove them from the ambit of the fundamental principle of free movement. Article 50 does not require that the service be paid for by those for whom it is performed. Furthermore, for the purposes of Article 50, the essential characteristic of remuneration lies in the fact that it constitutes consideration for the service in question. The Court stated that "in the present cases, the payments made by the sickness insurance funds under the contractual arrangements provided for by the ZFW,[18] albeit set at a flat rate, are indeed the consideration for the hospital services and unquestionably represent remuneration for the hospital which receives them and which is engaged in an activity of an economic character".[19]

In his opinion in *Smits and Peerbooms* AG Colomer had argued that hospital services do not fall within the ambit of Article 50 EC, when they are provided in kind and free of charge under the relevant sickness insurance scheme. He pointed at the fundamental difference between the Dutch situation, where there is no remuneration within the meaning of Article 50 EC where the patient receives care in a hospital infrastructure without having to pay for it himself or where all or part of the amount he pays is reimbursed to him, and the situation in *Kohll*,[20] where patients are free to choose their doctor or specialist and have to pay directly for treatment provided.[21]

That Article 49 EC may be relevant for the health insurance sector as well can be deduced from the *Freskot* case. Even though this case involved an insurance scheme for farmers e.g. in the event of damage caused by natural risks, managed by the Greek organisation for agricultural insurance, a private legal person wholly owned by the state, the Court's reasoning can also apply to health insurance schemes.[22] Benefits by health insurers will then probably not fall within the scope of Articles 49 and 50 EC, if the contribution is imposed by the legislature and levied by e.g. a tax authority; insurable risks, however, may fall within the scope of the provision on services, where the implementation of an insurance scheme constitutes a restriction on health insurers established in another Member State offering their insurance services against the risks in question.

The environment

Environmental policy is neither spared by the Community rules on free movement. The *Walloon Waste* case makes clear that waste is considered a good within the meaning of Articles 28-30 EC. According to Belgium the total ban on the disposal or storage of waste from other Member States imposed by the Region of Wallonia would not fall within the scope of the Treaty as waste did not

---

[18] Ziekenfondswet, Sickness Insurance Law.

[19] Case C-157/99, *Smits and Peerbooms*, paragraph 58.

[20] Case C-158/96, *Kohll*.

[21] Opinion AG Colomer in Case C-157/99, *Smits and Peerbooms*, paragraphs 35-50.

[22] Case C-355/00, *Freskot AE*.

constitute goods within the meaning of Article 28 EC. The Belgian Government argued that waste which was not recyclable and not reusable had no intrinsic commercial value and thus could not be the subject of a sale. Operations for the disposal or tipping of such waste came under the Treaty provisions on the freedom to provide services. The ECJ in response to that argument considered that objects which are shipped across a frontier for the purposes of commercial transactions, are subject to Article 28 EC, whatever the nature of those transactions. Moreover, the distinction between recyclable and non-recyclable waste is particularly difficult to apply in practice, especially with respect to controls at frontiers. That distinction is based on factors which are uncertain and liable to change in the course of time according to technical progress. Furthermore, whether waste is recyclable or not also depends on the cost of the recycling process and consequently on whether its proposed re-utilisation is viable, with the result that classification of waste is necessarily subjective and depends on variable factors.[23]

The fact that the disposal of non-recyclable waste was not regarded as a service, which, according to AG Jacobs in this case, would otherwise lead to the undesirable outcome that the free movement of goods is limited to products having only a positive value, shows the important if not nearly exclusionary role of the Treaty provisions on goods in the environmental field.

Consumer policy

The application *ratione materiae* of the free movement rules in the field of consumer policy appears rather self-evident, as consumers are generally persons who buy goods and services. The scope of application *ratione materiae* becomes particularly relevant where certain activities in particularly sensitive areas are involved; here Member States may want to retain the right to protect consumers in full by prohibiting these activities or by imposing stringent conditions upon the exercise of these activities, irrespective of the impact of such legislation on intra-Community trade. In the *Schindler* case, for example, concerning national legislation prohibiting certain lotteries the question was raised whether lotteries form an economic activity within the meaning of Article 49 EC. The Court held that "it is also the case that like amateur sport, a lottery may provide entertainment for the players who participate. However, that recreational aspect of the lottery does not take it out of the realm of the provision of services. Not only does it give the players, if not always a win, at least the hope of a win, it also yields a gain for the operator [...]."[24]

---

23 Case C-2/90, *Commission v. Belgium*, paragraphs 25-28.

24 Case C-275/92, *Schindler*, paragraph 34.

Culture

In the *Italian Arts Treasures* case the Italian government argued that the EEC Treaty was concluded to create an economic community, not a community in articles of an artistic, historic or ethnographic interest.[25] The Court rebutted this argument while considering that the interpretation of the term goods cannot be affected by the characteristics, which distinguished the articles covered by Italian law from other merchandise. Consequently art treasures had to be considered goods within the meaning of Treaty. The same reasoning applies to other cultural goods, such as books, even though books "might be considered as an expression of a cultural and spiritual state of society, regardless the fact whether the centre of gravity is situated in the educational or political field".[26] In the *Commission v. France* case the question arose whether newspapers and periodicals can be considered goods within the meaning of the EC Treaty. Here it was argued that newspapers and periodicals were products which served as vehicles for political, social and cultural information. The question was answered in the affirmative.[27]

In the *Sacchi* case the Court held that television signals should be regarded as a provision of services within the meaning of Article 49 EC.[28] The Italian government had argued that broadcasting companies do not exercise economic powers, but comprise an institution that has cultural and informative objectives. AG *Reischl* in his opinion had admitted that the application of Community law to television is subject to limitations, because "television is without doubt a means of mass-communication of great cultural and educational significance, an instrument which on account of its effect, is particularly capable of influencing public opinion".[29]

2.2 The personal scope

The Treaty provisions on free movement are primarily aimed at measures adopted by Member States. Nevertheless, the provisions may not only apply to actions taken by public authorities.[30] The extent to which the Treaty provisions on free movement are relevant for *Community* measures and therefore also directed at Community Institutions, will be discussed in Chapter 4.

---

25 Case 24/68, *Commission v. Italy.*

26 Sparr (1991), p. 103.

27 Case 269/83, *Commission v. France.*

28 Case 155/73, *Sacchi*, paragraph 7.

29 Opinion of AG Reischl in Case 155/73, *Sacchi.*

30 See also K. Mortelmans, Towards convergence in the application of the rules on free movement and on competition? *CMLRev.*, 2001, pp. 634-635.

Workers

The personal scope of application of the Treaty provision on workers is very broad. This appears first and foremost from the Court's judgment in *Angonese*.[31] In the *Angonese* case Article 39 EC was invoked against a private banking undertaking. The Court considered that conduct of the *Cassa di Risparmio*, which was grounded originally in a national collective agreement but in which adherence to the terms of the agreement were optional, fell within the scope of Article 39 EC. In this case the Court went a step further than in *Bosman*, which involved transfer rules that constituted an obstacle to the free movement of workers and that were set up and issued by a private organisation, the UEFA (and FIFA).[32] *Angonese* does not only extend the reach of Community law even more deeply in employment law, since now all private employers in all Member States must apply Community law standards to migrant workers whilst not being obliged to do so for home nationals,[33] it also reinforces the horizontal direct effect of Article 39 EC.

Establishment and services

The personal scope of application of the Treaty provisions on establishment and services seems more limited in comparison with workers; nonetheless from the case law it appears that these provisions are also addressed to rules set up by private organisations having considerable decision-making authority. The *Wouters* case, involving decisions by the Bar of the Netherlands (*Nederlandse Orde van Advocaten*), makes clear that the Treaty provisions on freedom of establishment are addressed to semi-public/semi-private organisations. This case will be further discussed in Chapter 3.[34]

The *Deliège* and *Walrave Koch* cases, for example, make clear that rules set up by sporting associations may be challenged on the basis of Article 49 EC.[35]

Goods

By contrast, the provisions on the free movement of goods do not seem to have horizontal direct effect.[36] According to the Court in *Sapod Audic* regarding the obligation to mark the packaging by affixing the 'Green Dot Logo', which derived from a more general obligation to identify the packaging laid down in national legislation, this obligation "arises out of a private contract between the parties to the main proceedings. Such a contractual provision cannot be regarded as a barrier to trade for the purposes of Article 28 of the Treaty since it

---

[31] Case C-281/98, *Angonese*.

[32] Case C-415/93, *Bosman*.

[33] See also annotation R. Lane and N.Nic Shuibhne, *CMLRev.*, 2000, p. 1244.

[34] Case C-309/99, *Wouters*; see Chapter 3, section 4.1.2.4.

[35] Joined Cases C-51/96 and C-191/97, *Deliège* and Case 36/74, *Walrave Koch*.

[36] Barnard (2004), p. 90.

was not imposed by a Member State but agreed between individuals."[37] For these types of restrictions, the competition rules may be relevant (see Chapter 3).

Nonetheless, a Member State may still be responsible under Article 28 EC for abstaining from taking action against national actions by *private* persons, who have as their objective the obstruction of the free movement of goods. In the *Spanish Strawberries* case the Court ruled that Article 28 EC in conjunction with the principle of Community loyalty as laid down in Article 10 EC requires that Member States must take all necessary and appropriate measures to ensure that the fundamental freedom of movement of goods is respected in their territory.[38] France had failed to take all necessary measures to prevent obstruction by actions of French farmers of the free movement of fruit and vegetables. The actions consisted of the interception of lorries transporting agricultural products in France, the destruction of their loads, violence against lorry drivers, threats against French supermarkets selling agricultural products from other Member States and damaging products on display in shops. In the light of a number of specific factors and given the frequency and seriousness of the incidents cited by the Commission, the Court concluded that the measures adopted by the French government were manifestly inadequate to ensure freedom of intra-Community trade in agricultural products.[39]

This ruling has been confirmed in *Schmidberger*, which involved a demonstration in Austria of an environmental group resulting in the complete closure of a major transit route, the Brenner motorway, for almost 30 hours. The Court held Austria responsible for the consequential restriction of the free movement of goods under Articles 10 and 28 EC.[40]

Hence, the Treaty provision on goods (Article 28 EC) clearly has no horizontal direct effect, but can be given a similar effect, albeit indirectly, through the application of Article 10 EC.

Capital

With regard to the Treaty provisions on capital it is still unsure whether they have horizontal direct effect and can be invoked against private organisations as well.[41]

---

37 C-159/00, *Sapod Audic*, paragraph 74; see also Case 8/74 *Dassonville*, paragraph 5.

38 Case C-265/95, *Commission v. France (Spanish Strawberries)*.

39 See also H. Temmink, From Danish Bottles to Danish Bees: The Dynamics of Free Movement of Goods and Environmental Protection – A Case Law Analysis, in: H. Somsen (Ed.), *Yearbook of European Environmental Law* (Oxford University Press, Oxford, 2000), p. 80.

40 Case C-112/00, *Schmidberger*.

41 Kapteyn & VerLoren van Themaat (2003), p. 633.

2.3 The territorial scope

The Treaty provisions on free movement will only apply, if intra-Community trade is affected. In other words, for a national measure to fall within the scope of one of the prohibitive provisions on free movement a trans-frontier element should be established. The fact that the rules on free movement do not apply to so-called internal situations may lead to reverse discrimination, i.e. a situation where domestic products, persons or services are treated less favourably than products, persons or services from other Member States. In addition, where stricter national rules on matters such as establishment or minimum prices are circumvented by using Articles 28 and 49 EC, the Court will not permit these Treaty provisions to be relied upon, if it appears that goods or services were exported in order to be re-imported and thereby to escape a legal requirement which they otherwise have to comply with – the application of U-turn constructions.[42] In that case the Member State is entitled to take measures to prevent nationals from attempting improperly to circumvent their national legislation or to prevent individuals from improperly or fraudulently taking advantage of provisions of Community law.[43] However, in the case of setting up a company in another Member State whose rules of company law are less restrictive, that conduct cannot constitute an abuse of the right of establishment. Any company that fulfils the prerequisites described in Article 48 EC is a beneficiary of the freedom of establishment.[44]

Whereas it appears at the outset to be impossible to invoke the free movement rules in internal situations, the Court seems, perhaps as a result of the operation of the internal market and the evolution of national and Community competition law,[45] nonetheless in some cases to have adopted a more subtle approach as regards the principle that Community law does not apply to internal situations. [46]

---

42 Kapteyn & VerLoren van Themaat (edited by L.W. Gormley) (1998), pp. 582-583.

43 See e.g. Case C-23/93, *TV 10*, paragraph 21.

44 Case C-212/97, *Centros*, paragraphs 19-27; see also annotation W.-H. Roth, *CMLRev.*, 2000, p. 149.

45 K. Mortelmans, Towards convergence in the application of the rules on free movement and on competition?, *CMLRev.*, 2001, p. 630; see also Chapter 3.

46 With regard to tariff barriers: Joined Cases C-485/93 and C-486/93, *Kos*; Joined Cases C-363/93 and 407-411/93, *Lancry*; with regard to Article 28 EC: Case C-184/96, *Commission v. France (Foie Gras)*; Case C-448/98, *Guimont*; Case C-254/98, *TK-Heimdienst Sass*; with regard to Article 39 EC: Case C-281/98, *Roman Angonese*: The fact that the Court did not address the 'appreciable Community element' in this case may also reflect an unwillingness to further compromise internal Member State autonomy and sensibilities: See annotation R. Lane and N.Nic Shuibhne, *CMLRev.*, 2000, p. 1243; regarding Article 56 EC: Joined Cases C-515/99, C-519/99 to C-524/99 and C-526/99 to C-540/99, *Reisch*.

2.4 Conclusions

Based on the foregoing it can first be concluded that the economic nature of the activity is decisive in determining the scope of the Treaty provisions on free movement. The purpose and effect of a distinction between categories of goods, services and persons, can thus not in principle be taken into account in the assessment of the applicability *ratione materiae* of the Treaty provisions on free movement, but may, as will be seen later, play a role in an assessment of the exceptions which are invoked to justify restrictions to free movement. This may only be different for activities like education, where courses are provided under the national education system.[47] This broad material scope of application of the free movement rules entails that the following question becomes most pertinent, i.e. the question to the scope of the *prohibitions* and the *exceptions* in relation to horizontal and flanking policies.

Furthermore, the personal scope of the free movement rules has not yet been conclusively defined. The provisions on the free movement of goods appear not to apply horizontally; rules set up by private organisations restricting the free movement of goods will therefore have to be assessed under the competition provisions.[48] The provisions on the free movement of persons and services, on the other hand, may also apply to actions by private organisations, although their exact scope of application remains unclear. The provisions on the free movement of workers appear to have the broadest personal scope of application.

3 The application of the free movement rules: the prohibitions

As stated before the fact that national measures are based upon horizontal and flanking policy considerations has no bearing on the *prima facie* applicability of the free movement rules. It is thus now necessary to focus on the prohibitions contained in the Treaty, essentially prohibiting Member States to restrict free trade and free movement. In this section the way in which the Court of Justice in its case law has interpreted the prohibitive Treaty provisions on free movement will be assessed. Tariff barriers prohibited by Articles 25 EC and 90 EC will only be briefly discussed at the end of this section.

47 Nonetheless the *Neri* case shows that courses provided by universities may fall within the material scope of application of the Treaty rules on free movement: Case C-153/02, *Valentina Neri*.

48 See also Chapter 3.

3.1 The prohibition: towards market access

The prohibitive rules on free movement are generally broadly applicable, covering distinctly as well as indistinctly applicable measures. The principle of non-discrimination on grounds of nationality is the cornerstone of the four freedoms.[49] The most severe restrictions on free movement are therefore national measures which apply with distinction to national products and foreign products, services and persons. The principle of non-discrimination still allows Member States to regulate goods, services, persons and capital on the condition that their regulation applies equally to home and host state goods, services, persons and capital. A requirement of non-discrimination does not seem to interfere with national regulatory autonomy.[50] The basic rule in the Court's case law is that discriminatory restrictions may only be justified by an exception laid down in the Treaty.

3.1.1 Indistinctly applicable measures

The *Dassonville* case and subsequent cases, in particular *Cassis de Dijon*,[51] entail that not only discriminatory or distinctly applicable measures, but also indistinctly applicable product requirements are caught by the prohibition on restricting trade in goods as contained in Article 28 EC.[52] In *Dassonville* the Court held that "all trading rules enacted by Member States which are capable of hindering, directly or indirectly, actually or potentially, intra-Community trade are to be considered as measures having an equivalent effect to quantitative restrictions"[53]. *Dassonville* makes clear that the legal commitment to free trade and free movement entails a regime which is directed at prohibiting any unjustified obstacle to trade rather than at merely eliminating discrimination and protectionism.[54]

In the context of the provisions on services and persons, the Court made clear that these provisions also apply to indistinctly applicable measures. In the *Säger* case the Court held that "Article 49 requires not only the elimination of all discrimination against a person providing services on the grounds of his nationality, but also the abolition of any restriction, even if it applies without distinction to national providers of services and to those of other Member States,

---

49 Barnard (2004), p. 18.

50 Barnard (2004), p. 18.

51 Case 120/78, *REWE-Zentral v. Bundesmonopolverwaltung (Cassis de Dijon)*.

52 Barnard (2004), p. 92; Oliver (assisted by Malcolm Jarvis) (2003), pp. 115-118.

53 Case 8/74, *Dassonville*, paragraph 5.

54 See J.H.H. Weiler on the dispute which cut to the heart of the international trade regime, The Constitution of the Common Market Place, in: P. Craig and G. de Búrca (Eds), *The Evolution of EU Law* (Oxford University Press, Oxford, 1999), p. 352.

when it is liable to prohibit or otherwise impede the activities of a provider of services established in another Member State where he lawfully provides similar services".[55] In the *Gebhard* case, concerning national restrictions on lawyers' freedom of establishment, the Court held that "it follows [...] from the Court's case law that national measures liable to hinder or make less attractive the exercise of fundamental freedoms guaranteed by the Treaty must fulfil four conditions: they must be applied in a non-discriminatory manner; they must be suitable for securing the attainment of the objective which they pursue; and they must not go beyond what is necessary in order to attain it".[56] The *Bosman* ruling indicates a similarly broad interpretation of Article 39 EC. The Court examined whether the transfer system formed an *obstacle to freedom of movement of workers* and held that "provisions which preclude or deter a national of a Member State from leaving his country of origin in order to exercise his right to freedom of movement therefore constitute an obstacle to that freedom even if they apply without regard to the nationality of the workers."[57]

A *de minimis* rule does not apply to the provisions on free movement.[58] In the *Danish Bees* case concerning a ban on keeping nectar-gathering bees other than the subspecies *Apis Mellifera mellifera* (brown bee) on the small island of Læsø the Danish government argued that the measure fell outside Article 28 EC since it covered only 0.3% of Danish territory. The Court ruled that the measure fell under Article 28 EC, but it did not address this *de minimis* argument.[59] Nevertheless in some cases certain measures were considered to fall outside the scope of Article 28 EC because the effects on intra-Community trade were too uncertain or indirect.[60]

3.1.2 Towards a market access based test

Rather than extending the concept of selling arrangement, which was introduced in the *Keck* case in respect of the free movement of goods and which will be discussed hereafter, the Court has always preferred to adopt a

55 Case C-76/90, *Säger v. Dennemeyer.*

56 Case C-55/94, *Gebhard*, paragraph 37; see also Case C-19/92, *Kraus*, where the Court considered a mere obstacle to the right of establishment as incompatible with Article 43 EC.

57 Case C-415/93, *Bosman*, paragraph 96.

58 Joined Cases 177 and 178/82, *Van de Haar.* In Case C-412/93, *Leclerc-TF 1*, AG Jacobs proposed to apply a *de minimis* rule in the context of Article 28 EC as an alternative to the *Keck* route. The Court did not follow his suggestion.

59 Case C-67/97, *Bluhme (Danish Bees)*; Ch. Denys, European Court of Justice: Case Report, *EELR*, 1999, p. 87. See also P. Oliver, Some further reflections on the scope of Articles 28-30 (ex 30-36) EC, *CMLRev.*, 1999, p. 790.

60 Case C-379/92, *Peralta*; see also K. Mortelmans, Towards convergence in the application of the rules on free movement and on competition, *CMLRev.*, 2001, p. 634.

market access based test in the context of the free movement of persons and services.[61] But also in the context of the free movement of goods the market access based test plays an increasingly important role, which is shown by cases like *TK Heimdienst Sass* and *Doc Morris*.

The *TK-Heimdienst Sass* case entails a more refined and sophisticated approach to market circumstances legislation. The Court's analysis of the applicability of Article 28 EC to an Austrian provision which provided that sales on rounds of certain grocery products could be carried on only by traders who had a permanent establishment in that administrative district or in a municipality adjacent thereto, is a step in the direction of a market access based test. It held that such legislation did not affect in the same manner the marketing of domestic products and that of products from other Member States.[62] In order for goods from other Member States to enjoy the same access to the market of the Member State of importation as domestic products, they have to bear additional costs.[63]

In *Doc Morris* the Court embroidered on this line of reasoning.[64] This case involved German legislation restricting the sale of medicinal products for human use to pharmacies established in Germany, thereby prohibiting the importation of these medicines by way of mail order through pharmacies established in other Member States in response to individual orders placed by consumers over the internet. Doc Morris had a pharmacy in the Netherlands and offered medicines for sale over the internet, for which activities a licence was obtained in the Netherlands. While German pharmacies could also sell their medicines over the internet, according to the Court "...for pharmacies not established in Germany, the internet provides a more significant way to gain direct access to the German market. A prohibition which has a greater impact on pharmacies established outside the German territory could *impede access to the market* for products from other Member States more than it impedes access for domestic products."[65]

The market access based test first developed within the context of persons and services. In the *Alpine Investment* case Dutch rules prohibiting cold calling were considered as *directly affecting access* to the market in services in other Member States.[66] In the *Bosman* case, the UEFA regulation was regarded as directly affecting football players' access to the employment market in other Member States.[67] In *Smits en Peerbooms, Vanbraekel* and *Mac Quen* concerning

---

[61] Barnard (2004), pp. 238-240; see also Luijendijk (2005), p. 166. In Case C-405/98, *Gourmet International*, the Court had the possibility to extend its *Keck* approach to the free movement of services, but did not do so.

[62] Case C-254/98, *TK-Heimdienst Sass*, paragraph 25; See annotation E. Spaventa, *CMLRev.*, 2000, p. 1266.

[63] Case C-254/98, *TK-Heimdienst Sass*, paragraph 26.

[64] Case C-322/01, *0800 Doc Morris NV*.

[65] Case C-322/01, *0800 Doc Morris NV*, paragraph 74.

[66] Case C-384/93, *Alpine Investments*.

[67] See *supra* Case C-415/93, *Bosman*.

the application of the free movement rules to the health care sector, the Court also used a market access based test to determine whether the free movement of services and freedom of establishment were restricted.[68] In *Smits en Peerbooms* the Court concluded that national rules, providing that a person insured under the sickness insurance fund requires prior authorisation from this insurance fund in order to claim his entitlement to benefits from a person or establishment outside the Netherlands, "deter, or even prevent, insured persons from applying to providers of medical services established in other Member States and this constitutes, both for insured persons and service providers, a barrier to freedom to provide services".[69] The Court hereby referred to its judgment in *Kohll* concerning the refusal by the Luxembourg health insurance fund to reimburse the costs for a medical treatment in Germany.[70] In the *Vanbraekel* case the Court held that "the fact that a person has a lower level of cover when he receives hospital treatment in another Member State than when he undergoes the same treatment in the Member State in which he is insured may deter, or even prevent, that person from applying to providers of medical services established in another Member States and constitutes, both for insured persons and for service providers, a barrier to freedom to provide services".[71] In *Mac Quen* concerning Belgian legislation prohibiting opticians from carrying out certain optical examinations the Court referred to it's ruling in *Gebhard*.[72]

The case law shows that market access has become the main criterion for adjudicating national legislation under the prohibitive rules on free movement, which entails that national rules preventing or hindering market access are unlawful, irrespective of whether they discriminate against other products, services, persons or capital.[73]

3.2 Selling arrangements

The foregoing shows that the Court has generally embraced a broad interpretation of the prohibitive Treaty provisions on free movement. With regard to certain national measures regulating selling arrangements, though, the much-debated *Keck* case introduced at the time a turning point in the case law on the free movement of goods.[74] In this case the Court placed national rules

---

68 See also annotation J.W. van de Gronden, *SEW*, 2001, pp. 319-331.

69 Case C-157/99, *Smits and Peerbooms*.

70 Case C-158/96, *Kohll*; see also annotation R. Giesen, *CMLRev.*, 1999, pp. 841-850.

71 Case C-368/98, *Vanbraekel*.

72 Case C-108/96, *Mac Quen*, paragraphs 25 and 26.

73 Barnard (2004), p. 19 and pp. 256-261: Spaventa, however, prefers to describe the Court's case law in terms of granting an individual right to exercise an economic activity free of disproportionate regulation rather than in terms of market access: E. Spaventa, From *Gebhard* to *Carpenter*: Towards a (non-)economic European constitution, *CMLRev.*, 2004, pp. 743-773.

74 Joined Cases C-267/91 and 268/91, *Keck*.

on selling arrangements outside the scope of Article 28 EC, provided that these rules apply to all affected traders operating within the national territory and provided that they affect in the same manner, in law and in fact, the marketing of domestic products and those from other Member States. Here the legal commitment to free trade appears to entail the abolition of discrimination, or protectionism, but no more.[75] *Keck* makes clear that Article 28 EC does not necessarily seek to liberalise economic activities within a Member State, or rather that not all market interventions hinder market access.[76] Where national rules address particularly local interests, such as the opening hours for shops or the prohibition of resale at a loss, the impact on trade must be assumed negligible.

In several cases before *Keck*, in particular the *Sunday Trading* cases,[77] the Court was confronted with essentially internally conflicting interests which could not be solved with reference to its *Dassonville* jurisprudence. Whether legislation restricting sales on Sundays was proportionate was a question which led to different decisions adopted by the British courts. In other words, the Court had left the 'hot potatoe' in the hands of the national courts.[78] The point of departure after *Keck* is that certain national rules on resale at a loss;[79] on advertising;[80] concerning the exclusive right for retailers to sell certain goods;[81] and on shop closing legislation[82] have been held by the Court to restrict or prohibit certain selling arrangements. These type of rules should be distinguished from product related measures, or product requirements, for which the *Dassonville* case law continues to be relevant.

From the perspective of horizontal and flanking policies regulating certain selling arrangements there is, according to the *Keck* methodology, no need to invoke a justification ground under the Treaty or under the rule of reason. The question then is to what extent *Keck* is really relevant for horizontal and flanking policies. From the Court's case law it appears that *Keck* cannot be relied upon for a national measure to fall outside the scope of Article 28 EC just like that. Where in the *Greek Baby Food* case the requirement to sell baby food in a pharmacy was

---

75 At dawn, just before the Court gave its judgment in *Keck* AG Tesauro, in his search to the rationale behind the Court's case law, asked himself the following question: "is Article 30 (now Article 28 EC) a provision which seeks to liberalise trade between Member States, or quite simply does it seek to liberalise the pursuit of economic activities within a Member State as well?" AG Tesauro in Case C-292/92, *Hünermund*, see: G. Tesauro, The Community's Internal Market in the light of the Recent Case-law of the Court of Justice, *Yearbook of European Law*, 1996, p. 5.

76 S. Weatherill, After *Keck*: Some thoughts on how to clarify the clarification, *CMLRev.*, 1996, p. 896.

77 For example Case C-145/88, *Torfaen*.

78 Maduro (1998), p. 33.

79 Joined Cases C-267/91 and 268/91, *Keck*.

80 Case C-292/92, *Hünermund*; Case C-412/93, *Leclerc-TF 1*; Joined Cases C-34/95, C-35/95 and C-36/95, *De Agostini*.

81 Case C-391/92, *Commission v. Greek (Baby Food)*; Case C-387/93, *Banchero*; C-162/97, *Gunnar Nilsson*.

82 Joined Cases C-401/92 and 402/92, *'t Heukske*; Joined Cases C-69/93 and 258/93, *Punto Casa*.

regarded as a selling arrangement and fell outside the scope of Article 28 EC, because the Greek measure did not regulate the characteristics of the concerned products,[83] in the previously discussed *Doc Morris* case, the requirement to sell medicines in pharmacies for public health reasons was considered to affect market access and hence fell within the scope of Article 28 EC.

Furthermore, where the measure even slightly bears on the content of the product, it is considered product-related and cannot be regarded as concerned with a selling arrangement. This appears from *Familiapress*, where the Court held that Austrian legislation prohibiting certain prize competitions in periodicals for maintenance of press diversity, even though directed against a certain method of sales promotion, nevertheless bears on the actual content of the product, in so far as the competitions in question form an integral part of the magazine in which they appear.[84] In the *Danish Bees* case the Danish government argued that the prohibition on keeping certain bees on the island of Læsø should be regarded as relating to a selling arrangement within the meaning of the *Keck* judgment. The Court, however, found that the legislation was product-related and did not concern the conditions of sale.[85]

The importance of *Keck* should thus be placed into perspective. The fact that the *Keck* reasoning is difficult to apply in practice is most notably shown by the cases on advertising rules. In *De Agostini* the Court held that it could not be excluded that an outright prohibition of a type of promotion for a product lawfully sold in another Member State may have a greater impact on products from Member States. Apparently not all advertising rules should be regarded as provisions regulating selling arrangements. The *Gourmet* ruling has confirmed this.[86] In this case the Court denied the application of the *Keck* formula to a Swedish law prohibiting the advertising of alcoholic beverages. Under the Swedish Alcohol Advertising Law commercial advertising of alcoholic beverages (more than 2.25% of alcohol by volume) in the press, on radio or on television is in principle prohibited. GIP publishes the periodical Gourmet containing advertisements for alcoholic beverages (wine and whisky) placed by importers, which, according to the Consumer Ombudsman, constitutes advertising within the meaning of the Alcohol Advertising Law. The Court held that "a prohibition of all advertising directed at consumers in the form of advertisements in the press, on the radio and on television, the direct mailing of unsolicited material or the placing of posters on the public highway is liable to impede access to the market by products from other Member States more than it impedes access by domestic

---

[83] This case was particularly criticised as regards the implications of the *Keck* ruling: see: S. Weatherill, After *Keck*: Some thoughts on how to clarify the clarification, *CMLRev.*, 1996, p. 888; annotation J.H. Jans, *SEW*, 1996, p. 386.

[84] Case C-368/95, *Familiapress.*

[85] Case C-67/97, *Bluhme (Danish Bees).*

[86] Case C-405/98, *Gourmet International.*

products, with which consumers are instantly more familiar".[87] Since it affected the marketing of products from other Member States more heavily than the marketing of domestic products, the second requirement of *Keck* – provided that the national rules affect in the same manner in fact the marketing of domestic products and those from other Member States – had not been fulfilled and the Swedish provision fell within the scope of Article 28 EC.[88]

The *Gourmet* case as well as the previously discussed *TK Heimdienst Sass* and *Doc Morris* cases make clear that the Court is increasingly prepared to work with a market access based test within the context of Article 28 EC. The outcome of the case law is that if a measure is classified as product requirement, it will be presumed to impede market access, which has been referred to as the *per se illegal* approach; if, on the other hand, the measure is classified as a selling arrangement, the presumption will be that it does not restrict market access, which has been referred to as the *per se legal* approach. This presumption can be rebutted, if it is shown (in fact) that the national law in question hinders market access.[89]

3.3 Inherent restrictions

Until now it appears that within the framework of the prohibitions little or no account can be taken of horizontal and flanking policy considerations. This could be different in case of the inherent restriction approach. From the case law in the field of sport and Community law, it appears that certain rules laid down by sporting associations will not be considered a restriction within the meaning of Article 49 EC, if they are inherent in the conduct of a sports event.[90] In the *Deliège* case preliminary questions were raised on the interpretation of the Treaty provisions on services (in particular Article 49 EC) and competition (Articles 81 and 82 EC) with regard to the refusal by the French and Belgian Judo leagues to select Christelle Deliège to participate in the Paris International Judo Tournament in the under-52 kg category. In contrast with *Bosman* the selection rules at issue were not considered to determine the conditions governing access to the labour market by professional sportsmen. The Court held that "although selection rules like those at issue in the main

87 Case C-405/98, *Gourmet International*, paragraph 21.

88 Most recently, the Court in *Burmanjer* was even willing to return to its old case law on 'hypothetical situations' in respect of a Belgian law that had clearly been qualified as a selling arrangement by making the itinerant sale of subscriptions to periodicals subject to prior authorisation. According to the Court even if it were established that market access for products from other Member States could be affected, the effects of the Belgian law would still be too insignificant and uncertain for them to hinder trade between Member States. It will have to be awaited whether the Court pursues this line of reasoning in future case law: Case C-20/03, *Burmanjer*.

89 Barnard (2004), p. 143.

90 Joined Cases C-51/96 and C-191/97, *Deliège*.

proceedings inevitably have the effect of limiting the number of participants in a tournament, such a limitation is *inherent in the conduct of an international high-level sports event,* which *necessarily* involves certain selection rules or criteria being adopted. Such rules may not therefore *in themselves* be regarded as constituting a restriction on the freedom to provide services prohibited by Article 49 of the Treaty (my Italics)." The Court did not answer the questions on Articles 81 and 82 EC.

The status of this approach with regard to the free movement rules is somewhat unclear. In the *Lehtonen* case, which ruling came two days later, the Court also referred to objective reasons concerning only sport, but came to the conclusion that rules of the Basketball Federation prohibiting a basketball club from fielding players from other Member States in matches in the national championship, where the transfer has taken place after a specified date, nevertheless formed an obstacle to the free movement workers.[91]

Where in *Deliège* non-discriminatory rules that do no substantially hinder market access, were concerned, which from the interest of subsidiarity should fall outside the prohibitive scope of Community law,[92] in *Lehtonen* rules that hindered market access and fell within the scope of the prohibitions, hence needing to be justified, were concerned. Apparently a distinction must be made between rules laid down by sporting associations that are inherent in the conduct of the sports event, where objectives of sport override objectives of an economic nature, and rules of sporting associations that affect market access and therefore restrict the free movement of persons, but may nevertheless be justified on non-economic grounds relating to sport as such.[93] With regard to the first type of rules (*Deliège*) it is not necessary to invoke a justification ground and consequently to prove that the rules are necessary and proportionate since they are not considered a restriction on free movement in the first place.

Hence, the scope of application of the inherent restriction approach remains limited to those situations where certain types of rules are involved which do not substantially restrict market access; furthermore, the need for this approach in the context of free movement, where a possibility exists to invoke non-economic justification grounds, is much less pertinent than in the context of the competition rules, where explicit exception grounds for horizontal and flanking policy interests do not, or only hardly exist (see hereafter Chapter 3).

---

91 Case C-176/96, *Lehtonen*; see also annotation K.J.M. Mortelmans and M.G. Wezenbeek-Geuke, *SEW*, 2000, p. 425.

92 Barnard (2004), p. 240.

93 Vogelaar (2000).

3.4 Article 29 EC and the exportation of goods

Article 29 EC plays a much less predominant role than Article 28 EC and is therefore only briefly referred to. Contrary to Article 28 EC on imports, Article 29 EC on exports only prohibits distinctly applicable measures. Member States may have several motives to restrict the exportation of goods,[94] for example, to secure supplies of a certain product,[95] to protect the preservation of works of art for the nation, to protect the environment, or to protect the life and health of animals.[96] The *Groenveld* ruling makes clear that Article 29 EC should be more restrictively interpreted than Article 28 on imports.[97] The Court held that "Article 29 concerns national measures which have as their specific object or effect the restriction of patterns of exports and thereby the establishment of a difference between the domestic trade of a Member State and its export trade in such a way as to provide a particular advantage for national production or for the domestic market of the state in question at the expense of the production or the trade of other Member States".[98]

The *Groenveld* formula has been applied in subsequent case law, such as the *Dusseldorp* case,[99] which concerned a Dutch measure banning the export of oil filters and waste to Germany, and the *Compassion* case involving a ban or restriction on the export of live calves from one Member State to another Member State.[100] The consequence of the Court's case law is that the rule of reason exceptions in principle do not apply to export restrictions. Article 30 EC, on the other hand, continues to be relevant for possible justification of national measures restricting exports.

---

94 Oliver (assisted by Malcolm Jarvis) (2003), pp. 138-139: he mentions five possible motives for Member States to restrict the exportation of goods: A desire to ensure supplies; the protection of jobs in processing industries; the prevention of parallel exports; the maintenance of the quality of exports and the preservation of works of art for the nation.

95 Case 72/83, *Campus Oil.*

96 E.g. Case C-5/94, *Hedley Lomas*; Case C-1/96, *Compassion.*

97 Some authors are in favour of this more restrictive approach, like: Oliver (assisted by Malcolm Jarvis) (2003), pp. 140-141; the question is whether the case law on the free movement of persons and services, which provisions do not distinguish between 'exports' and 'imports', should not be followed in respect of goods as well: Barnard (2004), pp. 152-153; Kapteyn & VerLoren van Themaat (2003), pp. 540-541.

98 Case 15/79, *Groenveld.*

99 Case C-203/96, *Dusseldorp*, paragraph 42.

100 Case C-1/96, *Compassion*; see also Case C-47/90, *Delhaize* and Case C-388/95, *Belgium v. Spain (Rioja)*, where the Court held that the obligation to bottle Rioja wine in the region of production establishes a difference of treatment between trade within a Member State and its export trade within the meaning of Article 29 EC; This was confirmed in Case 237/82, *Jongeneel Kaas*, where the Court considered that certain quality requirements on exports fell within the scope of application of Article 29 EC.

3.5 Tariff barriers

Articles 25 and 90 EC address tariff barriers; whereas Article 25 EC is concerned with charges imposed on goods by reason of the fact that they cross a frontier, Article 90 EC deals with internal taxation; barriers which are created on the basis of a system of internal dues.

3.5.1 Article 25 EC

According to Article 23 EC the Community is based on a customs union. This implies, according to Article 25 EC, that "customs duties on imports and all charges having equivalent effect shall be prohibited between Member States. This prohibition shall also apply to customs duties of a fiscal nature."

Charges having equivalent effect have been defined by the Court as "any pecuniary charge, however small, whatever its designation and mode of application imposed unilaterally on domestic or foreign goods by reason of the fact that they cross a frontier even if it is not imposed for the benefit of the State, is not discriminatory or protective in effect and if the product on which the charge is imposed is not in competition with the domestic product".[101]

Article 25 EC contains an absolute prohibition; there are only three situations which cannot really be considered as exception but which do not fall within the definition of customs duty or charge having equivalent effect:

- Payments made for administrative services provided for the importer;
- Charges for compliance with mandatory inspections required by Community law;
- Charges that should be considered internal taxation.

Apparently, there is no place for the consideration of horizontal and flanking policy interests within the scope of Article 25 EC. The exceptions contained in Article 30 EC, like the protection of public health, cannot be invoked in respect of Article 25 EC.[102]

3.5.2 Article 90 EC

Contrary to Article 25 EC, horizontal and flanking policy interests may, as appears from the case law, play a role within the context of Article 90 EC, prohibiting both directly and indirectly discriminatory taxes on goods. Fiscal measures may be an important instrument of horizontal and

---

[101] Case 24/68, *Commission v. Italy*.

[102] Case 46/76, *Bauhuis*.

flanking policies: apart from the fact that they are an effective revenue-raising mechanism, they may also reflect social, health and environmental concerns.[103]

In *Outokumpu Oy* the Court makes explicit that environmental considerations may constitute, within the framework of Article 90 EC, an objective justification for fiscal national legislation, even though in this case the Finnish law on excise duty on certain sources of energy could not be justified. The Court ruled that a differential tax system, with variable rates of duty according to the environmental friendliness of the production method, violated Article 90 EC, because imported electricity was in some cases more heavily taxed than domestic electricity. For imported electricity a flat rate of duty was applied, which corresponded to the average rate levied on electricity produced in Finland. For electricity produced in Finland, the duties varied according to the production method. According to the Finnish government in view of the unusual commodity which electricity is, differential rates cannot sensibly be applied to imported electricity, because of the impossibility of identifying the source, and consequently the method of production, once it has entered the distribution network.

The tax system could, however, not be justified, because the Finnish legislation at issue did not give the importer the opportunity to demonstrate that the electricity imported had been produced by a particular method. The Court did refer to the difficulty of determining the precise method of production of imported electricity and hence the primary energy sources, but nevertheless considered that the Finnish legislation was disproportionate. The reasoning of the Court leaves the door open in terms of burden of proof for importers of foreign electricity, by suggesting that the requirement of a certificate of origin as to the method of production of electricity demonstrated by importers of electricity, is an alternative and more proportionate measure than the application of a flat-rate duty on imported electricity. This suggests that directly discriminatory ecological tax legislation may, under certain strict conditions, be upheld under Article 90 EC.[104]

3.6 Conclusions

Generally it seems that there is little scope for the consideration of horizontal and flanking policy interests under the Treaty provisions addressing tariff barriers. Only within the context of Article 90 EC may horizontal and

[103] See also Ch. Denys, European Court of Justice: Case Report, *EELR*, 1998, p. 285. According to the Commission in its *Communication on the sixth environmental action programme: Environment 2010: Our future, Our choice*, "environmental taxes can be highly effective in both cost and environmental terms [...]. They also provide incentives for companies to research and invest in more-environmentally friendly or less resource intensive technologies. This makes them particularly attractive for problems of a long-term nature." (COM(2001) 31 final, p. 15).

[104] Ch. Denys, European Court of Justice: Case Report, *EELR*, 1998, pp. 285-286.

flanking policy reasons play a role. Although the case law is still evolving in this respect, the Court seems to suggest that at least environmental policy reasons could justify discriminatory, but proportionate, tax barriers.

Within the scope of the other prohibitive Treaty rules on free movement there is hardly any room to take account of horizontal and flanking policy interests. The *Keck* jurisprudence, which application so far is limited to Article 28 EC, appears to be of only little relevance to horizontal and flanking policies; this may be different in the case of so-called inherent restrictions. The scope of this doctrine in respect of the free movement rules, however, is rather limited. The emphasis in the case law on market access has at least the potential to bring numerous national horizontal and flanking policy measures within the ambit of the prohibitive Treaty rules on free movement.

4 The application of the free movement rules: the exceptions

A national measure restricting market access within the meaning of the free movement rules will not necessarily have to be removed, if it can be justified by an exception laid down in the Treaty or under the rule of reason as formulated in the case law of the Court. In this chapter the focus of attention is laid upon the relationship between the exceptions and national measures protecting *national* horizontal and flanking policy interests within the territory of the regulating state. Since states are increasingly willing to take action to protect e.g. the environment or welfare of animals outside their territory, the question of the extent to which the exceptions can be invoked for *externally directed* trade measures has become increasingly pertinent.

Extra-territorial protection impinges upon the sovereignty of states and may threaten the decentralised decision-making structure in the internal market.[105] There is, however, a common responsibility reflected by the Treaty towards the protection of horizontal and flanking policies.[106] Since this issue of extra-territorial protection of horizontal and flanking policy interests is highly contentious, it will only be briefly mentioned within the context of the respective horizontal and flanking policy fields, but not be further assessed.

4.1 The scope of the Treaty exceptions

The Treaty provides for a limited number of justification grounds, which can be invoked for both distinctly and indistinctly applicable measures. According to Article 30 EC the provisions of Articles 28 and 29 EC

105 W.-H. Roth, Altruistische Interessenwahrnehmung im Binnenmarkt – Eine Skizze, in: *Festschrift für Wolfgang Fikentscher zum 70. Geburtstag* (Mohr Siebeck, Tübingen, 1998), p. 723.

106 Sevenster (1998).

shall not preclude prohibitions or restrictions on imports, exports or goods in transit justified on grounds of public morality, public policy, public security, the protection of health and life of humans, animals or plants, the protection of national treasures possessing artistic, historic or archaeological value, or the protection of industrial and commercial property. To be justified on the basis of Article 30 EC a national provision must:

- Fall within one of the grounds of justification set out in the first sentence of Article 30 EC; and must
- Not constitute arbitrary discrimination or a disguised restriction on trade between Member States.[107]

Article 39(3) EC contains particular exceptions – public policy, public security and public health – for restrictions on the free movement of workers. Article 46 EC contains justification grounds (public policy, public security and public health) for restrictions on the freedom of establishment, and the free movement of services (in conjunction with Article 55 EC).

The Court has often held that the fact that these Treaty provisions form exceptions to the free movement rules entails that they have to be interpreted restrictively.[108] It will be seen to what extent this still goes true. The question of whether Member States' discretion to invoke the Treaty exceptions is indeed still severely restricted will be further answered in Chapters 5 and 6.

Furthermore, the Treaty provisions contain an exhaustive list of exceptions. They cannot be extended to cover other horizontal and flanking policy interests than are mentioned in the respective provisions. The protection of the living environment, for example, is not included in the list of exceptions contained in Article 30 EC. Environmental measures will therefore only be justified on the basis of Article 30 EC, if they have a direct influence on the protection of humans, animals or plants.[109]

4.2 Overriding requirements of public interest

Contrary to the Treaty provisions, the 'rule of reason' exceptions or mandatory requirements, or increasingly called overriding requirements of public interest, developed in the case law and do not form a closed class of justification grounds, but allow the Court to add new justification grounds whenever deemed necessary. The material scope is wider and therefore offers Member

[107] Oliver (assisted by Malcolm Jarvis) (2003), p. 216.

[108] Case 46/76, *Bauhuis*.

[109] See also H. Temmink, From Danish Bottles to Danish Bees: The Dynamics of Free Movement of Goods and Environmental Protection – A Case Law Analysis, in: H. Somsen (Ed.), *Yearbook of European Environmental Law* (Oxford University Press, Oxford, 2000), p. 87. See, for example, Case C-203/96, *Dusseldorp* and Case C-389/96, *Aher Waggon*.

States more latitude to take protective measures than the Treaty exceptions did. The rule of reason was introduced in the *Dassonville* case[110] and further specified and clarified in the *Cassis de Dijon* case[111] and subsequent cases. In *Dassonville* the Court held that "in the absence of a Community system guaranteeing for consumers the authenticity of a product's designation of origin, if a Member State takes measures to prevent unfair practices in this connection, it is subject to the condition that these measures should be *reasonable* and that the means of proof required should not act as a hindrance to trade between Member States and should in consequence be accessible to all Community nationals" (my Italics).

In *Cassis de Dijon* the Court accepted that mandatory requirements related in particular to the effectiveness of fiscal supervision, the protection of public health, the fairness of commercial transactions and the defence of the consumer might justify restrictions on intra-Community trade: "Obstacles to movement within the Community resulting in disparities between the national laws relating to the marketing of the products in question must be accepted in so far as those provisions may be recognised as being necessary in order to satisfy mandatory requirements relating in particular to the effectiveness of fiscal supervision, the protection of health, the fairness of commercial transactions and the defence of the consumer."[112]

Accordingly, Member States may restrict intra-Community trade for motives other than those mentioned in Article 30 EC, provided that the measure applies without distinction and that no Community harmonisation measure has been adopted. In later case law other horizontal and flanking policy interests have been added to the list of mandatory requirements, such as the protection of the environment, the protection of pluralism in the audio-visual sector, the protection of a language or the maintenance of press diversity (see hereafter).

4.3 Conditions for invoking the exceptions

There are three conditions that have to be fulfilled in order to successfully rely upon either the Treaty exceptions or overriding requirements of public interest: first, recourse to the exceptions will in principle be excluded, if the subject matter has already been covered by a harmonisation measure; second the protected interest must be 'non-economic', and third and very important, the principle of proportionality must be respected.

---

110 Case 8/74, *Dassonville*.

111 Case 120/78, *Cassis de Dijon*.

112 Case 120/78, *Cassis de Dijon*, paragraph 8.

4.3.1 No harmonisation measure

In the *Tedeschi* case the Court held that "where [...] Community Directives provide for the harmonisation of the measures necessary to ensure the protection of animal and human health and establish Community procedures to check that they are observed, recourse to Article 30 is no longer justified and the appropriate checks must be carried out and the measures of protection adopted within the framework outlined by the harmonising directive".[113] The introduction of harmonisation measures in a certain area in principle removes the availability of justification grounds under the Treaty exceptions or under the rule of reason. Pending harmonisation the Treaty rules on free movement apply to national trade barriers. Once harmonisation has been achieved recourse to the exceptions or the rule of reason is thus excluded.

Depending on the expiring of the implementation period, on the exhaustive nature of the harmonisation measure and the harmonisation technique that is used, the scope of reserved powers of Member States following harmonisation can be determined. This will be discussed more extensively in Chapter 4.

4.3.2 Non-economic interests

The Treaty exceptions and the mandatory requirements are essentially directed 'to eventualities of a non-economic kind'. However, where measures are equally based on economic and non-economic grounds, the Court may regard them as justifiable. The *Campus Oil* case concerned an Irish measure requiring importers to purchase petroleum products from the one remaining Irish refinery, particularly to ensure essential supplies, in the event of a crisis. The nature of the measure was also clearly economic for it served to keep the refinery in operation. The Court confirmed that Article 30 EC refers to non-economic matters, but went on by stating "however in the light of seriousness of the consequences that an interruption in supplies of petroleum products may have for a country's existence, the aim of ensuring a minimum supply of petroleum products at all times is to be regarded as transcending purely economic considerations and thus as capable as constituting an objective covered by the concept of public security".[114] Economic interests are thus taken into account in deciding whether an infringement of Article 28 EC can be justified on the basis of Article 30 EC.[115]

In *Evans Medical* the Court held that a restriction could not be justified by the Member State's wish to safeguard the survival of an undertaking.[116] Never-

---

[113] Case 5/77, *Tedeschi*, paragraph 35; see also, for example, Case 148/78, *Ratti* and Case 15/83, *Denkavit*.

[114] Case 72/83, *Campus Oil*,.

[115] K. Mortelmans, Towards convergence in application of the rules on free movement and competition, *CMLRev.*, 2001, p. 637.

[116] Case C-324/93, *Evans Medical*; see also Case C 238/82, *Duphar.*

theless, "the need to ensure that a country has reliable supplies for essential medical purposes may under Article 30 of the Treaty justify a barrier to intra-Community trade if that objective is one of protecting health and life of humans". It appears that where aims of a purely economic nature are predominant, the measure will not be justified.[117]

It remains difficult, however, to draw a dividing line between economic and non-economic aims. In the *Bond van Adverteerders* case the Court refused to accept that provisions on advertising in the Dutch media law were also intended to pursue objectives of a cultural nature. The national measures at issue restricted the relaying of advertisements broadcast from other Member States and were therefore discriminatory. The only exception available was Article 46 EC, in particular the ground of public policy. According to the Court, the rules resulted in the protection of the revenue of STER (the association for television advertisements), so they are construed in a manner that their aim is economic.[118] It was therefore not possible to rely on Articles 46 and 55 EC. With similar arguments the Court refused to justify a Spanish distribution scheme for the fostering of Spanish film production on the basis of Article 46 EC, since the measure should be regarded as economic.[119]

The condition that only non-economic interests can be invoked to justify trade restrictions can be particularly problematic in the field of export of waste. Member States prohibit the export of waste to ensure that their own installations can operate profitably. In *Dusseldorp* the Netherlands argued that an export ban on oil filters was necessary in order to ensure sufficient raw materials and business to enable AVR Chemie, responsible for waste management, to operate in a profitable manner and to ensure a sufficient supply of oil filters for use as fuel.[120] According to the Court, though, this argument should be rejected since settled case law supported the view that purely economic aims cannot justify barriers to the fundamental principle of the free movement of goods. In *Sydhavnens Sten and Grus* the Court seems to be milder by acknowledging that not all restrictions on export of waste can be justified on environmental grounds. It is noteworthy that the Court takes a different approach to the profitability of the undertakings in the two areas of free movement and competition. In the context of Article 29 EC (*Dusseldorp*) an export ban to guarantee profitability could not be justified on environmental grounds, whereas an exclusive right to guarantee profitability in the context of Article 86 EC (*Sydhavnens*) could be justified on

[117] Oliver (assisted by Malcolm Jarvis) (2003), p. 236.

[118] Case 352/85, *Bond van Adverteerders.*

[119] Case C-17/92, *Fedicine.*

[120] Case C-203/96, *Dusseldorp.*

environmental grounds, because the profitability of national undertakings was instrumental to the objective of environmental protection.[121]

In *Smits and Peerbooms*, however, the Court admitted that economic reasons were instrumental to the objective of protection of public health and could justify restrictions on the free movement of medical services. In this case a Dutch court referred preliminary questions to the Court of Justice on the interpretation of Article 49 EC in relation with the Dutch Law on sickness funds. It essentially asked whether Article 49 EC precludes legislation of a Member State which makes the assumption of the costs of care provided in a hospital in another Member State conditional upon prior authorisation by the sickness insurance fund with which the insured person is registered. Authorisation will only be granted if the following two conditions are met. First, the proposed treatment must be among the benefits for which the insured person can claim entitlement, which means that the treatment must be regarded as normal in the professional circles concerned. Second, the treatment abroad must be necessary in terms of the medical condition of the person concerned, which supposes that adequate care cannot be provided without undue delay by a care provider which has entered into an agreement with a sickness insurance fund in the first Member State.

According to the Court it can be seen from the contracting system in the Netherlands that planning (e.g. for the number of hospitals, their geographical distribution, the mode of their organisation and the equipment they are fitted out with) broadly meets a variety of concerns, such as the aim to ensure that there is sufficient and permanent access to a balanced range of high quality hospital treatment and the desire to control costs and prevent any wastage of financial, technical and human resources.[122] The fact that the Court accepted this 'forward-planning argument' as a legitimate reason to restrict the free movement of medical services is remarkable, because it may lead to the protection of the national market of hospital treatment from markets in other Member States.[123]

---

[121] N. Notaro, European Community Waste Movements: the Copenhagen Waste Case, *EELR*, 2000, p. 311; see also H. Temmink, From Danish Bottles to Danish Bees: The Dynamics of Free Movement of Goods and Environmental Protection – A Case Law Analysis, in: H. Somsen (Ed.), *Yearbook of European Environmental Law* (Oxford University Press, Oxford, 2000), p. 95 and K. Mortelmans, Towards convergence in the application of the rules on free movement and on competition, *CMLRev.*, 2001, p. 644.

[122] Case C-157/99, *Smits and Peerbooms*, paragraphs 76-79.

[123] See also annotation J.W. van de Gronden, *SEW*, 2001, p. 328. In paragraph 53 of the Joined Opinion in Cases C-120/95, *Decker* and C-158/96, *Kohll*, AG Tesauro states with regard to the exception ground of safeguarding the financial stability of the hospital system that "while it is true that the Court has on occasion categorically dismissed economic aims put forward to justify indistinctly applicable measures (as well), it is also apparent, on a closer reading of the relevant judgments, that economic aims are indeed justifiable, where far from being an end in themselves, they are crucial to the operation of the system in question or affect interests of vital importance to the State".

The overall result of the case law is that where it is clear that economic aims are crucial for the realisation of 'non-economic' aims, they are justifiable. Purely economic arguments, however, can never serve as a justification within the context of the free movement rules.[124] What matters is whether the national measure has a protectionist motive or purpose to be accepted under Community law. Thereby it is essential that the national state gives clear and relevant arguments that its measure truly serves horizontal and flanking policy aims, which may not have been the case in the *Dusseldorp* case.[125]

4.3.3 Proportionality

Apart from the condition that the national measure must be non-economic in nature, the measure must also be necessary and proportionate to its aim. The proportionality test plays a principal role in balancing horizontal and flanking policy interests with the requirements of free movement.

The proportionality test may contain the following three elements. Firstly, there must be a causal connection between the measure adopted and the aim pursued, that is to say the measure is relevant or pertinent. It is important for the Court to assess whether the national measure truly aims at protecting horizontal and flanking policy interests, or has a more protectionist motive. Secondly, there is no alternative to it, which is less restrictive of one of the four freedoms. This criterion of the least restrictive alternative means that the national measure must not be capable of being replaced by an alternative rule, which is equally useful but less restrictive to one of the freedoms. Within this context the principle of mutual recognition or doctrine of functional parallelism plays a significant role. The foundations of the doctrine of mutual recognition were laid down in *Cassis de Dijon*: "There is therefore no valid reason why, provided that they have been lawfully produced and marketed in one of the Member States, alcoholic beverages should not be introduced into any other Member State".[126] The idea is that every Member State must respect the traditions of other Member States and that, consequently, once a product has been lawfully produced and marketed in one Member State, it is entitled to free circulation within the Community save in exceptional circumstances.[127] If a Member

---

[124] Case C-398/98, *Commission v. Greece*, paragraph 30. The Greek government had argued that the objective of maintaining a stock of petroleum products on Greek territory was necessary for reasons of public security, since otherwise the refineries' fundamental right to economic freedom would be excessively restricted if they were required to store the minimum stocks of petroleum products, and thus assume an obligation of the marketing companies, if the latter were not required in return to purchase their supplies from those refineries (at paragraph 21).

[125] See with regard to the Dutch government's reasoning under Article 86(2) EC: Vedder (2003), pp.271-276; see also Chapter 3, section 3.2.3.

[126] Case 120/78, *Cassis de Dijon*, paragraph 14.

[127] Weatherill and Beaumont (1999), p. 569.

State insists on a different standard than the State where the product or service has been lawfully marketed, it will have adopted a measure which is not the least restrictive alternative possible.[128]

Lastly, there must be a relationship of proportionality between the obstacle introduced, on the one hand, and, on the other hand, the objective pursued thereby and its actual attainment. This element is generally considered to refer to the principle of proportionality *stricto sensu*, or the *Angemessenheit* of the national measure.[129] It means that a national measure will be regarded disproportionate, if the restriction caused is out of proportion to the aim sought by or the result brought about by the national rule.[130]

Whereas it will probably not be too difficult for the Court to deal with the first element of the proportionality test, the third element will be the most problematic, as it requires the Court to balance various conflicting interests, such as the functioning of the internal market against the protection of horizontal and flanking concerns.[131] The level of the protection of the environment, for example, will then be balanced against the harm to intra-Community trade.[132] This suggests that the Court controls whether the level of protection chosen by a Member State is reasonable and when the level of protection is perceived as unreasonable the Court will reduce it.[133] As will be seen hereafter, the Court rarely applies all three elements and sometimes even passes over the question of proportionality. It will also depend on the availability of sufficient factual information whether the Court settles the issue itself (in direct actions), or whether it leaves it to national courts to decide on the matter (in preliminary rulings).[134] Furthermore, the Court must be reluctant in putting itself in the place of the legislature, which may be overcome using marginal review and respecting the policy discretion of the legislature.

The application of the proportionality principle in the context of the free movement rules has an additional dimension, as it involves a question of separation of powers between the European Community and its Member States. This becomes particularly apparent when the Court in applying the third element of proportionality determines the degree of protection and then balances this

---

128 J.H.H. Weiler, The Constitution of the Common Market Place, in: P. Craig and G. de Búrca, *The Evolution of EU Law* (Oxford University Press, Oxford, 1999), p. 367.

129 See in the context of goods in particular the Opinion of AG Van Gerven in Case C-169/89, *Gourmetterie Van den Burg*; See also J.H. Jans, Proportionality revisited, *LIEI*, 2000, p. 241.

130 See Opinion of AG Van Gerven in Case C-159/90, *Grogan*, paragraph 27.

131 J. H. Jans, Proportionality revisited, *LIEI*, 2000, p. 241.

132 Geradin (1997), p. 27.

133 Geradin (1997), p. 28.

134 H. Temmink, From Danish Bottles to Danish Bees: The Dynamics of Free Movement of Goods and Environmental Protection – A Case Law Analysis, in: H. Somsen (Ed.), *Yearbook of European Environmental Law* (Oxford University Press, Oxford, 2000), p. 35.

against the interest of market integration. In this legal context the principle of proportionality has two constitutional implications: concerning the relationship between the judiciary and the legislature in general and concerning the relationship between European Community and its Member States.[135] This is different from the application of the proportionality principle to *Community* measures, where the second element, i.e. the relationship between the European Community and its Member States is not really relevant and the Court favours a more self-restraint approach to the application of the proportionality principle (see Chapter 4).

4.4 The protection of horizontal and flanking policy interests

In this section it will be seen how the Court of Justice in its case law has balanced the protection of in particular the environment, consumers, public health and culture with the requirements of free movement. First, the relevance of the Treaty exceptions to each horizontal and flanking policy will be assessed and then the relevance of the 'rule of reason', or overriding requirements of public interest; thereafter it will be seen how the Court has applied the conditions of non-discrimination and proportionality.

4.4.1 The protection of the environment

The protection of the environment is not included as a specific exception ground in the Treaty provisions on free movement; nonetheless the Court has accepted that environmental policy reasons may justify restrictions on free movement. The cases that will be discussed here involve the protection of the domestic environment and not the extra-territorial protection of the environment, which the Court is very reluctant to accept.[136] It is even unclear whether, in case of extra-territorial effects of a national environmental measure being necessary for the protection of domestic interests, the measure may be upheld on environmental grounds, the 'boomerang theory'.[137]

---

[135] J. H. Jans, Proportionality revisited, *LIEI*, 2000, p. 242.

[136] In the field of the environment the question of extra-territoriality can also be related to the concept of environmental citizenship. If environmental identity is increasingly European or global, there will be pressure to enlarge the scope of (extra-territorial) environmental action: Ch. Hilson, Greening Citizenship: Boundaries of Membership and the Environment, *Journal of Environmental Law*, 2001, p. 335.

[137] See, for example, Case C-422/92, *Commission v. Germany*. In this case the Court addressed the question of justification of a restriction on the export of dangerous waste and hinted at the possibility to justify export restrictions if the disposal of hazardous waste in another Member State, particularly an adjacent Member State, could have serious environmental consequences in Germany. The questions in this case were, however, particularly concerned with the interpretation of provisions of the waste directives, and not with the interpretation of a Treaty provision on free movement.

4.4.1.1 The protection of health and life of humans, animals or plants: Article 30 EC

Article 30 EC is interpreted narrowly excluding situations which do not *directly* threaten the protection of health and life of humans, animals and plants. In the *Walloon Waste* case it was held that "so far as the environment is concerned, it should be observed that waste has a special characteristic. The accumulation of waste, even before it becomes a health hazard, constitutes a threat to the environment because of the limited capacity of each region or locality for receiving it".[138] In *Dusseldorp* the Court considered that a restriction on exporting oil filters could not be justified by Article 30, if the processing of oil filters in other Member States and their shipment over a greater distance did not pose a threat to the health and life of humans.[139]

By contrast, excessive noise emissions *can* form a threat to human health; Article 30 EC could therefore justify restrictions on those emissions.[140] Biocides, which are used to combat organisms harmful to human and animal health and liable to damage natural or manufactured products, inevitably contain dangerous substances. A prohibition to market these products may therefore be justifiable under Article 30 EC.[141] Similarly where plant protection products entail an actual health risk for humans, animals or plants, Article 30 EC may be invoked to justify restrictions on the import or marketing of those products. [142]

National measures aimed at the protection of welfare of animals are also justifiable in the light of Article 30 EC.[143] In *Danish Bees* the Court appears to have approved of a wider interpretation of Article 30 EC.[144] In that case a Danish measure designed to protect the brown bee on the small and remote island of Læsø was considered to preserve an indigenous animal population with distinct characteristics thereby contributing to the maintenance of bio-diversity and

138 Case C-2/90, *Commission v. Belgium (Walloon Waste)*; see also in particular the opinion of the Advocate-General who states that the import of non-dangerous waste cannot be restricted on the basis of protection of health and life of humans. At the most the import of non-dangerous waste could threaten the 'quality of life'.

139 Case C-203/96, *Dusseldorp*; see also Case C-209/98, *Sydhavnens Sten & Grus*.

140 Case C-389/96, *Aher Waggon*.

141 Case C-400/96, *Harpegnies*.

142 See, for example, Case 272/80, *Frans-Nederlandse Maatschappij voor Biologische Producten*.

143 E.g. Case C-1/96, *Compassion*; Case C-5/94, *Hedley Lomas*; Case C-350/97, *Monsees*; in the Constitution for Europe an integration clause in respect of animal welfare has been included in Article III-5a (under the provisions of general application) stipulating the following: "In formulating and implementing the Union's agriculture, fisheries, transport, internal market, research and technological development and space policies, the Union and the Member States shall pay full regard to the welfare requirements of animals, as sentient beings, while respecting the legislative and administrative provisions and customs of Member States relating in particular to religious rites, cultural traditions and regional heritage."

144 Jans (2000), p. 244.

therefore justifiable on the basis of Article 30 EC.[145] Nevertheless, distinctly applicable measures, which are more generally aimed at the protection of the environment, remain excluded from the scope of Article 30 EC.[146]

4.4.1.2 The protection of the environment as overriding requirement of public interest

The development of environmental protection under the rule of reason has been long into being. After *Inter-Huiles*[147] and *ADBHU*[148] the Court in *Danish Bottles* finally accepted environmental requirements as justifiable barriers to interstate trade, and explicitly stated that the protection of the environment is *a mandatory requirement which may limit the application of Article 30 (now Article 28 EC) of the treaty.*[149] Since then the case law has further developed with judgments like *Walloon Waste* and *PreussenElektra.*

4.4.1.3 The condition that environmental measures should apply without distinction

As stated above, it is well established case law that mandatory requirements, unlike the grounds of justification in Article 30 EC, may not be relied upon to justify national measures which are not applicable to domestic and imported products without distinction. In several cases, though, the Court in its interpretation of Article 28 EC follows a classic pattern, nevertheless upholding distinctly applicable national measures on environmental grounds.

In *Walloon Waste* the Court addressed the question of whether a regional measure prohibiting the storage, tipping or dumping of waste from other Member States or from Belgian regions other than Wallonia, could be justified by Community law. The Commission alleged the breach of two Community directives on waste: Directive 75/442 set out a general framework for waste and Directive 84/631 provided for a system of supervision and control of hazard-

---

[145] Case C-67/97, *Bluhme (Danish Bees)*; see Oliver (assisted by Malcolm Jarvis) (2003), p. 279: the protection of health and life of animals extends to animal welfare, and the following categories of animal or plant protection may be considered: the protection of rare or endangered species; the prevention of animal or plant diseases, in particular where those diseases may have harmful consequences for breeders or other persons with a commercial interest; and animal welfare.

[146] According to Webster's dictionary the environment can be defined as the circumstances, objects or conditions by which one is surrounded; the complex of physical, chemical and biotic factors (as climate, soil and living things) that act upon an organism or an ecological community and ultimately determine its form and survival.

[147] Case 172/82, *Inter-Huiles.*

[148] Case 240/83, *ADBHU.*

[149] Case 302/86, *Commission v. Denmark (Danish Bottles).*

ous waste.[150] The Walloon measure did not distinguish between hazardous and non-hazardous waste. After it had been established that Directive 75/442 did not refer to trade in waste between Member States and that the Walloon measure, in so far as it concerned hazardous waste, was not consistent with Directive 84/631, the Court examined whether the Belgian rules in question were in breach of Articles 28-30 EC, as far as these rules related to waste which is not covered by Directive 84/631, i.e. non-dangerous waste.

The Court held the following: "Imperative requirements can indeed be taken into account only in the case of measures which apply without distinction to both domestic and imported products. However, in assessing whether or not the barrier in question is discriminatory, account must be taken of the particular nature of waste. The principle that environmental damage should as a matter of priority be remedied at source, laid down by Article 174 (2) of the Treaty as a basis for action by the Community relating to the environment, entails that it is for each region, municipality or other local authority to take appropriate steps to ensure that its own waste is collected, treated and disposed of; it must accordingly be disposed of as close as possible to the place where it is produced, in order to limit as far as possible the transport of waste."[151] The principle of 'rectification at source' is in accordance with the principles of self-sufficiency and proximity as laid down in the 1989 Basel Convention on the Control of Transboundary Movement of Hazardous Waste and their Disposal. As a result, waste produced in Wallonia was distinguishable from waste produced outside Wallonia. In this way a distinctly applicable measure was framed by the Court into an indistinctly applicable measure.

In *Dusseldorp* the Dutch government argued that the export restrictions on oil filters could be justified, *inter alia* by an imperative requirement related to the protection of the environment. Although the Court rejects the measure in view of its economic nature, the Court did not rule out the possibility of justifying a discriminatory restriction on exporting waste for reasons relating to the protection of the environment.[152] In the *Sydhavnens* case, which concerned a measure adopted by the Municipality of Copenhagen to grant three waste processors the exclusive right to process building waste produced within the Municipality of Copenhagen, thereby excluding the waste processing company Sydhavnens Sten and Grus from processing this type of non-dangerous waste, the Court referred to its ruling in *Dusseldorp* and held that "the protection of the environment cannot serve to justify *any* restriction on exports, particularly in the case

---

150 Directive 75/442, OJ 1975, L 194/39 (as amended); Directive 84/631 is replaced by Regulation 259/93, OJ 1993, L 30/1.

151 Case C-2/90, *Commission v. Belgium (Walloon Waste)*, paragraph 34.

152 Case C-203/96, *Dusseldorp*. H. Temmink, From Danish Bottles to Danish Bees: The Dynamics of Free Movement of Goods and Environmental Protection – A Case Law Analysis, in: H. Somsen (Ed.), *Yearbook of European Environmental Law* (Oxford University Press, Oxford, 2000), p. 92.

of waste destined for recovery".[153] This means that some restrictions on exports, which are by their very nature discriminatory, can be justified on the basis of a mandatory requirement.[154]

Aher Waggon concerned German legislation which made registration in the national territory of aircraft previously registered in another Member State conditional upon compliance with stricter noise standards than those laid down in a Community directive. Here the Court, without examining the character of the measure, came to the conclusion that the legislation could be justified on environmental grounds.[155] The non-discriminatory nature of the measure was not unambiguous, for aircraft that had already obtained registration in Germany before the measure was adopted could retain that registration; aircraft registered in other Member States could not.[156]

The *PreussenElektra* case demonstrated an increasing willingness by the Court to take environmental principles into account, even at the cost of the principle of non-discrimination. In fact it is the first time that the Court has explicitly referred to the integration principle (Article 6 EC) and the possibility of justifying national discriminatory measures. Nevertheless, the Court failed to address the question of whether the German measure at issue was an (in) distinctly applicable measure which could therefore be justified by imperative requirements of environmental protection. AG Jacobs in his Opinion had explicitly asked the Court to clarify its position on this matter and held – whilst referring to the integration principle contained in Article 6 EC – that it must be possible for environmental measures which are inherently liable to be found discriminatory precisely because they are based on environmental principles (e.g. environmental damage should as a matter of principle be rectified at source) to be justified, and this should not be excluded.[157] In this case preliminary questions were raised by the Landgericht Kiel on the compatibility of the German *Stromeinspeisungsgesetz* with the Treaty provisions on state aid (Article 87 EC, see Chapter 3, section 3) and on the free movement of goods (Article 28 EC).[158]

---

153 Case C-209/98, *Sydhavnens Sten & Grus.*

154 See also N. Notaro, European Community Waste Movements: the Copenhagen Waste Case, *EELR*, 2000, p. 311.

155 Case C-389/96, *Aher Waggon.*

156 See H. Temmink, From Danish Bottles to Danish Bees: The Dynamics of Free Movement of Goods and Environmental Protection – A Case Law Analysis, in: H. Somsen (Ed.), *Yearbook of European Environmental Law* (Oxford University Press, Oxford, 2000), pp. 91-92; Opinion of AG Jacobs Case C-389/96, *Aher Waggon*, paragraph 227.

157 See the Opinion of AG Jacobs in Case C-389/96, *Aher Waggon*, paragraph 232.

158 Case C-379/98, *PreussenElektra*; see, for example, annotation B.J. Drijber, *SEW*, 2001, p. 400-403; A Goossens and S. Emmerechts, *CMLRev.*, 2001, pp. 991-1010; S. de Vries: European Court of Justice: Case Report, *EELR*, 2001, p. 193-205.

The *Stromeinspeisungsgesetz* requires electricity supply undertakings which operate a general supply network to purchase electricity from renewable sources within their area of supply and at a fixed minimum price. The *Stromeinspeisungsgesetz* treats electricity of domestic origin differently from imported electricity. After all, electricity produced from renewable sources in Germany benefits from the purchase obligation at a minimum price. The same type of electricity from neighbouring Member States, however, does not.[159] According to the Court in order to determine whether the purchase obligation can nevertheless be considered compatible with Article 28 EC, account must be taken of the aim of the provision and of the particular features of the electricity market. The *Stromeinspeisungsgesetz* is intended to promote renewable sources of energy and is therefore useful for the protection of the environment in so far as it contributes to the reduction of emissions of greenhouse gasses. Before the Court concludes that the *Stromeinspeisungsgesetz* is compatible with Article 28 EC on environmental grounds, it refers to the importance of the objective to reduce greenhouse gasses, both internationally and in the context of the Community, and furthermore refers to the obligation to integrate environmental protection requirements into the definition and implementation of other Community policies, which is now transferred by the Treaty of Amsterdam, in a slightly modified form, to Article 6 of the Treaty, which appears in Part One, headed 'Principles' (paragraph 76).

Preussen Elektra is illustrative for the Court's willingness to uphold national discriminatory measures for environmental reasons, irrespective of the fact that environmental protection grounds are not mentioned by Article 30 EC. The integration principle, which the Court for the first time explicitly referred to in relation to the possibility to justify national discriminatory measures, seems to serve the gap between Article 30 EC, the text of which remained unchanged since 1957, and the rule of reason; it requires the degree of protection of the environmental to be similar to the protection of interests mentioned by Article 30 EC.[160]

4.4.1.4 The proportionality test: the assessment of environmental measures

Whether a national measure restricting trade will eventually be justified depends on the proportionality of the measure. In the *PreussenElektra* case the Court in fact avoids assessing the proportionality of the *Stromeinspeisungsgesetz*. By referring to the Commission's proposal for a Directive on the promotion of renewable energy sources in the internal market,[161] the Court

---

[159] See paragraph 221 of the Opinion of AG Jacobs in Case C-379/98, *PreussenElektra*.

[160] S. de Vries, European Court of Justice Case Report, *EELR*, 2001, pp. 204-205.

[161] OJ 2000, C 311/320.

implicitly acknowledges that the purchase obligation on German electricity producers is necessary and proportionate to its aim. According to the Court, it is, after all, very difficult to determine the origin of electricity and in particular the source from which it was generated. In adopting this approach the Court takes a more favourable position on the *Stromeinspeisungsgesetz* than it did on the Finnish law on excise duty on certain sources of energy in the *Outokumpu Oy* case.

A reference to secondary (and international) legislation was made in *Danish Bees* as well. On the basis of the Rio Convention and secondary Community law on bio-diversity, the Court concluded that the measure in question was appropriate in relation to the aim pursued. In *Monsees* the Court considered Austrian legislation requiring that animals intended for slaughter should be transported to the nearest suitable domestic abattoir disproportionate since less restrictive measures were conceivable, as the provisions in Directive 95/29 on maximum journey times, conditions of transport, animals' feeding and watering intervals, minimum rest periods and loading densities demonstrated. The Directive provided, according to the Court, sufficient grounds for applying the test of the least restrictive alternative.[162] The result was that the level of protection of the welfare of animals in Austria could, in the light of the Directive, not prevail over the interest of the free movement of goods.[163] The application of the second element of the proportionality test could therefore also lead to a reduction of the level of protection sought by a Member State.

In the *Danish Bottles* case the Court in a more explicit way applied the proportionality test and partly questioned the proportionality *stricto sensu* of a Danish environmental measure, which stipulated that manufacturers must market beer and soft drinks only in re-usable containers.[164] The containers must be approved by the national agency for the protection of the environment, which may refuse approval of new kinds of containers, especially if it considers that a certain container is technically unsuitable for a system for returning them, or that the return system envisaged does not ensure that a sufficient proportion of containers are actually re-used, or if a container of equal capacity, which is both available and suitable for the same use, has already been approved. However, these rules were amended in such a way that, provided that a deposit-return-system was established, non-approved containers, except for any form of metal container, may be used for quantities not exceeding 3000 hectolitres a year per producer and for drinks which are sold by foreign producers in order to test the market. The Court held that measures adopted to protect the environment must not "go beyond the inevitable restrictions which are justified by the

---

162 Case C-350/97, *Monsees*; see also Case C-389/96, *Aher Waggon*, on the impact of Directive 80/51 on noise nuisance caused by aircraft, which provides only for minimum harmonisation.

163 See also J. Langer and J. Wiers, De eeuwige strijd tussen het goederenverkeer, milieubescherming en het evenredigheidsbeginsel: Oostenrijks slachtvee en opnieuw flessen en blikjes uit Denemarken, *Milieu & Recht*, 2001, p. 64.

164 Case 302/86, *Commission v. Denmark (Danish Bottles)*.

pursuit of the objective of environmental protection. It is therefore necessary to examine whether all restrictions which the contested rules impose on the free movement of goods are necessary to achieve the objectives pursued by those rules."[165] It regarded the deposit-and-return system as an "indispensable element of a system intended to ensure the re-use of containers and therefore appears necessary to achieve the aims pursued by the contested rules. That being so, the restrictions which it imposes on the free movement of goods cannot be regarded as disproportionate."[166]

With regard to the second part of the Danish measure, the Court considered that, before the amendments, foreign producers who still wished to sell their products in Denmark would be obliged to manufacture or purchase containers of an already approved type, which would involve substantial additional costs for them and make the importation of their products into Denmark very difficult. Then it examined the amendments and came to the conclusion that "in those circumstances, a restriction of the quantity of the products which may be marketed by importers is disproportionate to the objective pursued".[167]

But the Court did not consider the deposit-and-return system as unreasonable, for this system was proportionate and consequently justified. The restriction of the quantity of the products, which may be marketed by importers, however, was considered disproportionate to the objective pursued. The Court admitted, though, that such a licence requirement ensures a maximum rate of re-use and therefore a considerable degree of protection of the environment since empty containers can be returned to any retailer of beverages. By accepting that this licence requirement ensures a high level of environmental protection, yet considering it disproportionate to the objective of environmental protection, the Court in effect balanced the *level* of environmental protection against the restriction on the free movement of goods, and reduced the level the Member State could choose.[168]

---

[165] Case 302/86, *Commission v. Denmark (Danish Bottles)*, paragraphs 11 and 12.

[166] Case 302/86, *Commission v. Denmark (Danish Bottles)*, paragraph 13.

[167] Case 302/86, *Commission v. Denmark (Danish Bottles)*, paragraphs 17 and 21. AG Slynn in his Opinion in Case 302/86, *Commission v. Denmark* states the following: "I accept, as Denmark contends, that it achieves the highest standard of environmental protection in respect of the collection of containers, though it obviously accepts the risk of certain kinds of bottle or container being left around the countryside. [...] Yet it does not seem to me that Denmark must succeed in its application... There has to be a balancing of interests between the free movement of goods and environmental protection, even if in achieving the balance the high standard of the protection sought has to be reduced. The level of protection sought must be a *reasonable* level."

[168] Geradin (1997), p. 27. In his Opinion in Case C-169/89, *Gourmetterie Van den Burg* AG Van Gerven pursued a similar line of thought as regards the proportionality test. According to Van Gerven an absolute ban on the import of red grouse in the Netherlands was only able to make small contributions to the protection of the red grouse birds. The import ban was therefore disproportionate in the light of the restrictive effect on trade.

In *Spitz* the Court had to rule on a national environmental measure on packaging and packaging waste as well. This case involved a German measure based on the 'Verpackungs Verordnung' requiring producers and distributors using non-reusable packaging to charge a deposit on mineral water, beer and soft drinks, to recover the empty packaging and to leave the waste collection-system (e.g. Der Grüne Punkt), on which basis the obligation to charge the deposit would be exempted. This requirement was imposed only after the proportion of reusable packaging on the German market fell below a certain percentage (72%).

After having assessed the scope of the packaging and packaging waste Directive 94/62 (see also Chapter 4) in relation to this measure, the Court held that the Directive did not preclude national packaging waste management systems from being assessed in the light of Article 28 EC. By referring to the above-mentioned *Danish Bottles* case, the Court held that the German measure violated Article 28 EC, since it affected the marketing of drinks from other Member States more heavily than the marketing of drinks in Germany; producers established outside Germany use considerably more non-reusable packaging than German producers.

The Court then considered whether the German rules were indispensable for the protection of the environment, which they were since they contributed towards reducing the amount of waste to be disposed of. However, the condition that no less restrictive means were available was more difficult to fulfil. According to the Court, the measure which makes the establishment of a deposit and return system dependent on a packaging use rate, which is certainly advantageous from an ecological point of view, complies with the principle of proportionality only if it gives the producers and distributors a reasonable transitional period to adapt thereto; furthermore, at the time when the packaging waste management system changes, every producer and distributor concerned can actually participate in an operational system.

Compared with *Danish Bottles* however, the Court did not really question the level of environmental protection pursued by the German authorities; it rather focused on the second element of proportionality, or whether the establishment of a deposit and return system was really necessary to attain the objective of reducing the amount of packaging waste on the German market. This would be the case only if the two conditions of reasonable transitional period and participation in an operational system were fulfilled.[169] The balancing approach adopted in *Danish Bottles* may therefore indeed have been an isolated instance.[169] The strict application of the second element of proportionality makes nonetheless clear that national environmental product rules are nonetheless still subject to a high level of scrutiny by the Court.

[169] Case C-309/02, *Radlberger & Spitz*.

[169a] Geradin (1997), p. 62.

4.4.2 The protection of consumers

Similarly to the field of the environment, consumer protection is not explicitly included in the Treaty as an exception ground to free movement. The protection of consumers and the conditions under which Member States may uphold national consumer laws restricting free movement have first and foremost been developed in the case law of the Court. Also here the cases discussed involve the protection of domestic consumers. Extra-territorial protection may for example occur where a prohibition in one Member State on the use of certain methods of sales promotion to consumers in other Member States has an impact on the protection of consumers outside the territory of the regulating state. It generally seems that whenever the protection of out of state interests have a domestic connotation, the Court is more willing to uphold such measures, or, like in *Alpine Investments*, rephrases an extra-territorial measure designed to protect consumers in other Member States into a measure protecting the domestic interest of the reputation of the Dutch financial market.[170]

4.4.2.1 The protection of health and safety of consumers

Since consumer protection is concerned with the exposure of individuals, as consumers, to risks which face any of us in everyday life, it is also concerned with health and safety risks. Health and safety are grounds of justification for restrictions to free movement as recognised in the Treaty in Articles 30 and 46 EC. The relevance of these provisions for the protection of public health will be discussed in the following section. The case law shows that where a national measure is designed to protect (sensitive) consumers from a health risk, Article 30 EC may be invoked.[171]

4.4.2.2 The protection of consumers as overriding requirement of public interest

Consumers are persons who buy goods and services.[172] The consumer in the Brussels Convention on Jurisdiction and Enforcement of Judgments has been defined as the person who concludes a contract for a use which can be regarded as being outside his trade or profession. Community directives correspond to this definition of consumer, but they limit, contrary to the

---

[170] Case C-384/93, *Alpine Investments*. The Court held in paragraph 43 that "although the protection of consumers in the other Member States is not, as such, a matter for the Netherlands authorities, the nature and extent of that protection does none the less have a direct effect on the good reputation of the Netherlands financial services".

[171] Case 97/83, *Melkunie*; Case 53/80, *Eyssen*.

[172] Oxford Advanced Learner's Dictionary.

Convention, the notion of consumer to natural persons.[173] Consumer protection originates from mandatory civil rules in favour of consumers. Even though the notion of consumers as a separate group that needs particular attention has only recently developed,[174] the protection of the economic interests of consumers has now a prominent place in the list of mandatory requirements developed under the rule of reason. In *Cassis de Dijon* the Court held that national laws which give rise to obstacles to the free movement of goods must be accepted in so far as these provisions may be recognised as being necessary to satisfy mandatory requirements relating *inter alia* to the *defence of the consumer* and the fairness of commercial transactions.[175] This recognition of the protection of the consumer as mandatory requirement has had the result that Member States are allowed to uphold their national protective measures, as long as the national legislation applies to domestic products and imported products alike.

Although the Court has formulated a general justification ground, it depends on the context of each case which particular consumer has to be protected. Since national consumer protection law may impede free movement, which in itself is designed to advance the consumer interest, the Court has developed its own notion of consumer interest.[176] The basic notion of consumer in Community law is that the consumer is considered an individual who can, if provided with the necessary information, make his own choices and defend his own interests. In *GB-INNO-BM* the Court held that "Article 28 cannot be interpreted as meaning that national legislation which denies the consumer access to certain kinds of information may be justified by mandatory requirements concerning consumer protection".[177] This is also referred to as the notion of 'reasonably circumspect consumer' considering the Court's perception "that most consumers are sufficiently robust and well-informed to take care of themselves in the market place".[178]

---

[173] J. Stuyck, European consumer law after the Treaty of Amsterdam: Consumer policy in or beyond the internal market?, *CMLRev.*, 2000, p 376.

[174] J. Stuyck, European consumer law after the Treaty of Amsterdam: Consumer policy in or beyond the internal market?, *CMLRev.*, 2000, pp. 368-369.

[175] Case 120/78, *Cassis de Dijon*.

[176] Weatherill (1997), p. 41; see for the notion of consumer in Community law: K. Mortelmans and S. Watson, The notion of the consumer in community law: a lottery?, *TvC*, 1995, pp. 229-246; S. Weatherill, Recent case law concerning the free movement of goods: mapping the frontiers of market deregulation, *CMLRev.*, 1999, pp. 51-85.

[177] Case C-362/88, *GB-INNO-BM*, paragraph 18. In his opinion AG Lenz emphasised the importance of information – in the form of advertisements – for consumers: "Information should only be withheld from the consumer for his own protection for *convincing* reasons. After all, it must be assumed that any accurate information can only be useful to the consumer" (paragraph 34).

[178] Weatherill and Beaumont (1999), pp.699-702.

In some cases, however, the Court is prepared to accept that certain specific groups of consumers need protection. The proportionality test serves to unmask protectionist measures from measures which are appropriate and proportionate to the objective of consumer protection, or measures which deny consumers their capacity to make informed choices from measures that are aimed to protect particularly vulnerable consumers who are misled by marketing practices.

4.4.2.3 The condition that consumer protection measures should apply without distinction

It may be justifiable under the Treaty provisions for national discriminatory laws to seek the protection of the health or safety interests of consumers. But if economic interests of consumers are involved, for national measures to be justifiable under the rule of reason they must be indistinctly applicable. Even where national consumer measures do not discriminate, but are merely based on domestic cultural perceptions, these measures are hardly eligible for justification on consumer protection grounds. The German law requiring Cassis-type of liqueurs be stronger than was demanded in France may have been inspired by local preferences and traditions, protecting consumers against relatively weak (French) Cassis, but had the result that French Cassis-de-Dijon was excluded from the German market.[179] The notion of reasonably circumspect consumer departs from the presumption that consumers decide on the basis of adequate information which products are to be preferred.

The *De Agostini* ruling suggests that the basic rule of national measures being indistinctly applicable does not necessarily apply always. Under Swedish law (*Marknadsföringslag*) the Marknadsdomstol may prohibit a trader who, in the marketing of goods, services or other commodities, engaged in advertising or any other activity which, by being contrary to good commercial practice or otherwise, is unfair towards consumers or other traders, from continuing so to act or from engaging in other similar activity. De Agostini whose main business is the publication of magazines advertised on television the magazine *Allt om dinosaurier* (everything about dinosaurs). The Consumer Ombudsman applied to the Marknadsdomstol under Article 2 of the Marketing Practices Act for an order prohibiting De Agostini from marketing this magazine on the ground that the advertising in question was designed to attract the attention of children under 12 years of age (CC-34/95). The other cases (C-35/95 and C-36/95) concern the activities of TV-Shop which business was presenting products in television spots whereafter the customer could buy the product by telephone. The products concerned were skin-care products and the detergent *Astonish*.

Even though the *Keck* ruling may be applicable in this case since legislation prohibiting television advertising in a particular sector concerns selling arrangements in that it prohibits a particular form of promotion of a particular

[179] Weatherill and Beaumont (1999), p. 698.

method of marketing products, it cannot, according to the Court, be excluded that an outright ban, applying in one Member State, of a type of promotion of a product which is lawfully sold there might have a greater impact on products from other Member States. The second condition of *Keck* might not have been fulfilled, which was for the national court to determine. Nevertheless, the Court went on by stating that "it is for the national court to determine whether the ban is necessary to satisfy overriding requirements of general public importance or one of the aims listed in Article 30 of the EC Treaty if it is proportionate to that purpose and if those aims or requirements could not have been attained or fulfilled by measures less restrictive of intra-Community trade. Further, according to settled case-law, fair trading and the protection of consumers in general are overriding requirements of general public importance which may justify obstacles to the free movement of goods."[180]

Hence, the Court implicitly recognised that a potentially discriminatory national measure may be justified by reasons related to the protection of consumers. The Court, contrary to AG Jacobs, did not refer to the condition that measures should apply without distinction for the rule of reason to apply, and failed to explain why a flexible approach may have been desirable in this case.[181] AG Jacobs also accepted that the second condition of *Keck* was probably not fulfilled in this case. Consequently, it remains unclear whether the Swedish ban on advertising should be considered as discriminatory and therefore should not be justifiable under the rule of reason. The Court's reasoning certainly does not exclude the possibility for a more flexible approach to distinctly applicable measures. In the field of free movement of services, though, several indirectly discriminatory measures, such as licence requirements or the requirement of establishment for a service provider, were in some cases justified on grounds related to the protection of consumers.[182]

Nonetheless, it remains highly contentious whether in general national discriminatory consumer laws may be justifiable on consumer protection grounds. At least the link between justifying discriminatory measures in general and justifying discriminatory consumer protection measures in particular remains more hypothetical in comparison with discriminatory environmental measures. There is no similar judgment like *Preussen Elektra* in respect of consumer policy. The field of consumer policy is considerably diffuse and it depends on the case at hand whether the Court will opt for a more flexible approach.

---

180 Joined Cases C-34/95, C-35/95 and C-36/95, *De Agostini*, paragraphs 45 and 46.

181 Opinion of AG Jacobs in Joined Cases C-34/95, C-35/95 and C-36/95, *De Agostini*, paragraph 101.

182 For example Case 205/84, *Commission v. Germany (German Insurance)*: In paragraph 29 the Court refers to imperative reasons which may justify establishment requirements restricting the free movement of services without mentioning the condition that the measure should apply without distinction.

4.4.2.4 The proportionality test: the assessment of consumer protection measures

With regard to the intensity of the proportionality test and the degree of consumer protection a Member State seeks to attain a distinction can be made between the following three types of cases:
- Measures that restrict consumer choice and the provision of information to consumers;
- Measures that protect the economic interests of (particularly vulnerable) consumers;
- Measures that restrict activities in particularly sensitive areas, like gambling or insurance.

As will be seen, the principle of mutual recognition plays a significant role in assessing the proportionality of a trade restrictive measure.

Consumer choice and the provision of information

The Court relies on the capacity of the consumer to process information and make informed choices about available products and services.[183] As stated above the Court departs from the notion of reasonably circumspect consumer. In the *Gut Springenheide* case the Court was asked to define the concept of consumer to be used as a standard for determining whether a statement designed to promote sales of eggs is likely to mislead the purchaser. According to the Court the national court must take into account the presumed expectations of an average consumer who is reasonably well informed and reasonably circumspect.[184] In several cases relating to misleading advertising, the Court refused to accept measures aimed at protecting the consumer whose intelligence and attention is less than average.[185] In *Mars*, for example, the question arose as to whether a German prohibition of the marketing of Mars ice-cream bars presented in wrappers marked "+10%" constituted a measure having equivalent effect and could be justified by reasons related to the protection of consumers against misleading information. According to the German government the "+ 10%" marking may lead the consumer to think that the new product is being offered at a price identical to that at which the old product was sold. Furthermore the "+10%" marking induces the consumers to believe, by the band bearing the "+10%" marking, which occupies more than 10% of the total surface area of the wrapping. The Court, however, held that this justification could not be accepted: "Reasonably circumspect consumers may be deemed to know that there is not necessarily a

---

183 Weatherill (1997), p. 48.

184 Case C-210/96, *Gut Springenheide.*

185 J. Stuyck, European consumer law after the Treaty of Amsterdam: Consumer Policy in or beyond the internal market?, *CMLRev.*, 2000, p. 392.

link between the size of publicity marking relating to an increase in a product's quantity and the size of that product."[186]

The strong belief in the consumer as an active and critical information-seeker at the cost of some consumers being possibly misled as to the characteristics of certain products is also reflected by the *Clinique* ruling.[187] Here, a German law prohibiting the use of the name *Clinique* for the marketing of a cosmetic product could not be justified on grounds of consumer protection. The products were ordinarily marketed in other Member States under the name *Clinique.* Besides the clinical or medical connotations of the word *Clinique* were not sufficient to make the word so misleading as to justify the prohibition of its use. The prohibition therefore did not appear to be necessary to satisfy the requirements of consumer protection and the health of humans. The Court thus rejected the notion that confusion suffered by German consumers could be sufficient to justify a prohibition to use the name *Clinique.*

In cases on the free movement of foodstuffs the Court applies the second element of the proportionality test more clearly. Where national rules require the use of certain ingredients or additives in the manufacture of certain products the Court will regard these rules often as disproportionate or unnecessary restrictions to free movement. Instead, appropriate labelling could sufficiently inform consumers about differences between various products. In *Drei Glocken* Italian rules required the use of durum wheat only for the manufacture of pasta products.[188] The Court found these rules disproportionate since it remained possible for the Italian authorities to restrict the description "pasta made from drurum wheat" to "pasta made exclusively from drurum wheat", and adequately inform the consumer.[189]

Similarly in *Guimont* French rules on the marketing of Emmenthal cheese, reserving the designation of Emmenthal for cheeses with a hard dry rind, were considered incompatible with Article 28 EC and could not be justified on consumer protection grounds.[190] Where the approach of the Court in cases on the free movement of foodstuffs could be criticised for its finding that labelling is more proportionate to the aim of consumer protection and the free movement of goods, where doubt has been casted on the fact that consumers actually read or even comprehend labelling disclosures,[191] it also stimulates cross border trade in products that consumers are not familiar with.

---

[186] Case C-470/93, *Mars*, paragraph 24.

[187] Case C-315/92, *Clinique*; see also Howells & Weatherill (2005), p. 116.

[188] Case 407/85, *Drei Glocken.*

[189] AG Mancini's argument of Italian consumers not being adequately informed by labels about production of differently constituted pasta in other states, given the depth of cultural expectation in Italy about pasta, was not followed by the Court.

[190] Case C-448/98, *Guimont.*

[191] For example C. MacMaolain, Free movement of foodstuffs, quality requirements and consumer protection: have the Court and the Commission both got it wrong?, *ELRev.*, 2001, p. 422.

The Court's perception of consumers as being reasonably circumspect has been criticised.[192] Differences in linguistic, social and cultural conditions may have the result that something which does not mislead consumers in one country may do so in another according to AG Gulmann in the *Clinique* case.[193] One state may regard something as unsafe or unintelligible, whereas another state may not, confirming that Community law does not force regulatory protection down to the lowest common denominator among the Member States. Furthermore, the lack of homogeneity among the traditions of the Member States may cause something harmless in one state to have a different impact in another state.[194] The Opinion of AG Gulmann in *Clinique* reveals the remarkable difference between the activist approach of the Court considerably restricting Member States' discretion in determining the level of protection they deem necessary, and the more reluctant attitude of the Advocate General in favour of the vulnerable consumer. The case law on the informed or reasonably circumspect consumer implies that the Court finally establishes the level of consumer protection.[195]

The importance of consumer choice even in more sensitive areas like banking has been reinforced in the *Caixa-Bank France* case.[196] This case involved a French measure prohibiting credit institutions, in this case a French subsidiary of a Spanish company, from remunerating sight accounts in euros opened by residents of France. The Court acknowledged that the French prohibition was necessary for maintaining basic banking services without charge, as the introduction of remuneration for sight accounts would increase operating costs of banks and as a consequence would increase charges for banking services currently provided free and hence for the protection of consumers. Nonetheless, it regarded the measure disproportionate, as consumers are prevented from choosing between an unremunerated sight account with certain basic banking services remaining free of charge and a remunerated sight account with banking services being charged for. The measure was also considered suitable for the encouragement of long-term saving, but was nevertheless disproportionate without further explanation by the Court.

Hence, in the context of reviewing national consumer laws a Community notion of consumers has emerged with a strong emphasis on information. The

---

192 The "information paradigm" according to G. Howells and T. Wilhelmsson, EC consumer law; has it come of age?, *ELRev.*, 2003, pp. 380-382.

193 Opinion of AG Gulmann in Case C-315/92, *Clinique*, paragraph 25. See also with regard to different consumer cultures: T. Wilhelmsson, The Abuse of the "Confident Consumer" as a Justification for EC Consumer Law, *Journal of Consumer Policy*, 2004, p. 328.

194 S. Weatherill, Recent case law concerning the free movement of goods: mapping the frontiers of market deregulation, *CMLRev.*, 1999, p. 60.

195 J.H.Jans, Proportionality revisited, *LIEI*, 2000, p. 252.

196 Case C-442/02, *Caixa-Bank France*.

focus on the more "ordinary confident consumers", for whom it can also be questioned whether information provision may not be a panacea,[197] does not always allow for the highest level of protection.[198]

Protecting the economic interests of consumers

In some cases the Court is more willing to uphold national consumer measures restricting trade, in particular to protect consumers who are seen as particularly vulnerable, considering the circumstances, or considering the fact that they are simply not in a position to make reasonably informed choices. In *Oosthoek* the Court held a Dutch law which controlled the offer for sales promotion purposes of free gifts to buyers of encyclopaedias as to contribute to consumer protection and fair trading, for "it is undeniable that the offering of free gifts as a means of sales promotion may mislead consumers as to the real prices of certain products and distort the conditions on which genuine competition is based".[199] It has also been accepted in case law that a particular group of vulnerable consumers may need extra protection.

The *Buet* case involved a French measure prohibiting canvassing in connection with the sale of educational material.[200] According to the Court "it is common ground that the French legislature adopted the prohibition of canvassing in question out of concern to protect consumers against the risk of ill-considered purchasers. However, as the Court has repeatedly held, such rules must be proportionate to the goals pursued, and if a Member State has at his disposal less restrictive means of obtaining the same goals, it is under an obligation to make use of them." "In that respect canvassing at private dwellings exposes the potential customer to the risk of making an ill-considered purchase. To guard against that risk it is *normally* sufficient to ensure that purchasers have the right to cancel a contract concluded in their home."[201] Apparently, in normal situations a right of cancellation is sufficient for the protection of consumers. This case did, according to the Court, not reflect a normal situation: "It is necessary, however, to point out that there is a greater risk of an ill-considered purchase when the canvassing is for enrolment for a course of instruction or the sale of educational material. The potential purchaser often belongs to a category of people who, for one reason or another, are behind with their education and are seeking to catch up. That makes them *particularly vulnerable* when faced with a salesman of educational material [...]. Finally, it needs to be stressed that since teaching is not a consumer product in daily use, an ill-considered purchase could cause the purchaser harm *other* than financial loss that could be *longer*

[197] G. Howells and T. Wilhelmsson, EC Consumer Law: has it come of age?, *ELRev.*, 2003, p. 381.

[198] Weatherill (1997), p. 58.

[199] Case 286/81, *Oosthoek*, paragraph 16.

[200] Case 382/87, *Buet*.

[201] Case 382/87, *Buet*, paragraphs 11 and 12.

lasting [italics added by the author]."[202] The Court concluded that the ban on canvassing was necessary at private dwellings in particular to protect vulnerable consumers. As a result there were no less restrictive means available.

Measures that restrict activities in particularly sensitive areas

The Court allows Member States a considerable margin of discretion where the specific nature of the activity requires so. In *Schindler* the Court was requested to judge upon a British law prohibiting the holding of certain lotteries with the provisions on the free movement of goods and services.[203] As lottery activities were not regarded as activities related to goods, but as services within the meaning of the Treaty, the Court only considered the questions on Articles 49 and 46 EC (in conjunction with Article 55 EC). According to the Court "given the peculiar nature of lotteries, which has been stressed by many Member States, those considerations are such as to justify restrictions, as regards Article 49 of the Treaty, which may go so far as to prohibit lotteries in a Member State".[204] "Those particular factors justify national authorities having a sufficient degree of latitude to determine what is required to protect the players and, more generally, in the light of the special social and cultural features of each Member State, to maintain order in society, as regards the manner in which lotteries are operated [...], it is for them to assess not only whether it is necessary to restrict the activities of lotteries but also whether they should be prohibited, provided that those restrictions are not discriminatory. When a Member State prohibits in its territory *large-scale lotteries and in particular the advertising and distribution of tickets for that type of lottery*, [...]. Such a prohibition is a necessary part of the protection which that Member State seeks to secure in its territory in relation to lotteries [italics added by the author]."[205]

In this case the Court was not prepared to test the necessity of the measure, if the matter was sufficiently sensitive.[206] Member States have an adequate degree of latitude to determine what measures are required, and the Court leaves it to the Member States whether less restrictive means are available.

In *Läärä* and *Zenatti* the Court refined the *Schindler* ruling to some extent by referring to the proportionality requirement. In *Läärä* the legality of a Finnish law providing that games of chance may only be organised with the authorisation of the administrative authorities and for the purpose of collecting funds for charity or for another non-profit activity provided for by law was challenged. The Court held that the law constituted a restriction to the freedom to provide services to the extent that such legislation prevented operators from other Member States from making gaming machines available to the public with a

[202] Case 382/87, *Buet*, paragraphs 13 and 14.

[203] Case C-275/92, *Schindler*.

[204] Case C-275/92, *Schindler*, paragraph 59.

[205] Case C-275/92, *Schindler*, paragraphs 61 and 62.

[206] J.H. Jans, Proportionality revisited, *LIEI*, 2000, p. 245.

view to their use for payment. However, the Finnish legislation responded to "the concern to limit exploitation of the human passion for gambling, to avoid the risk of crime and fraud to which the activities concerned give rise and to authorise those activities only with a view to the collection of funds for charity or for other benevolent purposes".[207] Referring to its judgment in *Schindler* the Court held that it is up to the Member States to determine the extent of protection on its territory with regard to lotteries and other forms of gambling: "In those circumstances, the mere fact that a Member State has opted for a system of protection which differs from that adopted by another Member State cannot affect the assessment of the need for, and proportionality of, the provisions enacted to that end. Those provisions must be assessed solely by reference to the objectives pursued by the national authorities of the Member State concerned and the level of protection which they are intended to provide."[208] The question of what measure would be preferable to achieve these objectives is a matter for the Member State, provided that the choice made in that regard should not be disproportionate to the aim pursued.

In *Zenatti* the Court pursued a similar line of thought with regard to an Italian law permitting the organisation of betting on sporting events where the taking of bets is a precondition for the competition to take place.[209] Only two undertakings had been granted special rights to take such bets in Italy. According to the Court the Italian legislation could be justified on public interest grounds, provided that the national legislation responded effectively to the objectives pursued by the Member State. The requirements in *Läära* that the choice between different measures must be proportionate, and in *Zenatti* that national legislation has to respond effectively to the objectives pursued are references to a marginal assessment by the Court of the proportionality of the measures concerned.[210]

In *Gambelli*, however, the Court makes clear that not all restrictions on gambling are necessarily proportionate.[211] This case involved an Italian law prohibiting on pain of criminal penalties persons other than those having received a concession or authorisation from engaging into activities of collecting, taking, booking and forwarding offers of bets, in particular bets on sporting events. Intermediaries who facilitated the provision of services by a British bookmaker faced up to one year imprisonment for having unlawfully organised bets. The Court cast doubt about the proportionality of the imposition of such a penalty, particularly considering the fact that betting is encouraged in the context of games organised by licensed authorities.

---

207 Case C-124/97, *Läära*, paragraph 32.

208 Case C-124/97, *Läära*, paragraph 36.

209 Case C-67/98, *Zenatti*.

210 See also annotation G. Straetmans, *CMLRev.*, 2000, p. 1001.

211 Case C-243/01, *Gambelli*.

These lottery cases make the following clear. Contrary to *Schindler* and *Läärä*, the Court does not apply the proportionality test itself in *Zenatti*, but leaves it to the national court. Furthermore, different justification grounds were held applicable in all three cases, but leading to the same result: restrictions on gambling were justified. *Gambelli* shows that each case has to be assessed individually. Where betting is more acceptable, and organised through licenses, the national court has to carefully establish whether the conditions of obtaining a licence satisfy the principle of non-discrimination and whether severe prohibitions on non-licensed companies facilitating betting or offering betting services are really necessary in the light of the propagated aims. In other words, "if Member States demonstrate that national restrictions bring about a genuine diminution of the gambling opportunities, the Court will continue to apply a relaxed proportionality test [...]. In case of excess [...] the Court is now prepared to apply a strict proportionality test."[212]

The *German Insurance* case shows how the Court applied the proportionality test while it took into account the sensitive nature of the regulated area. The Court accepted that the insurance sector is a very sensitive area particularly because of the *specific nature of the service* provided by the insurer, which is linked to future events, the occurrence of which, or at least the timing of which, is uncertain at the time when the contract is concluded.[213] The German *Sicherungsaufsichtsgesetz* provided that insurance companies which wished to provide services in Germany in relation to direct insurance business must be established and authorised in Germany. The Court examined whether the public interest (protection of consumers) was not already protected by the rules of the State of establishment and whether the same result could not be obtained by less restrictive means. According to the Court the public interest was not sufficiently protected by the Member State of establishment. The authorisation procedure could "provide an effective means of ensuring the supervision which, having regard to the foregoing considerations, is justified on grounds relating to the protection of the consumer both as a policy holder and as an insured person".[214] The requirement of establishment, however, was not considered indispensable, unless it concerned compulsory insurance or insurance for which the insurer either maintains a permanent presence equivalent to an agency or branch, or directs his business entirely or principally towards the territory of the Federal Republic of Germany.

The self-restraint in the application of the proportionality test, also compared to the proportionality test employed in other consumer cases, can be explained by the particularly sensitive nature of the area concerned where Member States

---

212 Annotation G. Straetmans, *CMLRev.*, 2004, p. 1424.

213 Case 205/84, *Commission v. Germany (German Insurance)*.

214 Case 205/84, *Commission v. Germany (German Insurance)*, paragraph 46.

are primarily competent to take action.[215] However, these cases may be limited, as is shown, for example, by the earlier discussed *Caixa-Bank France* case, where the notion of consumer as reasonably circumspect European citizen has been emphasised also in relation to banking activities.[216]

4.4.3 The protection of public health

Public health is a varied policy field, which can be roughly distinguished in public health in the strict sense, including the prevention of diseases and the protection of consumers' health on the one hand, and health care on the other, being part of a Member State's social security scheme.[217] National measures in both areas have become subject to the Court's scrutiny under the free movement rules.

The cases discussed involve the domestic protection of public health and not the extra-territorial protection of health, although here also the question of extra-territorial protection may be relevant. For example, the guarantee of a sickness insurance fund that medical care in another Member State should be of a certain quality has also effects on the treatment of patients in that state.

4.4.3.1 The protection of public health as Treaty exception

The protection of health of humans is mentioned in Article 30 EC as a ground for justifying restrictions to the free movement of goods. Article 39(3) EC includes public health as justification ground in the context of the free movement of workers. Similarly, Article 46 EC provides for a public health exception to restrictions on the freedom of establishment, and the free movement of services (in conjunction with Article 55 EC).

Public health stricto sensu

Article 30 EC covers national public health legislation regulating dangerous products, medicines or other health aspects of goods, such as measures to

---

[215] J.H. Jans, Proportionality revisited, *LIEI*, 2000, p. 250. According to Barnard there may be two explanations for the Court's approach: "The judicial deference towards the Member States may partly be explained by the fact that, in these cases involving an activity which is legal in one State but illegal in another, the Court is wary of imposing the values of the majority of the States (where lotteries are lawful, albeit highly regulated) on the minority (where lotteries are unlawful). Another explanation is that these cases concern the situation of a service which moves but the provider and the recipient do not" (Barnard 2004, p. 354).

[216] Case C-442/02, *Caixa-Bank France*.

[217] See in general: V. G. Hatzopoulos, *Killing* national health and insurance systems but *healing* patients? The European market for health care services after the judgments of the ECJ in *Vanbraekel* and *Peerbooms*, *CMLRev.*, 2002, pp. 683-729.

reduce alcohol consumption.[218] The assurance of the quality of medical products is an objective covered by Article 30 EC as well.[219]

According to the Court in the *De Peijper* case, "health and the life of humans rank first among the property of interests protected by Article 30 and it is for the Member States, within the limits imposed by the Treaty, to decide what degree of protection they intend to assure and in particular how strict the checks to be carried out are to be".[220] This would suggest that health measures have some measure of priority over other (economic and horizontal and flanking) interests.

The mere existence of a health risk is sufficient proof for a Member State's action against products which may form a real danger to human health. If there is a genuine health risk, no matter how slight the risk is, measures to guard against such a risk may be justifiable under Article 30 EC.[221] Nevertheless, the risk must be measured not according to the general conjecture but on the basis of relevant scientific research.[222] This is in accordance with the precautionary principle, according to which this principle and the role of scientific evidence will be discussed hereafter, within the context of the proportionality test.

Health care

The protection of public health in the context of the free movement of services and persons – Articles 39(3) EC and 46 EC (in conjunction with Article 55 EC) includes the maintenance of the quality of medical treatment, or the maintenance of a treatment facility or medical service on national territory. According to case law the objective of maintaining a balanced medical and hospital service open to all may also fall within the derogations of grounds of public health under Article 46 EC, in so far as it contributes to the attainment of a high level of health protection.[223]

4.4.3.2 The safeguarding of the financial stability of a health care system as overriding requirement of public interest

Since the Treaty exceptions do not explicitly refer to health care, it is important to look at the case law in order to assess the extent to which safeguarding the health care system may constitute an overriding requirement of public interest. In the *Kohll* and *Decker* cases[224] as well as the *Smits and*

---

[218] See for an overview, Oliver (assisted by Malcolm Jarvis) (2003), pp. 255-279.

[219] Case C-120/95, *Decker.*

[220] Case 104/75, *De Peijper.*

[221] Oliver (assisted by Malcolm Jarvis) (2003), p. 256; Case 97/83, *Melkunie.*

[222] Case C-17/93, *Van der Velde.* See also Ch. Joerges, Integrating Scientific Expertise into Regulatory Decision-Making, EUI Working Paper RSC No. 96/10, p. 11.

[223] Case C-158/96, *Kohll*, paragraph 50; Case C-157/99, *Smits and Peerbooms*, paragraph 73.

Peerbooms, Vanbraekel and *Müller-Fauré* cases[225] the risk of seriously undermining the financial balance of the social security system, or more in particular the safeguarding of the financial stability of the health care system, was recognised as a mandatory requirement or overriding general-interest reason that may justify restrictions on the free movement of goods and services. According to AG Tesauro in his opinion in the *Kohll* and *Decker* cases "it is beyond dispute that the preservation of the financial stability of the social security system, which is indeed the essential aim of the measure in question, is not an end in itself but a means which contributes (at least) to providing insured persons with services of a certain standard in terms of both quantity and quality. If the financial balance of the system were upset, the level of health protection could deteriorate with obvious and inevitable adverse repercussions, particularly for insured persons belonging to the weakest strata of society."[226]

Whereas here clearly recognised as a separate justification ground, the objective of protecting the financial balance of the social security system and in particular the safeguarding of the financial stability of the health care system could have been derived from the public health exception as laid down in Articles 30 and 46 EC.[227] Nevertheless, the Court has chosen to refer to this ground separately as overriding general interest reason, even though it recognised that the objective of maintaining a balanced medical and hospital service open to all, which may fall within the public health exception of Article 46 EC, is intrinsically linked to the method of financing the social security system.[228]

4.4.3.3 (No) condition that health measures should apply without distinction

Distinctly applicable measures in the field of public health are thus justifiable on the basis of the derogations provided for in the Treaty. The safeguarding of the financial stability of the health sector, however, is an overriding requirement of public interest, which can, according to established case law, only be invoked for indistinctly applicable measures. However, as in the field of environmental protection, the Court follows a classic pattern, but has nevertheless upheld distinctly applicable national measures on grounds related to the financing of the social security system.

In *Kohll* and *Decker* the Court accepted that a potentially discriminatory measure could be justifiable by reasons related to the general interest. In Luxembourg under the *Code des Assurance Sociales* prior authorisation from

---

224 Case C-158/96, *Kohll*, paragraph 21; Case C-120/95, *Decker*, paragraph 39.

225 Case C-157/99, *Smits and Peerbooms*, paragraph 73; Case C-368/98, *Vanbraekel*, paragraph 47.

226 Opinion AG Tesauro, paragraph 53.

227 See also annotation R. Giesen, *CMLRev.*, 1999, p. 846.

228 Case C-157/99, *Smits and Peerbooms* and more clearly Case C-385/99, *Müller-Fauré*.

the competent social security institution is needed for the reimbursement of the costs for a treatment abroad, with the exception of emergency treatment received in the event of illness or accident abroad. Mr Kohll, a Luxembourg national, made a request for authorisation for the treatment of his daughter by an orthodontist established in Trier, Germany, which request was rejected by the *Union des Caisses de Maladie.* Since the reimbursement of the costs of medical services provided in other Member States is subject to an authorisation procedure contrary to medical services provided in Luxembourg, the legislation can be considered discriminatory. The Court did not touch upon the question of whether the Luxembourg legislation must be qualified as an (in)distinctly applicable measure which could therefore be justified by imperative requirements relating to the safeguarding of the financial stability of the health sector. Instead, it held that such rules deter insured persons from approaching providers of medical services established in another Member State and constitute a barrier to freedom to provide services.[229] According to AG Tesauro, though, the measure at issue should have been regarded as indistinctly applicable. He argued that the measure did not prescribe, at least not formally and directly, different rules for providers of services established in another Member State. He referred to the Court's ruling in *Bachmann* on a national measure that made the deductibility of certain contributions subject to the condition that they were paid in the Member State itself, which could be justified in the interest of the cohesion of the national tax system, thereby classifying the measure as indistinctly applicable. Eventually, it was not really necessary for the Court to deal with the condition of discrimination, as the Court came to the conclusion that the reimbursement of the costs of dental treatment provided in other Member States in accordance with the tariff of the state of insurance has no significant effect on the financing of the social security system.[230]

Similarly, in *Smits and Peerbooms, Vanbraekel* and *Müller-Fauré* the Court did not question the potentially discriminatory character of the national legislation. It referred to its jugdment in *Kohll* and held that the rules at issue deterred insured persons and service providers to apply to providers of medical services in other Member States and therefore constituted a barrier to the free movement of services.[231] It follows from this case law that the principle of non-discrimina-

[229] Case C-158/96, *Kohll*, paragraph 35.

[230] See also annotation J. Stuyck, *SEW,* 1999, p. 261. By contrast, in Case C-484/93 *Svensson*, a Luxembourg rule restricting interest rate subsidies in respect of the construction, acquisition or improvement of housing to persons who have taken out a loan from a credit institution approved in Luxembourg was considered discriminatory and could therefore only be justifiable on the general interest grounds referred to in Article 46 EC (in conjunction with Article 55 EC). Consequently, differences remain in respect of how the condition of non-discrimination must be interpreted, and to what extent the discriminatory character of a national measure excludes the possibility of invoking mandatory requirements.

[231] Case C-157/99, *Smits and Peerbooms*, paragraph 69; Case C-368/98, *Vanbraekel*, paragraph 45; Case C-385/99, *Müller-Fauré*, paragraph 44.

tion is not a real condition for successfully relying on overriding requirements of public interest in relation to health care. The reasons are probably the important status of public health, including the safeguarding of the health care systems of the Member States, which should allow at least for indirect discrimination, as well as the limited powers of the Community under Article 152 EC to regulate public health at Community level, including a prohibition to harmonise national health laws.

4.4.3.4 The proportionality test: the assessment of public health measures

The proportionality test applies equally to the Treaty exception and public health as overriding requirement of public interest. A distinction can be made between measures within the context of health care, where proportionality serves to set limits on Member States' possibilities to restrict cross-border health care, and measures protecting public health *stricto sensu* more generally, where scientific evidence and the precautionary principle play an important role.

Health care

In *Kohll* the Court concluded that the Luxembourg measure could neither be justified on grounds related to the financing of the social security system, nor on grounds related to public health. The fact that the costs of a treatment in another Member State were reimbursed in accordance with the tariff of the state of insurance had no significant effect on the financing of the social security system made the measure inappropriate to achieve this objective. Furthermore, the Luxembourg rules could not be justified on grounds of public health in order to protect the quality of medical services in other Member States, because this objective was guaranteed by Community harmonisation measures on the mutual recognition of diplomas and qualifications for doctors and dentists. With regard to the objective of maintaining a balanced medical and hospital service open to all, it was not proved that the rules were indispensable for the attainment of this objective. Consequently, the Court did not need to embark on the second and third elements of proportionality.

In *Smits and Peerbooms* and *Müller-Fauré* the Court distinguished between intramural care (hospital services) and extramural care (non-hospital services).[232] The requirement of prior authorisation can in principle only be justified in the case of intramural care, and not of extramural care, following the Court's ruling in *Kohll*.

The Court then accepted that a prior authorisation requirement might be appropriate to safeguard the financial balance of the social security system and the attainment of a high level of health protection. Whether the authorisation

[232] Case C-157/99, *Smits and Peerbooms*; Case C-385/99, *Müller-Fauré*. See also annotations A.P. van der Mei, *LIEI*, 2004, pp. 57-67 and M. Flear, *CMLRev.*, 2004, pp. 209-233.

requirement could eventually be justified, depended on conditions attached to the grant of such an authorisation. In *Müller-Fauré* the Court affirmed the view presented in *Smits and Peerbooms* that prior authorisation can be refused only if the same or equally effective treatment can be obtained without undue delay from an establishment with which the insured person's sickness insurance fund has contractual arrangements.[233] According to the Court in *Müller-Fauré* this implies first that the degree of pain or the nature of a patient's disability, for example to carry out a professional activity, has to be taken into account and second that "a refusal to grant prior authorisation which is based not on fear of wastage resulting from hospital overcapacity but solely on the ground that there are waiting lists on national territory for the hospital treatment concerned, without account being taken of the specific circumstances attaching to the patient's medical condition, cannot amount to a properly justified restriction on the freedom to provide services".[234] Hence, the Court in *Müller-Fauré* appears to have somewhat limited the discretionary power of the state to require prior authorisation for receiving medical care. Furthermore, from a sweeping statement at the end of the judgment the Court makes clear that health care systems cannot be immune from the application of the free movement rules. According to the Court "first, achievement of the fundamental freedoms guaranteed by the Treaty inevitably requires Member States to make some adjustments to their national systems of social security. It does not follow that this would undermine their sovereign powers in this field. It is sufficient in this regard to look to the adjustments which they have had to make to their social security legislation in order to comply with Regulation No 1408/71 [...]. [...] Second, a medical service does not cease to be a provision of services because it is paid for by a national health service or by a system providing benefits in kind."[235]

Public health stricto sensu

Measures aimed at the protection of public health in general must be based on scientific evidence. Scientific data are relevant in assessing the proportionality of a national health measure restricting free movement. Mere references to the potential risks for human health do generally not suffice to justify the imposition of stricter rules on the basis of Article 30 EC: "Account must also be taken of the findings of international scientific research and in particular the work of the Community's Scientific Committee for Food, the Codex Alimentarius Committee of the FAO and the World Health Organization."[236] In the above-mentioned *Smits and Peerbooms* case the first condition, attached to the grant of authorisation, must be assessed in the light of *international* scientific evidence.

[233] Case C-157/99, *Smits and Peerbooms*, paragraph 103.

[234] Case C-385/99, *Müller-Fauré*, paragraph 92.

[235] Case C-385/99, *Müller-Fauré*, paragraphs 102 and 103; see Van de Gronden (2004), pp. 15-16.

[236] Case 178/84, *Commission v. Germany (Reinheitsgebot)*, paragraph 52.

The test based on international scientific information is dynamic as appears from the *Mac Quen* case. According to the Court the assessment of the risks to public health which might result if opticians were authorised to carry out certain eyesight examinations is liable to change with the passage of time, particularly as a result of technical and scientific progress. The Court referred to the situation in Germany where opticians are authorised to carry out certain examinations of their clients' eyesight. Apparently, the level of protection in another Member State may play a role in the context of the rule of reason or a Treaty exception.[237]

The principle of mutual recognition plays a role in this context as well. In *Frans-Nederlandse Maatschappij voor Biologische Producten* the Court held that "it follows from Art. 28 EC in conjunction with Article 30 EC that a Member State is not prohibited from requiring plant protection products to be subject to prior approval, even if those products have already been approved in another Member State. The authorities of the importing State are however not entitled unnecessarily to require technical or chemical analyses or laboratory tests when the same analyses or tests have already been carried out in another Member State and the results are available to those authorities or may at their request be placed at their disposal."[238]

Generally the Court allows Member States considerable leeway in adopting public health measures. In *Kemikalieninspektionen* a Swedish ban on the use of thrichloroethylene, a substance which can be used for degreasing and drying, was considered appropriate and necessary for the protection of public health as mentioned in Article 30 EC. According to the Court "taking account of the latest medical research on the subject, and also the difficulty of establishing the threshold above which exposure to trichloroethylene poses a serious health risk to humans, given the present state of the research, there is no evidence in this case to justify a conclusion by the Court that national legislation such as that at issue in the case in the main proceedings goes beyond what is necessary to achieve the objective in view".[239] The Court referred to the International Cancer Research Agency's evidence that trichloroethylene is a carcinogen. Furthermore, the Court took into account that the system of individual exemptions granted subject to conditions were appropriate and necessary in that it offered increased protection for workers, whilst at the same time taking account of the undertakings' requirements in the matter of continuity.

If the safety of a product is subject to genuine scientific doubt then the state is entitled to protect its public from this product. Where, for example, the data available at the present stage of scientific research do not make it possible to determine with certainty when the number of micro-organisms on a food product represent a danger to health, it is for the Member States to decide the level

[237] Case C-108/96, *Mac Quen*, paragraph 36; see annotation J.W. van de Gronden, *SEW*, 2001, p. 329.

[238] Case 272/80, *Frans-Nederlandse Maatschappij voor Biologische Producten*, paragraph 16.

[239] Case C-473/98, *Kemikalieninspektionen*, paragraph 45.

they consider acceptable to ensure that human life and health are protected.[240] In *Eyssen* the Netherlands had banned the use of nisin, a preservative, in processed cheese.[241] Research into the effects of nisin for public health had been undertaken by international and national research bodies. Some sources suggested that nisin should be banned as being harmful to public health whilst others suggested that nisin was perfectly safe. At the background dietary habits in different states also played a role in assessing the level of risk presented by nisin consumption. Consequently, real doubt about a product's safety may justify restrictive action under Article 30 EC even if other states have formed a different view.[242] As appears from *Mac Quen*, however, other Member States' views can be taken into account if in the passage of time the risk to public health has changed as a result of technical progress and scientific development.

In *Commission v. Denmark* the Court explicitly referred to the precautionary principle in respect of a Danish law allowing for the marketing of foodstuffs enriched with nutrients only if such enrichment met a need in the Danish population.[243] In examining whether the Danish law being restrictive of the free movement of goods under Article 28 EC could nevertheless be justified on grounds of public health as mentioned in Article 30 EC the Court held that a prohibition on the marketing of foodstuffs to which nutrients have been added must be based on a detailed assessment of the risk to public health.[244] According to the Court "in many cases, the assessment of those factors will demonstrate that there is a high degree of scientific and practical uncertainty in that regard. A proper application of the precautionary principle presupposes, in the first place, the identification of the potentially negative consequences for health of the proposed addition of nutrients, and, secondly, a comprehensive assessment of the risk to health based on the most reliable scientific data available and the most recent results of international research." "Where it proves to be impossible to determine with certainty the existence or extent of the alleged risk because of the insufficiency, inconclusiveness or imprecision of the results of studies conducted, but the likelihood of real harm to public health persists should the risk materialise, the precautionary principle justifies the adoption of restrictive measures."[245] In this case the Danish measures were eventually considered disproportionate and could not be upheld on grounds relating to the protection of public health.[246]

---

240 Case 97/83, *Melkunie*; Case C-375/90, *Commission v. Greece.*

241 Case 53/80, *Eyssen.*

242 Weatherill and Beaumont (1999), p. 539.

243 Case C-192/01, *Commission v. Denmark.*

244 Case C-192/01, *Commission v. Denmark*, paragraph 47.

245 Case C-192/01, *Commission v. Denmark*, paragraphs 51 and 52.

246 For that matter, according to the Court the absence of a nutritional need also does not in itself justify a complete ban on the marketing of foodstuffs or food supplements: Joined Cases C-211/03, C-299/03 and C-316/03 to C-318/03, *HLH Wahrenvertriebs GmbH and Orthica BV.*

Hence, it must be concluded that the principle of precaution, although not mentioned in the public health paragraph in the Treaty (Article 152 EC), plays an important role in assessing the proportionality of national health measures under Article 30 EC. It also explains the rather cautious approach of the Court to national health matters; as stated by the Court in *Commission v. Denmark* the precautionary principle requires that where scientific evidence is insufficient, inconclusive or uncertain, Member States may take measures when there are reasonable grounds for concern that the potentially dangerous effects on public health may be inconsistent with the level of protection sought. This definition is used by the Commission as well.[247]

4.4.4 The protection of culture

Cultural policy is very diverse covering various subjects like media, art, language, plurality of the press and media, the support of books and reading etc. Since Article 30 EC only refers to the protection of national treasures, and the other Treaty exceptions do not refer to culture or cultural policy at all, this provision will be dealt with first. Article 46 EC, the Treaty exception for restrictions on the free movement of services, may be relevant in the field of broadcasting and will be discussed thereafter. Lastly, culture as overriding requirement of public interest will be touched upon.

4.4.4.1 The protection of national treasures possessing artistic, historic or archaeological value: Article 30 EC

"Since Member States' laws and practices on the protection of works of art are an ill-matched assortment, this fact being explained by divergent interests and cultural traditions, the notion of national treasures is not easy to define." This is stated by the Commission in its first report on the consideration of cultural aspects in European Community action.[248] It appears that Member States are, in the absence of relevant case law, free to define national treasures, which is, according to the different language versions (*Kulturgut von künstlerischem Wert, Patrimonio artistico, Artistiek bezit, Treasures, Trésors*) plausible.[249] The *Italian Art Treasures* case involved an export restriction on art

[247] Oliver (assisted by Malcolm Jarvis) (2003), p. 256; See Commission's Communication on the precautionary principle, COM(2000) 1 final. See also J. Scott and E. Vos, The Juridification of Uncertainty: Observations on the Ambivalence of the Precautionary Principle within the EU and the WTO, in: Ch. Joerges and R. Dehousse (Eds), *Good Governance in Europe's Integrated Market* (Oxford University Press, Oxford, 2002), pp. 260-265.

[248] COM(96) 160 final, chapter V.

[249] Loman, Mortelmans, Post and Watson (1992), p. 46; Uhl (1993), p. 115; A. Mattera, La libre circulation des oeuvres d'art à l'intérieur de la Communauté et la protection des trésors nationaux ayant une valeur artistique, historique ou archéologique, *Revue du Marché Unique Européen*, 1993, p. 22. The Court is

treasures.[250] However, that restriction took the form of an export tax. The Court held that Article 30 EC cannot be used to justify tax measures. There is no case law on this subject which provides for an interpretation of Article 30 EC.[251]

The term *treasures* indicates that the work of art must be of special importance.[252] It does not concern any cultural product, such as books,[253] but objects possessing a particular value with respect to humanity, because of their uniqueness, their importance, and their manifestation of the artistic genius or as evidence of the past.[254] This interpretation does not exclude works of art from contemporary artists,[255] however; it is probable that only in exceptional circumstances, contemporary artists will satisfy this test.[256] The term *national* treasures does not necessarily relate to the nationality of the artist. A *Van Gogh* painting which has been acquired by the British museum in London could otherwise not be protected as national treasure within the meaning of Article 30 EC by the authorities of the United Kingdom. The term national treasures should therefore be understood as cultural objects which form part of the culture or civilisation of a Member State, its traditions, its history and values, regardless of the place where the object was created or the nationality of the creator.[257]

Directive 93/7 on the return of cultural objects unlawfully removed from the territory of a Member State as well as the international Unidroit Convention of 1995, which operates on the basis of private law and provides direct access to the courts of one state by the owner of a stolen cultural object or by a state from

certainly aware that these cultural objects are different: A. Biondi, The Gardener and other Stories: the Peregrinations of Cultural Artefacts within the European Union, in: R. Craufurd Smith (Ed.), *Culture and European Union Law* (Oxford University Press, Oxford, 2004), pp. 155-156.

250 Case 7/68, *Commission v. Italy.*

251 Oliver (assisted by Malcolm Jarvis) (2003), p. 285.

252 Oliver (assisted by Malcolm Jarvis) (2003), p. 286.

253 Case 229/83, *Leclerc.* Article 30 EC should be interpreted restrictively. The protection of creativity and cultural diversity in the realm of publishing are not mentioned in Article 30 EC.

254 See also A. Mattera, La libre circulation des oeuvres d'art à l'intérieur de la Communauté et la protection des trésors nationaux ayant une valeur artistique, historique ou archéologique, *Revue du Marché Unique Européen*, 1993, p. 23.

255 Sparr (1991), p. 92: "Es liegt im Ergebnis also wohl eher an der Experten, dass sie häufig die Bedeutung erst nachträglich erkennen und nicht am tatsächlichen künstlerischen Wert des Werkes. Daraus lässt sich schliessen, dass Artikel 36 EWG-Vertrag auch auf zeitgenössische Kunstwerke angewandt werden kann."

256 A. Mattera, La libre circulation des oeuvres d'art à l'intérieur de la Communauté et la protection des trésors nationaux ayant une valeur artistique, historique ou archéologique, *Revue du Marché Unique Européen*, 1993, p. 24; Oliver (assisted by Malcolm Jarvis) (2003), p. 287.

257 A. Mattera, La libre circulation des oeuvres d'art à l'intérieur de la Communauté et la protection des trésors nationaux ayant une valeur artistique, historique ou archéologique, *Revue du Marché Unique Européen*, 1993, p. 23; Oliver (assisted by Malcolm Jarvis) (2003), p. 287.

which it has been illicitly exported, could be of further guidance.[258] The Directive refers to Article 30 EC and national treasures, while it recognises Member States' competence under national law to define whether works of art are considered as national treasures, but it also provides a list of categories of cultural objects in the annex to the directive. Even though this list is not intended to define objects as national treasures within the meaning of Article 30 EC, it may still be used by the Court of Justice as aid to the interpretation of Article 30 EC.[259] The cultural objects the Directive refers to are national treasures defined by Member States within the meaning of Article 30 EC and cultural objects listed in the annex to the Directive or form part of public collections listed in the inventories of museums, archives or libraries' conservation collection or the inventories of ecclesiastical institutions. The annex contains a heterogeneous list, including paintings, sculptures, old books etc. For each category a minimum age and/or value is required.

Article 2 of the Unidroit Convention on Stolen and Illegally Exported Cultural Objects (1995) contains a general clause reading: "For the purposes of this Convention, cultural objects are those which, on religious or secular grounds, are of importance for archaeology, prehistory, history, literature, art or science and belong to one of the categories listed in the Annex to this Convention." The Annex mirrors to a large extent the Annex to the UNESCO 1970 Convention, which deals with the problem of illicit traffic by means of administrative procedures and state action. However, there are significant differences. The cultural objects do not have to be specifically designated by each state. This protects cultural property of states which do not have a system of classification of movables, most notably the United States and the United Kingdom.

The Annex does not or hardly set requirements regarding the value or age of cultural objects. It has therefore been argued that the definition is too wide. But the scope of this definition does not wholly extend to *illegally exported* cultural objects.[260]

The scope of the Unidroit Convention seems thus much broader than the Council Directive 93/7. Whereas contemporary artists, for example, could satisfy the test of the Unidroit Convention, they may not fulfil the conditions as to age and values of paintings and sculptures set by the Directive. These two legal instruments will return in Chapter 4.

---

[258] Directive 93/7, OJ 1993, L 74/74; see also Prott (1997).

[259] Oliver (assisted by Malcolm Jarvis) (2003), p. 286.

[260] Prott (1997), pp. 26-27.

4.4.4.2 Culture and public policy: Article 46 EC

In the *Bond van Adverteerders* case the public policy exception as laid down in Article 46 EC was invoked by the Dutch government to justify national discriminatory measures restricting advertisements broadcast from other Member States.[261] The Court did not rule out the possibility to rely on the public policy ground for the justification of measures of a cultural nature. Nevertheless it regarded the Dutch measures as disproportionate and therefore not justifiable under Article 46 EC. It held that "[...] the Netherlands government has stated that, in the final analysis, the prohibitions on advertising and subtitling have a non-economic objective, namely that of maintaining the non-commercial and, thereby, pluralistic nature of the Netherlands broadcasting system [...]. It is sufficient to observe in that regard that the measures taken by virtue of that article must not be disproportionate to the intended objective. As an exception to a fundamental principle of the Treaty, Article 46 of the Treaty must be interpreted in such a way that its effects are limited to what is necessary in order to protect the interests which it seeks to safeguard."[262] AG Mancini, however, had explicitly rejected the possibility to extend Article 46 EC as to include the safeguarding of a pluralistic, non-commercial television system through the financing of broadcasting organisations considering the Court's strictness in interpreting the public policy ground in Article 46 EC. Invoking grounds of public policy presupposes the "existence of a genuine and sufficiently serious threat to the requirements of public policy affecting one of the fundamental interests of society".[263]

In the *Fedicine* case the Spanish government invoked Articles 46 and 55 EC for the justification of a discriminatory distribution scheme for the fostering of Spanish film production.[264] Since the measure served an economic aim recourse to Article 46 EC was not justified. Even though the Court pointed at the fact that Article 46 EC does not include culture, it nevertheless examined the possible application of Article 46 EC to a cultural measure.

In *ERT* the Greek government invoked Article 46 EC for the justification of a national measure granting a monopoly to an organisation for the broadcasting of national programmes and programmes from other Member States.[265] The Court rejected the argument of the Greek government that only limited numbers of channels were available and admitting more organisations to these channels would cause disturbance. It also considered that Member States can only invoke Article 46 EC if the national measure is in accordance with general principles of law and in particular with fundamental rights, like the freedom of expression.[266]

---

[261] Case 352/85, *Bond van Adverteerders.*

[262] Case 352/85, *Bond van Adverteerders,* paragraphs 35 and 36.

[263] Case 30/77, *Bouchereau,* paragraph 35.

[264] Case C-17/92, *Fedicine.*

[265] Case C-260/89, *ERT.*

[266] Case C-260/89, *ERT,* paragraph 43.

4.4.4.3 Culture as overriding requirement of public interest

On the basis of its rule of reason case law the Court has gradually accepted more and more exception grounds for cultural measures. These include measures which have as their objectives the encouragement of a cinematographic work,[267] the preserving of a pluralistic and non-commercial public service television system,[268] the guarantee of a certain quality of the programmes,[269] the adoption of a policy for the promotion of a language of a Member State[270] or the protection of the pluriformity of the press.[271]

The Court was asked in a number of cases to reconsider the balance struck by the Community legislator between the free movement of goods and consumer protection regarding Community provisions on the use of language in labelling. The *Meyhui*,[272] *Peeters I*[273] and *Peeters II*[274] cases concern both protection of consumers' right to be well informed as the policy to protect various languages within the territory of the Member State. In the *Tourist Guide* cases the Court accepted that public interests in respect of the exploitation of national treasures may be a ground for justifying restrictions of the freedom to provide services.[275]

4.4.4.4 (No) condition that cultural measures should apply without distinction

At the outset it is clear that national measures to promote the use of a (regional) language may have discriminatory effects towards products, services or persons from other Member States. If the classic legal approach to mandatory requirements is followed, however, distinctly applicable measures will not be justifiable on cultural grounds. Several cases indicate, though, that the Court does not always follow its standard *Cassis de Dijon* approach concerning the application of the rule of reason in the cultural field.

---

[267] Joined Cases 60 and 61/84, *Cinéthèque*.

[268] Case C-288/89, *Collectieve Antennevoorziening Gouda*.

[269] Case C-353/89, *Commission v. The Netherlands (Media law)*.

[270] Case 379/87, *Groener*.

[271] Case C-368/95, *Familiapress*.

[272] Case C-51/93, *Meyhui*.

[273] Case C-369/89, *Peeters I*.

[274] Case C-85/94, *Peeters II*.

[275] Case C-154/89, *Commission v. France*; Case C-180/89, *Commission v. Italy*; Case C-198/89, *Commission v. Greece*.

Language policy

In *Groener* the Court considered a policy designed to promote the use of a language as a means of expressing national identity and culture a mandatory requirement that may justify a distinctly applicable measure restricting the free movement of workers.[276] Even though *Groener* cannot really be qualified as a 'rule of reason case', as the Court was engaged in an interpretation of a provision of Regulation 1612/68 (Article 3(1)), it is still relevant because the Court made clear that it is willing to take account of legitimate interests of the Member States concerning the protection of a national language.[277] Mrs. Groener, a Dutch art teacher, was employed on a part-time basis by the College of Marketing and Design in Dublin. When she applied for a permanent full-time post as a lecturer in art at that college, this was refused as she did not possess a certificate showing her proficiency in the Irish language or an equivalent qualification recognised by the Minister. The knowledge of the Irish language, however, was not necessary for the performance of the duties concerned, since all teaching was conducted in English.

According to the Court the "obligation to prove a knowledge of the Irish language imposed by the national provisions in question applies without distinction to Irish and other Community nationals [...]".[278] Since language requirements may affect non-nationals to a greater extent than nationals, they may also be seen as a form of indirect or *de facto* discrimination. Article 3(1) of Regulation 1612/68 only allows for the imposition of conditions relating to linguistic knowledge required by reason of nature of the post to be fulfilled. But: in the case of *Groener* the knowledge of Irish was not necessary for the performance of her duties. The language requirement at issue may therefore have a much greater impact on non-nationals with a completely different cultural background. This concerns people who could not otherwise take up employment compared to nationals, for whom it is not unreasonable to learn their language in order to preserve their own cultural heritage.[279] Concerning the principle of non-discrimination the Court held further that "...the principle of non-discrimination precludes the imposition of any requirement that the linguistic knowledge in question must have been acquired within the national territory. It also implies that the national of other Member States should have an opportunity to retake the oral examination, in the event of their having previously failed it, when they again apply for a post of assistant or lecturer."[280]

---

[276] Case 379/87, *Groener.*

[277] See also Loman, Mortelmans, Post and Watson (1992), p. 66; see also B. de Witte, Language Law of the European Union: Protecting or Eroding Linguistic Diversity?, in: R. Craufurd Smith, *Culture and European Union Law* (Oxford University Press, Oxford, 2004), pp. 224-229. For a critical view with regard to the fact that the ECJ did not consider Ireland's policy to promote the Irish language under Article 39 EC see: Creech (2005), p. 103.

[278] Case 379/87, *Groener,* paragraph 13.

[279] Loman, Mortelmans, Post and Watson (1992), p. 58.

[280] Case 379/87, *Groener,* paragraph 23.

The *Groener* ruling was confirmed in *Angonese* where the requirement to obtain a language certificate was considered to put nationals of other Member States at a disadvantage by comparison with residents of the province of Bolzano. The Court held that "a requirement, such as the one at issue in the main proceedings, making the right to take part in a recruitment competition conditional upon possession of a language diploma that may be obtained in only one province of a Member State and not allowing any other equivalent evidence could be justified only if it were based on objective factors unrelated to the nationality of the persons concerned if it were in proportion to the aim legitimately pursued. The Court has ruled that the principle of non-discrimination precludes any requirement that the linguistic knowledge in question must have been acquired within the national territory. It follows that, where an employer makes a person's admission to a recruitment competition subject to a requirement to provide evidence of his linguistic knowledge exclusively by means of one particular diploma, such as the Certificate, issued only in one particular province of a Member State, that requirement constitutes discrimination on grounds of nationality contrary to Article 39 of the EC Treaty."[281]

In *Bickel and Franz*, another case on the free movement of persons and language rules, the opposite situation occurred. An Austrian lorry driver (Mr. Bickel) and a German tourist (Mr. Franz) were both charged with criminal offences in Italy. Before the Italian Court they declared that they had no knowledge of Italian and relied on the rules for the protection of the German-speaking community of the Province of Bolzano, which provided that the German language has the same status as the Italian language and that the German-speaking citizens of the Province of Bolzano were entitled to use their own language in relations with the judicial and administrative authorities based in that province. The Italian court was uncertain whether these rules should, under Community law, be extended to nationals of other Member States visiting the province and referred the case to the Court of Justice. According to the Court "rules which make the right, in a defined area, to have criminal proceedings conducted in the language of the person concerned conditional on that person being resident in that area, favour nationals of the host State by comparison with nationals of other Member States exercising their right of free movement and therefore run counter to the principle of non-discrimination laid down in Article 12 of the Treaty. A residence requirement of that kind can be justified only if it is based on objective considerations independent of the nationality of the persons concerned and is proportionate to the legitimate aim of the national provisions."[282]

---

[281] Case C-281/98, *Roman Angonese*, paragraphs 42-44.

[282] Case C-274/96, *Bickel and Franz*, paragraphs 26 and 27; see also annotation H. Luijendijk, *SEW*, 1999, pp. 346-350.

These cases on the relationship between language rules and the Treaty provisions on free movement show that indirectly discriminatory measures, contrary to overtly discriminatory measures, to protect a national language can, within the context of the free movement of workers, be justified on cultural grounds.

The plurality of the media

Also within the context of the free movement of services it is unclear to what extent the condition that only indistinctly applicable measures can be justified on public interest grounds is applicable at all. In the *Media law* case the possibly discriminatory effects of the provisions in Dutch law obliging the use of technical resources of one organisation, the NOPB (Netherlands Broadcasting Production Company), for the production of radio and television programmes, and the conditions in the Media law relating to the structure of broadcasting bodies established in other Member States and relating to advertising were not examined by the Court.[283] In *Bond van Adverteerders*, on the other hand, the Court explicitly held that national measures which restricted the relaying of advertisements broadcast from other Member States were discriminatory and could therefore only be justified if they could be brought within the scope of an express derogation in the Treaty.[284]

The protection of national treasures

In the *Tourist Guide* cases licence requirements imposed on tourist guides accompanying groups of tourists from one Member State to another were considered justifiable on grounds related to the exploitation of the national artistic and archaeological treasures, but were nevertheless disproportionate to their aim.[285]

Book pricing

Within the context of the free movement of goods, the judgments in *Leclerc* and *Cinéthèque* are more in line with the classic legal doctrine on mandatory requirements.[286] In *Leclerc* a French Act, the *Loi Lang*, was involved which required publishers and importers of books to fix retail prices for the books which they publish or import. It was up to the retailers to determine the effective price, but this had to be between 95% and 100% of the price set up by the publishers or importers. For imported books published in France the price fixed by the importer was not allowed to be less than the price fixed by the publisher. According to the Court the legislation made it impossible for any importer to

[283] Case C-353/89, *Commission v. The Netherlands (Media law).*

[284] Case 352/85, *Bond van Adverteerders.*

[285] Case C-154/89, *Commission v. France,* Case C-180/89, *Commission v. Italy* and Case C-198/89, *Commission v. Greece.*

[286] Case 229/83, *Leclerc*; Joined Cases 60 and 61/84, *Cinéthèque.*

charge a retail price which is more adequate in the light of the cost price in the country of origin. As it created separate rules for imported books, it was liable to impede trade between Member States. Given the discriminatory character of the law recourse to Article 30 EC would be the only possibility for the justification of the price measure. However, since neither the safeguarding of consumer interests, nor the protection of creativity in the realm of publishing is mentioned in Article 30 EC, the law was held incompatible with Article 28 EC.

Cinema

In *Cinéthèque* a French measure which determined that cinematographic works irrespective of their origin which were being shown in French cinemas could not be exploited simultaneously in the form of videocassettes. This law was clearly indistinctly applicable and could therefore be justified on grounds related to the encouragement of the creation of cinematographic works by means of a system giving priority, for a limited period, to the distribution of such works through the cinemas.

The fact, though, that many cultural measures lead to discrimination may necessitate a flexible approach by the Court. Culture is after all closely related to a country or region. In his Opinion in the *Fedicine* case AG Van Gerven considered that measures adopted for the protection of cultural heritage will not infrequently involve a direct or indirect advantage for its own artists or cultural institutions, e.g. the establishment of a film or literature prize or other encouragement of artists or artistic societies. He advocated an analogue application of Article 30 EC, which has to be interpreted broadly, to restrictions on the freedom to provide services.[287] However, where a national measure clearly discriminates it will still be subject to strict scrutiny by the Court. In the *Commission v. Spain* case for example the Court held a Spanish measure granting their own nationals free admission to museums, where nationals of other Member States more than 21 years of age were required to pay an entrance fee, to contravene the principle of non-discrimination and the free movement of services.[288]

4.4.4.5 The proportionality test: the assessment of cultural measures

Like in case of the horizontal and flanking policies discussed above, the scope for national cultural policy eventually depends on the proportionality test as well.

---

[287] Opinion of AG Van Gerven in Case C-17/92, *Fedicine*.

[288] Case C-45/93, *Commission v. Spain*; see also Case C-388/01, *Musea (I)*, where the Italian government is accused by the Commission of imposing discriminatory charges for the admission to public museums, monuments, galleries, archaeological digs, parks and gardens in Italy to the detriment of foreign tourists who are not resident in such areas and do not fulfil the same age requirement.

The plurality of the media

In the *Media law* case the Court was not convinced that provisions in the Media law were proportionate to the objective of maintaining pluralism in the media sector. With regard to the condition relating to the structure of broadcasting bodies established in other Member States the Court held that "...it should be observed that there is no necessary connection between such a cultural policy and the conditions relating to the structure of foreign broadcasting bodies. In order to ensure pluralism in the audio-visual sector it is not indispensable for the national legislation to require broadcasting bodies established in other Member States to align themselves on the Dutch model should they intend to broadcast programmes containing advertisements intended for the Dutch public. In order to secure pluralism which it wishes to maintain the Netherlands government may very well confine itself to formulating the statutes of its own bodies in an appropriate manner."[289] With regard to the obligation to have all or some programmes produced by the NOPB the Court applied the second element of the proportionality requirement and held that the Netherlands went beyond the objective pursued: "if it is genuinely in the interest of those bodies to spend all or a proportion of their funds with the NOPB and hence cannot be capable of justifying that obligation".[290]

Language

The case law on language rules shows that Member States have considerable latitude in protecting and fostering their own language. Nevertheless the Court has been careful to stress that the protection of a linguistic minority is a legitimate objective per se, which is *prima facie* justified. Member States' language policy still has to be held up to the light of the principle of proportionality. AG Jacobs in his Opinion in *Bickel and Franz* points at the irony in this case, where the Italian government preferred the proceedings to be conducted in Italian via the use of interpreters: "refusing the use of German to visitors does not in any way serve [the aim of protecting a linguistic minority]. If anything, it has the reverse effect: it reinforces Italian as the principal language even in the predominantly German-speaking region of Bolzano."[291]

Press diversity

The *Familiapress* case is a good example of a case where the Court indicated the ground rules of the proportionality test and left the actual examination of the facts to the national court.[292] In 1992 Austria deregulated the field of

---

[289] Case C-353/89, *Commission v. The Netherlands (Media law)*, paragraph 42.

[290] Case C-353/89, *Commission v. The Netherlands (Media law)*, paragraph 31.

[291] Annotation R. Lane and N. Nic Shuibhne, *CMLRev.*, 2000, pp. 1246-1247.

[292] Case C-368/95, *Familiapress*; See also J.H. Jans, Proportionality revisited, *LIEI*, 2000, p. 247; however, according to Bavasso in his annotation, the Court is imposing on the national court an excessively onerous task, *CMLRev.*, 1998, p. 1425.

competition by the enactment of the 'Law on Deregulation of Competition', and liberalised *inter alia* the organisation of price competitions. Out of fear that small publishers would not be able to compete with the big ones and to resist cut throat competition, the law was amended to exclude the press from the application of the provisions on price competition. In Austria the market share of the largest press group was 54,5%. This is extremely high compared to, for example, Germany (23,9%) and the United Kingdom (34,7%). Accordingly, the main reason for excluding the press sector from price competition was the maintenance of press diversity.

An Austrian newspaper publisher, Familiapress, brought an action against Heinrich Bauer Verlag, a German newspaper publisher, before the Austrian court claiming that Bauer had acted against the Austrian Law on Unfair Competition. Bauer had published its weekly magazine Laura in Austria containing cross word puzzles which offered winners a prize of DM 500. The Austrian court referred the case to the Court of Justice to examine the compatibility of the law with Article 28 EC. First, the Court held that the law constituted a measure having equivalent effect to a quantitative restriction within the meaning of Article 28 EC. The Court then considered whether the aim to maintain press diversity was an overriding requirement for the purposes of Article 28 EC. This was the first case where the maintenance of press diversity was considered a mandatory requirement justifying restrictions on the free movement of goods. However, the maintenance of press diversity may justify limitations in so far as they are prescribed by law and necessary in a democratic society, and should be interpreted in the light of the European Convention for the Protection of Human Rights and Fundamental Freedoms.[293] Furthermore, in order to assess whether less restrictive measures were available the Court pointed out several conditions which the Austrian court had to examine: The Austrian press market needs to be defined, the market share of individual publishers or press groups has to be determined and the extent to which the product concerned can be replaced by papers which do not offer prizes has to be assessed, taking into account all relevant factors. The Court also provided alternatives, such as blacking out or removing the page on which the prize competition appears in copies intended for Austria, or a statement that readers in Austria do not qualify for a chance to win a prize.

The Court distinguished the approach from *Schindler* along the lines of AG Tesauro.[294] The large scale lotteries in *Schindler* cannot be compared with the small contests and modest prizes in *Familiapress*. The fact that Member States should be granted a wide discretion to determine the necessary requirements for protecting players and maintaining order in society does not apply to every game

[293] Case C-368/95, *Familiapress*, paragraphs 24-26.

[294] Case C-275/92, *Schindler*; see also the section on consumer protection above.

irrespective its scale. Consequently the nature of the interest to be protected is relevant to the manner in which the proportionality test will be applied.[295]

4.5 Conclusions

In its 'rule of reason' the Court of Justice has offered a considerable number of exception grounds to the prohibitive rules on free movement. It has thereby explicitly given weight to the consideration of horizontal and flanking policy interests in the application of the free movement rules to national measures aimed at safeguarding these interests where the Treaty itself does not provide for this possibility. Hence, it seems undisputed on the basis of the Court's case law that Member States may at the outset and under the conditions of non-discrimination and proportionality restrict free movement for the protection of horizontal and flanking policy interests, at least within their own territory; but this is not or only to a very limited extent the case for 'extra-territorial' horizontal and flanking measures, an issue which will not be further analysed here.

It appears that the justification of a national measure eventually depends on the principle of proportionality. The first two elements of proportionality, i.e. the existence of a causal connection between the aim pursued and the measure adopted and the fact that there is no alternative to it that is less restrictive to trade, are particularly relevant. The application of the proportionality principle also allows the Court to take into account important principles of horizontal and flanking policies, like the precautionary principle, or even the integration principle. Domestic preferences based on cultural differences between regions or Member States, and the fact that certain activities are restrictively regulated due to their sensitive nature from a consumer point of view can also be considered under an assessment of the proportionality of a national measure.

Contrary to the proportionality principle, the relevance of the principle of non-discrimination for invoking the 'rule of reason' exceptions, or overriding requirements of public interest, is less clear, certainly in the field of the environment. Even though it is often mentioned alongside proportionality as one of the conditions for invoking these exception grounds, it does not seem be a hard condition considering the many possibilities to justify at least indirectly discriminatory measures for horizontal and flanking policy purposes within the context of the free movement of persons and services, and considering the recent developments in the environmental field (*Preussen Elektra*).

[295] J.H. Jans, Proportionality revisited, *LIEI*, 2000, p. 246.

CHAPTER 3

The Application of the Competition Rules

1 Introduction: the growing relevance of competition law

Tendencies of privatisation, liberalisation and deregulation in most Member States of the European Union have drawn more attention to the function of competition rules, also in the field of horizontal and flanking policies.[1] Liberalisation policies aim at opening up the market to competition, more efficiency and lower prices for consumers. In addition the use of market-based and other economic instruments rather than traditional command and control instruments for the realisation of horizontal and flanking policy objectives has become increasingly important. The Commission has regularly encouraged the use of such instruments in various fields of horizontal and flanking policies, most notably in the area of environmental protection.[2] In its sixth environmental action programme the Commission states that "it is currently examining new methods of governance, including alternatives to traditional regulation such as voluntary commitments and agreements, which could improve the ability of enterprises to innovate and to change".[3] The Commission's Green Paper on Corporate Social Responsibility generally confirms this approach, since corporate social responsibility, which is a concept whereby companies voluntarily decide to contribute to a better society and a cleaner environment by integrating social and environmental concerns in their business operations, may, according to the Commission, contribute to the development of the European economy.[4] Contracts, such as environmental contracts, are one manifestation of a co-operative approach to attain these objectives.

Meanwhile the application of the EC rules on competition (Articles 81-88 EC) in various policy areas entails that Member States as well as private parties are limited to enact measures with 'non-competition' objectives, such as environmental protection, cultural objectives and objectives of public health, but with economic, anti-competitive consequences. It is less evident, however, to what extent such measures may be upheld on grounds relating to horizontal and flanking policies. The problem of tension, therefore, essentially involves the following two elements:

- The existence of a restriction of competition, whether as a result of practices by undertakings or as a result of state action;
- The existence of some kind of justification in terms of a (recognised) horizontal and flanking policy purpose.

1 With regard to privatisation and Community law in general: W. Devroe, Privatization and Community Law: Neutrality versus Policy, *CMLRev.*, 1997, pp. 267-306.

2 See the 5th Environment Action Programme 'Towards Sustainability', OJ 1993, C138/5.

3 The 6th Environment Action Programme 'Environment 2010-Our future, Our choice', COM(2001) 31 final.

4 Green Paper Promoting a European Framework for Corporate Social Responsibility, COM(2001) 366 final; see also L. Bergkamp, Corporate Governance and Social Responsibility: A New Sustainability Paradigm, *EELR*, 2002, pp. 136-152.

In this chapter an analysis will be made of how horizontal and flanking policy objectives are taken into account in the Community's competition policy. We will not only look at the Community's policy with respect to cartels, abusive behaviour of dominant firms and mergers, but also at the application of the state aid rules, rules on exclusive and special rights and the useful effect doctrine as developed in the Court's jurisprudence. Since the relationship between horizontal and flanking policy objectives and competition policy is evolving, it will be useful to sometimes refer to Dutch competition policy specifically in the field of health care. Here the Community legislature lacks substantial powers to harmonise the national laws of the Member States, whereas they remain primarily competent to take action. It is therefore interesting to look at some of the decisions adopted by the Netherlands Competition Authority in this area.[5]

Whereas the free movement rules are primarily aimed at measures adopted by Member States, the Treaty provisions on competition, i.e. Articles 81 and 82 EC, and the Merger Regulation are addressed to undertakings. Some provisions, though, are also aimed at measures adopted by Member States: Article 86(1) EC may apply where Member States grant exclusive or special rights to undertakings; Article 87 EC is applicable where Member States grant state aids to undertakings and the combined Articles 3(1) sub g, 10 and 81 or 82 EC may be applicable where Member States enact measures which render the competition rules ineffective. The exemption of Article 86(2) EC for undertakings entrusted with services of general economic interest can be invoked by (public) undertakings as well as Member States.

Since public authorities of the Member State are assumed to be the most obvious institutions to protect horizontal and flanking policy interests, which are *public* interests, the competition rules directed at Member States are first being discussed. The reason analysing Article 86 EC at this stage as well is twofold. The first paragraph of this provision is directed at Member States and furthermore, the concept of services of general interest contained in the second paragraph, which provision is relevant to both companies and Member States, clearly covers public interests, or horizontal and flanking policy interests as well (section 3). The cartel prohibition (Article 81 EC), the prohibition of the abuse of a dominant position (Article 82 EC) and the Merger Regulation (139/2004), in other words the competition rules directed at companies, will be analysed in the following section (section 4). Before the existence of a restriction can be established, the material, personal and territorial scope of the competition rules need to be assessed first (section 2).

---

5 See also J. van de Gronden, Purchasing Care: Economic Activity or Service of General (Economic) Interest?, *ECLR*, 2004, pp. 87-94.

2 In general: the material, personal and territorial scope of the competition rules

Similarly to what was said before in respect of the free movement rules (see Chapter 2), the assessment of the material, personal and territorial scope of application of the competition rules is essential in that it becomes apparent whether restrictions on competition for horizontal and flanking policy purposes will be exposed to Community law in the first place. If it appears that the competition rules are not applicable, no dispute and hence no problem of tension will arise within the context of competition law.

2.1 The material scope

The EC competition rules involve a system of prohibitive rules to prevent that competition could be distorted within the internal market. Irrespective of their aim restrictions on competition will therefore in principle fall within the material scope of the competition rules. This is somewhat different in the field of sport. According to the Court of First Instance in the *Meca-Medina* case purely sporting legislation may have nothing to do with economic activity or with economic relationships of competition, with the result that it does not fall within the scope of Articles 81 and 82 EC.[6] This case involved anti-doping rules implemented by the International Swimming Federation (FINA), which according to the CFI did not fall within the scope of Article 81 EC. Whether the CFI did not in fact apply an 'inherent restriction approach' is a question that will be dealt with in section 4.1.2.4. *Meca-Medina* shows that the concept of economic activity is not infinite, and must sometimes be restrictively interpreted.

Environmental agreements are covered by Article 81 EC as, according to the Commission, "it is clear that agreements which restrict competition continue to be prohibited by Article 81(1), even if parties invoke environmental protection in order to justify them".[7] In the field of public health and in particular in the pharmaceutical product sector Community competition law plays a role as well.[8] Agreements between pharmaceutical undertakings with regard to vaccines for human use are an example.[9] In the *Sodemare* case the Court has implicitly made clear that Articles 81 and 82 EC apply *ratione materiae* in areas such as the health care sector since it simply applied these provisions without examining whether private non-profit-making bodies engaged in health care activities were to be classified as undertakings.[10] However, where health insurance is involved,

---

6 Case T-313/02, *Meca-Medina*.

7 XXIIIrd Competition Report from the Commission, COM(94) 161, point 77.

8 Report of the Commission on the integration of health protection requirements in Community policies, COM(95) 196 final, p. 11.

9 Commission Decision 94/770, *Pasteur Mérieux-Merck*, OJ 1994, L 309/1.

10 Case C-70/95, *Sodemare and Others v. Regione Lombardia*, paragraph 43.

the Court has adopted a more restricted approach as appears most notably from the *AOK* judgment, wherein the German sickness funds were considered to be undertakings (see hereafter, section 2.2).

The competition rules cover all areas of the economy, but certain sectors have a special position, like agriculture and transport.[11] In *Brentjens* the Court held that agreements concluded in the context of collective negotiations between management and labour in pursuit of social policy objectives must, by virtue of their nature and purpose, be regarded as falling outside the scope of Article 81(1) EC.[12] As AG Jacobs had stressed in his opinion in *Pavlov* and the Court confirmed in its judgment, the exception must be limited to collective agreements concluded between the social partners which by their *nature* and *purpose* fall outside the scope of applicability *ratione materiae* of the competition rules.

Pavlov concerned questions relating to the compulsory membership of an occupational pension fund set up by the Dutch Medical Specialist Association (LSV), a liberal profession's representative body. The Treaty itself promotes close co-operation between Member States in the social field and provides that the Commission must endeavour to develop the dialogue between management and labour at European level which could, if the two sides consider it desirable, lead to relations based on agreement. Therefore the second condition of the *nature* of the agreement must, as appears from *Pavlov,* also be fulfilled. According to AG Jacobs "in order to enjoy antitrust immunity a given agreement must not only pursue a social purpose, but must also be of a particular *nature,* namely a collective agreement reached after collective bargaining between management and labour".[13] The Court held that "such exclusion from the scope of Article 81(1) of the Treaty cannot be applied to an agreement which [...] is not concluded in the context of collective bargaining between employers and employees. On this point, it should be emphasised that the Treaty contains no provisions, like Articles 118 and 118b of the EC Treaty (Articles 117 to 120 of the EC Treaty have been replaced by Articles 136 EC to 143 EC) or Articles 1 and 4 of the Agreement on Social policy (OJ 1992 C 191, p. 91), encouraging members of the liberal professions to conclude collective agreements with a view to improving their terms of employment and working conditions and providing that, at the request of a member of the professions, such agreements be made compulsory by the public authorities, for all the members of the professions in question."[14]

Since the agreements in *Pavlov* were not concluded between the social partners, but by parties which are considered to constitute associations of undertakings, they therefore fell within the ambit of Article 81 EC.[15]

---

11 Jones and Sufrin (2004), pp. 92-93.

12 Joined Cases C-115/97, C-116/97 and C-117/97, *Brentjens*, paragraph 57.

13 Opinion of AG Jacobs in Joined Cases C-180/98 to C-184/98, *Pavlov,* paragraph 98; see also E. Loozen, Pavlov en Van der Woude: meer dan een Pavlov-reactie?, *NTER*, 2000, pp. 301-307.

14 Joined Cases C-180/98 to C-184/98, *Pavlov,* paragraphs 68 and 69.

15 See also K. Mortelmans, Towards convergence in the application of the rules on free movement and on competition, *CMLRev.*, 2001, p. 629.

Agreements or restrictive practices pursuing horizontal and flanking policy goals have, contrary to collective labour agreements, not been granted a special status by the *Treaty*. Nevertheless, various policy documents – 'soft law instruments' – refer to and encourage the conclusion of agreements to pursue horizontal and flanking policy goals.[16] This is particularly true in the field of the environment, where the potential of environmental agreements to contribute to environmental policy objectives is widely recognised.[17] Hence, if the word *Treaty* is to be understood literally, i.e. how the Court's jurisprudence should be understood, agreements including horizontal and flanking policy goals are not *by their nature* sheltered from the application of the competition rules. Any different view would entail that the applicability of the competition rules depends on the interpretation of policy documents presented by the Community Institutions, which would jeopardise the application of the competition rules and as a consequence cause considerable legal uncertainty. Whenever agreements pursuing horizontal and flanking policy aims have (potential) harmful effects on competition in the market they should in principle not be excluded from the scope of Article 81(1) EC. Horizontal and flanking policies involve the market for goods and services, contrary to social policy, which involves the labour market, where trade unions and employers' organisations are involved in collective bargaining. The collective agreement is a co-ordinated attempt to influence the political decision-making and would not appear to distort competition.[18]

Naturally, where horizontal and flanking policy considerations are included in collective labour agreements, the *Brentjens* jurisprudence will be relevant. In the field of public health, for example, where an agreement concluded in the form of a collective agreement between the social partners establishes a health care insurance scheme, this agreement may fall outside the scope of Article 81(1) EC. Such an agreement would contribute to improving the working conditions of the employees, not only by ensuring that they have the necessary means to meet medical expenses, but also by reducing the costs which, in the absence of a collective agreement, would have to be borne by the employees.[19]

Similarly to the broad material scope of Articles 81 and 82 EC, Article 87 EC, the provision on state aids, also applies *ratione materiae* to horizontal and flanking policies; according to the Court the social character of the measure is not

---

16 More generally: Green Paper Promoting a European framework for Corporate Social Responsibility, COM(2001) 366.

17 See, for example: Communication from the Commission on Environmental Agreements within the Framework of the Action Plan on the Simplification and Improvement of the Regulatory Environment, COM(2002) 412 final; The 5th and 6th Environment Action Programme; Commission Recommendation 96/733 concerning Environmental Agreements implementing Community directives, OJ 1996, L 333/59.

18 Annotation L. Gyselen, *CMLRev.*, 2000, pp. 441-442.

19 Case C-222/98, *Van der Woude*, paragraphs 24 and 25.

sufficient to exclude it outright from being categorised as aid for the purposes of Article 87 of the Treaty.[20]

2.2 The personal scope

Of central importance for the assessment of the scope of application of the competition rules is the concept of undertaking, which is not defined in the EC Treaty, but has been broadly interpreted by the Court of Justice.

2.2.1 The concept of undertaking in general

According to the definition provided by the Court in *Höfner* and subsequent cases the concept of undertaking encompasses "every entity engaged in an economic activity, regardless the legal status of the entity and the way it is financed".[21] This definition raises two questions. First what must be understood by 'economic activity'; second: how broadly should this definition be interpreted.[22] The functional character of the concept of undertaking, which implies that the type of activity performed rather than the characteristics of the actors which perform it is relevant, the social objectives associated with it, or the regulatory or funding arrangements to which it is subject in a particular Member State,[23] entail that all sorts of horizontal and flanking activities can be brought within the ambit of the competition rules. Nevertheless, according to the case law of the Court of Justice certain activities cannot be characterised as economic and are therefore excluded from the scope of application of the competition rules; the rules on competition do not apply to an activity (i) which is connected with the exercise of the powers of a public authority; or (ii) which by its nature, its aim and the rules to which it is subject does not belong to the sphere of economic activity.[24]

Regarding (i) if the undertaking is engaged in a task in the public interest which forms part of the essential functions of the state, it will not be regarded as undertaking within the meaning of the Treaty. The *Diego Cali* case involved the payment to be made by Cali for anti-pollution surveillance exercised by SEPG

---

[20] Case C-241/94, *France v. Commission*, paragraph 21.

[21] Case C-41/90, *Höfner and Elser*, paragraph 21 and Joined Cases C-159/91 and C-160/91, *Poucet*, paragraph 17; see more generally Bellamy & Child (Edited by P.M. Roth QC) (2001), p. 45; Jones and Sufrin (2004), pp. 107-127.

[22] A. Winterstein, Nailing the Jellyfish: Social Security and Competition Law, *ECLR*, 1999, p. 325; V. Louri, Undertaking as a Jurisdictional Element for the Application of the EC Competition Rules, *LIEI*, 2002, p. 146.

[23] Opinion of AG Jacobs of 22 May 2003 in Joined Cases C-264/01, C-306/01, C-354/01 and C-355/01, *AOK Bundesverband*, paragraph 25.

[24] Case C-309/99, *Wouters*, paragraph 57.

(*SpA Porto Petroli di Genova*, a private undertaking holding an exclusive right) in relation to the loading and unloading of acetone products transported by Cali in the oil port of Genoa. The Court held that "anti-pollution surveillance for which SEPG was responsible in the oil port of Genoa is a task in the public interest which forms part of the essential functions of the state as regards protection of the environment in maritime areas. Such surveillance is connected by its nature, its aim and the rules to which it is subject with the exercise of powers relating to the protection of the environment which are typically those of a public authority. It is not of an economic nature justifying the application of the Treaty rules on competition."[25] Other organisations which have been considered by the Court as organisation entrusted with the operation of a public service are local authorities granting concessions for funeral services[26] and Eurocontrol, an air traffic control organisation in charge of maintaining and improving air navigation safety.[27]

Regarding (ii) the competition rules may not be held applicable for certain bodies that fulfil a social function. This is particularly so in the field of social security where the principle of solidarity plays a key role. The Court has on a case by case basis assessed whether social security schemes should be considered as economic activities. According to the Court's judgment in *Cisal* it depends on three elements for a body to fulfil a social function: the social aim of the insurance scheme, the principle of solidarity – contributions are not systematically proportionate to the risk insured and the amount of benefits is not necessarily proportionate to the insured person's earnings – and the activity of the body is subject to supervision by the state and the amount of benefits is, in the last resort, fixed by the state.[28]

The Court thus gives particular weight to the principle of solidarity and the fact that the insurance scheme managed by the body is subject to supervision by the state. The Institute performs an exclusively social function and its activity is therefore not economic within the meaning of the competition rules. It pursued its line of thought set out in the earlier *Poucet* ruling, where it held that French bodies administering sickness and maternity insurance schemes for self-employed persons engaged in non-agricultural occupations and the basic pension scheme for skilled traders were not to be classified as undertakings for the purpose of competition law.[29]

Where certain social security schemes, however, are optional and based on the principle of capitalisation and providing benefits of which level depends on the amount of contributions paid and the financial results of the undertakings

---

25 Case C-343/95, *Diego Cali*, paragraphs 22 and 23.

26 Case 30/87, *Bodson*.

27 Case C-364/92, *SAT Fluggesellschaft v. Eurocontrol*.

28 Case C-218/00, *Cisal*, paragraphs 37 to 44.

29 Joined Cases C-159/91 and C-161/91, *Poucet and Pistre*.

they, according to the Court in *FFSA*, constitute economic activities and are therefore subject to the competition rules.[30] The fact that they are non-profit-making and the manifestations of solidarity do not deprive them from the application of the competition rules.[31] On the basis of this case law it must be concluded that where the legislator chooses to introduce market elements in primarily non-economic, or rather social (security) areas, the competition rules will be applicable. This conclusion may have been premature; the Court in the *AOK* case has now once again reinforced the important role of the solidarity principle in determining the applicability of the competition rules in the health care sector, even in a situation of (potential) competition between sickness funds and between sickness funds and health insurers.[32] This judgment will be discussed in the following section within the context of public health.

The consequence of the Court's approach is that at least before the judgment in *AOK* a distinction could be made between undertakings that exercise typically public law powers, undertakings that fulfil an exclusively social function (Poucet, Cisal) and undertakings that are engaged in economic activities, i.e. undertakings which have the possibility to set their own market strategy and which activities are in real or potential competition with activities of other undertakings (FFSA and Brentjens).[33] In *AOK*, though, the Court has laid more emphasis on the principle of solidarity; furthermore, therefore this judgment has blurred the distinction between organisations fulfilling an exclusively social function and undertakings managing social security schemes but being engaged in economic activities.

Hence it does not follow from *Diego Cali "a contrario* that activities outside the realm of *imperium* are all bound to be economic and to fall within the scope of the competition rules".[34] Neither is the decisive criterion whether the activity can, at least in principle, be carried out by a private undertaking in order to

---

30 Case C-244/94, *Fédération Française des Sociétés d'Assurance.*

31 Joined Cases C-115/97, C-116/97 and C-117/97, *Brentjens*; Joined Cases C-180/98 to C-184/98, *Pavlov.*

32 Joined Cases C-264/01, C-306/01, C-354/01 and C-355/01, *AOK Bundesverband.*

33 The Court carefully examines the characteristics of the activities employed by the respective institutes to determine the extent of competition: A. Winterstein, Nailing the Jellyfish: Social Security and Competition Law, *ECLR*, 1999, p. 325.

34 Annotation L. Gyselen, *CMLRev.*, 2000, pp. 439-440: According to Gyselen the degree of solidarity is not a helpful criterion to determine whether certain organisations carry out economic activities. The question is not whether a certain entity is an undertaking, but whether a certain activity can be qualified as economic. Hence, it is according to him more logical to distinguish between activities which by virtue of their *imperium* fall outside the scope of the competition rules, i.e. if they are pursued by entities pursuant to their special prerogatives as sovereign regulators, and activities which fall within the scope of the competition rules, including activities pursued by entities administering a social protection regime.

make profits.[35] In the field of social security the Court instead focuses upon the important role of the solidarity principle, to determine whether certain bodies or organisations should be qualified as undertakings.[36]

Horizontal and flanking policy interests, except health care (see hereafter, section 2.2.2), by their very nature, do not really play a role in assessing the personal scope of application of the competition rules. In the case of *Diego Cali* or *Poucet* horizontal and flanking policy interests can only be taken into account in the wake of the Court's judgment. Activities pursued by organisations with a view to attain horizontal and flanking policy goals are all bound to be economic and are thus not sheltered from the application of the competition rules.

2.2.2 Horizontal and flanking activities

The social aim may not in itself be sufficient to preclude the activity from being classified as non-economic, neither is the fact that an undertaking fulfils horizontal and flanking tasks material, provided that they are engaged in an economic activity. The dual nature of horizontal and flanking policies entails that organisations pursuing horizontal and flanking policy concerns are generally not sheltered from the application of the competition rules. Certain activities can either belong to the prerogatives of the state or can be primarily non-economic (see above), they are nonetheless excluded from the application of the competition rules. Since the state increasingly allows certain organisations pursuing horizontal and flanking policy aims more discretion in setting their own market strategy, the relevance of competition law will grow as their activities will automatically fall within the scope *ratione personae* of the competition rules. The question is how much room for competition is sufficient for an organisation to qualify as undertaking and how as a consequence the

---

35 See, however, Opinion AG Jacobs in Joined Cases C-264/01, C-306/01, C-354/01 and C-355/01, *AOK Bundesverband*, paragraph 27, where he states that "in assessing whether an activity is economic in character, the basic test appears to me to be whether it could, at least in principle, be carried on by a private undertaking in order to make profits. If there were no possibility of a private undertaking carrying on a given activity, there would be no purpose in applying the competition rules to it." But in the following paragraph he states: "However, the application of that test in relation to certain fields of activity is by no means straightforward, and the Court has developed a more elaborate set of criteria to assist in the assessment. Of particular relevance for present purposes, there is now a considerable body of case-law concerning the proper classification of pension and social insurance schemes."

36 See also J. van de Gronden, Purchasing Care: Economic Activity or Service of General (Economic) Interest?, *ECLR*, 2004, pp. 87-94: he distinguishes between the abstract approach as in *Diego Cali*, and the concrete approach which can be found in cases like *Poucet* and *Brentjens*. Buendia Sierra criticises the approach of the ECJ in *Poucet* and submits that economic activities are activities that can be substituted by a private service, or, in other words those activities which can be privatised: Buendia Sierra (1999), p. 59.

dividing line between economic and non-economic activities must be determined in cases involving horizontal and flanking policy activities.[37]

Culture

Cultural organisations will thus not be sheltered from the application of the competition rules, if these organisations are engaged in economic activities. Television undertakings cannot be sheltered from the application of the competition rules as argued by the Italian and German governments in the *Sacchi* case, because they fulfil a task which concerns the public and is of a cultural and informative nature.[38] Similarly, the Commission considered that performances of artists fall within the scope of the competition rules as artists can be considered undertakings within the meaning of Article 81 EC when they commercially exploit their artistic achievements. In this case a number of artists, four leading opera singers performing Don Carlos at La Scala, Milan, had concluded an exclusive contract with the company UNITEL producing films for television. The Commission regarded this exclusive contract as possibly preventing performers (artists) from exploiting their achievements in other ways in other Member States.[39] Architects can probably also be considered as undertakings, since they perform professional services for which they receive remuneration.[40]

Public health

The question concerning the personal scope of application of the competition rules is mainly relevant in the field of health care, being part of the social security system of a Member State. The Court held in *Pavlov* that self-employed medical specialists could be regarded as undertakings. According to the Court "the medical specialists who are members of the National Association of Specialists of the Royal Netherlands Society for the Promotion of Medicine ('LSV') provide, in their capacity as self-employed economic operators, services on a market, namely the market in specialist medical services. They are paid by their patients for the services they provide and assume the financial risks attached to the pursuit of their activity."[41] In *Ambulanz Glöckner* the Court held

---

37 The relevance of this question has been reinforced by the Court's judgment in *AOK*: See S. Belhaj and J. van de Gronden, Some Room for Competition Does Not Make a Sickness Fund An Undertaking. Is EC Competition Law Applicable to the Health Care Sector? (Joined Cases C-264/01, C-306/01, C-453/01 and C-355/01 *AOK*), *ECLR*, 2004, p. 686.

38 Case 155/73, *Sacchi*.

39 Commission Decision 78/516, *RAI/UNITEL*, OJ 1978, L 157/39.

40 Case C-221/99, *Conte*: the Court did not answer the question of the Italian Court whether architects constitute undertakings since it concluded that the Italian legislation did not promote the creation of anti-competitive agreements having regard to the freedom of architects to set the fees for certain services they perform.

41 Joined Cases C-180/98 to C-184/98, *Pavlov*, paragraph 76. This also applies to medical practitioners specialising in dentistry: Case C-172/03, *Heiser*, paragraph 26.

that medical aid organisations to which the public authorities have delegated the task of providing the public ambulance service should be regarded as undertakings: "In the present case, the medical aid organisations provide services, for remuneration from users, on the market for emergency transport services and patient transport services. Such activities have not always been, and are not necessarily, carried on by such organisations or by public authorities. According to the documents before the Court, in the past Ambulanz Glöckner has itself provided both types of service. The provision of such services therefore constitutes an economic activity for the purposes of the application of the competition rules laid down by the Treaty."[42]

Hospitals and clinics may also be regarded as undertakings, since they are economic entities providing health care services for remuneration. This appears *inter alia* from the Commission's draft decision on the application of Article 86 EC to state aid in the form of public service compensation, wherein it states that hospitals should benefit from the *exemption* from notification of state aid.[43] In *Peerbooms* and *VanBraekel* the Court held within the context of the free movement rules that there is no need to distinguish between care provided in a hospital environment and care provided outside such environment (see Chapter 2). It is questionable whether public hospitals, where health services are genuinely offered for free, should be considered as undertakings. In Chapter 2 it was held that the organisation of a public education system probably remains outside the scope of the Treaty provisions on free movement.[44] In its Communication on services of general interest in Europe the Commission states that services such as national education are also excluded from the application of competition and internal market rules.[45]

Where medical professions, medical aid organisations and hospitals may be considered as undertakings,[46] this is more contentious in respect of sickness funds. With regard to sickness funds the situation seems to be complicated. As stated above, if a non-profit organisation manages an (optional) insurance scheme that operates according to the principle of capitalisation and is placed in a position to make decisions which generate effects in the market, it may be regarded as an undertaking within the meaning of Articles 81 and 82 EC, even

---

[42] Case C-475/99, *Ambulanz Glöckner*, paragraph 20.

[43] The draft decision can be found at: http://www.europa.eu.int/comm/competition/state_aid/others/.

[44] See Chapter 2, section 2.1.1.

[45] OJ 2001, C 17/4, p. 9; see G. Davies, Welfare as a Service, *LIEI*, 2002, pp. 27-40. See also the Commission's Green Paper on Services of General Interest, COM (2003) 270 final, p. 15. In the White Paper on services of general interest the Commission announced that it will submit a communication on social and health services of general interest in the course of 2005, COM (2004) 374 final, p. 17.

[46] See also V.G. Hatzopoulos, *Killing* national health and insurance systems but *healing* patients? The European Market for health care services after the judgments of the ECJ in *Vanbraekel* and *Peerbooms*, *CMLRev.*, 2002, pp. 714-715.

if the scheme exhibits certain features of solidarity.[47] On this basis, for example, the Netherlands Competition Authority has held that the Dutch sickness funds operating in an environment of regulated competition should be considered as undertakings with regard to the management of the insurance scheme and the purchasing of care.[48] Nonetheless, in some cases it was decided to refrain from applying the competition rules to the health care sector. In *Fenin* the Court of First Instance held that the organisations managing the Spanish Sistema Nacional de Salud (SNS, National health care system) in purchasing medical goods and equipment should not be considered undertakings as far as these purchasing activities are concerned, even though the Court recognised that an entity purchasing large quantities of products may possess very considerable economic power.[49] Decisive was whether the goods and services purchased were used by these bodies as part of an economic activity, which was not the case since the insurance activities of the Spanish National Health Service were not of an economic nature.[50]

In *AOK* the Court reinforced the important role of the solidarity principle in social security cases by concluding that the German *Krankenkassen* (sickness funds) ought not to be considered as undertakings irrespective of the existence of (potential) competition between sickness funds and between private insurers and sickness funds. Crucial for the Court were the absence of profit making, the obligatory character of the benefits and the risk equalisation scheme, which implies that funds whose health expenditure is high because they insure less healthy people (high risks) are compensated for those risks by funds to which more healthy persons are affiliated.[51] Thereby the Court took a different view than AG Jacobs, who, based on the previous case law, came to the conclusion that the German sickness funds should be considered as undertakings, since they are in a degree of price competition with one another, since there is some potential for the funds to compete in terms of services which they offer and since sickness funds and private health insurers are clearly in competition with

47 Case C-244/94, *FFSA*: "A non-profit organisation which manages an old-age insurance scheme intended to supplement a basic compulsory scheme, established by law as an optional scheme and operating according to the principle of capitalization in keeping with the rules laid down by the authorities in particular with regard to conditions for membership, contributes and benefits, is an undertaking within the meaning of Article 81 et seq. of the Treaty."

48 J. van de Gronden, Purchasing Care: Economic Activity or Service of General (Economic) Interest?, *ECLR*, 2004, p. 91.

49 Case T-319/99, *FENIN*.

50 J. van de Gronden, Purchasing Care: Economic Activity or Service of General (Economic) Interest?, *ECLR*, 2004, p. 91.

51 S. Belhaj and J. van de Gronden, Some Room for Competition Does Not Make a Sickness Fund An Undertaking. Is EC Competition Law Applicable to the Health Care Sector? (Joined Cases C-264/01, C-306/01, C-453/01 and C-355/01 *AOK*), *ECLR*, 2004, p. 684.

one another for the business of those employees who are not obliged to take out statutory health insurance.[52]

As a result of *AOK* the degree of solidarity seems even more essential in determining the scope *ratione personae* of the competition rules in the field of health care. Whether the extent to which a degree of competition has been introduced into the health insurance sector is still a relevant factor in the Court's assessment of the concept of undertaking, and if so, how much competition will be necessary to trigger the application of competition law, need to be awaited.[53] "The question whether certain sickness funds are to be regarded as undertakings will continue to require a case-by-case analysis."[54] Another and more consistent solution as presented by AG Jacobs would have been to conclude on the basis of the existing body of case law that the German sickness funds are undertakings, but that their conduct can still be justified under Article 86(2) EC, which allows the Court to take into account the special features of the health care sector.[55]

Environment

Undertakings operating in the field of the environment are also not spared by the EC rules on competition. An undertaking operating on the market for refillable bottles has to respect the competition provisions.[56] Waste disposal plants are undertakings within the meaning of Articles 81 and 82 EC.[57] Hence the question whether organisations or companies operating in the field of the environment are subject to the competition rules is not really pertinent; it is generally assumed that they are, which is also shown by the *DSD* case. *Duales System Deutschland AG* (DSD) which has been the only undertaking operating an exemption system for taking back packaging throughout Germany, brought an action for annulment of the Commission decision stipulating that DSD had abused its dominant position.[58] This case concerns interlocutory proceedings before the President of the Court of First Instance.[59] In these proceedings

---

52 Opinion of AG Jacobs of 22 May 2003 in Joined Cases C-264/01, C-306/01, C-354/01 and C-355/01, *AOK Bundesverband*, paragraphs 37-42.

53 See for the application of the competition rules to the Dutch health care system before the *AOK* judgment: Sluijs (2004).

54 Annotation B.J. Drijber, *CMLRev.*, 2005, p. 530.

55 S. Belhaj and J. van de Gronden, Some Room for Competition Does Not Make a Sickness Fund An Undertaking. Is EC Competition Law Applicable to the Health Care Sector? (Joined Cases C-264/01, C-306/01, C-453/01 and C-355/01 *AOK*), *ECLR*, 2004, pp. 686-687. For a more positive response to the Court's judgment in *AOK*, see: M. Krajewski and M. Farley, Limited competition in national health systems and the application of competition law: the *AOK Bundesverband* case, *ELRev.*, 2004, pp. 842-851.

56 Commission Decision in the *Spa Monopole*-case, XXIIIrd Competition Report, p. 240.

57 Case C-203/96, *Dusseldorp*.

58 Commission Decision 2001/463, OJ 2001, L 166/1.

59 Case T-151/01 R, *Der Grüne Punkt – Duales System Deutschland AG*.

neither the Commission nor the President of the Court of First Instance touch upon the question of whether DSD should be regarded as an undertaking.[60]

The *Diego Cali* ruling, however, shows that activities of some organisations in charge of accomplishing environmental duties do not fall within the scope of the competition rules.[61] In this case the tariffs established by SPEG for anti-pollution surveillance formed an integral part of its surveillance task and did not therefore constitute an abuse of a dominant position.

Consumer policy

Consumer associations themselves will normally be excluded from the application of the competition rules, since they are not engaged in economic activities.[62] Consumers are concerned with the satisfaction of their private needs and not with offering goods and services in a given market.[63] The question to the scope of the concept of undertaking, however, is in a more general sense relevant for the area of consumer policy, which does not only encompass the promotion of economic interests of consumers, but also consumer policy in its broad sense, including health, safety and information disclosure.[64] Where institutes have been granted by the state the possibility to set their own market strategy, it is important that the competition authority has the power to prohibit practices that inhibit on consumer interests, such as the interest to have optimal free choice. On the other hand excess of competition may lead to inefficiency and deception.[65] If socially valuable state monopolies become subject to competition law, the benefit of increased competition may have to be weighed against the cost of diminished consumer protection.[66] In assessing the economic character of the activity concerned, health, safety or environmental aspects of consumer policy play – at the background – a role in the Court's case law. For example, air navigation control as exercised by Eurocontrol designed to protect the users of air transport and the populations affected by aircraft flying over

60 Similarly Commission Decision 2001/663, *Eco-Emballages*, OJ 2001, L 233/37.

61 Case C-343/95, *Diego Cali*.

62 See also Communication from the Commission "Services of general interest in Europe", OJ 2001, C 17/4, p. 9.

63 Case C-35/96, *Commission v. Italy (CNSD)*, paragraph 36; see also Reich and Micklitz (2003), p. 159.

64 Compare the more narrow assessment of the relationship between competition law and consumer protection by Cseres (2005), p. 270: she makes a clear distinction between the promotion of consumers' economic interests as one of the core values of competition policy and the health, safety and information disclosure as public policy goals which may be recognised in competition cases, but will not represent overriding concerns.

65 See also N. Reich, Competition law and the consumer, in: L. Gormley (Ed.), *Current and future perspectives on EC competition law: a tribute to professor M.R. Mok* (Kluwer Law International, London, The Hague [etc.], 1997), p. 127.

66 See Howells and Weatherill (2005), p. 555.

them, was not considered to constitute an economic activity within the meaning of the competition rules.[67]

2.3 The territorial scope

The Community provisions on competition only apply if intra-Community trade is affected. With regard to Article 81(1) EC the Court held in the *STM* case that "it must be possible to foresee with a sufficient degree of probability on the basis of a set of objective factors of law or of fact that the agreement in question may have an influence, direct or indirect, actual or potential on the pattern of trade between Member States".[68] This interpretation clearly approaches the definition of measures having equivalent effect in *Dassonville* (see Chapter 2).

The criterion of affecting intra-Community trade must be flexibly interpreted, not only within the context of Article 81 EC, but also within the context of other provisions on competition such as Articles 86 and 87 EC. This has the consequence that even agreements concluded within a Member State will fall within the scope of Article 81 EC, if they extend over the whole territory of a Member State and thereby protect national production.[69] However, the mere fact that an agreement covers a particular Member State is not in itself sufficient for finding that trade has been affected.[70] Furthermore, even if the facts of the case seem confined to one Member State, so-called internal situations, Article 86 EC may be held applicable as becomes apparent from the Court's judgment in *Höfner.* Here the Court applied Article 86 EC in respect of the legal monopoly held by the German *Bundesanstalt für Arbeit*, whereas the provisions on the free movement of services were held inapplicable.[71]

The territorial scope of application of the EC competition rules depends on the type of product or service involved. In the case of book pricing agreements language is a natural factor, which can limit the relevant market to the national state, or to the states sharing the same language. In other words, the free trade in books between Member States will be restricted by language barriers rather than by other factors.[72] It is therefore unlikely that national systems of book

---

67 Case C-364/92, *Eurocontrol*. The activities of Eurocontrol were connected with the exercise of powers relating to the control and supervision of air space which are typically those of a public authority.

68 Case 56/65, *Société Technique Minière*; see Guidelines on the effect on trade concept contained in Articles 81 and 82 of the Treaty, OJ 2004, C 101/81, paragraph 24.

69 Case 8/72, *Vereeniging van Cementhandelaren*.

70 See also Joined Cases C-215/96 and C-216/96, *Carlo Bagnasco*, where national agreements in the financial services sector covering a whole Member State – *in casu* uniform bank conditions laid down by the Italian Banking Association – were not regarded to affect trade between Member States.

71 Case C-41/90, *Höfner and Elser*; see also K. Mortelmans, Towards convergence in the application of the rules on free movement and on competition, *CMLRev.*, 2001, p.630.

72 Everling, Rürup and Füssel (1997), p. 38.

pricing agreements will hold up the economic interpenetration and will protect domestic production. The Commission will not apply Article 81 EC to national systems of fixed book prices, if this system has no appreciable effect on competition and trade. This appears from the Commission's investigation into the effect of the Dutch system of fixed book prices on intra-Community trade. The Commission held that it was no longer up to her to decide on the applicability of the EC competition rules to fixed book prices in the Netherlands.[73]

In the field of health care the territorial scope of the Community competition rules is also limited. The relevant geographical health care market may be regional or local rather than national, particularly in the case of general practitioners, pharmacists or hospitals, all of whom need to be near their health care provider.[74] In other fields of horizontal and flanking policies, the territorial scope is broader and the relevant geographical market may extend to the national territory or beyond, as in the field of the environment.[75] Where the territorial scope of the EC competition rules is limited, the national competition rules may be applicable. Hence, contrary to the rules on free movement, where trade between Member States is not affected, cartels and other restrictive practices will not be tolerated but remain subject to supervision by the national competition authority.

The jurisdiction of the European Commission is not limited to prohibiting restrictions of competition resulting from actions by undertakings established within the European Community. There are three ways in which a connection between the activity concerned and the territory of the European Community can be established so as to provide for international jurisdiction.[76] First, the presence and activities of a subsidiary in the Community bring the entire group under Community jurisdiction as a single undertaking (single economic entity). Second, the implementation in the Community of agreements, concerted practices, or abuses of dominant positions conceived abroad by foreign undertakings brings them within Community jurisdiction. Third, the effects of agreements conceived abroad by foreign undertakings in the Community bring the agreements under Community jurisdiction. The application of the effects doctrine has been particularly controversial.[77] Consequently, the rules on competition,

---

73 Press release IP/99/668, 9 September 1999.

74 J.W. van de Gronden, Mededingingsrecht en gezondheidszorg, *M&M*, 2001, p. 268.

75 Waste collection and recycling schemes as for example set up by DSD often extend to the national territory.

76 See also Faull & Nikpay (1999), pp. 100-101.

77 Case T-102/96, *Gencor*, paragraphs 90-92: The Court of First Instance applied the effects doctrine under the Merger Regulation whilst holding that the "application of the Regulation is justified under public international law when it is foreseeable that a proposed concentration will have an immediate and substantial effect in the Community". "[...] It is therefore necessary to verify whether the three criteria of immediate, substantial and foreseeable effect are satisfied in this case."

which nevertheless have consequences within the Community, may explicitly apply to restrictive practices outside the territory of the European Community.

2.4 Conclusions

The broad material, personal and territorial scope of application of the competition rules implies that horizontal and flanking policy interests can hardly play a role in determining whether the competition rules are applicable to organisations pursuing horizontal and flanking policy aims. Due to the dual character of horizontal and flanking policies and due to the broad definition of economic activity provided for by the Court of Justice horizontal and flanking policies are not spared by the competition rules from the outset. This is different only where either certain organisations pursue non-economic activities, based on the principle of solidarity, or where certain activities are classified as belonging to the prerogatives of the state (by virtue of their *imperium*). However, in these situations they are not horizontal and flanking policy interests, but the social character of the activity concerned and the solidarity principle (*Poucet, FENIN, AOK*), or the fact that the activity typically involves tasks of a public authority (*Diego Cali*), that play a decisive role in determining the scope of application of the competition rules. In situations where the activities of certain entities are of a mixed "social/economic" character the competition rules are probably applicable (*FFSA, Brentjens*), although *AOK* has put this into perspective. Hence, horizontal and flanking policy interests stay in the background and may merely profit by other factors that are decisive for the applicability of the competition rules.

3 The application of the competition rules and the Member States

As stated in the introduction the fact that Member States are in the first place involved in pursuing horizontal and flanking policy aims pleads in favour of first assessing the relationship between the competition rules directed at Member States and horizontal and flanking policies. These rules are either laid down in the Treaty, i.e. Articles 87-89 EC (state aids) and Article 86 EC (exclusive rights), which will be discussed in the following sections (3.1 and 3.2), or have been developed in the Court's case law, i.e. the useful effect doctrine, which will be discussed in section 3.3.

3.1 Article 87 EC: the prohibition on state aids

As stated above the fact that measures adopted by undertakings or Member States are based upon horizontal and flanking policy considerations has no bearing on the *prima facie* applicability of the competition rules. Hence, it is now necessary to focus on the prohibitive Treaty rules, like Article 87 EC on state aids, and the respective requirements that need to be met for national measures to fall within the scope of the prohibition contained in Article 87 EC. Considering the special role of public service undertakings in the Member States and in the Community, as well as the fact that these undertakings are normally financially compensated for their public service tasks, a distinction is made between aid granted to 'normal' undertakings and aid granted to public service undertakings.

3.1.1 The grant of aid for horizontal and flanking policy reasons

Through various different measures and for a number of reasons, including the attainment of horizontal and flanking policy goals, national states grant financial assistance to undertakings. The preservation of various forms of cultural expression is dependent on the receipt of external support. Aid schemes may be set up to support individual artists by organising exhibitions of their work or by purchasing their work. Entry fees to theatres, drama and ballet performances may be wholly or partly subsidised by the state. Financial assistance is also provided for the production of films and other audio-visual productions, as well as for the maintenance of a system of public service broadcasting. Furthermore the publication of literature can be stimulated and encouraged by subsidising editors or awarding grants to authors.[78] In the field of the environment aid schemes are set up to encourage energy conservation, to support investment in new, environmentally friendly products and production processes, to support a sound treatment of waste products etc.[79] A particular problem arising here is that through the grant of state aids, the public bears the costs of pollution, which, according to the 'polluter pays principle', should be borne by the polluter. In the area of public health, financial benefits may be awarded both for research and development e.g. to develop new and better medicines, and also for the organisation of the public health sector, for example to hospitals or health insurance funds.[80] Naturally the consumer will benefit from financial assistance given to undertakings for horizontal and flanking purposes if, as a result, better products and services are offered on the market. On the other hand, consumer interests may not always be protected by state aid measures. If effective competition is distorted, the provision of good quality products for a reasonable price is assumed to be in danger.

---

78 Loman, Mortelmans, Post and Watson (1992), p. 123.

79 Jans (2000), p. 295.

80 See also V.G. Hatzopoulos, *Killing* national health and insurance systems but *healing* patients? The European Market for health care services after the judgments of the ECJ in *Vanbraekel* and *Peerbooms*, *CMLRev.*, 2002, pp. 714-715.

3.1.2 The scope of Article 87(1) EC: the concept of aid in relation to'normal undertakings'

In all the above mentioned situations Article 87 EC on state aids may be relevant, which provides that "any aid granted by a Member State or through State resources in any form whatsoever which distorts or threatens to distort competition by favouring certain undertakings or the production of certain goods shall insofar as it affects trade between Member States, be incompatible with the common market". If aid can be considered as state aid within the meaning of this Article, it will have to be notified to the Commission pursuant to Article 88 EC. The horizontal and flanking aim of the measure is not in itself sufficient to exclude the measure from classification as aid for the purposes of Article 87 EC.[81] The Court adopts a functional approach whereby the aims of the aid scheme can be taken into account under Article 87(2) or Article 87(3) EC.

For these measures to fall within the scope of Article 87(1) EC it is not necessary that they involve positive benefits for the undertakings concerned. According to the ECJ the concept of aid "encompasses not only positive benefits, such as subsidies, but also interventions which, in various forms, mitigate the charges which are normally included in the budget of an undertaking, and which, without therefore being subsidies in the strict sense of the word, are of the same character and have the same effect".[82] This includes a variety of aid schemes, from tax exemptions to direct subsidies.[83] What is relevant, though, is that the aid has been granted by the state or through state resources.

Furthermore, these types of aid must favour certain *specific* undertakings. The concept of undertaking is discussed before (section 2.2). Only aid given to organisations which cannot be defined as undertakings, such as aid given to public non-profit making higher education or research establishments, will normally not qualify as state aid.[84] This requirement of specificity entails that general aid schemes will not fall within the definition of state aid.

Finally, the company must have obtained a financial advantage that it would not have received in the normal course of business. The question whether financial benefits given to public service undertakings will be regarded as state aids will be dealt with separately (see hereafter, section 3.1.3).

---

81 See V.G. Hatzopoulos, *Killing* national health and insurance systems but *healing* patients? The European Market for health care services after the judgments of the ECJ in *Vanbraekel* and *Peerbooms*, *CMLRev.*, 2002, p. 714.

82 Case C-39/94, *SFEI v. La Poste*, paragraph 58. See also Case 30/59, *Steenkolenmijnen v. High Authority*.

83 In the field of the environment we can think of fixed minimum prices to support renewable energy, tax exemptions, support for research and development, green levies to finance support schemes, quota-based systems: see also F.B. Krieglstein, Renewable Energy Schemes and EC State Aids Provisions, *EELR*, 2001, p. 52.

84 Community framework for State aid for research and development, OJ 1996, C 45/5, paragraph 2.4.

Aid granted by the state or through state resources: Preussen Elektra

Irrespective horizontal and flanking policy goals, all these types of aid can be granted either directly by the public authorities or indirectly through other public or private bodies.[85] The first important issue therefore is to know whether the financial benefits are indeed granted by the state or through state resources as required by Article 87(1) EC. The condition of 'granted through state resources' is subject to various interpretations as appears from the Court of Justice's case law. The extensive interpretation of Article 87(1) EC entails that any measure which confers economic advantages on specific undertakings, and which is the result of conduct attributable to the state, constitutes state aid independently of whether it involves any financial burden for the state.

The second and narrower interpretation entails that the measure at issue must necessarily cost the state money and financing through public resources is a constitutive element of the definition of state aid.[86]

In *Preussen Elektra* the Court opted for the second and narrower view and held that financing through state resources remains a necessary element of the concept of state aid: "In this case, the obligation imposed on private electricity supply undertakings to purchase electricity produced from renewable energy sources at fixed minimum prices does not involve any direct or indirect transfer of state resources to undertakings which produce that type of electricity." "In those circumstances, the fact that the purchase obligation is imposed by statute and confers an undeniable advantage on certain undertakings is not capable of conferring upon it the character of state aid within the meaning of Article 87(1) of the Treaty."[87]

This case, which was introduced in Chapter 2, section 4.4.1, involved the *Stromeinspeisungsgesetz*, a German law on feeding electricity from renewable energy sources into the public grid and containing a compensation mechanism applying to cases where the electricity from renewable sources exceeded 5% of the total electricity supplied to the undertaking, in which cases the upstream network operator must compensate the undertaking for the supplementary costs caused by the purchase obligation. The question regarding the relationship between this law and the free movement of goods has already been discussed in Chapter 2. The first question of the German court was whether the German law, constituted state aid in favour of producers of electricity from renewable energy sources. This question should, according to the Court of Justice, as seen above, be answered in the negative.

According to the Commission, though, a narrow approach to the concept of state aid may lead to a risk of circumvention of state aid rules and the tempta-

---

85 For example Case 82/77, *Van Tiggele* and C-379/98, *Preussen Elektra AG.*

86 Opinion of AG Jacobs in C-379/98, *Preussen Elektra AG*, paragraphs 115-116; see also S. de Vries, European Court of Justice: Case Report, *EELR*, 2001, pp. 193-205.

87 Case C-379/98, *Preussen Elektra AG*, paragraphs 59 and 61.

tion for Member States to devise schemes, which confer economic advantages on certain undertakings but nevertheless escape the Commission's control under Article 88 EC. The Court should therefore give more weight to the objectives of the rule of state aid and their overall effectiveness.[88] In the line of this approach the Commission designated the *Stromeinspeisungsgesetz* 1990 as state aid, but approved it on the basis of its slight impact on intra-Community trade and competition. The Commission referred to the Council recommendation of 8 November 1988 on promoting co-operation between public utilities and auto-producers of electricity.[89] In 1999, the Commission initiated a procedure under Article 88(2) EC in respect of the Law on the electricity tax, which included an increase in the purchase price of electricity from renewable sources. After the withdrawal of the *Stromeinspeisungsgesetz*, the Commission decided to close its procedure.[90]

Preussen Elektra is in the first place relevant for environmental policy. The fact that Member States must have a considerable margin of discretion in the field of renewable energy is favoured by current Community policy efforts to promote electricity from renewable sources. The Directive on the promotion of electricity from renewable energy sources in the internal electricity market explicitly allows Member States to adopt various individual measures supporting renewable energy sources, which will, according to Article 4, be monitored by the Commission.[91] The Commission's Communication on the sixth environmental action programme makes clear that tackling climate change is one of the main concerns of Community environmental policy.[92] The new Community Guidelines on state aid for environmental protection are also relevant.[93] The Commission takes a favourable position on measures that promote the use of electricity from renewable energy sources. The present case, however, makes clear that minimum price schemes, such as the *Stromeinspeisungsgesetz*, which cannot be qualified as state aid, no longer have to be notified to the Commission, subject to these guidelines.

In a decision on an agreement between car producers, car importers and dismantling and recycling companies, which the Dutch government declared generally binding on all car producers and importers, the Netherlands and the

---

88 In legal literature it has been suggested that there is no *a priori* reason why national maximum and minimum price schemes intended to favour a particular sector should not be characterised as State aid for the purposes of Article 87: see Hancher, Ottervanger and Slot (1999), p. 26.

89 OJ 1988, L 335/29.

90 OJ 2001, C 117/8.

91 Directive 2001/77 of 27 September 2001, OJ 2001, L 283/33.

92 Communication from the Commission to the Council, the European Parliament, the Economic and Social Committee and the Committee of the Regions on the sixth environment action programme of the European Community, COM(2001) 31 final.

93 OJ 2001, C 37/3.

organisation for the dismantling of cars – ARN – referred to *Preussen Elektra* and argued that the levies collected do not constitute state resources.[94] Under this agreement car producers and importers have to pay a fee to finance a fund to pay for the dismantling of cars. A private executive organisation (ARN) grants premiums in respect of parts of car wrecks that cannot be dismantled or collected profitably. According to the Commission the ARN system differs from the system in *Preussen Elektra*. Here there is an intermediary organisation responsible for the management of the resources and a fund to which the charges are paid. The proceeds of the charge are being used only for the collection and recycling of the materials; distribution of profits to the participating companies is prohibited. Because of these characteristics, according to the Commission, the charge can be compared to a parafiscal charge, but should nevertheless not be considered to be state aid, due to the fact that the law imposes an obligation for the car manufacturers and importers to produce results rather than to contribute to the ARN system.[95] Even though the Commission comes to the conclusion that there is no state aid, it still seems to enhance a wider notion of the term 'granted through state resources' than the Court does. ARN is a private executive organisation and cannot simply be compared to an organisation established by the state as in the case *Steinike*, the judgment of the Court referred to by the Commission in its decision. Furthermore, now the Court seems to have enhanced the narrow interpretation of 'granted through state resources', the Commission cannot simply set aside the constitutive condition that it must cost the state money. The fact that here the ARN manages the resources makes it doubtful that this condition is fulfilled.[96] In *Pearle* the Court came to the conclusion that compulsory levies imposed by public bodies upon its members, which are companies trading in optical equipment, for the funding of an advertising campaign benefiting its members, cannot constitute state aid within the meaning of Article 87 EC.[97] Would it not be more obvious for the Commission in the *ARN* case to examine the applicability of Article 10, in conjunction with Articles 3(1) sub g and 81 EC, in respect of the decision to declare the agreement generally binding on all companies in the market (see hereafter, section 3.3.1).

The Court's choice in *Preussen Elektra* for the second and narrower interpretation is significant not only for the field of the environment, but also for other

---

94 The Law on Environmental Management gives the Minister for Housing, Planning and The Environment the power to declare an agreement generally binding. If an agreement is declared generally binding, all importers and producers of cars in the Netherlands will have to pay the fee for dismantling the cars, unless an exemption from this obligation has been granted by the Minister.

95 Commission Decision 2002/204, OJ 2002, L 68/18, paragraph 69; see also Case 78/76, Steinike.

96 Compare AG Jacobs in his opinion in C-379/98, *Preussen Elektra AG*; see also H.H.B. Vedder, Verwijderingssysteem voor autowrakken houdt geen staatssteun in *NTER*, 2002, p. 147.

97 Case C-345/02, *Pearle*.

horizontal and flanking policies since it allows Member States more latitude in choosing different instruments for the achievement of horizontal and flanking policy objectives. If national measures are not financed through state resources, they do not have to be notified to the Commission pursuant to Article 88(3) EC. An extensive reading of Article 87 EC would, as AG Jacobs argues, bring practically all national legislation regulating relationships between enterprises within the scope of the state aid rules (paragraph 157). The argument of certain aid schemes being immunised against European checks and balances does not seem to be very convincing,[98] particularly because other Treaty provisions may be applicable, most notably the provisions on free movement. Nevertheless, it must be admitted that generally – and not only in the field of state aid – the Court takes a rather cautious and formal position as regards state action that may jeopardise the application of the competition rules (see hereafter, in the context of Article 86 EC and the useful effect doctrine).

In the field of public health, for example, national health care systems, which are partly privately financed, or which involve a mutual system of health care services without state expenditure, will probably also escape the application of the state aid rules. The creation of a monopoly for the provision of ambulance services, for remuneration from users, on the market for emergency transport services and patient transport services, will also not fall within the scope of Article 87 EC.[99] Where payment facilities are granted directly by public bodies, such as national social security organisations, the national measure may qualify as state aid.[100]

In the field of culture the significance of *Preussen Elektra* has also been acknowledged by the Commission. It states that the legal obligations imposed by Member States upon TV broadcasters to invest in audiovisual production do not constitute state aid, where these investments provide a reasonable compensation to broadcasters. The extent to which these legal obligations may be considered state aid as such has to be considered in view of the development of the Court's jurisprudence after *Preussen Elektra*.[101]

---

98 See also M. Bronckers and R. van der Vlies, The European Court's *PreussenElektra* Judgement: Tensions Between E.U. Principles and National Renewable Energy Initiatives, *ECLR*, 2001, pp. 464-465.

99 Case C-475/99, *Ambulanz Glöckner.*

100 See also V.G. Hatzopoulos, *Killing* national health and insurance systems but *healing* patients? The European Market for health care services after the judgments of the ECJ in *Vanbraekel* and *Peerbooms*, *CMLRev.*, 2002, p. 715.

101 See Communication on certain legal aspects relating to cinematographic and other audiovisual works, p. 8, COM(2001) 534 final.

Favouring certain specific undertakings

Measures that take the form of general infrastructure, e.g. the provision of theatres and sport facilities, or that generally pursue horizontal and flanking policy objectives without benefiting a particular industry are unlikely to fall within the definition of state aid.[102] In such cases the criterion of specificity is not met. These measures should be considered as general economic measures taken by the state not directed at assisting specific industries and therefore fall outside the scope of Article 87 EC.[103] In its first report on the consideration of cultural aspects in European Community action the Commission regards certain types of aid granted to activities which are offered to all the potential beneficiaries in a Member State, such as theatres and art galleries, as not problematic in the light of Article 87(1) EC.[104] General aid measures in the cultural field do not meet the criterion of specificity and cannot qualify as state aid within the meaning of Article 87(1) EC.[105] If the measure benefits certain groups of undertakings, a particular sector of the economy or a particular region within a Member State, it will fulfil the condition of specificity. For example, aid schemes for the stimulation of film production can be considered to favour a certain specific undertaking.

General measures designed to promote and protect public health do not qualify as state aid either. Financial measures, however, that contribute to the development of a health insurance system affordable for everybody may qualify as state aid, if these measures are granted through state resources and benefit health insurers.[106] Public support granted to certain hospitals will also meet the criterion of specificity.[107] Tax deductions for medical practitioners, and not only for those specialising in a certain medical field like dentistry, will also fulfil the condition of selectivity.[108]

In the 1994 Guidelines on state aid for environmental protection it was stated that aid for publicity campaigns to increase general environmental awareness and provide specific information about, for example, selective waste collection, conservation of natural resources or environmentally friendly products may not fall within Article 87(1) EC at all where they are so general in scope and distant from the marketplace as not to confer an identifiable financial benefit

[102] Hancher, Ottervanger & Slot (1999), p. 80.

[103] D'Sa, (1998), p. 10. Quigley & Collins (2003), p. 49.

[104] COM 96 (160) def.

[105] Ch. Koenig and J. Kühling, Mitgliedstaatliche Kulturförderung und gemeinschaftrechtliche Beihilfekontrolle *EuZW*, 2000, p. 199. See also Hancher, Ottervanger and Slot (1999), pp. 29-30.

[106] See also with regard to the Dutch governmental plans for the reform of the health care system: Drijber and De Groot (2002), pp. 35-36. The *Altmark* judgment is particularly relevant for state funding of the health care system: see also Van de Gronden (2004), pp. 56-58.

[107] Case N 543/2001, Capital Allowances for Hospitals in Ireland.

[108] Case C-172/03, *Heiser*, paragraph 41.

on specific firms.[109] Measures to encourage final consumers – whether they are firms or individuals – to purchase environmentally friendly products will, for example, not fall within Article 87(1) EC if they do not confer a tangible financial benefit on particular firms.

Measures that provide a financial benefit for a certain sector of the economy, however, can be considered as state aid, according to the Court's judgment in *Adria-Wien Pipeline GmbH*.[110] This case involved Austrian legislation providing a rebate of energy taxes charged on supplies of natural gas and electricity exclusively to undertakings whose activity is shown to consist primarily in the production of goods – the manufacture sector. The Austrian government argued that this type of measure is based on objective criteria and benefits a very large number of undertakings. It does not have the selective nature which would trigger the application of Article 87(1) EC. The Court came to another conclusion. It considered *inter alia* that "the ecological considerations underlying the national legislation at issue do not justify treating the consumption of natural gas or electricity by undertakings supplying services differently than the consumption of such energy by undertakings manufacturing goods. Energy consumption by each of those sectors is equally damaging to the environment. It follows from the foregoing considerations that, although objective, the criterion applied by the national legislation at issue is not justified by the nature or the general scheme of that legislation, so that it cannot save the measure at issue from being in the nature of state aid."

Where a tax exemption for environmental or other public policy purposes does not provide selective advantages to certain undertakings it will not be regarded as state aid by the Commission. This was the case for a Dutch exemption of tax levied on waste for dredging sludge. The objective was to improve public water ways and therefore maintain, or even increase dredging.[111]

The examples show that the requirement of specificity does not seem to be really helpful in keeping horizontal and flanking policy measures outside the ambit of Article 87(1) EC. On the contrary, since financial aids will often be given to a specific industry, or a certain sector of the economy, *inter alia* for the realisation of horizontal and flanking policy aims, the criterion of specificity pleads against the unconditional state funding of horizontal and flanking activities pursued by undertakings. This is different where financial aids are granted to public service undertakings, which will be considered below.

---

109 OJ 1994, C 72/39.

110 Case C-143/99, *Adria-Wien*. See also Ch. Golfinopoulos, Concept of Selectivity Criterion in State Aid Definition Following the *Adria-Wien* Judgment – Measures Justified by the "Nature or General Scheme of a System", *ECLR*, 2003, pp. 543-549.

111 Case N 574/2004, Exemption from the waste tax for dredging sludge; see also Press Release, IP/05/135 of 3 February 2005.

3.1.3 The scope of Article 87(1) EC: the concept of aid in relation to 'public service undertakings'

A particularly important issue in the current debate on the Community's state aid policy involves the assessment of state aid to undertakings entrusted with the performance of services of general economic interest, which have been regarded as playing a fundamental function in all the Member States.[112] The state will grant financial benefits to these undertakings to compensate their public service obligations imposed upon them *inter alia* to contribute to the attainment of horizontal and flanking objectives.

Public service broadcasters are given financial support in order to face up to rising costs of expenditure in a competitive audio-visual market. In most Member States the licence fee has constituted the basic means of financing public service broadcasting. This enables national broadcasting companies to carry out their particular public mission, i.e. *inter alia* to provide quality programmes for all citizens, including minority interest groups, an objective of cultural policy.[113] The important role of public service broadcasters in Europe is also emphasised by the protocol on public service broadcasting annexed to the Treaty of Amsterdam.

Companies that are given exclusive rights for the collection or disposal of waste are granted indemnities for the services they perform. If medical specialists, sickness funds, hospitals and ambulance services are considered undertakings entrusted with public service tasks, similar questions will arise as to the financing of these services and the compatibility of national measures with the state aid rules.[114] In the *Ferring* case questions arose as to the compatibility of a French measure granting tax advantages to wholesale distributors not subject to payment of a tax that laboraties were required to pay on their direct sales to pharmacies, which were entrusted with public service obligations (see hereafter).[115]

---

[112] See Report from the Commission on the state of play in the work on the guidelines for State aid and services of general economic interest (SGEI) <http://www.europa.eu.int/comm/competition/>.

[113] See also Experts Meeting on Public Service Broadcasting in Europe – Amsterdam 17/18 February 1997, by the Netherlands Ministry of Education, Culture and Sciences and the NOS (*Nederlandse Omroep Stichting*). In this report various views are presented on the role of public service broadcasting in the European Union.

[114] See also 'Advies van de Interdepartementale Commissie Europees Recht (ICER) over Europeesrechtelijke aspecten van een stelsel van ziektekostenverzekeringen', ICER 2001-3/31a. Where a national law, for example, applies to all medical and paramedical services without regard to the nature of the service supplied or the nature of the costs incurred there is probably no question of compensation of public service tasks: Case C-172/03, *Heiser.*

[115] Case C-53/00, *Ferring SA*.

Public service undertakings may have been granted a significant role also in other horizontal and flanking policy areas. In its report "on the state of play in the work on the guidelines for state aid and services of general economic interest (SGEIs)" the Commission states that the introduction and development of services of general economic interest is in the interest of consumers and contributes to the objectives set out in Article 153 EC.[116] Even in the field of education if certain schools or institutions of higher education are considered to be undertakings and are entrusted with public service duties, similar questions as to the financing of educational services intended for the whole population will arise. The question in all these cases is whether financial benefits to public service undertakings should be considered as state aid and fall within the scope of Article 87(1) EC in the first place, or whether they are considered to be state aids and need to be justified in the light of the horizontal and flanking policy duties imposed upon them.

The situation before Altmark*: the 'state aid approach'*

In the jurisprudence of the ECJ there are two approaches, the state aid approach and the compensation approach, to be found to the question how financial benefits to public service undertakings should be assessed.[117] The state aid approach implies that state funding to a public service undertaking is to be regarded as state aid within the meaning of Article 87(1) EC. The Court of First Instance followed this approach in the cases *FFSA* and *SIC*.[118] In the *FFSA* case the CFI regarded tax concessions granted to the French post, a public service undertaking, to constitute state aid within the meaning of Article 87 EC.

In the *SIC* case, which is particularly interesting for the subject matter, the CFI came to a similar conclusion. In this case the CFI annulled a decision of the Commission, which had applied the compensation approach and thus regarded a system of financing for the Portuguese public television channels not to constitute state aid.[119] According to the Commission, since the Portuguese public television channels have to meet obligations imposed by the public authorities which the private channels are not required to perform – coverage of the entire national territory, coverage of the autonomous regions of Madeira and the Azores, keeping of audio-visual archives, co-operation with countries whose official language is Portuguese, the making available of broadcasting time for religious programmes, the provision of an international channel, the financing of a public theatre and the maintaining of offices and correspondents in areas where private channels do not operate –, it was decided that the state measures merely offset additional costs. It concluded that the financial advan-

[116] COM(2002) 636 final.

[117] See also Opinion of AG Jacobs in Case C-126/01, *GEMO SA*, paragraphs 94 and 95.

[118] Case T-106/95, *FFSA et al v. Commission*; Case T-46/97, *SIC SA v. Commission*.

[119] Competition Report 1996, p. 242.

tage resulting from the transfers did not exceed what was strictly necessary in order to meet public service obligations and consequently did not constitute state aid within the meaning of Article 87(1) EC. The CFI, however, followed a more effect-oriented approach and stated that in order to determine whether a state measure constitutes aid, it is necessary to establish that the recipient undertaking receives an economic advantage, which it would not have obtained under normal conditions. According to the CFI, Article 87(1) EC does not distinguish between measures of state intervention by reference to their causes or aims, but defines them in relation to their effects. The fact that a financial advantage is granted to an undertaking by the public authorities in order to offset the cost of public service obligations which that undertaking is claimed to have assumed, has no bearing on the classification of that measure as aid within the meaning of Article 87(1) EC. In fact the Commission should have taken recourse to Article 86(2) EC.[120] For that matter, the CFI did not refer to the protocol on public service broadcasting, which had recently been adopted.

With a view to this ruling in 1999 the Commission approved the financing of two German public interest channels 'Kinderkanal' and 'Phoenix', because Germany did not abuse its competence by defining a children channel and an event and documentation channel with the specific features above, as part of the public service remit of broadcasting. The Commission therefore concluded that the conditions of Article 86(2) EC were fulfilled.[121] The launch of a 24-hour news service by the BBC, similarly to the German channels funded solely by a licence fee, was also considered to be justified on the basis of Article 86(2) EC.[122]

In response to these cases the Commission published a Communication in 2001 on the application of the state aid rules to public service broadcasting, based on the state aid approach.[123] In this Communication the following principles on which basis state funding of public service broadcasting can be approved under Article 86(2) EC are set out:

- *The service in question must be a service of general economic interest and clearly defined as such by the Member State (definition);*
  Here the role of the Commission is in principle limited to checking. The question is what is actually a public service task, which has become increasingly relevant as a result of rapid technological developments. May, for example, new services or other side tasks of public service broadcasters also be covered by this definition, like Internet services? The Communication says that this is possible, but the extent to which remains unclear; is the Internet not a neighbouring market where public service broadcasters

[120] Case T-46/97, *SIC SA v. Commission*, paragraphs 78-84.

[121] Press release DN: IP/99/132, see also Competition Report 1999, p. 104-105.

[122] Competition Report 1999, p. 105.

[123] OJ 2001, C 320/5; see also P. Kreijger, De financiering van de publieke omroep in Europa: nieuw beleid van de Europese Commissie, *Mediaforum*, 2003, pp. 82-87.

should occupy a special position?
In any event the Member State will have to lay down these side tasks clearly in national legislation. I-mode and SMS services provided by a public service broadcaster against remuneration will probably not qualify as public services. This appears from the Commission's preliminary observations in the pending case on ad-hoc measures to Dutch public broadcasters and the NOB.[124]

- *The undertaking in question must be explicitly entrusted by the Member State with the provision of that service (entrustment);* The public service remit should be entrusted by means of an official act and the provision of public service should be monitored by a body in charge of supervision;
- *The proportionality requirement implies that state aid does not exceed the net costs of the public service mission, taking into account other direct and indirect revenues derived from the public service mission.*

To some extent these conditions resemble the conditions formulated by the ECJ in *Altmark* (see hereafter). Even though it appears that the Commission confines itself to a marginal review of systems funding public service broadcasters, which has been welcomed by commentators, it will nevertheless carefully examine whether the public service tasks have been explicitly laid down in national legislation. The problem is that tasks of public service broadcasters are mostly in a general manner referred to in national legislation, which makes the quantification of public service broadcasting tasks extremely difficult, if not impossible.[125] It may then be necessary for the Member State to prove for the Commission the necessity and special characteristics of certain services to qualify as services of general economic interest. The Commission's approach is in accordance with the judgment in *FFSA* where the CFI held that the Commission must be allowed a certain discretion in deciding which method it uses to apply the exemption of Article 86(2) EC which implies that the Commission is only entitled to carry out a general economic assessment of the economic conditions in which the undertaking performs its activities.[126] The *SIC* case may have been the exception, since the public service tasks were specifically and clearly laid down in Portuguese legislation. Furthermore and at first sight the Commission's approach has so far been in the spirit of the protocol on public service broadcasting.[127]

---

[124] OJ 2004, C 61/8.

[125] Ch. Koenig and J. Kühling, Mitgliedstaatliche Kulturförderung und gemeinschaftrechtliche Beihilfekontrolle, *EuZW*, 2000, p. 198.

[126] Case T-106/95, *FFSA et al v. Commission*; appeal was dismissed in Case C-174/97P, *FFSA et al v. Commission*.

[127] See with regard to the Commission's policy before the 'Broadcasting Communication': R. Craufurd Smith, State Support for Public Service Broadcasting: The Position Under European Community Law, *LIEI*, 2001, pp. 3-22.

Lastly, the proportionality test allows the Commission to examine whether public service tasks are not over-compensated, which is a difficult task, particularly when the specific costs of public service tasks are not clearly laid down in national law.[128]

The situation after Altmark*: the 'compensation approach'*

The compensation approach implies that state funding of services of general interest amounts to state aid within the meaning of Article 87(1) EC only if and to the extent that the economic advantage it provides exceeds an appropriate remuneration of such additional costs. The Court of Justice followed this approach in the *ABDHU* case and the *Ferring* case and most recently the ECJ seems to have confirmed this approach in the *Altmark* case. In *ABDHU* the ECJ held that indemnities granted by a Member State to undertakings collecting or disposing of waste oils did not constitute aid within the meaning of Article 87 EC, but rather consideration for services performed by such undertakings.[129] In the *Ferring* case the ECJ held that a tax exemption for wholesale distributors of medicines did not constitute state aid within the meaning of Article 87(1) EC.[130] Under the French legislation a tax was levied on pharmaceutical laboratories for the sale of medicines and not on sales of medicines by wholesale distributors, which are under a duty of public service which is not imposed on pharmaceutical laboratories. According to the Court of Justice "[...] provided that the tax on direct sales imposed on pharmaceutical laboratories corresponds to the additional costs actually incurred by wholesale distributors in discharging their public service obligations, not assessing wholesale distributors to the tax may be regarded as compensation for the services they provide and hence not state aid within the meaning of Article 87 of the Treaty".[131] For that matter in the *Gemo* case, a system providing farmers and slaughterhouses with the free collection and disposal of animal carcasses and slaughterhouse waste, was considered to be state aid, since the service for the collection and disposal of animal carcasses and slaughterhouse waste constituted a benefit relieving farmers and slaughterhouses, which are not entrusted with public service obligations, of an expense which should properly be covered by their budget.[132]

[128] This may imply that the Commission's review should be limited to supervising the bookkeeping of obtained public means: K. Mortelmans and R. Wezenbeek-Geuke, Staatssteun in de Nederlandse omroepsector en de artikelen 92-93 EG Verdrag, *Mediaforum*, 1997, pp. 104-112. However, even supervising the bookkeeping of obtained public means may be problematic since the specific costs for public service tasks are not always calculated and written down: *see* Ch. Koenig and J. Kühling, Mitgliedstaatliche Kulturförderung und gemeinschaftrechtliche Beihilfekontrolle, *EuZW*, 2000, p. 198. This also appears from the pending case on ad-hoc measures for Dutch public broadcasters and NOB, OJ 2004, C 61/8, paragraph 96.

[129] Case 240/83, *ADBHU*, paragraph 18.

[130] Case C-53/00, *Ferring SA*.

[131] Case C-53/00, *Ferring SA*, paragraph 27.

[132] Case C-126/01, *GEMO SA*.

In his conclusion in the *Altmark* case AG Léger advised the ECJ to reverse its judgment in *Ferring* and to return to the state aid approach as followed by the CFI. The ECJ did not follow Léger's opinion and eventually decided the argument in favour of the compensation approach. This case involved licences and subsidies granted to Altmark for scheduled bus transport services; the case is also significant for financial benefits given to public service undertakings engaged in horizontal and flanking policy activities. The ECJ held that "where a state measure must be regarded as compensation for the services provided by the recipient undertakings in order to discharge public service obligations, so that the undertakings do not enjoy a real financial advantage and the measure does not have the effect of putting them in a more favourable competitive position than the undertakings competing with them, such a measure is not caught by Article 87(1) of the Treaty".[133] In addition four conditions have to be fulfilled for such compensation to fall outside the scope of Article 87(1) EC:

- The recipient undertaking must actually have public service obligations to discharge and the obligations must be clearly defined;
- The parameters on the basis of which the compensation is calculated must be established in advance in an objective and transparent manner;
- The compensation may not exceed what is necessary to cover all or part of the costs incurred in the discharge of public service obligations, taking into account the relevant receipts and a reasonable profit;
- Where the undertaking is not chosen pursuant to a public procurement procedure, the level of compensation needed must be determined on the basis of an analysis of the costs which a typical undertaking would have incurred in discharging those obligations.

Now that the ECJ clearly opted for the compensation approach the abovementioned cases may have to be assessed differently. By adopting a Decision and Community Framework for state aid in the form of public service compensation an attempt has been made by the Commission to offer more clarification in this matter.[134] In addition an amendment to the Commission Transparency Directive clarifies that companies receiving compensation and operating on both public service and other markets must have separate accounts for their different activities.[135] In the Decision the Commission spells out the conditions based on the *Altmark* case under which public service compensation consti-

[133] Case C-280/00, *Altmark Trans*, paragraph 87.

[134] The Decision on the application of Article 86(2) of the Treaty to state aid in the form of public service compensation granted to certain undertakings entrusted with the operation of services of general economic interest, and the Community Framework for state aid in the form of public service compensation can be found at: www.europa.eu.int/comm/competition/state_aid.

[135] Directive 80/723 on the transparency of financial relations between Member States and public undertakings, OJ 1980, L 195/35; see also Press Release IP/05/937.

tutes state aid compatible with Article 86(2) EC and exempts such aid from the notification requirement. The Decision will apply to public service undertakings whose turnover is limited, and which meet the *Altmark* criteria. Furthermore, according to Article 2(b) of the Decision public service compensation granted to hospitals and social housing undertakings carrying out services of general economic interest also benefits from the Decision irrespective of the turnover (see also section 3.1.5.4).

The purpose of the Community Framework is to specify under what conditions public service compensation that constitutes state aid can nevertheless be compatible with the common market or in accordance with Article 86(2) EC. For the public service broadcasting sector, the Commission's Communication remains relevant.

Hence, in the example of financing public service broadcasting the financial benefits should – before *Altmark* – have been notified to the Commission and must comply with the conditions of the 'Broadcasting Communication'.

After *Altmark*, it has become more complicated. First, one should try to fulfil the conditions laid down in *Altmark* to prevent notification; if one does not succeed, another option is to remain within the framework of the Decision (maximum turnover) without notifying the aid; third, if this does not work out, the aid scheme will have to be notified to the Commission and will have to comply with the conditions of the 'Broadcasting Communication'.[136]

It appears that in any event the Commission continues to carefully examine state funding of public service (broadcasting) undertakings, and whether there is no question of *overcompensation*, as appears from the *BBC-Digital Curriculum* case[137] and the pending case on ad-hoc measures for Dutch public broadcasters and NOB.[138] In *BBC-Digital Curriculum* the Commission held that one of the conditions of *Altmark* was not fulfilled and that as a result the aid scheme should be considered state aid within the meaning of Article 87(1) EC. Since the service, i.e. an extensive online service aimed for use in schools and homes and provided by BBC, was not awarded as a result of an open public procurement procedure, the fourth condition of *Altmark* was not fulfilled; nonetheless, the Commission concluded with reference to the 'Broadcasting Communication' that the aid scheme was justified under Article 86(2) EC.

In another case concerning the public service obligation imposed on the Electricity Supply Board (ESB) in Ireland the Commission concluded that since ESB had not been selected in a public procurement procedure, the fourth condition of *Altmark* had not been fulfilled and the measure therefore did not escape the qualification of state aid.[139]

---

[136] B. Hessel, Ontwikkelingen rond staatssteun en diensten van algemeen economisch belang na het Altmark-arrest, published at: www.europadecentraal.nl.

[137] Case N 37/2003, *BBC Digital Curriculum*.

[138] OJ 2004, C 61/8.

[139] Case N 143/2004, *Public Service Obligation – Electricity Supply Board (ESB)*.

Comments on the compensation approach

There are several arguments pleading in favour of the compensation approach. First, the concept of state aid only applies to measures which provide an economic advantage and distort or threaten to distort competition. There are no obvious reasons why those requirements should not apply where state funding of services of general economic interest is involved.[140] Second, there will be state aid only if and to the extent that the remuneration paid exceeds what is appropriate, which analysis is also applicable where the state purchases services which are to be provided to the collectivity. Third, the procedural implications of the state aid approach, in particular the notification requirement and the standstill requirement in Article 88(3) EC, might seriously disrupt the provision of services of general interest through private undertakings.[141] With regard to services of general interest it will be difficult or even impossible to wait for prior authorisation by the Commission. The duty of notification and the standstill period under the state aid approach may therefore cause considerable problems for the Member State in providing services of general interest, particularly in (politically) sensitive areas such as the area of health care. If the compensation approach were followed, numerous financial aid schemes to health insurance funds would escape the requirement of notification.[142]

There are also more substantive arguments in favour of the state aid approach. First, the Commission would still be able to control whether the services in issue in fact constitute services of general interest, whether the services have been entrusted to the undertaking concerned and whether the financing of these services affects trade between Member States. Second, the Member State would not be able to conceal potentially harmful measures by escaping the duty of notification. Third, the state aid approach is more consistent with the parallel analysis in two steps of measures which infringe Article 86(1) EC read in conjunction with other Treaty provisions (see hereafter, section 3.2),

[140] The approach of the Court of Justice in *Ferring* seems to underline the fact that the special character of public service broadcasters, i.e. to provide for programmes aimed at all citizens, implies that the Commission cannot simply compare public service broadcasters with commercial undertakings which objectives are to make profits; see also H. Zeinstra and H. van der Plas, Het Protocol bij het Verdrag van Amsterdam inzake de financiering van publieke omroepen, *Mediaforum*, 1997, p. 125.

[141] The ruling in *Altmark* enhances the decentralised control of financial public service obligations by national courts: J.A. Winter, Re(de)fining the notion of State aid in Article 87(1) of the EC Treaty, *CMLRev.*, 2004, p. 501.

[142] It has been argued that in *Altmark* the Court has offered Member States a choice: "to gain an easier life by compliance with advance openness and transparency or to forgo this and risk having to sustain a justification exercise under Article 86(2) somewhere": M. Ross, The Europeanization of Public Service Supervision: Harnessing Competition and Citizenship?, in P. Eeckhout and T. Tridimas (Eds), *Yearbook of European Law* (Oxford University Press, Oxford, 2004), p. 307.

and which can be justified by Article 86(2) EC.[143] Furthermore, Article 16 EC by using the words "without prejudice to the rules governing state aid provided in Articles 73, 86 and 87 of the Treaty..." suggests that Article 87 EC is applicable to state action in favour of services of general economic interest.[144]

There are two further compelling reasons why the approach of the ECJ in *Altmark* can be criticised, particularly from the perspective of horizontal and flanking policies. First, the judgment has the *appearance* to provide Member States with more discretion to pursue horizontal and flanking policy interests in this manner, yet the Commission will continue to examine state aid measures, whether they meet the four requirements laid down in *Altmark*. Second, the fact that our economies are regulated economies, where, apart from particular public service tasks, also various horizontal and flanking policy obligations are imposed on companies, entails that for public service undertakings no specific exception should be made.[145] Similarly to aids granted for horizontal and flanking policy purposes, which generally need to be exempted under Article 87(3) EC, aids granted to public service undertakings should in principle also be subject to notification and justification under Article 86(2) EC. The state aid approach and the corresponding review of aid schemes to public service companies under Article 86(2) EC provides the Community with a mechanism that could *guarantee* that state-granted compensation will be proportional to the public service remit as defined by the Member State. In other words, Article 86(2) EC should not be interpreted as a limited derogation from the state aid rules, but as an endorsement of horizontal and flanking policy considerations subject to only a marginal review of the Commission and the courts.[146]

Certainly, the procedural arguments cannot and should not be overlooked. If however, the Commission continues to carefully examine state aid schemes to public service undertakings, as is the case in the area of public service broadcasting, it becomes questionable whether *Altmark* really serves the provision of

143 See also K. Mortelmans and R. Wezenbeek-Geuke, Staatssteun in de Nederlandse omroepsector en de artikelen 92-93 EG Verdrag, *Mediaforum*, 1997, pp. 104-112; Article 87(1) EC does not distinguish between public service broadcasters and commercial undertakings. The special nature of public service broadcasters can, however, be taken into account under Article 86(2) EC as is shown by the Commission's guidelines in response to the German and British fund systems.

144 These arguments partly derive from the Opinion of AG Jacobs in Case C-126/01, *GEMO SA*.

145 The Commission's assessment should then be restricted to analysing whether the State-granted compensation does not exceed the net costs of the particular task assigned to the public service company, and whether as a result of extra costs exceeding extra revenue the public service would not be offered by the undertaking in question: see P. Nicolaides, Distortive Effects of Compensatory Aid Measures: A Note on the Economics of the *Ferring* judgment, *ECLR*, 2002, pp. 317-318.

146 See also Communication from the Commission on Services of general interest in Europe, OJ 2001, C17/4, at p. 22; see also P. Nicolaides, Distortive Effects of Compensatory Aid Measures: A Note on the Economics of the *Ferring* judgment, *ECLR*, 2002, p. 319.

public services in the end. After all if a Member State implements the aid before such an authorisation has been granted, the aid will be illegal with all the consequences of that illegality.[147]

3.1.4 The distortion of competition and trade

Member States have a duty to notify the aid before the Commission demonstrated the actual effect which that aid has on competition and on trade between Member States. Another interpretation would, according to the CFI, "ultimately favour Member States which pay aid without complying with the duty to notify the aid laid down in Article 88(3) EC, to the detriment of those which notify the aid at the proposal stage".[148] Hence, it must now be determined when competition and trade within the context of Article 87(1) EC have been restricted.

De minimis *aid*

If state aids meet the requirements set out above but do not have an appreciable effect on trade and competition between Member States, they will not fall within the scope of application of Article 87(1) EC. Even though the Court originally seemed to reject a *de minimis* rule for state aids, the Commission's approach has been different.[149] In 1996 the Commission adopted a notice on *de minimis* rule for state aid, which laid down the ceilings for aid covered by this rule. Below the threshold figure – 100.000 ECU – Article 87(1) EC could not be said to apply, so that the measure no longer had to be notified to the Commission in advance.[150] The Commission's approach has formally been recognised by Regulation 994/98.[151] Now, the *de minimis* rule is laid down in Regulation 69/2001, which provides for a similar threshold figure of 100.000 Euro over a three years time period.[152] This figure applies to any one enterprise, which means that

---

[147] See also the Opinion of AG Jacobs in Case C-126/01, *GEMO SA*.

[148] Joined Cases T-116/01 and T-118/01, *P&O European Ferries (Vizcaya) SA*, paragraph 142.

[149] Quigley & Collins (2003), pp. 63-66. Hancher, Ottervanger & Slot (1999), p. 38; Before 1996, the Commission had not objected to a fund set up in the Netherlands to subsidize the publication and translation of literary works (Nederlands literair productie- en vertalingenfonds) inter alia because it had a negligible effect on trade between Member States, see Loman, Mortelmans, Post and Watson (1992), p. 128.

[150] Commission notice on the *de minimis* rule for State aid, OJ 1996, C 68/6.

[151] OJ 1998, L 142/1; Regulation on the application of Articles 87 and 88 of the EC Treaty to categories of Horizontal State aid. Article 2 of this Regulation allows the Commission to declare by Regulation that certain aids fall outside the scope of Article 87(1), because they do not exceed a certain fixed amount over a given period of time.

[152] Commission Regulation 69/2001 on the application of Articles 87 and 88 of the EC Treaty to *de minimis* aid, OJ 2001, L 10/30.

local governments will have some margin of discretion in granting financial benefits to undertakings.[153] According to article 1 the Regulation does not apply to aid granted to undertakings in the transport sector, aid to export-related activities and aid contingent upon the use of domestic over imported goods. Generally, though, aid granted by, for example, local communities for horizontal and flanking purposes to small and medium sized undertakings could benefit from this notice. For small and medium sized undertakings a specific Regulation has been adopted which stipulates that under certain conditions aid granted to small and medium-sized undertakings is compatible with the common market and is not subject to the notification requirement of Article 88(3) EC.[154]

Outside this regulatory framework the Commission regards aid which is granted at a local level to locally operating enterprises only as not to distort competition and trade. For example, an annual grant made to the private operator of a swimming pool in Dorsten did not affect trade between Member States and consequently did not constitute state aid within the meaning of Article 87(1) EC, since the sporting facility is essentially used by inhabitants of the town and surrounding area.[155] In its *Renove* decision, the Commission regarded a Spanish aid regime for the purchase of commercial vehicles, the objective of which was to facilitate the renewal of the commercial fleet in Spain with regard to safety and environmental protection, not to fall within the scope of Article 87(1) EC, where *inter alia* the aid was granted to small undertakings and natural persons operating at a local level, and where small vehicles typically used for very short journeys were subsidised.[156] However, with regard to other recipients of the aid scheme, having transport as their main business or only as an auxiliary, the Commission considered that the measure could be regarded as state aid strengthening the financial position of those undertakings and affecting trade between Member States within the meaning of Article 87(1) EC. The Commission treated transport companies and non-transport companies alike, which entailed that, since the *de minimis* rule does not apply to the transport sector, aid given to non-transport companies could not benefit from the *de minimis* rule. This part of the decision was annulled by the ECJ in the case *Spain v. Commission*, since, according to the Court, the Commission should have examined whether the aid to non-transport companies could fall within the *de minimis* rule.[157]

In the field of public health, an Irish measure which provided for a tax benefit for individuals investing in the construction, extension and refurbishment

[153] Hessel and Neven (2001), p. 102.

[154] Commission Regulation 70/2001 on the application of Articles 87 and 88 of the EC Treaty to State Aid to small and medium-sized enterprises, OJ 2001, L 10/33.

[155] Case N-258/2000; see also Press Release IP/00/1509 of 21 December 2002.

[156] Commission Decision 98/693, OJ 1998, L 329/23.

[157] Case C-351/98, *Spain v. Commission*.

of hospitals was not incompatible with Article 87(1) EC. The hospitals must set aside some of their capacity for public health care. The Commission concluded that the measure confers an advantage on those hospitals which are thus able to develop their activities, but will essentially benefit local hospitals, where there is undercapacity, and will not result in the construction of hospital complexes likely to attract clients from other Member States. Accordingly, the measure did not affect trade between Member States.[158]

In the field of culture it should be noted that, according to the Commission, the restoration of existing monuments and landmarks of cultural and historical value (heritage aid) does not in itself affect trade between Member States.[159]

Aids that distort competition and trade

In the *Philip Morris* case the Court ruled that in order to establish whether aid is (in)compatible with Article 87 EC it is necessary to consider whether the aid strengthens the position of an undertaking compared to other undertakings competing in intra-Community trade.[160] The Commission's approach under the state aid rules is rather formal. The Commission does not need to conduct a *thorough* market analysis, but it remains unclear what market analysis suffices for state aid to be incompatible with Article 87(1) EC. The Guidelines on the definition of the relevant market which are relevant for Articles 81 and 82 EC will not normally extend to the assessment of state aid cases.[161] In the *Philip Morris* case Philip Morris argued that the criteria for deciding whether competition restrictions fall under Articles 81 and 82 EC should also apply to Article 87(1) EC. The Commission must therefore first determine the relevant market, and then must assess how far the aid in question in a given case affects relations between competitors, which was rejected by the Court. In the *Leeuwarder Papierenfabriek* case, though, the Court held that "[...] even if in certain cases the very circumstances in which the aid is granted are sufficient to show that the aid is capable of affecting trade between Member States and of distorting or threatening to distort competition, the Commission must at least set out those circumstances in the statement of reasons for its decision".[162]

A similarly broad approach has been adopted towards the criterion of effect on trade. It is, for example, not necessary for the aid to be considered as affecting trade between Member States that the enterprise actually exports its products.[163] In its decisions on state aid for the promotion of film production, the Commission assumed that, even though films produced within a Member State are

[158] Case N-543/2001, *Capital Allowances for Hospitals in Ireland.*

[159] Case N 560/01 and NN 17/02, *United Kingdom Brighton West Pier*, paragraph 34.

[160] Case 730/79, *Philip Morris.*

[161] Hancher, Ottervanger and Slot (1999), p. 37.

[162] Joined Cases 296/82 and 318/82, *Leeuwarder Papierfabriek.*

[163] Hancher, Ottervanger & Slot (1999), p. 39.

primarily directed at the state nationals, they could be exported to other Member States as well, which is sufficient for Article 87 EC to apply.[164]

That the definition of the relevant market plays some role in assessing state aid measures appears from several decisions of the Commission also in relation to aids for horizontal and flanking policy reasons. In its decision concerning aid granted by the Italian government to the paper manufacturer Cartiere del Garda to safeguard the environment and to reorganise land in the productive sector, for example, the Commission stated that there is competition between manufacturers of paper and their products are traded between Member States. The fact that Cartiera del Garda received financial aid for the realisation of extra production capacity at Mori instead of extending its production capacity at Riva for environmental reasons does not alter the conclusion that compensation of these investment costs constitutes state aid.[165] In order to establish whether financial aid strengthens the company's position as compared to others competing in intra-Community trade a reference to the relevant market is therefore necessary. Nevertheless, the Commission does not provide for a thorough market analysis.

In its decision concerning state aid in favour of CELF – Coopérative d'exportation du livre français – for the handling of small orders of French books from foreign booksellers the Commission held that notwithstanding constraints imposed by language and culture, books aided through various schemes may be in competition with books on the same subject or in the same category for which no aid has been granted. Without examining the book market in detail, the Commission came to the conclusion that the subsidy granted to CELF constituted state aid within the meaning of Article 87 EC.[166] A market analysis of the book market was conducted, however, within the context of Article 87(3) sub d EC, in other words, in order to examine whether the cultural exception could be applied in this case (see hereafter, section 3.1.5.5).

The rather formal approach under Article 87(1) EC as compared to the more economic approach under Articles 81(1) and 82 EC (see section 4) implies that there is hardly room to take account of horizontal and flanking policy interests under Article 87(1) EC, which brings the exceptions contained in Articles 87(2) EC and 87(3) EC to the fore. As has been shown, the situation is different for aids granted to public service undertakings. Here the Court of Justice adopts a particularly favourable approach towards such aid schemes, which are designed to contribute to the protection of public interests through the establishment of public service undertakings (see above).

---

164 See Commission Communication on certain legal aspects relating to cinematographic and other audiovisual works, COM(2001), 534 final; see for example Case N 496/2004 on aid by the Flemish Community to cinematographic and audiovisual production; see also Ch. Koenig and J. Kühling, Mitgliedstaatliche Kulturförderung und gemeinschaftrechtliche Beihilfekontrolle, *EuZW*, 2000, p. 200.

165 Commission Decision 93/564, OJ 1993, L 273/51.

166 OJ 1999, L 44/37.

3.1.5 The exceptions: state aids that can be justified for horizontal and flanking policy reasons

Aid that is incompatible with Article 87(1) EC may, after having been notified to the Commission, obtain an exemption under the conditions laid down in Articles 87(2) EC and 87(3) EC. Before the cases on state aid in the fields of the environment, consumer protection, public health and culture will be discussed (section 3.1.5.2 and further), the scope of Articles 87(2) EC and 87(3) EC needs to be assessed in a more general sense.

In the following sections the exceptions and the extent to which horizontal and flanking policy interests can be taken into account will be discussed first; hereafter the important role of the proportionality principle in balancing distortions of competition with horizontal and flanking policy interests is dealt with.

3.1.5.1 The scope of Articles 87(2) and 87(3) EC

Articles 87(2) and 87(3) EC do not, apart from Articles 87(2) sub a on aid for individual consumers and 87(3) sub d EC on culture, explicitly refer to horizontal and flanking objectives. Hence, the question is whether and if so to what extent, the Commission in granting an exemption may nonetheless take horizontal and flanking policy interests into account.

The exceptions of Articles 87(2) and 87(3) EC

Article 87(2) EC contains a list of categories of aids that are automatically exempted from the prohibition in Article 87(1) EC. Exemption is automatic if the Commission considers that the aid falls within one of these categories. During the negotiations on the Maastricht Treaty the German Länder have, obviously without success, tried to include culture in the second paragraph of Article 87, so that aids for cultural purposes would be automatically exempted.[167] Now, Article 87(3) sub d EC states that aid to promote culture and heritage conservation *may* be compatible with the common market, where such aid does not affect trading conditions and competition in the Community to an extent that is contrary to the common interest. For that matter, as stated before, Article 87(3) EC does not refer to other objectives of horizontal and flanking policies. This has, however, not withheld the Commission from exempting state aids on such grounds.

Article 87(3) sub b and Article 87(3) sub c EC have been the main grounds of justification for horizontal and flanking state aids. Cultural subsidies could be justified on the basis of Article 87(3) sub c before the introduction of Article 87(3) sub d EC. Article 87(3) sub b EC provides that aid to promote the execution

---

167 M. Niedobitek, Die Kulturelle Dimension im Vertrag über die Europäische Union, *EuR*, 1995, pp. 374-375.

of an important project of common European interest or to remedy a serious disturbance in the economy of a Member State may be considered compatible with the common market. This provision was originally used as grounds for justifying environmental aids. Now, the Community Guidelines on environmental state aids and the Community framework for state aid for research and development refer to both Article 87(3) sub b and 87(3) sub c EC, but Article 87(3) sub c EC seems to have become the main provision for exemption.[168] The latter provides that aid to facilitate the development of certain economic activities or of certain economic areas, where such aid does not adversely affect trading conditions to an extent contrary to the common interest, may be considered compatible with the common market.

The difference between the two provisions is explained by the Commission in paragraph 73 of its Guidelines on environmental state aids: "Aid to promote the execution of important projects of common European interests which are an environmental priority and will often have beneficial effects beyond the frontiers of the Member State(s) concerned can be authorised under the exemption provided for in Article 87(3)(b) of the EC Treaty. However, the aid must be necessary for the project to proceed, and the project must be specific, well defined and qualitatively important and must make an exemplary and clearly identifiable contribution to the common European interest. When this exemption is applied, the Commission may authorise aid at higher rates than the limits laid down for aid authorised pursuant to Article 87(3)(c)." On the one hand, Article 87(3) sub b EC allows for aids at higher rates than Article 87(3) sub c EC, on the other hand the conditions of application seem more stringent.[169]

By Council Regulation 994/98 the Commission is authorised to adopt block exemption regulations for certain categories of horizontal State aid, i.e. aid in favour of small and medium-sized enterprises, research and development, environmental protection and employment and training.[170] Only for aid in favour of small and medium-sized enterprises and for training aid – and apart from the *de minimis* Regulation – has the Commission so far adopted block exemption regulations. In its State Aid Action Plan the Commission states that it intends to adopt a general block exemption regulation to exempt certain categories of aid from the obligation to notify the Commission.[171] The advantages of a block

[168] Community guidelines on State aid for environmental protection, OJ 2001, C 37/3; Community framework for State aid for research and development, OJ 1996, C 45/6. With regard to environmental State aids see also G. van Calster, Greening the E.C.'s State Aid and Tax Regimes, *ECLR*, 2000, pp. 294-314.

[169] G. van Calster, Greening the E.C.'s State Aid and Tax Regimes, *ECLR*, 2000, p. 297.

[170] Council Regulation 994/98, OJ 1998, L 142/1.

[171] According to the Commission the regulation will be based on the principle that State aid policy should focus on the most distortive types of aid and that it should set clear 'positive' and 'negative' priorities: State Aid Action Plan – Less and better targeted State aid: a roadmap for State aid reform 2005-2009, point 35, to be found at: http://www.europa.eu.int/comm/competition/state_aid/others/action_plan/.

exemption regulation are, according to the Council, that they can be applied directly by the national courts which will increase transparency and legal certainty and that they offer more efficient supervision and simplified administration since these aid categories are in principle exempted from the notification requirement under Article 88(3) EC. Whereas the Guidelines on state aid for environmental protection definitely provide more legal certainty, they do not have a similarly broad scope of application as block exemption regulations have.

The proportionality test

In declaring state aid compatible with the common market under Article 87(3) EC the Commission will have to balance the adverse effects on competition and intra-Community trade with the positive effects for the interests mentioned in Article 87(3) EC. In this respect the proportionality principle plays a principal role. According to the Commission, the following factors, which are connected to this principle, are relevant in reviewing state aid measures under Article 87(3) EC:

- The aid must promote or further a project that is in the Community interest as a whole;
- The aid must be necessary for the achievement of this result, and in its absence the objective could not have been obtained otherwise. In other words, there must be a causal connection between the measure and the aim pursued. The company must be incited to take some action, which they otherwise would not have taken. This is also referred to as the compensatory justification criterion. The contribution to the company must be over and above the effects of the normal play of the market forces;[172]
- The duration, intensity and scope of the aid must be proportional to the importance of the intended result.[173]

A few remarks with regard to the above-mentioned factors must be made. First, the Community interest may include national interests as well. National measures that benefit the domestic cultural industry, for example, are eligible for an exemption based on Article 87(3) sub d EC. Particularly in the field of culture a certain degree of territorialisation will be unavoidable (see hereafter). However, state aid measures that clearly discriminate vis à vis products from other Member States will probably not be considered compatible with the common market as appears from the *Biofuels* decision. In its decision on tax exemptions for biofuels in France the Commission refused to give an exemption on the basis of Article 87(3) EC, since the tax exemption only applied to biofuels produced from certain basic products.[174] The measure therefore discriminated

[172] Case 730/79, *Philip Morris.*

[173] See Hancher, Ottervanger & Slot (1999), p. 73.

[174] Commission Decision 97/542, OJ 1997, L 222/26.

against biofuels made from other basic products that could be technically appropriate for the production of biofuels, but which were grown mainly outside France. As a consequence, biofuels imported from other Member States and produced from other basic products were subject to a higher tax. The following amended biofuel aid scheme was approved by the Commission under Article 88(3) EC (see hereafter).[175]

Second, the two other factors mentioned above refer to the necessity and the proportionality *stricto sensu* of the state aid measure, whereby the Commission will sometimes need to define the relevant market to assess the impact of the state aid measure on competition and trade and to compare that impact on competition and trade with the importance of the intended aim of the measure.

3.1.5.2 The environment

In the field of environmental state aids the Commission's approach under Article 87(3) EC has been further elaborated and clarified in Guidelines. A particular problem here involves the application of the polluter pays principle.

The protection of the environment as an exception: the Guidelines

The 2001 Guidelines on state aid for environmental protection generally offer, in the absence of a specific Treaty provision of state aids for environmental protection, a comprehensive set of rules and clear guidance as to the Commission's position with regard to such state aids. In reviewing the former 1994 Guidelines the Commission has not chosen to adopt a block exemption regulation for environmental state aids. This could have been an option since nowadays more environmental problems are known than at the time of the adoption of the Guidelines in 1994.[176] In its State Aid Action Plan (2005-2009) the Commission announces that it might consider to exempt certain environmental measures under the new general block exemption from the obligation to notify the aid.[177] Nevertheless, the Guidelines should not merely be considered as an

---

[175] This decision was partly annulled by the CFI in Case T-184/97, *BP Chemicals* where the decision related to measures of the scheme concerning the ETBE-sector (ETBE: Ethyl Tert-Butyl Ether). The Commission infringed Article 8(2) of Directive 92/81 (as amended) which provides that 'without prejudice to other Community provisions, Member States may apply total or partial exemptions or reductions in the rate of duty to mineral oils used under fiscal control: ...(d) in the field of pilot projects for the technological development of more environmentally-friendly products and in particular in relation to fuels from renewable resources' (amended by Directive 94/74, OJ 1994, L 365/46).

[176] See also H.H.B. Vedder, The New Community Guidelines for Environmental Protection – Integrating Environment and Competition?, *ECLR*, 2001, pp. 366-367: he wonders whether a block exemption regulation would ever be the right tool considering the dynamic nature of this matter.

[177] State Aid Action Plan – Less and better targeted State aid: a roadmap for State aid reform 2005-2009, point 46, to be found at: http://www.europa.eu.int/comm/competition/state_aid/others/action_plan/.

instrument of 'soft law' with a purely informative character; the Commission's margin of discretion to develop a policy in the field of environmental state aids is definitely limited by the Guidelines.[178]

The 1994 Guidelines were the first instrument setting out the Commission's approach towards environmental state aids.[179] In these Guidelines the Commission recognised the dilemma between the application of the polluter pays principle on the one hand and the grant of environmental state aids on the other hand, and therefore regarded state aids as the second best solution in situations where the polluter pays principle was not yet fully applied.[180] The polluter pays principle may actually have been the reason to prefer Guidelines to a block exemption regulation, since Guidelines do not take away the obligation for Member States to notify their environmental aid schemes to the Commission. The Commission's original view has always been that the use of Guidelines had to be a transitional stage, paving the way for the polluter pays principle. State aid in this area was to gradually disappear.[181] With the adoption of the 2001 Guidelines, the Community's policy seems to be much more structural and long lasting, even though they will cease to be applicable on 31 December 2007. However, the Commission may amend them before this date on the basis of important competition policy or environmental policy considerations or in order to take account of other Community policies or international commitments. The Commission has thus provided a flexible instrument since the Guidelines can be amended at any time.

In the introductory chapter of the 2001 Guidelines the Commission states that whereas the granting of state aids is at odds with the polluter pays principle, such aid may nonetheless be justified if necessary to ensure environmental protection and sustainable development without having disproportionate effects on competition and economic growth (point 5). In fact there are two main principles which form the basis of these Guidelines. Apart from the polluter pays principle, the integration principle laid down in Article 6 EC is referred to in the Guidelines. This entails that whereas state aids is at odds with the polluter pays principle, such aids may nonetheless be justified in two instances. Firstly, state aids represent a temporary second-best solution by encouraging firms to adapt to certain standards. Secondly, state aids may be used as an incentive for firms to improve on standards or, in the absence of standards, to further invest in the reduction of pollution.[182] In other words, the Guidelines allow Member States,

[178] Case C-351/98, *Spain v. Commission*; see annotation G. van Calster, *SEW*, 2003, p. 40; see also Case C-409/00, *Spain v. Commission*, paragraph 95.

[179] Before 1994 the Commission's policy was laid down in environmental frameworks which were not published in the Official Journal but could only be found in the Reports on Competition: see G. van Calster, Greening the E.C.'s State Aid and Tax Regimes, *ECLR*, 2000, p. 296.

[180] For the polluter pays principle, see Chapter 1.

[181] See also G. van Calster, Greening the E.C.'s State Aid and Tax Regimes, *ECLR*, 2000, p. 296.

[182] Point 18 of the Guidelines; see also H.H.B. Vedder, The New Community Guidelines for Environmental Protection – Integrating Environment and Competition?, *ECLR*, 2001, p. 367.

under certain conditions, to speed up environmental protection via governmental incentives and aim to strike a balance between requirements of competition and environmental policy.[183]

Apart from aids granted specifically for environmental purposes, aids granted for other purposes in sectors like agriculture, transport or energy should at least not have negative side effects for the environment. Cases in the fields of agriculture and transport will be not be further discussed here. It is suggested, however, that in these areas aid schemes, whether at a Community or national level, should be diverted as to meet environmental protection requirements and the polluter pays principle.[184]

The proportionality test

The application of the proportionality test to state aids in the field of the environment has been made concrete by the Commission through the adoption of the Guidelines. In point 1.6 of the Guidelines it is stated that "the Commission's approach in these guidelines therefore consists in determining whether, and under what conditions, state aid may be regarded as necessary to ensure environmental protection and sustainable development without having disproportionate effects on competition and economic growth". The criteria laid down in the Guidelines help the Commission to appraise environmental aids and to determine possible disproportionate effects on competition and trade. Generally, aid for the protection of the environment is justifiable, but the proportionality of the measure depends on the type of aid schemes adopted by the national state.

In the Guidelines a distinction is made in the following types of state aid schemes. First, aid for investment in land, buildings, plant and equipment intended to reduce or eliminate pollution or to protect the environment can be exempted, provided that the investment is strictly necessary to attain environmental objectives. This means that the investment costs must be strictly confined to the extra investment costs necessary to meet environmental objectives. Investment aid can be distinguished in aid to help firms adapt to new mandatory standards (generally up to the level of 15% gross of the eligible costs, with a bonus of 10% for SME's), aid to encourage firms to improve on mandatory environmental standards (up to 30% gross of the eligible costs, with a bonus of 10% for SME's) and aid in the absence of mandatory standards (similarly to aid for improvement). In comparison with the 1994 Guidelines, the following is apparent. The Kyoto Protocol and the Community's interest in the development of electricity from renewable energy sources are clearly reflected in

[183] G. van Calster, Greening the E.C.'s State Aid and Tax Regimes, *ECLR*, 2000, p. 298; See also the 6th Environmnent Action Programme 'Environment 2010-Our future, Our choice', COM(2001) 31 final, p. 19.

[184] See Dhondt (2003).

the Guidelines. Aid for energy-related investments is now subject to a clear set of rules. Furthermore, apart from SME's, firms cannot qualify anymore for investment aid for adapting to compulsory standards.

Second, aid for horizontal measures – for advisory/consultancy services in the environmental field – may be granted under the block exemption regulation for SME's.[185] No reference is made anymore to aid for information activities, training and advisory services, which probably does not confer identifiable benefits on specific firms and will therefore fall outside the scope of Article 87(1) EC (see above).

Third, operating aid may be exempted, but only under strict conditions. Operating aid is almost always prohibited under Article 87 EC. Aid for the management of waste or aid in the energy-saving field may only be exempted where it is shown to be absolutely necessary. For aid in the form of tax reductions or exemptions a distinction is made between taxation schemes that have an origin in a Community decision, and national taxation schemes. Furthermore the Guidelines include a number of criteria on which basis it will be assessed whether the tax reductions or exemptions can be exempted. For the production of renewable energy, operating aid will usually be allowable under the Guidelines if it covers the difference between the market price for energy and the costs for producing energy from renewable energy sources. The Commission then distinguishes between four options of state aid for the production of renewable energy.

The Guidelines partly codify the decision practice of the Commission on state aids in environmental matters, which is illustrative as to how the Commission seeks to balance environmental concerns with requirements of competition. The decision on aid granted by the Netherlands for the construction of a hydrogen peroxide plant in Delfzijl (province of Groningen), for example, shows how the Commission applies the proportionality test in this field. The aid scheme provided a financial contribution towards the costs of constructing a hydrogen peroxide plant in Delfzijl and the aid was to be paid under the Regional Investment Project Subsidies Order. Since the aid exceeded the maximum level of admissible aid under this regional aid scheme, the aid could only be justifiable on other grounds, which were environmental grounds. The Dutch government brought forward that since the company is established in a nature conservation area which is protected under both Community law and domestic legislation with strict mandatory environmental standards in force, the aid scheme served to compensate the extra investment costs necessary to meet these strict environmental requirements. By referring to the 1994 Guidelines, the Commission emphasised that it only allows aid up to the ceiling of 30% gross of the eligible costs in cases where the measures being taken are very substantially beyond the compulsory standards. According to the Commission

[185] Regulation 70/2001, OJ 2001, L 10/33.

the Dutch government had not demonstrated that the company had gone beyond the requirement of domestic environmental legislation, nor had they shown that the aid is in proportion to the investment or to the extent to which standards have been exceeded.[186]

The Commission thus intends to apply the criteria laid down in the Guidelines strictly and state aid will only be approved if the environmental benefits outweigh the impact on competition.[187] In the decision in *Cartiera del Garda* the Commission makes clear that where a Member State grants aid to a company to relocate the company to a new site, the Member State has to demonstrate that the aid is absolutely necessary to prevent the firm from investing in the present site, for environmental reasons.[188] Other, perhaps hidden objectives, such as objectives of employment, may not outweigh environmental objectives of the aid scheme. Furthermore, the Commission will take account of the polluter pays principle. The present Guidelines now provide a relatively clear guidance in cases on land rehabilitation and plant relocation.

3.1.5.3 Consumer protection

A Community policy in respect of state aid for reasons of consumer protection can hardly said to have developed yet; nevertheless, Article 87(2) sub a EC includes an explicit reference to consumers.

The protection of consumers as an exception

Article 87(2) sub a EC explicitly refers to aid having a social character granted to individual consumers. The aid must be granted to individual consumers and not undertakings.[189] For example, measures designed to lower the prices for bread which are given to undertakings and which do not directly benefit consumers, will not fall within the scope of Article 87(2) sub a EC.[190] A German measure designed to give a tax relief to individual consumers purchasing cars fitted with pollution reduction devices could, according to the Commission, be exempted by Article 87(2) sub a EC, but only if it did not result in discrimination as to the origin of the products, contrary to Article 28 EC.[191] Apart from this provision, aid granted for research and development projects to develop safer products is also in the interest of consumers. Of course, from the perspective of sustainable consumption environmental aid is also beneficial to consumers. It

---

[186] Commission Decision 98/384, OJ 1998, L 171/36.

[187] D. Geradin, EC Competition Law and Environmental Protection: Conflict or Compatibility?, in: H. Somsen (Ed.), *Yearbook of European Environmental Law* (Oxford University Press, Oxford, 2002), p. 153.

[188] Commission Decision 93/564, OJ 1993, L 273/51.

[189] Hancher, Ottervanger & Slot (1999), p. 70.

[190] Hessel & Neven (2001), p. 134.

[191] Hessel & Neven (2001), p. 70.

can however, be concluded that compared to the other areas of horizontal and flanking policy, there is hardly any Community policy developed in this field.

The proportionality test

Exemption on the basis of Article 87(2) EC is automatic if the Commission considers that the aid falls within one of the categories.[192] Nevertheless, the aid remains subject to Commission control and needs to be notified to qualify for an automatic exemption. The proportionality test, if one can speak of a proportionality test in this context, is extremely limited and merely involves an assessment of the causal link between the national measure and the aim pursued.

3.1.5.4 Public health

A distinction can be made between state aid in the health care sector and state aid for the protection of public health *stricto sensu*. Articles 87(2) and 87(3) EC do not contain explicit references either to health care or to the protection of public health in general.

Health care

Regarding domestic aid schemes in the health care sector, it is unclear to what extent Article 87 EC may be applicable. If it is assumed that certain organisations active in the health care sector, such as hospitals and sickness funds, should be considered as public service undertakings, the mere compensation for the costs related to their public service tasks will probably not be considered as state aid within the meaning of Article 87 EC (see above). According to Article 2(b) of the Commission's Decision on the application of Article 86(2) of the Treaty to state aid in the form of public service compensation, public service compensation granted to hospitals that carry out activities involving services of general economic interests does not have to be notified to the Commission.[193] Article 87 EC will then be irrelevant.

In the *BUPA* case the Commission had to establish whether the risk equalisation scheme (RES) in the Irish health insurance market constituted state aid within the meaning of Article 87 EC.[194] The Irish health care system is characterised by a free universal public health service, and a private system by way of voluntary private medical insurance. Risk equalisation aims at neutralising differences in health insurers' costs that arise due to variations in their risk profiles, which results in cash transfers from insurers with healthier than average risk profiles to those with less favourable risk profiles.[195] The Commission

---

[192] Hancher, Ottervanger & Slot (1999), p. 69.

[193] The decision can be found at: www.europa.eu.int/comm/competition/state_aid. See also above, section 3.1.3.

[194] Case N 46/2003, *Risk equalisation scheme in the Irish health insurance market.*

[195] Case N 46/2003, *Risk equalisation scheme in the Irish health insurance market*, paragraph 17.

comes to the following conclusion: "Taking into account that health care issues come primarily under the responsibility of the Member States, that national governments are in principle free to impose regulations with a view to promote the public good, that the RES is necessary for the stability of a community related health insurance market and given that the scheme, as it is designed involves payments which are limited to the minimum necessary to neutralise differences in health insurers' risk profiles, the Commission considers that the RES is justified as a compensation for obligations imposed on all insurers in the Irish health insurance market, which qualify as SGEI. Therefore, the RES does not constitute state aid within the meaning of Article 87(1) of the Treaty or if it were assumed that compensation for extra costs of services of general economic interest constituted state aid within the meaning of Article 87(1) of the Treaty, these aid elements could be considered compatible with the common market pursuant to Article 86(2) of the Treaty."[196]

The European Commission also takes a favourable approach to public funding for the new Dutch health insurance system, which is carried out by private insurance companies that are required to offer basic health insurance to all citizens (public service obligation). According to the Commission's press release the setting up of a risk equalisation scheme between insurers and the granting of start-up capital to certain insurers to support the transformation of the system does not distort competition and can therefore be authorised.[197]

Whether over-compensation would still be justifiable under Article 87(2) or 87(3) EC is unclear; Article 86(2) EC could probably not serve as an exception. According to the Court in *Ferring* Article 86(2) EC does not cover a tax advantage enjoyed by public service undertakings (wholesale distributors of medicines) in so far as that advantage exceeds the additional costs of performing the public service (see also above, section 3.1.3).[198]

The protection of public health stricto sensu

Regarding other aid schemes designed to promote or protect public health in a general way, Article 87 EC will be relevant. Article 87(3) EC does not contain a specific reference to public health; neither has the Commission adopted specific Guidelines for the appraisal of aid schemes for reasons of public health. State aid that generally contributes to public health, however, can be exempted on the basis of Article 87(3) sub c EC. This particularly appears from the Commission decision on a Swedish aid scheme to improve the indoor environment. According to the Commission the Guidelines on environmental protection could not apply to aid aimed at the indoor environment, but given its contribution to public

[196] Case N 46/2003, *Risk equalisation scheme in the Irish health insurance market*, paragraphs 60 and 61.

[197] IP/05/531.

[198] Case C-53/00, *Ferring*, paragraphs 32 and 33.

health, the protection of workers' health and safety and environmental policy, which are Community objectives of common interest it can be approved on the basis of Article 87(3) sub c EC.[199] The Commission refers thereby to Articles 137, 152 and 174 of the EC Treaty. The Commission hereby directly incorporates *inter alia* the objective of public health into Article 87(3) sub c EC by referring to the Treaty provisions on horizontal and flanking policies.

The Community Framework for state aid for research and development is also relevant for the field of public health, for example where aid has been awarded for the development of new medicines, or for other research and development programmes aimed at promoting and protecting public health. The Commission approved a Dutch aid measure to stimulate a long-term research programme at Shell Chemicals BV, a joint initiative by the Dutch government and Shell Chemicals. The research programme could result in new materials, a better understanding of the nature and/or composition of materials and product streams and a better understanding of how certain molecular structures interact with human cells. According to the Commission the programme complied with the Community Framework on state aid for research and development.[200] With regard to aid to the pharmaceutical sector, financial support for pharmaceutical innovation may be subject to the Community Framework for research and development. In a Report of the Working Group on "Pharmaceuticals and Public Health" of the High Level Committee on Health, giving advice to the Commission, the Working Group states that in order to make efficacious, high quality and safe medicines readily accessible Member States must provide resources needed to cover the costs of medicines and must support the development of new medicines, which depends mainly on the ability of a market-based multinational manufacturing industry to invest in research and development.[201]

Where state aids to the pharmaceutical sector allow for a particular advantage to the domestic industry, for example by imposing levies on imports from other Member States, this amounts to discrimination, which is not acceptable under Article 87 EC.[202]

The proportionality test

The application of the proportionality test in the field of state aids for public health reasons is less concrete compared to the area of environmental state aids. The Commission has not provided specific Guidelines for state aids for public health reasons, neither is it conceivable that it will give these Guidelines in the nearby future. For the health care sector, as stated above, Article 86(2) EC may

---

[199] Commission Decision 2000/733, OJ 2000, L 295/30.

[200] XXIXth Competition Report 1999, pt. 247, p. 91.

[201] Report of 28 March 2000.

[202] Commission Decision 95/456 on a Greek aid scheme in the pharmaceutical sector financed by means of levies and other related products, OJ 1995, L 265/30.

be relevant; with regard to public health *stricto sensu*, Article 87(3) EC forms the framework of review; regarding the (pharmaceutical) product sector, the framework on state aid for research and development is available.

The Community Framework on state aid for research and development distinguishes between fundamental research, industrial research and pre-competitive development activity. The closer the research and development is to the market, the more significant may be the distortive effect of the state aid. According to the Commission in its *Orlistat* decision, even in the pharmaceutical sector where product development times are long, categorising a research project as fundamental research, industrial research or pre-competitive development activity is open to a wide range of interpretations. Particular account needs to be taken regarding the existing state-of-the art technology and technology trends.[203] In this decision on the proposal of Austria to award aid to the Hoffman-La Roche company for the development of the drug 'Orlistat', designed for the treatment of pathological obesity, the Commission did not accept the scheme as eligible for funding within the meaning of the Community framework, since the development of the drug Orlistat is typical of drug development in the pharmaceutical industry, and therefore constituted normal operations in progress for the company at the time the project began.[204] In other words, the aid scheme must be necessary for the development of a new medicine, which would not otherwise be developed by the company. Similarly to the Guidelines on state aid for environmental protection, the Community Framework on state aids for research and development also reflects the proportionality test carried out by the Commission in assessing the compatibility of state aid schemes with the common market.

In its decision on the Swedish aid scheme to improve the indoor environment the Commission came to the conclusion that "the measure will promote the development of public health in line with the Community policy in this field. Given, in addition, the very low budget of the scheme and since the eligible costs and the aid intensity of the grant are the same as those of the already approved measures of the scheme, it can be concluded that the aid will facilitate the development of certain activities without adversely affecting trading conditions to an extent contrary to the common interest." In particular the Commission referred to Article 152 EC, two Council Resolutions of 1999 in the field of public health,[205] one of which refers to the integration clause, Decision 1296/1999 adopting a programme for Community action on pollution-related diseases in the context of the framework for action in the field of public health,[206] a Commu-

---

[203] Commission Decision 98/251, OJ 1998, L 103/28, p. 32.

[204] Commission Decision 98/251, OJ 1998, L 103/28, p. 33.

[205] Council Resolution of 8 June 1999 on the future Community action in the field of public health, OJ C 2000/1; Council Resolution of 18 November 1999 on ensuring health protection in all Community policies and activities, OJ 2000, C 86/3.

[206] OJ 1999, L 155/7.

nication by the Commission on the health strategy of the European Community and a proposal for the adoption of a Community action programme in the field of public health.[207] The Commission takes a favourable approach to national initiatives that contribute to the attainment of objectives, which are considered important at Community level. Without really examining the proportionality of the Swedish aid scheme, the Commission in fact implicitly acknowledges that the measure is necessary and proportionate to its aim by referring to Treaty provisions and Community initiatives in the field of public health.

The above-mentioned decisions are examples of how the Commission balances public health interests *stricto sensu* with the state aid rules; regarding health care the compensation approach, or the application of Article 86(2) EC play a particularly important role.

3.1.5.5 Culture

Article 87(3) sub d EC provides for a specific exception for aid in the field of culture.

The protection of culture as an exception: Article 87(3) sub d EC

According to this provision aid to promote culture and heritage conservation may be considered to be compatible with the common market. Regarding heritage conservation, the aids must pursue a genuine cultural objective as well.[208] Measures that protect the cultural heritage or that create beneficial conditions or guarantees that each citizen has access to art and culture may fall under this exception. The inclusion of this paragraph in the Treaty (Maastricht) led to the question what types of cultural aids fall within the scope of Article 87(3) sub d EC and which measures should be justified under Article 87(3) sub c EC. The general opinion was that 'mixed' economic and cultural activities, such as film production, would be considered under sub c and that purely cultural activities, in particular artistic activities which strongly rely on language, such as literary pursuits and drama, would be eligible for an exemption under sub d.[209] Nevertheless, the Commission applied Article 87(3) sub d EC to both state aid for film production and to aid for the export of books. The aim of the measure, though, must be predominantly cultural, and not economic or industrial. The scope of Article 87(3) sub d EC is nevertheless broad and includes various cultural aims, which are traditionally considered to fall within the scope of a Member State's cultural policy.[210]

---

[207] COM(2000) 285 final.

[208] See Case N 560/01 and NN 17/02, *United Kingdom Brighton West Pier*, paragraph 37.

[209] Loman, Mortelmans, Post and Watson (1992), p. 192; Schmall (1996), p. 257.

[210] Ch. Koenig and J. Kühling, Mitgliedstaatliche Kulturförderung und gemeinschaftrechtliche Beihilfekontrolle, *EuZW*, 2000, p. 201.

Furthermore, Article 87(3) sub d EC should be interpreted in the light of Article 151 EC and follows naturally from the integration clause contained in Article 151(4) EC. For that matter, the Commission refers to the integration clause in its decisions on state aid for film production. From this it appears that the Commission takes a particularly favourable approach towards cultural aids, which has been commented as an application of state aid rules in *favorem culturae.*[211]

The proportionality test

No Guidelines comparable to the Guidelines in the environmental field exist with regard to the cultural sector. But for state aids in the audio-visual sector the application of the proportionality test had been made more concrete in the Commission decision on the French automatic aid scheme to film production. Here the Commission formulated a number of compatibility criteria for state aid to cinema and TV production. These criteria are also mentioned in the Communication from the Commission on certain legal aspects relating to cinematographic and other audio-visual works and are as follows:[212]

- The aid is directed to a cultural product. Each Member State must ensure that the content of the aided production is cultural according to verifiable national criteria, in compliance with the application of the subsidiarity principle;
- The producer must be free to spend at least 20% of the film budget in other Member States, without suffering any reduction in the aid given under the scheme. 80% of the production budget may thus be spent in the own Member State;
- Aid intensity must in principle be limited to 50% of the production budget with a view to stimulating normal commercial activities and avoiding a bidding contest between Member States. Difficult and low budget films, which definition is established according to national parameters – in accordance with the subsidiarity principle –, are excluded from this limit;
- Aid for specific filmmaking activities are not allowed in order to ensure that the aid has a neutral incentive effect.

According to the Commission in its Communication, a certain degree of territorialisation, i.e. the requirement that a certain part of the film production budget will be spent on their own territory, may be necessary to ensure the continued presence of the human skills and technical expertise required for cultural creation. Nevertheless territoriality requirements fragment the internal market for the provision of goods and services for audio-visual production. Furthermore,

[211] Ch. Koenig and J. Kühling, Mitgliedstaatliche Kulturförderung und gemeinschaftrechtliche Beihilfekontrolle, *EuZW*, 2000, p. 201.

[212] COM(2001) 534 final.

territoriality requirements, according to the Commission, exceeding what may be judged acceptable under the necessity and proportionality criteria go beyond the strict limits of cultural promotion and aim basically at industrial objectives. An example is the aids granted by the Greek government to the film industry for the production of Greek films. The Greek government underlined that the particular nature of the film industry as an expression of cultural values should allow for certain measures based on the criteria of nationality. The Commission held that a selective aid programme for the film industry can be evaluated under cultural criteria as long as the quantitative criteria for the aid scheme apply equally to Greek nationals and nationals of other Member States. The problem here was that there was no possibility for nationals of other Member States to work as producers or take part in the production of assisted films.[213]

Member States should be encouraged to reduce national preferences for the sectors providing items for a film production budget. Still, the Commission may regard aid intensities higher than 50% necessary in cases other than difficult and low budget films due to the limited geographic extension of certain languages and cultures, and given the limited circulation of those cultural products within the Community and world markets.[214] The compatibility criteria, according to the Commission, strike a balance between the aims of cultural creation, the development of EC audio-visual production and the respect of the EC rules on state aid.

In other areas of culture the state aid rules are relevant as well, for example where a Member State grants aid to support the export of books. An example provides the *SIDE* case that concerned certain aids granted by the French Ministry of Culture to CELF (Coopérative d'Exportation du Livre Français) for the export of French books. In its first decision the Commission considered that the aids in question had a cultural aim and that competition in the book sector was special and therefore authorised the aid.[215] The subsidies granted to CELF are intended to offset the extra costs involved in handling small orders from booksellers established abroad. The grant of these subsidies helps to spread the French language and to propogate French language literature. SIDE (Société Internationale de Diffusion et d'Edition), an agency company established in France, mainly exports French books to other Member States (and to states

---

[213] Commission Decision of 21 December 1988, OJ 1989, L 208/38.

[214] Decision of 21 December 1988, p. 9. The Commission refers in this Communication to its review of aid schemes to film production in various Member States, which reveals the following features:
- There is a great diversity of aid schemes with EC both in terms of aid type and scope;
- Many of the schemes contained provisions contrary to the general legality principle;
- Very few Member States impose territoriality requirements in order to qualify for aid;
- Only exceptionally, Member States grant State aid level higher than 50% of the film costs;
- The exceptions to this latter finding normally fall under the "difficult and low budget film"category.

[215] OJ 1993, C 174/6.

outside the Community). Since the procedure of Article 88(2) EC had not been followed, SIDE asked the Court of First Instance to annul the Commission's decision, which it did. According to the Court, notwithstanding the cultural aim of the subsidy, the Commission should not have relied solely on the information provided to it during the preliminary examination, but should have initiated the procedure under Article 88(2) EC in order to ascertain its assessment was correct.[216]

After having opened the procedure of Article 88(2) EC, the Commission adopted a new decision in favour of state aid to CELF and considered that the aid could be approved under Article 87(3) sub d EC, the cultural exception. In a procedure brought before the Court of First Instance by SIDE, the Court once again annulled the decision of the Commission, since the Commission failed to correctly define the relevant market for the export of French-language books.[217] According to the Court in order to establish whether competition is affected to an extent that is contrary to the common interest for the purposes of Article 87(3) sub d EC, it is necessary to first consider the definition of the market in question. The Commission defined the market as being that for the export of French-language books in general. It should, however, have been examined whether the market for the handling of *small* orders of such books forms a separate market. They failed to do so, even though the Commission's definition of the relevant market is contradicted by the justification for the aid in question, i.e. the aid granted to CELF enables it to meet orders which publishers or their associated distributors do not consider it profitable to satisfy, given the increased transport costs and the total value of the order it involved and that among the various operators involved in the distribution of books, agents, who deal only with retailers or organisations but not with the final consumer, enable orders which publishers or their distributors consider unremunerative to be satisfied.[218] According to the Court in selecting the export market for French-language books in general as the reference market, the Commission was unable to assess the true impact of the aid on competition. In its latest decision the Commission comes to the conclusion that the aid did not distort competition on the *export agency market* to an extent contrary to the common interest.[219]

In applying the cultural exception the Commission apparently cannot simply ignore the effects of state aid measures on competition and intra-Community trade. In the case of *CELF* the proportionality of cultural aims could only be assessed after the Commission had provided a market analysis. The causal link between the state aid measure and the cultural aim is not sufficient for the measure to be eligible for an exemption. Otherwise, the cultural exception

[216] Case T-49/93, *SIDE v. Commission.*

[217] Case T-155/98, *SIDE v. Commission* (2).

[218] Case T-155/98, *SIDE v. Commission* (2), paragraph 60.

[219] Commission Decision 2005/26, *Coopérative d'exportation du livre français (CELF)*, OJ 2005, L 85/27.

should have been given a place in Article 87(2) EC. The decision in CELF makes it particularly visible that an overall approach to state aids in the cultural field is lacking. This lack of clear guidance causes legal insecurity since it will be difficult to assess Member States' discretion in granting state aids for cultural purposes. A suggestion is to bring general cultural policy into line with audio-visual policy, where compatibility criteria have been established to strike a balance between the cultural aims of audiovisual policy and the respect of the EC rules on state aid. Here the proportionality test has been applied more clearly and thus more in accordance with Article 87(3) sub d EC. Nevertheless, the above-mentioned examples reveal a strong willingness of the Commission to apply the cultural exception.

3.1.6 Conclusions

The assessment of state aids for horizontal and flanking policy purposes has developed differently according to substantive differences that exist between horizontal and flanking policies involved. This becomes particularly visible through the application of the proportionality test under Article 87(3) EC, in two ways. First, due to substantive differences between horizontal and flanking policies the compatibility of state aids with the Treaty provisions is assessed in a different way; the dilemma between environmental state aids and the 'polluter pays principle' does not exist in respect of cultural state aids; in the field of culture it is more difficult if not impossible to really *integrate* cultural consideration into state aid policy.[220]

Second and in relation with the foregoing, the application of the proportionality test in the field of the environment, probably due to the 'polluter pays principle' has been visualised through a set of comprehensive Guidelines. No similar Guidelines have been drafted for other areas of horizontal and flanking policies.

3.2 Article 86 EC: public undertakings and exclusive rights

Apart from granting state aids Member States may also pursue horizontal and flanking policy aims through the establishment of legal monopolies. In the relationship between the national state and competition law Article 86 EC plays a particularly interesting role. Article 86(1) EC is directed at Member States, but it does not make clear how state action should be assessed eventually. It merely contains a reference to the (competition) provisions such as Articles 81 and 82 EC which do contain substantive criteria. Article 86(2) EC, the justification ground, can be invoked by both the national state as well as undertakings.

---

[220] Vedder (2003), p. 351.

3.2.1 The scope of Article 86(1) EC: the concept of exclusive rights in relation to horizontal and flanking activities

Exclusive or special rights are granted to undertakings for the exercise of a specific economic activity, a concept which was discussed before (see section 2), and which includes activities in the field of culture, public health or the protection of the environment. Undertakings may, for example, be granted an exclusive right for the broadcasting of certain television programmes for cultural reasons, for the collection and disposal of waste for environmental reasons or for the performance of certain health care services or for providing a nationwide health insurance scheme for public health reasons. If horizontal and flanking policy aims are pursued through the grant of exclusive or special rights, Article 86 EC will be relevant. Article 86(1) EC provides that: "In the case of public undertakings and undertakings to which Member States grant special or exclusive rights, Member States shall neither enact nor maintain in force any measure contrary to the rules contained in this Treaty, in particular to those rules provided for in Article 12 and Articles 81 to 89".[221]

An exclusive right has been defined as "a measure taken by a Member State in the exercise of its functions as a public authority, by which exclusivity is granted through any legal instrument in favour of a single undertaking, public or private, such exclusivity being for the exercise of a given economic activity in a given territory for a given period of time".[222] Special rights are rights granted by a Member State to a limited number of undertakings to provide a service or undertake an activity.[223] The Court, however, has also qualified such rights, granted to a limited number of undertakings, as exclusive rights.[224] Exclusive or special rights can be granted to both public and private undertakings. The *VTM* case is an example of an exclusive right granted to a private undertaking. VTM (Vlaamse Televisie Maatschappij), a private Dutch-language television company

---

[221] Article 2 of Directive 80/723 on the transparency of financial relations between Member States and public undertakings defines the concept of public undertaking as follows: "any undertaking over which the public authorities may exercise directly or indirectly a dominant influence by virtue of their ownership of it, their financial participation therein, or the rules which govern it. A dominant influence on the part of the public authorities shall be presumed when these authorities directly, or indirectly in relation to an undertaking: (a) hold the major part of the undertaking's subscribed capital; or (b) control the majority of the votes attaching to shares issued by the undertakings; or (c) can appoint more than half of the members of the undertaking's administrative, managerial or supervisory body." OJ 1980, L 195/35; as stated above (section 3.1.3) the directive will be amended with a view to clarify that companies receiving compensation and operating on both public service and other markets must have separate accounts for their different activities: Press Release IP/05/937.

[222] Buendia Sierra (1999), p. 6.

[223] See for a definition: Directive 94/46, OJ 1994, L 268/15.

[224] Case C-209/98, *Sydhavnens FFAD*; see in particular Opinion of AG Léger, paragraph 53.

established in Flanders, was approved as the only private television company authorised to broadcast to the Flemish community as a whole for a period of 18 years and authorised to broadcast television advertising.[225]

3.2.2 Exclusive rights and the competition rules: different approaches in the case law

Article 86(1) EC seeks to provide a balance between the objective of free competition (Article 3(g) EC) and the right of property ownership as laid down in Article 295 EC, which states that the Treaty shall not prejudice the Member States' rules on property ownership.[226] The allocation of exclusive rights to (public) undertakings, on the other hand, is subject to certain conditions. In a series of cases the Court has sought to clarify this provision, but in fact has adopted opposite approaches. In the literature the following four different approaches have been identified:
- Absolute sovereignty approach;
- Absolute competition approach;
- Limited sovereignty approach;
- Limited competition approach.[227]

From the perspective of horizontal and flanking policies it is relevant to know which approach will be adopted by the Court, for the need to invoke a justification ground, Article 86(2) EC is dependent upon this. What will become clear, however, is that horizontal and flanking policy interests are considered services of general economic interests, which makes the question to the approach adopted under Article 86(1) EC less pertinent. Under the absolute sovereignty approach the creation of legal monopolies would not be problematic in the light of Article 86(1) EC and cannot be condemned. A distinction is made between the existence of exclusive rights and the exercise of such rights. But this approach was rejected by the Court.[228] The absolute competition approach, on the other hand, assumes that the very creation of a legal monopoly enables the company to abuse its dominant position, with no possibility to assess the legality of such monopoly, for example, under Article 86(2) EC. This approach is not only damaging for those undertakings granted exclusive rights for the performance of certain horizontal and flanking policy tasks, it is also inconsistent with

[225] Case T-266/97, *Vlaamse Televisie Maatschappij NV*, paragraphs 8 and 9.

[226] D. Edward and M. Hoskins, Article 90: Deregulation and EC Law; Reflections arising from the XVI Fide Conference, *CMLRev.*, 1995, p. 158.

[227] D. Edward and M. Hoskins, Article 90: Deregulation and EC Law; Reflections arising from the XVI Fide Conference, *CMLRev.*, 1995, p. 158; see also L. Hancher, Community, State and Market, in: P. Craig and G. de Búrca (Eds), *The Evolution of EU Law* (Oxford University Press, Oxford, 1999), p. 727.

[228] Case C-202/88, *France v. Commission*.

Article 86(2) EC. In the *ERT* case, for example, the Court held that the grant of exclusive rights to a state radio and television company was a breach of Article 86(1), "where those rights are liable to create a situation in which that undertaking is led to infringe Article 82 of the Treaty by virtue of a discriminatory broadcasting policy which favours its own programmes".[229] In spite of the fact that the facts of the case suggested that the Greek rules obliged ERT to pursue a discriminatory policy, the Court found it sufficient that the mere grant of exclusive rights to ERT placed it in a position where they might pursue such a policy.[230] It should be noted that the Court referred to the national court for the examination to the exception possibility of Article 86(2) EC.

In the Court's case law particular support can be found for the limited sovereignty approach and the limited competition approach. But the limited competition approach implies that the creation of a legal monopoly will necessarily produce restrictive effects and should only be permitted if there is a justification ground.[231] This approach can be found in, for example, the *Sacchi* case involving the establishment of a legal monopoly for radio and television, and in particular in the *Corbeau* case, which concerned a Belgian law granting a legal monopoly to the Belgian post, the *Régie des Postes*.[232] In *Corbeau* the Court used the following formula: "Thus Art. 86(1) of the Treaty provides that in the case of public undertakings to which Member States grant special or exclusive rights, they are neither to enact nor to maintain in force any measure contrary to the rules contained in the Treaty with regard to competition. That provision must be read in conjunction with Article 86(2) which provides that undertakings entrusted with the operation of services of general economic interest are to be subject to the rules on competition in so far as the application of such rules does not obstruct the performance, in law or in fact, of the particular tasks assigned to them." On the one hand the Court affirms the useful effect rule from *ERT* that Member States must not maintain or adopt measures which could deprive Article 86 of its effectiveness, on the other hand it reiterates the earlier *Sacchi* judgement by holding that where the creation of a monopoly can be justified, in casu on the basis of Article 86(2), it is not incompatible with Article 86(1) EC.[233] Under this approach there is no possibility to take account of horizontal and flanking policy considerations in the application of Article 86(1) EC. The focus of attention is put on the second paragraph of Article 86 EC.

---

229 For example: Case C-320/91, *Corbeau*.

230 D. Edward and M. Hoskins, Article 90: Deregulation and EC Law; Reflections arising from the XVI Fide Conference, *CMLRev.*, 1995, p. 162.

231 D. Edward and M. Hoskins, Article 90: Deregulation and EC Law; Reflections arising from the XVI Fide Conference, *CMLRev.*, 1995, p. 164.

232 Case C-320/91, *Corbeau*.

233 D. Edward and M. Hoskins, Article 90: Deregulation and EC Law; Reflections arising from the XVI Fide Conference, *CMLRev.*, 1995, p. 165; see also annotation L. Hancher, *CMLRev.*, 1994, pp. 105-122.

The limited sovereignty approach was confirmed in e.g. the *Höfner* case and implies that the existence of a legal monopoly as such is not illegal, only its abuse, and provides the Member State with more leeway to grant exclusive rights to an undertaking without necessarily having to justify these rights. A Member State will infringe Article 86(1) EC only if, in merely exercising the exclusive right granted to it, the undertaking cannot avoid abusing it. Even though under this approach the national state has more discretion in establishing legal monopolies for horizontal and flanking policy reasons, these reasons can nevertheless only play a role in the wake of a primarily competition law assessment under the first paragraph of Article 86 EC, for example, in the definition of the relevant market or the assessment of abusive behaviour.

A clear distinction between these two approaches, however, cannot always follow from the case law. In the *Sydhavnens* case the Court, after having examined the existence of a dominant position, continued to examine whether the exercise of the exclusive rights by the undertakings concerned led to an abuse of a dominant position.[234] This case involved exclusive rights granted by the Municipality of Copenhagen to three companies for the collection and recovery of building waste and the compatibility of the Danish legislation with the Treaty provisions on free movement (Article 29 EC) and competition (Article 86 EC) and with the EC rules on waste laid down in the Waste Framework Directive and the Regulation on the Transfrontier Shipments of Waste.[235] The background of the Regulation of the Municipality of Copenhagen and the corresponding grant of exclusive rights to only three companies was the very small percentage of non-hazardous building waste being recovered from the Copenhagen region and the fact that this region produced one third of the building waste in Denmark. The Court seems to suggest that it must first be examined whether the exclusive right does lead to an abuse of a dominant position, after it had stated that the grant of an exclusive right over part of the national territory for environmental purposes, such as establishing the capacity necessary for the recycling of building waste, does not in itself constitute an abuse of a dominant position; this is in conformity with the limited sovereignty approach. Despite this suggestion, the Court leaves the question of abuse and moves on to the possible justification under Article 86(2) EC.

In *Dusseldorp*, though, the Court concluded that an exclusive right granted by the Dutch state to the waste plant AVR-Chemie for the incineration of dangerous waste constituted a breach of Article 86(1) EC.[236] This case concerned the obligation to deliver oil filters – waste for recovery – to AVR-Chemie, even though the quality of processing available in another Member State was comparable to that performed by the national undertaking. According to the Court

[234] Case C-209/98, *Sydhavnens FFAD.*

[235] Regulation 259/93, OJ 1993, L 30/1.

[236] Case C-203/96, *Dusseldorp.*

this obligation had the effect of favouring the national undertaking by enabling it to process waste intended for further processing by a third undertaking and it therefore resulted in the restriction of outlets in a manner contrary to Article 86(1) EC. In *Sydhavnens* this argument was also brought forward by the applicant, but the Court stepped over it, thereby implicitly rejecting the structural notion of abuse, i.e. that a change in the market – the exclusion of competitors – as a result of the grant of an exclusive right, would be sufficient for a breach of Article 86(1) EC.[237]

In *Ambulanz Glöckner* the Court explicitly and extensively dealt with the applicability of Article 86(1) EC to medical aid organisations before it turned to Article 86(2) EC.[238] This case involved the refusal by the Landkreis Südwestpfalz (Germany) to renew authorisation for the provision of ambulance transport services by the private undertaking Ambulanz Glöckner. Under German law medical aid organisations are entrusted with the public ambulance service; non-emergency transport of patients may be carried out by private undertakings, but authorisation will be refused, if it is likely to have an adverse effect on an effective public ambulance service. This implies that only if there is full utilisation of the capacities available to medical aid organisations, private undertakings will be authorised to carry out the task of patient transport services, which is more lucrative than providing emergency services. In practice this amounts to granting medical aid organisations a monopoly on the market for emergency and patient transport services.

The Court first deals with the question whether medical aid organisations occupy a dominant position on a substantial part of the common market, and how this market should be defined; then it continued by carefully assessing whether the medical aid organisations were led to abuse their dominant position; the application of German legislation enabled them to restrict access to the market for patient transport services. The fact that an ancillary transport activity which could be carried out by other (private) undertakings, like Ambulanz Glöckner, was reserved to the medical aid organisations constituted an abuse of a dominant position within the meaning of Article 82 EC, according to the Court.

The approach of the Court in *Ambulanz Glöckner* as well as in *Sydhavnens* towards Article 86 EC corresponds to the limited sovereignty approach rather than to the limited competition approach. This entails that both Articles 86(1) EC and 86(2) EC continue to be relevant for an assessment of exclusive rights granted to undertakings for horizontal and flanking policy reasons. Nonetheless, the fact that the requirements of Article 86(1) EC will often be met as well as the fact that horizontal and flanking policy interests can only be taken into

---

[237] See also Vedder (2003), pp. 260-261: he argues that the outcome of the case can probably be explained on the basis of the facts underlying the case.

[238] Case C-475/99, *Ambulanz Glöckner.*

account in the wake of the Court's analysis, make the application of the exception, i.e. Article 86(2) EC, pertinent. It is therefore important to assess to what extent horizontal and flanking policy interests can fall within the scope of Article 86(2) EC and may directly justify state action leading to a restriction of competition.

3.2.3 Article 86(2) EC: the justification for public service undertakings

Where Member States grant exclusive or special rights to undertakings for the management of horizontal and flanking policy interests, such rights may be justified if the conditions of Article 86(2) EC are fulfilled. As stated above, even when it is still relevant to determine whether the exclusive right is contrary to Article 86(1) EC, the emphasis is eventually laid on the justifiability of the right in the light of Article 86(2) EC. Hence Article 86(2) EC has considerable importance in balancing Member States' interference with the competition rules and the supply of services of general interest, or in other words in the choice between market values and other values.

Before turning to the particular relevance of Article 86(2) EC in the fields of the environment, consumer protection, public health and culture, it is first necessary to look at Article 86(2) EC more generally.

3.2.3.1 The scope of Article 86(2) EC in general

According to Article 86(2) EC "undertakings entrusted with the operation of services of general economic interest or having the character of a revenue producing monopoly shall be subject to the rules contained in this Treaty, in particular the rules on competition; insofar as the application of such rules does not obstruct the performance, in law or in fact, of the particular tasks assigned to them. The development of trade must not be affected to such an extent as would be contrary to the interests of the Community."

From this provision it appears that two general conditions must be fulfilled: the undertaking must be entrusted with services of general economic interest; and the proportionality principle must be respected.

Services of general (economic) interest

Article 86(2) EC is not only relevant for Article 86(1) EC, but also for other Treaty provisions like Article 31 EC on state monopolies of a commercial character (electricity cases), Article 87 EC on state aids (see above), Article 82 EC on the abuse of a dominant position and also Article 81 EC on cartels.[239] In its

[239] In Case C-393/92, *Almelo v. NV Energiebedrijf IJsselmij*, the Court of Justice admitted the possibility to invoke Article 86(2) EC for restrictive practices contrary to Article 81(1) EC.

decision in Navewa-Anseau, the Commission examined the possibility to invoke Article 86(2) EC for a restrictive agreement making the attachment of conformity labels to washing machines and dishwashers compulsory, but came to conclusion that the proportionality requirement was not fulfilled (see hereafter). The objective of the agreement was "to prevent, in the interest of public health, any deterioration in the quality of water supplied due to contamination or pollution, particularly when washing machines or dishwashers are connected to the drinking-water supply".[240] The *Métropole* judgment (1996) of the Court of First Instance makes clear that the public service tasks as mentioned by Article 86(2) EC can also play a role in granting an exemption on the basis of Article 81(3) EC, but only if all the conditions of Article 81(3) EC are fulfilled (see section 4.1.3.5).[241] Consequently, the potential of Article 86(2) EC as an exception ground for horizontal and flanking policy objectives reaches far beyond Article 86(2) EC.

Article 86(2) EC contains an exception for undertakings entrusted with the operation of services of general economic interest, but can be invoked by undertakings as well as by the national state. The term 'general *economic* interest' is not defined. According to the Commission in its Green Paper on Services of General Interest services of general *economic* interest refer to market services which are subjected to specific service obligations by virtue of a general interest criterion. *Services of general interest* cover market and non-market services.[242] The term *public service* is, according to the Commission, ambiguous, since it may refer either to the actual body providing the service or to the general interest role assigned to the body concerned. The definition and guarantee of *universal service*, yet another term, ensures that the continuous accessibility and quality of established services is maintained for all users and consumers during the process of passing from monopoly provision to openly competitive markets.[243] In various documents the Commission seems to prefer the term services of general interest.[244] Both the terms services of general economic interest and services of general interest appear to include horizontal and flanking policy interests. In fact the Court seems to regard the adjective 'economic' to be redundant.[245] As will be seen, though, the term general (economic) interests also allows for national restrictions which are based on economic reasoning and seems to have a broader scope than the exceptions to the rules on free movement, which are basically of a purely non-economic nature.

---

[240] Commission Decision 82/371, OJ 1982, L 167/39.

[241] Joined Cases T-528/93, T-542/93, T-543/93 and T-546/93, *Métropole Télévision*; see also Joined Cases T-185/00, T-216/00, T-299/00 and T-300/00, *ERU*.

[242] COM(2003) 270 final, pp. 6-7.

[243] Report to the Laeken European Council on Services of General Interest, COM(2001) 598 final.

[244] See also Communication from the Commission on Services of general interest in Europe, OJ 2001, C 17/4.

[245] Buendia Sierra (1999), p. 278.

The Member State has a margin of discretion in how to determine and organise public service tasks.[246] The Commission states in its Report on the state of play in the work on the Guidelines for state aid and services of general economic interest (SGEIs) that "SGEIs perform a fundamental function in all Member States, which, in the absence of Community rules in the matter, have wide discretionary powers when it comes to defining the nature and extent of the services they wish to introduce in the light of their political choices. It is for each Member State to decide what is the most appropriate level at which to define the services that the general public needs: the central, regional or local level." In its earlier Communication on services of general interest in Europe the Commission states that "Member States' freedom to define means that Member States are primarily responsible for defining what they regard as services of general economic interest on the basis of the specific features of the market." "Whether a service is to be regarded as a service of general interest and how it should be operated are issues that are first and foremost decided locally."[247] In its White Paper the Commission rather speaks of a shared responsibility of the Union and the public authorities of the Member States, but *detailed* definition of services to be provided and delivery of those services remain the responsibility of the Member States (my Italics).[248] The Commission welcomes the amendment of provisions of the current Article 16 EC as proposed by the Constitution, providing a legal basis for Community action in the field of services of general economic interest (see later, Chapter 6).[249] It has been shown earlier that the Commission in the field of state aid for public service undertakings, in particular public broadcasting undertakings, carefully examines whether and how the service of general economic interest has been defined in national legislation (see section 3.1.3).

The undertaking must be 'entrusted' with the operation of services of general economic interest by a public authority. That public authority must grant that assignment in the exercise of its functions as a public authority.[250] Whether this requires an act of public authority or merely a contract laying down the reciprocal obligations of the undertaking and the Member States is unclear, even though, it is generally assumed, also by the Commission, that an official document such as a contract suffices. More important from the perspective of maxi-

[246] L. Hancher, Community, State and Market, in: P. Craig and G. de Búrca (Eds), *The Evolution of EU Law* (Oxford University Press, Oxford, 1999), p. 733.

[247] See Communication from the Commission on Services of general interest in Europe, OJ 2001, C 17/4, paragraph 22.

[248] COM(2004) 374 final, paragraph 2.

[249] The Commission announced in its White Paper that it will re-examine the feasibility of and the need for a framework law for services of general interest on the entry into force of the Constitutional Treaty: COM(2004) 374 final, paragraph 4.1.

[250] Buendia Sierra (1999), p. 284.

mum transparency and legal certainty is that it is clear from the legal document that the undertaking in question has really been granted public service tasks. In the *VTM* decision on the exclusive right to the private Flemish broadcasting company VTM for the broadcasting of advertisements the Commission came to the conclusion that VTM could not be regarded as an undertaking for the purposes of Article 86(2) EC. The provisions of the Flemish media legislation (Codex) contained only general requirements in respect of VTM's programme content. They did not, according to the Commission, point to the conclusion that VTM had been given the task to carry out one of the Flemish Community's cultural policies. That responsibility had been given to the public television corporation BRTN, which is required to provide airtime to political parties and various schools of thought.[251] In the *CELF* case (see above, section 3.1.5.5) the French government also referred to Article 86(2) EC for the justification of state aid in favour of CELF. According to the Commission, the French government had failed to demonstrate that the service performed by CELF in handling small orders of French books from foreign booksellers is based on any legal or administrative act, since the acts referred to by the French government are acts concerned with the book sector in general.[252] In its latest decision concerning CELF the Commission did not really dispute the possibility to rely on Article 86(2) EC, but simply held that since the aid scheme was compatible with Article 87(3) sub d EC there was no need to further assess the subsidised activities of CELF under Article 86(2) EC. Furthermore, it held that the *Altmark* conditions had not been fulfilled, as *inter alia* the parameters on which basis the compensation was calculated had not been established in advance.[253]

Finally, the importance of services of general interest in Community law is underlined by Article 16 EC which reads as follows: "Without prejudice to Articles 73, 86 and 87, and given the place occupied by services of general economic interest in the shared values of the Union as well as their local role in promoting social and territorial cohesion, the Community and the Member States, each within their respective powers and within the scope of application of this Treaty, shall take care that such services operate on the basis of principles and conditions which enable them to fulfil their missions." Article 16 EC in its relationship with Article 86(2) EC merely articulates the value of services of general interest to Member States and to the Community. Apart from this, Article 16 EC has an independent role and function in Community law.[254] The additional value of Article 16 EC is twofold. First it makes clear that the function of services of general interest stretches beyond the field of competition; Article 16 EC can

---

[251] Commission Decision 97/606 of 26 June 1997, OJ 1997, L 244/18.

[252] Commission Decision 99/133, OJ 1999, L 44/37.

[253] Commission Decision 2005/262, OJ 2005, L 85/27, paragraphs 247 and 248.

[254] See also M. Ross, Article 16 E.C. and services of general interest: from derogation to obligation?, *ELRev.*, 2000, pp. 22-38.

possibly play a role where no other Treaty provision is available to justify actions by the national state which have an effect on the internal market. Furthermore, it imposes an obligation on the Community to further develop and clarify the meaning of services of general interest. Second, it entails that the traditional approach to interpret derogations from the free movement and competition rules restrictively should be abandoned.[255]

The proportionality test

If a certain undertaking is deemed to be entrusted with the performance of horizontal and flanking tasks, the exclusive rights granted to it must be necessary for the undertaking to perform its general interest tasks. In other words such national measures have to fulfil the condition of proportionality. As stated before in relation with Article 86 EC, in fact the legality of exclusive rights eventually depends on how the proportionality test is being applied. A similarly crucial role for the principle of proportionality can be seen in the context of the mandatory requirements and the free movement rules (Chapter 2). Generally the first two elements of the proportionality test will be applied, i.e. the question of suitability or of the existence of a causal connection between the measure and aim pursued (i), and the question of whether the measure is necessary to attain the objective or whether no less restrictive means are available (ii). In an infringement procedure it will be the Commission's task to come up with alternative forms of providing these services, which are less restrictive than the establishment of a legal monopoly in a certain area.[256]

Regarding (i) Article 86(2) EC allows for the justification of market and non-market services by virtue of a general interest criterion. Economic aims are part of the eventually more general aim to fulfil public service obligations. Article 86(2) EC therefore seems to have a wider scope than the mandatory requirements within the context of the free movement rules which are of a non-economic nature, even though the case law of the Court is evolving in this respect (see Chapter 2). For example, in the *Sydhavnens* case an exclusive right to guarantee profitability of the waste management undertakings concerned in the context of Article 86(2) EC could be justified on environmental grounds, since the profitability of national undertakings was instrumental to the objective of environmental protection. In *Dusseldorp* this argument could not be used to justify an export restriction in the context of Article 29 EC.[257] In the field of public health, the maintenance of financial stability in the health care sector

[255] M. Ross, Article 16 E.C. and services of general interest: from derogation to obligation?, *ELRev.*, 2000, p. 38.

[256] See for example Case C-157/94, *Commission v. Netherlands.* See also L. Hancher, Community, State and Market, in: P. Craig and G. de Búrca (Eds), *The Evolution of EU Law* (Oxford University Press, Oxford, 1999), p. 733.

[257] Case C-203/96, *Dusseldorp.*

can surely be taken into account under Article 86(2) EC, which is less clear for Article 46 EC. Nevertheless, through an extensive interpretation of Article 46 EC and the concept of public health the Court has been able to take into account these economic considerations within the context of free movement rules.

Regarding (ii) in its Communication on services of general interest the Commission refers to the proportionality test under Article 86(2) EC, which "implies that the means used to fulfil the general interest mission shall not create unnecessary distortions of trade. [...] The performance of the service of general economic interest must be ensured and the entrusted undertakings must be able to carry the specific burden and the net extra costs of the particular tasks assigned to them. [...] The principles formulated in Article 86 allow for a flexible and context-sensitive balance that takes account of the Member States' different circumstances and objectives as well as the technical constraints that may vary from one sector to another."[258] The Commission thus seems to enhance a rather flexible approach towards the proportionality test under Article 86(2) EC that seems to be in accordance with the present approach of the Court and with Article 16 EC, which reinforces the value of services of general interest within Community law.

Nevertheless, a stricter, less flexible application of the proportionality test can be found in the case law of the Court and in the decision practice of the Commission as well. The problem with regard to this stricter approach is that, in case of exclusive rights granted to an undertaking, the creation of a legal monopoly itself will be questioned, which may leave the Member State with no other possibility than to use other legal instruments such as state aid measures which could be challenged under other provisions of Community law, such as Article 87 EC. In *Dusseldorp*, for example, the Court held that Article 86(2) EC could be relied on if it was shown that, without the contested measure, the undertaking would be unable to carry out its task and that the objective of sound waste management could not be achieved equally well by other means.[259]According to the Commission in its decision in *Navewa-Anseau* involving an agreement by water-supply undertakings on the use of a conformity label for washing machines and dishwashers, "a possible limitation of the application of the rules on competition can be envisaged only in the event that the undertaking concerned has no other technically and economically feasible means of performing its particular task".[260] Furthermore, in the search for the least restrictive means it is not sufficient, according to the Commission, that the performance of the particular task becomes more complicated. This implies that only where the application of the competition rules makes it impossible for the undertaking to perform its task, Article 86(2) EC could be relied upon.

---

[258] OJ 2001, C 17/4, p. 8, points 23 and 24.

[259] Case C-203/96, *Dusseldorp*, paragraph 67; see also M. Ross, Article 16 E.C. and services of general interest: from derogation to obligation?, *ELRev.*, 2000, 22-38.

[260] Commission Decision 82/371/EEC, Navewa-Anseau, OJ 1982, L 167/39, paragraph 66.

The strict test of obstructing the performance or making impossible the performance of a public service task was probably inspired by the ideology of market building: the exceptions should be construed narrowly, the conditions to invoke the exceptions should be applied strictly.[261] The *Corbeau* judgment led to a more flexible application of the proportionality test.[262] Here the Court held in respect of Article 86(2) EC that "the question which falls to be considered is therefore the extent to which a restriction on competition or even the exclusion of all competition from other economic operators is necessary in order to allow the holder of the exclusive right to perform the task of general interest and in particular to have the benefit of economically acceptable conditions".[263] No more is the economic viability of the undertaking a minimum requirement for Article 86(2) EC to apply. This approach was confirmed in the *Sydhavnens* case, which will be discussed below.[264]

Finally, regarding state aids granted to public service undertakings, the Commission's approach in respect of public service broadcasters shows that the review of state aids under Article 86(2) EC is limited to the question whether the national state has abused its powers to grant financial benefits to public service broadcasters, in other words state aids are also only subject to marginal review under Article 86(2) EC.

3.2.3.2 The environment

Environmental tasks as tasks of general interest

Regarding the environmental field Article 86(2) EC is particularly relevant for the waste sector. In the *Almelo* case the Court for the first time refers to the environment within the context of Article 86(2) EC.[265] From the *Dusseldorp* judgment it could be concluded that exclusive rights granted to undertakings for the accomplishment of certain environmental tasks could benefit from the exemption of Article 86(2) EC.[266] It remained unclear, how-

---

[261] See also L.M. Soriano, How proportionate should anti-competitive State intervention be?, *ELRev.*, 2003, p. 121.

[262] See Buendia Sierra (1999), p. 320.

[263] Case C-320/91, *Corbeau*, paragraph 16.

[264] How the proportionality test should be applied in the context of a restrictive agreement concluded between public service undertakings is less clear. The Commission's Communication suggests that a flexible approach is desirable regardless of the type of measure involved. AG Jacobs in his opinion in the *AOK* case confirms this view: Opinion of AG Jacobs in Joined Cases C-264/01, C-306/01, C-354/01 and C-355/01, *AOK Bundesverband*.

[265] Case C-393/92, *Almelo v. NV Energiebedrijf Ijsselmij*. Since Case 172/82, *Inter-Huiles*, it was already considered possible that environmental protection activities can form the subject of a service of general economic interest: see Vedder (2003), p. 270.

[266] Case C-203/96, *Dusseldorp*.

ever, whether waste treatment undertakings and, more generally, undertakings entrusted with environmental tasks could be considered as undertakings entrusted with the performance of services of general economic interest.[267] In the *Sydhavnens* case, though, the Court for the first time makes it explicit that where a service is designed to deal with an environmental problem this service should be considered as a service of general economic interest for the purposes of Article 86(2) EC.[268] Thus Article 86(2) EC incorporates environmental considerations; the protection of the environment appears to be recognised as an independent objective justifiable under Article 86(2) EC.

The proportionality test

In the *Dusseldorp* case the Court regarded the prohibition by the Dutch government to export oil filters – waste for recovery – and the corresponding obligation to deliver the oil filters to AVR Chemie, which obtained an exclusive right to incinerate dangerous waste, as contrary to Article 86(1) EC. This obligation could be justified by Article 86(2) EC, if it was shown to the national court that the objective to reduce the costs of the undertaking responsible for the incineration of dangerous waste and thereby enabling it to be economically viable, could not be achieved equally well by other means. The Court thus leaves the assessment of the proportionality of the Dutch measures entirely to the national court. What is interesting here is that the Court accepts the possibility to rely on Article 86(2) EC in case of infringement of Article 86(1) EC, similar arguments cannot contribute to justifying measures having equivalent effect to quantitative export restrictions within the context of Article 29 EC (see Chapter 2).

In *Sydhavnens* the Court dealt more extensively with the question of proportionality and abandoned its strict approach adopted in *Dusseldorp*. First, it held that "[...] it is necessary to consider whether the exclusive right granted to the three undertakings is necessary for them to be able to perform the tasks of general economic interest which has been assigned to them under economically acceptable conditions".[269] According to the Court this was the case, since the exclusive rights were necessary to face a serious environmental problem, namely the burial of most building waste in the ground when it could have been recycled. Besides, the grant of an exclusive right was limited in time and in space. Less restrictive measures, such as rules, which merely required undertakings to have their waste recycled, were no alternative, because there was not sufficient capacity to process that waste. In this case the Court explicitly deals

[267] D. Geradin, EC Competition Law and Environmental Protection: Conflict or Compatibility?, in: H. Somsen (Ed.), *Yearbook of European Environmental Law* (Oxford University Press, Oxford, 2002), p. 141.

[268] Case C-209/98, *Sydhavnens FFAD*.

[269] Case C-209/98, *Sydhavnens FFAD*, paragraph 77.

with the proportionality of the Danish measure and with the first two elements of the proportionality test, namely the element of causal connection between the measure concerned and the interest pursued, and the element of the least restrictive alternative. The fact that in this case the exclusive rights were limited in time and space probably means that open-ended exclusive rights are disproportional.[270]

3.2.3.3 Consumer protection

The protection of consumers as an exception

The interest of consumers forms an essential part of the concept of services of general economic interests. For consumers a guarantee of universal access, high quality and affordability constitute the basis of their needs.[271] Particularly the liberalisation of certain service sectors, such as telecommunication and energy, has important ramifications for the protection of consumers.

The formulation of universal service obligations is essential to maintain services of minimum quality to which consumers have access at an affordable price. In the electricity cases the Court held that the concept of service of general economic interest covers the activity of an undertaking which "must ensure that throughout the territory in respect of which the concession is granted, all consumers, whether local distributors or end-users, receive uninterrupted supplies of electricity in sufficient quantities to meet demand at any given time, at uniform tariff rates and on terms which may not vary save in accordance with objective criteria applicable to all consumers".[272]

The proportionality test

According to the Commission in its Communication on services of general interest the efficient provision of services of general interest should be seen as a key element in the European model of society. The double interest of consumers in having access to universal services of a high quality on the one hand, and being able to receive specific services at affordable prices on the other hand is reflected by the proportionality test as applied by the Court since *Corbeau*. From a consumer perspective the effect of a flexible application of the proportionality test is twofold. On the one hand, the Court seeks to guarantee public service undertakings to perform their public service tasks under economically acceptable conditions, on the other hand public service undertakings should

[270] D. Geradin, EC Competition Law and Environmental Protection: Conflict or Compatibility?, in: H. Somsen (Ed.), *Yearbook of European Environmental Law* (Oxford University Press, Oxford, 2002), p. 143.

[271] See Communication from the Commission on Services of general interest in Europe, OJ 2001, C 17/4, paragraph 10.

[272] For example Case C-393/92, *Almelo v. NV Energiebedrijf IJsselmij*, paragraph 48.

not prevent other undertakings to offer consumers specific services for which there is a demand. Besides the national measure should not create a situation in which the public service undertaking is not always able to satisfy the demand of consumers.

3.2.3.4 Public health

Health services as services of general interest

Article 86(2) EC can be a useful justification ground for health care services provided by health insurers,[273] health insurance funds or hospitals, provided they qualify as undertakings and are subject to the competition rules. Health care services accessible to all under reasonable conditions of time and price, are important services of general interest and should therefore fall within the scope of Article 86(2) EC.[274] The fact that under the new Dutch health insurance scheme, for example, private health insurers that carry out the insurance system will be obliged by the Dutch government to accept all citizens and will be prevented from differentiating premiums makes them, according to the Commission, public service undertakings.[275]

In *Ambulanz Glöckner* the Court of Justice considered that medical aid organisations are entrusted with a task of general economic interest, consisting of the provision of a permanent standby service of transporting sick or injured persons in emergencies throughout the territory concerned, at uniform rates and on similar quality conditions, without regard to the particular situations or to the degree of economic profitability of each individual operation.[276]

In its White Paper on services of general interest the Commission stipulates that social services of general interest, including health services, have a specific role to play as an integral part of the European model of society. They are based on the principle of solidarity and are person-centred.[277]

---

[273] With regard to the German sickness funds see, however, Joined Cases C-264/01, C-306/01, C-354/01 and C-355/01, *AOK Bundesverband* and section 2.2.1 of this Chapter. AG Jacobs in his opinion in the *AOK* case held that "there is no doubt in my mind that German sickness funds are charged with such a service, namely in the provision of a solidarity-based system of statutory health insurance" (paragraph 87).

[274] See V.G. Hatzopoulos, *Killing* national health and insurance systems but *healing* patients? The European Market for health care services after the judgments of the ECJ in *Vanbraekel* and *Peerbooms*, *CMLRev.*, 2002, p. 726.

[275] See Press Release from the European Commission, IP/05/531.

[276] Case C-475/99, *Ambulanz Glöckner*, paragraph 55.

[277] COM(2004) 374 final, paragraph 4.4; the Commission announced that it will submit a Communication on social and health services of general interest in the course of 2005.

The proportionality test

In *Ambulanz Glöckner* the Court applies a similar proportionality test as it does in *Corbeau* and *Sydhavnens*. According to the Court "the question to be determined, therefore, is whether the restriction of competition is necessary to enable the holder of the exclusive right to perform its task of general interest in economically acceptable conditions". The performance of services in conditions of economic equilibrium "presupposes that it will be possible to offset less profitable sectors against the profitable sectors and hence justifies a restriction of competition from individual undertakings in economically profitable sectors". In this case it was shown that the revenue from non-emergency transport helped to cover the costs of providing emergency ambulance services. Furthermore, the services provided by the medical aid organisations were not regarded as dissociable. Non-emergency transport services are traditionally closely linked to the provision of public ambulance service, according to the Court. The Court added to this that only where it is shown that the medical aid organisations in question were manifestly unable to satisfy the demand for emergency ambulance services, Article 86(2) EC could not be relied upon.

In this respect it is interesting to refer to the *Duphar* case as discussed in Chapter 2, which also provides evidence that the Court seems willing to leave Member States a rather large margin of discretion in adopting measures in the field of health care.[278]

3.2.3.5 Culture

The protection of culture as an exception

Article 86(2) EC plays a particularly important role in the field of public service broadcasting. In the already mentioned *Sacchi* case the Court implicitly made clear that public service undertakings granted with exclusive rights for considerations of public interests could benefit from an exception to Article 86(1) EC. In the *ERT* case the Court referred to the national court to examine whether Article 86(2) EC could be relied upon to justify the exclusive concession by the Greek state to ERT for the broadcasting of national television programmes and the general reception and transmission of programmes from other Member States.[279] In the context of the free movement rules the Court has recognised the preservation of a pluralistic and non-commercial public service television system as a legitimate ground to uphold national measures that restrict the free movement of services (see Chapter 2).

---

[278] Case 238/82, *Duphar.* According to Gyselen, though, "the Court's *obiter dictum* about Member State discretion in *Duphar* might therefore be a useful starting point, but can hardly provide an "alpha and omega" for the assessment of State measures in the area of social protection under Article 86(2)": *CMLRev.*, 2000, p. 447.

[279] Case C-260/89, *ERT.*

The protocol on the system of public broadcasting reinforces the value of the public service remit in the field of broadcasting and its role as exception to the competition rules in the Treaty. In addition the objective of pluralism in the media and the guarantee of a wide availability of programmes for all citizens in society, including minority groups, is generally regarded by the Member States as to be attained by a public service broadcasting system.

The proportionality test

In the *VTM* case the Belgian authorities did not rely on Article 86(2) EC for the justification of the advertising monopoly.[280] As stated before, the Commission denied the possibility to invoke Article 86(2) EC in respect of an undertaking, which has not explicitly been granted public service tasks by the national state. The Commission held that such an advertising monopoly could, within the context of Article 43 EC, be justifiable on cultural grounds, but it did not find the necessary relationship – causal link – between the cultural aim and the grant of exclusive rights. The peculiarity of this case is that the advertising monopoly served an aim beyond the objective of a plural television system, namely the preservation of plurality of the press. Similarly, this argument would probably not have been accepted under Article 86(2) EC, if this provision were applicable in this case.

In the *Sacchi* and *ERT* cases the Court adopted a strict approach to the second element of the proportionality test, but as was stated before, this strict approach has been left by the Court in *Corbeau* and subsequent cases (see above, section 3.2.3.1). This more flexible approach by the Court is more in keeping with Article 16 EC and the protocol on public service broadcasting. In addition the Commission's approach to financing public service broadcasting reinforces the idea of a less strict and more flexible proportionality test.

Article 86(2) EC may possibly also play a role in the context of agreements concluded between public service broadcasters. In the *Métropole (I)* case the Court of First Instance implicitly made clear that Article 86(2) EC can be relevant where agreements are concluded between public service broadcasters that restrict competition within the meaning of Article 81(1) EC.[281] In Europe most public broadcasting companies are members of the non-profit-making association European Broadcasting Union (EBU). They must fulfil certain conditions for membership: the broadcasting organisation is under the obligation to cover the entire population, to provide a varied and balanced programming for all sections of the population, including a fair share of the programmes catering for special or minority interests of various sections of the public etc. After EBU's refusal to grant 'Screensport' a sublicence for the broadcasting of sports

[280] See also P. Valcke, Autopsie van VTM monopolie leidt niet tot nieuwe resultaten, *Mediaforum*, 2000, pp. 2-6.

[281] Joined Cases T-528/93, T-542/93, T-543/93 and T-546/93, *Métropole Télévision*.

events, it delivered complaints at the Commission, which eventually provided an exemption of the EBU agreements on the basis of Article 81(3) EC on 11 June 1993.[282] According to the CFI the basis of the Commission's reasoning and the final decision was the concept of 'particular public mission' of the EBU. According to the Court this public mission is characterised by the "obligation to provide varied programming including cultural, educational, scientific and minority programmes without any commercial appeal and to cover the entire national population irrespective of the costs". It finds these elements to form part of the general economic interest which is included in Article 86(2) EC and factors which come within the ambit of this provision cannot in this case constitute a criterion for the application of Article 81(3) EC. Instead the Commission should have shown that such considerations of a 'particular public mission' required exclusivity of rights to transmit sports events, and that the requirement of indispensability was fulfilled. The Court thus accepts that the Commission based its decision on considerations related to the general interest, and more in particular cultural reasons. The requirements of Article 81(3) EC, however, must be met and cannot simply be set aside.

On 10 May 2000 the Commission adopted a new decision granting an exemption on the basis of Article 81(3) EC, which was again annulled by the CFI in *Métropole (II)*.[283] In this case however, the CFI does not pay any attention at all to the role of the general interest of pluralism and culture within the context of Article 81(3) EC; instead it focused on the fourth condition of Article 81(3) EC, i.e. that competition should not be eliminated in respect of a substantial part of the relevant market.[284]

3.2.4 Conclusions

Even though the approach of the ECJ towards Article 86(1) EC has not always been consistent, this has not led to a degrading of standards of protection of horizontal and flanking policy interests. In fact the generally well-known Community law adage 'the prohibition must be applied broadly, the exceptions restrictively', does not appear to apply to Article 86 EC. The Court in applying Articles 86(1) and 86(2) EC conducts a balancing approach where much weight is given to the consideration of horizontal and flanking policy interests. This is not surprising taking into account the special status of services of general interest in Community law as is also emphasised by Article 16 EC.

---

282 Commission Decision 93/403, OJ 1993, L 279/23.

283 Joined Cases T-185/00, T-216/00, T-299/00 and T-300/00, *Métropole (M6)*.

284 According to Bailey the two *Métropole* cases indicate a trend to a more conscientious and robust view by the CFI of whether the Commission has lawfully applied Article 81(3) EC: D. Bailey, Scope of judicial review under Article 81 EC, *CMLRev.*, 2004, p. 1351.

3.3 Articles 3(1) sub g, 10 and 81 & 82 EC

The use of so-called convenants or 'self-regulatory' instruments has increasingly become important in realising horizontal and flanking policy aims, most notably in the field of the environment. Instead of the more traditional command and control legislation, other more market-based instruments can be used to involve industry in the process of setting targets and solving horizontal and flanking policy problems. This provides a more flexible regulatory regime and may therefore be more efficient and effective.[285] Nevertheless, traditional, but more flexible regulation, remains necessary to set a legal framework, which can be supported by alternative forms of regulation (see Chapter 4).

3.3.1 The useful effect doctrine

Not only for the field of the environment, but also for other areas of horizontal and flanking policies is such an approach increasingly significant. But the problem is that if the national state is involved in these forms of co-operation between companies to attain objectives of horizontal and flanking policies, its involvement will possibly run counter to the Treaty provisions on competition. There are several ways in which the Member State may enact measures which render the competition provisions ineffective. For example, the government may take action or threaten to pass legislation, the government may participate in the agreements involved, or the government enacts legislation which promotes or reinforces anti-competitive agreements or concerted practices.[286] The new norm, or useful effect rule of Articles 3g, 10 and 81 or 82 EC, which implies that Member States are under an obligation to abstain from any measures which could jeopardise the attainment of undistorted competition and thus neither to enact nor to maintain anti-competitive state regulation,[287] makes constraints on Member States' choice to rely on forms of self-regulation and co-operation between companies.

The useful effect rule was developed in the jurisprudence of the Court of Justice to deal with state measures which have a trade and competition restrictive effect, but which do not fall within a specific provision in the Treaty.[288] In the *GB-Inno-BM v. ATAB* case the Court held that, although Articles 81 and 82

---

285 See for example the Commission's 5th environmental action programme, Towards Sustainability, OJ 1993, C 138/5, p. 16.

286 Regarding this distinction and environmental law: see Jans (2000), pp. 251-252.

287 C.-M. Chung, The Relationship between Sate Regulation and EC Competition Law: Two Proposals for a coherent approach, *ECLR*, 1995, p. 87.

288 For the term 'new norm' or 'useful effect rule' see K. Mortelmans, Towards convergence in the application of the rules on free movement and on competition?, *CMLRev.*, 2001, p. 619 and Vedder (2003), p. 237.

EC are directed at undertakings, Member States authorities' are under an obligation not to detract from the useful effect of these provisions. This follows from Article 10 EC in connection with Article 81 EC.[288a] Later case law shows that an approach based on the *effet utile* principle has been forced to give up territory to a more formalistic approach. In the *Van Eycke* case, the Court held that Articles 81 EC and 82 EC in conjunction with Article 10 EC prohibit a Member State to require or favour the adoption of agreements, to reinforce their effects, or deprive its own legislation of its official character by delegating to private traders responsibility for taking decisions affecting the economic sphere.[289] Any measure that renders the competition provisions *ineffective* is in principle incompatible with the Treaty. That will, however, only be the case if a direct link between the state regulation and the anti-competitive agreement can be shown according to the Court in the *Meng* and *Ohra* cases.[290] Instead of assessing whether a national measure has *in casu* the result that Article 81 EC is deprived of its effectiveness, national measures are now reviewed on the basis of the criterion whether a Member State requires or favours the adoption of agreements contrary to Article 81 EC. The criterion of favouring the adoption of agreements suggests that a causal link between state action and distortion of competition must be established.[291] It also implies that the intention or will of the Member States is relevant to assess whether Articles 3(1) sub g. 10 and 81 are violated, without considering the effects on competition.[292]

Where legislative provisions oblige companies to engage in restrictive practices, the useful effect rule would probably be violated. Where, on the other hand, companies are merely permitted by law to conclude restrictive agreements, the useful effect rule would not be violated.[293] Where legislation has no real link to the practices of undertakings, this legislation will not fall within the scope of the new norm. Where certain practices required by law do not fall within the scope of application of Article 81 or 82 EC, the useful effect rule will

[288a] Case 13/77, *GB-Inno-BM v. ATAB*.

[289] Case 267/86, *Van Eycke v. Aspa*, paragraph 16 and Case C-35/96, *Commission v. Italy (CNSD)*, paragraphs 53 and 54.

[290] Case C-2/91, *Meng* and Case C-245/91, *Ohra*.

[291] N. Reich, The "November Revolution" of the European Court of Justice: *Keck, Meng* and *Audi* revisited, *CMLRev.*, 1994, p. 489.

[292] C.-M. Chung, The Relationship between Sate Regulation and EC Competition Law: Two Proposals for a coherent approach, *ECLR*, 1995, p. 89.

[293] This may lead to unsatisfactory outcomes: see N. Reich, The "November Revolution" of the European Court of Justice: *Keck, Meng* and *Audi* revisited, *CMLRev.*, 1994, pp. 489-491; see also C.-M. Chung, The Relationship between Sate Regulation and EC Competition Law: Two Proposals for a coherent approach, *ECLR*, 1995, p. 90: "Ironically this case law could give absolute exemption to the national regulation which absolutely abolishes any room for voluntary behaviour and competition on the part of the undertakings and no exemption to the not so bad state regulation which leaves some scope for competition."

also not be violated. The simple fact that legislation has an impact on competition, for example, because it imposes strict environmental standards on its own nationals, or where it directly regulates the prices of certain products, will not be sufficient to establish a breach of Articles 3(1)(g), 10 and 81 or 82 EC.[294] In the *Peralta* case that concerned Italian legislation prohibiting vessels from discharging harmful substances into the sea, the Court held that Articles 3(1)(g), 10 and 81 EC could not be relied on. The Italian legislation "does not require or foster anti-competitive conduct since the prohibition which it lays down is sufficient in itself. Nor does it reinforce the effects of a pre-existing agreement".[295] However, other Treaty provisions, such as Article 28 EC on the free movement of goods, may be applicable in these situations.

Environmental protection

Particularly in the field of the environment where the use of self-regulatory instruments is encouraged this process of substituting traditional and sometimes inefficient command and control legislation by alternative and more efficient instruments should not be frustrated by the application of the useful effect doctrine. Nevertheless, the theory presented above implies that in some cases legislation entrusting companies with the duty to adopt environmental standards that will be binding for the industry may be incompatible with the useful effect rule, provided that the agreements are contrary to Article 81 EC. Delegation of powers to the industry to set environmental standards, reinforcing the restrictive effects of environmental agreements in national legislation or extending the effects of environmental agreements to third parties are examples of state intervention that possibly runs counter to the useful effect rule.[296]

The useful effect doctrine may be particularly relevant for the Netherlands where the Environmental Management Act provides for a possibility to declare an agreement between the majority of the members of an industry on a waste disposal fee to be generally binding for the entire sector, if this is in the interest of the efficient disposal of waste materials.[297]

---

[294] See also D. Geradin, EC Competition Law and Environmental Protection: Conflict or Compatibility?, in: H. Somsen (Ed.), *Yearbook of European Environmental Law* (Oxford University Press, Oxford, 2002), p. 133.

[295] Case C-379/92, *Peralta*, paragraph 22.

[296] D. Geradin, EC Competition Law and the Environmental Protection: Conflict or Compatibility?, in: H. Somsen (Ed.), *Yearbook of European Environmental Law* (Oxford University Press, Oxford, 2002), p. 134.

[297] Vedder (2003), p. 237; see also NMa and Dte Annual Report 2000, p. 62; J.W. van de Gronden, Milieu en mededinging: is milieubescherming alleen een publieke taak of ook onderdeel van de producentenverantwoordelijkheid?, in: J.W. van de Gronden and K.J.M. Mortelmans (Eds), *Mededinging en niet-economische belangen*, (Kluwer, Deventer, 2001), p. 143.

Culture

In the field of culture the useful effect doctrine particularly plays a role in the area of resale price maintenance for books. If national legislation obliges publishers and booksellers to set up a system of fixed prices for books, Articles 3(1)g, 10 and 81 and 82 EC may be violated. In the Netherlands a law has been adopted that requires publishers and booksellers to fix a retail price for books.[298] The immediate cause for this legislation is that the current private law system of resale price maintenance for books had obtained an exemption from the Dutch competition rules until 2005.[299] After 2005 the agreements would probably be held incompatible with the cartel prohibition laid down in Article 6 of the Competition Act. Their future existence is therefore highly uncertain. The aims of providing a legal basis for resale price maintenance in the book sector are, according to explanatory memorandum, *inter alia* to provide for a wide availability of books, a wide variety of titles, diversity of information and broad accessibility to books after 2005 also. The law applies only to books written in the Dutch or Frisian language.

The Dutch law on fixed prices for books resembles to some extent the French *Loi Lang* which was subject to a procedure before the Court in the *Leclerc* case, which judgment was confirmed in *Echirolles*.[300] In *Leclerc* the Court held that since purely national systems and practices in the book trade have not yet been made subject to a Community competition policy, Member States' obligations under Article 10 EC in conjunction with Articles 3(1) g and 81 EC are not specific enough to preclude them from enacting legislation which requires publishers and importers to fix retail prices for books.[301] Nevertheless, in several cases the Court and the Commission have pronounced themselves on trans-national book price maintenance agreements which are considered unacceptable under Article 81 EC (see hereafter section 4.1.3.5). The Commission, however, has made clear that it will not touch upon purely national systems of book pricing. Where fixed prices for books also apply to imported books, there will be an effect on intra-Community trade and Article 81 EC will be applicable. According to the Commission in the *Sammelrevers* case fixed prices may have to be complied with only where the exportation and re-importation of the books were designed solely to evade the price maintenance agreements.[302] As will be seen the Commission's

[298] Wet van 9 november 2004, houdende regels omtrent de vaste boekenprijs (Wet op de vaste boekenprijs, 'Law on fixed book prices'), *Stb.* 600.

[299] On behalf of the Minister of Education, Culture and Sciences, the Minister of Economic Affairs has granted an exemption from the prohibition on vertical price fixing (Article 9e of the former Dutch Law on Competition – WEM). After the Competition Act came into force the legal ground for this exemption remained valid and the resale price maintenance system should not be challenged under Article 6 of the Competition Act until 2005: decision NMa in case 1561, *Free Record Shop-KVB*, 25 November 1999.

[300] Case C-9/99, *Échirolles Distribution SA*.

[301] Case 229/83, *Leclerc*, paragraph 20.

[302] Notice pursuant to Article 19(3) of Council Regulation No 17 concerning an application for negative clearance or exemption under Article 81(3) of the EC Treaty, OJ 2000 C 162/25, at p. 26.

policy with regard to resale price maintenance for books has, particularly after *Sammelrevers*, to a considerable extent taken shape, which means that, considering the Court's reasoning in *Leclerc*, it would be possible to apply the useful effect doctrine to national legislation requiring publishers and booksellers to set fixed prices for books.

Whether the Dutch law on fixed book prices is in accordance with the useful effect doctrine is uncertain.[303] The original law proposal contained a requirement for importers of books to take account of the price recommended or fixed by publishers established in another state, which after consultation of the Commission has changed in a mere obligation for importers of Dutch language books to establish a fixed price, thereby providing them to take account of import advantages and the original price.[304] The duty to fix a price for publishers and the obligation for booksellers to respect this price directly derives from the law itself. It does not require or favour the adoption of restrictive agreements within the meaning of *Meng* and *Ohra*, but makes the conclusion of those agreements superfluous.[305] Nevertheless, the fixed prices apply to all Dutch language books, including books imported from Belgium. The system put in place by the national legislation has thus clearly cross-border effects. Where the proposed legislation intends, however, to prevent U-turn constructions for books published in the Netherlands, it should not be caught by the useful effect doctrine, at least if the Commission's approach in the *Sammelrevers* case were followed.[306]

Public health

Where the national state requires or favours the adoption of restrictive agreements between health insurance funds on the one hand and health care providers and hospitals on the other hand state action may be subject to the combined application of Articles 3(1)(g), 10 and 81 EC. [307] The *Pavlov* case involved a decision by the National Association of Specialists of the Royal Netherlands Society for the Promotion of Medicine (LSV) to set up a supplementary pension fund, which affiliation was made compulsory by the Netherlands authorities.[308]

---

303 See J. Houdijk, De nieuwe Wet op de vaste boekenprijs: immuun voor het mededingingsrecht?, *Mediaforum*, 2005, pp. 148-156; see for a more positive view and a reaction on Houdijk's article: B.J. Drijber, Reactie op: De Wet op de vaste boekenprijs en het mededingingsrecht, *Mediaforum*, 2005, pp. 232-234.

304 Advisory Opinion of the European Commission (DG Competition) of 2 August 2004, at: www.vasteboekenprijs.nl.

305 B.J. Drijber, Kroniek 2002: stilte voor de storm?, *M&M*, 2003, p. 74.

306 Mok makes no distinction between these two types of cross-border effects of the proposed regulation: M.R. Mok, Naar een wettelijke vaste boekenprijs? Een initiatiefvoorstel, *Ondernemingsrecht*, 2003, p. 6.

307 See also V.G. Hatzopoulos, *Killing* national health and insurance systems but *healing* patients? The European Market for health care services after the judgments of the ECJ, in *Vanbraekel* and *Peerbooms*, *CMLRev.*, 2002, p. 713.

308 Joined Cases C-180/98 to C-184/98, *Pavlov a.o.*

The Court concluded that the useful effect doctrine was not violated, since the decision by the medical specialists to set up a pension fund and to apply to the public authorities for a decision making membership compulsory, did not appreciably distort competition within the meaning of Article 81(1) EC (see also hereafter, section 3.3.2 and section 4.1.2.2).

Furthermore, where national rules place health care providers in a dominant position and as a result they abuse their dominant position Articles 3(1) sub g, 10 and 82 EC may be violated. In the *Sodemare* case it was not proved that the Italian rules, which made the conclusion of contracts with local health and welfare centres conditional on the private operator being non-profit making, placed these individual undertakings in a (collective) dominant position. The conclusion of such contracts was necessary for the reimbursement of the costs of providing social welfare services of a health care nature.[309]

3.3.2 Exceptions

Considering the lack of cases no distinction is being made here between the respective horizontal and flanking policy fields of the environment, consumer protection, public health and culture. No specific exception ground seems to be available for the combined application of Article 3g, 10 and 81 or 82 EC. However, if the underlying restrictive agreement can be exempted on the basis of Article 81(3) EC, the state will not act contrary to Articles 3g, 10 and 81 EC. The problem remains that Article 81(3) EC is not designed to apply to activities of public bodies, and when certain arrangements are declared generally binding, the requirement that a minimum degree of competition must remain in tact will probably not be fulfilled.[310] Furthermore, where the national state is involved in setting up systems of resale price maintenance, it is highly unlikely that an exemption for these agreements can be obtained under Article 81(3) EC (see section 4.1.3).

In *Pavlov* AG Jacobs presents an alternative general interest exception for anti-competitive state regulation, arguing that "in every competition law system the rules defining the respective responsibilities of the state and the professions are of crucial importance if that system wants to strike the right balance between the prevention of anticompetitive practices and the preservation of regulatory autonomy in the professions". In his view, measures taken by Member States comply with Article 10 EC where they are taken in pursuit of a legitimate and clearly defined public interest objective, although they reinforce the restrictive effects of a an agreement between undertakings. AG Jacobs also stated that in some cases Article 86(2) EC might be held applicable, whereas in

---

[309] Case C-70/95, *Sodemare*.

[310] See K. Mortelmans, Towards convergence in the application of the rules on free movement and on competition, *CMLRev.*, 2001, p. 643.

the present cases the decree rendering affiliation compulsory would be justified on social grounds.

The problem with the Court's case law is that many laws would automatically have to be declared contrary to Articles 10 and 81 EC, yet on grounds of public interest the state might have good reasons to reinforce or legitimise the anti-competitive effects of these laws. Accordingly, he concluded that Articles 10 and 81 EC were not infringed.[311]

The suggestion that governmental action with anti-competitive effects may be justifiable on public interest grounds seems inspired by the Court's case law on the rule of reason (Chapter 2). It also bears a certain resemblance to the application of Article 86(2) EC, which provision may be applicable to anti-competitive state regulation as well, according to AG Jacobs. He proposes a presumption of illegality for state action reinforcing restrictive effects of cartels, which can be rebutted if the state action is justified on public interest grounds. The reason for this approach is that it would otherwise not be possible to challenge governmental action under Article 10 EC or agreements between undertakings, where the restrictive effects are the result of state intervention and where the agreements are not restrictive enough to be caught by Article 81(1) EC. According to AG Léger in the *Wouters* case, where the Court considers that an agreement is not contrary to Article 81(1) EC and as a consequence the state measure imposing, encouraging or reinforcing its effects is automatically compatible with the provisions of Article 10 and 81 EC, this automatism is not in keeping with economic reality. There are a number of cases where agreements may not in themselves be contrary to Article 81(1) EC, but where the state measure strengthening the effect of that conduct leads to an appreciable restriction of competition.[312]

The Court in *Pavlov* was receptive to the Advocate General's suggestion for a general interest exception for anti-competitive state regulation in the social domain, as appears from the following considerations: "As for the request, made to the public authorities by an organisation representing the members of a profession, to make membership of the occupational pension fund it has set up compulsory, it is made under a scheme identical to those existing under the national law of a number of countries concerning the exercise of regulatory authority in the social domain. Such regimes are designed to promote the creation of supplementary pensions of the second type and include a number of safeguards whose observance the competent Minister must ensure, so that a request by the members of a profession for membership to be made compulsory cannot constitute an infringement of Article 81(1) of the Treaty." [313] Apparently Member States have a certain margin of discretion in the 'social domain' to impose,

311 Opinion of AG Jacobs in Joined Cases C-180/98 to C-184/98, *Pavlov*, paragraphs 162-165.

312 Opinion of AG Léger in Case C-309/99, *Wouters*, paragraph 207.

313 Joined Cases C-180/98 to C-184/98, *Pavlov*, paragraph 98.

encourage or reinforce the effects of a restrictive agreement within the context of the useful effect rule. This development in the case law leads to the question whether state intervention for the attainment of horizontal and flanking policy objectives could also be justified on public interest grounds, even if state action imposes, encourages or reinforces the effects of a restrictive agreement. When the protection of the environment, culture or public health are the main reasons for the state to support anti-competitive conduct on the part of private individuals, a general interest exception should also apply to agreements in these fields. According to AG Jacobs "[...] even where concertation between private actors (for example in social or environmental matters) analysed in isolation restricts competition within the meaning of Article 81(1), the state might have legitimate reasons to reinforce and officialise on public interest grounds the effects of that concertation".[314]

3.3.3 The relevance of the useful effect doctrine for national competition authorities

The importance of the useful effect doctrine has been further reinforced by the Court's judgment in *CIF*, stipulating that the national competition authorities must declare inapplicable national law that violates the useful effect rule.[315] In 1923 CIF, a consortium of Italian match manufacturers, was granted an exclusive right to produce and sell matches in the Italian market. The Ministry of Finance was in charge of establishing the sales price of matches, whereas representatives of the match manufacturers and an official of the State Monopolies Board set rules for the allocation of production quotas. In 1994 the monopoly of CIF was abolished; the state remained responsible for setting the sales price of matches. After complaint by a German undertaking the Italian competition authority came to the conclusion that for the period before liberalisation, the Italian state violated Articles 10, 3(g) and 81(1) EC by requiring match manufacturers to be a member of CIF; the manufactures infringed Article 81(1) EC by allocating production quotas. For the period after liberalisation, the match manufacturers were considered entirely responsible for their behaviour. After appeal with the Court, one of the two questions referred to the Court of Justice was whether the competition authority had the competence to disapply national law that legitimises or reinforces the anti-competitive effects of the behaviour of CIF.

The fact that the Court held that national competition authorities are under a duty to disapply national law which is contrary to the useful effect doctrine, has important ramifications for the national state regulating horizontal and flanking policy interests through alternative and sometimes more flexible regulation.

314 Opinion of AG Jacobs in Joined Cases C-180/98 to C-184/98, *Pavlov*, paragraph 164.

315 Case C-198/01, *Consorzio Industrie Fiammiferi (CIF)*.

The judgment also raises new questions (i) as to the scope of power of a national competition authority to disapply national laws and, more fundamentally, (ii) as to the fact that administrative organs have far reaching powers to disapply national laws, similarly to the courts.

Regarding (i), should the national competition authority in assessing the anti-competitive effects of national legislation also take into account public or horizontal and flanking policy interests?[316] As has been seen in the foregoing section, it is rather unclear to what extent exception grounds can be invoked for the justification of anti-competitive laws. That a national competition authority is, however, allowed to reconcile contradictions between other objectives laid down in the Treaty in applying national competition law appears from the Court's judgment in *Milk Marque*.[317] This case involved the abuse of a dominant position by Milk Marque, a farmers' co-operative society engaged in the collection, distribution and supply of milk in the United Kingdom. According to the Court national competition authorities may apply national competition rules also in an area governed by the common organisation of the market in milk and milk products, however, they must not compromise the objectives of that common organisation.[318]

This case could be applied by analogy to the application of the competition rules to national laws violating the useful effect doctrine, but this violation being justifiable on grounds of horizontal and flanking policies. After all the Commission is obliged to consider horizontal and flanking policy interests in applying the competition rules based on the integration clauses laid down in the Treaty (see Chapter 6).[319]

Regarding (ii) national competition authorities are not only bound to disapply national law violating the useful effect doctrine, they are in fact empowered to do so, which the Commission itself is not. The judgment may therefore provide a further incentive to decentralise EC competition law.[320] Furthermore, even where national law does not grant administrative organs powers to disapply national laws, which is reserved to the judiciary, the primacy and direct effect of Community law nonetheless entail that competition authorities must do so. The power of the national competition authorities to disapply anti-competitive legislation complements the power of national courts to disapply laws which infringe the rules on free movement (see Chapter 2). The problem is, however, that national competition authorities do not have the competence to ask the Court of Justice for a preliminary ruling.[321]

316 See annotation B.J. Drijber and W.T. Algera, *M&M*, 2003, pp. 250-252.

317 Case C-137/00, *Milk Marque*.

318 Case C-137/00, *Milk Marque*, paragraphs 57-94.

319 Annotation B.J. Drijber and W.T. Algera, (2003) *M&M*, nr. 7/8, p. 251.

320 Annotation P. Nebbia, *CMLRev.*, 2004, p. 846.

321 Annotation P. Nebbia, *CMLRev.*, 2004, p. 846.

3.3.4 Conclusions

The problem with the useful effect doctrine is twofold: first its scope of application with respect to state action is not entirely clear; second and particularly important for the subject matter there is no explicit exception ground. It should be admitted that also in the context of the free movement rules the ECJ managed to develop a rule of reason in the absence of an explicit Treaty exception for certain public interests. Nevertheless it is still worrying that no judgment exists where the ECJ explicitly pronounces on this issue, particularly considering the fact that with a view to *CIF* national competition authorities are bound to disapply national laws that violate the useful effect doctrine. Apart from the suggestion of the AG in *Pavlov* to introduce a type of rule of reason in this field, there are two other possibilities: First Article 86(2) EC, which is not really designed to offer private firms without an explicit public service task protection from the application of the competition rules and second Article 16 EC, a catch all provision, which may be able to fill the lacuna in the Treaty, particularly in these 'grey areas' where government and private firms mutually pursue public interests. In any event, the proportionality test, which plays an essential role in balancing horizontal and flanking policy considerations with the respect for the state aid rules and the other competition rules, has not yet been under discussion here.

4 The application of the competition rules and undertakings

In the foregoing sections the competition rules which involve state action were discussed. Due to the involvement of the national state the state can, at least to a considerable extent, be held accountable for the achievement of horizontal and flanking policy objectives. The fact that companies voluntarily decide to contribute to social and other public aims is, as stated in the introduction of this chapter, promoted by the Commission as well, for example in its green paper on promoting a European framework for Corporate Social Responsibility,[322] but also in other documents relating to specific areas of horizontal and flanking policies. Action by undertakings may, if leading to restrictions of competition, come into conflict with the competition rules, which are laid down in Article 81 EC (cartel prohibition, see hereafter section 4.1), Article 82 EC (abuse of a dominant position, section 4.2) or the Merger Regulation (section 4.3).

---

[322] COM(2001) 366 final.

4.1 Article 81 EC: the cartel prohibition

In this section it will be analysed how competition policy responds to restrictive practices of undertakings within the meaning of Article 81 EC and to what extent horizontal and flanking policy considerations can play a role in this policy.[323] After an introduction, the important notion of restriction of competition within the meaning of Article 81(1) EC will be discussed. As stated before, the fact that horizontal and flanking policy considerations have in principle no bearing on the *prima facie* applicability of Article 81 EC, makes the assessment of the notion of restriction of competition even more pertinent.[324] This section then concludes with the possibilities to justify restrictions on competition on horizontal and flanking policy grounds.

4.1.1 Introduction

Companies may strive for a cartel solution and include horizontal and flanking policy considerations into their activities for a variety of reasons. The most obvious reason is that companies expect to benefit from co-operation more than from traditional policy instruments.[325] It can be argued as opposed to the idea of corporate governance and social responsibility that companies have "only one social responsibility, and that is their responsibility towards their shareholders to maximize profits within the limits set by law".[326] Arguably it cannot be guaranteed that co-operation between companies is in line with the public interest and will lead to the attainment of horizontal and flanking policy objectives.[327] But corporate governance and social responsibility appeals to the companies' sense of social responsibility; it suggests that companies are able to effectively and – more efficiently than governments – achieve public interest objectives, and aims to ensure that companies integrate horizontal and flank-

---

[323] According to Gilliams a notice that would set guidelines precluding any non-competition concerns being taken into account when applying Article 81(3) EC was to be expected in connection with 1/2003: H. Gilliams, Modernisation: from policy to practice, *ELRev.*, 2003, p. 466. Meanwhile this notice has been adopted: Notice on "Guidelines on the application of Article 81(3) of the Treaty", OJ 2004, C 101/97, which will be discussed hereafter.

[324] This is different where collective labour agreements are involved, for example, in the health care sector, or where certain organisations entrusted with horizontal and flanking policy tasks should not be considered as undertakings.

[325] See also J.A. Maks, The "New" Horizontal Agreements Approach in the EU: an "economic" assessment, paper presented at the Workshop on "Reform of EC Competition Policy Jointly organised by EIPA and HWWA", 10-11 December 2001, Maastricht, p. 11.

[326] L. Bergkamp, Corporate Governance and Social Responsibility: A New Sustainability Paradigm, *EELR*, 2002, p. 146.

[327] L. Bergkamp, Corporate Governance and Social Responsibility: A New Sustainability Paradigm, *EELR*, 2002, p. 149.

ing policy considerations into their activities. Not only the government, but also companies have an important role in society in achieving public aims. The theory of corporate governance therefore implies that not only self-interest would cause the company to engage in restrictive practices, but due to the company's role in society, the public interest as well.

Examples of cartels in the field of the environment are environmental agreements with a view to develop environmentally friendly products or with the aim to reduce environmental effects to a minimum, or agreements that aim to protect the environment by using the same production process.[328] In the field of public health pharmaceutical companies may conclude agreements in the sphere of research and development for the development of new medicines. Health care providers and health insurance companies conclude agreements in the field of health care. Book price agreements are an example of an instrument of self-regulation with the aim to pursue cultural aims. In the media sector agreements are concluded between public service broadcasters for the broadcasting of certain major events, which are considered in the public interest. From a consumer perspective agreements on quality standards generally or on the improvement of safety and environmental standards in particular are relevant. If these agreements contain restrictive clauses and affect trade between Member States Article 81 EC will be applicable

4.1.2 Article 81(1) EC: the restriction of competition

Essential in determining whether agreements or restrictive practices fall within the prohibition of Article 81(1) EC is the concept of 'restriction of competition'.

4.1.2.1 The object or effect to restrict competition

In order to assess whether an agreement restricts competition within the meaning of Article 81(1) EC a distinction is made between agreements having as their object the restriction of competition and agreements having as their effect the restriction of competition. Furthermore, the impact on competition differs depending on the type of agreement, whether the agreement involves horizontal or vertical restraints.[329] In *Consten & Grundig* the Court made

---

[328] Jans (2000), p. 273.

[329] Contrary to horizontal agreements, it has not always been self-evident that vertical agreements are harmful to competition and should be prohibited as a consequence. There is great controversy about the extent to which vertical agreements are actually economically harmful and hence whether the competition rules have been applied correctly in the field. Particularly Bork is an exponent of the view that vertical agreements are not at all harmful to competition and should therefore be lawful. According to him vertical price fixing, vertical market division and all vertical restraints are beneficial to consumers and should for that reason be completely lawful: Bork (1978), pp. 297-298.

explicit that vertical agreements relating to inter-brand competition are covered by Article 81 EC.[330]

The object

Agreements containing obvious restrictions of competition such as price fixing, market sharing or the control of outlets have the object to restrict competition and will normally fall within the scope of Article 81(1) EC, provided that they restrict trade between Member States.[331] As opposed to hard-core restrictions for some restrictions of conduct it can be quite clear that they do not have an anti-competitive effect. Where an undertaking uses its right to conclude an agreement with another undertaking of its choice, competition will not be distorted. For example, where a health insurance undertaking concludes an agreement with a provider of health care of its choice, the cartel prohibition will not apply.[332] With respect to the environmental field, where agreements leave a large degree of discretion as to the means of achieving an environmental objective the competition rules will not apply. The Commission took the view in the *ACEA* decision that the agreement between members of the Association of European Automobile Manufacturers (ACEA) to reduce CO_2 emissions from new passenger cars by a target of 25% by 2008 did not infringe Article 81(1) EC.[333] From the Guidelines on the applicability of Article 81 of the EC Treaty to horizontal co-operation agreements it appears that not all environmental agreements fall under Article 81(1) EC.[334] Irrespective of the market share of the parties, some agreements will not restrict competition to an appreciable extent if no precise individual obligation is placed upon the parties or if they are loosely committed to contributing to the attainment of a sector-wide environmental target. In this latter case, according to the Commission, the assessment will

[330] Joined Cases 56/64 and 58/64, *Consten and Grundig*. The approach of the Court towards vertical agreements can at least partly be explained by the nature of the EC competition rules, i.e. that they are not only aimed at the attainment of workable competition, but more in particular also at market integration.

[331] See, for example, Joined Cases T-374/94, T-375/94, T-384/94 and T-388/94, *European Night Services*.

[332] See, for example, decision of the NMa in Case 407/882, Amicon, paragraph 67.

[333] XXVIIIth Competition Report, paragraph 132. See also Commission Communication on implementing the Community strategy to reduce carbon dioxide emissions from cars (COM(1998) 495), Bulletin EU 7/8-1998. J. Bongaerts, Carbon Dioxide Emissions and Cars: An Environmental Agreement at EU Level, *EELR*, 1999, p. 101. The Commission's position has, however, been criticised for disregarding the potential anti-competitive risks of the agreement. The ANCEA agreement may lead to a significant degree of co-operation between market participants. Negotiations over the 25% target may prove a fertile ground for collusive behaviour, and the existence of a bundle of agreements designed to control or reduce CO_2 emissions from automobiles could strengthen the anti-competitive effect of each individual agreement: D. Geradin, EC Competition Law and Environmental Protection: Conflict or Compatibility?, in: H. Somsen (Ed.), *Yearbook of European Environmental Law* (Oxford University Press, Oxford, 2002), p. 192.

[334] OJ 2001, C 3/2, points 184-187.

focus on the discretion left to the parties as to the means that are technically and economically available in order to attain the environmental objective agreed upon. The more varied such means, the less appreciable the potential restrictive effects. Similarly, agreements setting the environmental performance of products or processes that do not appreciably affect product and production diversity in the relevant market or whose importance is marginal for influencing purchase decisions do not fall under Article 81(1) EC. From a consumer perspective these Guidelines are also relevant, since they also apply to commercialisation agreements and agreements on standards, where the parties to the agreement want to distinguish themselves from a qualitative perspective.[335]

The effect

With regard to the assessment of agreements which have the effect of restricting competition the Court of First Instance held in *European Night Services* that "account should be taken of the actual conditions in which it functions, in particular the economic context in which the undertakings operate, the products or services covered by the agreement and the actual structure of the market concerned, unless it is an agreement containing obvious restrictions of competition such as price fixing, market-sharing or the control of outlets. In the latter case, such restrictions may be weighed against their claimed pro-competitive effects only in the context of Article 81(3) of the Treaty with a view of granting an exemption from the prohibition in Article 81(1)."[336] Agreements merely having the effect of restricting competition will be subject to a carefully conducted economic analysis of the effect on competition, which is necessary to assess their compatibility with Article 81(1) EC.[337]

As part of the modernisation programme of EC competition policy, several changes have taken place with regard to the analysis of vertical and horizontal agreements. The originally heavily criticised formalistic and legalistic approach

[335] Commercialisation agreements involve co-operation between competitors in the selling, distribution or promotion of their products and agreements on standards have as their primary objective the definition of technical or quality requirements with which current of future products, production processes or methods may comply. Agreements on standards which set no obligation to comply with the standard or which are parts of a wider agreement to ensure compatibility of products do, according to the Commission, not restrict competition, where participation in standard setting is unrestricted and transparent, OJ 2001, C 3/ 2, point 163.

[336] Joined cases T-374/94, T-375/94, T-384/94 and T-388/94, *European Night Services Ltd.*, paragraph 136.

[337] The Court hereby leaves scope for the consideration of pro-competitive effects under Article 81(1) EC, see Bellamy & Child (2001), p. 88; it is, however, highly disputed whether this economic approach should be understood as an implicit application of the rule of reason: Faull & Nikpay (1999), p. 93. According to Jones and Sufrin only the *negative or restrictive* effects that result from an agreement can be considered under Article 81(1) EC, since the CFI in *Métropole* held that the weighing of *beneficial* effects should take place at the stage of Article 81(3) EC: Jones and Sufrin (2004), p. 212.

by the Commission towards vertical agreements[338] and, to a lesser extent, horizontal agreements has been put in place by a supposedly more economic approach, particularly since the adoption of Regulation 2790/99 providing a new block exemption for vertical agreements.[339] In addition the Commission published Guidelines on Vertical Restraints, which are also relevant for the assessment of vertical agreements under Article 81(1) EC.[340] With respect to horizontal agreements the Commission adopted two new block exemption regulations[341] and Guidelines on Horizontal Co-operation Agreements.[342] The new block exemption regulations and the Guidelines reflect the Commission's willingness to take more account of the economic context wherein companies operate and conclude agreements. Within this context three issues must be further explored: the notion of appreciability (or *de minimis*), the 'rule of reason' and the 'inherent restriction approach'.

4.1.2.2 Appreciability or *De minimis*

In *Völk v. Vervaecke* the Court established the principle that an agreement falls outside Article 81(1) EC where it is unlikely to affect trade or to restrict competition between Member States to an appreciable extent.[343] The requirement that an agreement should have an appreciable effect on competition and trade, also referred to as the *de minimis* requirement, first and foremost relates to the size of the parties concerned and their market share. This is also considered as the *quantitative* notion of appreciability. In addition the *qualitative* notion of appreciability, also referred to as the concept based on 'effective competition'[344] suggests that undertakings compete on various aspects of a product, such as price, quality, service or guarantee.[345] Both the qualitative and qualitative notion of appreciability are used to assess the extent to which competition in a certain market is restricted and are thus based on competition arguments.

---

338 For example B.E. Hawk, System Failure: Vertical restraints and EC competition law, *CMLRev.*, 1995, pp. 973-989.

339 OJ 1999, L 336/21.

340 OJ 2000, C 291/1.

341 For specialisation agreements, Regulation 2685/2000, OJ 2000, L 304/3; For research and development, Regulation 2659/2000, OJ 2000, L 304/7.

342 OJ 2001, C 3/2.

343 Case 5/69, *Völk v. Vervaecke.*

344 See also C.E. Zandvliet, Note: Fixed Book Prices in the Netherlands and the European Union: A Challenge for Community Competition Law, *Columbia Journal of European Law*, 1997/1998, p. 423.

345 See also H.H.B. Vedder, Collectieve verwijderingssystemen en het mededingingsrecht, in: J.W. van de Gronden and K.J.M. Mortelmans, *Mededinging en niet-economische belangen* (Kluwer, Deventer, 2001), p. 219.

An appraisal of the appreciable effect of an agreement necessitates an analysis of the relevant product or service market as well as of the position and importance of parties on the relevant market, i.e. the product or service market and geographical market in which the product or service competes. The Commission specified the *de minimis* rule in its Notice on Agreements of Minor Importance,[346] which was replaced by a new Notice in 2001.[347] From this Notice it appears that the appreciable extent of a restriction will be established on the basis of market shares and turnover (in respect of small and medium sized undertakings) of the undertakings concerned.[348]

The qualitative notion of appreciability implies that agreements on price, where their effect on competition in a certain market is limited, may fall outside the scope of application of Article 81(1) EC. In *Pavlov* the Court held that a decision standardising in part the costs and the supplementary pension benefits of medical specialists restricts competition as far as it concerns one cost factor of specialist medical services, but the restrictive effects of such a decision on the specialist medical services are limited. The Court therefore came to the conclusion that the decision did not appreciably restrict competition within the common market.[349]

The qualitative notion of appreciability may be used as an argument to bring price fixing agreements pursuing horizontal and flanking policy goals outside the ambit of Article 81(1) EC. In the *VBVB/VBBB* case concerning the Flemish-Dutch resale price maintenance system for books the applicants argued that price competition is but one aspect of competition in the book retail sector. According to them the price elasticity of books, as goods, is minimal, so that other facets of competition have a predominant interest in comparison with price. In this connection the applicants mention the variety of supply, the diversity of stock held by bookshops, the speed with which orders are executed, and the services offered to consumers by way of information and advice as other facets of competition.[350] Their view was supported by the supposedly special

---

[346] OJ 1997, C 372/13.

[347] OJ 2001, C 368/13.

[348] A distinction is made between horizontal and vertical agreements. According to the Commission the recent Notice reflects a more economic approach and raises the market share threshold to 10% market share for agreements between competitors (horizontal agreements) and to 15% for agreements between non-competitors (vertical agreements). This quantitative definition of appreciability serves only as a guideline in individual cases. Even agreements which exceed the threshold may still have a negligible effect on trade or competition. The Court of First Instance has also rejected the possibility to automatically apply Article 81(1) EC to agreements when the market shares of the parties exceed the thresholds in the Commission's Notice: Joined Cases T-374/94, T-375/94, T-384/94 and T-388/94, *European Night Services.*

[349] Joined Cases C-180/98 to C-184/98, *Pavlov*, paragraphs 93-97.

[350] Joined Cases 43/82 and 63/82, *VBVB/VBBB v. Commission*, paragraph 41.

nature or structure of the book market. The Court's judgment could, however, only relate to the restrictive effects of the *trans-national* agreement on trade between the markets in Dutch-language books in the Netherlands and Belgium. The applicants' argument had not been brought forward in respect of an agreement operating at the national level and therefore remained an unsettled point of Community competition law.[351]

In the field of the environment agreements involving recycling contributions and environmental surcharges could be held to fall outside the scope of Article 81 EC where the recycling contribution determines only a minor percentage of the price of the product and should therefore not be considered to restrict competition to an appreciable extent.[352]

This qualitative notion of appreciability touches upon the question whether price competition in itself is an aim of competition policy. The Court in *Metro I* recognised that price competition is not an absolute objective of EC competition law.[353] As far as consumer interest is concerned, price competition will not be the only objective, but must be balanced with other elements of a healthy functioning of markets, such as the protection of quality expectations of consumers, safeguarding know how and good will (franchise agreements) and encouraging dealers to invest in the after sales service whilst at the same time excluding free riding. The Commission and the Court have, however, insisted on prohibiting vertical price agreements.[354] The cases on environmental agreements show that the mere insistence on price competition may well be contrary to imperative demands on sustainable consumption and therefore be detrimental to ecological concerns.[355] After all price arrangements in recycling schemes may also contribute to the environmental awareness of consumers.[356] The *VOTOB* case, for example, which will be discussed in section 4.1.3.2 and which in fact concerned a horizontal price agreement, has been referred to as a missed opportunity for

---

351 Joined Cases 43/82 and 63/82, *VBVB/VBBB v. Commission*, paragraph 44; see also C.E. Zandvliet, Note: Fixed Book Prices in the Netherlands and the European Union: A Challenge for Community Competition Law, *Columbia Journal of European Law*, 1997/1998, p. 423.

352 See also also H.H.B. Vedder, Collectieve verwijderingssystemen en het mededingingsrecht, in: J.W. van de Gronden and K.J.M. Mortelmans (Eds), *Mededinging en niet-economische belangen* (Kluwer, Deventer, 2001), p. 219; Vedder (2003), p. 145.

353 Case 26/76, *Metro/Saba*.

354 (Contrary to the courts in the US.) N. Reich, Competition law and the consumer, in: L. Gormley (Ed.), *Current and future perspectives on EC competition law: a tribute to professor M.R. Mok* (Kluwer Law International, London, The Hague [etc.],1997), p. 132.

355 Regarding imperative demands of sustainable consumption and competition policy: N. Reich, Competition Law and the Consumer, in: L. Gormley (Ed), *Current and future perspectives on EC competition law: a tribute to professor M.R. Mok* (Kluwer Law International, London, The Hague [etc.], 1997), p. 128.

356 S. de Vries, Consumer Interests and the Dutch Competition Act: an ambivalent relationship?, *TvC*, 2002, p. 166.

the Commission to integrate environmental considerations into its decision practice.[357]

Through the notion of appreciability agreements also including horizontal and flanking policy interests may fall outside the scope of application of Article 81(1) EC. Nevertheless, the discussion whether competition has been restricted to an appreciable extent, in a quantitative or qualitative sense, is not honed to the integration of horizontal and flanking policy interests in Article 81(1) EC or with the balancing of horizontal and flanking policy interests with a restriction of competition within the framework of Article 81(1) EC as such, but rather with determining the effect on competition in a given market of certain types of agreements.

4.1.2.3 The rule of reason

Until now it appears that within the framework of Article 81(1) EC little or no account can be taken of horizontal and flanking policy considerations. This could be different in case the 'rule of reason' were applicable to Article 81(1) EC. The problem with the application of the rule of reason is twofold, however. First, the rule of reason, which stems from US anti-trust law, is based on economic reasoning and involves a balancing approach within the context of Article 81(1) EC; if the economic advantages of an agreement means that the agreement is pro-competitive overall, it will fall outside Article 81(1) EC.[358] Second, it is unsure and highly controversial whether and to what extent the rule of reason can be applied in the context of EC competition law.

An example where the application of a rule of reason may benefit (part of) agreements, which pursue horizontal and flanking policy aims, is the Commission decision in the *DSD* case. In this case the Commission examined a number of agreements notified by Der Grüne Punkt – Duales System Deutschland AG (hereafter DSD), which operates a countrywide system for the collection and recovery of sales packaging in Germany, on their compatibility with Article 81 EC. With regard to the service agreement, i.e. the agreement on the establishment and operation of a system for the collection and sorting of used sales packaging, the Commission considered with reference to the Packaging Ordinance, which is the legislative framework in Germany in this respect, that the collection and recovery of plastic and composite packaging introduced a

---

357 XXIInd Competition Report 1992; see in particular F.O.W. Vogelaar, Towards an Improved Integration of EC Environmental Policy and EC Competition Policy: An Interim Report, in: B.E. Hawk (Ed.), *Annual Proceedings of the Fordham Corporate Law Institute – International Antitrust Law & Policy 1994* (Kluwer Law International, The Hague, 1995), p. 554; L. Gyselen, The emerging interface between competition policy and environmental policy in the EC, in: J. Cameron, P. Demaret and D Geradin (Eds), *Trade and the Environment – The Search for a Balance* (Cameron May, London, 1994), p. 252.

358 Bellamy & Child (2001), p. 77.

new area for business activity. This positive economic effect of the agreement outweighed the restrictive effect of the agreement caused by the provision that the collector of plastic and composite packaging was not entitled to commercially exploit this packaging himself. The collector could pass on packaging to third parties, guarantor, only free of charge.[359] This approach is in line with the Guidelines on the applicability of Article 81 EC to horizontal co-operation agreements. In paragraph 187 the Commission mentions that "agreements which give rise to genuine market creation, for instance recycling agreements, will not generally restrict competition...".[360] Another example is the *Eco-Emballages* decision, involving contracts concluded between Eco-Emballages and various other parties in France. According to the Commission, the scheme did not contravene Article 81(1) EC taking into account the particular circumstances on the French market and the fact that the system enabled local authorities to have their waste recycled.[361]

The Community courts seem to disagree whether Article 81(1) EC allows the application of the rule of reason. In the *European Night Services* case the Court of First Instance rejects the possibility to apply the rule of reason within the context of Article 81(1) EC.[362] This was confirmed by the ruling in *Métropole*. Here a group of French television companies had formed a joint venture to challenge Canal +, the market leader in the French TV-market for pay television. They notified the agreement to the Commission, which imposed conditions under Article 81(3) EC. According to the parties to the joint venture, the Commission should have balanced the pro- and anti-competitive elements of the agreement under Article 81(1) EC, which was rejected by the Court of First Instance which held that this balancing should take place within the framework of Article 81(3) EC.[363] The Court of Justice, on the other hand, has never explicitly referred to the rule of reason as such, but has in fact in several cases adopted a balancing approach under Article 81(1) EC.[364]

In its White Paper on the modernisation of the rules implementing Articles 81 and 82 the Commission states that if more systematic use were made

---

359 Commission Decision 2001/837, OJ 2001, L 319/1, paragraphs 47, 112 and 114; the provision in the service agreement that the collector enjoys exclusivity as regards the collection and sorting services for DSD in a designated area was considered to restrict competition to an appreciable extent.

360 OJ 2001, C 3/24.

361 Commission Decision 2001/663, *Eco-Emballages*, OJ 2001, L 233/37, paragraphs 80-81.

362 Joined Cases T-374/94, T-375/94, T-384/94 and T-388/94, *European Night Services*.

363 Case T-112/99, *Métropole Télévision et al v. Commission*.

364 See, for example, Case 26/76, *Metro/Saba*; in this ruling the Court recognises the fact that the reduction of the number of economic entities on the market does not necessarily diminish the intensity of competition on the relevant market. Co-ordination between undertakings can also lead to a more balanced market structure and even to an increase of competition: Stuyck, Waelbroeck, Van Reeken, Noë and Vogelaar (2000), p. 27.

under Article 81(1) EC of an analysis of the pro- and anti-competitive aspects of a restrictive agreement, Article 81(3) EC would be cast aside, whereas any such change could be made only through revision of the Treaty.[365] Nevertheless, the Commission admitted that in fact it had applied the rule of reason. In the Guidelines on the application of Article 81(3) of the Treaty, though, the Commission states that Article 81(3) EC "expressly acknowledges that restrictive agreements may generate objective economic benefits so as to outweigh the negative effects of the restriction of competition".[366]

In any event the Court and the Commission seem to be willing to apply a more 'economic' approach under Article 81(1) EC Under this approach the pro- and anti-competitive aspects of the agreement will be implicitly balanced.[367] An economic analysis of the restrictive agreements within the context of Article 81(1) EC, however, will not directly benefit agreements involving horizontal and flanking policy considerations. Here the focus is laid on competition considerations and not on the agreement's contribution to the attainment of horizontal and flanking policy aims.

4.1.2.4 Inherent restrictions

If certain restrictions of competition are considered necessary and appropriate for the proper functioning of a certain organisation or system, they may be regarded as not problematic in view of Article 81(1) EC.[368] An example is the case *Gøttrup-Klim* where the Court considered the rules of a Danish agricultural purchasing co-operative, which had the object of providing its members with farm supplies at the lowest prices, held that "in order to escape the prohibition laid down in Article 81(1) of the Treaty, the restrictions imposed on members by the statutes of co-operative purchasing organisations must be limited to what is necessary to ensure that the co-operative functions properly and maintains its contractual power in relation to producers". [369]

---

[365] COM (99) 101 final, paragraph 57

[366] OJ 2004, C 101/97, paragraph 33.

[367] Faull & Nikpay (1999), p. 93.

[368] The term 'inherent restriction' is used by Van de Gronden and Mortelmans (Eds) (2001), pp. 318-323.

[369] Case C-250/92, *Gøttrup-Klim*, paragraph 35. This case is usually mentioned within the context of the doctrine of ancillary restraints, relating to restrictions on the conduct of the parties ancillary, or objectively necessary, to the operation of a pro-competitive or non-restrictive agreement. See Jones and Sufrin (2004), p. 216; Goyder (2003), p. 101. However, the reasoning of the Court in *Gøttrup-Klim* seems to go beyond the doctrine of ancillary restraints, since the Court in its assessment of the rules in the light of the cartel prohibition included the economic situation of the relevant markets.

Sport

That the inherent restriction approach can be relevant for horizontal and flanking policy activities was particularly shown by the *UEFA* decision of the Commission and the opinions of AG Alber and Cosmas in *Lehtonen* and *Deliège*. They suggested that this approach, already employed in the context of the free movement of sportsmen (see Chapter 2), could also be applied in the field of sports and competition law.[370] It entails that certain rules, which may have a restrictive effect on competition, nevertheless cannot be regarded as a restriction because they are inherent to the particular nature of the activity. The *UEFA* referred to the Opinion of AG Alber in *Lehtonen* and argued that the EC competition rules shall not be assessed in the abstract and that they are always depending on the economic conditions in the relevant markets. Rules restricting freedom of action which by their effect are necessary for the creation of competition on the relevant market can therefore be compatible with Articles 81 and 82 of the EC Treaty, so long as they are necessary and appropriate to attain this objective. The Commission held the following: "Taking into account that what the Court of Justice has recognised in the *Bosman* case as legitimate objectives in view of the considerable social importance of football in the Community, the Commission considers that the restrictions imposed by the rule may escape the prohibition laid down in Article 81(1) of the Treaty. In order to establish whether this preliminary conclusion can be upheld or not, the Commission has to know if such restrictions are limited to what is necessary to preserve the integrity of the UEFA club competitions and to ensure the uncertainty as to results."[371]

In the *Meca-Medina* case, which was introduced before in section 2.1, the CFI placed anti-doping legislation adopted by the International Swimming Federation (FINA) outside the scope of Articles 81 and 49 EC (see Chapter 2). In this case the CFI referred to *inter alia Deliège* where an inherent restriction approach had been adopted, as well as to the Commission's conclusion wherein it had unmistakenly adopted an inherent restriction approach. Nonetheless, the CFI clearly held that a prohibition of doping is based on purely sporting considerations and therefore has nothing to do with any economic consideration, meaning that these rules cannot come within the scope of Articles 49, 81 and 82 EC.[372] Furthermore, the CFI distinguished this type of legislation from the legislation at issue in *Wouters* concerning market conduct and applied to an essentially economic activity (see hereafter).[373]

In any event, this judgment reinforces the dichotomy created in reviewing the rules set up by sporting associations under competition law. Certain rules

370 Case C-176/96, *Lehtonen*; Joined Cases C-51/96 and C-191/97, *Deliège*.

371 Communication made pursuant to Article 19(3) of Council Regulation No. 17, OJ 1999, C 363/2, paragraph 8.

372 Case T-313/02, *Meca-Medina*, paragraph 47.

373 Case T-313/02, *Meca-Medina*, paragraph 65.

that are inherent in the conduct of a sports event, where sports interests are more important than economic interests, and which are directed at the safeguarding of club competitions, do not appear to be prohibited by Article 81(1) EC.[374] On the one hand, the *Meca-Medina* judgment makes clear, which is in particular relevant to horizontal and flanking policies, that not all (self-)regulatory instruments do automatically come within the scope of the EC Treaty; with regard to Article 81(1) EC the legal and economic context must be carefully examined to determine whether the rules at issue do really intend to restrict competition.

On the other hand, rules regulating the economic aspects of sport do fall within the scope of Article 81(1) EC and will have to meet the conditions mentioned in Article 81(3) EC.[375] A few months later the same chamber of the CFI as in *Meca-Medina* delivered its judgment in *Piau* concerning the FIFA rules requiring a licence for the profession of players' agents. According to the CFI in *Piau* these rules did constitute a barrier to access to that economic activity and therefore necessarily affected competition within the meaning of Article 81(1) EC.[376] Remarkably, both the Commission and the CFI coupled the 'inherent restriction approach' in this case to Article 81(3) EC, the exception.[377] In fact they stepped over the review of the FIFA rules under Article 81(1) EC, whether the requirement of a licence for players' agents was inherently necessary and proportionate to protect the clubs and players, which was indeed the case according to the Commission, and instead made an assessment of the justifiability of these rules under Article 81(3) EC.

Professional services

Not only in the sports sector, but also in the market for professional services has this approach been adopted by the Commission and the Court. As AG Jacobs stated in his opinions in *Brentjens* and *Pavlov* the typical features of a certain market must be taken into account under an assessment of the application of the competition rules. In cases involving specific sectors or specific categories of agreements the Court 'has gone beyond a mechanistic approach and has adopted a more searching analysis' according to AG Jacobs.[378]

In *Pavlov* the market for professional services determines the framework within which the regulations of undertakings will be assessed in the light of

[374] For a critical assessment of the Court's and Commission's attitude to sporting interests, see: Stephen Weatherill, "Fair Play Please!": Recent developments in the application of EC law to sport, *CMLRev.*, 2003, pp. 51-93.

[375] Vogelaar (2000), p. 28.

[376] Case T-193/02, *Piau*, paragraph 101.

[377] Case T-193/02, *Piau*, paragraph 100.

[378] Opinion of AG Jacobs in Case C-67/96, *Albany*, Joined Cases C-115/97, C-116/97 and C-117/97, *Brentjens* and Case C-219/97, *Drijvende Bokken*, paragraph 252.

competition law.[379] From an economic point of view the markets for professional services differ in two respects from normal markets for goods and services. First there are the externalities; the quality of the services plays a crucial role, since professionals not only serve their clients, but also provide benefits to the wider public, which means that society has an extra interest in keeping the average quality of their services high. Second, there is a problem of asymmetric information, which problem is particularly acute in the professions because of the nature of their highly technical services. Apart from the economic perspective, from a legal point of view in many states regulatory powers have been delegated to professional bodies, which may even be governed by public law. Therefore, owing to the heterogeneity of the professions and the specificities of the markets on which they operate no general formula can be applied and it will be necessary to assess carefully in each case whether a given restriction of conduct leads for the market in issue in fact to a restriction of competition within the meaning of Article 81 EC.

In the *EPI* decision which involved the code of conduct of the European Patent Office (EPO) the Commission regarded the prohibition for members to charge fees related to the outcome of the service provided as not covered by Article 81(1) EC. According to the Commission "even if in other circumstances it might constitute a restriction of competition to prohibit fees from being determined according to outcome, it is necessary in the economic and legal context specific to the profession in question in order to guarantee impartiality on the part of representatives and to ensure the proper functioning of EPO".[380] Apparently even price agreements may, according to the Commission in *EPI*, benefit from the inherent restriction approach.

The Wouters *case: a step further?*

A step further in the above-mentioned development was the Court's judgment in *Wouters*. This case involved decisions by the Bar of the Netherlands (*Nederlandse Orde van Advocaten*) prohibiting lawyers from practising as members of the Bar in full partnership with accountants. These decisions were based on a regulation which, in order to guarantee the independence and loyalty to the client of members of the Bar who provide legal assistance in conjunction with members of liberal professions, adopts universally binding rules governing the formation of multidisciplinary partnerships. According to the Court this regulation (*Samenwerkingsverordening*) has an adverse effect on competition and may affect trade between Member States. As it prevents clients to turn to a single structure for a large part of services necessary for the organisation, management and operation of their business, it cannot satisfy the needs created by the increasing interpenetration of national markets and it prevents econo-

[379] Opinion of AG Jacobs in Joined Cases C-180/98 to C-184/98, *Pavlov*, paragraphs 83 to 89.

[380] Commission Decision 1999/267, *EPI* (code of conduct), OJ 1999, L 106/14, point 35.

mies of scale resulting from such multidisciplinary partnerships which might have positive effects on the costs of services.[381]

Nevertheless, the Court regards the restrictions on competition necessary for the proper practice of the legal profession as organised in the Member State concerned. According to the Court "not every agreement between undertakings or any decision of an association of undertakings which restricts the freedom of action of the parties or of one of them necessarily falls within the prohibition laid down in Article 81(1) of the Treaty. For the purposes of application of that provision in a particular case, account must first of all be taken of the overall context in which the decision of the association of undertakings was taken or produces its effects. More particularly, account must be taken of its objectives, which are here connected with the need to make rules relating to organisation, qualifications, professional ethics, supervision and liability, in order to ensure that the ultimate consumers of legal services and the sound administration of justice are provided with the necessary guarantees in relation to the integrity and experience. It has then to be considered whether the consequential effects restrictive of competition are inherent in the pursuit of those objectives."[382]

The peculiarity of *Wouters* is that whilst the Court at first sight seems to endorse an inherent restriction approach, it in fact applies a Cassis-type or European-style[383] rule of reason to justify certain restrictions on competition within the framework of Article 81(1) EC. Here the Court did not come to the conclusion that eventually competition is not restricted because of the inherent characteristics of the profession in question, but concluded that competition was restricted but nevertheless justified on the basis of public interest grounds.[384] In any event, Article 81(1) EC was not violated and recourse to a Treaty exception ground, such as Article 81(3) EC or Article 86(2) EC was not necessary. In this respect the judgment is very interesting from the aspect of convergence between the competition rules and the rules on free movement.[385]

In paragraphs 119-123 the Court deals with the question whether the regulation is compatible with the freedom to provide services and the freedom of establishment. First, the Court confirms that Articles 43 and 49 EC are also directed at associations or organisations not governed by public law, and have thus horizontal direct effect. Second, the Court states that "on the assumption that the provisions concerning the right of establishment and/or freedom to provide services are applicable to a prohibition of any multi-disciplinary partner-

381 Case C-309/99, *Wouters*, paragraphs 87-89.

382 Case C-309/99, *Wouters*, paragraph 97.

383 See also G. Monti, Article 81 EC and public policy, *CMLRev.*, 2002, p. 1088.

384 J.W. van de Gronden en K.J.M. Mortelmans, Wouters: is het beroep van advocaat een aparte tak van sport?, *AA*, 2002, p. 459.

385 See with regard to this issue of convergence: K Mortelmans, Towards convergence in the application of the rules on free movement and on competition?, *CMLRev.*, 2001, pp. 613-649.

ships between members of the Bar and accountants such as that laid down in the 1993 Regulation and that that regulation constitutes a restriction on one or both of those freedoms, that restriction would in any event appear to be justified for the reasons set out in paragraphs 97 to 109 above. The answer to be given to the seventh, eight and ninth questions must therefore be that it is not contrary to Articles 43 and 49 of the Treaty for a national regulation such as the 1993 Regulation to prohibit any multi-disciplinary partnership between members of the Bar and accountants, since that regulation could reasonably be considered to be necessary for the proper practice of the legal profession, as organised in the country concerned."[386]

The consequences for horizontal and flanking policy considerations

The *Wouters* judgment leads to the question whether the inherent restriction approach as it has been applied here, can in a more general sense be useful for agreements containing horizontal and flanking policy considerations in general and, if so, which types of competitive restraints should benefit from this approach. Similarly to sports a distinction could be made between the inherent characteristics of environmental agreements, cultural agreements or agreements in the healthcare sector and primarily commercial considerations contained in such agreements.[387] For example, would codes of conduct outside the market for professional services on important ethical questions with regard to the application of biotechnology in health care for medical advances or in agriculture for the creation of genetically modified plant crops be able to benefit from this approach? Rules set up by the biotechnology industry and possibly other operators in this field which involve gene testing, regeneration of human organs or genetically modified plants will then not be prohibited by Article 81(1) EC. Self-regulation may be an important instrument to help to develop biotechnology in harmony with ethical values and societal goals. In a Communication from the Commission on Life Sciences and biotechnology it is stated that "the Commission will work with public and private partners to identify areas where it is possible to establish consensus on ethical guidelines/standards or best practice. Areas might include stem cell research, biobans, xenotransplantation, genetic testing and use of animals in research. Such guidelines could, when appropriate, take the form of self-regulatory initiatives in the scientific community and industry."[388]

With regard to the cultural sector the German government argued in the *Binon* case that the special market in newspapers and periodicals required a modification of the competition rules, whereas price fixing was absolutely neces-

[386] Case C-309/99, *Wouters*, paragraphs 122 & 123.

[387] Vogelaar (2000), pp. 28-32.

[388] See also with regard to biotechnology in Europe: Communication from the Commission on Life Sciences and biotechnology – A Strategy for Europe, COM(2002)27 final.

sary for maintaining an effective distribution system.[389] This case involved the establishment of a selective distribution system by the Belgian company 'Agence et messageries de la Presse' (AMP) and publishers of newspapers and periodicals, whereby every new retail outlet was subject to a prior recognition procedure and whereby AMP was reserved to fix the prices which retailers had to respect. Similarly, in the *VBVB/VBBB* case which involved a collective vertical price agreement between Dutch and Flemish associations of publishers and booksellers the applicants argued that the Commission in its decision had failed to have regard for the special structure of the book market and the specific nature of books.[390] Furthermore it appears from the Court's ruling in *Publishers' Association* on the Net Book Agreements that the Commission should have taken into account a decision of the UK Restrictive Practices Court and more in particular the situation on the Irish book market and the fact that the United Kingdom and Ireland formed one language area. The Net Book Agreements contained common rules for the application and enforcement of retail prices for books of which the publisher decided to regard them as net books. The selling conditions also applied to books on the Irish market.[391]

These examples make clear that the question as to the scope of the *Wouters* jugdment outside the field of professional services is pertinent. So far the approach of the Court in *Wouters*, where it explicitly balanced the acknowledged restriction of competition with the stated public interests within the framework of Article 81(1) EC, has remained an isolated incident.[392] One conclusion might be that Articles 81(1) and 81(3) EC "have been conflated and operated as if they were a single provision", particularly with a view to the modernisation programme and the new Regulation 1/2003 which abolished the Commission's monopoly of granting an individual exemption.[393] More important, however, are the particularities of the markets of professional services and the fact that they are characterised by assymetric information which may have induced the Court to take this position.[394] In the grey area between state regulation and private

---

[389] Case 243/83, *Binon*.

[390] Joined Cases 43/82 and 63/82, *VBVB/VBBB*, paragraph 41.

[391] Case C-360/92 P, *Publishers' Association*. The negative decision of the Commission led first to a procedure before the Court of First Instance, which judgment was challenged before the Court of Justice, which eventually annulled the Commission's decision.

[392] "Wouters is hard to square with previous case law and again re-opens the debate as to exactly how much analysis is required under Article 81(1)", according to Jones and Sufrin (2004), p. 230.

[393] Goyder (2003), pp. 94-95.

[394] Annotation A.J. Vossestein, *CMLRev.*, 2002, p. 857: he refers to an opinion of the Supreme Court of the US in California Dental Association v. Federal Trade Commission [526 U.S. 756 (1999)], where the Supreme Court required more extensive examination by the Court of Appeals of the advertising restrictions of a dental association, as the advertising restrictions, restricting difficult-to-verify claims about quality or patient comfort, had a plausible pro-competitive effect by preventing misleading or false claims that distort the market.

initiatives of professional organisations the Court had to find a way to allow the NOVA to set up rules to protect their own profession and ultimately the consumers of legal services, without coming into conflict with the cartel prohibition. The particularities of a certain sector, however, plays a role in a more general sense in the context of Article 81(1) EC and the implications of Wouters may therefore stretch well beyond the market for professional services, as confirmed by the Commission's approach towards the sports sector. After all, the application of Article 81(1) EC is always conditioned by the particular context in which rules are set up and agreements are concluded.[395] Hence, the *Wouters* ruling remains relevant for the consideration of horizontal and flanking policy interests within the framework of Article 81(1) EC, but is limited to the economic context wherein the arrangements are made. To accept that *Wouters* has important ramifications for the balancing of horizontal and flanking policy considerations with restrictions of competition in a more general sense would blur the distinction between Article 81(1) EC and Article 81(3) EC, which is still relevant according to the case law of the Community courts and the opinion of the Commission.[396]

4.1.3 Exemptions: restrictive practices that can be justified for horizontal and flanking policy reasons

The foregoing shows that the possibilities to take account of horizontal and flanking policy considerations under the cartel prohibition of Article 81(1) EC are limited. The question therefore as to the scope of the exemptions, in particular Article 81(3) EC, has become pertinent. Regulation 1/2003 introduced the 'exception légale', or direct applicability of Article 81(3) EC as from 1 May 2004. Not only the Commission, but also the national competition authorities and the national courts are empowered to apply Article 81(3) EC.

4.1.3.1 The scope of Article 81(3) EC

The grounds for exemption will first be introduced, i.e. to what extent horizontal and flanking policy considerations can be brought within the ambit of Article 81(3) EC in the first place. Second, if an agreement serves objectives which satisfy the conditions of Article 81(3) EC, it must still be indispensable to the achievement of the objectives or, in other words, the agreement must be proportionate to the propagated aims. This requirement has played

---

395 S. Weatherill, "Fair Play Please!": Recent developments in the application of EC law to sport, *CMLRev.*, 2003, p. 82.

396 Vossestein argues that even though it appears that the Court in Wouters balances public interests with anti-competitive behaviour, the Court still had competitive considerations in mind: annotation A.J. Vossestein, *CMLRev.*, 2002, p. 859. See also Guidelines on the application of Article 81(3), OJ 2004, C 101/97, paragraph 11.

an essential role in the decision practice of the Commission.[397] In this section therefore the focus will be laid upon the grounds for exemption and the application of the proportionality test, similarly to the assessment of the exceptions to free movement (see Chapter 2).

Grounds for exemption

If an agreement is considered to restrict competition and trade within the meaning of Article 81(1) EC, it may still be exempted on the basis of Article 81(3) EC, but only if the following four cumulative conditions are met:

- the agreement, decision or concerted practice contributes to improving the production of goods or to promoting technical or economic progress;
- it allows consumers a fair share of the resulting benefit;
- the restriction of competition is indispensable to the attainment of the objectives;
- competition shall not be eliminated in respect of a substantial part of the products in question.

Apart from a reference to the consumer, who should be given a fair share of the benefit resulting from a restrictive agreement and who is not even necessarily the final consumer,[398] there is no mention of other horizontal and flanking policy interests in Article 81(3) EC. One interpretation of Article 81(3) EC is therefore that it only allows for the balancing of the restrictive effects of an agreement with the enhancement of efficiency. Article 81(3) EC would merely permit improvements of economic efficiency to obtain an exemption. A broader view suggests, however, that Article 81(3) EC stretches beyond economic efficiency and includes other policies and non-competition considerations.[399] Or in the words of some economists, it includes a broader welfare concept, not only productive efficiency, but also other benefits which are relevant to consumer welfare.[400] Despite the lack of an explicit reference in Article 81(3) itself, the Commission has been able to extend the ambit of Article 81(3) EC whilst taking into consideration cultural interests, public health interests, environmental interests and other 'non-competition' interests and hence seems to enhance, at least to some extent, the broader view. In particular the condition that agreements which contribute to improving the production or distribution of goods may include horizontal and flanking policy considerations.

---

397 Jones and Sufrin (2004), p. 242.

398 J. Stuyck, The consumer and European competition policy in the past and next decade, *TvC*, 2002, p. 155.

399 See also Whish (2001), pp. 125-128: He suggests that Article 81(3) ought to be interpreted in a narrow rather than a broad manner, also with a view to the decentralisation of competition policy.

400 G. Monti, Article 81 EC and public policy, *CMLRev.*, 2002, p. 1065.

Regarding sport the *Piau* case is interesting. In this case the Commission considered that the objective of raising professional and ethical standards for the occupation of players' agent falls within the scope of Article 81(3) EC. Strangely enough the CFI upheld the Commission's decision, whilst on the one hand recognising in paragraph 100 that the Commission's decision was based on the reasoning that the inherent restriction of the licence system was necessary and proportionate to protect the players and the clubs, yet on the other hand considering in paragraph 105 of the judgment that the Commission's decision was in fact not based on arguments relating to the specificity of sport, but on purely economic grounds.[401]

Several arguments plead in favour of the broader view to Article 81(3) EC. Firstly, the integration clauses, requiring the Commission to take other than purely competition goals into account in its competition policy (see chapter 1), entail that horizontal and flanking policy considerations must be given more weight by the Commission in applying Article 81(3) EC to restrictive agreements.[402] As stated in the first chapter, what is unclear, however, is to what extent these aims of horizontal and flanking policies must contribute to granting an exemption and what significance horizontal and flanking policy considerations should have in the decision making process.[403] With regard to environmental agreements it can be submitted that the economic conditions in Article 81(3) EC must by reason of Article 6 EC be interpreted in an environmentally friendly manner.[404]

Secondly, the Court itself has confirmed that the application of Article 81(3) EC to agreements may involve other than purely competition interests.[405] In the *Metro I* case the Court held that an agreement, which constitutes a stabilizing factor with regard to the provision of employment, improves the general conditions of production and comes within the framework of the objectives of Article 81(3) EC.[406] The Court hereby indicates that broader than purely economic objectives may play a role in the proportionality test under Article 81(3) EC. The Court of First Instance went a step further whilst explicitly recognising that

---

[401] Case T-193/02, *Piau*, paragraphs 62, 100 and 105. Meanwhile an appeal has been lodged by Piau against this judgment: Case C-171/05 P, *Piau (2)*.

[402] See also Faull & Nikpay (1999), p. 108.

[403] See also G. Monti, Article 81 EC and public policy, *CMLRev.*, 2002, p. 1070.

[404] Ehle speaks of 'ökologische-qualitatieve Auslegung': Ehle (1996), p. 153.

[405] Jones and Sufrin (2004), p. 233.

[406] Case 26/76, *Metro/Saba*, paragraph 43; see also with regard to the environment: F.O.W. Vogelaar, Towards an Improved Integration of EC Environmental Policy and EC Competition Policy: An Interim Report, in: B.E. Hawk (Ed.), *Annual Proceedings of the Fordham Corporate Law Institute – International Antitrust Law & Policy 1994* (Kluwer Law International, The Hague, 1995), pp. 529-563.

Article 81(3) EC may also include general interests and cultural reasons. In the *Métropole* judgment the CFI held:

> *"Admittedly, in the context of an overall assessment, the Commission is entitled to base itself on considerations connected with the pursuit of the public interest in order to grant exemption under Article 81(3) of the Treaty."*[407]

Thirdly, in his opinion in the *Albany, Brentjens* and *Drijvende bokken* cases AG Jacobs also underlines the possibility to balance different interests within the context of Article 81(3) EC. According to him "both the Court and the Commission have on occasions recognised the possibility of taking account of social grounds in that context, in particular by interpreting the conditions of Article 81(3) broadly so as to include concerns for employment".[408]

The willingness of the Community courts as well as the Commission to take horizontal and flanking policy interests into account under Article 81(3) EC has, however, not (yet) resulted in the development of legislation or even soft law instruments to clarify under which conditions co-operation between firms for the attainment of public interests may be exempted, except for the field of the environment (see hereafter, section 4.1.3.2). The scope of Article 81(3) EC will therefore be considered separately for each horizontal and flanking policy field. The block exemption regulations that have been adopted for certain categories of vertical and horizontal agreements do not refer to horizontal and flanking policy interests and are therefore only indirectly relevant. With regard to vertical agreements Commission Regulation 2790/1999 is relevant which, contrary to the former block exemption regulations, applies to all vertical restraints, with the exception of distribution agreements for motor vehicles.[409] It differs from the previous regulations particularly because it is less formalistic and more economically oriented. Where, for example, the supplier (or the buyer in case of vertical supply obligations) does not have a market share of more than 30 percent, the block exemption will be applicable The block exemption regulation only contains a black list of clauses that are prohibited – Article 4. Vertical agreements pursuing horizontal and flanking policy aims may thus benefit from this block exemption regulation, if the market share of the supplier (or buyer) remains below 30 percent, and if the agreement does not contain black clauses as mentioned in Article 4, such as clauses which amount to absolute territorial protection or price fixing. Depending on the market share therefore, agreements

---

407 Joined Cases T-528/93, T-542/93, T-543/93 and T-546/93, *Métropole Télévision (Métropole I)*, paragraph 118.

408 Opinion AG Jacobs in Case C-67/96, *Albany*, Joined Cases C-115/97, C-116/97 and C-117/97, *Brentjens* and Case C-219/97, *Drijvende Bokken*, paragraph 193.

409 Commission Regulation No 2790/1999 on the application of Article 81(3) of the Treaty to categories of vertical agreements and concerted practices, OJ 1999, L 336/21.

containing provisions which stipulate that the supplier employs environmentally friendly processes or which require the franchisees of a manufacturer of environmentally friendly products to operate in an environmentally friendly manner could benefit from this block exemption. Book price agreements, however, will not benefit from the block exemption as they have the object to restrict price competition, which restraint is black-listed.

Furthermore, block exemption regulations have been issued for horizontal agreements, namely specialisation agreements and research and development agreements.[410] The block exemption for research and development agreements may, for example, be relevant for agreements in the pharmaceutical product sector as well as for environmental agreements. The exemption also includes a market share threshold and applies where the combined market share of the participating companies does not exceed 25% (Article 4). Agreements containing hardcore restrictions such as price fixing, limiting the freedom of parties to conduct research in unconnected fields, the limitation of output of sales etc. (Article 5) cannot benefit from the block exemption.

Standards of adjudication: the principle of proportionality

An agreement will only be exempted from the cartel prohibition, if the four cumulative conditions are fulfilled. With regard to the first condition, an improvement must show objective advantages, which compensate the disadvantages of the agreement for competition. A causal connection must exist between the agreement and the pursued improvement. Regarding the second condition, consumers must benefit from the agreement. Consumers include all users of goods and services being private individuals and undertakings. Agreements could have direct benefits for consumers or potential benefits for consumers, which will be passed on to them depending on the situation on the market and disadvantages for consumers.[411] Once these positive conditions are fulfilled, which involves an assessment of the aims of the agreement and the causal connection between the restrictions on competition and the aims pursued, the third condition, the indispensability of the restrictions, needs to be analysed. This requirement goes beyond the establishment of a mere causal link between the agreement and the aims pursued, as it involves the question whether no less restrictive means are available to pursue similar aims.[412] This essentially entails that, similarly to the exceptions to the rules on free movement, agreements will only be exempted, if they do not go any further than is deemed necessary for the achievement of the objective pursued. In other words the proportionality

[410] Commission Regulation No 2658/2000 on the application of Article 81(3) of the Treaty to categories of specialisation agreements, OJ 2000, L 304/3; Commission Regulation No 2659/2000 on the application of Article 81(3) of the Treaty to categories of research and development agreements, OJ 2000, L 304/7.

[411] Bellamy & Child (2001), pp. 172-174.

[412] Bellamy & Child (2001), p. 174.

principle plays a role within the context of Article 81(3) EC as well. The fourth condition requires that real or potential competition in the market must be maintained. As will be shown by the following examples this 'rigid conceptual framework' has not withheld the Commission from taking into account horizontal and flanking policy considerations. Nevertheless their status within the context of Article 81(3) EC is still unsettled.

4.1.3.2 The environment

Environmental protection as ground for exemption

The decision practice of the Commission makes clear that environmental protection requirements may form a ground for exemption under Article 81(3) EC.[413] The first condition of Article 81(3) EC includes the improvement of the quality of the product. A relevant criterion may therefore also be the improvement of the *environmental* quality of the product, which might relate to an environmental friendly production process or use of a product, or a less polluting form of disposal.[414] Particularly a flexible interpretation of the term technical and economic progress has made it possible that environmental interests are taken into account under Article 81(3) EC.[415] In 1983, for example, the Commission declared that the carbon-gas technology contributed more to the attainment of environmental protection than the direct burning of coal. On the basis of *inter alia* this ground the Commission decided that the co-operation agreement for the purpose of developing this technique contributes to the promotion of technical and economic progress.[416] In the *DSD* decision the Commission held that the service agreements concluded between DSD, the only extensive tack-back and exemption system for used sales packaging, and the collectors, offers a high level of environmental protection. According to the Commission "regular collection from private final consumers of used sales packaging [...] gives direct practical effect to environmental objectives".[417] The exclusivity clause in the service agreement has several beneficial effects: It makes possible for the parties to plan the provision of services on a long-term basis and to organise it reliably; there are positive network effects; requirements are met in a sensitive area previously organised under public law. This all leads to the conclusion that the service agreement and the exclusivity clause contrib-

---

[413] See also Vedder (2003), pp. 159-174.

[414] Jans (2000),p. 278: He also refers to the 'life-cycle approach' which is a central feature of both national and European product policy.

[415] D. Geradin, EC Competition Law and the Environmental Protection: Conflict or Compatibility?, in: H. Somsen (Ed.), *Yearbook of European Environmental Law* (Oxford University Press, Oxford, 2002), p. 124.

[416] *KSB/Goulds/Lowara/ITT*, Commission Decision on a stainless steel component of centrifugal pumps, OJ 1991, L 19/25.

[417] Commission Decision 2001/837, OJ 2001, L 319/1, paragraph 144.

ute to improving the production of goods and promoting technical or economic progress. Thus environmental benefits are in this way aligned with benefits for the production of goods and technical and economic progress within the meaning of Article 81(3) EC. It is furthermore interesting that the Commission takes into account the fact that this area is a sensitive area which was previously organised under public law.

In several decisions the Commission aligned environmental benefits with a fair share for the consumer, like in *Exxon/Shell*, where the Commission indicated that environmental advantages in question "will be perceived as beneficial by many consumers at a time when the limitation of natural resources and threats to the environment are of increasing public concern".[418] In *DSD* the Commission regards not only the cost savings as a result of the scale and scope advantages achievable by the service agreement to benefit consumers, but also the improvement in environmental quality by the reduction in the volume of packaging.[419]

In *CECED* the Commission explicitly recognised environmental benefits as directly beneficial to consumers.[420] This decision involved an agreement for domestic washing machines set up by members of CECED, an association that comprises manufacturers of domestic appliances and national trade associations not to manufacture and import washing machines that do not meet a certain standard of energy efficiency. In order to assess whether an exemption should be granted, the Commission makes a distinction between individual economic benefits and collective environmental benefits. Regarding the individual economic benefits, even though the minimum price of washing machines is likely to increase, the price of washing machines in categories A and B, which are most efficient, is likely to decrease. Regarding the collective environmental benefits, the Commission refers to Article 174 EC including the principle that environmental damage should be rectified at source and states that "on the basis of reasonable assumptions, the benefits to society brought about by the CECED agreement appear to be more than seven times greater than the increased purchase costs of more energy-efficient washing machines. Such environmental results would adequately allow consumers a fair share of the benefits, even if no benefits accrued to individual purchasers of machines."[421] A similar approach can be found in the Guidelines on horizontal co-operation agreements where it is stated that "environmental agreements caught by Article 81(1) may attain economic benefits which, either at individual or aggregate consumer level,

---

418 Commission Decision 94/322, OJ 1994, L 144/20, paragraph 71.

419 Commission Decision 2001/837, OJ 2001, L 319/1, paragraph 148.

420 Commission Decision 2000/475, OJ 2000, L 187/47.

421 Commission Decision 2000/475, OJ 2000, L 187/47, paragraph 56; according to Maks the benefits for consumers are not at all clear, see J.A. Hans Maks, The "New" Horizontal Agreements Approach in the EU: an "economic" assessment, paper presented at the Workshop on Reform of EC Competition Policy Jointly organised by EIPA and HWWA, 10-11 December 2001, Maastricht, p. 15.

outweigh their negative effects on competition. To fulfil this condition there must be net benefits in terms of reduced environmental pressure resulting from the agreement, as compared to a baseline where no action is taken. In other words, the expected economic benefits must outweigh the costs."[422]

The *CECED* decision and the Guidelines obviously show that environmental protection requirements can be integrated into the definition and implementation of Community competition policy. Unfortunately, the Commission omits to refer to the integration principle as laid down in Article 6 EC, which would provide a more explicit legal basis to integrate environmental protection requirements into Article 81(3) EC.[423] Hence the extent to which environmental protection forms an (independent) ground of exemption remains not entirely clear, although the *CECED* decision is a step in the direction of directly balancing environmental aims with restrictions on competition. In fact the economic value of environmental benefits is now just as relevant to consumer welfare as productive efficiency.[424]

The proportionality test: the assessment of environmental agreements

In several decisions the Commission has been able to develop criteria for assessing environmental agreements under Article 81(3) EC. In the much-discussed *VOTOB* case the Commission refused to grant an exemption for a horizontal price fixing agreement. This case involved a uniform environmental charge, which was applied by the members of VOTOB, a Dutch association consisting of independent companies that offer tank storage facilities to third parties. The uniform fee was meant to cover the costs of the investments required to reduce vapour emissions from the members' storage tanks and to be paid by their customers. In 1989 the VOTOB members entered into a convenant concluded with the Dutch government, thereby accepting considerable reductions in the emission standards which apply to storage of volatile chemical and mineral oil products. VOTOB had hoped to obtain a tax relief from the Dutch government to finance 30% of its investment costs;, the government refused, however, and the VOTOB members had to organise the financing themselves. Firstly, the Commission declared the agreement to be contrary to Article 81(1) EC, because the agreement demanded a uniform charge – the environmental charge – to cover the costs of the investments required to reduce vapour emissions from the members' storage tanks and to be paid by their customers. Secondly, the agreement did not meet the requirements of Article 81(3) EC, and in fact the charge was considered disproportional to the aim of environmental protection. First, the surcharge is fixed and all members of VOTOB have to

[422] Guidelines on horizontal co-operation agreements, OJ 2001, C 3/2, paragraph 193.

[423] H.H.B. Vedder, De onvermijdelijke confrontatie – maar ook integratie? Over wasmachines, groene punten en auto's, *NTER*, 2000, p. 236.

[424] G. Monti, Article 81 EC and public policy, *CMLRev.*, 2002, p. 1075.

apply the charge regardless of their considerations. The separate invoicing of the charge makes it look like a tax or government imposed levy, rather than a negotiable component of the sales price. Competition on this price element is thus excluded. Second, the surcharge is uniform thus ignoring differences in each member's circumstances, which discourages members of VOTOB to seek more cost-efficient environmentally friendly investments. Eventually the case was settled after an agreement was reached between the VOTOB members and the Commission to incorporate the costs of their investments in their tariffs on an individual basis and to make clear for their clients that the surcharge forms a negotiable component of the tariff by abandoning the separate invoice.

Hence, the environment would thus have been better served by competition instead. Regardless of convincing arguments of the parties in this case, it may have been too early for the Commission to integrate environmental concerns in its decision practice.[425] After the 'convenant' between VOTOB and the Dutch government had been concluded, VOTOB asked for a tax relief. But the Dutch government told VOTOB to organise the financing themselves. The consequential surcharge was identical to the foregone tax relief (state aid), which would be permissible under the state aid Guidelines on the environment.[426] This aid program would have assisted the VOTOB members in complying with the 'convenant'. The problem here is that the VOTOB-agreements obviously concerned horizontal price fixing, a hard-core restriction, and thus regarded as disproportionate by the Commission. If VOTOB members had individually fixed an environmental surcharge in order to finance their convenant obligations, the agreement could probably have been granted an exemption on the basis of Article 81(3) EC.

In the Guidelines on horizontal co-operation agreements the Commission takes a more moderate approach towards uniform charges for waste collection. It does not exclude the possibility that agreements including uniform fees are eligible for an exemption, as long as it is shown that no other alternative means of attaining the expected environmental benefits exist which are less economically or financially costly.[427] In the recently adopted Directive on waste electrical and electronic equipment (WEEE), it is explicitly recognised that recycling schemes may be collectively organised and financed and that, for a transitional period, the costs of collection, treatment and disposal in an environmentally

---

[425] F.O.W. Vogelaar, Towards an Improved Integration of EC Environmental Policy and EC Competition Policy: An Interim Report, in: B.E. Hawk (Ed.), *Annual Proceedings of the Fordham Corporate Law Institute – International Antitrust Law and Policy 1994* (Kluwer Law International, The Hague, 1995), p. 549 et seq.

[426] L. Gyselen, The emerging interface between competition policy and environmental policy in the EC, in: J. Cameron, P. Demaret and D. Geradin (Eds), *Trade and the environment – the search for a balance* (Cameron May, London, 1995), at p. 252.

[427] Guidelines on horizontal co-operation agreements, OJ 2001, C 3/2, paragraph 196.

sound way may be declared separately.[428] Hence, the Directive explicitly recognises the self-regulatory approach in this respect. The WEEE Directive requires Member States to ensure that producers provide for the financing of collection, treatment, recovery and environmentally sound disposal of WEEE from private households. According to article 8 of the Directive producers can choose to fulfil this obligation either individually or by joining a collective scheme. Furthermore, the costs of collection, treatment and environmentally sound disposal shall not be shown separately to purchasers at the time of sale of new products. Nevertheless, during a transitional period producers are allowed to show the costs separately, which shall not exceed the actual costs incurred. The transitional period for imposing separate uniform fees seems to provide the producers with a means to attain the objective of a high level of collection, recovery and treatment of historical waste. Hence sustainable consumption is used as a means to attain greater environmental benefits.[429] This does not take away the producer responsibility for financing the management of the waste from his own products as stated in the preamble of the Directive.[430]

In examining whether the service agreement including the exclusivity clause concluded between *DSD* and the collectors was eventually justified in the light of Article 81(3) EC, the Commission argued that without the exclusivity clause it would not have been possible to set up a countrywide system of collection and that particularly in view of the packaging ordinance and the first time that such a large scale tack-back and exemption system has been set up, an exemption on the basis of Article 81(3) EC is justified. Nevertheless, in the future the Commission will not regard lifetime service agreements justified, but will consider agreements of up to three years reasonable and economically justified.[431]

In the *CECED* case the Commission examines whether there are no less restrictive alternatives that would be capable of delivering similar reductions of consumption of energy by washing machines. Three examples of possibly less restrictive alternatives are accordingly analysed by the Commission: the parties could limit the agreement to setting a more stringent industry-wide target; information campaigns could be used by the parties to the agreement and they could focus more on fulfilling EU eco-label criteria.[432] Non of these alternative measures would, according to the Commission, equally contribute to the attainment of environmental benefits as the present agreement does. It

[428] Directive 2002/96 on waste electrical and electronic equipment, OJ 2003, L 37/24, in particular article 8 thereof; see also Directive 2002/95 on the restriction of the use of certain hazardous substances in electrical and electronic equipment, OJ 2003, L 37/19.

[429] Compare H.H.B. Vedder with regard to the approach of the NMa in the case Stichting Wit – en Bruingoed, *M&M*, 2001, p. 257.

[430] Vedder (2003), p. 179.

[431] Commission Decision 2001/837, OJ 2001, L 319/1, paragraphs 156 and 157.

[432] Commission Decision 2000/475, OJ 2000, L 187/47, paragraphs 58-63.

can be concluded that the Commission was apparently quite eager to grant an exemption without providing for an in debt assessment of the proportionality of the measure. The necessity test employed in *CECED* can be compared to the application of the proportionality test in the context of free movement. The Commission does not intend to question the level of protection envisaged by the parties or, in other words, it does not question the proportionality *stricto sensu* of the agreement.[433] What is particularly important, though, is that collective environmental benefits will be taken into account to assess the proportionality of an agreement.[434] Furthermore, the cost-benefit analysis incorporates the assessment of the agreement's environmental impact in an objective manner.[435]

4.1.3.3 Consumer protection

The protection of consumers as ground for exemption

Contrary to the environmental field, the consumer is explicitly mentioned by Article 81(3) EC. As will be considered below in several decisions the Commission has sought to align environmental interests with consumer interests. The consumer within the context of Article 81(3) EC does not necessarily refer to the end-user only, but to all customers, meaning not only the consumers within the Member State concerned by the agreement, but all consumers throughout the Community.[436] Article 81(3) EC does not necessarily focus on a rather narrow consumer perspective, taking into account the economic interests of consumers, it has been increasingly important to assess the relationship between consumer interest and competition policy from a broader perspective, taking into account health and safety of consumers and the imperative demands of sustainable consumption.[437] Furthermore, apart from the fact that the consumer is mentioned by Article 81(3) EC, the condition that the agreement contributes to technical and economic progress also includes consumer

---

433 Vedder (2003), p. 177.

434 D. Geradin, EC Competition Law and Environmental Protection: Conflict or Compatibility?, in: H. Somsen (Ed.), *Yearbook of European Environmental Law* (Oxford University Press, Oxford, 2002), p. 132.

435 D. Geradin, EC Competition Law and Environmental Protection: Conflict or Compatibility?, in: H. Somsen (Ed.), *Yearbook of European Environmental Law* (Oxford University Press, Oxford, 2002), p. 132; G. Monti, Article 81 EC and public policy, *CMLRev.*, 2002, p. 1075.

436 Faull & Nikpay (1999), p. 111.

437 See also G. Monti, Article 81 EC and public policy, *CMLRev.*, 2002, p. 1075; S. de Vries, Consumer Interests and the Dutch Competition Act: an ambivalent relationship?, *TvC*, 2002, p. 161; see also Cseres (2005), pp. 258-261. Cseres, however, notes at p. 270 that "consumer protection in its broad meaning is not a goal of competition policy. Consumer measures concerning health, safety and information disclosure are public policy considerations that may be analysed or even recognised in competition cases but will not represent overriding concerns."

protection. This is the case where technological improvement may include better service or increased safety for the consumer.[438]

It can be disputed whether indirect benefits fall under the second condition of Article 81(3) EC like environmental benefits for society, which would adequately allow consumers a fair share of the benefits, even if no benefits accrued to individual persons of washing machines (see above). The conclusion of the Commission in *CECED* has been criticised, because Article 81(3) EC requires the assessment of direct benefits to consumers and not to the public as a whole.[439] Environmental protection can, however, also be considered as directly beneficial.[440] For that matter, in *Exxon/Shell* the Commission considered that the environmental advantages "will be perceived as beneficial by many consumers at a time when the limitation of natural resources and threats to the environment are of increasing public concern".[441]

The proportionality test: the assessment of agreements with a view to the interest of consumers

Restrictions on competition must be indispensable to the attainment of *inter alia* benefits which are passed on to consumers. However, the Commission does not often consider the consumer benefit as a separately identifiable interest, but rather identifies consumer advantages as part of the economic advantages of the co-operation.[442] Several decisions in the field of the environment as discussed before, such as *CECED* and *DSD*, indicate that the Commission will not always regard the reduction of costs for consumers as a constitutive element of the indispensability requirement; also the improvement of environmental quality may be considered beneficial to consumers, even if – in the short run – this may lead to price increases.

Agreements are particularly beneficial to consumers where they result in a new product or better services for them. In *Olivetti-Digital* the Commission considered that the restrictive obligations in a co-operation agreement between Olivetti and Digital in the field of computer systems were indispensable because they were the only way in which the identified benefits to consumers could be ensured.[443] According to the agreement Digital was to make available to Olivetti its AXP technology and Olivetti would commit itself to the Alpha AXP technology for all its computer platform offerings and related software except the line

[438] Commission Decision 94/89, *Asahi/Saint-Gobain*, on agreements aimed at research and development in a bi-layer technology and products derived therefrom for safety glazing in, for example, cars, OJ 1994, L 354/87, paragraphs 24-26; see also G. Monti, Article 81 EC and public policy, *CMLRev.*, 2002, p. 1075.

[439] G. Monti, Article 81 EC and public policy, *CMLRev.*, 2002, p. 1077.

[440] Bellamy & Child (2001), p. 172.

[441] Commission Decision 94/332, OJ 1994, L 144/20.

[442] Howells and Weatherill (2005), p. 534.

[443] Commission Decision 94/771, OJ 1994, L 309/24.

of products based on Intel-type microprocessors. Particularly the purchase commitment to this technology would restrict competition within the meaning of Article 81(1) EC, but thanks to this commitment Digital would be able to produce more of the innovative product Alpha AXP at lower cost which is beneficial to consumers.

Another example is the *P&O Stena Line* case which involved the creation of a joint venture (P&O Stena Line) by the companies P&O and Stena Line AB for the ferry operations on the Short French Sea and Belgian Straits. According to the Commission this would lead to an increase in the frequency of crossings and to major cost savings which is in the interest of consumers. Lesser forms of co-operation would according to the Commission be unlikely to lead to the same benefits.[444]

4.1.3.4 Public health

As stated before in respect of the competition rules and the state the field of public health encompasses health care and public health *stricto sensu.*

The protection of public health stricto sensu *as ground for exemption*

According to the Commission competition policy is particularly relevant for the pharmaceutical product sector. Funding of research and development may be an incentive for stronger co-operation between undertakings. On the ground that the agreements or restrictive practices by undertakings pursue benefits for public health in general or benefits for the health of a particular group of persons the Commission may grant an exemption on the basis of Article 81(3) EC, referring to the condition of promoting technical or economic progress. In the *Pasteur Mérieux-Merck* case the Commission regarded an agreement relating to activities in human vaccines to contribute to technical progress and improvements in distribution.[445] This case involved the agreements adopted by Pasteur Mérieux Sérums et Vaccins and Merck & Co. Inc. with a view to jointly organise their existing activities in the field of human vaccines and some related business. The Commission examined whether the agreement fell within the scope of Article 81(3) EC and could be granted an exemption. It recognised that the agreement led to a qualitative promotion of technical progress, which consisted of advantages in the field of health. Furthermore, with regard to benefits to the consumer the Commission considered that the achievement of technical progress and improvements in distribution respond to a *genuine public health concern*. According to the Commission the development of accurate, stable and

---

[444] Commission Decision 99/421, OJ 1999, L 163/61.

[445] Commission Decision 94/770, OJ 1994, L 309/1.

easy to administer vaccines are beneficial for public health, and therefore also for consumers.[446]

Arguments related to the protection of public health can thus be taken into account within the context of Article 81(3) EC.

Health care policy considerations as grounds for exemption

Where Community competition policy plays an obvious role in the pharmaceutical product sector, however, this role is less evident in the health care sector. The question that has until now been left unanswered is whether health care policy considerations can also be taken into account under Article 81(3) EC. The applicability *ratione materiae* and *ratione personae* of the competition rules to the health care sector is not self-evident, particularly since the Court's judgment in *AOK*. The Court has demonstrated a willingness to take into account the special features of the health care sector already at the first stage of the assessment under Article 81 EC;[447] the question as to the scope of Article 81(3) EC has therefore, at least with regard to health insurance, become less imminent. The decisions taken in a collective manner by the (German) sickness funds, however, must be consistent with the rules on free movement.[448]

If health care organisations are nonetheless to be regarded as undertakings, Article 86(2) EC will be an exception ground, since they are entrusted with general interest tasks (see above, section 3.2.3.4). If, on the other hand, agreements are concluded between, for example, private health insurers or between general practitioners, Article 86(2) EC will probably not apply; instead the conditions of Article 81(3) EC will have to be fulfilled. It can be argued that at least on the basis of the integration clause health care considerations must play a role in the assessment of a restrictive agreement under Article 81(3) EC.

Apart from the *AOK* case there are no cases on the relationship between public health and Article 81 EC. The decision practice of the Netherlands Competition Authority (NMa) may therefore be illustrative as to how health policy considerations can or cannot play a role in the application of the Competition Act. The NMa Guidelines for the health care sector state what agreements restrain competition and what agreements may obtain an exemption.[449] Remark-

---

[446] Commission Decision 94/770, OJ 1994, L309/1, paragraphs 83- 89.

[447] S. Belhaj and J. W. van de Gronden, Some Room for Competition Does Not Make a Sickness Fund An Undertaking. Is EC Competition Law Applicable to the Health Care Sector? (Joined cases C-264/01, C-306/01, C-453/01 and C-355/01, *AOK*), *ECLR*, 2004, p..686; M. Krajewski and M. Farley, Limited competition in national health systems and the application of competition law: the *AOK Bundesverband* case, *ELRev.*, 2004, p. 849.

[448] The sickness funds in determining the maximum amount of reimbursement for medical products in a collective manner in fact comply with the strict criteria set by German legislation and may therefore contravene Article 28 EC. However, it will be difficult to prove that such (price) measures will eventually violate Article 28 EC: annotation B.J. Drijber, *CMLRev.*, 2005, pp. 530-531.

[449] www.nma-org.nl; see also press release, "NMa Approves Guidelines for the Healthcare Sector", 25 October 2002.

ably, though, they do not refer to public health policy considerations within the framework of Article 17 CA. In fact the NMa seems to have a rather narrow and certainly economically-oriented view towards the conditions of Article 17 CA. This becomes particularly clear from the decision in *Zorgverzekeraars Nederland-Solidariteitsprotocol.*[450] This case involved the so-called 'Solidarity protocol' set up by the members of the Dutch association for private health insurers (ZN), which contains both a provision for a range of premiums (premiebandbreedte-regeling) as well as a provision for the relationship between collective and individual contracts of health insurers to prevent that collective contracts are financed by the higher premiums normally requested for individual contracts (premium subsidy scheme, or premiesubsidieregeling). According to the 'premiebandbreedte-regeling' the premiums to be paid by the highest age category of policyholders should not be more than 150% of the premium to be paid by a 20 year old policyholder with less health risks. The health insurers argued that the aim of the 'premiebandbreedte-regeling' is essentially to prevent the further increase of premiums to be paid by the elderly and to give transparency in the management of insurances. The aim of the 'premiesubsidieregeling' is to strengthen the solidarity between individually and collectively insured policyholders, which is beneficial for society as a whole. According to the health insurers these aims contribute to the promotion of technical and economic progress, the first condition of Article 17 CA. However, the NMa did not accept these arguments and came to the conclusion that neither the 'premiebandbreedte-regeling' contributes to the promotion of technical and economic progress and that it is not up to the insurers to decide what range of premiums is in the interest of society, nor does the 'premiesubsidieregeling', since it was not proved that this provision would lead to lower premiums for individual products.[451] Particularly the view of the NMa that it is not up to private insurers to restrict competition for the benefit of society calls to mind the former approach of the Commission in the Dutch-Flemish book pricing case, the *VBBB/VBVB* case, where the Commission held that it is not up to private undertakings to engage in cultural questions (see hereafter, section 4.1.3.5), and strongly contrasts with the present approach of the Commission and the jurisprudence of the Court leaving more scope for other non-competition and – for the society beneficial – public interests.

---

450 Case 2605/31, *Zorgverzekeraars Nederland – Solidariteitsprotocol,* 16 December 2002. See also Van de Gronden (2004), p. 45.

451 Case 2605/31, paragraphs 116-137; see with regard to the critical attitude of the NMa to self-regulation in the health care sector: Van de Gronden (2004), p. 45.

The proportionality test: the assessment of agreements in the field of public health stricto sensu

The *Pasteur Mérieux-Merck* case provides an example of how the Commission assesses the indispensability of an agreement in the field of public health. The establishment of a joint venture with a view to organize their activities in the area of human vaccines was, according to the Commission, the only mechanism flexible enough to develop a wide range of vaccines adapted to the needs of different European countries. The more far-reaching co-operation through the establishment of a joint venture would enable the parties to adapt to unforeseen or new circumstances resulting from the continuous exchange of information between the parties.[452]

The proportionality test: the assessment of agreements in the health care sector

With regard to agreements adopted in the health care sector the decision practice of the NMa and the Guidelines show to what extent agreements between organizations active in the market of health care infringe the cartel prohibition of Article 6 CA and could be exempted under Article 17 CA.[453] With regard to horizontal agreements between healthcare providers and health insurers the Guidelines distinguish between agreements which contain hardcore restrictions, such as agreements on prices and tariffs, agreements to divide markets and coordinated boycott campaigns, which are incompatible with Article 6 CA and are not eligible for an exemption, agreements which normally do not restrict competition within the meaning of Article 6 CA, agreements which fall within the scope of a block exemption and other forms of horizontal co-operation which may lead to a restriction of competition. With regard to vertical agreements in the health care sector the Guidelines distinguish between agreements which infringe Article 6 CA and can normally not obtain an exemption, such as vertical price fixing or absolute territorial protection, agreements which fall within the scope of a block exemption and other forms of co-operation which may lead to a restriction of competition.

In the decision in *Zorgverzekeraars Nederland-Solidariteitsprotocol* the NMa argued that the health insurers had not proven that there were no less restrictive means available to attain the objective of premium solidarity. Does this imply that if the health insurers had been able to show that the 'premiebandbreedteregeling' en de 'premiesubsidieregeling' were the only means available to attain this objective, the NMa would have granted an exemption?[454] The references made by the NMa to relevant literature, where alternatives for the Solidarity protocol are presented, and to legislation suggest, however, that the NMa was not really convinced from the outset that the Solidarity protocol was proportional to its aims.

---

[452] Commission Decision 94/770, OJ 1994, L 309/1, paragraphs 91-94.

[453] Richtsnoeren voor de zorgsector (Guidelines for the health care sector), to be found at: www.nma-org.nl.

[454] Annotation J.W. van de Gronden, *RZA*, 2003, pp. 246-249.

4.1.3.5 Culture

The protection of culture as ground for exemption

Article 81 EC has played a particularly important role in the context of book pricing agreements. Depending on the type of agreement, cultural arguments play a role in the assessment of compliance of restrictive agreements with the conditions of Article 81(3) EC. Cultural interests are, however, very diverse and include the protection of public service broadcasting, the promotion of distribution and production of books, the plurality of the media etc. In the field of resale price maintenance for books, the Commission is extremely reluctant to even consider cultural interests within the context of Article 81(3) EC, whereas in the field of public service broadcasting restrictive agreements are almost without hesitation exempted from the cartel prohibition on cultural grounds. The difference in assessment can be explained at least partly by the fact that vertical price agreements are considered as hardcore restrictions which are, regardless of the aim of the agreements, generally not eligible for an exemption. Nevertheless, the decisions on book pricing agreements show that the Commission's attitude has slightly changed over the years. It is now clear that national systems of fixed book prices are, according to the Commission, not incompatible with Community law, even if provisions are made to prevent the re-importation of books undermining the national price cartel.

In the field of book pricing agreements cultural arguments may play a role in the context of the first condition, the agreement must contribute to an improvement of the production and distribution of goods. The Commission has never found evidence that such agreements indeed do contribute to an improvement of the production and distribution of books. Does the Commission hereby implicitly acknowledge that cultural concerns play a role in granting an exemption on the basis of Article 81(3) EC? The remark of the Commission in the *VBVB/VBBB* case on a trans-national book pricing agreement in the Dutch language area – that it is not up to private undertakings to engage in cultural questions – has not been repeated in following decisions.[455] Arguments in favour of resale price maintenance for books point at the protection of small booksellers against larger businesses which may sell books at strongly reduced prices, at the possibility of offering a wide selection of titles, and at the argument of cross-subsidization, whereby less popular books are subsidised by the more profitable ones.[456] In legal and economic literature the effectiveness of resale

---

[455] Commission Decision 82/123, VBVB/VBBB, OJ 1982, L 54/36.

[456] The main economic arguments in favour of book price agreements can be summarised as follows:

- they reduce distribution costs per unit of sales;
- resale price maintenance may lead to wider display and encourage wider stockholding;
- if resale price maintenance leads to lower costs, this must also benefit the consumers.

The main reasons against are:

price maintenance is heavily debated. Proponents of fixed prices for books point to the definite cultural risks of abolishing a system of fixed prices for books as opposed to the hypothetical economic risks of maintaining such a system.[457] Others argue, for example, that fixed book prices are merely an artificial means designed to sustain an expensive system run by retailers.[458] In *VBBB/VBVB* Advocate-General VerLoren van Themaat more profoundly addressed the cultural question, but eventually came to the conclusion that cultural consequences of an agreement can only be taken into account in a negative sense; that no cultural values are destroyed. Besides there can never be any question of an absolute priority of cultural over economic considerations. The Court of Justice finally held that the specific nature of books as an object of trade may justify certain special conditions in the matter of distribution and price.[459] In spite of the negative outcome of the case, it appears to have been a first step in the direction of cultural arguments contributing to an exemption on the basis of Article 81(3) EC.

In the *Sammelrevers* case on the German-Austrian system of fixed book prices the Commission in its provisional conclusion acknowledges the importance of books as cultural medium, but maintains its view that book price agreements cannot qualify for an exemption under Article 81(3) EC.[460] Nevertheless, the fact that the promotion of the distribution and production of books is an aim which directly falls within the scope of Article 81(3) EC is beyond doubt. However, the problem is, according to the Commission, first that it cannot be proved that a causal connection exists between a system of fixed prices and its cultural aim and second, that there are other less restrictive systems available to improve the distribution and production of books (see hereafter). Meanwhile the cross-border agreements for price fixing between Austrian publishers and German booksellers and between German publishers and Austrian booksellers have been abolished. A new German system of fixed book prices limited to agreements between German publishers and German booksellers was notified to the Commission. German books re-imported into Germany from another

---

- the elimination of price competition tends to reduce efficiency;
- in stead of price competition, other forms of competition may originate such as service competition which the consumer is obliged to pay for;
- resale price maintenance may facilitate collusion among producers themselves.

From Fishwick (1989): he made a thorough analysis of the economic implications of the Net Book Agreement. For that matter in some Member States fixed book prices may be more economically beneficial, whereas in others this may not be the case: Langbein (1989), p. 123.

457 See also Opinion of AG Darmon in Case 229/83, *Leclerc*; see, for example, Everling (1997), pp. 1-61.

458 Mok, Naar een wettelijke vaste boekenprijs? Een initiatiefvoorstel, *Ondernemingsrecht*, 2003, p. 7. See for a critical but subtle view also: M. Appelman and M. Canoy, Notes and communications – Horses for courses: why Europe should not harmonise its book prices, *De Economist*, 2002, pp. 583-600.

459 Joined Cases 43/82 and 63/82, *VBVB/VBBB*.

460 DN: IP/98/30.

Member State are in principle not subject to the retail price maintenance, unless it is clear that these books were exported from Germany solely for the purpose of being re-imported in order to circumvent the *Sammelrevers* price system – the so-called U-turn construction (see in the context of the free movement rules, Chapter 2). The Commission did not object to this system since it had no appreciable effect on trade between Member States and therefore did not fall under Article 81(1) EC.[461]

Apparently the call from the Council to take account of the integration clause as laid down in Article 151(4) EC and the cultural aspects of trans-national book price agreements was not answered by the Commission.[462] The approach of the Commission is more in line with the Council resolution on the application of national fixed book-price systems, wherein the Commission is called upon to pay particular attention to *inter alia* the risk of the development of evasion.[463] On the one hand it can be argued that the Commission takes account of the national cultural interest, from a perspective of subsidiarity, since national book price agreements are tolerated, even if they contain provisions to prevent evasion. On the other hand the approach of the Commission can be criticised as formalistic, or jurisdictional.[464] The Commission is not willing to really integrate cultural interests in Article 81(3) EC where book price agreements are involved.

In contrast where public service broadcasting is involved the cultural arguments have been given considerably more weight in the application of Article 81(3) EC to restrictive agreements. This most notably appears from the *Métropole* case (see also section 4.1.3.1).[465] Two commercial broadcasting companies applied for membership of the EBU, the European Broadcasting Union, with a view to get access to Eurovision programmes. But their application was refused because they did not meet the following criteria for membership:

- The broadcasting organisation is under an obligation to cover the entire population;
- They are under an obligation to provide a varied and balanced program-

[461] Notice pursuant to Article 19(3) of Council Regulation No 17 concerning an application for negative clearance or exemption under Article 81(3) of the EC Treaty (Sammelrevers and Einzelreverse), OJ 2000, C 162/25.

[462] Council Resolution on fixed book prices in homogeneous cross-border linguistic areas, OJ 1999, C42/3; see also S. de Vries, Cultuur en mededinging: harmonie of dissonantie?, in: J.W. van de Gronden and K.J.M. Mortelmans (Eds), *Mededinging en niet-economische belangen* (Kluwer, Deventer, 2001), p. 107.

[463] OJ 2001, C 73/5.

[464] G. Monti, Article 81 EC and public policy, *CMLRev.*, 2002, pp. 1085-1086: he regards the decision problematic both from a legal perspective, since the German system affects trade between Member States on the basis of the Court's jurisprudence, as well as from a policy perspective, since the decision is jurisdictional rather than an example of the Commission's willingness to confront the market versus culture debate.

[465] Joined Cases T-528/93, T-542/93, T-543/93 and T-546/93, *Métropole Télévision (Métropole I)*; see also M.G. Wezenbeek-Geuke, Métropole Télévision e.a.; de strijd om de sportprogramma's, *NTER*, 1996, p. 241.

ming for all sections of the population, including a fair share of the programmes catering for special or minority interests of various sections of the public, irrespective of the ratio of the programmes broadcast;
- They actually produce under their own editorial control a substantial proportion of the programmes broadcast.

In the following procedure, the Commission provided an exemption of the EBU agreements under Article 81(3) EC and held that the particular features of the economic sector in which the – public or private – undertakings operate and the burdens to and incumbent upon them should be taken into account under Article 81(3) EC, without prejudice to the specific provisions of Article 86(2) EC. On appeal the CFI argued that, even though the Commission may base its decision on considerations related to the general interest, and more in particular cultural reasons, the Commission had brought factors of Article 86(2) EC within the ambit of Article 81(3) EC, without examining the conditions of this provision. As a consequence the Court annulled the Commission's decision.

In the following decision of 2000 the Commission in its assessment of the Eurovision system under Article 81(3) EC once again took into account cultural and sports interests. Regarding the improvement of the distribution of goods, the Commission held that "without the Eurovision rules which lead to the sharing of rights and the alternation of the transmission of an event by the members concerned, there would be less coverage of the event in question. [...] This sharing means that the alternating members can guarantee quasi-permanent coverage of the sporting event in question, for example, of the Olympic Games."[466] Furthermore, the Commission held with regard to the benefit of the Eurovision system to consumers that "as a result of the joint acquisition of rights, the participants in the Eurovision system can show more and higher quality sports programmes, both popular sports and minority sports, to European television viewers. In particular, national participants in the joint acquisition from smaller countries can provide their chair viewers with a broad range of international sporting events with a commentary in their own language and tailored to their specific national interests."[467] Hence, the conditions of Article 81(3) EC were broadly interpreted, so as to take into account the cultural interest and the interest of society as a whole in the broadcasting of major sports events. Nevertheless, the Court of First Instance also annulled this decision, without considering the horizontal and flanking policy aims of the Eurovision system.[468]

---

[466] Commission Decision 2000/400, *Eurovision*, OJ 2000, L 151/18, paragraph 88.

[467] Commission Decision 2000/400, *Eurovision*, OJ 2000, L 151/18, paragraph 91.

[468] Joined Cases T-185/00, T-216/00, T-299/00 and T-300/00, *Métropole II*; see also J. van de Gronden & K. Mortelmans, Mededinging en algemene belangen: welke signalen geeft de Europese rechter in de Eurovisiezaak?, *Mediaforum*, 2003, pp. 11-20. According to Bailey the two *Métropole* cases indicate a trend to a more conscientious and robust review by the CFI of whether the Commission has lawfully applied Article 81(3) EC: David Bailey, Scope of judicial review under Article 81 EC, *CMLRev.*, 2004, p. 1351.

Cultural interests can thus play a role within the context of Article 81(3) EC, but, as shown by the cases on resale price maintenance for books and the recent judgment of the CFI in *Métropole II*, the significance of cultural policy considerations in the application of Article 81(3) EC to restrictive agreements is not always recognised. From the first *Métropole I* judgment it can be seen that cultural interest goals are relevant within the context of Article 81(3) EC but cannot outweigh the indispensability requirements.[469]

The assessment of cultural agreements: the proportionality test

How the proportionality test can play a significant role in the assessment of book price agreements within the context of Article 81(3) EC is particularly shown by the Commission's notice on the *Sammelrevers* case. First, it was held that no causal connection exists between a system of fixed prices and the improvement in the production and distribution of books. Within this context the Commission refers to countries where fixed prices have been abolished, such as Sweden, Belgium, Finland and the United Kingdom, and where, according to the Commission, the production and distribution of books have not been damaged. This reference is rather odd. In Sweden, for example, a discussion started some years ago as to the possible re-introduction of a fixed price for books,[470] whereas in the United Kingdom recent studies show that the abolishment of fixed prices did not result in lower, but overall higher prices of books.[471] Second, the Commission refers to alternative systems which may be equally effective, but less restrictive to competition: "The Commission takes the view that alternative mechanisms are available which are less objectionable from the point of view of competition policy: publishers and booksellers could contribute to a fund to support more demanding literary works; targeted and selective direct aid could be given; discounts could be quality-based rather than quantity-based; or indeed there could be a selective distribution system designed to encourage works with a strong cultural element." Unfortunately, since the Commission adopted no formal decision these arguments were not examined in detail.

The generally rigid approach of the Commission in the field of book pricing agreements does not always correspond to the approach of the Court. The latter does not regard it as self-evident that resale price maintenance could never contribute to the aims mentioned by Article 81(3) EC. In the *Binon* case concerning the establishment of a selective distribution system for newspapers and magazines, the Court made clear that if price fixing "constitutes the sole method by which a wide selection of newspapers and periodicals is available to readers,

---

[469] Goyder (2003), at p. 134.

[470] See also Boken i Tiden – Betänkande från utredningen om boken och kulturtidskriften, *SOU* 1997: 141.

[471] See also R. Mulder, Beleid wereldwijd – Boekenprijzen in het Verenigd Koninkrijk, *ESB*, 1999, p. 455; he refers to Fishwick (1998); see also Langbein (1989).

the Commission must take account of those factors when examining an agreement for the purposes of Article 81(3)".[472] According to the Court in the *Publishers Association* case the Commission should have examined the decision of the UK Restrictive Practices Court, and more in particular the situation on the Irish market.[473] The Restrictive Practices Court had held that a collective enforcement system was necessary for the maintenance of fixed prices. Moreover the Commission should have considered that the United Kingdom and Ireland form one language area. Furthermore the Court held that the reference to the VBVB/VBBB-case is "manifestly inappropriate", as the system designed by the Dutch and Flemish associations of booksellers and publishers differed from the system set up by the Net Book Agreements (NBA). The NBA provide uniform standard conditions for the sale of books at a fixed price, which apply only if the publishers choose to market a book as a net book. The VBVB/VBBB-agreement, on the other hand, concerned a collective resale price maintenance scheme, including an obligation for publishers to fix a retail price. This formal difference did not seem to be proved by the facts though.[474]

In the *Eurovision* decision the Commission examined whether the Eurovision rules were necessary to guarantee the solidarity between the members of EBU. According to the Commission "if the EBU members were forced to negotiate separately for television rights, were not to agree on the sharing of the rights or were not to offer the signal free of charge, the solidarity system would be jeopardised and with it all the objectives in terms of improvement of distribution and benefits to consumers".[475] The Court of First Instance only implicitly touched upon the question of proportionality by examining whether the Commission rightly assessed the fourth condition of Article 81(3) EC. In its judgment on the first decision in *Métropole* the CFI held that the Commission should have shown that considerations of the particular public mission required exclusivity of rights to transmit sports events, and that the requirement of indispensability should be fulfilled. According to the Court the Commission's decision should have been based on a minimum of actual economic data. Thus the Court in fact required the Commission to carefully assess the proportionality of the EBU membership rules.

4.1.4 Conclusions

The cartel prohibition of Article 81(1) EC leaves little scope for the consideration of horizontal and flanking policy interests. Within the context of a broader economic assessment of restrictive agreements horizontal and

[472] Case 243/83, *Binon*.

[473] Case C-360/92 P, *Publishers' Association*.

[474] Annotation M.R. Mok, *SEW*, 1996, p. 141: He noted that a vast majority of publishers regarded their books as net-books: 94%.

[475] Commission Decision 2000/400, OJ 2000, L 151/18, paragraph 94.

flanking policy concerns can only play a modest role in the background. However, the inherent restriction approach and in particular the *Wouters* judgment undoubtedly allow for the consideration of horizontal and flanking policy aims within the framework of Article 81(1) EC. The 'Cassis-type rule of reason' in *Wouters* even potentially opens the door wide open to all kinds of public interests being brought into Article 81(1) EC; nonetheless, the implications of this judgment seem so far limited to the sector of professional services.

At the same time more weight is increasingly being given to the consideration of horizontal and flanking policy goals in the application of Article 81(3) EC. In the field of the environment this development has been most remarkable culminating in the Guidelines on horizontal co-operation agreements and the *CECED* decision. At the same time we see that in other areas the significance of horizontal and flanking policy goals within the context of Article 81(3) EC is less clear due to a number of reasons. With regard to agreements in the field of *public health*, particularly where they concern the provision of health care, the application of competition rules to this sector is still in its infancy. So far it can be concluded from the practice of the Dutch Competition Authority that, according to its view where competition between health care institutions is made possible, the competition rules apply as they do to other (normal) sectors of the economy. The *AOK* judgment may, at least in respect of the health insurance sector, have put this view into perspective.

Cultural policy considerations may also contribute to granting an exemption, but in whatever degree remains unclear. The cases on book pricing agreements seem to suggest that not cultural arguments but other more formal or jurisdictional arguments have induced the Commission to eventually tolerate national book pricing agreements. The Commission seems to have chosen to leave national book pricing agreements to the discretion of the national authorities in the Member States. The more striking is therefore the approach of the Commission with regard to public service broadcasting, where it was very eager to apply Article 81(3) EC to the restrictive practices of public service broadcasters. In any event the integration clause requires an assessment of the impact of restrictive agreements on culture also in the case of book pricing agreements. The Commission cannot ignore the cultural arguments which are raised in the context of Article 81(3) EC by simply stating that it is not up to private companies to engage in cultural matters.

The crucial question is therefore how restrictions on competition should be balanced with horizontal and flanking policy considerations. There is an important difference between applying Article 81(3) EC and the exceptions to free movement. In applying Article 81(3) EC the Commission "must operate within a rigid conceptual framework which [...] requires the restriction to pass [...] a cumulative series of four separate tests".[476] In applying the exceptions to restric-

[476] Goyder (2003), p. 127.

tions on free movement the Court applies a balancing test with a key role for the principle of proportionality. Compared with this balancing exercise how rigid is then the conceptual framework of Article 81(3) EC? It has been submitted that the proportionality test plays an essential role also in the context of Article 81(3) EC. The difference is, however, that the Commission cannot restrain itself by merely balancing the public interest goals of the agreement with its restrictive effects on competition, but should at least conduct some economic assessment by examining the efficiency gains of the agreement (*Métropole I* case). This entails a proportionality test *stricto sensu* whereby an exemption will not be granted if the level of protecting horizontal and flanking policy interests is unreasonable in the light of the restriction of competition (see also Chapter 2, section 4.3.3). In its Guidelines on the application of Article 81(3) of the Treaty the Commission admits that a strict approach is desirable: "Goals pursued by other Treaty provisions can be taken into account to the extent that they can be subsumed under the four conditions of Article 81(3)."[477] If the Commission acts beyond this policy of subsuming general interest goals under the four conditions, the Court will probably blow the whistle on the Commission.

4.2 Article 82: the prohibition on abuse of a dominant position

In this section it will be shown whether and if so to what extent in the application of Article 82 EC, which prohibits the abuse of a dominant position by one or more undertakings, horizontal and flanking policy considerations can be taken into account. The fact that unilateral action by individual firms also aims at the realisation of horizontal and flanking policy goals has, however, no bearing on the *prima facie* applicability of Article 82 EC. As stated before, irrespective of their aim, such activities will fall within the personal and material scope of the competition rules.

In the following and after a few examples of unilateral action where horizontal and flanking policy considerations play a role, the concepts of dominance and abuse will be considered. Article 82 EC does not, contrary to Article 81 EC, contain an explicit exception for abusive behaviour.

4.2.1 The scope of Article 82 EC: abusive behaviour and horizontal and flanking policy considerations.

A broadcasting company having a monopoly over television programme information, may make abuse of its dominant position if it refuses to licence this information to third parties. An undertaking operating an extensive system for the collection and recovery of sales packaging (DSD, see hereafter) and having a dominant position, will be required to refrain from excessive

[477] OJ 2004, C 101/97, paragraph 42.

pricing or predatory pricing and may be required to give access to third parties to their collection and recycling scheme. Pharmaceutical companies using intellectual property rights to prevent newcomers from entering the market may make abuse of their dominant position.[478] Abuse of a dominant position may also occur where a dominant firm provides a broad range of market research, marketing, and sales management services to the pharmaceutical industry based on a 'brick structure', which is protected by national copyright law and is essential for competing on a given market, and for which the firm refuses to grant licence.[479] Health care institutions purchasing care from health care providers, such as doctors, are often in a dominant position. If they do not offer all doctors the option to enter into contracts with them, they may make abuse of their dominant position.[480] Undertakings granted with exclusive rights for the performance of horizontal and flanking activities have a legal monopoly and are therefore considered to be in a dominant position within the meaning of Article 82 EC. These are just a few examples of situations where Article 82 EC could play a role, and where horizontal and flanking policy considerations, such as the maintenance of a plural media system, the protection of the environment and public health concerns, can be brought to the fore.

4.2.2 The abuse of a dominant position

Article 82 EC prohibits the abuse of a dominant position within the common market or in a substantial part of it insofar as it may affect trade between Member States. Article 82 EC places particular obligations on undertakings having a dominant position, or according to the ECJ in *Michelin* "the undertaking concerned has a special responsibility not to allow its conduct to impair genuine undistorted competition in the common market".[481] In assessing whether the two conditions of dominance and abuse are fulfilled on the basis of economic factors, there is hardly room to take account of horizontal and flanking policy considerations under Article 82 EC. Nevertheless, there are two possibilities to take to some extent account of horizontal and flanking policy considerations within the context of Article 82 EC:[482] first, the concept of 'objective justification' entails that conduct which appears to be abusive, will not be prohibited by Article 82 EC, if objectively justified; and second, Article 86(2) EC is relevant for dominant firms entrusted with tasks of general economic

[478] Mossialos & McKee (with W. Palm, B. Karl and F. Marhold) (2002), p. 175.

[479] Case C-418/01, *IMS Health*.

[480] Mossialos & McKee (with W. Palm, B. Karl and F. Marhold) (2002), p. 178.

[481] Case 322/81, *Michelin*, paragraph 57.

[482] Whether the inherent restriction approach which was developed within the context of Article 81 EC also applies to Article 82 EC is unsure. The considerations of the Court in Case C-250/92, *Gøttrup-Klim*, paragraph 50, may confirm this view.

interests. This provision was extensively discussed before and will therefore not be dealt with at this stage.

4.2.2.1 Dominance

The concept of dominance is defined in case law as "a position of economic strength enjoyed by an undertaking which enables it to prevent effective competition being maintained on the relevant market by giving it the power to behave to an appreciable extent independently of its competitors, customers and ultimately of its consumers".[483] In order to determine whether a company has a dominant position within the meaning of Article 82 EC it is first necessary to define the relevant market, which consists of the product market and the geographic market.

The product market

According to the Commission notice on the definition of the relevant market for the purposes of Community competition law the relevant product market "comprises all those products and/or services which are regarded as interchangeable or substitutable by the consumer, by reason of the products characteristics, their prices and their intended use".[484] Substitutability is the most important factor for the definition of the relevant product market. Substitutability can be determined from the demand side perspective, what products in particular consumers consider as substitutable, and from the supply side perspective, whether it is possible to switch production in the short term and whether the producer incurs significant risks or costs by switching its production.

Hence, the relevant product market is defined according to economic factors. Horizontal and flanking policy concerns could within this economic context also play a role in the definition of the relevant market. In the field of the environment, for example, if an undertaking seeks to distinguish its environmentally friendly products from other products, it is less likely for these products to be interchangeable with other environmentally more harmful products. The relevant product market would then be the market for environmentally friendly or eco-products, which implies that the undertaking involved is more likely to have a dominant position within the meaning of Article 82 EC.[485] Eventually, though, the consumer's willingness to pay more for the production costs of an environmentally friendly product will decide whether there can be a separate product market. Environmental concerns may also play a role from the perspective of the

---

[483] Case 85/76, *Hoffman-La Roche*, paragraph 38.

[484] OJ 1997, C 372/5, point 7.

[485] H.G. Sevenster and H.H.B. Vedder, Integreren of concurreren?, *SEW*, 2000, p. 8.

supply side substitutability. The production of an environmentally friendly product may require a completely different method of production, which indicates a separate product market for environmentally friendly products.[486] In the field of waste the product market is also narrowly defined, depending on special characteristics of waste, the technical characteristics of the market and the legislative framework.[487] In *Dusseldorp* the exclusive right granted to AVR Chemie for the processing of waste oil implied that AVR Chemie occupied a statutory monopoly, whereas in *Sydhavnens* the ECJ did not find it self-evident that three waste collection undertakings granted with exclusive rights occupied a statutory monopoly in the field of building waste.[488]

In the field of culture the relevant product market for books, for example, should from a consumer perspective be narrowly defined as well. Most books do not directly compete with each other, because they are not similar due to their different and original content.[489] From the demand side perspective books are therefore hardly substitutable; from the supply side perspective this is different, since publishers might be able to produce various different titles without incurring additional costs.

Apart from the above-mentioned economic factors the regulatory framework may have an impact on the definition of the relevant product market as well. In the *DSD* case the Commission referred to the German Packaging Ordinance which offered the undertakings in question two options for fulfilling their obligation to take back and recover used sales packaging: the individual collective system – the 'self-management' solution – and the joined exemption system. The latter was used to set up DSD, the only undertaking in Germany which operates an extensive exemption system for the collection and recovery of sales packaging. According to the Commission the exemption system should be distinguished from the 'self-management' system on the market for organising the take-back and recovery of used sales packaging collected from private final consumers. The 'self-management' system requires the packaging to be taken back at the place where it was supplied; consumers should thus bring back their packaging to the place where they bought the product, which is highly unlikely since a majority of consumers is accustomed to dispose of waste close to their homes. This only for certain combinations of packaging and collection points, the self-management system enables recovery rates in accordance with the Ordinance. Manufacturers and distributors can thus only be released from this system by joining the exemption system provided by DSD. According to the Commission this is one reason to assume limited substitutability between the

---

[486] Vedder (2003), p. 203.

[487] Vedder (2003), p. 205.

[488] Case C-203/96, *Dusseldorp* and Case C-209/98, *Sydhavnens FFAD*. See also paragraph 3.

[489] This may be different for books containing objective information, like encyclopaedias and dictionaries: Albers (1999), p. 246.

two systems. Since DSD is the only undertaking with respect to the exemption system, this resulted in a market share of 100%.[490] In the field of health care the regulatory framework plays first and foremost a role in defining whether health care organisations are to be considered undertakings within the meaning of Articles 81 and 82 EC, and second, if so, on what market they compete with other undertakings.

The geographic market

The relevant geographic market is defined as the "area in which the undertakings concerned are involved in the supply and demand of the products and services, in which the conditions of competition are sufficiently homogeneous and which can be distinguished from neighbouring areas because the conditions of competition are appreciably different in those areas".[491] What was stated before with regard to book pricing agreements, that language is a natural factor which delimits the relevant geographic market to the national market, is also relevant in the context of Article 82 EC.

With regard to the health care sector the markets are often regional; even in situations where health insurance funds in a given region have a market share of 100%, they do not necessarily have a dominant position considering the power of collectively organised purchasers of care, like medical practitioners, physiotherapists etc.[492]

This is different for the environmental field, e.g. due to cross-border effects of pollution. In the field of waste, for example, the Court held that the municipality of Copenhagen was a substantial part of the common market within the meaning of Article 82 EC. However, also here consumer preferences and differing environmental standards play a role in defining the relevant geographic market.[493]

4.2.2.2 Abuse

A dominant position as such is not prohibited by Article 82 EC. The abuse of a dominant position results in a violation of Article 82 EC. According to the Court in the *Hoffman-La Roche* case "the concept of abuse is an objective concept relating to the behaviour of an undertaking in a dominant position which is such as to influence the structure of a market where, as a result of the very presence of the undertaking in question, the degree of competition is weakened and which, through recourse to methods different from those which condition normal competition in products or services on the basis of the

[490] Commission Decision 2001/463, OJ 2001, L 166/1, paragraphs 65-86.

[491] Commission notice on the definition of the relevant market, OJ 1997, C 372/5, point 8.

[492] J.W. van de Gronden, Mededingingsrecht en gezondheidszorg, *M&M*, 2001, p. 275.

[493] Vedder (2003), p. 204.

transactions of commercial operators, has the effect of hindering the maintenance of the degree of competition still existing in the market of the growth of that competition".[494] Generally a distinction is made between conduct which is exploitative of the dominant position, which is unfair or unreasonable towards those persons who depend on the dominant firm for the supply or acquisition of the relevant goods or services, and exclusionary conduct, which economic effect is further to reduce or to impede effective competition by excluding actual or potential competitors.[495] The concept of abuse rules out the possibility of an exemption similar to Article 81(3) EC,[496] although, as will be seen hereafter, certain behaviour may be considered justified and therefore not abusive in the light of Article 82 EC.

Exploitative conduct

An example of exploitative conduct is charging unfair prices. According to the Commission this was the case in *DSD*, whenever DSD demanded a licence fee because a producer had placed a green dot on his packaging, whereas the producer would not actually use the DSD system to retrieve and recycle packaging. Another example is applying discriminatory and unfair conditions. A dominant firm that wants to encourage environmentally friendly products or production processes and therefore requires its supplier only to supply products that meet certain environmental criteria, or charges higher prices to suppliers that are environmentally unfriendly may amount to abusive behaviour.[497] These suppliers may argue that unfair or discriminatory conditions have been imposed upon them. It could also be argued that the behaviour to be supplied with high quality products is not abusive. With the increasing importance of Integrated Product Policy (IPP) as a quality management tool it is admitted that the environmental performance of a product is an essential part of its overall quality.[498] In its Communication on Integrated Product Policy the Commission states the following: "The private sector can demand greener products and greener production processes from their suppliers. They have considerable potential to influence the market for greener products, should they choose to do so, through, for example, demanding a certified environmental management system [...]."[499]

---

[494] Case 85/76, *Hoffman-La Roche*, paragraph 91.

[495] Bellamy & Child (2001), p. 721.

[496] Vedder (2003), p. 207.

[497] Vedder (2003), p. 211.

[498] D. Geradin, EC Competition Law and Environmental Protection: Conflict or Compatibility?, in: *Yearbook of European Environmental Law* (Oxford University Press, Oxford, 2002), pp. 117-154; see also R. Jacobs, EEC Competition Law and the Protection of the Environment, *LIEI*, 1993, p. 37.

[499] Communication from the Commission to the Council and the European Parliament, Integrated Product Policy – Building on Environmental Life-Cycle Thinking, COM(2003) 302 final, p. 13; see also Green Paper on Integrated Product Policy, COM (2001)68 final.

In the field of public health, similar questions may arise where health care institutions or health insurance funds, if considered undertakings, do not offer all health care providers contracts with them.[500] Objective quality requirements imposed on health care providers will probably not be considered abusive.[501] Closely linked to price discrimination are fidelity rebates to bind customers to a particular supplier over a long period, like in the *Hoffman La Roche* case, where Hoffman La Roche was accused of abusing its dominant position in the vitamin market.[502] Pharmaceutical companies dividing various national markets in medicines between its subsidiaries, which practice is capable of affecting the competitive position of third parties, may also make abuse of their dominant position. However, the refusal to sell or change its delivery policy would not automatically imply that a dominant firm violates Article 82 EC.[503]

Exclusionary conduct: the example of essential facilities

The doctrine of essential facilities has been used to require dominant firms to give access to an essential facility, like weekly radio and television schedules, a collection and recycling scheme for waste or a 'brick structure' for sales data for pharmaceutical products. The *Magill* judgment involved the refusal by RTE (the Irish radio and television authority) to licence weekly radio and television schedules to Magill, an organisation which wished to publish a weekly television guide containing these schedules. At the material time, no comprehensive weekly television guide was available on the market in Ireland or in Northern Ireland. On appeal to the judgment of the CFI the ECJ held that "the appellants' refusal to provide basic information by relying on national copyright provisions thus prevented the appearance of a new product, a comprehensive weekly guide to television programmes, which the appellants did not offer and for which there was a potential consumer demand. Such refusal constitutes an abuse under heading (b) of the second paragraph of Article 82 of the Treaty. Second, there was no justification for such refusal either in the activity of television broadcasting or in that of publishing television magazines. Third, and finally, as the Court of First Instance also held, the appellants, by their conduct, reserved to themselves the secondary market of weekly television guides by excluding all competition on that market since they denied access to the basic information which is the raw material indispensable for the compilation of such a guide."[504]

The condition that the reliance on national copyright provisions prevents *the appearance of a new product* has been reinforced by the Court's judgment in

[500] Mossialos & McKee (With W. Palm, B. Karl and F. Marhold) (2002), p. 178.

[501] See also within the context of Article 24 CA: NMa Richtsnoeren voor de zorgsector (2002), p. 60.

[502] Case 85/76, *Hoffman-La Roche.*

[503] Case T-41/96 *Bayer AG*, paragraph 180. The judgment of the CFI has been confirmed by the ECJ in Joined Cases C-2/01 P and C-3/01 P, *Bundesverband der Arzneimittel-Importeure eV.*

[504] Joined cases C-241/91 P and C-242/91 P, *RTE and ITP (Magill)*, paragraphs 54-56.

IMS Health.[505] This case involved the alleged refusal by IMS Health providing data on regional sales of pharmaceutical products in Germany to pharmaceutical laboratories formatted according to the 1860 brick structure, to grant a licence to NDC to use its brick structure. It appeared that this structure had become the normal industry standard to which clients adapted their information and distribution systems. The question was whether this refusal to licence the brick structure by IMS Health, protected by an intellectual property right, constituted an abuse of a dominant position within the meaning of Article 82 EC. After all it was extremely difficult, if not impossible, for NDC to market its data on pharmaceutical products to potential clients, being accustomed to the IMS Health brick structure. According to the Court, though, "the refusal by an undertaking in a dominant position to allow access to a product protected by an intellectual property right, where that product is indispensable for operating on a secondary market, may be regarded as abusive only where the undertaking which requested the licence does not intend to limit itself essentially to duplicating the goods or services already offered on the secondary market by the owner of the intellectual property right, but intends to produce new goods or services not offered by the owner of the right and for which there is a potential consumer demand".[506]

After *Magill* and *IMS Health* it appears that only in exceptional circumstances would competition law prevail over intellectual property rights. Otherwise the primary purpose of Article 82 EC would be ignored, which is to prevent the distortion of competition, and especially to safeguard the interests of consumers, rather than to protect the position of particular competitors. [507]

The situation is different in respect of products or services which are not protected by intellectual property rights. The prevention of the appearance

---

[505] According to Jones and Sufrin there are two ways of looking at this judgment: on the one hand the judgment appears to "come down firmly on the side of the intellectual property holder"; on the other hand, the nature of the new product requirement is such that it depends on the application of the national courts and national competition authorities of these conditions to the facts of the case whether the requirement is actually met: Jones and Sufrin (2004), pp. 508-509. Perhaps the outcome of the Microsoft proceedings could give further clarification on this issue: Cases T-201/04 R(1) and (2), *Microsoft Corporation*. In these cases the application for interim measures by Microsoft have been dismissed by the President of the Court of First Instance.

[506] Case C-418/01, *IMS Health*, paragraph 49. See also Annotation V. Hatzopoulos, *CMLRev.*, 2004, pp. 1613-1638.

[507] See the President of the Court of First Instance in Case T-184/01 R, *IMS Health Inc*, paragraph 145 (see also Opinion of AG Jacobs in *Bronner*, paragraph 58). The Commission had adopted a decision invoking the doctrine of essential facilities to take interim measures under which IMS would be forced to give immediate licence of the "brick system" for pharmaceuticals, however, the President of the CFI overruled the Commission's order, which was upheld by the President of the ECJ. The President of the CFI did cast serious doubts as to the applicability of *Magill* to this case.

of a new product is not a condition for invoking the essential facility doctrine in these cases. Here the *Bronner* case is relevant, involving the refusal by an Austrian publisher of daily newspapers, Mediaprint, to include Bronner, publisher of a single daily newspaper with a market share of only 3.6 percent in its home delivery service against payment of reasonable remuneration.[508] According to the Court this refusal could only involve an abuse of a dominant position within the meaning of Article 82 EC, if certain conditions were met: "the refusal of the service comprised in home delivery be likely to eliminate all competition in the daily newspaper market on the part of the person requesting the service and that such refusal be incapable of being objectively justified, but also that the service in itself be indispensable to carrying on that person's business, inasmuch as there is no actual or potential substitute in existence for that home-delivery scheme".[509] The Court followed A-G Jacobs opinion, who advised the Court not to extend the doctrine in an undesirable manner.[510] *Bronner* suggests that in general the essential facilities doctrine should be applied with caution.[511]

In the field of the environment, the doctrine of essential facilities has played a role where undertakings refuse to give access to a collection or recycling scheme. In *Spa/GDB* the Commission considered that the refusal by GDB (Genossenschaft Deutsche Brunnen – German association of mineral water producers) to grant access to the pool of standardized reusable glass bottles set up by GDB "hindered access by foreign water producers to the German market restricting competition and appreciably affecting inter-State trade within the meaning of Articles 81 and 82 of the EC Treaty. Furthermore, in view of the dominant position of the GDB in the market for mineral water containers, its refusal to grant foreign water producers access to its pool, despite the fact that such access was essential in order to be able to compete effectively in the mineral water market, constituted an abuse of a dominant position within the meaning of Article 82 of the Treaty."[512] What the outcome of the case would be if the judgment in *Bronner* had been delivered before, is unsure. In case of non-duplicable recycling schemes, the doctrine of essential facilities can be used to force the dominant firms to grant third parties access to these schemes.[513]

---

508 Case C-7/97, *Bronner*.

509 Case C-7/97, *Bronner*, paragraph 41.

510 Case C-7/97, *Bronner*.

511 S. de Vries, Cultuur en mededinging: harmonie of dissonantie?, in: J.W. van de Gronden and K.J.M. Mortelmans (Eds), *Mededinging en niet-economische belangen* (Kluwer, Deventer, 2001), p. 119; it is argued that after *Bronner* the essential facilities doctrine is more difficult to invoke: Goyder (2003), p. 320; the *Magill* case was described by the ECJ in *Bronner* as an exceptional case: see Whish (2001), p. 613 and 617.

512 Competition Report 1993, paragraph 240; see also Vedder (2003), p. 213.

513 D. Geradin, EC Competition law and Environmental Protection: Conflict or Compatibility?, in: H. Somsen (Ed.), *Yearbook of European Environmental Law* (Oxford University Press, Oxford, 2002), p. 138.

Present systems, like the *DSD* system, are differently structured, so that making abuse of the system as a barrier to entry for foreign manufacturers is increasingly unlikely.[514]

These examples are not particular to the context of horizontal and flanking policies. The fact that the concept of abuse is objective and neutral implies that horizontal and flanking policy considerations shall in principle have no impact on its definition. Nevertheless, there are, albeit limited ones, possibilities to take account of horizontal and flanking policy considerations also within the framework of Article 82 EC.

4.2.2.3 The objective justification

Behaviour that is objectively justified will not be considered abusive within the meaning of Article 82 EC. This will normally be the case where the anti-competitive effects are kept to the minimum necessary for the attainment of some economic advantage.[515] Thus the test of objective justification is primarily concerned with competition interests, and appears at first sight not really useful for balancing horizontal and flanking policy interests with competition interests. In other words justifying abusive practices on the basis of general economic welfare similarly to Article 81(3) EC seems difficult and limited.[516] Nevertheless, in several cases parties advanced this justification for, for example, maintaining an extensive collection and recycling scheme (DSD) or for ensuring effective security at football matches (Football World Cup).[517]

In the *DSD* case *DSD* argued that its abusive behaviour was objectively justified for a number of reasons.[518] The German Packaging Ordinance compelled DSD to act as it did and allowed DSD to prevent using the green dot mark for packaging not collected through the DSD system. Furthermore, DSD relied on trade-mark law and argued that the trade mark necessarily loses its identifying power where it is carried on packaging which is not exempted from the take-back obligation or is to be collected by a competing system. Both arguments were rejected by the Commission, who maintained that DSD abused its dominant position.

The Commission decision on the 1998 Football World Cup is also relevant in this respect.[519] The Commission found the ticketing arrangements relating

[514] Vedder (2003), p. 214.

[515] Faull & Nikpay (1999), p. 163.

[516] Faull & Nikpay (1999), p. 149.

[517] The *Hilti* case suggests that a dominant firm may rely on safety policy considerations for the justification of its abusive behaviour, even though the arguments were rejected by the Commission, which decision was upheld by the Court of First Instance: Commission Decision 88/138, OJ 1988, L 65/19; Case T-30/89, *Hilti AG v. Commission*.

[518] Commission Decision 2001/463, OJ 2001, L 166/1 (*DSD*), paragraphs 136-153.

[519] Commission Decision 2000/12, OJ 2000, L 5/55 (*1998 Football World Cup*).

to the sale to the general public in 1996 and 1997 of entry tickets for the 1998 Football World Cup finals tournament by the 'Comité français d'organisation de la Coupe du monde de football 1998' (CFO) to be abusive on the basis of Article 82 EC. According to the Commission the behaviour of CFO had the effect of imposing unfair trading conditions on residents outside France, which resulted in a limitation to the prejudice of those consumers. In fact the arrangements made by CFO resulted in discrimination on the basis of nationality and hence violated the fundamental principle of non-discrimination. One of the arguments brought forward by CFO to oppose the findings of the Commission was the principal concern of CFO to ensure that rival groups of supporters of teams participating in any given match were separated from one another in each of the World Cup stadiums. The Commission indeed accepted that "ensuring effective security at football matches is essential and may, in particular circumstances, justify the implementation of special ticket sales arrangements by tournament organisers".[520] Nonetheless, the Commission concluded that the arrangements were excessive and failed to contribute to maintaining or improving security at football matches.[521]

The earlier discussed *Piau* case may offer a possibility to justify practices which would otherwise be abusive. According to the CFI the fact that the licence requirement could obtain an exemption on the basis of Article 81(3) EC, because the restrictions on competition were only of a qualitative nature and were justifiable, entails that the FIFA, having a dominant position on the market of services provided by players' agents, does not make abuse of its dominant position.[522]

4.2.3 Conclusions

The possibilities to justify abusive behaviour for horizontal and flanking policy reasons are extremely limited. With regard to objective justification of abusive behaviour, this notion may include horizontal and flanking policy considerations. At least the Commission does not exclude the possibility that abusive practices may not be contrary to Article 82 EC, where they are justified on public interest grounds. Nevertheless, from the cases discussed above it appears that, regardless of the possibility of justifying abusive behaviour on public policy grounds, it will hardly ever be considered proportional. Objective justifications within the context of Article 82 EC are therefore not solid justifications for dominant firms using anti-competitive means to attain horizontal and flanking policy aims to rely upon. Another and more realistic justification ground is provided by Article 86(2) EC.

---

[520] Commission Decision 2000/12, paragraph 105.

[521] See also S. Weatherill, Fair Play Please: Recent developments in the application of EC law to sport, *CMLRev*, 2003, pp. 64-65.

[522] Case T-193/02, *Piau*, paragraphs 115-117.

4.3 Merger Regulation 139/2004

In 2001 the Commission published a Green Paper, wherein it proposed considerable changes to procedural, substantive and jurisdictional matters of the Merger Regulation. This eventually resulted in the adoption of a new Regulation, Regulation 139/2004 replacing Regulation 4064/89 (as amended).[523] One of the important issues discussed in the Green Paper was whether the substantive test for appraisal of mergers, the dominance test, should be revised and if so, how.[524] Regulation 139/2004 has indeed introduced a 'new' test for the appraisal of concentrations in Article 2 of the Regulation.

In the following, the scope of the Merger Regulation in relation to horizontal and flanking policies will be considered first; then the appraisal of concentrations on the basis of the test laid down in Article 2 of the Regulation. Lastly the exceptions laid down in Article 21(4) of the Merger Regulation will be discussed.

4.3.1 The scope of the Merger Regulation in relation to horizontal and flanking policies

According to Article 3 of the Merger Regulation concentrations may involve mergers, a change in control of parts or whole of the undertaking(s) and the creation of full-function joint ventures. Examples are where two media companies merge, or where a media corporation merges with an Internet firm, such as the well-known merger between TIME, a publishing and music company, and America Online, an Internet firm.[525] Mergers with a Community dimension must be notified to the Commission and will be prohibited if they create or strengthen a dominant position as a result of which competition would be significantly impeded. Meanwhile questions as regards the plurality of the media, freedom of speech and more generally the cultural quality of programmes will arise.[526] Mergers between pharmaceutical firms, health insurance funds or insurance companies providing health insurance,[527]or even between

[523] Council Regulation 139/2004, OJ 2004, L 24/1.

[524] COM (2001) 745/6 final.

[525] Case No COMP/M. 1845 – *AOL./TIME WARNER*.

[526] In the Netherlands the *cable* company UPC could have been seduced to buy the *broadcasting* company SBS 6 which would have raised various questions relating to cross-ownership and the plurality of the media: J. Alberts and J. van Barschot, Machtsgreep in medialand, *NRC Handelsblad*, 10 maart 2000, p. 3. With regard to convergence of media and information technology sectors and problems of cross-ownership and plurality of the media: G. Schuijt, Commissie Mediaconcentraties: toezicht overlaten aan NMa, *Mediaforum*, 1999, pp. 140-144; see also Commission's Green Paper on the Convergence of the Telecommunications, Media and Information Technology Sectors, and the Implications for Regulation, COM(97) 623 final.

[527] See for example Case No. IV/M.1453, the merger between AXA, providing insurance and related financial services and GRE, providing life and general insurance including particularly health insurance and related services.

hospitals, may have to be notified to the Commission and may raise questions relating to public health. The establishment of joint ventures in the field of waste based upon environmental considerations may have to be notified to the Commission under the Merger Regulation.

Concentrations with a Community dimension, which will be assessed according to the criteria mentioned in article 1 of the Merger Regulation (the combined turnover of the undertakings concerned), will have to be notified to the Commission.[528] In assessing whether a concentration will be considered incompatible with the common market, the concepts of dominant position and restriction of competition play essential roles. Hence, there seems little room for the consideration of horizontal and flanking policy interests in the appraisal of mergers. Nevertheless, at three instances horizontal and flanking policy interests could play a role in concentration control. First, they can play a role in the definition of the relevant market as has been discussed before in section 4.2.2.1 and will here only be briefly touched upon. Second, they can be taken into account under the appraisal of concentrations. The Commission is, according to Article 2(1) of the Merger Regulation, obliged to take into account the interests of the consumers and the development of technical and economic progress, criteria which are also included in Article 81(3) EC. This provision could be read in conjunction with the 23rd recital of the Merger Regulation, stipulating that "[...] the Commission must place its appraisal within the general framework of the achievement of the objectives referred to in Article 2 of the Treaty establishing the European Community and Article 2 of the Treaty on European Union".[529] Third, Article 21(4) of the Merger Regulation, which provides an exception to the rule that the Commission is solely competent to appraise mergers with a Community dimension, explicitly refers to public interests.

4.3.2 The appraisal of concentrations

Dominance still plays a central role in the appraisal of concentrations. However, the revision of the Merger Regulation and the introduction of the new test in Article 2 to determine if the merger leads to a significant impediment of competition, indicates it is not necessary that the merger leads to a dominant position.[530]

---

[528] See Article 4 of the Merger Regulation.

[529] See Vedder (2003) in respect of the former Merger Regulation, p. 230 and Jones and Sufrin (2004) in respect of the present Regulation, pp. 974-975.

[530] S. Voigt and A. Schmidt, The Commission's guidelines on horizontal mergers: Improvement or deterioration?, *CMLRev.*, 2004, pp. 1584-1585.

4.3.2.1 Dominance

The concept of dominance, familiar from Article 82 EC, plays a central role in the appraisal of concentrations. In paragraphs 1 and 4 of the Horizontal Merger Guidelines it is stated that "the creation or the strengthening of a dominant position is a primary form of such competitive harm" and provides "an important indication as to the standard of competitive harm that is applicable when determining whether a concentration is likely to impede effective competition to a significant degree".[531] Before a dominant position can be established the relevant product and geographic market must be defined.

The product market

As stated before in respect of Article 82 EC, horizontal and flanking policy considerations may – in the background – play a role in the definition of the relevant product market. For example, in the field of the environment the Commission has taken account of the specific characteristics of waste and the application of environmental legislation in this area. In the Case *Lyonnaise des Eaux/Northumbrian Water* the Commission makes a distinction between the collection and transport of non-hazardous waste, landfill disposal of waste, incineration and clinical waste disposal.[532]

The geographic market

In the cultural field the definition of the relevant geographic market is influenced by language and other cultural factors. These 'natural' factors may delimit the geographic market to the national market. This appears from several concentration cases in the field of media. In the *Kirch/Richemont/Telepiú* case, for example, the acquisition of joint control of Telepiu, providing broadcasting services in Italy, by Richemont and Kirch with the aim to enter the Italian pay-TV market did not, according to the Commission, give rise to competition problems.[533] The reason was that the television activities of the parties took place on separate geographic markets. According to the Commission conditions of competition vary considerably from one Member State to another for *inter alia* the following reasons:

- Programme rights to broadcast are purchased by television channels on a national or language basis;
- Rights to broadcast new films are subject to different rules in the Member States;
- Programme-mix of the main television channels in the Community is

---

531 OJ 2004, C 31/5.

532 Case IV/M. 567, paragraphs 14-18. See also Vedder (2003), p. 228.

533 Case IV/M.410, *Kirch/Richemont/Telepiu*. Kirch is active in film and television production and broadcasting in Germany, whereas Richemont operates in the Belgian, Dutch, Danish, Norwegian, Swedish and Finnish markets.

designed on the basis of cultural interests of a national or regional audience;

- Language differences hinder a wide expansion of television channels outside the home country.[534]

The *BskyB/KirchPayTV* case involved a concentration by which British Sky Broadcasting Group plc (BskyB) would acquire 24% of KirchPayTV from Kirch. Upon investigation of this concentration the Commission stated with regard to the geographic market for the acquisition of broadcasting rights that "although rights can be sourced from anywhere in the world and some operators acquire rights for more than one territory at a time, it has to be borne in mind that broadcasting rights are still acquired mainly on a national basis or, at the most, by language area. Thus the Commission has noted that film broadcasting rights are usually granted for a given language version and broadcasting area".[535] This is different for the broadcasting of some sporting events, such as the Olympic Games, which have a pan-European interest from the viewers' perspective.[536] The definition of the relevant geographic market is also relevant for the application of Article 9 of the Merger Regulation, which offers the possibility, upon request of a Member State, to refer a notified concentration to the competent authority of the Member State concerned in case competition will be significantly impeded on a market within that state. Another case involving the merger of Vía Digital's with Sogecable was referred to the Spanish Competition Authorities by the Commission under Article 9 of the Merger Regulation, because of the national character of the market for pay television. Hereby the Commission referred *inter alia* to language barriers and cultural factors.[537]

4.3.2.2 A significant impediment of competition

According to Article 2(2) and (3) a concentration is compatible with the common market if it "would not significantly impede effective competition in the common market or in a substantial part of it, in particular as a result of the creation or strengthening of a dominant position". Whether a concentration will be considered incompatible with the common market will in the first place be decided upon the basis of various competition considerations, whereby the definition of a dominant position plays a crucial, but not only, role (see above).[538] The Guidelines on the assessment of horizontal mergers are

[534] Case No IV/M.410, paragraph 17. See also N. Th. Nikolinakos, Mergers and Strategic Alliances in the Emerging Multi-Media Sector: The EU Competition Policy, *ECLR*, 2004, p. 626.

[535] Case No COMP/JV.37 , *BskyB/KirchPayTV*, paragraph 45.

[536] Case No COMP/JV.37 , *BskyB/KirchPayTV*, paragraph 46.

[537] COMP/M. 2845, *Sogecable/Canalsatélite Digital/Vía Digital*, paragraph 17 (see also IP/02/1216). This decision was upheld by the Court of First Instance in Joined Cases T-346/02 and T-347/02, *Cableuropa SA a.o.*

[538] Jones and Sufrin (2004), p. 916.

intended to provide guidance as to how the Commission assesses concentrations.[539] It appears that the Commission relies primarily on market shares and concentration ratios to aid its assessment of a case.[540] As stated above the Merger Regulation now contains an explicit reference to efficiencies as well, which will be considered below.[541]

The relationship between horizontal and flanking policies and the Merger Regulation is twofold. First, where the aim of concentrations is also the attainment of horizontal and flanking policy interests, the question is whether on the basis of these non-competition considerations concentrations can be allowed. Second, the prohibition of concentrations may also further the aims of horizontal and flanking policies, particularly in the field of culture and media policy. Concentrations that are harmful to competition are at the same time harmful to the realisation of non-competition objectives, where a limited number of media companies may curtail media pluralism, diversity and freedom of information.[542]

The prohibition of mergers and the plurality of the media

Dominance in the field of culture is often regarded as dangerous from a cultural, human rights and democratic perspective. It has been argued that "cultural conglomerates dominate substantial parts of cultural markets, specifically effecting the distribution, the promotion and the organisation of the reception of artistic creation" and that for that reason, from a democratic and human rights perspective a huge quantity of producers and distributors is necessary.[543] The Merger Regulation is in this respect an important instrument to prevent the creation of such cultural conglomerates, at least where competition considerations are at issue. But it did not withhold the Commission from approving the creation of the joint-venture 'SonyBMG' by Sony Corporation and Bertelsmann AG for their global recorded music business, which is considered threatening for cultural diversity by the independent music companies.[544]

539 OJ 2004, C 31/5.

540 Jones and Sufrin (2004), p. 926; S. Voigt and A. Schmidt, The Commission's guidelines on horizontal mergers: Improvement or deterioration?, *CMLRev.*, 2004, p. 1588.

541 See recital 29 of the Merger Regulation.

542 P. Lowe, Media Concentration and Convergence: Competition in Communications, Speech of 13 January 2004, to be found at: http://www.europa.eu.int/comm/competition/speeches/.

543 Smiers (2002), p. 9.

544 The Commission did not really discuss the question of cultural diversity: I. Wekstein-Steg, Le droit des concentrations appliqué au secteur des industries culturelles, *ERA-Forum*, 2005, p. 61. Case No COMP/M.3333, *Sony/BMG*. The Commission identified several competition concerns but nevertheless cleared the merger: see also P. Buigues and V. Rabassa, European perspective on the media sector: Competition versus regulation, July 2004, to be found at: www.idei.fr/doc/conf/rmm/buigues.pdf. Meanwhile the independent music companies (Impala et al.) have lodged an appeal against the Commission Decision

An example of a case where the Commission applied the Merger Regulation also with a view to sustain plurality of the media is the HMG-decision.[545] The Commission was requested by the Dutch government pursuant to Article 22 of the Merger Regulation to examine the proposed joint venture Holland Media Groep SA (HMG) between RTL4 SA (RTL), Vereniging Veronica Omroeporganisatie (Veronica) and Endemol Entertainment Holding BV (Endemol). The Commission concluded that the concentration would lead to the creation of a dominant position on the Dutch market for TV advertising and to the strengthening of an already existing dominant position of Endemol in the market for independent TV production, but nevertheless decided to approve the merger eventually. The main reason was the transformation of RTL 5 into a news channel, which was considered an appropriate and sufficient measure to restore effective competition in the Dutch TV advertising market.

The HMG-decision touches upon the limits of the application of the Merger Regulation in the field of media policy. From a competition perspective the Merger Regulation must prevent the creation of cultural conglomerates, but can it be used to serve wider goals of cultural plurality and safeguard the variety of ideas? In other words, is the Commission allowed to adopt a decision relating to the organisation and, even if indirectly, to the content of television programmes? In other cases the Commission merely focused on the sale of assets of media corporations, like in the case of Lagardère's acquisition of Vivendi Universal Publishing (VUP), which involved a merger between the two largest publishers of French-language books. According to the Commission this transaction led to competition problems on several markets for French-language books, but after certain commitments were made, including the sale of the Larousse publishing house and other assets of VUP, the Commission declared the concentration compatible with the common market.[546]

The meaning of the notion of 'plurality of the media' is after all twofold: first it refers to the number of publishers and independent newspapers or, in the field of broadcasting, to the number of independent broadcasting corporations; second, it refers to the independence of the editorial staff and the existence of smaller newspapers, which may only be guaranteed by large concentrations or, in the field of broadcasting, to the diversity of programme information and the cultural quality of television programmes. A tension may then develop between merger control on the one hand and the freedom of speech as laid down in the

(the first time that a merger decision in the entertainment sector has been appealed) with the Court of First Instance. They claim that the merger leads to market imbalances and is detrimental to the emergence of new artists, genres and creativity and hence to cultural diversity. See Case T-464/04, *Impala v. Commission (pending)*. See also www.impalasite.org.

545 Commission Decision 96/649, *RTL/Veronica/Endemol*, OJ 1996, L 294/14.

546 Case No COMP/M.2978, *Lagardère/Natexis/VUP*, 7 January 2004; see also press release IP/03/808.

constitutions of the Member States on the other hand.[547] In *HMG* HMG itself proposed to transform RTL 5 into a news channel.[548]

The approval of mergers on horizontal and flanking policy grounds

Article 2(1) sub b of the Merger Regulation allows the Commission to take into account the development of technical and economic progress provided that it is to the consumers' advantage and does not form an obstacle to competition. This is usually referred to as the 'efficiency defence', and shows similarities with the possibility of an exemption under Article 81(3) EC. An efficiency defence "would redeem a concentration which increases concentration and, prima facie significantly impedes effective competition, but which results in significant cost savings and economies of scale".[549] In this sense a concentration actually contributes to an increase in consumer welfare. In the Horizontal Merger Guidelines the Commission states "if the efficiencies generated by the merger are likely to enhance the ability and incentive of the merged entity to act pro-competitively for the benefit of consumers, thereby counteracting the adverse effects on competition which the merger might otherwise have".[550] It furthermore specifies the conditions for taking account of efficiencies:

- Consumers should not be worse off as a result of the merger (paragraph 79); not only cost savings, but also new or improved products may be beneficial for consumers;
- The efficiencies must be merger specific (paragraph 85);
- Efficiencies must be verifiable so that the Commission can be reasonably certain that the efficiencies are likely to materialise (paragraph 86).

These criteria together with the explicit reference to efficiencies in recital 29 of the Regulation have certainly reinforced the efficiency defence with regard to horizontal mergers. However, the lack of further specification of the criteria as

---

547 According to Lowe the freedom of information as well as diversity and pluralism, which are enshrined in Article 11 of the EU Charter on fundamental rights and Article 10 of the European Convention on Human Rights, have to be taken into account by the Commission also in the application of the Merger Regulation: P. Lowe, Media Concentration & Convergence: Competition in Communications, Speech delivered on 13 January 2004 at the Oxford Media Convention 2004, to be found at: http://europa.eu.int/comm/competition/speeches/text/sp2004_002_en.pdf.

548 On appeal the Court of First Instance did not touch upon this issue and left the Commission decision intact, Case T-221/95, *Endemol Entertainment*. In the Netherlands the Netherlands Competition Authority (NMa) was confronted with a similar problem in respect of the merger between Wegener Arcade and VNU Dagbladen: Case no. 1528, *Wegener Arcade-VNU Dagbladen*, decision of 13 March 2000; On appeal the Dutch court did touch upon this question: Case no. MEDED 00/874-*SIMO*, judgment of 20 September 2000.

549 Jones and Sufrin (2004), p. 949.

550 OJ 2004, C 31/5, paragraph 77.

well as the uncertainty whether the emergence of a dominant position can eventually be offset by possible efficiencies, make the status of efficiencies in merger control policy still unclear.[551]

Under the former Merger Regulation it has been submitted that the conditions for an efficiency defence were stricter than under Article 81(3) EC; whenever there was an obstacle to competition, the technical and economic benefits appeared to be irrelevant.[552] Hence, the possibilities to take account of horizontal and flanking policy considerations under Article 2(1) (b) were considerably limited. Nevertheless, the following cases show that the door had not been entirely closed for the consideration of non-competition interests.[553]

According to the CFI in the *Nestlé/Perrier* case "Article 2(1) (b) of Regulation No 4064/89 requires the Commission to draw up an economic balance for the concentration in question, which may, in some circumstances, entail considerations of a social nature, as is confirmed by the thirteenth recital in the preamble of the Regulation, which states that 'the Commission must place its appraisal within the general framework of the achievement of the objectives referred to in Article 2 of the Treaty, including that of strengthening the Community's economic and social cohesion, referred to in Article 130a'".[554] This case involved the takeover by Nestlé of Perrier which was, subject to conditions, approved by the Commission. The worker representation organisation brought an action for annulment of this decision because of fears of job losses. Thus the CFI now seems to suggest that also non-competition factors, in this case the social implications of the decision, can be included in the appraisal of mergers.

In the *Kali + Salz* case the Commission applied the 'failing company defence', which means that a company will withdraw from the market, in this case the formerly GDR owned company Mitteldeutsche Kali AG (MdK), if it is not taken over by a private company.[555] The decision was annulled by the ECJ, but the Commission's application of the 'failing company defence' was confirmed by the Court.[556] AG Tesauro more profoundly addressed the question whether

[551] S. Voigt and A. Schmidt, The Commission's guidelines on horizontal mergers: Improvement or deterioration?, *CMLRev.*, 2004, pp. 1592-1593. See also more in general regarding the role of efficiency claims in merger control policy: D. Gerard, Merger control policy: how to give meaningful consideration to efficiency claims?, *CMLRev.*, 2003, pp. 1367-1412.

[552] Whish (2001), p. 779; see also Commission Decision 2000/42, *Danish Crown/Vestjykse Slagterier*, OJ 2000, L 20/1. See also J. Schmidt, The new ECMR: "Significant Impediment" or "Significant Improvement?", *CMLRev.*, 2004, pp. 1571-1572.

[553] See also D. Banks, Non-Competition Factors and their Future Relevance under European Merger Law, *ECLR*, 1997, pp. 182-186.

[554] Case T-12/93, *Comité Central d'Enterprise de la Société Anonyme Vittel (Nestlé/Perrier)*, paragraph 39.

[555] Commission Decision 94/449, *Kali + Salz/MDK/Treuhand*, OJ 1994, L 186/38, paragraphs 77 and 95.

[556] Joined Cases C-68/94 and C-30/95, *French Republic and Société commerciale des potasses et de l'azote (SCPA) and Entreprise minière et chimique (EMC)*.

the appraisal of concentrations should only be based upon competition considerations. He considered that the Commission is justified to take account of objectives regarded equally fundamental by the Treaty, provided that the course of competition is not jeopardised and thereby refers to recital 13 of the Merger Regulation.[557]

The *BASF/Eurodiol/Pantochim* case involved the acquisition of sole control by BASF, a company with world-wide activities in the production and distribution of speciality chemicals and other chemical products, health and nutrition products, oil and gas, of Eurodiol and Pantochim, two chemical companies placed under a pre-bankruptcy regime in Belgium. BASF argued that the conditions for a failing company defence were met, since BASF would gain a comparable position even in the absence of the merger and that in any event the assets of the business in question would definitely exit the market. The Commission accepted this argument while *inter alia* considering that not only would the shutdown of the plants cause considerable additional costs when the plant is restarted, but also have considerable environmental risks, resulting from the sensitive production processes.

4.3.3 Exceptions: legitimate public interests in Article 21(4) of the Merger Regulation

Contrary to the other competition rules, the Merger Regulation explicitly refers to public, non-competition interests in article 21(4), which reads as follows:[558] "Notwithstanding paragraphs 2 and 3, Member States may take appropriate measures to protect legitimate interests other than those taken into consideration by this Regulation and compatible with the general principles and other provisions of Community law. Public security, plurality of the media and prudential rules shall be regarded as legitimate interests within the meaning of the first subparagraph. Any other public interest must be communicated to the Commission by the Member State concerned and shall be recognized by the Commission after an assessment of its compatibility with the general principles and other provisions of Community law before the measures referred to above may be taken. The Commission shall inform the Member State concerned of its decision within one month of that communication."

Hence, Member States remain entitled to apply their own legislation to protect legitimate interests other than those taken into account by the Merger Regulation and should be seen as an exception to the principle that the Commission is exclusively competent to apply the Merger Regulation to concentra-

[557] Opinion of AG Tesauro in Joined Cases C-68/94 and C-30/95, *French Republic and Société commerciale des potasses et de l'azote (SCPA) and Entreprise minière et chimique (EMC)*, paragraphs 50-57.

[558] Article 21(4) was Article 21(3) in the former Regulation 4064/89 (as amended).

tions with a Community dimension.[559] Since this provision is an exception to the general application of the Merger Regulation, it will be applied strictly.[560] Nevertheless, the provision makes it clear that it contains an open class of public interests, which may justify action by the national state.

Article 21(4) should be negatively interpreted, which means that Member States are only entitled to take action to condemn concentrations rather than to authorise them on these public interest grounds, which the Commission may have itself prohibited under the Merger Regulation.[561] Hence, from the perspective where concentrations having an effect on competition should be tolerated on horizontal and flanking policy grounds it is of limited interest.[562] Actually this provision is the opposite from the exceptions to the free movement rules, which permit Member States under certain conditions to derogate from the objective of the internal market on public interest grounds.[563] From the perspective of whether the prohibition of concentrations serve the wider aims of horizontal and flanking policies, though, Article 21(4) is relevant.

In *Newspaper Publishing* the UK authorities took action under Article 21(4) of the Merger Regulation to examine the joint acquisition of Newspaper Publishing plc by Promotora de Inforciones S.A. (PRISA), Editoriale l'Espresso S.p.A. (Espresso) and Mirror Group Newspapers plc (MGN), which was not opposed by the Commission under the Merger Regulation.[564] According to the Commission the proposed operation would not lead to the creation of a dominant position as a result of which competition would be significantly impeded in the common market or in a substantial part of it. The relevant product market is the market for national newspapers, which can be divided into three identifiable segments, the popular tabloids, the middle market titles and the quality segment. The relevant geographic market is the United Kingdom, according to the Commission, given the language and cultural specificities. Since the United Kingdom authorities were concerned to maintain the product differentiation, and since the proposed transaction involved issues such as the accurate presentation of news and free expression of opinion, for which the UK Secretary of State must grant formal consent under the relevant provisions of the UK Fair Trading Act, the exception of Article 21(4) was applied.

559 This may lead to conflicts between the Commission and the national competition authorities: Case No IV/M. 1616, *Champalinaud*, and R.H. Lauwaars, De verhouding tussen Europese en nationale fusiecontrole, *SEW*, 2002, pp. 228-231.

560 Whish (2001), at p. 764. See also with regard to plurality of the media, freedom of speech and competition policy: J. van den Beukel and A.J. Nieuwenhuis, Pluriformiteit in het mededingingsrecht, *Mediaforum*, 2000, pp. 116-124.

561 Goyder (2003), p. 372.

562 Vedder (2003), p. 232.

563 Jones and Sufrin (2004), p. 889.

564 Case No IV/M. 423, *Newspaper Publishing*.

In *Lyonnaise des Eaux/Northumbrian Water* the Commission also recognised under Article 21(4) of the Merger Regulation the legitimate interest of the United Kingdom authorities in applying the provisions of the Water Industry Act (as amended) to a concentration in the fields of water supply, sewerage services and waste management.[565] The proposed operation involved the acquisition of Northumbrian, which is principally engaged in the provision of water supply and sewerage services, by Lyonnaise, a French multinational mainly active in water distribution and waste water treatment, waste management, energy and construction. The Commission did not consider the proposed concentration problematic in the light of the Merger Regulation. The UK authorities, though, adopted a measure with respect to the tightening of price control in respect of the merged companies' water business and included the requirement that Lyonnaise will list all its United Kingdom water interests on the stock exchange.

For the Commission to grant its permission to Member States to apply their national laws the principles of proportionality and non-discrimination play an important role. In *Lyonnaise des Eaux/Northumbrian Water* the Commission held that the measures adopted on the basis of national law must be appropriate, proportional and non-discriminatory and more generally be in line with Community law. The notes annexed to the Merger Regulation, which are referred to in *Newspaper Publishing*, include the following passage concerning Article 21(4): "In application of the principle of necessity or efficacy and the rule of proportionality, measures which may be taken by Member States must satisfy the criterion of appropriateness for the objective and must be limited to the minimum of action necessary to ensure protection of the legitimate interest in question. The Member States must therefore choose, where alternatives exist, the measure which is objectively the least restrictive to achieve the end pursued." This application of the principle of proportionality resembles the proportionality test as employed under the free movement rules.

4.3.4 Conclusions

Similarly to Article 82 EC, the possibilities to take account of horizontal and flanking policy considerations under the Merger Regulation are rather limited. Horizontal and flanking policy considerations may only marginally carry some weight with the definition of the relevant market. The scope of the efficiency considerations contained in Article 2 and the recital of the Merger Regulation is not really clear. Even though the Commission's Horizontal Merger Guidelines suggest that the efficiency defence is similar to Article 81(3) EC, it probably has a narrower scope than Article 81(3) EC. In its Green Paper on Merger Review, the Commission supported the debate on how and to what

565 Case No IV/M. 567, *Lyonnaise des Eaux/Northumbrian Water.*

extent efficiencies that may result from mergers must play a role in the appraisal of mergers, but came to the conclusion that the present test suffices.[566] The cases referred to above, though, show that the extent to which non-competition and thus horizontal and flanking policy interests can play a role in the appraisal of mergers remains unclear. They also suggest that the 23rd recital of the Merger Regulation, which refers to other objectives of Community law contained in Articles 2 EC, should not be ignored completely. This leaves the door open for horizontal and flanking policy considerations, however, subsumed under the conditions of the Merger Regulation.

The prohibition of mergers may also coincide with horizontal and flanking policy considerations, most notably in the field of media policy. However, at the same time new questions arise concerning the delicate relationship between competition policy and the freedom of speech. The assessment of remedies under the Merger Regulation must not go beyond the Commission's discretion of power and result in an infringement of fundamental rights guaranteed by the constitutions of the Member States.[567] In the Netherlands, for example, a proposal has been made to include a specific test in the Competition Act which is applied by the Netherlands Competition Authority with a view to protect the plurality of the press. Concentrations in the press sector may not lead to higher market shares than 35%. The inclusion of a more 'substantive plurality test', however, is, according to the Dutch government, not possible considering the freedom of speech, which is laid down in Article 7 of the Constitution.[568]

Lastly, Article 21(4) of the Merger Regulation allows Member States to apply their own legislation for the protection of legitimate horizontal and flanking policy interests. This provision is important, because it explicitly refers to non-competition interests, which is unique for EC competition law. Furthermore, under the application of this provision the principle of proportionality plays a decisive role, similarly to the role it plays in the context of the free movement rules.

---

[566] COM(2001)745/6 final, pp. 40-41.

[567] Commission Notice on remedies acceptable under Council Regulation (EEC) No 4064/89 and under Commission Regulation (EC) No 447/98, OJ 2001, C 68/3. In the notice the Commission does not touch upon the assessment of remedies and the protection of fundamental rights, such as the freedom of speech.

[568] See Letter by the State Secretary for Education, Culture and Science, *TK* 2004-2005, 29 692, nr. 2.

CHAPTER 4

Harmonisation of Horizontal and Flanking Policies

1 Introduction

From the foregoing chapters it appears that a certain tension continues to exist between the free movement rules and competition rules on the one hand, and horizontal and flanking policy interests on the other hand. Neither judicial intervention nor intervention of the Commission in competition cases has proved to be sufficient to remove trade barriers and hence to completely lift the tension between free movement and horizontal and flanking policies.

In this chapter the possibilities the Community legislature has in resolving this tension are examined. As became clear from Chapter 2 the principle of proportionality plays a key role in the jurisprudence of the Court of Justice in defining the relationship between national horizontal and flanking policies and the Community rules on free movement. This principle allows Member States to pursue, within limits, horizontal and flanking policy interests, even though their policies impinge upon one of the four freedoms. Hence, where Member States have retained the right to invoke exceptions to the four freedoms legal barriers still exist in the form of discriminatory measures and restrictive measures as a result of differences between national horizontal and flanking policy measures. Harmonisation measures are put in place in areas regulated by Member States for the purpose of gradually removing still existing barriers to trade. This process of economic integration is referred to as *positive* integration and complements *negative* integration in the realisation of a Community wide internal market.[1] Hence, positive integration through harmonisation may be an important tool in removing the remaining tension between primary Community law and national legislation. So where primary Community law does not prove to be sufficient, harmonisation will be needed.[2] As will be seen, though,

1 See also Pelkmans (2001), p. 7: "*Negative integration* denotes the removal of discrimination in national economic rules and policies under joint surveillance. *Positive integration* refers to the transfer to common institutions, or the joint exercise, of at least some powers. In practice negative and positive integration will go together." Barnard refers to the decentralised model on the one hand, where Member States retain the freedom to regulate provided that they do not overstep the limits laid down by the Treaty, and the centralised model, where centralised standards are put in place to combat market failure: Barnard (2004), pp. 18-23. In the field of competition policy, however, the Community has not actively pursued the harmonisation process; a spontaneous harmonisation of national competition laws has resulted in a more uniform body of competition law throughout the European Community.

2 According to Weatherill "harmonisation has historically been driven by two separate rationales". The first rationale is connected to market-building, based on the assumption that market integration is promoted by harmonised rules; the second rationale is connected to 'non-market regulation', and also to meet unanimous demands of the Member States in the Council: see S. Weatherill, Why Harmonise?, in: T. Tridimas & P. Nebbia, *European Union Law for the Twenty-First Century – Rethinking the New Legal Order*, Volume 2, Internal Market and Free Movement Community Policies (Hart Publishing, Oxford and Portland, 2004), p. 11.

primary Community law remains relevant, albeit to a less intensive extent than with respect to national legislation, since harmonisation measures should, in principle, be in conformity with the free movement rules and general principles of Community law.

In the following sections and sub-sections the harmonisation of national laws in fields of horizontal and flanking policies is further explored. The point of departure is the process of harmonisation itself; according to Article 249 EC the Community legislature may, apart from decisions, use directives and regulations. Directives are binding as to the result to be achieved upon each Member State; regulations have a general application, are binding in their entirety and are directly applicable in all Member States. Neither the Community's legislature's choice of instrument (regulation or directive), nor the implementation of Community law by the Member States will be discussed here, since it has no bearing on the subject matter of this book, i.e. the problem of tension between the internal market and horizontal and flanking policies.

In section 2 the question whether there really is a directive that actually *harmonises* national legislation needs to be addressed. If so, in section 3 the techniques of harmonisation, in particular total harmonisation, minimum harmonisation and the 'new approach', will be considered. In sections 4 and 5 the possibilities of the Community legislature to take action in fields of horizontal and flanking policies are being assessed. Article 95 EC and other internal market legal bases will be introduced first. Article 95 EC is not only a general legal basis for internal market legislation, it also provides for harmonisation in the public interest, which most notably appears from Article 95(3) EC. Therefore, the legislative powers of the Community in the field of the internal market are first being assessed, before the specific powers concerning horizontal and flanking policies will be discussed. The focus of attention is laid upon the possibilities of the Community legislature to reconcile horizontal and flanking policy interests with the requirements of an internal market through the harmonisation of national laws. Examples of harmonisation measures, mostly in the field of the free movement of goods, which seek to reconcile these conflicting interests are used to illustrate this point. In section 5 the more specific legal bases for horizontal and flanking policies will be touched upon. Whereas Articles 153 EC and 175 EC provide the Community legislature with specific harmonisation powers in the fields of consumers and the environment respectively, Articles 151 EC and 152 EC principally prohibit harmonisation in the areas of culture and public health.

Finally, in section 6 the relationship between harmonisation and free movement will be assessed.

2 No 'real' harmonisation of national legislation

In order to assess the scope of Community harmonisation in a particular field, it is first necessary to examine whether and, if so to what extent, horizontal and flanking policies can be harmonised at Community level. The term harmonisation will here be used for legislative harmonisation that presupposes the establishment of common rules at Community level by the Community legislature. Harmonisation occurs where the Community legislature has taken over the task of regulating the market from the Member States.[3] This meaning of harmonisation excludes Community financial measures such as the structural funds, where no common norms have been established at Community level, but where criteria are set for the support of regions and certain policies. Furthermore, the Community's state aid policy or competition policy in general do not involve harmonisation. The decision practice of the Commission in the field of competition policy is an example of how the Commission fleshes out *negative integration* (see Chapter 3).

When the Community legislature has not adopted harmonisation measures in a given field, the national legislature remains competent. National measures will then have to be assessed in the light of primary Community law (see Chapter 2). In the following three situations, there is no harmonisation of national legislation:

- Some Treaty provisions (legal bases) expressly exclude the possibility to adopt harmonisation measures;
- Harmonisation is possible, but the Community legislature has not made use of this possibility or has done so only partially;
- Harmonisation is possible, but the Community legislature has used another instrument to attain the aim of market integration, like the principles of mutual recognition and home country control.

The exclusion of harmonisation

The Treaty provisions on culture and public health, for example, expressly exclude harmonisation of national legislation. According to Article 151(5) EC (culture) the Community may adopt incentive measures, *excluding any harmonisation* of the national laws and regulations of the Member States. According to Article 152(4) sub c EC (public health) the Community may adopt incentive measures designed to protect and improve human health, *excluding any harmonisation* of the laws and regulations of the Member States. Harmonisation is only allowed on the basis of Article 152(4) sub a and b EC, to set safety and quality standards for organs and blood products and in the veterinary and phytosanitary fields. The consequence is that Member States remain largely competent to

[3] Bernard (2002), p. 63.

legislate in these areas, but only within the boundaries set by primary Community law as explained in Chapter 2. This will be elaborated in section 5.3.

No or only partial use of the possibility to harmonise

The Community legislature may simply not have used, or is not intending to use, its powers to harmonise in a particular field. If the Community legislature has not adopted a harmonisation measure, or has not regulated a particular subject 'exhaustively', the national legislature remains competent to enact regulations regarding this subject. Exhaustive (or full) harmonisation implies that a particular subject is completely regulated at Community level.[4] If a Community measure is considered to regulate a certain field or matter 'exhaustively', the national state's legislation will have to be held up against the light of the relevant Community legislation; if the Community measure has not exhaustively regulated a particular subject, again primary Community law, in particular the free movement rules, would constitute the framework for review of national laws.[5]

It follows from in particular the *Tedeschi* case law that once the Community has exhaustively regulated a subject, the provisions of primary Community law, the Treaty rules on free movement and the exceptions, lose their significance. In the *Tedeschi* case the ECJ held that "where, in application of Article 94 of the Treaty,[6] Community Directives provide for the harmonisation of the measures necessary to ensure the protection of animal and human health and establish Community procedures to check that they are observed, recourse to Article 30 is no longer justified and the appropriate checks must be carried out and the measures of protection adopted within the framework outlined by the harmonizing Directive".[7] A similar line of reasoning was also followed by the ECJ in subsequent case law, for example *Walloon Waste*,[8] and the more recent case *Daimler Chrysler*, which involved the exhaustive harmonisation of rules for the shipment of dangerous waste brought about by Regulation 259/93.[9]

In *DocMorris*, which involved German legislation restricting Internet sales of medicines by pharmacies established in other Member States, the ECJ held that "a national measure in a sphere which has been subject of exhaustive harmonisation at Community level must be assessed in the light of the provisions of

---

4 P.J. Slot, Harmonisation, *ELRev.*, 1996, p. 382; K. Mortelmans, The relationship between the Treaty rules and Community measures for the establishment and functioning of the internal market – Towards a concordance rule, *CMLRev.*, 2002, p. 1327; P.J. Slot and G. Straetmans, Harmonisatie van wetgeving in de EG, *Tijdschrift voor privaatrecht*, 2003, p. 740.

5 P.J. Slot and G. Straetmans, Harmonisatie van wetgeving in de EG, *Tijdschrift voor privaatrecht*, 2003, p. 741.

6 The legal basis, in this particular case Article 94 EC, is not important; the harmonisation technique is.

7 Case 5/77, *Tedeschi*, paragraph 35.

8 Case C-2/90, *Commission v. Belgium (Walloon Waste)*.

9 Case C-324/99, *Daimler Chrysler.*

the harmonising measure and not those of the Treaty".[10] This approach is thus based on the principle of pre-emption.[11] This principle was interpreted by the ECJ in the *Simmenthal* case as not only entailing that national law conflicting with provisions of Community law are automatically inapplicable, but also that the valid adoption of new legislative measures is precluded.[12] The important consequence of this doctrine of pre-emption is that in principle Member States' powers to pursue horizontal and flanking policy aims in an area that has been exhaustively regulated by the Community are precluded. It may, however, not be as it seems, since the pre-emption of national legislation does not only depend on the exhaustive nature of Community legislation, but also on the harmonisation technique used by the Community legislature (minimum or total harmonisation, see hereafter, section 3). Whether Community legislation exhaustively regulates a certain subject, it is necessary, according to the ECJ in *Compassion*, to consider "not only their wording but also the context in which they occur and the objectives of the rules of which they are part". If the Community legislature does not safeguard a particular objective sufficiently, harmonisation may not be considered exhaustive.[13]

The use of other instruments than harmonisation

Instead of harmonising national laws, the Community legislature may seek to attain market integration through the application of the "principle of mutual recognition". Contrary to harmonisation as defined above, under the mutual recognition approach, Member States remain responsible and therefore it does not dispose of the tension between the internal market and horizontal and flanking policies.[14] This principle as discussed in Chapter 2 in the context of the *Cassis de Dijon* jurisprudence, has been "used" by the Community legislature in its legislative programme to facilitate free movement within the internal market.[15] In the Internal Market Strategy 2003-2006 the Commission still regards mutual recognition as corner stone of the Internal Market, despite its shortcomings in terms of absence of transparency, the lack of a commonly

10 Case C-322/01, *DocMorris*, paragraph 64.

11 K. Mortelmans, The relationship between the Treaty rules and Community measures for the establishment and functioning of the internal market – Towards a concordance rule, *CMLRev.*, 2002, p. 1328.

12 Case 106/77, *Simmenthal III*.

13 Case C-1/96, *Compassion*, paragraph 56: According to the ECJ it followed from the wording of the directive, its context, and the objectives which it pursues, that it lays down common minimum standards for the protection of calves that are confined for the purposes of rearing and fattening. Therefore "in adopting the directive the Community legislature laid down exhaustive common minimum standards".

14 See also Bernard (2002), p. 63.

15 See, for example, Directive 89/48 on a general system for the recognition of higher-education diplomas, OJ 1989, L 19/16; see also the proposed Directive on services in the internal market, COM(2004) 2 final/3, which will be discussed later.

agreed approach to evaluating whether levels of protection are equivalent and the lack of a clear procedure for a company to challenge a negative decision.[16]

The mutual recognition principle, also referred to as home country control principle, is generally accompanied by the harmonisation of general interests through the inclusion of common rules. An example is the Television without Frontiers Directive, which includes provision on the protection of minors, culture and advertising (see below, section 4.3.4). However, in the proposed Directive on services in the internal market, harmonisation is essentially limited to procedural aspects, like authorisation requirements for certain activities. Important features of the Directive are the principle of mutual recognition and country of origin, applying to nearly all types of services.[17] This Directive is relevant for horizontal and flanking policies, since Member States have lost the power to set additional standards regarding services which have been authorised by the home Member State, and will therefore be discussed in more detail in section 4.2.2.

In case the Community does not dispose of harmonisation powers, or has neither used, nor is willing to use its harmonisation powers, national laws could – within the context of a common market – also gradually grow closer to one another. This could be described as the process of 'spontaneous harmonisation', which is no harmonisation within the meaning of this chapter, because the Member States act on their own free will, not forced by some EC directive from above. This has, for example, occurred in the field of competition law.[18] In areas where harmonisation is expressly excluded, as in the fields of culture and public health, co-operation between Member States may, without the adoption of binding rules, lead to some form of spontaneous harmonisation. Examples are the pursuance of a Community cultural policy through the grant of subsidies or the introduction of a health insurance card within a broader framework of patient mobility and health care developments.[19]

---

16 Internal Market Strategy (2003-2006), COM(2003) 238 final, p. 7.

17 Proposal for a Directive of the European Parliament and of the Council on services in the internal market, COM(2004) 2 final/3. See for a critical analysis of the proposed Directive: B.J. Drijber, De bezems van Bolkestein, *NTER*, 2004, pp. 112-120.

18 Spontaneous harmonisation has neither been considered in Chapter 3 (The application of the Competition rules). Regarding spontaneous harmonisation, see: K. Mortelmans, Towards convergence in the application of the rules on free movement and on competition?, *CMLRev.*, 2001, pp. 613-649.

19 See with regard to culture: B. de Witte, The Cultural Dimension of Community Law, in: Academy of European Law (Ed.), *Collected Courses of the Academy of European Law*, Volume IV, Book 1 (Kluwer Law International, The Hague, 1995), pp. 293-294. Albers (1999), p. 358. R. Craufurd Smith, Community Intervention in the Cultural Field: Continuity or Change?, in: R. Craufurd Smith (Ed.), *Culture and European Union Law* (Oxford University Press, Oxford, 2004), pp. 19-78. With regard to patients mobility and health care and the introduction of a health insurance card (within the context of Regulation 1408/71) see the Communication from the Commission "Follow-up to the High level process of reflection on patient mobility and health care developments in the European Union", COM(2004) 301 final.

3 Harmonisation techniques

The technique of harmonisation eventually determines the scope of harmonisation and should therefore be distinguished from the question whether a certain Community measure provides for exhaustive harmonisation. Various techniques of harmonisation have been used to attain Community objectives, including optional harmonisation, partial harmonisation, alternative harmonisation, total harmonisation, minimum harmonisation, common policies and the so-called 'new approach'.[20]

The techniques of total and minimum harmonisation are in particular relevant for the relationship between horizontal and flanking policies and the internal market. Whereas total harmonisation entails that Member States merely implement the rules laid down in the directive, minimum harmonisation allows Member States to maintain or develop additional policies. The contrast between these two techniques is interesting for the tension between horizontal and flanking policies and the internal market. After all, in case of total harmonisation Member States merely implement Community legislation and fulfil the task of 'an executive agency'.[21] In case of minimum harmonisation, however, Member States, though implementing Community legislation, may also set *additional* standards.

The 'new approach' will also be considered here, since harmonisation is limited to essential health and safety standards.

3.1 Total harmonisation

In case of *total harmonisation* it is in principle not possible for the Member State to derogate from the provisions of the directive or regulation.[22] Total harmonisation, for example where goods are concerned, imposes a two-fold obligation on Member States:

- Member States are required to freely import and market goods complying with the directive; and
- Member States must prohibit the sale of goods not complying with the directive.[23] Consequently there is no scope for the adoption of national policies; the Member State is merely required to implement the provisions of the directive.

---

20 In general on these harmonisation techniques see also: Barnard (2004), pp. 506-526; P. J. Slot, Harmonisation, *ELRev.*, 1996, pp. 378-397.

21 See generally in respect of harmonisation: Bernard (2002), p. 63.

22 P.J. Slot and G. Straetmans, Harmonisatie van wetgeving in de EG, *Tijdschrift voor privaatrecht*, 2003, p. 722; P. J. Slot, Harmonisation, *ELRev.*, 1996, p. 382.

23 Oliver (assisted by Malcolm Jarvis) (2003), p. 478.

Particularly in the beginning of the Community's harmonisation programme total harmonisation was favoured as harmonisation technique. Later, other techniques of harmonisation, such as minimum harmonisation or the 'new approach' were used to provide for more flexibility and less detailed rules. Now it can be seen, however, that for the attainment of certain aims the Community returns to the technique of total harmonisation, in particular in the field of consumer policy (see below, section 4.3.2).[24]

3.2 Minimum harmonisation

In the case of *minimum harmonisation* minimum standards are set at the level of the Community, leaving the Member States free to maintain or introduce more stringent standards.[25] The more stringent standards applied by the Member State must nonetheless be in conformity with primary Community law, i.e. the free movement rules. Where the directive apart from a minimum provision also contains a free movement clause, e.g. stipulating that certain products complying with the provisions (i.e. minimum requirements) of the directive should be able to move freely within the Community, it will only be possible for Member States to set additional standards in respect of their own products. This was the case in *Gallaher* which involved Directive 89/622 on tobacco labelling requiring the health warning "Tobacco seriously damages health" to appear on cigarette packets. This warning had to cover at least 4 per cent of each large surface of the packet. By implementing the directive the United Kingdom had exceeded the 4 per cent requirement by providing that at least 6 per cent of the packet should be covered by the health warning. At the same time imported products which complied with the 4 per cent requirement of the directive were considered to comply with the requirements of British law as well.[26] This in fact amounted to 'reverse' discrimination of the British tobacco industry, which is still possible within the context of Community law.[27] A similar free movement clause has been included in Article 13(1) of the new Tobacco Directive, Directive 2001/37 concerning the manufacture, presentation and sale of tobacco products.[28]

However, in case of a directive containing minimum standards, but *no* free movement clause, a Member State may apply its more stringent rules to *all*

---

[24] P.J. Slot and G. Straetmans, Harmonisatie van wetgeving in de EG, *Tijdschrift voor privaatrecht*, 2003, pp. 722-726. Cseres (2005), p. 219.

[25] See, for example, M. Dougan, Minimum harmonization and the internal market, *CMLRev.*, 2000, p. 853.

[26] See Case C-11/92, *Gallaher.* See also Case C-222/91, *Philip Morris Belgium*. Annotation G. Robert, *CMLRev.*, 1994, pp. 165-171.

[27] Barnard (2004), pp. 517-520.

[28] OJ 2001, L 194/26.

products. This was at issue in the *Aher-Waggon* case, where the German authorities refused to register a Danish propeller-driven Piper aircraft on the ground that it exceeded the noise limits permitted in Germany.[29] Whereas the Danish plane complied with the noise emission standards laid down in a Community Directive, it exceeded the German requirements, these being more stringent than the relevant Community standards. Since the Community Directive merely laid down minimum requirements and did not contain a free movement clause, Germany was allowed to apply its more stringent standards also to aircraft from other Member States, subject to the condition that the standards complied with primary Community law, in particular the free movement of goods.

Minimum harmonisation may, apart from the Community harmonisation measure itself, also be prescribed by Treaty provisions, like Articles 176 EC (environment) or 153(5) EC (consumer protection). Articles 95(4, 5) EC provides for a conditional possibility for Member States to maintain or take additional measures under supervision of the Commission. This provision is relevant where a directive based on Article 95 EC provides for *total* harmonisation; otherwise a Member State does not need the derogation contained in Articles 95(4, 5) EC.

Article 176 EC and Article 153(5) EC

According to Article 176 EC "the protective measures adopted pursuant to Article 175 shall not prevent any Member State from maintaining or introducing more stringent protective measures. Such measures must be compatible with this Treaty. They shall be notified to the Commission." This means that Member States may, even after the Community has issued a harmonisation measure on the basis of Article 175 EC, continue to apply more stringent standards in the field of the environment, provided that these measure comply with the Treaty, in particular provisions on free movement.

Whether Article 176 EC can also be invoked by a Member State to apply more stringent measures, even where the subject matter has been subject to a total harmonisation measure, remains contentious.[30] In *Dusseldorp*, which involved the question whether principles of self-sufficiency and proximity could be applied to waste for recovery, given that Regulation 259/93 only provided for this in respect of waste for disposal, the ECJ did not explicitly rule on this matter, but held the Dutch measures, which were more stringent than the Regulation, nevertheless not justifiable in the light of the free movement of goods.[31] It is submitted that Article 176 EC remains relevant, even after the Community legislature has adopted a total harmonisation measure.

---

29 Case C-389/96, *Aher-Waggon*.

30 Jans (2000), pp. 117-120.

31 Case C-203/96, *Dusseldorp*.

The duty to notify the national measures according to Article 176 EC is no standstill requirement contrary to the notification requirement under Article 95 EC (see hereafter). This means that non-notification will not preclude the application of national, more stringent, measures.[32] Similar conclusions must be drawn in respect of Article 153(5) EC, the provision allowing Member States to maintain or introduce more stringent consumer protective measures.

Article 95(4, 5 & 8) EC

The mere possibility of escape from harmonisation measures based on Article 95 EC mainly to compensate the qualified majority procedure,[33] has been heavily criticised in legal literature.[34]

In Article 95(4) EC it is stipulated that "if, after the adoption by the Council or by the Commission of a harmonisation measure, a Member State deems it necessary to maintain national provisions on grounds of major needs referred to in Article 30 EC, or relating to the protection of the environment or the working environment, it shall notify the Commission of these provisions as well as the grounds for maintaining them".

According to Article 95(5) EC "[...] if, after the adoption by the Council or the Commission of a harmonisation measure, a Member State deems it necessary to introduce national provisions based on new scientific evidence relating to the protection of the environment or the working environment on grounds of a problem specific to that Member State arising after the adoption of the harmonisation measure, it shall notify the Commission of the envisaged provisions as well as the grounds for introducing them".

The requirements to rely on this provision are, compared to Articles 153(5) and 176 EC, rather strict, indicating that Article 95 EC is after all concerned with the *internal market*.[35] There are several limitations to the use of the derogation contained in Article 95 EC. Firstly, the conditions laid down in paragraphs 4, 5 and 6 are cumulative. This means that if any one of those conditions is not met, the application of Article 95(4-5) EC must be rejected without there being a need to examine the others.[36] It appears from the decisions adopted by the Commission pursuant to this provision that the Commission indeed seriously looks at the conditions.[37]

---

[32] Jans (2000), p. 121. Van de Gronden (1998), p. 442.

[33] Barnard (2004), p. 504.

[34] See also Oliver (assisted by Malcolm Jarvis) (2003), p. 465.

[35] See with respect to the former Article 100a(4) EC: Case C-319/97, *Kortas*. See also H. Sevenster, The Environmental Guarantee After Amsterdam: Does the Emperor Have New Clothes, in: H. Somsen (Ed.), *Yearbook of European Environmental Law* (Oxford University Press, Oxford, 2000), pp. 291-310; Oliver (assisted by Malcolm Jarvis) (2003), p. 467; Barnard (2004), pp. 504-506.

[36] Case C-3/00, *Commission v. Denmark*, paragraph 118.

[37] See, for example, Commission Decision concerning national provisions on the use of azodyes notified by Germany under Article 95(4) EC, OJ 2003, L 311/46 (Commission did not approve of the German

Secondly, the notification requirement must, according to the Court's case law, be considered as a *standstill* requirement, meaning that national provisions cannot be applied until they have been approved by the Commission.[38] As stated above this is not the case for Articles 176 EC and 153(5) EC.[39] Article 95(4-10) can in this respect be compared with the standstill obligation contained in the State aid provision of Article 88 EC. The reason is, according to the ECJ in the *Kortas* case, which involved a Swedish ban on the use of a colorant (E124, which was approved by a Community directive) because of alleged health risks, that otherwise harmonisation measures would be rendered ineffective if Member States retained the right unilaterally to apply national rules derogating from those measures.[40] After all, Article 95(4-10) EC contains a specific procedure with a particular role for the Commission precisely to prevent that the internal market realised by secondary legislation should not be undermined by national measures. The starting point for Article 176 EC, or Article 153(5) EC, is not the internal market with integration and uniformity as guiding values, but the protection of the environment, or the protection of consumers.[41]

Finally, more stringent measures cannot be applied in respect of *all* horizontal and flanking policy interests. Article 95(4) EC is limited to the protection of the environment, the working environment and interests mentioned in Article 30 EC, including the protection of public health and national treasures. Neither consumer protection nor the protection of cultural interests constitute grounds for the maintenance of more stringent measures. Article 95(5) EC is limited to the protection of the environment and working environment only. Consumer

measures, because Germany could not demonstrate that more stringent measures were necessary than the Community Directive 76/769 on certain dangerous substances and preparations (as amended by Directive 2003/53)); see also Commission Decision concerning national provisions on the use of short chloronited paraffins notified by the Netherlands under Article 95(4) EC, OJ 2004, L 1/20 (Commission only partially approved of the Netherlands more stringent measures); Case C-3/00, *Commission v. Denmark* involved the protection of public health, i.e. the prohibition by Denmark of the use of sulphites, nitrites and nitrates as food additives.

38 Case C-41/93, *France v. Commission (PCP)*, paragraph 30.

39 See for Article 176 EC: Jans (2000), pp. 120-121.

40 Case C-319/97, *Kortas*; Jans (2000), p. 128. See also H. Sevenster, The Environmental Guarantee After Amsterdam: Does the Emperor Have New Clothes? in: H. Somsen (Ed.), *Yearbook of European Environmental Law* (Oxford University Press, Oxford 2000), pp. 296-298.

41 Compare the judgment of the Court in Case 380/87, *Balsamo*, where the Court held that Article 3(2) of Directive 75/442 on waste merely contained the obligation for Member States to inform the Commission in good time not only of draft rules concerning *inter alia* the use of products which might be a source of technical difficulties as regards disposal or lead to excessive disposal costs, but also of draft rules designed to encourage *inter alia* the prevention, recycling and processing of waste. Failure by the Member States to observe their obligation to give prior notice does not in itself render unlawful the rules thus adopted, according to the Court in paragraph 22. See also Van de Gronden (1998), p. 444.

protection, the protection of public health or cultural interests are excluded from the scope of this provision. The reason that the grounds under which Article 95(5) EC can be invoked are more limited is that, according to the Court in the *Commission v. Denmark* case, the adoption of new legislation under Article 95(5) EC is more likely to jeopardise harmonisation than the application of existing standards under Article 95(4) EC, which the Community legislature knows of.[42]

A special and different derogation is provided by Article 95(8) EC stipulating the following: "When a Member State raises a specific problem on public health in a field which has been subject of prior harmonisation measures, it shall bring it to the attention of the Commission which shall immediately examine whether to propose appropriate measures to the Council." This provision is interesting since, as stated above, Article 95(5) EC does not mention public health as ground for *introducing* more stringent national standards. Article 95(8) EC explicitly concerns public health and in a way gives Member States a certain right of initiative on which basis the Commission has a duty to further examine whether action in this area is necessary.[43]

Article 95(8) EC, which so far seems to have attracted only little attention, raises at least two intriguing questions. Firstly, does Article 95(8) EC merely allow the *Community legislature* to propose an adaptation of the harmonisation measure, or does it also, but implicitly, offer the *Member State* the possibility to take action first and before the Community legislature to deal with a specific health problem? On the one hand, the fact that public health is not included in Article 95(5) EC as derogation ground suggests that only the Community can take concrete action. On the other hand, it seems illogical and highly unsatisfactory that a Member State in case of a specific health problem has no possibility to introduce measures unilaterally – it has to wait a considerable time until the Community legislature has taken action –, whilst in case of an environmental problem it can take such action under Article 95(5) EC.[44]

Secondly, Article 95(8) EC may encourage the Community legislature to take action in the field of public health on the basis of Article 95 EC, so within the context of the internal market. Hence, this provision underlines the potentially broad scope of application of Article 95 EC also in the field of public health, as embraced by the Court in the *Tobacco* cases (see hereafter, section 4.2.4).

---

[42] Case C-3/00, *Commission v. Denmark*, paragraph 57; see Barnard (2004), p. 505.

[43] Von der Groeben and Schwarze (Eds); Schriftleitung: A. Bardenhewer-Rating (2003), p. 1469.

[44] Sevenster considers it bizarre that the environment and even the working environment should enjoy preferential status over public health: H. Sevenster, The Environmental Guarantee after Amsterdam: Does the Emperor Have New Clothes? in: H. Somsen (Ed.), *Yearbook of European Environmental Law* (Oxford University Press, Oxford, 2002), p. 309. The fact that environmental protection enjoys a preferential status does not seem to be in accordance with the Court's approach under the free movement rules where according to the Court's case law, the protection of public health ranks first among the interests mentioned in Article 30 EC: see Chapter 2, section 4.4.3.1.

Considering the possibilities to derogate from a harmonisation measure on the basis of Article 95(4, 5 and perhaps 8) EC, it must be concluded that the procedure laid down in Article 95 EC severely constrains the potential to apply more stringent national measures and also in practice seems a hurdle for Member States.[45] Furthermore, even though Article 95 EC has also been used for the adoption of *minimum* harmonisation directives, it has been suggested that the availability of special derogation rules "may indicate that, generally speaking, total harmonisation should be the way towards the establishment and functioning of the internal market."[46] This statement becomes more relevant now the Court in the *Tobacco Advertising* case implicitly discourages the use of the technique of minimum harmonisation (see hereafter, section 4.2.4).

3.3 The 'New Approach'

Under the 'new approach' harmonisation is limited to the establishment of essential safety requirements to be satisfied by all products if they are to be placed on the market. Standards, or technical specifications, are drawn up by competent 'standardization bodies' (e.g. CENELEC and CEN). Products which are in conformity with these specifications, are presumed to comply with the essential safety requirements, and must be suitable to be placed on the market without any obstacles. The 'new approach' was set out in a Council Resolution of 7 May 1985.[47] A good example of a 'new approach' directive is the Toys Directive concerning the safety of toys.[48] Article 2 of the Directive stipulates that "toys may be placed on the market only if they do not jeopardise the safety and or health of users and of third parties when they are used as intended or in a foreseeable way, bearing in mind the normal behaviour of children". Furthermore, Member States shall presume compliance with the essential requirements in respect of toys bearing the EC mark; these essential requirements are listed in an Annex to the Directive, without which compliance toys cannot be placed on the market. The Directive thus seeks to create an internal market for *safe* toys affording effective protection to consumers, especially children.

In the Internal Market Strategy 2003-2006, the Commission intends not only to effectively implement and improve the 'new approach', but also to better integrate environmental requirements in technical standards, which "can help to reduce the impact on the environment of products and also reduce the development of national legislation."[49]

---

45 Considering the fact that the provision has been applied relatively rarely: Barnard (2004), pp. 505-506.

46 P. Rott, Minimum harmonisation for the completion of the internal market? The example of consumer sales law, *CMLRev.*, 2003, p. 1109.

47 OJ 1985, C 136/1.

48 Directive 88/378, OJ 1988, L 187/1 (as amended by Directive 93/68, OJ 1993, L 220/1).

49 A Communication is scheduled for adoption by the end of the year.

The 'new approach' may on the one hand be seen as reducing protection given to consumers due to the absence of specific detailed standards; it may on the other hand be seen as a technique that combines total harmonisation of certain horizontal and flanking objectives, such as safety and health, with a flexible approach of means, i.e. standardisation.[50] That horizontal and flanking policy concerns may also play a role in the standardisation process itself becomes clear from the Commission's intention to draw more attention to the integration of environmental concerns.

4 Harmonisation within the framework of the internal market

In this section the possibilities to harmonise horizontal and flanking policy interests within the framework of the internal market are being further explored. After a general introduction of the internal market legal bases in the Treaty their potentially broad scope of application will be discussed (section 4.2). Examples will then be given of harmonisation measures based upon internal market legal bases in the areas of the environment, consumer protection, public health and culture (section 4.3).

4.1 Introduction

Before the introduction of the Single European Act (1986), which introduced Article 100a (now Article 95 EC) EEC in the Treaty, Article 100 (now Article 94 EC) EEC functioned more or less as sole legal basis for harmonisation measures, which also pursued horizontal and flanking policy aims. In addition Article 235 (now Article 308 EC) EEC providing the possibility to enact measures, "if action by the Community should prove necessary to attain, in the course of the operation of the common market one of the objectives of the Community", was used for unforeseen circumstances.[51] The economic orientation of the Community apparently did not seem to be a substantive handicap to the pursuit of horizontal and flanking policy objectives. This appears from measures which were previously adopted pursuant to Article 308 EC in the fields of, for example, the environment, like the Directive on the conservation of wild birds,[52] and consumer protection.[53]

---

50 Barnard (2004), p. 524.

51 P.J. Slot and G. Straetmans, Harmonisatie van wetgeving in de EG, *Tijdschrift voor privaatrecht*, 2003, p. 696.

52 Directive 79/409, OJ 1979, L 103/1.

53 For example Decision 86/138 concerning a demonstration project with a view to introducing a Community system of information on accidents involving consumer products, OJ 1986, L 109/23; see H.-W. Micklitz and S. Weatherill, Consumer Policy in the European Community: Before and After Maastricht, *Journal of Consumer Policy*, 1993, p. 291.

In fact "the objective of economic integration has proved a remarkably powerful incentive for the establishment of an environmental policy".[54] To some extent the same goes true for other horizontal and flanking policies. In that sense the fact that in particular the Treaty of Maastricht includes specific tasks for the Community to pursue horizontal and flanking policies at least partly represents a codification of activities having been pursued before on the basis of Articles 94, 95 and 308 EC. Nevertheless, activities were pursued piecemeal and not always satisfactorily.[55] Furthermore, as will be seen, the extent to which some horizontal and flanking policies have become Community policies varies considerably.

From a policy perspective, it is important to mention the Internal Market Strategy 2003-2006, in which the Commission makes clear that actions within the context of the internal market are necessary also in the fields of the environment, product safety (consumer protection) and health to ensure that economic development is sustainable, that (economic) interests of consumers are safeguarded and that the Internal Market can support national health systems.[56] Even though some of the criticism expressed with respect to the Action Plan for the Single Market (1997) may still be applicable, in particular where it concerns the possible conflict between the objective of simplifying the regulatory environment and the pursuance of horizontal and flanking policies,[57] the Commission seems aware of this while stating in its current Internal Market Strategy: "The quality of rules depends not only on making sure that the impacts of a measure have been checked before it is proposed and that it is well drafted, clear and proportionate to its objectives. Within the Internal Market, it also depends on choosing the right legislative technique or instrument – i.e. the one which will most effectively eliminate barriers to cross-border trade while serving public interests, such as health and safety and sustainable development, and respecting national diversity as possible."[58]

4.2 Legal bases for harmonisation within the context of the Internal Market

The Treaty contains various legal bases for the adoption of harmonisation measures with a view to achieve the internal market: particularly relevant are the Articles 95, 47(2), 55, 57 and 308 EC.

---

[54] H. Somsen, Dynamics, Process and Instruments of Environmental Decision-Making in the European Union, in: T. Jewell and J. Steele (Eds), *Law in Environmental Decision-Making* (Clarendon Press, Oxford, 1998), p. 165.

[55] R. Lane, New Community competences under the Maastricht Treaty, *CMLRev.*, 1993, p. 944.

[56] COM(2003) 238 final.

[57] K. Mortelmans, The common market, the internal market and the single market, what's in a market?, *CMLRev.*, 1998, p. 118.

[58] COM(2003)238 final, p. 25.

4.2.1 Article 95 EC

The main legal basis for internal market measures is obviously Article 95 EC, which since the Single European Act is the *lex specialis* in relation to Article 94 EC. It stipulates that the Council shall adopt measures for the approximation of provisions laid down by law, regulation or administrative action in Member States which have as their object the establishment and functioning of the internal market. According to paragraph 3 "the Commission, in its proposals envisaged in paragraph 1 concerning health, safety and environmental protection and consumer protection, will take as a base a high level of protection, taking account in particular of any new development based on scientific facts". It confirms that the aims of measures based upon Article 95 EC are twofold: the realisation and functioning of the internal market, and the safeguarding of general interests.[59]

Article 95 EC does not contain any general power for the Community legislature to harmonise national provisions. It sets out only the power to adopt harmonisation measures having as their object the establishment and functioning of the internal market, which must, as will be seen in section 4.2.4, on the basis of the *Tobacco* cases nevertheless be broadly interpreted.[60] Measures that are not connected to the internal market can in principle not be based on Article 95 EC. The Community is based on the principle of attributed powers as laid down in Article 7(1) EC: "Each institution shall act within the limits of the powers conferred upon it by this Treaty" and Article 5 EC: "The Community shall act within the limits of the powers conferred upon it by this Treaty and of the objectives assigned to it therein".

4.2.2 Articles 47(2), 55 and 57 EC

No reference to safeguarding certain interests in the general good similarly to Article 95(3) EC is made in other provisions providing for a legal basis for internal market legislation, such as Articles 40/42 EC (workers), 44/47 EC (establishment), 55 EC in conjunction with 47 EC (services) or 57 EC (capital). Nevertheless, the integration clauses contained in the various titles on horizontal and flanking policies require the Community legislature to take account of horizontal and flanking policy interests in harmonising on the basis of these provisions. Article 47(1) EC stipulates that the Council issues directives

---

59 In the *Tobacco Advertising* case the ECJ held that "[...] the third paragraph of Article 129(1) (now Article 152) provides that health requirements are to form a constituent part of the Community's other policies and Article 95(3) expressly requires that, in the process of harmonisation, a high level of human health protection is to be ensured": Case C-376/98, *Germany v. European Parliament and Council (Tobacco Advertising)*, paragraph 88.

60 See Opinion AG Geelhoed in Case C-491/01, *BAT/Imperial Tobacco*, paragraph 103.

for the mutual recognition of diplomas, certificates and other evidence of formal qualifications. Article 47(2) EC grants the power to enact directives concerning the taking up and pursuit of activities as self-employed persons. By means of Article 55 EC, Article 47(2) EC is also applicable in the field of services.

The above-mentioned proposal for a Directive on services in the Internal Market (see section 2) is an example of a harmonisation measure based on Articles 55 and 47(2) EC, which is in principle applicable to all types of services, including health services, funeral services, child care, tax services, security services etc.[61] It is a typical example of 'liberalisation' with an emphasis on the principle of mutual recognition, including home country control, for the incorporation and extension of the prohibitive Treaty provisions on services, yet with a limited number of exception grounds to the application of this principle in certain specific cases. It can therefore be – and has also been – strongly criticised for being far too 'liberal'. It will have to be awaited and seen whether, and if so how, the present proposal will become law.[62]

The reasons for criticising the initial proposal are various. Firstly, the key role for the country of origin principle in combination with the principle of mutual recognition may lead to a weakening of standards of protection at least in a number of Member States.[63] As stated above, the proposed Directive in principle applies to all types of services, including the more sensitive activities like health services, social services or audio-visual services, where important interests such as a high level of health protection, the maintenance of a health care system open to all, and the preservation of a pluralist broadcasting system are at stake. Certainly, the country of origin principle makes it possible to achieve the objective of guaranteeing the free movement of services, since providers of services are only subject to the national provisions of their Member States of origin (Article 16 of the Commission's proposal). Furthermore, the Member State shall not make access to a service activity or the exercise thereof subject to an authorisation, unless certain conditions mentioned in Article 9 are fulfilled. Hence, the possibilities for a Member State to supervise service providers are extremely limited. After all the proposed Directive does not foresee in a single licence for service activities, and a requirement of authorisation by the Member State is in principle prohibited.[64]

---

[61] B.J. Drijber, De bezems van Bolkestein, *NTER*, 2004, p. 114.

[62] See with regard to the concerns about the effects of the proposed Directive: Statement to the European Parliament on the Services Directive of 8 March by the European Commissioner for Internal Market and Services, McCreevy, Speech/05/149.

[63] See Press Release No 16/2005 of the European Economic and Social Committee, 7 February 2005. This will occur most likely in the northern and rich Member States, but not in Poland; Polish workers can now earn a decent living. From this perspective the Directive is not at all liberal.

[64] The question is also which Member State should be considered Member State of origin, for example, where larger corporations are concerned having their seat in one Member State and their principal place of business in another: see B.J. Drijber, De bezems van Bolkestein, *NTER*, 2004, p. 116.

A second point of criticism is the limited number of case-by-case derogations provided for in the proposed Directive, combined with the country of origin principle. Environmental protection, consumer protection or culture are not included in Article 19(1) of the present proposal; only the safety of services, including aspects related to public health, the exercise of a health profession and the protection of public policy, most notably the protection of minors, are mentioned by Article 19. The protection of the environment may only constitute a derogation from the country of origin principle, where the service provider moves to another Member State (Article 17). Furthermore, consumer protection is only mentioned in recital 68 of the preamble to the proposed Directive. This 'freezing' of justification grounds by the Directive not only does not correspond to the open class of exception grounds in the rule of reason jurisprudence of the Court of Justice (see Chapter 2), it is also contrary to the notion of harmonisation itself, which presupposes the regulation of general interests at the level of the Community.[65]

Thirdly, the possibilities to derogate from the country of origin principle for the reasons mentioned by Article 19 are further limited by the 'mutual assistance procedure' laid down in Article 37. According to this procedure the Member State of origin shall first have to be asked to check whether the service provider is operating lawfully; then both the Commission and the Member State of origin will have to be notified, if the recipient state intends to adopt measures. If the Commission regards the measure incompatible with Community law, it shall adopt a decision asking the Member State in question to refrain from adopting the measure. This procedure looks similar to the notification procedure under Article 95(4-10) EC, which, as stated above, severely constrains Member States' possibilities to adopt measures for the protection of horizontal and flanking policy interests.

The final point of criticism that must be made is that the Directive codifies the principles on cross-border health care as laid down in the Court's case law, in particular the judgment in *Müller-Fauré*.[66] According to Article 23 of the proposed Directive Member States are prohibited from making the assumption of the costs of non-hospital care in another state subject to the granting of authorisation, where the costs of that care, if it had been provided in their territory, would have been assumed by their social security system. For hospital care prior authorisation is still possible, and the conditions laid down in *Müller-Fauré*, which are now included in Article 23 of the present proposal, must be respected. The question is whether it is wise to lay down these conditions in a directive, when the case law of the Court in this field is still developing.[67] Furthermore, in Article 4(10) the Directive provides for a definition of hospital care. By provid-

[65] B.J. Drijber, De bezems van Bolkestein, *NTER*, 2004, p. 118.

[66] Case C-385/99, *Müller-Fauré*.

[67] B.J. Drijber, De bezems van Bolkestein, *NTER*, 2004, p. 119.

ing for this definition and by thus deciding on which health care activities may and which may not be subjected to prior authorisation, the Community legislature touches upon the organisation of health care, which, according to Article 152 EC, is reserved to the Member States (see section 4.3.3.2). Member States have indeed questioned this definition, and according to the Council, it should be explicitly clarified in the Directive that the Member State of affiliation must determine what concerns hospital and non-hospital care.[68] Whether the Directive will apply to the health care sector and social services is uncertain, however. According to the European Commissioner's Statement to the European Parliament, the Commissioner for the Internal Market and Services, the health sector should be excluded from the scope of the Directive all together.[69]

In conclusion one may wonder whether the proposal could be seen as a *harmonisation* measure at all. Clearly, and unfortunately from the perspective of horizontal and flanking policies, in this proposal the balance between horizontal and flanking policy interests and the internal market has been struck wrongly. Hence, the proposed Directive on services in the Internal Market does not, at least in its present form, meet the prerequisites of a true *harmonisation* measure.[70]

4.2.3 Article 308 EC

Article 308 EC provides: "If action by the Community should prove necessary to attain, in the course of the operation of the common market, one of the objectives of the Community and this Treaty has not provided the necessary powers, the Council shall, acting unanimously on a proposal from the Commission and after consulting the Assembly, take the appropriate measures." Article 308 EC is a *general* legal basis for harmonisation measures vis à vis the *specific* legal bases in the Treaty for harmonisation measures in fields of horizontal and flanking policies, which will be discussed in section 4.

The residual legislative authority of Article 308 EC has after the inclusion of powers in fields of horizontal and flanking policies been considerably reduced. Harmonisation measures, for example, in the field of the environment, which were previously based on Article 308 EC, have since the adoption of the Single European Act been based upon the *lex specialis* Article 175 EC.[71] Hence, Article

---

68 See also the Interinstitutional File of the Council of 16 July 2004 (11570/04), p. 5.

69 See Statement to the European Parliament on the Services Directive of 8 March by the European Commissioner for Internal Market and Services, McCreevy, Speech/05/149.

70 With regard to the question what type of measure should be considered a *harmonisation* measure, see also the pending case C-217/04, wherein the United Kingdom contests a Community Regulation setting up a European Network and Information Security Agency and based on Article 95 EC on the ground that it does not constitute harmonisation within the meaning of Article 95 EC. It should therefore have been based on Article 308 EC (OJ 2004, C 201/8).

71 Jans (2000), pp. 3-10.

308 EC can only be used for the regulation of certain activities, which fall within the scope of the objectives of the EC Treaty, but which have not been further elaborated in a specific title in the Treaty, like tourism, sports or civil protection.[72]

If indeed Article 308 EC may only be relied on as a legal basis of last resort, when no other legal basis in the Treaty is available,[73] Article 308 EC has lost most of its potentially additional value for the development of horizontal and flanking policies at Community level. Does this imply that Article 308 EC may not be used in situations which are not covered by Article 95 EC, but by another specific legal basis for horizontal and flanking policy measures, which explicitly prohibits the harmonisation of national laws? Theoretically, where *necessary* powers are lacking, e.g. the power to adopt harmonisation measures in the field of culture, to take action which is considered *necessary* for the realisation of, for example, cultural objectives as laid down in the Treaty, the Community may take recourse to Article 308 EC.[74] If, however, a measure falls, by reason of its content and aims, within the scope of, for example Article 151 EC, Article 308 EC may not be used to circumvent the prohibition of harmonisation contained in Article 151(5) EC, stipulating that "the Council [...] shall adopt incentive measures, excluding any harmonization of the laws and the regulations of the Member States".[75] Otherwise the useful effect of the prohibition to adopt harmonisation measures would be jeopardised.[76] Objectives of, for example, cultural policy which are not included in Article 151 EC, but fall within the scope of Article 2 EC and are of a more mixed economic nature, may nevertheless be pursued on the basis of Article 308 EC.[77] This means that Article 308 EC does not fill a regulatory gap in fields of horizontal and flanking policies. That this provision will not be used in this way can also be deduced from the Conclusions of the European Council at Edinburgh (1992).[78] Hence, Article 308 EC cannot serve as legal basis to relieve the tension between horizontal and flanking policies and the internal market.

---

72 Van Ooik (1999), p. 133.

73 Oliver (assisted by Malcolm Jarvis) (2003), p. 476.

74 See with respect to cultural policy: Albers (1999), p. 83 and p. 359.

75 Van Ooik (1999), p. 313.

76 See also Albers (1999), p. 359; M. Niedobitek, Die kulturelle Dimension im Vertrag über die Europäische Union, *EuR*, 1995, p. 364; B. de Witte, The Cultural Dimension of Community Law, in: Academy of European Law (Ed.), *Collected Courses of the Academy of European Law*, Volume IV, Book 1 (Kluwer Law International, The Hague, 1995), pp. 230-234.

77 Schmahl (1996), p. 234.

78 Bull. EC 12-1992. See also R. Lane, New Community competences under the Maastricht Treaty, *CMLRev.*, 1993, p. 979. In Opinion 2/94 the Court of Justice held that the Community does not have the competence to accede to the European Convention for the Protection of Human Rights and Fundamental Freedoms on the basis of Article 308 EC.

4.2.4 Snus, Cigarettes and commercials; the potential and limits of harmonisation on the basis of internal market provisions

In a number of cases the Court has been confronted with questions relating to the validity of two 'tobacco Directives', the Directive on advertising and sponsorship of tobacco products, which was annulled by the Court, and the Directive concerning the manufacture, presentation and sale of tobacco products, which was declared valid. Both Directives were based on the internal market legal basis of Article 95 EC (and some other legal bases, such as Articles 47 and 55 EC and 133 EC, but this did not change the procedure), but clearly aimed at the protection of consumer's health against the dangers of smoking and other use of tobacco products. Another case is pending before the Court and involves a new action for annulment of the revised Tobacco Advertising Directive lodged by Germany (see below, section 4.3.3.1).[79] The Court of Justice in a case concerning the validity of Directive 2002/46,[80] certain provisions of which prohibit the marketing of food supplements that do not comply with the directive, has recently confirmed the judgments in the *Tobacco* cases. According to the ECJ this Directive was also validly based on Article 95 EC, irrespective of the prohibitions to market food supplements that do not comply with the Directive and irrespective of the public health considerations that played a part in the formulation of these provisions.[81] The *Tobacco* cases will be discussed in more details below.

Tobacco, advertising and Snus

The *Tobacco advertising* case involved the successful action of annulment by Germany of the Directive on advertising and sponsorship of tobacco products, which was based upon Articles 100a, 57(2) and 66 EC (now Articles 95, 47(2) and 55 EC) and banned nearly all forms of advertising and sponsoring for tobacco products.[82] According to the Court a directive can be adopted on the basis of these provisions only if:

- the measure genuinely has as its object the improvement of the conditions for the functioning of the internal market;
- the measure has the aim and is designed to prevent the emergence of future obstacles, which are likely to occur; the mere finding of disparities between national rules and of the abstract risk of obstacles to the exer-

---

[79] Case C-380/03, *Germany v. European Parliament and Council*, OJ 2003, C 275/31 (pending).

[80] Directive 2002/46 relating to food supplements, OJ 2002, L 183/51.

[81] Joined Cases C-154/04 and C-155/04, *Alliance for Natural Health*, paragraphs 28-42.

[82] Case C-376/98, *Germany v. European Parliament and Council (Tobacco Advertising)*; Directive 98/43, OJ 1998, L 213/9.

> cise of fundamental freedoms or of distortions of competition does not suffice.[83]

Hence, measures must have as their object either the objective of removal of obstacles to the exercise of fundamental freedoms, *or* the removal of appreciable distortions of competition.[84] The ECJ added in paragraph 88 of its judgment that "[...] provided that the conditions for recourse to Articles 95, 47(2) and 55 as a legal basis are fulfilled, the Community legislature cannot be prevented from relying on that legal basis on the ground that public health protection is a decisive factor in the choices to be made. On the contrary, the third paragraph of Article 152(1) provides that health requirements are to form a constituent part of the Community's other policies and Article 95(3) expressly requires that, in the process of harmonisation, a high level of human health protection is to be ensured."

The *Tobacco Advertising* case could still be seen as a "significant step in the direction of a closer scrutiny of Community competence by the Court";[85] yet at the same time the judgment entails an extension of the scope of application of Article 95 EC in the field of public health; this latter aspect has in particular been confirmed in subsequent case law, i.e. the *BAT/Imperial Tobacco* case and the *Snus* cases. The *BAT/Imperial Tobacco* case involved questions relating to the validity of Directive 2001/37 on the manufacture, presentation and sale of tobacco products.[86] The Directive was adopted on the basis of Articles 95 and 133 EC (common commercial policy), which legal basis was contested

---

83 Case C-376/98, *Germany vs. European Parliament and Council (Tobacco Advertising)*, paragraphs 83 and 84.

84 The attainment of one of these two objectives is sufficient for the use of Article 95 EC: see annotation K.J.M. Mortelmans and R.H. van Ooik, *AA*, 2001, p. 121 and p. 123. In Case C-491/01, *BAT/Imperial Tobacco* AG Geelhoed summarises the Court's ruling in *Tobacco Advertising* as follows (paragraph 18): Article 95 EC can serve as legal basis, if the following requirements are met: Measures must improve the conditions for the establishment and functioning of the internal market; Article 95 EC does not confer any general power to regulate the internal market; measures must have as their object the removal of obstacles to the exercise of fundamental freedoms or the removal of distortions of competition; future obstacles to trade, which emergence must be probable, may be prevented by measures based on Article 95 EC; a directive may incorporate provisions which contribute only indirectly to the removal of obstacles; distortions of competition are relevant only if they are appreciable; a distortion of competition involves any restriction of forms of competition applicable to all market participants in a Member State, for instance through the fact that a particular course of action is prohibited. Such distortion does not by itself justify Article 95 EC as a legal basis for the general application to the entire EU of a stringent prohibition existing in one Member State.

85 Bernard (2002), p. 85.

86 Directive 2001/37, OJ 2001, L 194/26. Case C-491/01, *BAT/Imperial Tobacco.*

on *inter alia* the ground that the Directive, notwithstanding the statements in the recitals, is not intended to ensure the free movement of tobacco products but rather to ensure the protection of public health. Considering the exclusion of harmonisation in the field of public health laid down in Article 152(4) sub c EC, the Community did not have the power to adopt this Directive. But the Court came to the conclusion that the Directive was valid in its entirety. According to the Court, "the Directive genuinely has as its object the improvement of the conditions for the functioning of the internal market and it was, therefore, possible for it to be adopted on the basis of Article 95 EC, and it is no bar that the protection of public health was a decisive factor in the choices involved in the harmonising measures which it defines".[87] This is, according to the Court, not undermined by the fact that the Directive contains a prohibition to manufacture certain cigarettes.

Nevertheless, after this judgment, the Court was asked to rule on the validity of certain provisions contained in the same Directive 2001/37, which is most remarkable, as it had already declared this Directive valid in its entirety. In these *'Snus'* cases two prejudicial questions were raised regarding the validity of Article 8 of the Directive, prohibiting the placing on the market of tobacco products for oral use. One case involved a German prohibition on the marketing of tobacco products for oral use, in this case Swedish Snus marketed by Arnold André and imported by Swedish Match.[88] The other case involved a British prohibition of placing on the market of 'Snus', which Swedish Match wanted to market in the United Kingdom.[89] In this case the Court also dealt with the question of the relationship between the Directive and Article 28 EC, which will be discussed below in section 6.[90] "Snus is finely ground or cut tobacco sold loose or in small sachet portions and intended to be consumed by placing between the gum and the lip."[91]

Both national prohibitions were the result of the implementation of Directive 89/662, which was also at issue in the *Gallaher* case (see above, section 3.2), and which has now, together with the Tar Directive,[92] been replaced by Directive 2001/37. Article 8 of Directive 2001/37 provides that "Member States shall prohibit the placing on the market of tobacco for oral use, without prejudice of the Act of Accession...". This provision in the Act of Accession grants Sweden

87 Case C-491/01, *BAT/Imperial Tobacco*, paragraph 75.

88 Case C-434/02, *Arnold André*.

89 Case C-210/03, *Swedish Match*.

90 Other questions in this case concerned the infringement of the principle of non-discrimination; the infringement of the principle of proportionality; the infringement of Article 95(3) EC; the misuse of powers; the infringement of Article 253 and/or the duty to give reasons; infringement of the fundamental right to property.

91 Case C-434/02, *Arnold André*, paragraph 19.

92 Directive 90/239 concerning the maximum tar yield of cigarettes, OJ 1990, L 137/36.

a derogation from the provisions of the Directive. The reason for prohibiting tobacco products like Snus is, according to the Court whilst referring to the Directive, that this product can lead to nicotine addiction and can cause cancer of the mouth.[93] A prohibition on the marketing of such tobacco products is thus certainly dictated by reasons relating to the protection of public health. Nonetheless, also measures prohibiting the marketing of products could, according to the Court, be validly adopted within the context of the internal market and hence be based on Article 95 EC.[94] After all, there were at the time of adoption of the Directive differences between the laws of the Member States, some prohibiting the marketing of these tobacco products, others allowing them on the market. This reasoning, however, is somewhat flawed as the Court approached the question from the point of view of obstacles to free movement rather than of distortion of competition.[95] A total ban on 'Snus' can hardly be seen as contributing to free movement.[96]

The *Tobacco* cases are very important for the harmonisation of horizontal and flanking policies with a view to relieve and eventually resolve the tension between horizontal and flanking policies and the internal market for a number of reasons.

A broad scope of application of Article 95 EC in the fields of public health and culture

On the one hand the Court's ruling entails a *restriction* of the scope of application of Article 95 EC through the introduction of a type of 'appreciability' test. It is clear from the outset that not everything can or should be harmonised on the basis of Article 95 EC. It must at least be shown that trade between Member States has been affected according to the criteria set out above.[97] On the other hand, though, the Court's ruling clearly entails an *extension* of the scope of application of Article 95 EC, because once these threshold requirements have been met, the Community legislature has the power to intervene in any (horizontal and flanking policy) field regulated by Member States.[98] This is

---

93 Paragraph 47 of Case C-434/02, *Arnold André* and paragraph 49 of Case C-210/03, *Swedish Match*.

94 Case C-210/03, *Swedish Match*, paragraph 34 and Case C-434/02, *Arnold André*, paragraph 35.

95 See also annotation K.J.M. Mortelmans, *AA*, 2005, p. 170.

96 According to AG Geelhoed the prohibition diminishes enforcement costs and can even diminish the costs of the enforcement of regulations on related products. If Snus is not on the market, the effort to control the marketing of other smokeless tobacco products can be reduced. See also annotation T. Vandamme, *SEW*, 2005, p. 232.

97 According to Weatherill "...although the ruling puts the legislature on notice that it must offer more rigorous justification, the case is by no means fatal to the future vitality of the harmonisation programme": S. Weatherill, Why Harmonise, in: T. Tridimas & P. Nebbia, *European Union Law for the Twenty-First Century – Rethinking the New Legal Order*, Volume 2, Internal Market and Free Movement Community Policies (Hart Publishing, Oxford and Portland, 2004), p. 27.

98 A. Somek, Good news for a bad habit: tobacco, culture and the rule of law in the European Union, available at: http://www.somek.org/Lectures/KSchoolHandout.PDF, p. 4.

particularly relevant in areas where the Community does not dispose of specific harmonisation powers, as in the fields of public health or culture.

The purpose of the harmonisation measure has thus become irrelevant, in the sense that a directive or regulation does not necessarily have to pursue market interests as its first agenda. From *Tobacco Advertising* it becomes clear that even though some prohibitions on advertising could not be regulated on the basis of Article 95 EC, others can. This implies that Article 95 EC can be used to even *prohibit* trade in certain 'demerit' goods, which has been confirmed in *BAT/Imperial Tobacco*, where the ECJ held – as I already discussed above – that a prohibition to manufacture certain cigarettes is not a provision aimed directly at improving the conditions for the functioning of the internal market; nevertheless a measure adopted on the basis of Article 95 EC may incorporate such a provision as long as its purpose is to ensure that certain prohibitions concerning the internal market and imposed in pursuit of that object are not circumvented.[99] Furthermore, from *Snus* it appears that even a total ban on the marketing of a product may contribute to free trade, and can thus be validly based on Article 95 EC. This has been reinforced in the above-mentioned *'Food supplements'* case.[100]

Hence, the 'centre of gravity theory', which implies that the choice of the legal basis must be determined according to its main *object*, does not play a role where another and more specific Treaty provision cannot constitute an alternative legal basis for the *harmonisation* of horizontal and flanking policies.[101] This theory has, after the Court's judgments in the *Waste* cases, generally been regarded as guiding theory in determining the proper legal basis for the harmonisation of horizontal and flanking policy interests.[102] The centre of gravity theory, however, continues to play a role, but only where an alternative legal basis to Article 95 EC exists, as in the fields of environmental and consumer policy; hence, not in the fields of culture and public health, apart from Article 152 sub a and b EC.

---

[99] Case C-491/01, *BAT/Imperial Tobacco*, paragraph 82.

[100] Joined Cases C-154/04 and C-155/04, *Alliance for Natural Health.*

[101] According to AG Fennelly in Tobacco Advertising the dispute did not concern the choice between two legal bases, particularly due to the fact that Article 152(4) EC did not constitute an alternative, which made the reference to the 'centre of gravity theory' inappropriate. This implies that where viable alternatives to Article 95 EC et seq. exist, i.e. Community powers to adopt harmonisation measures, the centre of gravity theory remains relevant unimpaired. Where no alternatives exist, as in the field of public health, and if the threshold criteria are met, the centre of gravity theory will not be applicable and the Community will be able to adopt harmonisation measures on the basis of Article 95 EC et seq. The Community legislature will then have to duly motivate whether the conditions for the use of Article 95 et seq. have been fulfilled: paragraph 68 of the Opinion of AG Fennelly in Case C-376/98, *Germany v. European Parliament and Council (Tobacco Advertising).*

[102] See in general: Van Ooik (1999). See also section 4.3.1.

According to AG Fennelly in *Tobacco Advertising* it is sufficient for Article 95 EC to be applicable that the harmonisation measure regulates the movements of goods between Member States, thereby equalising conditions of competition: "the free movement of goods may well be facilitated by measures which prevent, restrict or burden the circulation of particular goods".[103] Interestingly, the AG refers hereby to *inter alia* the *Waste* cases.[104] Severe restrictions on the movements of waste are laid down in the Transfer of Waste Regulation, which is, however, not based on Article 95 EC, but on Article 175 EC (see below, section 5.1). This confirms the view that the 'centre of gravity theory' continues to play a role in the field of environmental policy, where Article 175 EC indeed provides for an alternative legal basis to harmonise environmental interests in order to resolve the tension between environmental policy and the internal market.

Thus, even if the Treaty does not provide for the necessary harmonising powers, Article 95 EC may still be used to pursue horizontal and flanking policies, provided the threshold criteria are met. For environmental and consumer policy, the Court's ruling in the *Tobacco* cases has no real additional value, since the Treaty provides for sufficiently alternative harmonisation powers in these areas.

The integration of horizontal and flanking policy interests in internal market law

The *Tobacco* cases are furthermore so important for the harmonisation of horizontal and flanking policies precisely because the Court makes clear that also within the context of internal market legal bases, like Article 95 EC, considerable weight should be granted to horizontal and flanking policy interests. The integration principle, requiring the Community legislature to pursue and protect horizontal and flanking policy interests also within the context of other policies, like internal market policy, has clearly contributed to this view. Since an integration clause has been included in the Treaty for the fields of the environment, public health, culture and consumers, what has been said by the Court in *Tobacco Advertising* and the other *Tobacco* cases in respect of public health is equally relevant for other horizontal and flanking policies.

The free movement clause: an incentive for total harmonisation

One of the grounds for declaring the Tobacco Advertising Directive as being invalidly based on Articles 95, 47(2) and 55 EC was, according to the Court "that the Directive contained no provision ensuring the free movement of products which conform to its provisions, in contrast to other directives allowing Member States to adopt stricter measures for the protection of general interest".[105] Direc-

[103] Opinion of AG Fennelly in Case C-376/98, *Germany v. European Parliament and Council (Tobacco Advertising)*, paragraph 86.

[104] Case C-155/91, *Commission v. Council* and Case C-187/93, *European Parliament v. Council.*

[105] Case C-376/98, *Germany v. European Parliament and Council (Tobacco Advertising)*, paragraph 104.

tive 2001/37 concerning the manufacture, presentation and sale of tobacco products, however, includes a free movement clause, which had been subject to a procedure in the *Gallaher* case (see above, section 3.2). By this reasoning the Court provides for an incentive to pursue *total* harmonisation on the basis of Article 95 EC.[106] *Minimum* harmonisation could, in combination with a market access or free movement clause, only be applied restrictively and, if applied, will probably lead to reverse discrimination.[107] This tendency towards total harmonisation can clearly be noticed in the field of consumer policy, where however, an alternative legal basis, i.e. Article 153 EC, exists (see below, section 4.3.2).[108]

This means that the tension between horizontal and flanking policies, for which also no specific harmonisation powers are granted in the Treaty, and the internal market could not only be *relieved* on the basis of internal market legal bases, it could also be *resolved* at Community level through integration and uniformity, now that the incentive to adopt minimum harmonisation measures on the basis of 95 EC has clearly diminished.

One problem remains and that is the extensive scope of application of Article 95 EC (and other internal market legal bases), which has in particular been reinforced by the ECJ's judgments in *BAT/Imperial Tobacco* and *Snus*, and the possible circumvention of the express exclusion of harmonisation laid down in Articles 152(4) EC (public health) and 151 EC (culture).[109] Even though the Court states that other legal bases may not be used to circumvent the express exclusion of harmonisation,[110] this has not at all been an obstacle to reinforce the broad

---

[106] See also H.-W. Micklitz, N. Reich and S. Weatherill, EU Treaty Revision and Consumer Protection, *Journal of Consumer Policy*, 2004, p. 375.

[107] S. Weatherill, Pre-emption, Harmonisation and the Distribution of Competence to Regulate the Internal Market, in: C. Barnard and J. Scott (Eds), *The Law of the Single European Market – Unpacking the Premises* (Hart Publishing, Oxford and Portland, 2002), at p. 60. Otherwise, see Case C-389/96, *Aher-Waggon*, which has been discussed in section 3.2 of this chapter.

[108] See Cseres (2005), p. 219; Howells and Weatherill (2005), p. 136; H.-W. Micklitz, N. Reich and S. Weatherill, EU Treaty Revision and Consumer Protection, *Journal of Consumer Policy*, 2004, p. 375: They refer, like Cseres, to rulings dealing with the impact of the Product Liability Directive (Directive 85/374), in particular Case C-183/00, *Gonzalez Sanchez*. In this case the ECJ held that since the Product Liability Directive is based on Article 94 EC, there is no possibility to derogate from the Directive on the basis of the Treaty. The minimum harmonisation provision contained in Article 153(5) EC only applies to measures adopted on the basis of Article 153 itself (paragraph 3b), and not to measures based on Article 95 EC. The possibility for Member States to adopt more stringent provisions than the Directive depends entirely on the content of the Directive itself, which does not contain a provision expressly authorising the Member States to adopt or to maintain more stringent provisions in matters in respect of which it makes a provision, in order to secure a higher level of consumer protection.

[109] See with regard to the prohibition of harmonisation laid down in Article 151 EC: R. Craufurd Smith, Community Intervention in the Cultural Field: Continuity of Change?, in: R. Craufurd Smith (Ed.), *Culture and European Union Law* (Oxford University Press, Oxford, 2004), p. 51.

[110] Case C-376/98, *Germany v. European Parliament and Council (Tobacco Advertising)*, paragraph 79.

scope of application of Article 95 EC also in the field of public health, motivated by the requirement laid down in Article 152 EC to integrate health requirements in other policies. Hence, the *Tobacco* cases appear to have a clear potential to undermine the prohibition of harmonisation as laid down in the Treaty provisions on public health and culture, at least in situations where the measure has an effect on intra-Community trade. The integration clauses hereby certainly restrict the scope of these provisions expressly excluding harmonisation.

4.3 Harmonisation of national horizontal and flanking policies on the basis of internal market legal bases

The following sections that analyse the harmonisation of national horizontal and flanking policies within the framework of the internal market, should from now on be assessed in the light of the Court's ruling in the *Tobacco* cases.

4.3.1 Environmental policy and the internal market

In the field of the environment the ECJ has had the possibility to decide on the relationship between Article 95 EC and Article 175 EC, which is the legal basis to take specific action in the field of the environment. The ECJ has made clear that indeed Article 95 EC can be used as legal basis to effectively pursue environmental objectives within the context of the internal market. In the *Titanium Dioxide* case, which involved the question whether the Directive on pollution caused by waste from the titanium dioxide industry should have been based upon Article 95 EC or Article 175 EC – recourse to both provisions, considering the fact that the Directive concerned both the internal market and the environment, was not possible due to different procedures – the ECJ explained its choice for Article 95 EC as follows.[111] First, the fact that pursuant to Article 130r (2) EEC (now Article 6 EC), environmental protection requirements shall be a component of the Community's other policies, implies that a Community measure cannot be covered by Article 175 EC merely because it also pursues objectives of environmental protection. Furthermore, provisions relating to the environment and health may be a burden upon the undertakings to which they apply and if there is no harmonisation, competition may be appreciably distorted. Article 95 EC is particularly appropriate to the attainment of the internal market. Finally, the ECJ referred to Article 95(3) EC, which indicates that the objectives of environmental protection referred to in Article 174 EC may be effectively pursued by means of harmonising measures adopted on the basis of Article 95 EC.[112]

---

111 Case C-300/89, *Commission v. Council (Titanium Dioxide)*.

112 Case C-300/89, *Commission v. Council (Titanium Dioxide)*, paragraphs 21-24.

After *Titanium Dioxide* the point of departure was that Article 95 EC was held to be broadly applicable in the field of the environment to all cross-border cases involving the free movement of goods or the conditions of competition in the internal market.[113] It was even advocated that Article 95 EC should be the principal if not only legal basis for Community environmental regulation, which also incorporates the objectives and principles mentioned by Article 174 EC.[114] In this respect a parallel can be drawn with the above-discussed *Tobacco Advertising* case. In later case law, the *Waste Framework Directive* case,[115] which was later confirmed by the *Transfer of Waste Regulation* case,[116] the ECJ made clear, though, that where in Community legislation the main focus has been laid upon the protection of the environment, Article 175 EC should be used as legal basis. Consequently the attention has partly shifted from Articles 94 and 95 EC as legal basis for environmental regulation to Article 175 EC, also including the power for the Community legislature to adopt harmonisation measures, but then specifically to implement environmental objectives and principles.

The 'centre of gravity theory' and the dispute on the choice of legal basis have become less pertinent due to the increased consistency between Articles 95 EC and 175 EC, now these provisions in principle both provide for the possibility to adopt harmonisation measures according to the co-decision procedure. Hence, whatever the outcome of an environmental case before the ECJ relating to choice of the legal basis will be, the Community remains competent to enact legislative measures under the same procedural rules. But it should be noted that in theory there are still important differences between Article 175(1) EC providing a qualified majority procedure and Article 175(2) EC providing unanimity for the adoption of environmental measures. Article 175(1) EC gives a legal basis for Community environmental legislation in general; Article 175(2) EC, although this provision seems of little practical use,[117] concerns specific provisions on environmental protection which either have an impact on, for example, land use or town and country planning in a Member State, or are closely connected to policy areas where Member States cannot simply give up 'sovereignty', like fiscal policy and energy policy.[118]

---

113 Geradin (1997), pp. 83-84.

114 R. Barents, Milieu en interne markt, *SEW*, 1993, pp. 5-29. See also for an overview of EC Environmental Law: L. Krämer, Thirty Years of EC Environmental Law: Perspectives and Prospects, in: H. Somsen (Ed.) *Yearbook of European Environmental Law*, 2002, pp. 156-182.

115 Case C-155/91, *Commission v. Council (Waste Directive)*.

116 Case C-187/93, *European Parliament v. Council (Transfer of Waste)*.

117 R.H. van Ooik, Bescherming van de Donau en de grondslagen van het Europese milieubeleid, *NTER*, 2001, p. 202.

118 See with regard to the relationship between Articles 175(1) and 175(2): Case C-36/98, *Spain v. Commission (Danube)* and R.H. van Ooik, Bescherming van de Donau en de grondslagen van het Europese milieubeleid, *NTER*, 2001, pp. 199-204.

Irrespective of the (theoretical) differences between Articles 175(1) and 175(2) EC, the choice of the proper legal basis remains relevant, since Article 176 EC, contrary to Article 95 EC, explicitly provides for minimum harmonisation without containing a standstill obligation. In addition the Community legislature may, considering the ruling in the *Tobacco* cases, be induced to adopt *total* harmonisation measures (see above, section 4.2.4). Article 95 EC furthermore only includes limited possibilities for a Member State to derogate from a harmonisation measure allowing the Commission to exclusively assess the adoption of more stringent standards (see above, section 3.2).[119] Hence, differences between Articles 95 EC and 175 EC continue to exist, a particularly important one is the scope of the minimum harmonisation provision laid down in Article 176 EC as compared to Article 95(4-5) EC.

The fact that Article 95 EC can very well be used as a legal basis for environmental measures is emphasised by paragraph 3, which refers to a high level of environmental protection which must be taken as a base for the Commission's legislative proposals and by the integration principle of Article 6 EC, requiring the Community legislature in adopting measures based on other legal bases to really integrate environmental considerations, thereby in particular taking account of the objectives and principles mentioned in Article 174 EC.[120] To give effect to this principle the Commission in its Internal Market Strategy 2003-2006 states that one of the priorities is to facilitate the free movement of goods, which should also entail a reduction of the impact on the environment of products.[121] It *inter alia* intends to adopt a Framework Directive on the eco-design of products and a Communication on a better integration of environmental requirements in technical standards, which are in line with the principles of Integrated Product Policy.[122]

In particular environmental product regulation (see below), which relates to the packaging of products or the (environmentally damaging) content of products, has been based on Article 95 EC, as well as measures which have an impact on trade and conditions of competition in a particular industry.[123]

---

119 See also H. Sevenster, The Environmental Guarantee after Amsterdam: Does the Emperor Have New Clothes? in: H. Somsen (Ed.), *Yearbook of European Environmental Law* (Oxford University Press, Oxford, 2002), pp 305-308.

120 Dhondt (2003).

121 COM(2003) 238 final.

122 See also COM(2001) 68 final; see the proposal for a Directive of the European Parliament and of the Council establishing a framework for the setting of Eco-design requirements of Energy-using Products, COM(2003) 453 final; see Opinion of the Commission on the European Parliament's amendments to the Council's common position, COM(2005) 219 final.

123 See Jans (2000), p. 53.

Packaging and packaging waste

The Directive on Packaging and Packaging Waste is a particularly good example of a Community harmonisation measure seeking to resolve the tension between the internal market and environmental protection, whereby the internal market provision of Article 95 EC has been chosen as proper legal basis.[124] The Directive is in accordance with the 'new approach' and brings about full harmonisation of the national measures on packaging management and packaging waste.[125] Furthermore, it exemplifies the Community's shift in the beginning of the 1990's from 'end of pipe' emissions controls towards the regulation of the environmental effects of products during their whole life cycle.[126] It therefore fits in with the Community's emphasis on integrated product policy.

The Directive aims at harmonising national measures concerning the management of packaging and packaging waste while providing for a high level of environmental protection. It thus includes two objectives: environmental protection and the functioning of the internal market, avoiding obstacles to trade and distortion of competition within the Community, which explains the use of Article 95 EC as legal basis. Where another but similar measure of integrated product policy includes environmental objectives that are more predominant, like the Directive on end-of-life vehicles, Article 175 EC is considered more appropriate as legal basis.[127]

In order to attain a high level of environmental protection Article 1(2) of the Directive stipulates that as a priority the production of packaging waste should be prevented, and additionally packaging waste should be re-used, recycled or recovered. Regarding prevention, Member States must ensure that preventive measures are taken in conformity with the objective of Article 1 of the Directive. Furthermore Member States shall encourage re-use systems of packaging in conformity with the Treaty, which means in conformity with Articles 28-30 EC. In other words, the organisation of national systems intended to encourage the reuse of packaging is therefore not the subject of full harmonisation, but has to be assessed in the light of primary Community law, i.e. Articles 28-30 EC. This appears from the Court's judgment in *Spitz* (see also Chapter 2).[128] In addition the Directive includes targets for recovery and recycling of packaging, but without including a clear ranking of waste management options.[129]

---

[124] Directive 94/62 on Packaging and Packaging Waste, OJ 1994, L 365/10.

[125] See also the Opinion of AG Colomer in Case C-246/99, *Commission v. Denmark*, paragraph 40: this case involved Danish measures prohibiting the use of certain packaging, like can and other single-use containers, which did, however, comply with the essential requirements of the Directive; the case was removed from the register on 11 September 2002 by Order of the President of the Court.

[126] I. Rose and G. Knighton, Integrated Product Policy: The New Approach to Environmental Regulation, *EELR*. 1999, p. 266.

[127] Directive 2000/53, OJ 2000, L 269/34.

[128] Case C-309/02, *Radlberger & Spitz*, paragraphs 52-59.

[129] The Packaging and Packaging Waste Directive has been extensively analysed by Haverland (1998).

Article 6(6) of the Directive provides for a limited – but still wider than Article 95(4-5) EC – possibility for Member States to set higher standards for recovery and recycling of packaging than are laid down in Article 6(1)(a) and (b) of the Directive. Firstly, the Member State must provide appropriate capacities for recycling and recovery; secondly, the national measures must avoid distortions of the internal market and may not hinder compliance by other Member States with the Directive; finally, the Member States must inform the Commission of the measures, which shall verify whether they are in conformity with these requirements, and whether they do not constitute an arbitrary means of discrimination or a disguised restriction of trade.

To ensure the free movement of packaging and packaging waste, packaging may only be placed on the market if it complies with the essential requirements included in Annex II of the Directive. As a consequence Article 18 of the Directive includes a market access or free movement clause: Member States shall not impede the placing on their market of packaging which satisfies the provisions of the Directive.

From these provisions it is clear that the Directive is an attempt to balance free movement of packaging and packaging waste with the prevention or reduction of packaging waste. The compromise which finally led to the adoption of this Directive, had made an originally exclusively environmental project from DG XI, laying down a hierarchy of waste management options, into a Directive with emphasis on both internal market and environmental considerations.[130] The Directive is currently under revision with a view to set a deadline by which new targets must be achieved in the acceding States.[131] The Directive may be criticised from an environmental perspective; nonetheless, where a common will exists to pursue a more stringent and protective environmental policy, by amending the Directive and, for example, including a hierarchy of waste management options, this will, considering the *Tobacco* cases, certainly be possible also within the context of Article 95 EC. Furthermore, this possibility is reinforced by the principle of integration as laid down in Article 6 EC.

4.3.2 Consumer policy and the internal market

Article 95 EC is the main legal basis for consumer policy measures.[132] Article 95 EC is also explicitly referred to in Article 153 EC, which provides for a specific legal basis in the field of consumer policy. There are no

---

130 See also Haverland (1998); Gehring (1995).

131 COM(2004) 127 final. See for practical problems relating to the implementation of the Directive: Haverland (1998).

132 J. Stuyck, European Consumer Law after the Treaty of Amsterdam: Consumer Policy in or beyond the internal market?, *CMLRev.*, 2000, p. 387; Reich and Micklitz (2003), p. 32; Callies and Ruffert (Eds); Bearbeitet von: H.-J. Blanke et al (2002), p. 1736.

cases in which the ECJ explicitly decided on the relationship between Article 95 EC and Article 153 EC. But Article 95 EC remains most relevant for the harmonisation of national consumer laws. There are several reasons for this. First, Article 153 EC itself refers to Article 95 EC as legal basis for consumer policy measures; a similar reference to the use of Article 95 EC as legal basis is lacking in other Treaty provisions on horizontal and flanking policies. Second and similar to the field of the environment, Article 95(3) EC also includes a reference to a high level of consumer protection which must be envisaged in the proposals of legislation based on this provision, emphasising the link between internal market policy and consumer protection.[133] In addition Article 153(2) EC (after the Treaty of Amsterdam) contains an integration clause, which was not included in the former Article 129a EC (Maastricht version), stipulating that consumer protection requirements shall be taken into account in defining and implementing other Community policies and activities. The last reason relates to the Community's (recent) preference for total harmonisation rather than minimum harmonisation.[134] Most consumer harmonisation measures based on Article 95 EC have, at least until now, followed the concept of minimum harmonisation.[135]

The Consumer Policy Strategy 2002-2006 stipulates the following three objectives of the Community's consumer policy: (i) a high *common* level of consumer protection, (ii) effective enforcement of consumer protection rules and (iii) involvement of consumer organisations in EU policies. According to the Commission these three objectives are designed to help achieving integration of consumer concerns into all other EU policies, to maximise the benefits of the single market for consumers and to prepare for enlargement.[136] Total harmonisation or a *common* level of consumer protection throughout the EU is an important means to achieve these objectives. The following developments have contributed towards this shift from minimum harmonisation to total harmonisation:[137]

- It appears that big differences still exist between Member States'

---

[133] Weatherill (1997), p. 18.

[134] See also P.J. Slot and G. Straetmans, Harmonisatie van wetgeving in de EG, *Tijdschrift voor Privaatrecht*, 2003, pp. 723-726; P. Rott, Minimum harmonisation for the completion of the internal market? The example of consumer sales law, *CMLRev.*, 2003, pp. 1108-1109. H.-W. Micklitz, N. Reich and S. Weatherill, EU Treaty Revision and Consumer Protection, *Journal of Consumer Policy*, 2004, p. 375; Cseres (2005), pp. 219-220.

[135] For an overview see: Weatherill (1997); J. Stuyck, European consumer law after the Treaty of Amsterdam: Consumer Policy in or beyond the internal market?, *CMLRev.*, 2000, pp. 367-400; Reich and Micklitz (2003).

[136] OJ 2002, C 137/2.

[137] See also Commissie voor Consumentenaangelegenheden ('Committee for Consumer Affairs'), Derde ontwerpadvies over het richtlijnvoorstel oneerlijke handelspraktijken, 11 February 2004 (Third concept-advisory report on the proposal for a Directive on unfair trading practices), pp. 32-33.

(consumer) laws, which has a negative impact on the functioning of the internal market as well as on consumer confidence, according to the Commission's Report on Consumer complaints in respect of distance selling and comparative advertising.[138]

- The Commission intends to harmonise national contract laws to improve coherence in the field of contract law and to stimulate the establishment of standard contract terms for the whole of the European Union.[139]
- The enlargement of the EU implies that the in practice still existing considerable differences in levels of consumer protection in the new Member States will lead to new distortions of competition and restrictions of trade within the internal market. A common solution might then be even more desirable.

The following examples of the Directive on unfair commercial practices and the Regulation on co-operation between national authorities responsible for the enforcement of consumer protection laws show how within the above-mentioned context the Community legislature seeks to improve the integration of consumer interests in its internal market policy.

The Directive on unfair commercial practices

The background of this Directive is the Green Paper on EU Consumer Protection, where the Commission intended to present a framework Directive containing a general duty in relation to unfair commercial practices as a possible basis for reform of EC consumer protection legislation.[140] The Directive is based on Article 95 EC, refers to Article 153 EC and in principle provides for total harmonisation.[141] However, it includes in Article 3, paragraphs 5 and 6, the possibility for Member States for a period of 6 years to apply national provisions which are more restrictive or prescriptive than this Directive and which implement directives containing minimum harmonisation clauses. There is even a possibility after review to prolong this derogation for a limited period.

According to the Commission in its original proposal the Directive "fully harmonises EU requirements relating to unfair business-to-consumer commercial practices and provides an appropriately high level of consumer protection. This is needed to address the internal market barriers caused by divergent national provisions and to provide the necessary support to consumer confi-

[138] COM(2000) 127 final.

[139] Communication from the Commission: A more coherent European contract law – An action plan COM(2003) 68 final.

[140] COM(2001) 531 final.

[141] Directive 2005/29 concerning unfair business-to-consumer commercial practices in the internal market and amending Directives 84/450, 97/7, 98/27 and 2002/65 and Regulation 2006/2004 (Unfair Commercial Practices Directive), OJ 2005, L 149/22.

dence to make a mutual recognition approach workable. Member States will not be able to use the minimum clauses in other directives to impose additional requirements in the field co-ordinated by this Directive."[142]

Apart from total harmonisation, notwithstanding the temporary derogation for Member States to set more stringent standards, the Directive shows the following features:

- It defines the conditions which determine whether a commercial practice is unfair.
- The initial proposal contained an internal market clause, providing that traders have to comply only with the requirements of the country of origin and preventing other Member States from imposing additional requirements on those traders who do so: principle of mutual recognition; the Directive has deleted the country of origin principle, but maintained the clause of free circulation of services or goods (Article 4 of the Directive).
- It contains a general prohibition covering unfair commercial practices and establishing three conditions for determining whether a practice is unfair. This prohibition will replace the existing divergent general clauses and principles in the Member States and define a common EU wide framework.
- It establishes the Court's average consumer, rather than the vulnerable or atypical consumer as benchmark consumer (see also Chapter 2); an explicit reference to the protection of the vulnerable consumer, however, has been included in Article 5, paragraph 3 of the Directive. For this 'clearly identifiable group of consumers' which are vulnerable to the commercial practice or underlying product because of their mental or physical infirmity, age or credulity in a way which the trader could reasonably be expected to foresee, commercial practices shall be assessed from the perspective of the average member of that group.
- Apart from the general prohibition, practices can be misleading or aggressive, which also means that they are unfair.
- The Directive contains a black list of commercial practices which are in all circumstances considered unfair.

Irrespective of practical issues, like whether not other factors, such as distance, language and culture discourage or prevent consumers from cross-border shopping, certain questions, which have not or hardly been dealt with by the Commission, remain pertinent.

The first comment that needs to be made concerns the choice of legal basis for this Directive. Article 95 EC is justifiable considering the encouragement of greater development of cross-border shopping by consumers by addressing internal market failures, even though the Commission in its impact assessment of

[142] COM (2003) 356 final, p. 8.

the Directive states that "the overall aim of the proposal is to fulfil the requirements of Treaty Articles 95 and 153 to put in place complete the internal market by removing barriers to the free movement of goods and services, and to provide a high level of consumer protection".[143] The Directive now contains a mere reference to Article 153 EC but no more, stipulating that the Community is to contribute to the attainment of a high level of consumer protection by the measures it adopts pursuant to Article 95 EC. The Consumer associations regretted this choice of legal basis and preferred Article 153 EC as (joint) legal basis, since measures based on Article 153 EC are minimum harmonisation measures.[144]

Another question relates to the interaction between the (framework) Directive with other Community consumer directives, which remains rather unclear.[145] According to the preamble, the Directive provides protection for consumers where there is no specific sectoral legislation. Where specific provisions do exist, they will take precedence.[146] Nonetheless, the possibility provided by Article 3, paragraph 5, of the Directive for Member States to apply during a period of six years more stringent national provisions also includes existing directives containing minimum harmonisation clauses. The question is whether this derogation implies that only during a period of six years time Member States may adopt more stringent provisions than laid down in the sectoral consumer directives containing minimum harmonisation clauses; should after this period these minimum directives be harmonised by the Community legislature at a sufficient high level of consumer protection?[147]

Lastly, an improvement is the introduction of a reference to the protection of more vulnerable consumers in the Directive by the Council. The condition though, that the trader must reasonably be able to foresee that such consumers are affected by a certain practice will need to be further clarified. Furthermore, the fact that as benchmark the average member of the group of vulnerable consumers is taken, puts the idea that this framework Directive really intends to take account of weaker consumers into perspective.

---

[143] Commission Staff Working Paper – Extended Impact Assessment on the Directive of the European Parliament and of the Council concerning unfair business-to-consumer commercial practices in the Internal Market, SEC(2003) 724, p. 9.

[144] See BEUC (The European Consumers' Organisation) comments on the Proposal for a Directive on Unfair Commercial Practices, 15 January 2004, BEUC/X/001/2004, to be found at: http://www.beuc.org/Content/Default.asp?PageID=146.

[145] Commission Staff Working Paper – Extended Impact Assessment on the Directive of the European Parliament and of the Council concerning unfair business-to-consumer commercial practices in the Internal Market, SEC(2003) 724, p. 23.

[146] Point 10 of the Directive on Unfair Commercial Practices. Cseres (2005), p. 231.

[147] As put forward by Sweden and Denmark in the Council: Interinstitutional File: 2003/0134, Brussels, 12 November 2004. They therefore did not support this proposal for a Directive on Unfair Commercial Practices.

The Regulation on co-operation between national authorities responsible for the enforcement of consumer protection laws

This Regulation will, according to the Commission, "help prevent unscrupulous traders from evading consumer protection authorities by targeting consumers living in other countries" and creates a EU-wide network of national enforcement authorities.[148] The Regulation in that sense complements the above-discussed Directive on unfair trading practices; it should provide for effective enforcement in cross-border cases, preventing sellers and suppliers to evade enforcement attempts by relocating within the Community and hence will, according to the Commission in its original proposal further increase the positive impacts of the framework Directive.[149]

The Regulation has been based on Article 95 EC, since, according to the recitals of the Regulation co-operation between public authorities responsible for enforcement of consumer protection also contributes to improving the functioning of the internal market.[150] It is nevertheless at least peculiar that the Regulation does not refer to the more specific Treaty provision of Article 153 EC, particularly since the Regulation is mainly concerned with the protection of consumer interests through the enforcement of consumer protection legislation by competent public authorities. This proves once more that Article 153 EC is of a clearly residual nature, leaving Article 95 EC to remain the main legal basis for the harmonisation of national consumer laws.

The Regulation requires Member States to designate competent authorities responsible for the application of the Regulation (Article 4); it provides for the exchange of information between the public authorities in case of an intra-Community infringement on request and without request, when a competent authority becomes aware of an intra-Community infringement, or reasonably suspects that such an infringement may occur (Article 7); it furthermore provides for enforcement measures (Article 8), effectiveness and responsibility (Article 11), protection of personal data, information exchange with third countries and enforcement co-operation at Community level (Article 16).

Conclusions regarding to the Directive and Regulation

In conclusion, the most striking feature of the present Community's consumer policy is the tendency towards total harmonisation. This preference for total harmonisation to minimum harmonisation can in particular for the field of consumer policy be explained as follows. As was shown in Chapter 2, the Court of Justice has in its jurisprudence developed a common notion of

[148] See Press Release, IP/04/1197 and Regulation 2006/2004 on co-operation between national authorities responsible for the enforcement of consumer protection laws (the Regulation on consumer protection co-operation), OJ 2004, L 364/1.

[149] See also point 2 of the initial proposal for this Regulation, COM(2003) 443 final.

[150] See in particular recital 2 of Regulation 2006/2004.

European consumer, the notion of informed consumer, who, if provided with adequate information, is capable of making his own choices and defending his own interests.[151] Hence, as point of departure must be taken the average *European* consumer, not the Swedish, Dutch, Italian, French or Polish consumers, which makes the use of the technique of total harmonisation in a European Union of 25 Member States, with increasing differences between national consumer laws even more pertinent.

Contrary to other horizontal and flanking policies, like environmental policy, where, for example, differing local and regional natural circumstances require different rules, which justifies regulatory diversity, the common European notion of consumer as *basis* for harmonisation justifies uniformity and makes regulatory experimentation by individual Member States less self-evident.[152] After all, consumers are, like companies, important market participants contributing to the integration of national markets. Total harmonisation may offer more legal certainty to consumers and at the same time contribute to cross-border trade.[153]

This is no pleading for a narrow version of Article 95 EC, incapable of promoting measures of consumer protection and leading the triumph of market freedom over market regulation;[154] on the contrary, it is a pleading for a broad version of Article 95 EC in the field of consumer policy, leading to an overall increase in consumer protection to the benefit of all consumers as required by Article 153 EC.

4.3.3 Public health and the internal market

Public health concerning *human* health, not animal health, is a varied policy field involving many issues. A distinction can roughly be made between public health in the strict sense, including the prevention of diseases, tobacco policy or more generally the protection of consumers' health, for which Community action is not that controversial, and national health care schemes, which form part of a Member State's social security system and which regulation at a Community level is much more contentious. This distinction is particularly relevant in assessing the harmonisation powers in the field of public health in general.

---

151 K. Mortelmans and S. Watson, The notion of consumer in community law: a lottery?, *TvC*, 1995, p. 233.

152 This is despite the fact that there may be other reasons pleading for minimum harmonisation, like adaptability and flexibility: see also BEUC comment on Unfair Commercial Practices, 15 January 2004, BEUC/X/001/2004, to be found at: http://www.beuc.org/Content/Default.asp?PageID=146.

153 R.W. de Vrey, Eerlijk is eerlijk: de consument voorop? Het richtlijnvoorstel 'oneerlijke handelspraktijken' nader bezien, *TvC*, 2004, p. 5.

154 This fear is expressed by H.-W. Micklitz and S. Weatherill, EU Treaty Revision and Consumer Protection, *Journal of Consumer Policy*, 2004, p. 376.

4.3.3.1 Public health *stricto sensu*

Article 95 EC is one of the main legal bases for health related measures adopted within the context of the internal market.[155] As stated before, the broad scope of application of Article 95 EC in the field of public health has been reinforced in the *Tobacco* cases and is confirmed by Article 95(8) EC which calls upon the Community legislature to take action on the basis of Article 95 in case of specific health problems (see section 3.2). The Commission should thereby, according to paragraph three of Article 95 EC, in its proposals take as a base a high level of health protection.

Other legal bases within the context of the internal market for health related measures are, for example, Articles 40, 47 and 55 EC (workers, services and establishment). Due to the impact of various policies on health, a combination of Treaty provisions may be used as legal basis for harmonisation measures; an example is provided by Regulation 1829/2003 on genetically modified food and feed, which is based on Articles 37 (agriculture), 95 (internal market) and 152(4)(b) EC (public health). Another example is Regulation 178/2002 establishing the European Food Safety Authority, which is based on Articles 37, 95, 133 and 152(4)(b) EC.[156]

Tobacco Advertising

Particularly relevant for the scope of Article 95 EC and other internal market legal bases in the field of public health are of course the *Tobacco* cases (see above, section 4.2.4). As stated before, on the one hand the possibilities to adopt harmonisation measures in the field of public health on the basis of Article 95 EC have been limited. In fact the Directive on Tobacco Advertising should, considering the fact that health interests play a predominant role, also have been based on Article 152 EC. On the other hand, where the threshold criteria are met,[157] the prohibition to harmonise contained in Article 152 EC may not withhold the Community from adopting harmonisation measures on the basis of other Treaty provisions, such as Article 95 EC. In that sense the rulings of the ECJ in the *Tobacco* cases are at least "an indirect confirmation that health protection is not a matter simply of national competence".[158]

According to the ECJ in *Tobacco Advertising*, certain advertising prohibitions could not be considered to help facilitating trade in products, such as the

---

[155] Callies and Ruffert (Eds); Bearbeitet von H.-J. Blanke et al(2002), p. 1728.

[156] OJ 2002, L 31/1.

[157] A. Somek, Good news for a bad habit: tobacco, culture and the rule of law in the European Union, available at: http://www.somek.org/Lectures/KSchoolHandout.PDF, p. 4; T.K. Hervey, 'Up in smoke? Community (anti-) tobacco law and policy, *ELRev.*, 2001, p. 119.

[158] T.K. Hervey, Community and national competence in health after tobacco advertising, *CMLRev.*, 2001, p. 1425.

prohibition of advertising on posters, parasols, ashtrays and other articles used in hotels, restaurants and cafés, and the prohibition of advertising spots in cinemas.[159] Hence, these prohibitions could not be based on Article 95 EC. The scope of application of Article 95 EC thus (partly) corresponds to the scope of application of Article 28 EC, which after *Keck* excludes certain rules on selling arrangements, including advertising rules (see also Chapter 2). In this respect the judgments in *Keck* and *Tobacco Advertising* can be seen as part of a process of redefining the internal market into a narrower concept.[160] The judgment in *Tobacco Advertising*, however, qualifies the effect of the *Keck* ruling by concluding that not all regulation of advertising rules, which admittedly do have an impact on trade in products, can be excluded from internal market legislation.[161] A qualification of *Keck* can also be found in other cases. In the field of public health the *DocMorris* case is relevant, which makes clear that the scope of the *Keck* doctrine is limited, particularly where new methods of cross-border sales of medicines, such as the Internet, are at stake (see also Chapter 2).[162] This means that in such cases Member States must rely on the protection of public health to justify restrictions on the free movement of goods, allowing the Community legislature to adopt measures on the basis of Article 95 EC safeguarding public health interests at a Community level. Due to the absence of an alternative legal basis, Article 95 EC should be used to harmonise public health interests in case of cross-border problems. The solution is thus to exclude from its scope activities that have a local impact, like a prohibition on tobacco advertising in bus stops, and to focus on cross-border effects of advertising for tobacco products with serious health implications. In other situations, for the harmonisation of health interests recourse must be taken to Article 152 EC, which, however, does not provide for this possibility.

More concretely the result of this case law has been that in the field of tobacco advertising, a new Directive has been adopted on the basis of the internal market Articles 47(2), 55 and 95 EC, indeed limiting the prohibition of advertising of tobacco products to the advertising and their promotion in the press and other printed publications, in radio broadcasting, in information society services and through tobacco related sponsorship, including the

---

[159] Case C-491/01, *BAT/Imperial Tobacco*, paragraph 99.

[160] See with regard to *Keck*: D. Chalmers, Repackaging the internal market the ramifications of the Keck judgment, *ELRev.*, 1994, p. 402; see also Bernard (2002), p. 85. According to Davies, however, *Keck* is only confined to Article 28 EC "and does not speak to the question of the scope of Art. 95". According to him selling arrangements could still be harmonised on the basis of Article 95 EC: G. Davies, Can selling arrangements be harmonised?, *ELRev.*, 2005, pp. 370-385. In my opinion the *Tobacco* cases suggest otherwise.

[161] K.J.M. Mortelmans and R.H. Van Ooik, Het Europese verbod op tabaksreclame: verbetering van de interne market of bescherming van de volksgezondheid?, *AA*, 2001, pp. 125-127.

[162] Case C-322/01, *DocMorris*, paragraph 73.

free distribution of tobacco products. The Directive contains a free movement clause.[163] As stated before, this Directive has also been challenged before the Court by Germany, arguing that it essentially concerns a public health measure which cannot be based on Article 95 EC.[164] At the same time, the Commission issued a proposal for a (non-binding) Council *Recommendation* on the prevention of smoking and on initiatives to improve tobacco control, which has now been adopted on the basis of Article 152 EC, in particular with a view to include forms of tobacco advertising, which could not be justified on the internal market rules given the Court's ruling in *Tobacco Advertising*.[165]

The authorisation and supervision of medicinal products for human and veterinary use and the establishment of a European Medicines Agency

Regulation 726/2004 improves the operation of the authorisation procedures for the placing of medicinal products on the market in the Community and amends certain administrative aspects of the European Agency for the Evaluation of Medicinal Products, which name is changed to European Medicines Agency. This Agency should provide the Community and Member States with scientific opinions on the quality, safety and efficacy of medicinal products. The Regulation is based on Articles 95 EC and 152(4)(b) EC and is just one of many examples of Community harmonisation measures in the field of pharmaceuticals.[166]

The Regulation clearly aims at completing the internal market for pharmaceuticals, yet also guaranteeing a high level of health protection for European citizens. This explains the choice for a dual legal basis, now Article 152(4)(b) EC stipulates that "the Council [...] shall contribute to the achievement of the objectives referred to in this Article through adopting by way of derogation from Article 37, measures in the veterinary and phytosanitary fields which have as their direct objective the protection of public health". Important features of the Regulation are that it provides for the opening of centralised authorisation procedure to more types of new medicines; it will become mandatory for medicines to treat AIDS, cancer, diabetes, neurodegenerative disorders and orphan diseases (see also the Annex); it aims to increase the availability and speed of access of new and innovative medicines to the European market by means of a 'fast track registration procedure' for products of significant therapeutic interest; in addition the possibility of a conditional marketing authorisation has been

---

163 See Articles 1 and 8 of Directive 2003/33 relating to the advertising and sponsorship of tobacco products, OJ 2003, L 152/16.

164 Case C-380/03, *Germany v. European Parliament and Council (Tobacco Advertising II)*, OJ 2003, C 275/31 (pending).

165 COM(2002) 303 final, at p. 4 (Commission proposal) and Council Recommendation of 2 December 2002 on the prevention of smoking and on initiatives to improve tobacco control, OJ 2003, L 22/31.

166 OJ 2004, L 136/1.

introduced, allowing for one-year authorisation to be granted provided that there is an important health benefit for the patients concerned. The Regulation also aims at increasing access to information and transparency for the benefit of patients. Scientific research plays an increasingly important role as well.

The objectives of public health, being predominant in the Regulation, fit in with the Court's approach in the *Tobacco* cases, allowing the Community legislature to make extensive use of Article 95 EC. The additional and specific legal basis for the harmonisation of national measures in veterinary and phytosanitary fields as laid down in Article 152(4)(b) EC in combination with the integration clause laid down in Article 152 EC, allow the Community legislature, by means of this Regulation, to relieve the tension between internal market and public health interests. However, the tension can be relieved only to a limited extent, since the possibilities for the Community legislature to legislate in this area are, according to the Regulation itself, not infinite. Article 1 of the Regulation stipulates that the provisions of the Regulation shall not affect the national authorities' powers as regards setting the prices of medicinal products or their inclusion in the scope of the national health system or social security schemes on the basis of health, economic or social conditions, thereby respecting the prohibition of harmonisation as laid down in Article 152 EC. According to Article 152(5) EC "Community action in the field of public health shall fully respect the responsibilities of the Member States for the organisation and delivery of health services and medical care". This does not mean that Member States have *carte blanche* in regulating the health care sector. The provisions on free movement set limits to the possibility to regulate in this area as was seen in Chapter 2.

4.3.3.2 Health care

Community action in the field of health care is (even) more contentious. Nevertheless, harmonisation measures adopted within the framework of the internal market may have an impact on national health care systems. The already mentioned proposal for a Directive on services in the internal market, for example, for the time being also applies to health services.[167] The aim of the proposed Directive is not only to enable service providers to freely provide services in other Member States, being only subject to the law of the country in which they are established (country of origin principle), but also to safeguard rights of recipients of services to use the services of service providers established elsewhere without being hampered by restrictive measures applying in their country of origin. With respect to recipients of health services, though,

[167] See point 7 of the explanatory memorandum of the proposal, COM(2004) 2 final/3, p. 19. As stated before in section 4.2.2 it is likely that the health care sector will be excluded from the scope of the Directive.

the proposed Directive provides for some restrictions on the rights of service recipients. In Article 23 of the proposed Directive the case law of the ECJ with regard to the free movement of health services and the requirement of prior authorisation to receive treatment in another Member State has been codified. This means that recipients of health care should in principle be able to go to another Member State in order to receive medical care there and to get their costs reimbursed to the extent that the costs of health care provided in their home state would have been reimbursed. As discussed in Chapter 2, according to the Court's jurisprudence and in particular the case *Müller-Fauré* a distinction ought to be made between hospital care and non-hospital care. As stated in section 4.2.2 the fact that the proposed Directive on services in the internal market includes a definition of hospital care is contentious, since the Community legislature hereby touches upon the organisation of the health care system, which, according to Article 152 EC, belongs to the competence of the Member States.

Where national health care systems include market elements and where costs of health services are partly covered by private insurance, Community law becomes relevant. The principle of mutual recognition has been used to attain an internal market for private insurance, based on single license and home country control principles allowing insurance companies based in a Member State to offer their products throughout the Community.[168] An example is Directive 92/49 on direct insurance.[169] This Directive is based on Articles 57(2) and 66 (now Articles 47(2) and 55 EC) and intends to make it easier, from the point of view of both the right of establishment and free movement of services, for insurance undertakings with head offices in the Community to cover risks situated within the Community. At the same time it intends to provide for adequate protection for policy holders.

Where health insurance is provided for by the state the Directive contains an exception. According to Article 2(2) that refers to Article 2(1)(d) of Directive 73/239, this Directive shall not apply to insurance forming part of a statutory system of social security.[170] The scope of this exception as well as the scope of application of the other provisions of the Directive relating to prior approval of policy conditions, of supervision, of prior authorisation by the home Member State etc. has been subject to case law and has been discussed in legal literature, in particular with a view to the possible consequences for national health insurance schemes which are partly or wholly carried out by private insurance undertakings.[171] According to the Court in *García* Article 2(2) excludes not merely

---

[168] G.J. Hamilton, Private Insurance for All in the Dutch Health Care System? *European Journal of Health Law*, 2003, p. 58.

[169] Directive 92/49, OJ 1992, L 228/1.

[170] OJ 1973, L 228/3.

[171] See, for example: Van de Gronden (2004); Mossialos & McKee (with Palm, Karl & Marhold) (2002), pp. 151-152.

social security organisations (undertakings or institutions) but also the types of insurance and operations which they provide in that capacity.[172]

Hence, in the field of public health a distinction is made between internal market and social security legislation. The ruling in *Tobacco Advertising* and the other *Tobacco* cases does not really put in jeopardy this distinction, but becomes relevant whenever health services are considered to fall within the scope of Articles 49 and 50 EC and hence will become subject to the rules of the internal market. The fact that the principle of mutual recognition applies to the sector of (private) insurance is in line with *Tobacco Advertising,* as it limits the possibilities of setting more stringent standards to the home state. This may seriously undermine the possibilities for Member States to regulate the health care sector, since more stringent or additional standards could not be applied in respect of, for example, health insurers established in another Member State. This could only be possible, if harmonisation were pursued on the basis of Article 152 EC, which should then include a similar minimum harmonisation clause as Article 176 EC or 153(5) EC. Harmonisation, however, is not possible due to the express exclusion of harmonisation of national health laws.

4.3.4 Cultural policy and the internal market

Cultural policy aims have also before the inclusion of Article 151 EC in the EC Treaty been pursued within the context of the internal market. The idea that Article 95 EC could very well be used as a legal basis for cultural measures is, similarly to the field of public health, more contentious than in case of environmental or consumer policy measures, particularly where Article 95 EC and other internal market legal bases could be used to circumvent the prohibition on harmonisation contained in Article 151 EC. For that matter Article 95 EC does not contain a reference to culture. This lacuna is to some extent filled by the integration clause contained in Article 151(4) EC. Nevertheless, where national measures have an impact on trade or competition within the internal market, Article 95 EC should be used to eliminate still existing trade barriers, irrespective of the prohibition of harmonisation as laid down in Article 151 EC.[173] The limits as well as the potential scope of application of Article 95 EC in fields of horizontal and flanking policies as set by the ECJ in the *Tobacco* cases are of course also relevant here.

An example of a rather controversial 'cultural' measure based on Article 95 EC is the Directive on the return of cultural objects unlawfully removed from the territory of a Member State.[174] This Directive concerns rules on the protection of cultural property within the European Community and complements

[172] Case C-238/94, *José García and others,* paragraph 10.

[173] Schmahll (1996), pp. 230-234; Albers (1999), p. 363.

[174] Directive 93/7, OJ 1993, L 74/74.

Regulation 3911/92 on the export of cultural goods, which is aimed at the protection of cultural goods with regard to trade with third countries and is also based on Article 133 EC.[175]

Other specific Treaty provisions providing for the harmonisation of 'cultural' measures (culturally-related) within the context of the internal market include Article 55 EC in conjunction with Article 47 EC for the harmonisation of services, which has been the legal basis for the 'Television without Frontiers Directive' adopted to facilitate the cross-border provision of television programmes.[176]

The return of cultural objects unlawfully removed from the territory of a Member State

The realisation of the internal market has led to some fear among Member States regarding possible conflicts between the aim of unrestricted intra-Community trade and their national art trade regulations. In other words, would the internal market lead to a deterioration of the artistic, historic or archaeological heritage of Member States? In response to this question the Commission drafted a Communication on the Protection of National Treasures Possessing Artistic, Historic or Archaeological Value: Needs Arising from the Abolition of Frontiers in 1992.[177] This finally led to the adoption of Council Regulation 3911/92 on the export of cultural goods and Council Directive 93/7 on the return of cultural objects unlawfully removed from the territory of a Member State.[178]

Directive 93/7 obliges Member States to return national treasures which have been removed unlawfully from their country of origin and which can be qualified as cultural objects within the meaning of the directive. The Directive, as well as the Regulation on the export of cultural goods, should both be considered as instruments that support Member States' action to prevent (an increase in) illegal art trade in and outside the Community. The Directive and Regulation were according to the Commission necessary since Member States had lost certain control mechanisms (customs controls) in the internal market to combat the illegal export of cultural goods.[179] The unlawful removal from the territory of a Member State involves as appears from article 1 of the Directive both stolen arts as well as cultural goods exported with the consent of the owner but in breach of export restrictions.[180]

---

175 Regulation 3911/92, OJ 1992, L 395/1.

176 Directive 89/552, OJ 1989, L 298/23 as amended by Directive 97/36, OJ 1997, L 202/60. For a general overview of EC cultural policy see: Albers (1999); Craufurd Smith (Ed.) (2004).

177 COM(89)594 final; see also, Loman, Mortelmans, Post and Watson (1992), pp. 174-176.

178 Council Regulation 3911/92, O.J. 1992, L 395/1; Council Directive 93/7, O.J. 1993, L 74/74.

179 COM(89) 594 final.

180 B. de Witte, The Cultural Dimension of Community Law, in: Academy of European Law (Ed.), *Collected Courses of the Academy of European Law*, Volume IV, Book 1 (Kluwer Law International, The Hague, 1995), p. 243.

The requesting Member State can only ask for the return of cultural objects which are national treasures within the meaning of Article 30 EC and which qualify as cultural objects as defined by the Annex to the Directive. The use of the term cultural 'objects', rather than 'goods' probably derives from the mixed nature of the objects: they are both national treasures as defined by the Member States as well as cultural goods mentioned in the Annex.[181] Even though Member States remain free to determine which goods are considered to be 'national treasures' within the meaning of Article 30 EC, the effect of this directive is that Member States have to accept each other's trade laws on cultural goods. The mutual recognition of national art measures has a wide influence, since Member States have to recognise the extra-territorial effects of legislation from other Member States. Legislation including a broad definition of national treasures which protects these articrafts from being exported (like in Italy), has to be accepted by Member States with a more liberal legal protection of cultural goods (for example in Germany).[182]

According to the Commission the Directive (as well as the Regulation) seeks to reconcile the fundamental principle of free movement of cultural goods with that of the protection of national treasures. Particularly due to the abolition of physical checks at the Community's internal borders, there was a need to provide for supplementary action to ensure adequate protection for cultural goods.[183] The Directive can therefore be seen as an instrument of common action preserving the shared cultural policy interests of the Member States,[184] but also as an instrument, which in fact leads to the territorialisation of art trade cultural policy. Since the Directive in fact enforces prohibitions to transfer cultural objects, the question has been raised as to whether the Directive is validly based upon Article 95 EC.[185] It should be noted, though, that notwith-

[181] B. de Witte, The Cultural Dimension of Community Law, in: Academy of European Law (Ed.), *Collected Courses of the Academy of European Law*, Volume IV, Book 1 (Kluwer Law International, The Hague, 1995), p. 244.

[182] W. Eberl, Probleme und Auswirkungen der EG-Vorschriften zum Kulturgüterschutz, *NVwZ*, 1994, p. 731; B. De Witte, The Cultural Dimension of Community Law, in: Academy of European Law (Ed.), *Collected Courses of the Academy of European Law*, Volume IV, Book 1 (Kluwer Law International, The Hague, 1995), p. 244.

[183] See also Report from the Commission on the implementation of Council Regulation 3911/92 on the export of cultural goods and Council Directive 93/7 on the return of cultural objects unlawfully removed from the territory of a Member State.

[184] B. De Witte, The Cultural Dimension of Community Law, in: Academy of European Law (Ed.), *Collected Courses of the Academy of European Law*, Volume IV, Book 1 (Kluwer Law International, The Hague, 1995), p. 274.

[185] W. Eberl, Probleme und Auswirkungen der EG-Vorschriften zum Kulturgüterschutz, *NVwZ*, 1994, p. 734; see with regard to nationalism versus internationalism: J.H. Merryman, Thinking About the Elgin Marbles, *Michigan Law Review*, 1985, p. 1881: the international dimension of culture, i.e. common cultural heritage, should also be taken into account; see also Uhl (1993), p. 154 et seq.

standing these important legal questions, in practice the procedure as laid down in the Directive has never been applied.[186]

What has been stated before with respect to public health policy, is equally relevant here. If the purpose of the Directive were to create an internal market for cultural goods, or a level playing field for the market of art treasures, precisely by preventing the free movement of unlawful or stolen art, it would in the words of AG Fennelly be sufficient for Article 95 EC to be applicable.[187] The fact that the Directive is also concerned with the protection of cultural interests is then less relevant.[188] The *Tobacco* judgments in that sense may save the Directive from nullity. After all the realisation of the internal market, in particular the abolition of physical checks at the internal borders, determines the level at which these cultural interests must be safeguarded, i.e. the level of the Community.[189] Hence the tension between cultural policy and the internal market has here been resolved within the context of Article 95 EC, which can now be justified by the cultural integration clause laid down in Article 151(4) EC.

The Television without Frontiers Directive

The recognition of television as a service within the meaning of Article 50 EC has brought national broadcasting regulation within the ambit of the Treaty.[190] The Court's *media* cases reveal the extent to which Community law has driven into the regulation of the national media (See also Chapter 2). The regulation of broadcasting activities, or the media in general, has always been the responsibility of the Member States. This is hardly surprising considering the impact of the press and television on society as a whole. Taking into account the hours that are spent daily in front of the television by European citizens, the influence of television on society and the shape of politics must be enormous.[191] The characteristics of television as means of mass communication with

[186] A. Biondi, The Gardener and other Stories: the Peregrinations of Cultural Artefacts within the European Union, in: R. Craufurd Smith (Ed.), *Culture and European Union Law* (Oxford University Press, Oxford, 2004), p.160.

[187] Opinion of AG Fennelly in Case C-376/98, *Germany v. European Parliament and Council (Tobacco Advertising)*, paragraph 86.

[188] A. Biondi, The merchant, the thief & the citizen: The circulation of works of art within the European Union, *CMLRev.*, 1997, pp. 1173-1195: Works of arts are goods within the meaning of Article 28 EC; however, they have always been considered as in a legal category of their own; virtually every modern State has adopted specific legislation dedicated to the protection of cultural objects: see also J. H. Merryman, The Public Interest in Culture Property, *California Law Review*, 1989, p. 339.

[189] See in the context of tobacco policy and public health: Opinion of AG Geelhoed in Case C-491/01, *BAT/Imperial Tobacco*, paragraph 106.

[190] See chapter 2.

[191] See also: E. Barendt, Towards a European Media Law? *MJ*, 1994, p. 41; M.J. Hahn, Eine Kulturelle Bereichsausnahme im Recht der WTO?, *ZaöRV*, 1996, pp. 315-352: From a cultural point of view free trade has the consequence of uniform television programmes which should, in the eyes of the states, be prevented by pursuing a cultural policy which goes beyond trade policy considerations.

a cultural and pedagogical meaning are recognised in national legislation, but may limit the free movement of television services at the level of the Community. Restrictions on access to the domestic television market, restrictions on television advertisements, the protection of national public service broadcasters, the protection of national television programmes and the protection of consumers, including minors may all impede the free movement of television services within the Community.

In 1989 the Community adopted the 'Television without Frontiers' Directive on the basis of Articles 47(2) and 55 EC in order to implement the free circulation of television programmes in the European Community.[192] An increasingly expanding television market and the will to preserve and strengthen the European audio-visual industry were strong incentives to adopt this Directive. In order to attain this objective Member States shall ensure the freedom of reception and must not restrict the retransmission of television broadcasts from other Member States on their territory for reasons which fall within the field co-ordinated by this Directive.[193]

Mainly due to technological developments the Directive has meanwhile been revised and amended by Directive 97/36.[194] The Directive provides *inter alia* for rules on advertising, sponsorship and teleshopping, on the protection of minors against harmful television programmes, the relationship between cinema and television, the broadcasting of major (sports) events and on 'quota' for the broadcasting of European programmes (Article 4).

According to the Commission the Directive gives due account of the audiovisual's cultural dimension: it reflects a synergy between economy and culture. Apart from the above-mentioned cultural aspects of the Directive, the relation between cinema and television as well as the broadcasting of major events, the Commission, in its 1st report on Article 151(4) EC particularly mentions two cultural aspects:

- The quota-provision ensures minimum representation of national and European cultures on European screens;
- Member States have to maintain certain national measures relating to linguistic policy.[195]

The preamble of the Directive refers to Article 151(4) EC and the promotion of European audio-visual products, which should, according to Article 4 of the

[192] Council Directive 89/552, O.J. 1989, L 298/23, amended by Council Directive 97/36, O.J. 1997, L 202/60.

[193] Case C-11/95, *Commission v. Belgium*; Case C-14/96, *Denuit*.

[194] See also B.J. Drijber, The revised television without frontiers directive: is it fit for the next century? *CMLRev.*, 1999, pp. 87-122.

[195] European Commission, First Report on the Consideration of Cultural Aspects in European Community Action, COM(96) 160 final (Part III – Audiovisual Policy).

Directive be attained by the establishment of quota for the broadcasting of European works: "Member States shall ensure *where practicable and by appropriate means* [italics added by the author] that broadcasters reserve for European works, within the meaning of Article 6, a majority proportion of their transmission time, excluding the time appointed to news, sports events, games, advertising, teletext services and teleshopping. This proportion, having regard to the broadcaster's informational, educational, cultural and entertainment responsibilities to its viewing public, should be achieved progressively, on the basis of suitable criteria." Article 4 has no compelling character because of the words "where practicable and by appropriate means" but is nevertheless 'legally binding' since it has been included in a harmonisation measure.[196]

The proposal to give Article 4 a more compelling character, *requiring* Member States to reserve time for European works, has not been accepted. Especially France turned out to be an advocate of an obligatory quota system.[197] The promotion of cultural and linguistic diversity and the strengthening of the European audio-visual industry, particularly vis à vis the American film and television industry, remain important elements of European audio-visual policy and will continue to play a role in future legislative proposals in relation with the Television without Frontiers Directive.[198] Nevertheless, the quota-provision

[196] The German Länder thus argued before the German Constitutional Court (Bundesverfassungsgericht) that their rights were infringed by the Bund during the adoption of the directive and held that the European Community did not dispose of a cultural competence, particularly with regard to the Quota-provision. The ruling of the Bundesverfassugsgericht implied that the Quota-provision would extend beyond the competence of the Community: see also U. Häde, BVerfG: Beteiligungsrechte der Länder und Verhalten des Bundes beim Zustandekommen von EG-Rechtsakten, *EuZW*, 1995, pp. 277-285; see also M. Herdegen, After the TV judgement of the German Constitutional Court: decision-making within the EU Council and the German Länder, *CMLRev.*, 1995, pp. 1369-1384.

[197] Germany and the United Kingdom were against the proposal. The United Kingdom stressed the need to ensure competitiveness while allowing new services to be introduced, whereas Germany underlined the need to main culture as a field of national action, in: Agence Europe No. 6421, 16 February 1995, at p. 7.

[198] Conclusions of the Council, OJ 2003, C 13/1. Safeguarding cultural diversity in relation to audio-visual services is an important aim of the EU in the WTO debate. In 2001 a Ministerial Conference on the WTO was held in Doha. It is known as the Doha Development Agenda (DDA). In February 2000, though, sectoral negotiations started in the World Trade Organisation, on agriculture (GATT), Intellectual property (TRIPS) and services (GATS). As far as services are concerned, these negotiations were laid down in the GATS treaty itself, the so-called 'built-in' agenda. The Conclusions adopted by the General Affairs Council of 26 October 1999, i.e. during the forthcoming WTO negotiations, the Union will ensure, as in the Uruguay Round, that the Community and its Member States maintain the possibility to preserve and develop their capacity to define and implement their cultural and audio-visual policies for the purpose of preserving their cultural diversity, form the negotiating mandate for the European Commission and are also valid for the negotiations on the built-in agenda. As far as audio-visual services are concerned, this mandate has also been confirmed for the DDA negotiations: http: //europa.eu.int/comm/avpolicy/extern/gats_en.htm.

contained in Articles 4 and 5 remains contentious. Its legality has been questioned from three different perspectives, namely the perspective of the legal basis, the perspective of the freedom of expression contained in Article 10 of the ECHR and the perspective of international trade law: trade in audio-visual products between the Community and the US.[199] The question of legal basis is particularly relevant here, for the Directive is based on Articles 47(2) EC and 55 EC, whereas the quota-provision constitutes a restriction on the free movement of television services for the sake of improving the knowledge and dissemination of European culture.

On the basis of the *Tobacco* cases and the integration principle as laid down in Article 151(4) EC it can be argued that the quota-provision is validly based on the internal market legal bases. Cultural interests may after all be harmonised on the basis of Articles 47(2) EC and 55 EC, once the threshold criteria are met, which is the case since the Directive provides for common rules to prevent distortions of competition. Once again the presumed broad scope of the internal market legal bases after the *Tobacco* cases justifies Community intervention also in the cultural field, which is good news for the *Community* legislature.

4.4 Conclusions

The foregoing shows that the Community legislature has harmonised horizontal and flanking policy interests within the context of the internal market. It has sometimes been able to deal with and eventually resolve the tension between horizontal and flanking policies and the internal market. This process of harmonisation has been reinforced by the *Tobacco* cases, endorsing a broad use of the internal market legal bases, like Article 95 EC, also in areas of horizontal and flanking policies. Article 95(3) EC, and for the field of public health Article 95(8) EC, furthermore confirm this. The question, however, is how broadly the Court's ruling in the *Tobacco* cases must be interpreted, and to what extent this ruling can contribute to resolving the tension between horizontal and flanking policies and the internal market, which will be dealt with in Chapters 5 and 6.

Generally two views are possible. The broader view suggests that, apart from the criterion of appreciability (threshold criteria), there are no limitations for the use of the Community's legislative powers under Article 95 EC and other internal market legal bases with a view to adopt harmonisation measures, also in areas where harmonisation on the basis of other and more specific legal bases is excluded. A confirmation of this view in respect of public health policy can be deduced from Article 95(8) EC, requiring the Community legislature to take legislative action in case of a specific health problem. This very broad view

199 B.J. Drijber, The revised television without frontiers directive: is it fit for the next century?, *CMLRev.*, 1999, pp. 108-113.

implies that even social security systems can be subject to harmonisation under the internal market legal bases.

A slightly narrower view, however, departs from the idea that there must be some limitations for the Community's legislative powers, also when the threshold criteria have been fulfilled, in particular in the area of health care. Even though the Court's ruling in the *Tobacco* cases clearly suggests that the objective of the harmonisation measure is not really relevant in deciding upon the proper legal basis, in particular when the more specific legal basis excludes harmonisation of national laws, Article 152 EC on public health does not merely exclude harmonisation; in paragraph 5 it is stipulated that Community action in the field of public health shall fully respect the responsibilities of the Member States for the organisation and delivery of health services and medical care. This less broad view implies that the boundaries of the *Tobacco* cases are defined by the organisation of the health care system. But there is an undetermined margin in between, wherein the Community legislature can make widely use of its powers under Article 95 EC and other internal market legal bases to harmonise horizontal and flanking policies.

5 Harmonisation beyond the internal market: specific legal bases

The discretionary power to harmonise national laws within the context of the internal market is, according to the jurisprudence of the ECJ, nonetheless limited. It must be established that there is somehow a certain link between inter-state trade, the objective of the common market and the measure concerned (*Tobacco Advertising* case). If this link cannot be shown, a specific Treaty provision must be identified for the Community to take legislative action, which is not always possible.

As will be seen here the Community has not been granted *de facto* a general competence; the nature and content of horizontal and flanking policies are defined in separate Treaty provisions. Different decision-making procedures apply and for some areas harmonisation is expressly excluded. This has also been referred to as the "variable geometry of norms and the complex instrument of different procedures".[200]

The specific Treaty provisions on, for example, environmental and consumer protection may furthermore and from a national state's perspective, be particularly relevant, where they permit the Member States to supplement harmonised Community regimes in a much wider range of cases than Article 95 EC does,

---

[200] R. Lane, New Community competences under the Maastricht Treaty, *CMLRev.*, 1993, p. 940; D. Chalmers, The Single Market: From Prima Donna to Journeyman, in: J. Shaw and G. More, *New Legal Dynamics of European Union* (Clarenden Press, Oxford 1995) at p. 70.

permitting additional Member States' measures only under carefully regulated circumstances.[201] The pre-emptive effect of harmonisation measures based on these specific provisions is as a consequence much less than the effect of measures based upon Article 95 EC.

5.1 Environmental policy as horizontal and flanking policy

According to Article 3(1) sub l the activities of the Community include a policy in the sphere of the environment.

5.1.1 The legal basis for environmental policy

Article 175 EC is the legal basis to take specific action to attain the objectives of environmental policy mentioned by Article 174 EC. The objectives of European environmental policy are:

- preserving, protecting and improving the quality of the environment
- protecting human health
- prudent and rational utilisation of natural resources
- promoting measures at international level to deal with regional or world-wide environmental problems.

According to Article 174(2) EC the principles on which European environmental policy is based are:

- a high level of environmental protection
- precautionary principle
- principle that preventive action should be taken
- principle that environmental damage should be rectified at source
- polluter pays principle

This Treaty provision designed particularly to protect the environment had already been included in the E(E)C Treaty since the Single European Act (1987). Since the adoption of the Treaty of Amsterdam co-decision has been the standard decision-making procedure for environmental legislation, apart from legislation in the areas mentioned in paragraph 2 of Article 175 EC (see above, section 4.3.1). From a substantive law perspective it is important to mention that since *Maastricht* the focus is laid upon sustainable development rather than sustainable growth as one of the objectives of the Community.

Article 175 EC clearly provides for the adoption of *harmonisation* measures specifically to attain objectives of environmental policy unconnected from the functioning of the internal market and has been a legal basis for many harmonisation measures ever since.[202] The power to adopt such environmental legisla-

[201] See also M. Dougan, Minimum harmonization and the internal market, *CMLRev.*, 2000, p. 883.

[202] See with regard to Article 175 EC: Jans (2000), pp. 44-50.

tion at a Community level was reinforced in the three cases, in which the ECJ had to decide on the relationship between Article 175 EC and Article 95 EC (see section 3.4.1). The attention shifted from Articles 94 and 95 EC as legal basis for environmental regulation to Article 175 EC in the *Waste Framework Directive* case[203], which was later confirmed in the *Transfer of Waste Regulation* case.[204] In other cases the ECJ was asked to draw the line between Article 175 EC and other Treaty provisions.[205]

Not only has the ECJ qualified its ruling in *Titanium Dioxide*, but it has also reinforced the role of Article 175 EC as legal base for harmonisation measures. The application of this so-called "centre of gravity theory" was made possible due to the inclusion of the co-decision procedure for the adoption of measures based on Article 175 EC by the Treaty of Maastricht. If the primary objective is the protection of the environment, the harmonisation measure will have to be based on Article 175 EC. In the *Transfer of Waste Regulation* case the ECJ held that Regulation 259/93 on the Transboundary movement of hazardous Wastes was properly based on Article 130s (now Article 175) EC, since the Regulation could not be regarded as seeking to implement the free movement of waste within the Community, but fell within the Community's environmental policy.[206]

5.1.2 An example of a harmonisation measure: the Transfer of Waste Regulation

The Transfer of Waste Regulation is a particularly good example of how in Community legislation based on Article 175 EC the tension between the internal market and environmental protection may be resolved while making a distinction between two categories of products: waste destined for disposal and waste destined for recovery.[207] Where waste destined for recov-

---

[203] Case C-155/91, *Commission v. Council.*

[204] Case C-187/93, *European Parliament v. Council.*

[205] In its Opinion 2/00, *Cartagena Protocol,* the ECJ was asked to establish the proper legal basis for the Cartagena Protocol on Biosafety, adopted by the conference of the parties to the Convention on Biological Diversity signed by the EC and its Member States on the Earth Summit in Rio de Janeiro. According to the ECJ the Cartagena protocol should be based on Article 175 EC and not on Article 133 EC (common commercial policy with exclusive competence for the Community), since "the main purpose or component is the protection of biological diversity against the harmful effects which could result from activities that involve dealing with living modified organisms (LMOs), in particular from their transboundary movement". (paragraph 34) The ECJ admitted, though, that provisions of the protocol relate to the transboundary movement of LMOs, however, the ECJ maintained the protocol's purpose is not to promote, facilitate or govern trade.

[206] Opinion 2/00, *Cartagena Protocol*, paragraph 23.

[207] Article 13 of Regulation 259/93 on the supervision and control of shipments of waste within, into and out of the European Community, OJ 1993, L 30/1.

ery and at the same time considered least harmful is concerned, the internal market provisions are normally applicable; where waste destined for disposal is at stake, the Regulation provides for a stringent regime of supervision and control of shipments of waste for the benefit of the environment.[208]

The Regulation involves interstate movements of wastes, and does not apply to movements of wastes within a Member State. The fact that the Regulation cannot be seen as to *facilitate* the free movement of wastes for disposal within the Community particularly appears from Article 4 of the Regulation, which allows Member States, in order to implement the principles of proximity, priority for recovery and self-sufficiency at Community and national levels, to prohibit systematically shipments of waste. Such measures shall immediately be notified to the Commission, which will inform the other Member States. This makes Member States, subject to supervision by the Commission, primarily responsible for the supervision and control of waste shipments.

Shipments of waste destined for recovery are, if the waste is included in the green list and hence considered least harmful, subject to a lighter regime and in principle to the rules on free movement. According to the Court in the *Dusseldorp* case "the difference in treatment between waste for disposal and waste for recovery reflects the different roles played by each type of waste in the development of the Community's environmental policy. By definition, only waste for recovery can contribute towards implementation of the principle of priority for recovery laid down in Article 4(3) of the Regulation. It was in order to encourage such recovery in the Community as a whole, in particular by eliciting the best technologies, that the Community legislature stipulated that waste of that type should be able to move freely between Member States for processing, provided that transport poses no threat to the environment. It therefore introduced for intra-Community shipment of that waste a more flexible procedure, which does not reflect the principles of self-sufficiency and proximity."[209]

Thus where waste destined for disposal is concerned the Regulation in fact renationalises the control of shipments of waste and thereby codifies the Court's ruling in the earlier discussed *Walloon Waste* case.[210] The importance of the Waste Regulation is therefore that it is apparently possible on the basis of Article 175 EC to implement the environmental principles contained in Article 174 EC through the adoption of harmonisation measures which restrict the functioning of the internal market.

[208] See in general: Veldkamp (1998).

[209] Case C-203/96, *Dusseldorp*, paragraph 33.

[210] Case C-2/90, *Commission v. Belgium (Walloon Waste)* (see Chapter 2). Annotation H. Sevenster and L. Hancher, *CMLRev.*, 1993, pp. 351-367. Geradin (1997), p. 124.

Hence, environmental protection measures could, far from the objective of market integration, lead to wholly Treaty conform legislation.[211] The tension between environmental policy and the internal market has thus been resolved through the adoption of far-reaching legislation, which is, as we have seen, made possible by Article 175 EC. In the light of the *Tobacco* cases, though, the adoption of such far-reaching legislation may also be possible in respect of other horizontal and flanking policies. The difference remains that in respect of environmental policy, the 'centre of gravity theory' applies, contrary to other horizontal and flanking policies for which harmonisation powers are lacking and where the threshold criteria (or appreciability test) are relevant.

5.2 Consumer policy as horizontal and flanking policy

Article 3(1) sub t EC states that the Community shall contribute to the strengthening of consumer protection. According to the Commission this implies that EC consumer policy should provide essential health and safety requirements, safeguard the economic interests of consumers and also empower consumers to understand policies that affect them.[212]

5.2.1 The legal basis for consumer policy

Article 153 EC, which was introduced by the Treaty of Maastricht, stipulates that the Community's objectives are to protect the health, safety and economic interests of consumers and to promote consumers' right to information, education and to organize themselves in order to safeguard their interests; the right to education and the right for consumers to organise themselves to safeguard their interests were included by the Treaty of Amsterdam. Article 153 EC does not provide for a right for consumers to their health, safety and to the protection of their economic interests. Such rights have to be elaborated in secondary law (harmonisation measures). The protection of health of consumers here is closely linked to the actual or potential use of goods and services, and does not involve general public health policy including the prevention of diseases, which is covered by Article 152 EC (see hereafter).[213]

---

[211] M. Schröder, Die steuernde und marktbergenzende Wirkung umweltschutzrelevanter Prinzipien des EG-Vertrages am Beispiel Abfallexportes, *NVwZ*, 1996, p. 837. In Joined Cases C-307/00 to C-311/00, *Oliehandel Koeweit BV*, preliminary questions were raised by the Netherlands Raad van State ('Council of State') also with regard to the interpretation of the export prohibition as laid down in Regulation 259/93 in the light of Article 29 EC. Due to an earlier judgment in Case C-6/00, *ASA Abfall Service*, where similar questions were raised, the Court proposed to give its decision by reasoned order and did not further deal with this question.

[212] Consumer policy strategy 2002-2006, OJ 2002, C 137/2.

[213] Callies and Ruffert (Eds); Bearbeitet von H.-J. Blanke (2002), p. 1734.

Article 153 EC is the legal basis to adopt measures which support, supplement and monitor the policy pursued by the Member States in order to attain the objectives mentioned above. Even though Article 153 EC provides the Community with specific powers to develop a Community consumer policy, the fact that the Community contributes to the policies of the Member States seems to suggest that its powers are of a more limited scope than in the field of the environment. It makes clear, though, that similarly to environmental policy the Community legislature shares its powers with the Member States and that the principle of subsidiarity plays a role here as well.[214] Nevertheless, the formulation used in Article 153 EC is peculiar. It suggests that on the basis of Article 153 EC Member States would have more powers to pursue consumer interests than they would have in the field of the environment on the basis of Article 175 EC. In the end, though, their powers are more limited due to the extensive use of Article 95 EC as legal basis for consumer policy measures with an increasing preference to use total harmonisation as harmonisation technique. Contrary to the other Treaty provisions on e.g. the environment, public health and culture, Article 153 EC itself refers to these two possibilities to take action in the interest of consumers (Article 153 (3) EC), probably due to the close link that exists between consumer matters and the internal market and the fact that the protection of consumers should first be pursued within the framework of the internal market.

The pre-Amsterdam provision of Article 129a EC (now Article 153 EC) referred to 'specific action' rather than 'measures' the Community could take to support and supplement the policy pursued by the Member States. Since the term 'specific action' was nowhere defined its scope remained unclear.[215] It was generally presumed though, that specific action included harmonisation measures, although, not by all Member States.[216] The reference to 'measures' in Article 153 EC now clarifies that consumer protection measures whose primary aim are not the completion of the internal market can be of a legislative nature,[217] which is confirmed by the legislative measures which have until now been adopted on the basis of Article 153 EC (see below).[218] It has also been suggested in literature that Article 153 EC could be used to adopt a similar Directive on tobacco advertising, which was annulled by the Court in the *Tobacco*

---

[214] Reich & Micklitz (2003), p. 23; Kapteyn & VerLoren van Themaat (2003), p. 940.

[215] H.A.G. Temmink, Het Europees consumentenbeleid van Maastricht naar Amsterdam en verder, *TvC*, 1997, p. 227.

[216] H.-W. Micklitz and S. Weatherill, Consumer Policy in the European Community: Before and after Maastricht, *Journal of Consumer Policy*, 1993, pp. 287-321.

[217] J. Stuyck, European consumer law after the Treaty of Amsterdam: Consumer Policy in or beyond the internal market?, *CMLRev.*, 2000, p. 387.

[218] See also Reich & Micklitz (2003), p. 34; Callies and Ruffert (Eds); Bearbeitet von H.-J. Blanke (2002), p. 1736.

Advertising case.[219] Article 153 EC provides the possibility to adopt measures of consumer protection "not subordinate to the dictates of internal market policy",[220] which may also restrict the functioning of the internal market.[221] Even though Article 153 EC clearly provides for a coherent legal framework for Community action in the field of consumer policy, which is not necessarily linked to the internal market process,[222] its additional value to the use of Article 95 EC, which continues to be the main legal basis for the harmonisation of national consumer laws, remains uncertain. Furthermore, despite the legal improvements, a political commitment is needed for specific consumer protection measures to further develop EC consumer policy.[223]

The question of which legal basis should be used is relevant, since measures adopted pursuant to Article 153 EC are, according to Article 153(5) EC, minimum harmonisation measures, whereas consumer protection is not mentioned in Article 95(4) EC as ground for the adoption of stricter national measures. Furthermore, contrary to Article 95(4) EC, Article 153(5) EC does not confer powers of decision on the Commission. As till now however, no cases which in particular touch upon the relationship between Article 95 EC and Article 153 EC and which may have clarified the scope of application of Article 153 EC, have been decided upon by the Court.

5.2.2 Measures adopted on the basis of Article 153 EC

So far Article 153 EC has been scarcely used as legal basis for harmonisation measures in the field of consumer policy.[224] Apparently and in contrast with Article 175 EC on the environment, the practical relevance of Article 153 EC has been extremely limited. The Commission neither in the Green Paper on consumer protection, nor in its most recent consumer policy strategy

---

[219] K.J.M. Mortelmans and R.H. van Ooik, Het Europese verbod op tabaksreclame: verbetering van de interne markt of bescherming van de volksgezondheid, *AA*, 2001, p. 128.

[220] Weatherill (1997), p. 25.

[221] According to Stuyck "measures of consumer protection which restrict the functioning of the market should be specifically justified": J. Stuyck, European Consumer Law after the Treaty of Amsterdam: Consumer Policy in or beyond the internal market?, *CMLRev.*, 2000, p. 400.

[222] See also Howells and Weatherill (2005), pp. 128-129.

[223] This political commitment has not been very significant according to G. Howells and T. Wilhelmsson, EC consumer law: has it come of age?, *ELRev.*, 2003, pp. 370-388.

[224] Decision 3092/94 introducing a Community system of information on home and leisure accidents (EHLASS), OJ 1994, L 331/1; Directive 98/6 on consumer protection in the indication of the prices of products offered to consumers, OJ 1998, L 80/27; Decision 276/1999, adopting a multi-annual Community action plan on promoting safer use of the Internet by combating illegal and harmful content on global networks, OJ 1999, L 33/1; Decision 283/1999, establishing a general framework for Community activities in favour of consumers, OJ 1999, L 34/1.

further defines the relationship between Articles 153 EC and 95 EC.[225] Article 153 EC will however, certainly be relevant for the establishment of a Community framework for *financing* Community actions in support of consumer policy.[226]

One of the measures adopted pursuant to Article 153 EC is the Directive on the indication of the prices of products offered to consumers.[227] The purpose of this Directive is, according to Article 1, to stipulate indication of the selling price and the price per unit of measurement of products offered by traders to consumers in order to improve consumer information and to facilitate comparison of prices. Apart from the aim of consumer protection, the homogeneous and transparent information on prices benefits not only consumers, but also businesses in the context of the internal market. In order to achieve these aims *inter alia* Article 4 of the Directive states that the selling price and the unit price must be unambiguous, easily identifiable and clearly legible. The Directive contains a minimum harmonisation clause in Article 10 stipulating that Member States shall not be prevented from adopting or maintaining provisions which are more favourable as regards consumer information and comparison of prices, without prejudice to their obligations under the Treaty.

Even though the Decision on introducing a Community system of information on home and leisure accidents is not in force anymore, it will nevertheless be briefly discussed here considering the lack of other examples of harmonisation measures based on Article 153 EC. By means of this Decision the Community provided for action to supplement and complement Member States' policy in this respect.[228] According to the Community legislature: "Whereas, although the management of consumer safety is primarily the responsibility of each Member State, Community financial involvement can help the Member States to overcome the problems of the actual collection of data at national level; whereas the Commission must therefore provide co-ordination and contribute to the homogeneous implementation of action taken at national level, by promoting the dissemination of information on home and leisure accidents to all the competent authorities." The principle of subsidiarity is clearly reflected in this Decision, as Member States are primarily responsible for the health and safety of consumers as well as for prevention of home and leisure accidents, whereas the Community, owing to the circulation of products which may be involved

[225] Green Paper on European Union Consumer Protection, COM(2001) 531 final; Consumer Policy Strategy, OJ 2002, C 137/2.

[226] Decision 20/2004, establishing a general framework for financing Community actions in support of consumer policy for the years 2004-2007, OJ 2004, L 5/1.

[227] Directive 98/6, OJ 1998, L 80/27; Nevertheless, considering the fact that price measures, if applicable without distinction, fall outside the prohibition of Article 28 EC, it is not surprising that Article 153 EC has been used as legal basis.

[228] Decision No 3092/94, OJ 1994, L 331/1.

in accidents in the internal market, provides for instruments to support the exchange of information. Where the safety of products is concerned, for example if products placed on the market puts in serious jeopardy the health and safety of consumers in a number of Member States, the Community may take action based on Article 95 EC.[229]

In contrast to environmental policy the legal basis of Article 153 EC has hardly been used to pursue harmonisation of consumer interests. Even though Article 153 EC in my view (see above) undoubtedly provides the Community legislature the competence to adopt harmonisation measures, its formulation, compared to Article 175 EC, seems to indicate that Article 153 EC has a subsidiary character. The question is therefore whether Article 153 EC could in fact be a suitable legal basis at all to resolve the tension between consumer protection and the internal market.[230] An answer to this question can still not be given due to the fact that Article 153 EC has hardly been used by the Community legislature.

5.3 Public health policy as horizontal and flanking policy

Article 3(1) sub p EC stipulates that the activities of the Community include a contribution to the attainment of a high level of health protection.

5.3.1 The legal basis for public health policy

According to Article 152(1) EC Community action shall complement national policies in improving public health, preventing human illness and diseases, and obviating sources of danger to human health. The Community shall also complement the Member States' action in reducing drugs related health damage, including information and prevention. Community activities are thus not only directed at the prevention of diseases, but also at the promotion of public health.[231] Article 152(2) EC makes clear that these objectives of public health policy should first be attained by the Member States through co-operation, and then, if necessary, the Community will support their action.

Article 152(4) EC sets out the procedures by which the Community legislature acts in the field of public health. Particularly due to the BSE and other crises in the field of animal health, and due to health scandals concerning blood and human organs, such as the distribution and transfusion of HIV-infected

---

229 Directive 2001/95 on general product safety, OJ 2002, L 11/4 (recasting Directive 92/59 on general product safety, OJ 1992, L 228/24). See also Case C-359/92, *Germany v. Council*.

230 Micklitz, Reich and Weatherill cast serious doubts over the use of Article 153 EC to advance consumer protection, in what they call a very feeble provision: H.-W. Micklitz, N. Reich and S. Weatherill, EU Treaty Revision and Consumer Protection, *Journal of Consumer Policy*, 2004, p. 376.

231 T.K. Hervey, Up in smoke? Community (anti-) tobacco law and policy, *ELRev.*, 2001, p. 1425.

blood and blood products, the pre-Amsterdam Article 129 EC was amended by the Treaty of Amsterdam.[232] Now basically two types of measures may be enacted by the Community on the basis of Article 152 EC: firstly, harmonisation measures for (a) setting high standards of quality and safety of organs and substances of human origin, blood and blood derivatives, with the possibility for Member States to set more stringent standards; even though one could imagine that such measures might just as well be adopted on the basis of Article 95 EC, if these substances can be considered goods within the meaning of Article 28 EC, the ethical and political connotation however, make these substances neither goods nor the object of commercialisation or consumption;[233] (b) in the veterinary and phytosanitary fields; after the BSE crisis, health-related measures in the field of agriculture have got an independent legal basis to combat more effectively such crises.[234]

Secondly, incentive measures, excluding harmonisation measures, which are designed to protect and improve public health.

Article 152(5) EC stipulates that Member States remain fully responsible for the organisation and delivery of health services and that the Community shall fully respect their responsibilities in this regard.

5.3.2 Measures adopted on the basis of Article 152 EC

In particular Article 152(4)(b) EC, providing the possibility to adopt harmonisation measures, has been widely used as legal basis for measures in the veterinary and phytosanitary fields.[235] Apart from the two possibilities mentioned in Article 152(4, sub a and b) EC, the adoption of harmonisation measures on the basis of this provision is excluded. Furthermore, the Community will only take action, which cannot be taken by individual Member States and in accordance with the principle of subsidiarity.[236] The debate[237] on a new direction for Community public health policy launched by the Community after

---

232 Kapteyn & VerLoren van Themaat (2003), p. 946; T.K. Hervey, Up in smoke? Community (anti-) tobacco law and policy, *ELRev.*, 2001, p. 1426.

233 T.K. Hervey, Up in smoke? Community (anti-) tobacco law and policy, *ELRev.*, 2001, p. 1426.

234 Callies and Ruffert (Eds); Bearbeitet von H.-J.Blanke (2002), p. 1725.

235 An interesting example of a harmonisation measure based on Article 152(4)(b) EC is Directive 2002/2 on compound feedingstuffs (OJ 2002, L 63/23). The Dutch Court of The Hague in a case brought by the Dutch Association of Compound Feedingstuffs Industry (Nevedi) cast serious doubts on the legal basis: see R.H. van Ooik and T.A.J.A. Vandamme, Schorsing van Europese regelgeving in Nederland – Kanttekeningen bij de Nevedi-uitspraak van de rechtbank Den Haag, *SEW*, 2005, pp. 60-69.

236 Decision 1786/2002, adopting a programme of Community action in the field of public health (2003-2008), OJ 2002, L 271/1.

237 COM(98) 230 final; see T.K. Hervey, Up in smoke? Community (anti-) tobacco law and policy, *ELRev.*, 2001, p. 1427.

the Treaty of Amsterdam had been adopted has eventually resulted in the health action programme 2003-2008.[238]

The action programme forms the basis for further Community action and for the development of a Community health strategy, even though the possibilities of taking legislative action in this field are limited. The programme has three main objectives: (i) to improve information and knowledge for the development of public health; (ii) to enhance the capability of responding rapidly and in a coordinated fashion the threats to health and (iii) to promote health and prevent disease through addressing health determinants across all policies and activities.

A financial framework has been established for the implementation of the programme. Each year the Community presents a work plan setting out the priorities for the work to be undertaken, including the allocation of resources. The priority areas for 2003 were (i) cross-cutting themes; (ii) health information; (iii) health threats and (iv) health determinants.[239] It is particularly interesting to look at the first priority area. Here the Commission touches upon issues of integrating health into other Community issues, for example by providing for health impact assessment, and of co-operation between Member States on health services, by setting up a high level process of reflection on patient mobility and future health care development in the EU (see also section 2.4.3).

What is however apparent from these programmes is that regardless of the establishment of a single financial framework with a single budgetary heading and regardless of the possibilities of taking supportive action to attain aims of health policy, Community intervention in the field of public health remains limited. Legislative action specifically in the field of public health may still only relate to setting standards of quality and safety of human organs, or to the veterinary and phytosanitary fields. An example with regard to the latter is the already mentioned Regulation laying down general principles and requirements of food law, establishing the European Food Safety Authority and laying down procedures in matters of food safety is based on several Treaty provisions including Article 152(4)(b) EC.[240]

Hence, if the Community legislature intends to harmonise certain health interests, but is unable to motivate why trade or competition have been appreciably affected, neither Article 95 EC, nor Article 152 EC could, in the light of *Tobacco Advertising*, serve as proper legal bases.

---

[238] OJ 2002,L 271/1.

[239] OJ 2003, C 62/21.

[240] Regulation 178/2002, OJ 2002, L 31/1; see also White Paper on Food Safety, COM(1999) 719 final.

5.4 Cultural policy

According to Article 3(1) sub q EC the activities of the Community include a contribution to education and training of quality and to the flowering of the cultures of the Member States.

5.4.1 The legal basis for cultural policy

Article 151 EC provides the Community the legal basis to take specific action in the field of culture.[241] According to Article 151(1) EC the Community shall contribute to the flowering of the cultures, while respecting their national and regional diversity and at the same time bringing the common cultural heritage to the fore. Action by the Community shall, according to paragraph 2, be aimed at encouraging co-operation between Member States and, if necessary supporting and supplementing their action in the following areas:

- improvement of the knowledge and dissemination of the culture and history of the European peoples;
- conservation and safeguarding of cultural heritage of European significance;
- non-commercial cultural exchanges;
- artistic and literary creation, including the audio-visual sector.

Article 151 EC was brought into the EC Treaty by the Treaty of Maastricht and its wording and structure reflects to a considerable extent the principle of subsidiarity. In order to attain the objectives of cultural policy the Council may adopt incentive measures and recommendations, however, harmonisation is expressly excluded. This is intended to guarantee that Community competence should not expand in the field of culture. Besides measures based on Article 151 EC can only be adopted by unanimity, which further restricts the development of a Community cultural policy.[242] The integration clause contained in Article 151(4) EC is particularly important here since those legislative measures touching upon issues of cultural policy will necessarily be based upon internal market provisions (see also section 2.4.4).

The reference to national and regional diversity implies that Article 151 EC does not envisage substituting national and regional cultures for a European culture. Although the notion of 'common cultural heritage' may support a cultural policy at Community level, cultural policy largely remains a national

---

[241] For an overview, see: Albers (1999), pp. 337-405 (with regard to the former Article 128 EC); R. Craufurd Smith, Community Intervention in the Cultural Field: Continuity or Change?, in: R. Craufurd Smith (Ed.), *Culture and European Union Law* (Oxford University Press, Oxford, 2004), pp. 49-68.

[242] R. Craufurd Smith, Community Intervention in the Cultural Field: Continuity or Change?, in: R. Craufurd Smith (Ed.), *Culture and European Union Law* (Oxford University Press, Oxford, 2004), p. 51.

affair where the Community legislature merely stays at the background. The lack of harmonisation powers in this field also implies that the possibility for the Community legislature to develop a Community cultural policy harmonising national provisions of cultural policy, unconnected with the internal market, is extremely limited. On the other hand, as stated before with regard to the *Tobacco* cases, the prohibition of harmonisation contained in Article 151 EC cannot be used to prevent the adoption of harmonisation measures on the basis of Article 95 EC et seq. In the case *Commission v. Belgium* regarding the Television without Frontiers Directive, the ECJ held that Article 151 EC should not harm the fundamental principles of the internal market.[243] Considering the limited possibilities offered by Article 151 EC itself Community cultural policy has mainly been developed on the basis of other Treaty provisions.[244] A Decision promoting linguistic diversity of the Community in the information society has, according to the Court, been validly based on Article 157 EC, the legal basis for industrial policy, since the promotion of linguistic diversity as main object of the programme should be seen within this context as essentially economic and incidentally as vehicle for culture. The European Parliament, however, had argued that the programme pursued a cultural object, based on the view that the Community's linguistic wealth forms part of the Community's cultural heritage.[245]

5.4.2 Measures adopted on the basis of Article 151 EC

Decision 508/2000 of the European Parliament and the Council establishes the Culture 2000 programme, a single financing and programming instrument for cultural co-operation.[246] The programme includes a number of (ambitious) objectives, such as the promotion of a cultural dialogue and of mutual knowledge of the culture and history of the European peoples, the promotion of creativity and transnational dissemination of culture, movement of artists etc., highlighting of cultural diversity, sharing the common cultural heritage, taking into account the role of culture in socio-economic development, recognition of culture as an economic factor and improved access and participation in culture.[247] The Annex distinguishes between the vertical approach (concerning one cultural field) and the horizontal approach (concerning several

[243] Case C-11/95, *Commission v. Belgium*.

[244] R. Craufurd Smith, Community Intervention in the Cultural Field: Continuity or Change?, in: R. Craufurd Smith (Ed.), *Culture and European Union Law* (Oxford University Press, Oxford, 2004), p. 64.

[245] Case C-42/97, *European Parliament v. Council*. See annotation R.H. van Ooik, *SEW*, 2001, pp. 283-286.

[246] Decision 508/2000, OJ 2000, L 63/1. Meanwhile the Commission has published a proposal for a Decision establishing the Culture 2007 programme (2007-2013), COM(2004) 469 final.

[247] See Article 1 of Decision 508/2000.

[248] COM(2004) 154 final.

cultural fields) towards the three cultural actions as laid down in Article 2 of the Decision:

- Specific innovative and/or experimental actions;
- Integrated actions covered by structured, multi-annual cultural co-operation agreements;
- Specific cultural events with a European and/or international dimension.

According to the Commission in its Communication "Making Citizenship Work: fostering European culture and diversity through programmes for Youth, Culture, Audiovisual and Civic Participation" the main goal of Community action in the field of culture is "to contribute to the flourishing of shared European cultural values on the basis of cultural co-operation between artists, cultural operators and cultural institutions". This implies multilateral rather than bilateral co-operation.[248]

The Commission has recently recognised that the Culture 2000 programme pursues too many objectives, given the limited financial resources. It therefore proposes for the Culture 2007 programme (2007-2013) to limit the objectives of cultural policy to three main aspects which should be given priority: the transnational mobility of people working in the cultural sector, the transnational circulation of art and artistic and cultural products and the promotion of intercultural dialogue. The focus is laid on the role of European citizens in the integration process; furthermore, the concept of 'European added value', meaning that projects must be on a sufficient scale and offer maximum added value at European level, remains an essential concept in the context of European cultural co-operation. The promotion of cultural diversity within the national context remains a matter for the Member State, which of course in doing so will have to respect the provisions of primary Community law (see Chapters 2 and 3).[249]

Clearly and even more so compared to the field of public health, the tension between culture and the internal market cannot be resolved by the Community legislature on the basis of Article 151 EC, considering the express exclusion of harmonisation of national laws. The only possibilities for the Community legislature would be either to use 'soft law' instruments with no (or limited) binding effects whilst Member States remain competent to enact their own laws and after the Council has reached a unanimous position, or, in the light of the *Tobacco* cases, to use internal market legal bases, but then only after having proven that the threshold criteria have been fulfilled. With a view to resolve the tension, only the second option is relevant.

---

[249] Proposal for a Decision of the European Parliament and the Council establishing the Culture 2007 programme, COM(2004) 469 final.

5.5 Conclusions

So far only Article 175 EC has provided a solid basis for the adoption of harmonisation measures that can clearly contribute to resolving the tension between environmental protection and the internal market. Article 153 EC is the other specific legal basis in the Treaty for harmonisation measures in the field of consumer protection. However, contrary to Article 175 EC, this provision has not only been scarcely used, it is also considered a 'feeble' provision, hardly suitable to promote measures of consumer protection.[250] The consumer associations also bring forward that the Commission has told them that due to its pragmatic nature and limited scope Article 153 EC is not a suitable provision to be used as legal basis for a legislative proposal.[251] Hence, according to the Community legislature, the harmonisation of consumer protection measures should in the first place be pursued within the context of the internal market, which is considering the Court's ruling in the *Tobacco* cases certainly possible.

The Treaty provisions on public health and culture offer only limited possibilities to the Community legislature to take action in these areas. In the field of culture, for example, many measures continue to be based on other Treaty provisions, because harmonisation is excluded and unanimous voting is required in the Council.[252] This practice has been endorsed indirectly by the Court's ruling in the *Tobacco* cases.

6 Harmonisation and free movement

Even after it has been established that the Community legislature is competent to enact harmonisation measures, and has in fact adopted harmonisation measures, the *validity* of these measures still depends on their conformity with general principles of law and primary Community law, i.e. the free movement rules. This question is relevant since the scope of action by the Community legislature in areas of horizontal and flanking policies may depend on the limits set by the Treaty provisions on free movement. The relationship between *national* measures and the free movement rules has been extensively discussed in Chapter 2. Do similar principles define the relationship between *Community* measures and the rules on free movement? In other words, what is the 'constitutional' status of the free movement provisions in Community law?

---

250 H.-W. Micklitz, N. Reich and S. Weatherill, EU Treaty Revision and Consumer Protection, *Journal of Consumer Policy*, 2004, p. 376.

251 They regret this very much: BEUC comments on Unfair Commercial Practices, 15 January 2004, BEUC/X/001/2004, to be found at: http://www.beuc.org/Content/Default.asp?PageID=146.

252 R. Craufurd Smith, Community Intervention in the Cultural Field: Continuity or Change, in: R. Craufurd Smith (Ed.), *Culture and European Union Law* (Oxford University Press, Oxford, 2004), pp. 64-65.

Tobacco Advertising has apart from providing a broad interpretation of Article 95 EC and other internal market legal bases, also shown the limits of the Community legislature's powers to regulate the internal market. Criteria have been laid down as to the valid adoption of measures on the basis of internal market legal bases. According to AG Geelhoed in his opinion in *BAT/Imperial Tobacco* three limits to the discretionary power of the Community legislature can be identified:

- The measure must contribute to the establishment of the common market;
- When removing the public interest from the power of the Member State, the Community legislature must take account of that interest without subordinating the level of protection to market-related interests;
- The role of the principle of proportionality.[253]

With regard to the second condition, i.e. public interests should not be made subordinate to market-related interests; a reference can be made to the integration principle as guiding principle of Community law. It is therefore highly disputable whether the above-discussed proposal for a Directive on Services in the Internal Market is in conformity with this condition, now the Directive in its present form is merely a liberalisation measure, but no more. As stated above, in this proposal the balance between horizontal and flanking policy interests has been struck wrongly.

According to AG Geelhoed in his Opinion in *BAT/Imperial Tobacco* "the Community legislature is faced with the same evaluation as the national legislatures which it is replacing. That evaluation must lead to certain prior conditions being attached to the economic freedom of market participants, under which equal account is taken of the freedom of market participants and of the need to protect specific public interests."[254] For example, the centralised authorisation procedure for certain new types of medicines as provided for by Regulation 726/2004 (see section 4.3.3.1) may be restrictive to the free movement of medicines and hence contravene Article 28 EC. At the same time the Regulation clearly aims at protecting public health by introducing a faster and more transparent authorisation procedure for the benefit of patients.

One of the basic cases with regard to the relationship between Community legislation and the free movement rules is *Ramel* in which the Court held that a provision of a regulation "in so far as it authorizes producer Member States

[253] Opinion of AG Geelhoed in Case C-491/01, *BAT/Imperial Tobacco*, paragraphs 117-121. The Court may deal with the principle of proportionality within the context of the application of the free movement rules, like in the case on food supplements: Joined Cases C-154/04 and C-155/04, *Alliance for Natural Health*, paragraphs 109-112. In his Opinion AG Geelhoed dealt with the proportionality principle separately and came to the conclusion, contrary to the Court, that the Directive infringed this principle.

[254] Opinion of AG Geelhoed in Case C-491/01, *BAT/Imperial Tobacco*, paragraph 118.

to prescribe and levy, in intra-Community trade [...], charges having an effect equivalent to customs duties, is incompatible with Article 13 (now withdrawn), in particular paragraph (2) thereof, and with Articles 38 to 46 (now Articles 32 to 38) of the Treaty and is consequently invalid".[255] The provision was not justifiable. Since *Ramel* and since the respective amendments of the EC Treaty the relationship between the rules on free movement and Community harmonisation measures has evolved over the years in various areas of horizontal and flanking policies.[256]

In the *Meyhui* case, which involved the field of consumer policy, the Court held that "it is settled case law that the prohibition of quantitative restrictions and of all measures having equivalent effect applies not only to national measures but also to measures adopted by the Community institutions".[257] This case involved a dispute between a crystal glass producer (Schott Zwiesel) and an importer of Schott's products in Belgium (Meyhui) regarding Schott's refusal to affix to its glass products a description in the language of the Member State where they are marketed. The Belgian court asked the ECJ whether Directive 69/493 on the composition, characteristics of manufacture and labelling of crystal glass products and all forms of publicity for those products is compatible with Article 28 EC. Annex I allows for the purposes of the description of this type of glass products only the language or languages of the country in which the product is marketed to be used. The Court answered that this provision in the Directive indeed constituted a barrier to intra-Community trade, which was, however, justifiable in the light of the protection of consumers. Since the measure chosen by the Community was not disproportionate to the goal pursued, the Community legislature had not exceeded the limits of its discretion in the framework of its powers of harmonisation.[258]

The ruling in *Meyhui* cited by AG Alber in the more recent cases on Parma ham and Grana Padano cheese seems to confirm the principle that Community measures as well as national measures should respect the four fundamental freedoms, but may in case of conflict also be justified.[259] In *Parma Ham* AG Alber concludes that the condition the Protected Designation of Origin Parma Ham may be used for sliced ham only if it is sliced, packaged and labelled in the region of production under the supervision of the 'Consorzio del Prosciutto di

---

[255] Joined Cases 80 and 81/77, *Ramel*, paragraph 38.

[256] See for an extensive discussion regarding the relationship between the Treaty rules and Community measures: K. Mortelmans, The relationship between the Treaty rules and Community measures for the establishment and functioning of the internal market – towards a concordance rule, *CMLRev.*, 2002, pp. 1303-1346.

[257] Case C-51/93, *Meyhui*, paragraph 11.

[258] According to Vandamme this case, where the Court in fact ignored the issue of compatibility with the internal market, should be deplored: Vandamme (2005), p. 187.

[259] Case C-108/01, *Parma Ham* and Case C-469/00, *Ravil*.

Parma' is contrary to Article 29 EC and cannot be justified on the basis of Article 30 EC on grounds of protection of industrial and commercial property or on the basis of structural policy considerations.[260] This condition was laid down in Commission Regulation 1107/96 on the registration of geographical indications and designations of origin specifying the rules laid down in Council Regulation 2081/92 on the protection of geographical indications and designations of origin for agricultural products and foodstuffs.[261] He advised the Court to declare the Commission Regulation invalid. Neither in *Parma Ham* nor in *Ravil* on Grana Pardano did the ECJ follow the AG's opinion and regarded the conditions in the Commission Regulation nevertheless contrary to Article 29 EC, but justified by Article 30 on grounds of protection of industrial and commercial property.

According to the ECJ the condition that Parma ham (or cheese) should be sliced and packaged in the region of production aims to safeguard the quality and authencity of the product. The ability to control this process helped to guarantee consumers a quality which they expected of such products.[262] According to AG Alber, though, consumer protection interests could have been met by appropriate labelling or inspections, which is less restrictive to trade and which is, as has been seen Chapter 2, often considered as viable alternative by the ECJ where *national* restrictive measures are at issue. Hence, where the Community has itself decided to protect certain distinctive domestic products from trade and competition, the ECJ seems to allow it a considerable degree of discretion in protecting this interest.[263]

In the *Safety High-Tech* case the ECJ ruled that the Regulation on substances which deplete the ozone layer providing *inter alia* for the prohibition of the use of hydrochlorfluorocarbons for fire-fighting was proportional to the aim of environmental protection as a result of which the provision was not invalid in the light of Article 28 EC.[264] In examining whether the proportionality test is fulfilled the ECJ seems, similarly to the *Parma Ham* and *Ravil* cases to award the Community legislature a considerable margin of discretion.

Where the principle that the Community Institutions too are obliged to respect the rules on free movement seems undisputed, the extent to which they have to do so is contentious. In academic literature different views are presented as to the question of whether the Community legislature should be bound in the same way as Member States to the Treaty rules on free movement.[265] The view

[260] Opinion of AG Alber in Case C-108/01, *Parma Ham*.

[261] OJ 1996, L 148/1; OJ 1992, L 208/1.

[262] Case C-108/01, *Parma Ham*, paragraphs 65 and 75 and 76.

[263] See R. Craufurd Smith, Community Intervention in the Cultural Field: Continuity or Change?, in: R. Craufurd Smith (Ed.), *Culture and European Union Law* (Oxford University Press, Oxford, 2004), pp. 56-57.

[264] Case C-284/95, *Safety High-Tech*.

[265] See in general: K. Mortelmans, The relationship between the Treaty rules and Community measures for the establishment and functioning of the internal market – towards a concordance rule, *CMLRev.*, 2002, pp. 1303-1346.

that the same rules apply to the Community legislature as to the Member States, which corresponds to AG Alber's view in *Parma Ham*, has not been followed by the ECJ. The more dominant view in academic literature that the Community is not bound in the same way as Member States are, but has a margin of discretion in issuing harmonisation measures to reconcile horizontal and flanking policy interests with the internal market is in line with the jurisprudence of the Court and also more in accordance with the Treaty, especially incorporating powers in horizontal and flanking policy areas and requirements to integrate these interests into other policies, like internal market policy.[266] The discretion of the Community legislature in doing so also appears from the Transfer of Waste Regulation. Unfortunately the ECJ left untouched the question of validity of Regulation 259/93 on the transboundary shipments of waste vis à vis Articles 28-30 EC in the *Daimler Chrysler* case, because the national court did not raise this issue.[267] This case involved the relationship between a national regulation prescribing that waste produced in the Land Baden-Württemberg must be sent to a treatment centre in Germany, with Regulation 259/93 and the free movement of goods.[268]

It does not mean that the Community legislature has carte blanche in adopting harmonisation measures restricting free movement within the internal market. Irrespective of the wide discretion the Community legislature enjoys, it must revert to horizontal and flanking policy considerations and must take as a basis a high level of protection of the *public* interest involved. For example in the field of public health, it should take account of scientific developments, it must in assessing the need to adopt health measures make an evaluation of health risks and it must have regard for the precautionary principle.[269] That also without clear scientific facts, or when scientific information does at least

---

[266] K. Mortelmans, The relationship between the Treaty rules and Community measures for the establishment and functioning of the internal market – towards a concordance rule, *CMLRev.*, 2002, p. 1315 *et seq.* H. Temmink, From Danish Bottles to Danish Bees: The Dynamics of Free Movement of Goods and Environmental Protection – A Case Law Analysis, in: H. Somsen (Ed.), *Yearbook of European Environmental Law* (Oxford University Press, Oxford, 2000), p. 71. Vandamme notes that it would have been more transparent if the Court held that in certain situations the Community legislator enjoys more discretion under Article 28 EC than the national legislator: Vandamme (2005), p. 187.

[267] Regulation 259/93, OJ 1993, L 30/1; G. van Calster, The free movement of waste after DaimlerChrysler, *ELRev.*, 2002, p. 613; see also Annotation J.W. van de Gronden and K.J.M. Mortelmans, *AA*, 2002, pp. 180-197.

[268] Case C-324/99, *Daimler Chrysler.*

[269] Opinion of AG Geelhoed in Case C-491/01, *BAT/Imperial Tobacco*, paragraph 120. See also J. Scott and E. Vos, The Juridification of Uncertainty: Observations on the Ambivalence of the Precautionary Principle within the EU and the WTO, in: Ch. Joerges and R. Dehousse (Eds), *Good Governance in Europe's Integrated Market*, Academy of European Law, European University Institute (Oxford University Press, Oxford, 2002), pp. 265-267.

not exclude the possibility of products presenting health risks, the Community legislature is allowed to adopt far-reaching legislation appears from the *Snus* cases and the recent *Alliance for Natural Health* case.[270] Interestingly, according to AG Geelhoed not the precautionary principle was at issue in *Snus* – there was no uncertainty about the health risks of Snus but about the effects of marketing Snus throughout the Community on the behaviour of mainly young people -, but the principle that preventive action should be taken.[271] Although the Court did not refer to this principle of preventive action in its judgment, in the end it reached the same conclusion as the AG: the prohibition of *Snus* as incorporated in the *Tobacco* Directive was proportionate to the protection of public health with a view to Article 95(3) EC and hence also with a view to Article 30 EC.[272]

Where a directive contains an export prohibition, which aims to protect *economic* interests, or has in other words a *protectionist* aim, which Member States are neither allowed to pursue, it must be declared invalid in the light of the free movement rules. The *Deposit Guarantees* case, for example, can therefore be criticised since the Court, although it rightly indicated that the objective of consumer protection is also relevant in the realm of Article 47(2) EC, nevertheless went so far as to confirm an export prohibition contained in an internal market measure, which was hardly justifiable.[273]

The conclusion is that the outcome of the few cases, which touch upon the relationship between harmonisation and free movement and which were brought before the Court, is, at least from the Community's perspective, positive. Due to the wide discretionary powers of the Community legislature, harmonisation measures will not easily violate the free movement rules. This 'positive news' for the Community legislature also means that, within the limits set by the Court, it may issue far-reaching legislation to pursue horizontal and flanking policy interests without being similarly threatened by the possible application of the free movement rules as Member States are.

[270] Case C-210/03, *Swedish Match*; Case C-434/02, *Arnold André*; Joined Cases C-154/04 and C-155/04, *Alliance for Natural Health* with an explicit reference to the precautionary principle in paragraph 68 of this judgment.

[271] This principle is laid down in the environmental paragraph, Article 174(2) EC, but also plays a role in the context of public health, allowing the Community to act in a preventive manner before it can be proved that Snus presents potential health risks: see Opinion AG Geelhoed in Cases C-434/02, *Arnold André* and C-210/03, *Swedish Match*, paragraphs 107-109.

[272] Case C-210/03, *Swedish Match*, paragraphs 58 and 61; see also annotation T. Vandamme, *SEW*, 2005, pp. 227-234.

[273] Annotation W.H. Roth, *CMLRev.*, 1998, p. 479. Vandamme (2005), pp. 182-183.

CHAPTER 5

Towards a Synthesis

1 Introduction

The mixed approach towards the development of horizontal and flanking policies at Community level is the starting point for a synthesis of the case law of the Court on free movement, the decision practice of the Commission in competition policy and secondary legislation. These three main sources of tension are brought together in this chapter with a view to establish whether a coherent legal approach can be developed in respect of the conflict between horizontal and flanking policies and the rules on free movement and competition.

Based on the main conclusions of the foregoing chapters, in the following sections an inventory is made of the way in which horizontal and flanking policy interests have been dealt with within the context of free movement (section 2), the competition rules directed at Member States (section 3) and the competition rules directed at undertakings (section 4). It will hereafter be possible to determine the extent to which a degree of coherence exists between the free movement rules, between the free movement rules and the competition rules, and between horizontal and flanking policies (section 5). This degree of coherence will be relevant for the solutions which will be presented in Chapter 6 concerning the problem of tension; it reveals whether uniformity in the case law of the Court on free movement, in the decision practice of the Commission and in Community secondary legislation has been and can be attained or is ultimately desirable, or whether the key to the problem lies precisely in the variety in these sources of tension.

2 Free movement

Free movement within the internal market cannot be attained through the process of negative integration, i.e. the application of the prohibitive rules, alone. Negative integration must be complemented by positive integration through the adoption of harmonisation measures by the Community legislature.[1]

The point of departure within the context of free movement is the public authority being involved in the drafting of horizontal and flanking policies. Public interests will either be pursued by national legislative bodies, thereby possibly infringing the Treaty provisions on free movement, or by the Community legislature in so far as it has taken over environmental, public health, consumer or cultural protection from national legislative bodies.

[1] This appears from Chapters 2 and 4.

2.1 Negative integration

National horizontal and flanking policies will easily come within the scope of application of the Treaty provisions on free movement.

2.1.1 Prohibitive rules

It appears from Chapter 2 that the prohibitive rules are broadly applicable. The role of the *Keck* case and the doctrine of 'inherent restrictions' are both limited in the context of the free movement rules.

A broad scope of application

The personal and material scope of application of the free movement rules have by means of the concept of economic activity been broadly interpreted as to include horizontal and flanking policy interests. With regard to the territorial scope a more subtle approach has been adopted by the ECJ.[2]

The prohibitive rules in the Treaty should be broadly interpreted as well, leaving no possibility to take account of horizontal and flanking policy interests, or for that matter to deal with the tension between these policy interests and the internal market, at this stage.[3] The scope of the prohibitive Treaty provisions on exports (Article 29 EC) and on internal taxation (Article 90 EC) is not so broad, since only discriminatory measures are prohibited.

The limited relevance of Keck and 'inherent restrictions'

There are two exceptions to the broad application of the Treaty provisions on free movement, which may be relevant for horizontal and flanking policies. Firstly, if domestic horizontal and flanking policies involve the regulation of selling arrangements, they will in principle not qualify as measures having equivalent effect and will therefore fall outside the scope of application of Article 28 EC.[4] The *Keck* jurisprudence is, however, of limited value to horizontal and flanking policies. The *Keck* ruling is only relevant within the context of Article 28 EC (free movement of goods). It can be seen that the market access based test, which has been applied under the other freedoms, plays an increasingly important role also in the context of the free movement of goods.[5] Furthermore, the starting point here is the type or form of national legislation, whether it restricts or prohibits certain selling arrangements, rather than its objectives, and hence whether national legislation aims at the protection of horizontal and flanking policy interests.

---

2 Chapter 2, section 2.

3 Chapter 2, section 3.2.

4 Joined Cases C-267 and C-268/91, *Keck and Mithouard*. See also Chapter 2, section 3.2.

Secondly, the Court has applied an *inherent restriction* approach within the context of free movement, but only in relation to sports (see the *Deliège* case). The scope of this approach within the field of free movement remains rather unclear and appears to be limited to specific sectors, such as sport.[6]

2.1.2 Exceptions

The Treaty exceptions and the rule of reason case law offer the possibility to justify measures falling within the scope of the prohibitive rules for horizontal and flanking policy reasons.

The importance of the exceptions

The broad scope of application of the prohibitive rules brings the exceptions to the fore, providing the possibility to justify national horizontal and flanking measures that restrict free movement. Hence, the tension between free movement rules and domestic horizontal and flanking policies should first and foremost be resolved within the context of the justification grounds, i.e. the Treaty exceptions and the rule of reason. The extent to which national bodies involved in the policy and law-making process and the European Court of Justice can contribute to controlling or resolving this problem of tension will be discussed in Chapter 6.[7]

The basic rule is that exceptions can only be invoked if horizontal and flanking measures seek to protect non-economic mandatory requirements, are necessary for the attainment of these objectives and are proportionate to their aims.[8] The ECJ has not always followed this rule systematically. Particularly in the field of the environment, but also in other horizontal and flanking policy fields, the condition that mandatory requirements can only be invoked in respect of non-discriminatory, or indistinctly applicable, measures seems increasingly irrelevant.

An important role for the principle of proportionality

The principle of proportionality plays a central role in assessing the justifiability of national restrictive measures implementing horizontal and flanking policies. Due to its twofold function in Community law – i.e. as principle for the

---

5 Chapter 2, section 3.1.2.

6 According to the Court's ruling in *Deliège* rules laid down by sporting associations that are inherent in the conduct of the sports event may not be considered to affect market access: Joined Cases C-51/96 and C-191/97, *Deliège*. See also Chapter 2, section 3.3. The inherent restriction approach is more relevant within the context of the competition rules, see: Chapter 3, section 4.1.2.4.

7 Chapter 6, sections 3 and 4.

8 Chapter 2, section 4.

relationship between the judiciary and the legislature and, particularly relevant here, as an important principle for the relationship between the European Community and the Member State – it allows for the balancing of the requirements of the internal market with the need to maintain a high level of protection of horizontal and flanking policy interests.

The proportionality test as introduced in Chapter 2 in respect of the free movement rules can contain three elements. The first element is that there must be a causal connection between the measure adopted and the aim pursued. The measure must be relevant or pertinent. The second element is that there is no alternative to it, which is less restrictive. The third element is proportionality *stricto sensu*, which requires an assessment of whether the restriction is not out of proportion to the aim sought or the result brought about.[9]

In particular the second element, the condition that there must be no less restrictive alternative available, plays a predominant role in assessing the proportionality of national measures.[10] Hence, the application of the proportionality test is extremely relevant for Member States as it eventually determines their margin of discretion to set standards on horizontal and flanking policies.[11]

2.2 Positive integration

The answer to the still existing legal barriers for trade as well as for safeguarding horizontal and flanking policy interests at a Community level is harmonisation of national laws.

2.2.1 Harmonisation contributes to solving the problem of tension

Harmonisation presupposes the adoption of common rules at Community level, which rules necessarily deal with horizontal and flanking policy interests previously regulated by the Member State. Hence, the development of horizontal and flanking policies at Community level has first occurred within the context of the internal market. In addition the Community disposes of specific harmonisation powers in the fields of consumer policy and the environment; harmonisation is excluded in the fields of culture and public health with the exception of measures based on Article 152(4) sub b and c EC.

In two situations Community legislation may not be relevant for the subject matter, as it does not, or only to a limited extent, dispose of the tension between free movement and horizontal and flanking policies. Firstly, instead of harmonising national laws, the Community legislature may 'use' the principles of mutual recognition and home country control in order to attain the aim of

9 Chapter 2, section 4.3.3; see also J.H. Jans, Proportionality revisited, *LIEI*, 2000, pp. 240-241.

10 Regarding this second element of the proportionality principle, see: Trimidas (1999), pp. 133-145.

11 See hereafter Chapter 6, sections 3 and 4.1.

market integration. The application of these principles do not contribute to a solution for the problem of tension, since Member States remain responsible and the Treaty provisions on free movement continue to be relevant.[12]

Secondly, the 'new approach' is of limited value as a harmonisation method for the harmonisation of horizontal and flanking policies, since it involves, in particular, the establishment of essential safety requirements for products, which have to be complied with if they are to be placed on the market. The 'new approach' tells us more about the flexibility of means, i.e. standardisation, than about the extent to which horizontal and flanking policies have been harmonised at Community level. This can be deduced from the techniques of total and minimum harmonisation.[13]

2.2.2 Minimum harmonisation

In the case of minimum harmonisation the problem of tension between free movement and horizontal and flanking policies can only be partially resolved, since after minimum harmonisation the free movement rules continue to be relevant for the more stringent measures adopted by the Member State. As was shown before in Chapter 4, minimum harmonisation occurs either because this technique has been laid down in the Treaty itself, i.e. in Article 176 EC for measures in the field of the environment and in Article 153(5) EC for measures in the field of consumer policy, or because a Community directive includes a minimum clause allowing Member States to adopt more stringent standards. Minimum harmonisation plays an important role in the context of horizontal and flanking policies. This is not unusual, since integration and uniformity may not be apt "as paramount guiding values in such realms and that space should be preserved for diverse local preferences and regulatory experimentation".[14]

The scope of minimum harmonisation may be limited however. First, a harmonisation measure, including a minimum clause as well as a free movement provision, allows the Member State to adopt more stringent standards, but only in respect of its own products or services, which may lead to reverse discrimination. Second, some measures, like the Transfer of Waste Regulation, may regulate a certain topic so extensively that it leaves little scope for additional national measures, even though the Treaty explicitly allows for this possibility (Article 176 EC).[15]

[12] Chapter 4, section 2.

[13] Chapter 4, section 3.

[14] S. Weatherill, Pre-emption, Harmonisation and the Distribution of Competence to Regulate the Internal Market, in: C. Barnard and J. Scott (Eds), *The Law of the Single European Market, Unpacking the Premises* (Hart, Oxford and Portland, 2002), p. 62.

[15] Regulation 259/93 on the supervision and control of shipments of waste within, into and out of the European Community, OJ 1993, L 30/1; see also Chapter 4, section 5.1.2.

2.2.3 Total harmonisation

The tension between free movement and horizontal and flanking policies can be resolved through total harmonisation of national laws, pre-empting Member States to set additional standards. An additional role for the Treaty provisions on free movement ceases to exist. Total harmonisation may also become increasingly relevant in the context of horizontal and flanking policies. Article 95 EC and other internal market legal bases like Article 47(2) EC[16] not only may have been broadly interpreted, they also give cause to the increasing use of the technique of total harmonisation, which had already been envisaged by the Community legislature in the field of consumer policy.[17] The ruling in *Tobacco Advertising* suggests that where Article 95 EC is used as legal basis the directive must contain a provision ensuring the free movement of products which conform to its provisions, hereby insisting on a pro-integrative model.[18] Stricter national rules applying to imported products can only be maintained according to the procedure contained in Articles 95(4-10) EC.[19] The possibilities to use the technique of minimum harmonisation on the basis of Article 95 EC are limited to setting more stringent standards to domestic products, possibly leading to reverse discrimination; not a very attractive perspective for the Member State.

2.2.4 A wide margin of discretion of the community legislature to pursue horizontal and flanking policy interests

Similar to the Member States, the Community legislature has to respect primary Community law as well, in particular the free movement rules and the principle of proportionality as laid down in Article 5 EC. Due to the wide discretionary powers of the Community legislature, harmonisation measures will not easily violate the free movement rules. From the case law of the ECJ it appears that the Community legislature may, more so than the Member States, take far-reaching measures severely restricting free movement, without being subject to a similar degree of scrutiny.[20]

With regard to the principle of proportionality, the review of Community measures as compared to national measures under the Treaty provisions on

---

16 See, for example, Directive 89/552, OJ 1989, L 298/23, amended by Directive 97/36, OJ 1997, L 202/60 (Television without Frontiers), Chapter 4, section 4.3.4.

17 Chapter 4, section 4.3.2.

18 Case C-376/98, *Germany v. European Parliament and Council (Tobacco Advertising).*

19 S. Weatherill, Pre-emption, Harmonisation and the Distribution of Competence to Regulate the Internal Market, in: C. Barnard and J, Scott (Eds), *The Law of the Single European Market, Unpacking the Premises* (Hart, Oxford and Portland, 2002), p. 62.

20 Chapter 4, section 6.

free movement, seems at first sight to be subject to a similar degree of scrutiny. Nevertheless, the case law also shows that in the end the ECJ will only exercise marginal review of Community harmonisation measures and will not, other than in case of national measures, put emphasis on the search for the least restrictive alternative.[21]

3 Competition and the Member States

Apart from the free movement rules, the Member States may also come into conflict with the competition rules and thereby jeopardise the objective of market integration, by granting exclusive rights to undertakings, by giving financial benefits to undertakings or by being involved in forms of co-operation between companies to attain objectives of horizontal and flanking policies. The Community legislature has not taken action in this field for reasons relating to horizontal and flanking policies.

3.1 Articles 86 and 87 EC

From Chapter 3 it appears that the problem with the useful effect rule of Articles 3g, 10 and 81 or 82 EC is twofold: its scope of application with respect to State action is not entirely clear and there is no explicit exception ground.[22] This is somewhat different in respect of Articles 86 and 87 EC.

3.1.1 The prohibitive rules

A broad scope of application

Due to the broad interpretation of the concept of undertaking (including the notion of economic activity) State aids for horizontal and flanking policy reasons are likely to fall within the scope of Article 87(1) EC.[23] The same applies to public monopolies and exclusive rights.

The question whether financial aid falls within the scope of the prohibitive rule of Article 87(1) EC is more pertinent than in the case of the prohibitive rules on free movement. After all, the fact that financial aid will always be considered to constitute an economic advantage, and hence State aid, is now, after *Altmark*, not self-evident. *Altmark* leaves some room for the consideration

---

[21] Chapter 4, section 6. See, for example, Joined Cases C-154/04 and C-155/04, *Alliance for Natural Health* where the Court dealt with the proportionality principle within the context of the free movement rules.

[22] Chapter 3, section 3.3.

[23] This entails that public financing of activities by public non-profit-making establishments are normally not regarded as State aids.

of horizontal and flanking policy interests within the context of the prohibitive rule, as one of the conditions is that public service compensation is proportionate, but is relevant only where public service undertakings are involved.[24] In that case there will be no need to invoke an exception ground and, provided that certain criteria are met, the financial aid will not have to be notified to the Commission.

With regard to Article 86(1) EC the Court has adopted various approaches to overcome the inherent conflict between Article 295 EC – the Treaty shall not prejudice Member States' right of property ownership – and the allocation of exclusive rights, which is subject to certain conditions. But this has not led to a degradation of standards of protection of horizontal and flanking policy interests. As a result of the 'limited sovereignty approach', the adage 'the prohibition must be applied broadly, the exceptions restrictively' does not appear to apply to Article 86 EC, contrary to the prohibitive rules on free movement.[25]

De minimis *aid*

Irrespective of the broad scope of application of Article 87 EC, financial aid that does not exceed a certain amount over a given period of time as laid down in Regulation 69/2001,[26] or aid granted at local level to only locally operating undertakings will not fall within the scope of the prohibitive provision of Article 87 EC. This *de minimis* rule, however, is only to a limited extent relevant for horizontal and flanking policies. Relevant is the fact that such aid schemes have no appreciable effect on competition and trade and not the objective of the aid scheme.

3.1.2 Exceptions

The importance of the exceptions

Once State aids are considered to fall within the scope of Article 87(1) EC – and apart from *'Altmark* situations' this will often be the case – the exceptions contained in Articles 87(2) and 87(3) EC become relevant. Even though Articles 87(2) EC and 87(3) EC do not explicitly refer to horizontal and flanking policy interests – apart from Articles 87(2) sub a (consumers) and 87(3) sub d EC (culture) – the Commission in granting an exemption takes

[24] Case C-280/00, *Altmark Trans*; see also Chapter 3, section 3.1.3: "The compensation may not exceed what is necessary to cover all or part of the costs incurred in the discharge of public service obligations."

[25] Under the limited sovereignty approach the existence of a legal monopoly is not illegal, only its abuse is. In the Court's case law particular support can be found for the limited sovereignty approach, as confirmed by the *Sydhavnens* case (Case C-209/98, *Sydhavnens FFAD*), as well as for the limited competition approach, which implies that the creation of a legal monopoly will necessarily produce restrictive effects and should thus only be permitted if there is a justification ground: Chapter 3, section 3.2.2.

[26] OJ 2001, L 10/30.

these interests into account. This appears most notably from the Community Guidelines on state aid for the protection of the environment.[27] In fact the Commission balances the attainment of horizontal and flanking objectives with the restriction on competition. If the environmental benefits outweigh the negative effects on competition, environmental aid will be tolerated.

An important role for the principle of proportionality

The principle of proportionality plays a central role and its application in the field of the environment has been visualised through a set of comprehensive Guidelines laid down in the guidelines on environmental state aids.[28] Regarding cultural subsidies the Commission has shown its willingness to give an exemption for State aids with cultural objectives, without necessarily providing a thorough legal and economic analysis under Article 87(3) EC.[29] Nevertheless, due to substantive differences between horizontal and flanking policies the compatibility of state aids with the Treaty provisions is assessed differently; the dilemma between environmental state aids and the 'polluter pays principle' does not exist in respect of cultural aids, which makes it more difficult, if not impossible to really integrate cultural considerations in state aid policy.

Article 86(2) EC

The case law also shows that services of general *economic* interests within the meaning of Article 86(2) EC include horizontal and flanking policy interests ('economic' has to be understood in its broad meaning). The ECJ, in applying Articles 86(1) and 86(2) EC, conducts a balancing approach. The principle of proportionality plays a role in this context as well, and the way it is applied suggests that much weight should be given to the consideration of horizontal and flanking policy interests.[30]

3.2 Community measures: no positive integration

The Community legislature has not adopted *harmonisation* measures in the field of state aids and horizontal and flanking policies. This would not be possible, since the Community's policy in this respect is at right angles with Member States' policies; the only possibility for the Community is to grant financial aid itself. Hence, there is no question of the Community legislature taking over the task of the Member State in regulating the state aid regime with a view to establish common rules at Community level. Even though the 'procedural Regulation' which lays down rules for the application of Article

---

27 OJ 2001, C 37/3.

28 OJ 2001, C 37/3; Chapter 3, section 3.1.5.2.

29 Chapter 3, section 3.1.5.5.

30 Chapter 3, section 3.2.3.

88 EC is an example of a Community measure, it merely elaborates on and further specifies the procedural rules and principles with regard to state aid as laid down in the Court's case law.[31] Furthermore, the guidelines and block exemption regulations cannot be considered as acts of positive integration, since they merely clarify the scope of Article 87 EC.

With the exception of sector specific legislation, there are no harmonisation measures in the field of exclusive rights. The Commission has issued a Communication and adopted a White Paper on services of general interest in which the role of services of general interest in the European Union is further explained.[32] Hence, the Treaty provisions on state aid and exclusive rights continue to remain the framework for review of national state aid measures and of the state's grant of exclusive rights to undertakings. Tensions between state aid provisions and the protection of horizontal and flanking policy interests should be dealt with within this framework.

4 Competition and undertakings

Where companies (private actors) for a variety of reasons decide to contribute voluntarily to horizontal and flanking policy aims, the competition rules, i.e. Articles 81 and 82 EC and the Merger Regulation, may be applicable. Actions by companies may lead to market fragmentation and distortions of competition, but their actions may be justifiable; the Community legislature has not adopted harmonisation measures for the sake of the internal market and the protection of horizontal and flanking policies in this field.

4.1 Articles 81, 82 EC and Merger Control

Due to their broad scope of application firms using anti-competitive means to attain horizontal and flanking policy objectives will easily come within the reach of the competition rules.

4.1.1 The prohibitive rules

A broad scope of application; Article 81(1) EC, Wouters and inherent restrictions

The broad concept of undertaking implies that horizontal and flanking policy interests easily fall within the scope of the competition rules as

[31] Regulation 659/1999, laying down detailed rules for the application of Article 93 of the EC Treaty (now Article 88 EC), OJ 1999, L 83/1.

[32] Communication from the Commission on Services of general interest in Europe, OJ 2001, C 17/4; White Paper, COM(2004), 374 final; see also Chapter 3, section 3.2.3.1.

well. The interpretation of the cartel prohibition laid down in Article 81(1) EC, though, leaves some, albeit limited, scope for the consideration of horizontal and flanking policy interests, in particular through the application of the 'inherent restriction approach', like in the earlier mentioned *Meca-Medina* case[33] and due to the Court's ruling in *Wouters*. In the latter case the ECJ may have opened the door to a Cassis-type of rule of reason within the framework of Article 81(1) EC. Nevertheless, the scope of *Wouters* is limited, since it would not include all horizontal and flanking policy interests and it would depend on the economic context and particularities of a certain market whether Article 81(1) EC were to apply.[34] The same goes true for the 'inherent restriction approach'.[35]

A broad scope of application of Article 82 EC

Horizontal and flanking policy interests may only to a very limited extent play a role in the context of Article 82 EC. Horizontal and flanking policy interests can play a role in determining the relevant product market, which is also relevant for the Community's merger control policy. Certain behaviour by dominant firms, which are also involved in activities of a horizontal and flanking nature, is not considered abusive, for example in the case of demanding high quality and environmentally friendly products from the supplier. It is questionable to what extent *Wouters* could apply to Article 82 EC.[36]

A broad scope of application of the Merger Regulation

Within the context of Merger Control horizontal and flanking policy considerations carry weight only at the background. The efficiency considerations should be interpreted restrictively. But the prohibition of mergers may coincide with horizontal and flanking policy considerations too, most notably in the field of media policy.[37]

4.1.2 Exceptions

A limited scope of the exceptions

From the foregoing it appears that for the problem of tension between horizontal and flanking policy interests and competition rules the exceptions, if available, are crucial. Increasingly more weight is being given to

---

33 Case T-313/02, *Meca-Medina and Majcen*; according to the CFI in section 42 of its judgment, the fact that "sporting legislation may have nothing to do with economic activity, with the result, according to the Court, that it does not fall within the scope of Articles 39 and 49 EC, means, also, that it has nothing to do with the economic relationships of competition, with the result that it also does not fall within the scope of Articles 81 EC and 82 EC".

34 Case C-309/99, *Wouters*.

35 For the *Wouters* case and the inherent restriction approach, see: Chapter 3, section 4.1.2.4.

36 Chapter 3, section 4.2.2.3.

37 Chapter 3, section 4.3.1.

the consideration of horizontal and flanking policy goals in the application of Article 81(3) EC to restrictive agreements.[38] In the field of the environment this development has been most remarkable, culminating in the guidelines on horizontal co-operation agreements and the CECED decision.[39] At the same time we see that in other areas the significance of horizontal and flanking policy goals within the context of Article 81(3) EC is less clear due to a number of reasons. With regard to agreements in the field of public health, particularly where they concern the provision of health care, the application of competition rules to this sector is still in its infancy. The cases on book pricing agreements seem to suggest that not cultural arguments but other more formal or jurisdictional arguments, i.e. whether the agreement has an effect on intra-Community trade, have induced the Commission to eventually tolerate national book pricing agreements.[40]

In case of Article 82 EC, the possibilities to justify abusive behaviour for horizontal and flanking policy reasons are extremely limited. Objective justifications within the context of Article 82 EC are no solid justifications for dominant firms using anti-competitive means to attain horizontal and flanking policy aims to rely upon. Another and more realistic justification ground is provided by Article 86(2) EC.[41]

The Merger Regulation does at one point explicitly refer to public interests: Article 21(4) offers Member States the possibility to take appropriate measures to protect legitimate interests other than those taken into consideration by the regulations, such as the plurality of the media. This provision is important, because it explicitly refers to non-competition interests, which is unique for EC competition law. Furthermore, under the application of this provision the principle of proportionality plays a decisive role, similar to the one in the context of the free movement rules.[42]

An important role for the principle of proportionality

The proportionality principle plays a central role in balancing horizontal and flanking policy considerations with restrictions on competition, if horizontal and flanking policy considerations are included in the exceptions to the prohibitive rules on competition in the first place. The conceptual framework of Article 81(3) EC is particularly rigid in comparison with the exceptions to free movement. The Commission cannot restrain itself by merely balancing the presumed public interest goals of the agreement with its restrictive effects on competition. It should at least conduct some economic assessment by examining the efficiency gains of the agreement. This entails a proportionality test *stricto sensu,*

[38] Chapter 3, section 4.1.3.

[39] Commission decision 2000/475, OJ 2000, L 187/47; see also Chapter 3, section 4.1.3.2.

[40] *Sammelrevers* case, DN: IP/98/30; see also Chapter 3, section 4.1.3.4.

[41] Chapter 3, section 4.2.2.4.

[42] Chapter 3, section 4.3.3.

whereby an exemption will not be granted if the level of protection of horizontal and flanking policy interests is unreasonable in the light of the restriction of competition.[43]

4.2 Community measures: no positive integration

There is no Community legislation with the purpose to harmonise national competition laws. What can be seen, though, is that a process of 'spontaneous harmonisation' has eventually led to similar competition rules throughout the EU, without the Community legislature being involved through the adoption of harmonisation measures.

Block exemption regulations, for example for vertical agreements, or guidelines on horizontal agreements merely clarify the scope of application of Article 81 EC for certain categories of agreements. The Guidelines on the application of Article 81(3) EC should also be placed within this category. Here the Commission had the chance to clarify whether and if so to what extent horizontal and flanking policy interests can be taken into account under Article 81(3) EC. Unfortunately it did not do so and thereby missed the opportunity to give further relieve to the tension between competition policy and horizontal and flanking policies. By stating that "goals pursued by other Treaty provisions can be taken into account to the extent that they can be subsumed under the four conditions of Article 81(3)" the Commission gives a much more restrictive interpretation of Article 81(3) EC than it does in the guidelines on horizontal co-operation agreements and in its *CECED* decision with regard to environmental agreements.[44]

5 Coherence or convergence?

On the basis of the foregoing the question is to what extent a coherent policy has been developed in respect of free movement and competition. A coherent policy may even imply convergence, when policies have become so similar, or even identical, that the same standards of adjudication are applicable and a comprehensive solution to the problem of tension can be found. The degree of coherence may also be implying to a lesser extent that various solutions may be found to solve the problem of tension in respect of free movement, competition and horizontal and flanking policies. Perhaps there is no question of coherence at all; the policies involved differ considerably, and too much, for

43 Chapter 3, section 4.1.4.

44 P. Lugard and L. Hancher, Honey, I shrunk the Article! A Critical Assessment of the Commission's Notice on Article 81(3) of the EC Treaty, *ECLR*, 2004, p. 418; see also Chapter 3, section 4.1.3 and hereafter, Chapter 6, section 4.2.4.

a consistent approach towards these policies. The degree of coherence and the extent to which convergence has taken place can be established by comparing the four freedoms, the four freedoms and the rules on competition, and the various horizontal and flanking policies involved.

5.1 The four freedoms

The convergence process between the rules on free movement is in an advanced phase.[45] This process of convergence has carried on through the following three main stages. The first stage involves the broad personal and material scope of application of the free movement rules. The second stage involves the broad interpretation of the prohibitive Treaty rules, which entails that both distinctly and indistinctly applicable measures are in principle prohibited. A market access based test has begun to emerge as a key test for all freedoms. This brings the relevance of the exceptions to the fore and marks the last and third stage. The third stage includes the development of the rule of reason for all freedoms, which provides Member States with the possibility, in addition to the Treaty exceptions, to enact measures that restrict free movement, but are nonetheless justifiable for reasons related to the general interest. The proportionality principle plays an important role in this phase. The consequence of this is that it has become increasingly irrelevant how an activity or situation should be classified under goods, services, capital or persons since their legal consequences are identical. This leads to more legal certainty and uniformity in the field of free movement. Differences relating to the specific nature of the economic factors involved can still be taken into account under the exceptions to free movement.[46] The proportionality principle, allowing for a certain degree of flexibility, can be used to 'fine-tune' these differences.[47] The process of convergence is further encouraged by the fact that the prohibitive rules mainly serve to prevent State protectionism and that the justification grounds within the context of the rules on free movement in principle are invoked by public authorities,

---

45 "[...] the principles governing the four freedoms have converged to a considerable extent – but not absolutely", see: P. Oliver and W.-H. Roth, The internal market and the four freedoms, *CMLRev.*, 2004, p. 440.

46 These differences continue to be relevant as common sense tells us that persons and products are different: P. Oliver and W.-H. Roth, The internal market and the four freedoms, *CMLRev.*, 2004, p. 441; see also J. Snell, And Then There Were Two: Products and Citizens in Community Law, in: T. Trimidas & P. Nebbia (Eds), *European Union Law for the Twenty-First Century – Rethinking the New Legal Order*, Volume 2, Internal Market and Free Movement Community Policies (Hart Publishing, Oxford and Portland, 2004), pp. 49-72.

47 Baquero Cruz (2002), p. 96. According to Baquero Cruz, though, the free movement of workers should be distinguished from the other freedoms to avoid their commodification. There are, however, sufficient indications that also within the context of workers, the ECJ adopts a similar approach as regards the other freedoms.

which are generally presumed to act in the interest and for the benefit of the *public*.

5.2 The four freedoms and the competition rules

The process of convergence here is in a less advanced stage, which is particularly important for the suggestions presented in Chapter 6 hereafter.[48] Nevertheless, similarities can be found in the way the Courts and the Commission have applied the rules on free movement and competition. This can be seen at the following three stages. Firstly, the broad concept of economic activity is relevant for both the competition rules and the free movement rules. Secondly, the Court has provided a broad interpretation of the prohibitive rules on competition emphasising that the aims of the competition rules and the free movement rules are intrinsically linked, i.e. concern the establishment of a common market. Furthermore, national cartels will fall within the scope of Article 81 EC, if they affect access to the national market. The broad scope of the prohibitive rules also entails that hard-core restrictions as well as soft restrictions or soft cartels may be prohibited, and brings the exceptions to the fore. Thirdly, the exceptions are also crucial and horizontal and flanking objectives can play a role in the application of Article 81(3) EC, or can be taken into account more explicitly under Articles 87(3) and 86(2) EC. The proportionality test will be applied in this phase as well. It will furthermore be interesting to see whether the decentralisation process and the direct effect of Article 81(3) EC will have an effect on this process of convergence. If the Court receives more preliminary references as a result of Article 81(3) EC being directly applicable, the Court could show a more activist approach, thereby leaving its limited judicial review of Commission decisions.[49]

Irrespective of these general similarities, more coherence exists between the application of the state aid rules, the rules on public monopolies and the rules on free movement, than it does between the competition rules directed at undertakings and the free movement rules. Under Article 87(3) EC, either explicitly through Article 87(3) sub d EC (culture), or implicitly by guidelines (environmental aids) the Commission clearly considers horizontal and flanking policy interests as independent grounds for exempting state aids. Article 86(2) EC also leaves considerable scope for the incorporation of horizontal and flank-

48 K. Mortelmans, Towards convergence in the application of the rules on free movement and on competition?, *CMLRev.*, 2001, pp. 613-649. Baquero Cruz refers to procedural reasons for the blurring between the scopes of competition and free movement as well in: Baquero Cruz (2002), p. 103.

49 Baquero Cruz (2002), p. 102. This review is limited to manifest errors of assessment, because complex economic facts are involved and the Commission has a degree of administrative discretion. The Court could also oblige the Commission to take more account of the integration principle, incorporating horizontal and flanking policy considerations into its decisions.

ing policy concerns. That is much less clear in the case of Article 81(3) EC; on the one hand the Commission's decision practice and guidelines on horizontal co-operation agreements suggest that horizontal and flanking policy interests are also very important (perhaps even of equal value) for the exemption of cartels, whereas on the other hand the recent guidelines on Article 81(3) EC still regard such interests as subordinate to the competition interests mentioned in 81(3) EC.[50]

5.3 Horizontal and flanking policies

The EC Treaty provides various possibilities to develop horizontal and flanking policies at the level of the Community. In particular the judgments of the ECJ in the *Tobacco* cases make clear that the use of Article 95 EC and other internal market legal bases, if sufficiently motivated, may not be restricted to purely internal market legislation.[51] In this respect the Court's judgment contributes to further coherence between different horizontal and flanking policies, since cultural and public health policies may now easily be pursued through harmonisation of national laws as well, albeit within the context of the internal market.

Furthermore, a common approach to horizontal and flanking policies can be found in the Treaty. These policies are mainly based on the principle of subsidiarity and are, to a more or lesser extent, shared with the Member States. Regardless of this common approach, a closer look at the Treaty as well as at the development of horizontal and flanking policies in Community law reveals a mixed approach. In fact, there is no question of a process of convergence between the various horizontal and flanking policies, which can be explained as follows.

First, horizontal and flanking policies are being pursued and regulated at different levels of law-making (decision-making). At the level of the Community the powers to regulate in these areas are fleshed out differently. In the fields of consumer policy and environmental policy, the Community shares its powers with the Member States, whereas in the fields of culture and public health Member States are primarily competent to take action. At the level of the national state horizontal and flanking policies may be pursued by the central government, or rather by regions and/or even local authorities. In Germany, for example, the *Länder* are in principle responsible for cultural policy affairs, which explains their criticism on the revision of the Television without Frontiers Directive and the proposed compulsory quota system (see Chapter 4). Hence, horizon-

---

50 Chapter 3, section 4.1.3.

51 Case C-376/98, *Germany v. European Parliament and Council (Tobacco Advertising)*; Case C-491/01, *BAT/Imperial Tobacco*; Case C-434/02, *Arnold André*; Case C-210/03, *Swedish Match*. This has been confirmed by the Court in the *'Food Supplements'* case: Joined Cases C-154/04 and C-155/04, *Alliance for Natural Health*. See also Chapter 4, section 4.2.4.

tal and flanking policy interests are looked upon from different perspectives, the perspective of the local government, of the regions within a national state, of the central government or from the perspective of the Community. The principle of subsidiarity plays an important role here.

Second, inherently substantive differences between horizontal and flanking policies entail different approaches to these policies. Within the context of the Treaty provisions on free movement, the Court has held that public health ranks first among the interests mentioned in Article 30 EC.[52] By contrast, regarding the protection of the economic interests of consumers the Court departs from a common European notion of reasonably circumspect consumer, and not necessarily from the weakest consumer, who requires a higher level of protection afforded by the Member State. From the Treaty provisions on horizontal and flanking policies, it also appears that from a Community law perspective a gradation can be made as regards the significance of the interests involved. Environmental policy as well as consumer policy can be pursued by the Community legislature on the basis of specific legislative powers. Nevertheless it seems that the consumer policy paragraph is, through its more careful formulation, of a more subsidiary nature than the environmental paragraph. In other words, consumer policy should first and foremost be pursued within the context of the internal market based on Article 95 EC. The general importance of public health including the attention given to certain specific health problems related to, for example, the BSE crisis, has led to an amendment of Article 152 EC, now allowing the Community legislature to adopt harmonisation measures in this area.[53] This also applies to the area of blood products and human organs. The cultural paragraph, however, has been left unchanged and harmonisation remains excluded for all aspects of cultural policy within the realm of Article 151 EC.

6 The tension between horizontal and flanking policies and the internal market

Apparently the degree of coherence is not everywhere the same. No comprehensive solution to the tension between horizontal and flanking policies and the internal market has yet been found. Tensions continue to exist, which can be explained by the opposing aims of maintaining a degree of regulatory autonomy from the Member State's perspective on the one hand and of adopting a common approach necessary for the creation of a Community-wide internal market from the Community's perspective on the other. These two different perspectives will be further explained in the following sections.

52 Case 104/75, *De Peijper*; see also Chapter 2, section 4.4.3.1.

53 Chapter 4, section 5.3.2.

6.1 The perspective of the Member State

Protecting domestic horizontal and flanking policy interests

The Member State's main concern is to protect horizontal and flanking policy interests, the environment, public health, culture or consumers, according to its own will and to the fullest extent, without necessarily having to take account of the requirements of the internal market. This interest in maintaining regulatory diversity and in protecting domestic interests clearly conflicts with the interest of the Community in realising a Community-wide internal market through the application of the free movement rules and the competition rules. In other words, the Member State's desire to protect horizontal and flanking policy interests is and continues to be at right angles to the Community requirements of free movement and competition.

Free movement

It appears from Chapter 2 that, due to the broad personal and material scope as well as the broad scope of the prohibitive rules, the internal market rules are certainly applicable to horizontal and flanking policies. For national horizontal and flanking policies having an impact on free movement to be upheld, the focus must be laid on the exceptions.

Due to the development of a rule of reason in addition to the Treaty exceptions, a wide range of exception grounds is now available for Member States to justify horizontal and flanking policies. However, these exceptions are in principle not available for national measures discriminating on grounds of nationality; furthermore they have been, depending on the application of the proportionality test, restrictively interpreted as well. Hence, recourse to an exception ground for horizontal and flanking policies may still be difficult.

The competition rules

Similar to the free movement rules, Chapter 3 makes clear that the competition rules apply broadly and clearly include horizontal and flanking policy interests, through the broad concept of undertaking and corresponding notion of economic activity. Hence, the focus of attention must also be laid upon the exceptions.

The problem here is that, apart from Article 87(3) sub d EC, the exceptions to the competition rules do not contain an explicit reference to horizontal and flanking policy interests. Consequently it remains uncertain to what extent horizontal and flanking policy interests may contribute to the grant of an exemption, or to the application of the exception of Article 81(3) EC. Furthermore and in particular within the context of Article 81(3) EC the proportionality test has been applied stringently. This is less the case in the areas of state aid (Article 87(3) EC) and of services of general economic interests (Article 86(2) EC).[54] Hence,

[54] For a detailed analysis of the application of the proportionality test in these areas, see: Chapter 3, in particular sections 3.1.5, 3.2.3, 4.1.3.

recourse to an exception ground appears to be much more problematic here than in the context of free movement. Exception grounds for horizontal and flanking policy interests may simply not be available, and even if they were, they would have to be restrictively interpreted and applied.

Some degree of coherence

In section 5 it has been concluded that the convergence process between the *rules on free movement* is in an advanced stage. Nevertheless, full recourse to the exception grounds is not always possible. Even though the Court of Justice has taken Member States' concerns in protecting domestic horizontal and flanking policies to the fullest extent seriously, it has also imposed either more or less stringent conditions upon the State to successfully rely on justification grounds. So far attempts to protect out-of-state interests have not been successful.[55]

At the adoption of horizontal and flanking policies Member States may choose between various regulatory instruments, like, for example, command and control regulation, whereby certain standards are imposed by law or self-regulation, leaving the protection of horizontal and flanking policy interests up to private parties. From the Member State's perspective the protection of horizontal and flanking policy interests would therefore be served best by a coherent approach to the *free movement rules and the rules on competition*, which provides a comprehensive solution to the conflict between horizontal and flanking policies and the internal market. This 'seamless web approach' would be in accordance with the case law on the rules on free movement and would guarantee that the horizontal and flanking dimension of competition policy is duly implemented.[56]

However, as is suggested above, the degree of coherence between the free movement rules on the one hand and the competition rules on the other is much less than that between the free movement rules. The fact that convergence is problematic and disputable here can be explained by the presumed private interest of private companies, as opposed to the presumed public interest of public authorities. This manifests itself by the way in which the proportionality test is carried out. Where *private* actors are concerned, recourse to *public* interest exception grounds is the most contentious. The margin of discretion to pursue horizontal and flanking policy interests within the context of Article 81(3) EC is therefore very limited. All three elements of the proportionality test will have to be fulfilled for an agreement to benefit from the exception of Article 81(3) EC.[57] It can be seen, though, that in the field of the environment, private actors seem

55 See also P. Oliver and W.-H. Roth, The internal market and the four freedoms, *CMLRev.*, 2004, pp. 407-441.

56 L. Gyselen, The Emerging Interface between Competition Policy and Environmental Policy in the EC, in: J. Cameron, P. Demaret & D. Geradin (Eds), *Trade & The Environment – The Search for a Balance* (Cameron May, London, 1994), p. 245.

57 Chapter 3, section 4.1.3.

to have more leeway to pursue environmental policy interests through the adoption of agreements (see above).

Where semi-public/semi-private associations are involved, the situation is different. The case law here is still in its infancy, but the *Wouters* judgment as well as the Commission's Report on Competition in Professional Services show that where specific public interests and the protection of consumers are at stake, self-regulatory initiatives may be justifiable provided that no less restrictive measures are available.[58]

Where public undertakings entrusted with tasks of general interest are involved, the specific exception ground of Article 86(2) EC is available; here the Court has applied a more flexible approach towards proportionality, which may nevertheless require an assessment of whether no less restrictive measure was available.[59]

Where *public authorities* are involved, in case of application of the free movement rules, the Court will focus on whether no less restrictive alternatives are available to attain the same horizontal and flanking policy objective, guaranteeing a similar level of protection.[60] If the state decides to grant financial aid to undertakings for the protection of horizontal and flanking policy interests, recourse to the exception of Article 87(3) EC will probably be possible. The way in which the proportionality principle will be applied has either been elaborated in a comprehensive set of guidelines, like in the field of the environment, or must be assessed on a case-by-case basis.[61]

6.2 The perspective of the Community

The Community wide internal market and the pursuance of horizontal and flanking policies

The answer to the problem of tension may be the harmonisation of national laws. After all, from Chapter 4 it appears in particular that the Community legislature's interest in the realisation of a Community-wide internal market through harmonisation generally goes together with the pursuance of horizontal and flanking policy interests.[62] From the Community's perspective

58 Case C-309/99, *Wouters*. Report on Competition in Professional Services, COM (2004) 83 final. For a more detailed discussion see Chapter 3, section 4.1.2.4.

59 Chapter 3, section 3.2.3.

60 Chapter 2, section 4 *et seq.*

61 Chapter 3, section 3.1.5.

62 This may not always be the case: see for example the proposal for a Directive on services in the Internal Market (COM(2004) 2 final/3). This proposal was criticised for not having met the prerequisites of a true harmonisation measure; from the perspective of horizontal and flanking policies the balance between horizontal and flanking policy interests and the internal market has been struck wrongly: see Chapter 4, section 4.2.2.

the tension could therefore be resolved if horizontal and flanking policies are pursued at the level of the Community, or rather become 'Community policies'. This has not happened and is – at least for the time being – not likely to happen. Member States are seeking to prevent the extension of Community powers in certain policy areas, like public health and culture. In fact there is a paradox of Member States wishing to remain primarily competent in certain areas of horizontal and flanking policies and the negative integration process 'spoiling the whole game'. It appears from Chapter 4 that this is partly the result of the positive integration process as well, since horizontal and flanking policies, for which no specific legal basis is available, can also be harmonised 'through the backdoor', i.e. by using the broadly applicable internal market legal bases as reinforced by the Court in *Tobacco Advertising*.

No real coherence

Notwithstanding a common approach to horizontal and flanking policies in the Treaty, there is no real coherence between the various horizontal and flanking policies, i.e. between environmental, public health, consumer and cultural policies. The differences between environmental, public health, consumer and cultural interests have been explained by the fact that horizontal and flanking policies are regulated at different levels of law-making, and because there are inherently substantive differences between horizontal and flanking policies. The reason why convergence is problematic and disputable here is that with a view to the principle of subsidiarity, horizontal and flanking policies have been and must be fleshed out differently.

CHAPTER 6

Closer Harmony

1 Introduction

The synthesis in Chapter 5 reveals the unavoidability of the law having a certain 'messiness' in dealing with fundamental tensions, like the tension between horizontal and flanking policies and the internal market. Messiness, though, is not the same as chaos.[1] In other words, no convergence or little convergence does not necessarily mean that no coherence does or can exist. Therefore suggestions will be made that must contribute to further coherence and the achievement of closer harmony between free movement, competition and horizontal and flanking policies, against which background the problem of tension could be controlled or even ultimately resolved.

The example of books, introduced in the first chapter of this book, can be used to illustrate in a more general sense the problem of tension between free movement, competition and horizontal and flanking policies. Books are cultural products, but at the same time they are commercial goods within the meaning of Articles 28-30 EC. Whereas the regulation of the book market may have an effect on the free movement of goods and on competition, the objective of this regulation is often of a cultural nature, i.e. to support books as a cultural medium, which is an objective of cultural policy, falling within the field of horizontal and flanking policies.

Furthermore, the example of books shows the importance of general principles of Community law in balancing the opposite interests of free movement and competition and horizontal and flanking policies. These principles of Community law, which have also been introduced in the first chapter, are relevant for the bodies that are involved in the policy and law-making process at Community and national levels, and will be briefly recapitulated here.

The *integration principle* is addressed to the Community institutions and has been laid down in the various Treaty paragraphs on horizontal and flanking policies as well as in Article 6 EC with respect to the environment, requiring that environmental, public health, consumer and cultural interests are really integrated into internal market policy.

The *principle of Community loyalty*, another important principle for the achievement of closer harmony, has been laid down in Article 10 EC and is, contrary to the principle of integration, specifically addressed to the Member States.

---

1 The words 'messiness' and 'chaos' have been used in the context of the tension between free trade and local regulatory policies by D.E. Farber and R.E. Hudec, Gatt Legal Restraints on Domestic Environmental Regulations, in: J.N.Bhagwati and R.E. Hudec (Eds), *Fair Trade and Harmonization – Prerequisites for Free Trade*, Volume II (The MIT Press, Cambridge,1996), p. 84.

The *principle of proportionality* as ground for the review of measures derogating from the rules on free movement and competition is addressed to both the Member States and the Community legislature.

Against this background, it will be assessed how closer harmony can be attained from the perspective of the Member State (section 3), the perspective of the Community (section 4) and the perspective of the Community as constitutional legislator (section 5). Regarding the latter suggestions for amendments to the Treaty will be presented as ultimate remedy for the problem of tension. The various bodies of the Member State and the Community that are involved in the policy and law-making process have distinct roles in dealing with the problem of tension. Suggestions for the achievement of closer harmony are therefore specifically addressed to those bodies. At the level of the Member State these are the national legislature (section 3.1), the national competition authorities (section 3.2) and the national courts (section 3.3). At the level of the European Community these are the European Court of Justice (section 4.1), the European Commission (section 4.2) and the Community legislature (section 4.3).

2 The example of books

"Libris satiari nequeo"[2]

In respect of one type of product, books, different regulatory instruments can be used to pursue the same cultural objective. But it should be noted that the example of books is not all embracing and merely gives an *idea* of the bodies that are involved in the policy and law-making process at national and European levels and how they are confronted with the application of Community law.

2.1 Supporting books as cultural product at national level

Depending on the type of regulatory instrument, its use by the Member State may be either more or less problematic in the light of Community law.

Vertical price fixing agreements

The most commonly used instrument in Europe has been the instrument of 'self-regulation', i.e. vertical book pricing agreements between publishers and booksellers. But as was shown in Chapter 3 the Commission has always considered price fixing agreements with cross-border effects to violate the cartel prohibition of Article 81(1) EC and has not granted an exemption to such

[2] F. Petrarca (1304-1374): "From books I never get enough." Petrarca is considered to be the first modern European, and also the first modern European *lawyer.*

agreements on the basis of Article 81(3) EC. In fact, price restraints imposed by private actors are simply not proportionate in the light of Article 81(3) EC and cultural aims have not been recognised as grounds for exemption; rather formal, jurisdictional arguments have contributed to the Commission's view in *Sammelrevers* that purely national book price fixing agreements will not be considered problematic in the light of Article 81 EC.[3]

Is the Commission's remark that in the *VBVB/VBBB* case on the trans-book pricing agreement in the Dutch language area it is not up to private undertakings to engage in cultural questions, still valid? And could the Commission have opted for another approach? The point of departure for the Commission could be the homogeneous language area rather than the territorial border in assessing book price agreements under Article 81 EC. Transnational book price agreements in a single language area would then be presumed to fall *prima facie* outside the scope of Article 81(1) EC because they lead to more, instead of less, competition on the book market and they do not affect trade in a homogeneous language area. The Commission takes Article 151(4) EC into account by interpreting the criterion of affecting intra-Community trade in terms of language boundaries, rather than in terms of territorial borders.[4]

Another and more likely solution is to take account of homogeneous language areas under Article 81(3) EC. In addition it will be very difficult for the Commission to compare the various transnational book price systems, as national cultures between Member States differ to a considerable extent. In some Member States and homogeneous language areas fixed prices may have beneficial effects, whereas in others free prices help to increase the sale of books.[5]

Nonetheless, if a Member State chooses not to intervene through the adoption of legislation, private initiatives, in this case by publishers and booksellers, will almost certainly come up against a high wall of resistance, whether it be Article 81 EC or the cartel prohibition laid down in national competition law, unless they involve 'softer cartels' or other harmless instruments as suggested by the Commission in the *Sammelrevers* case.

Regulating book prices by law

Another option is to regulate book prices by law. When it in the Netherlands became clear that book pricing agreements would either fall within the scope of Article 81 EC or within the scope of Article 6 of the Netherlands Competition Act and would not be eligible for an exemption, it was decided to intervene

---

3 This applies even if books exported solely for the purpose of being re-imported in order to circumvent the national price fixing system are subject to fixed retail prices (the so-called U-turn construction): see Chapter 3, section 4.1.3.5.

4 Everling (1997), p. 39.

5 Langbein (1989), p. 123.

through the adoption of legislation.[6] A law has been adopted that requires publishers and booksellers to fix a retail price for books.[7] The background is to avoid possible conflicts with the competition rules. Nevertheless, the law must still be in accordance with the EC Treaty rules on free movement and, particularly relevant in this case, with the useful effect doctrine as developed in the case law of the Court of Justice.[8] After having consulted the Netherlands Competition Authority ('NMa')[9] and the European Commission (DG Competition),[10] Article 3 of the initial proposal requiring importers of books to take account of the price recommended or fixed by publishers established in another State was modified, now merely requiring importers of Dutch language books to establish a fixed price, thereby providing them to take account of import advantages and the original price.

Whereas the compatibility of price regulation by law with the useful effect doctrine may still be uncertain, this is less so with Article 28 EC on the free movement of goods. Based on the case law and contrary to agreements on prices being *per se* prohibited by Article 81 EC, price regulation by *law* is not really that problematic under Article 28 EC, unless a distinction is made between imported products and domestic products. This was the case in *Leclerc* where the French law on fixed book prices, the 'Loi Lang' required importers to fix the price of imported books. Hence, there was no possibility to take account of the cost price in the state in which the book was published, a possibility existing on the basis of the present Dutch law.[11]

State aids

A third option, which was also suggested by the Commission in the *Sammelrevers* case, is to grant financial aid to support the publication, distribution or, for example, the export of books. In this case it is likely that an exemption will

---

6 Article 6 of the Netherlands Competition Act is the equivalent of Article 81 EC.

7 Wet van 9 november 2004, houdende regels omtrent de vaste boekenprijs (Wet op de vaste boekenprijs, *Law on fixed book prices*), *Stb.* 600. See also Chapter 3, section 3.3.

8 See Chapter 2, section 4.4.4 and Chapter 3, section 3.3.1.

9 Advisory opinion of the d-g NMa of 22 April 2004 at www.vasteboekenprijs.nl. According to the 'NMa' the Netherlands Competition Act will not be applicable to the law proposal on fixed book prices, since the obligation for the publisher to establish a fixed price for booksellers as well as the obligation for booksellers to apply that price directly follows from the law itself. However, the 'NMa' held that the law proposal, considering its effect on inter-state trade, as Article 3 applies to imports, may well be in conflict with the useful effect doctrine, i.e. Articles 10 Jo. 81 EC. Furthermore, in particular Article 12 of the initial law proposal providing the possibility to conclude price fixing agreements would have competition law consequences.

10 Advisory opinion of the European Commission (DG Competition) of 2 August 2004 at: www.vasteboekenprijs.nl.

11 Case 229/83, *Leclerc v. Au Blé Vert*. See also Chapter 2, section 4.4.4.4.

be granted on the basis of Article 87(3) sub d EC. The Commission has shown a strong willingness to apply the cultural exception, but case law of the Court makes clear that the proportionality principle cannot be ignored.[12]

2.2 Supporting books as cultural product at Community level

There are various ways in which the Community legislature could support books as cultural products, for example, by adopting a directive or a regulation or by granting subsidies or other financial incentives.

Intervention through harmonisation

It is not conceivable that the Community will adopt a regulation or directive on fixed book prices, at least not within the foreseeable time.[13]

The idea for a common approach to the problem of book prices by the Community legislature arose for the first time in 1985, when the Commission presented various alternatives for the regulation of book prices at Community level. However, up till now the Commission has never drafted a proposal for a directive or regulation in the field of fixed book prices. In 2001 the European Parliament adopted a resolution with recommendations to the Commission on the drawing-up of a Directive based on Article 95 EC on the fixing of book prices.[14] This Directive would only provide a legal basis for Member States wishing to pursue book price fixing systems either by law or by contractual agreements. On the basis of this Directive Member States that do not wish to adopt a system for book price fixing will not be required to do so.

According to the European Parliament the use of Article 95 EC as legal basis for this proposal can be justified as it provides the possibility, contrary to the Commission's practice on book pricing systems, to subject domestic booksellers to similar conditions of competition as those applying to importers, exporters and re-importers of books; in other words, the detailed rules on prevention of circumvention of national price fixing systems as well as, for example, the possibility for publishers in one Member State to enter contractual agreements concluded in another Member State.

Whereas the use of Article 95 EC for cultural measures also may have been reinforced by the Court's ruling in the *Tobacco* cases,[15] it is unsure and disput-

---

[12] Cases T-49/93, *SIDE v. Commission* and T-155/98, *SIDE v. Commission* (2); see also Chapter 3, section 3.1.5.5.

[13] See also M. Appelman & M. Canoy, Notes and Communications: Horses for courses: why Europe should not harmonise its book policies, *De Economist*, 2002, pp. 583-600.

[14] European Parliament resolution with recommendations to the Commission on the drawing-up of a directive of the European Parliament and of the Council on the fixing of book prices (2001/2061(INI)).

[15] Case C-376/98, *Germany v. European Parliament and Council (Tobacco Advertising)*; Case C-491/01, *BAT/Imperial Tobacco*; Case C-434/02, *Arnold André*; Case C-210/03, *Swedish Match*. This approach is confirmed by the Court in Joined Cases C-154/04 and C-155/04, *Alliance for Natural Health*. See also Chapter 4, section 4.2.4.

able whether the threshold criteria would be fulfilled here, since there is no real harmonisation of national laws; rather the status quo is maintained. This proposal would merely partly codify the decision practice of the Commission.

Subsidies

Article 151 EC empowers the Community to take action in the cultural field, e.g. by means of subsidies or information programmes, and requires the Community to attain objectives of a cultural nature. But harmonisation on the basis of this provision is excluded. The Community could, for example within the framework of the Culture 2000 programme, which includes the support of projects aimed at improving access to books and reading, grant subsidies to support the dissemination of books in cross-border language areas.[16] Subsidies granted by the Community are not subject to Community review, which is reserved for aid granted by Member States under Article 87 EC.

2.3 What does this example tell us?

The example of books makes clear firstly that even though the predominantly cultural objective of supporting books as cultural medium is similar for different forms of intervention in the book market by different regulatory bodies, their discretionary powers to intervene in the market is not akin and depends on the application of individual Treaty provisions. Private actors have hardly any, or no possibility at all, to impose *price* measures under Article 81 EC. If their conduct is contrary to Article 81(1) EC, but can nevertheless be exempted on the basis of Article 81(3) EC, they will be faced with the proportionality principle, which is rigidly applied. Since in the following the emphasis is laid upon regulatory instruments used by the Member State or the Community, the suggestions are addressed to the institutions involved in the policy-making and law-making process and not to private actors, i.e. individual undertakings.

Secondly, the example shows that from the perspective of the Member State the possibilities to choose between various regulatory instruments to pursue cultural, or for that matter other horizontal and flanking policy interests, are not unlimited. If the Member State opts for the instrument of self-regulation, it will have to realise the sometimes limited room for manoeuvre for private actors under Article 81 EC to pursue cultural, or other horizontal and flanking policy interests. If the Member State chooses not to use the instrument of self-regulation, but instead opts for another form of regulation, it will have to take account of the Treaty rules on free movement, or perhaps the useful effect doctrine.

If the Member State decides to give financial aid to the book sector for cultural policy reasons, the Treaty provisions on state aid have to be respected.

---

16 Decision No 508/2000 of the European Parliament and of the Council of 14 February 2000 establishing the Culture 2000 programme, OJ 2000, L 63/1.

In all these situations the exceptions to the prohibitive provisions are brought to the fore with an essential role for the principle of proportionality in seeking to resolve the tension. On the basis of the proportionality principle Member States are required to take account of Community interests, ensuring that national measures are proportionate to their propagated cultural or other horizontal and flanking policy objectives.

More generally, the requirement to take account of Community interests can also be deduced from the principle of Community loyalty. This principle becomes particularly relevant where the tension cannot be resolved on the basis of the proportionality principle alone, always requiring the bodies involved in the policy and law-making process to prevent possible conflicts with Community law.

Thirdly, the example makes clear that from the Community's perspective the cultural aim of a Community measure does not necessarily curtail the Community's power to legislate on the basis of Article 95 EC. The Community legislature has, however, a strong duty to motivate its legislation, which has been reinforced by the Court's ruling in *Tobacco Advertising*.[17] If it cannot be motivated why Article 95 EC should be used as legal basis, the Community can only resort to 'soft law instruments' or financial instruments in the field of culture. Although less stringently applied than in respect of Member State action, Community harmonisation measures must also be proportionate.

3 Closer harmony: the perspective of the Member State

If confronted with the application of the rules on free movement and competition, what can various national bodies involved in the policy-making and regulatory process do to attain closer harmony between the internal market rules and horizontal and flanking policies? There are generally two ways that may lead to more coherence in respect of the tension between horizontal and flanking policies and internal market policy and hence to closer harmony: one way is based upon the principle of proportionality, the other upon the principle of Community loyalty. These principles are relevant for the national legislature being involved in the law-making process, the national competition authorities being involved in the policy-making process and in carrying out competition law, and the national courts in carrying out the law and controlling the legislature.

As can be seen from the foregoing chapters, the principle of proportionality plays a particularly significant role in the balancing of national horizontal and flanking policies with the internal market and the competition rules;

[17] Case C-376/98, *Germany v. European Parliament and Council (Tobacco Advertising)*; see also Chapter 4, section 4.2.4.

the suggestions based on the principle of proportionality and addressed to the national legislature will therefore be presented first, followed by suggestions based on the Community loyalty principle (hereafter, sections 3.1.1 and 3.1.2). The Community loyalty principle is particularly relevant for the national competition authorities which, as a result of Regulation 1/2003, are confronted with the application of EC competition law and onsequently have to co-operate closely with each other and with the European Commission to prevent inconsistencies in the application of the EC competition rules (section 3.2.1). Due to the direct applicability of Article 81(3) EC, the national competition authorities will now also be confronted with a balancing exercise previously conducted by the Commission under Article 81(3) EC and consequently with the application of the proportionality principle (section 3.2.2). The same goes true for the national courts having to respect the Community loyalty principle and the principle of proportionality whilst being confronted with the application of Articles 81 and 82 EC as well as with the free movement rules having direct effect (sections 3.3.1 and 3.3.2).

3.1 The national legislature

The national legislature has to be aware of the importance of both the proportionality principle and the principle of Community loyalty in drafting national laws that may have an impact on free movement and competition.

3.1.1 Realising the importance of the proportionality principle

In respect of horizontal and flanking policies having an impact on free movement and competition the focus of attention is laid upon the application of the exception grounds; hence, the national legislature must give considerable weight to the proportionality principle first. In the following the two extreme situations are distinguished, i.e. the national legislature when intervening through command and control regulation facing the application of the free movement rules, and the national legislature when abstaining from regulatory action facing the application of the competition rules.

3.1.1.1 Introduction

The application of the proportionality test in respect of national laws restricting free movement in particular entails whether the least restrictive alternative instrument has been found by the Member State.[18] Member States are under a constant obligation to examine on a case-by-case basis whether no

[18] Chapter 2, in particular section 4.3.3; Chapter 5, section 2.

measures less restrictive to free movement are available.[19] Where private actors are involved, the proportionality test carried out under Article 81(3) EC may be even more stringent.

Based on the synthesis presented in Chapter 5 two factors are particularly relevant for the application of the proportionality principle as an instrument to balance horizontal and flanking policies with the requirements of the internal market. First, the application of the proportionality test depends on the horizontal and flanking policy interest at stake, whether it involves environmental, public health, consumer or cultural interests; second, it depends on the intensity of the regulatory instrument used by the national legislature, to what extent private actors, semi-public/semi-private actors, or public actors are involved in the regulatory process.

3.1.1.2 The horizontal and flanking policy interest at stake

A certain hierarchy of horizontal and flanking policy interests within the context of the free movement rules

The Court of Justice has indicated in its case law that some horizontal and flanking policy interests are particularly important thereby leaving Member States with a considerable margin of discretion to pursue these interests.[20] Special importance has been given to the protection of public health, which makes it particularly attractive for Member States to argue that their law can be justified on public health grounds. The protection of health and life of humans, which according to the case law also covers health care, is included in the Treaty as an exception ground, as in Article 30 EC as well.

To some extent the same goes true for the protection of the environment, considering the ECJ's willingness to uphold national discriminatory measures for the sake of the environment. Nonetheless, the protection of the environment has not (yet) been included in the Treaty as justification ground.

By contrast, in the field of consumer policy, excluding sensitive issues as gambling etc. the Court of Justice has always departed from a reasonable level of consumer protection and from the notion of the consumer as a beneficiary of the internal market process. Nevertheless the gambling cases show that even though different justification grounds may be brought forward by the Member State, the Court may choose only one as applicable. The result is that restrictions on gambling are permitted, and that Member States have considerable leeway to impose restrictions on gambling.[21]

---

19 Case C-239/02, *Douwe Egberts*, paragraph 43.

20 K.J.M. Mortelmans, Botsende algemene belangen en de werking van de interne markt, *SEW* 2004, pp. 247-248. With regard to Article 3 of the EC Treaty (tasks and activities), see: J. Basedow, Zielkonflikte und Zielhierarchien im Vertrag über die EG, in: O. Due, M. Lutter & J. Schwarze (Eds), *Festschrift für Ulrich Everling* (Nomos Verlagsgesellschaft, Baden-Baden, 1995), pp. 49-68.

21 Chapter 2, section 4.4.2.4. See with regard to the 'gambling cases': J. H. Jans, Proportionality revisited, *LIEI*, 2000, p. 250.

In the field of culture, a policy area which also primarily has been promoted by the Member States, the Court may put more self-restraint in the application of the proportionality test as well, for example in the 'language cases', but it has not always done so.[22]

Consequently, the national legislature may seek to wrap up national legislation as measures of public health or environmental policy in order to improve their chance of success in upholding the law, if national legislation is challenged before national courts, by the Commission or before the Court of Justice. Conversely, if a Member State, for example, wishes to stimulate the purchase of safe plastic and non-recyclable bottles of a high quality and to ban the more environmentally friendly *glass* bottles of lesser, but sufficiently safe quality, the measure might not be justifiable on grounds of consumer protection; not only might the policy be in conflict with Article 28 EC, but also with principles of environmental policy and Article 6 EC, the integration principle (see also hereafter, section 4.1).

Hence, in drafting horizontal and flanking policies it is essential to clearly lay down the purpose of the national measure as well as to extensively motivate why the measure contributes to that purpose. Arguments relating to the protection of public health and the protection of the environment may find a more ready ear with the Court of Justice than arguments relating to the protection of consumers or culture.

The status of horizontal and flanking policy interests remains less clear in the context of competition policy

Where the competition rules directed at Member States are concerned, there is more clarity with regard to the significance of horizontal and flanking policy interests, than where the 'traditional' competition rules addressed to undertakings are concerned.

In the field of competition policy it appears that the Commission has been willing to consider, in particular, *environmental* agreements restricting competition as being necessary and proportionate to the aims of environmental protection and competition. In the field of the environment this development has been most remarkable, considering the Commission's decision in *CECED,* which is the finest example in which the Commission explicitly incorporates environmental aims into Article 81(3) EC as well as applies, in particular, the second element of the proportionality test, i.e. whether no alternative measure were available to equally contribute to the environmental benefits, to an agreement between private undertakings.[23] In other areas, though, the significance of horizontal and flanking policy goals within the context of Article 81(3) EC is much less clear.

---

[22] Chapter 2, section 4.4.4.5.

[23] Commission Decision 2000/475, OJ 2000, L 187/47; Chapter 3, section 4.1.3.2.

This means that where the national legislature wants to take recourse to alternative, more economic-oriented, instruments rather than traditional command and control regulation, its chances of success to uphold such instruments in the light of the competition rules may be higher in the field of the environment than in other horizontal and flanking policy fields, like culture or consumer policy. Most notably in the field of the environment there has been a trend towards an increased use of economic instruments, despite the fact that traditional command and control regulation continues to dominate the environmental field.[24]

With regard to books self-regulation has always been considered an important instrument as support to them as cultural products; the voluntary fixing of prices by publishers and booksellers has therefore been accepted under national laws in several Member States.

3.1.1.3 Choosing the least restrictive alternative

Not only the status of horizontal and flanking policy interests, but also the regulatory instrument used is relevant for the application of the proportionality principle. The national legislature has to be aware of these differences in the application of the proportionality principle, when they choose the type of intervention and the instrument to promote and protect horizontal and flanking policy interests. Within this context it appears that there are still possibilities, depending on the degree of intervention and type of instrument, to pursue horizontal and flanking policies either through (command and control) regulation or through self-regulation.

National legislation that is particularly problematic in the light of free movement

National rules on product standards are generally considered to restrict intra-Community trade; the same goes true for national measures restricting access to the market in services, or forming an obstacle to the free movement of workers. If a national authority (or regional or local) decides to intervene through command and control instruments in a certain field, for example, through banning the use of a certain product, it will have to realise that such instruments would probably be in conflict with the free movement of goods, in particular Article 28 EC. Accordingly, in order to be justifiable, it must be proved that the law in question is necessary for the protected interest involved, as well as that it is proportionate to the aim pursued. The national authority must ascertain itself whether no less restrictive means than an absolute ban

---

[24] M. A. Heldeweg, R.J.G.H. Seerden and K. Deketelaere, Public Environmental Law in Europe; a comparative search for a *ius commune, EELR*, 2004, pp. 84-85. See also the sixth environment action programme of the European Community: 'Environment 2010: Our future, Our choice', COM(2001) 31 final, in particular section 2.3: Encouraging the Market to Work for the Environment.

on the use of a certain product were available to protect the interest at stake. If an import ban seeks to protect public health and is based on sound scientific evidence, or if there is genuine scientific doubt, the Court will probably uphold the ban. If an import ban merely seeks to protect consumers' interests, the ECJ will almost certainly come to the conclusion that less restrictive alternatives are available, for example measures requiring producers to provide consumers with sufficient product information.[25]

National legislation that is not problematic in the light of free movement

If the public authority decides to impose certain price restrictions on products, it will probably not act contrary to Article 28 EC, unless the price measure has discriminatory effects. The fixing of maximum prices, minimum prices or a ban on retail sales at a loss will not constitute measures having equivalent effect, if they are applicable without distinction to imported and domestic products. Resale price maintenance for books will probably only be caught by Article 28 EC whenever the retail price is fixed by the importer (see section 2 and the example of books).[26]

Self-regulation that is particularly problematic in the light of competition

By contrast price restrictions imposed by private actors will almost certainly be prohibited by Article 81(1) EC and will hardly ever be eligible for an exemption pursuant to Article 81(3) EC (see section 2 and the example of books). Hence, certain practices, which are acceptable under the free movement rules, may not, or only under limited and sometimes even exceptional circumstances be justifiable on the basis of Article 81(3) EC.

Self-regulation that is not problematic in the light of competition

On the other hand, certain types of national measures that are likely to infringe the free movement rules may not at all be problematic in the light of the cartel prohibition. Quality standards and product requirements, for example, are generally not considered to restrict competition within the meaning of Article 81(1) EC as long as participation in standard setting is unrestricted and transparent, market access is not affected and competition between competitors not excluded.

Furthermore, qualitative restrictions have generally also been placed outside the scope of the prohibition of Article 81(1) EC, provided they do not contain hard core restrictions.[27] Where agreements that restrict competition on one cost factor of certain services may in reality have insignificant effects on the market for these services, Article 81(1) EC will probably not be violated.[28] Professional

[25] Chapter 2, section 4.4.2.4.

[26] Oliver (assisted by Malcolm Jarvis) (2003), pp. 202-203. See also Chapter 2, section 4.4.4.4.

[27] Chapter 3, section 4.1.2.

[28] Joined Cases C-180/98 to C-184/98, *Pavlov*; see also Chapter 3, section 4.1.2.2.

rules set up by semi-public/semi-private organisations will generally not be prohibited on the basis of Article 81(1) EC, if they are necessary to attain certain objectives which are connected to the need to make rules relating to organisation, qualifications, professional ethics, supervision and liability.[29] Rules set up by sporting associations concerning questions of purely sporting interests also fall outside the scope of application of Article 81(1) EC.[30]

In sum, if it is decided to abstain from command and control instruments and to opt for the instrument of self-regulation instead, leaving private actors a considerable margin of discretion to adopt voluntary agreements for the attainment of horizontal and flanking policy aims, the national legislature will have to realise that the cartel prohibition may come in its way. Nonetheless, it may not always be as it looks. Although the possibilities for private companies to make arrangements for the protection of horizontal and flanking policies may have been considerably reduced by the application of the EC competition rules, the use of self-regulation as instrument for horizontal and flanking policies is, as shown above, not wholly excluded.

3.1.2 Respecting the Community loyalty principle

The foregoing sections have shown that balancing the opposing interests of horizontal and flanking policies on the one hand and of free movement and competition on the other is a difficult and delicate exercise. The example of books is illustrative in this respect. Against this background it is essential that conflicts between Community rules on free movement and competition and domestic horizontal and flanking policies are prevented; the Community loyalty principle becomes relevant, as on the basis of this principle the national legislature cannot simply sit still; it will have to actively contribute to the removal of barriers to trade and competition.[31]

There are various practical ways at different levels of law-making, national or European, how the Community loyalty principle could be complied with by the national legislature with a view to achieve closer harmony. In the following sections different ways of exchanging information with a view to loyal co-operation are being discussed according to their level of intensity.

3.1.2.1 The exchange of information at national level

Examples of tools contributing to the exchange of information at national level are information and communication, co-operation between the

---

[29] Case C-309/99, *Wouters*; see also Chapter 3, section 4.1.2.4.

[30] Case T-313/02, *Meca-Medina*.

[31] See, for example, in the context of the free movement of goods: Case C-265/95, *Commission v. France (Spanish Strawberries)* and Case C-112/00, *Schmidberger*; Chapter 2, section 2.2.

bodies and national departments involved in the policy and law-making process as well as screening of national law proposals by its effects on Community law.

Information and communication

Information and communication are essential tools for the creation of more awareness of the relevance of Community law among national policy officials working either at national, regional or local levels of the State's administration.[32] The regional level is particularly important in a federal State like Germany where the *Länder* are competent to regulate in certain fields of horizontal and flanking policies such as culture. In Belgium where the state-regions carry the most important environmental powers, regional legislation is considered to be of equal importance to federal law.[33]

Information can be exchanged in various ways: By *training* policy officials who are involved in the development of horizontal and flanking policies, in the field of European Community law; by *informing* policy officials more generally about recent developments in Community law; by organising regular *meetings* where recent developments in Community law and their relevance for a particular policy field are being discussed; by rotating policy officials from various departments in order to increase their knowledge of and understanding in other horizontal and flanking policies and in other policy fields, like competition policy.[34] Another suggestion is to send national policy officials on secondment to the European Commission.

Co-operation

A step further is close co-operation between the various departments of a national government involved in trade policies and the development of horizontal and flanking policies in order to get to know and understand the implications of their policies for Community law and vice versa, to prevent future conflicts and to create conditions for the development of mutually supportive instruments.[35] Special inter-ministerial committees could be established to co-ordinate their actions with a view to European law.[36]

---

32 Information could, for example, be provided through the establishment of a centre of expertise in the field of European law, in individual departments, or in a specific department, such as the department of International and European affairs, being responsible for distributing the relevant information to the other 'spending and caring' departments involved in the pursuance of horizontal and flanking policies.

33 See with regard to environmental policy: M. A. Heldeweg, R.J.G.H. Seerden and K. R. Deketelaere, Public environmental law in Europe; a comparative search for a *ius commune*, *EELR*, 2004, p. 80.

34 K.J.M. Mortelmans, Milieubeleid en mededingingsrecht: onvermijdelijke confrontatie en gewenste integratie, *NTER*, 2000, p. 27.

35 Examples are the abolition of environmentally harmful state aids and the support of eco-efficient innovations giving economic and ecological benefits: see also the Presidency Conclusions Informal Environment Council, 16-18 July 2004, "Clean, Clever and Competitive", where at Community level

In a federation, like Germany, it is essential that the regions (*Länder*) closely co-operate with the federal government (*Bund*) in fields of horizontal and flanking policies. If certain policies, like cultural policy, belong to the competence of the *Länder*, it must be clear through close co-operation with the federal government to what extent Community law limits their discretionary power to take action in the cultural field. Otherwise serious conflicts will arise between the federal government and the *Länder*, as the dispute regarding the inclusion of a (legally binding) quota provision in the Television without Frontiers Directive before the German Constitutional Court has shown.[37]

Co-operation may sometimes be difficult or even impossible. Co-operation between the Netherlands Competition authority and departments involved in developing horizontal and flanking policies, for example, regarding the way in which horizontal and flanking policy interests can be incorporated in individual cases is not considered desirable and will, after the NMa has gained its independence from the Ministry of Economic Affairs, not be possible.[38] The decision-making process would otherwise become too much influenced by political preferences.[39] At the level of the Community, however, there are less barriers for these forms of co-operation. After all, the European Commission decides as 'board' – jointly – also in competition cases, meaning that Commissioners of other departments may be involved in the decision-making process as well. The Commission's final decision is drafted by DG Competition and "adopted by majority vote by the Commission, on a proposal of the Competition Commissioner, and after consultation with the Legal Service and sometimes other Commission services, as well as the Advisory Committee, composed of the officials of the Member States".[40]

---

it is proposed that the Environment Council should create alliances with other Councils for creating supportive conditions for eco-efficient innovations. This is in my opinion also relevant for the national government and the various departments involved.

36 See with regard to problems of participation of Ministries in the implementation of EU legislation in the Netherlands and the need for a permanent centre of co-ordination: V.J.J.M. Bekkers, A.J.C. de Moor-van Vught and W. Voermans, Going Dutch: problems and policies concerning the implementation of EU legislation in the Netherlands, in: P. Craig and C. Harlow, *Lawmaking in the European Union* (London, The Hague, Boston, 1998), pp. 474 and 477.

37 See Chapter 4, section 4.3.4.

38 See also with regard to the Netherlands Competition Authority and its possible status as independent administrative authority: W.T. Algera, Is de ZBO-Status voor de NMa nu al wenselijk?, in: J.W. van de Gronden and R.J.G.M. Widdershoven (Eds), *Mededingingsautoriteiten als zelfstandig bestuursorgaan: onafhankelijk toezicht?* (Kluwer, Deventer, 2002), pp. 93-143.

39 See also letter by the Minister of Economic Affairs regarding the independent status of the NMa, *TK* 2003-2004, 27 639 A.

40 W.P.J. Wils, The Combination of the Investigative and Prosecutorial Function and the Adjudicative Function in EC Antitrust Enforcement: A Legal and Economic Analysis, *World Competition*, 2004, p. 203.

Screening

A Community law impact assessment implies that each law proposal will have to be assessed by its effects on Community law. This should help to prevent future conflicts between national legislation serving horizontal and flanking policy interests and the rules on free movement and competition and, as a consequence, to prevent that this legislation eventually has to be withdrawn. Already at an early stage of the law-making process an assessment should be made by the respective policy-makers of the possible impact legislative proposals will have on Community law. Screening of law proposals requires close co-ordination with other departments, in particular the Ministry of Economic Affairs, as well as with the European Institutions, in particular the European Commission (see hereafter, section 3.1.2.2).

It is interesting to see that the proposal for a Directive on services in the Internal Market requires Member States to screen national measures that may restrict the free movement of services. This entails a nation-wide evaluation of national legislation.[41] National legislation will be treated with a fine comb.[42] According to the proposed Directive Member States will have to remove barriers to the freedom of establishment and the free movement of services, if these barriers are mentioned on a list of prohibited restrictions incorporated in the Directive; Member States must also screen national laws on their suitability and proportionality, and national laws may not *de iure* or *de facto* discriminate against undertakings from other Member States; lastly, several conditions are imposed upon the grant of licences for the access to and performance of certain service activities.

In developing horizontal and flanking policies the Member States must take into account the limits Community law imposes on the adoption of regulatory instruments. The Dutch law on fixed book prices provides another example of how national law proposals can be screened on its compatibility with Community law. The law proposal on fixed book prices has been screened 'horizontally', by consulting the Netherlands Competition Authority, as well as 'vertically', by consulting the European Commission, on its effects on Community law (see hereafter).

3.1.2.2 The exchange of information at European level

Apart from exchanging information at national level, it is essential that information is also exchanged between the Community institutions and the national legislature.

41 At least according to the Dutch government: see letter by the Minister of Economic Affairs, *TK* 2003-2004, 21 501-30, nr. 59, p. 4.

42 Drijber refers to the 'operatie stofkam', in: B.J. Drijber, De bezems van Bolkestein, *NTER*, 2004, p. 115.; see Chapter 4, section 4.2.2.

The Member States co-operating within the Council

In the first place information between Member States at European level on issues of horizontal and flanking policies can be exchanged within the Council, as this body is responsible for decision-making and co-ordination. The Council can be used as a 'platform' to exchange information regarding the possible impact of national legislative initiatives on European law and vice versa.[43]

The Member States and the Court of Justice

Pursuant to Article 40 of the Statute of the Court of Justice Member States may intervene in cases before the Court. In this way Member States are not only more involved in important cases which may have an impact on national horizontal and flanking policies, they can also seek to influence the Court's judgment in favour of the protection of horizontal and flanking policy interests.[44] This is furthermore reinforced by the possibility, pursuant to Article 23 of the Statute, to submit oral and written observations to the Court.

Screening

As stated above the European Commission, DG Competition, was asked to give its opinion on the compatibility of the Dutch law proposal on fixed prices for books with Community law, in particular the EC rules on competition. According to the Commission, Article 3 of the original proposal requiring importers of books to take account of the price recommended or fixed by publishers established in another State would violate Article 10 in conjunction with Article 81(1) EC (the useful effect doctrine).[45]

This informal way of consulting the European Commission may help to prevent possible conflicts with Community law. In its advisory report on the Dutch law proposal the Commission also advises the national legislature to contact the DG Internal Market to assess the compatibility of the law proposal with Article 28 EC on the free movement of goods.

3.2 The national competition authorities

Since the national competition authorities are involved in the *application* of the EC and national competition rules, and not in the law-making process, they are first and foremost confronted with the Community loyalty prin-

---

43 Even though the Council is a single body, it works in different configurations, which are attended by the Ministers of the areas concerned.

44 Protocol on the Statute of the Court of Justice annexed to the Treaty on European Union, to the Treaty establishing the European Community and to the Treaty establishing the European Atomic Energy Community.

45 Advisory Opinion of the European Commission (DG Competition) of 2 August 2004 at: www.vasteboekenprijs.nl.

ciple. However, considering the fact that national competition authorities may have to apply Article 81(3) EC or Article 86(2) EC, the principle of proportionality is relevant to them as well.

3.2.1 Respecting the Community loyalty principle

Hence, in applying EC competition rules as well as national competition rules to horizontal and flanking policy activities the national competition authorities ('NCAs') have to respect the Community loyalty principle. Actually, from Article 10 EC the ECJ has deduced that there are mutual obligations for Member States and European Institutions of loyal co-operation.[46] This duty of loyal co-operation at European level is visualised for both the national competition authorities and national courts through the co-operation procedures laid down in Regulation 1/2003, which are further elaborated by the Commission notices on co-operation (see hereafter). The duty of loyal co-operation has become particularly relevant after the adoption of Regulation 1/2003.[47] Article 3 of this Regulation provides that where agreements may affect trade between Member States, Articles 81 and 82 EC have to be applied in combination with national competition rules. The direct applicability of Article 81(3) EC pursuant to Article 1 of Regulation 1/2003 entails that the NCAs become involved in a balancing exercise that was previously conducted solely by the Commission.

3.2.1.1 The exchange of information at national level

Not only do national competition authorities have to apply EC competition rules to actions by private actors, they also have to disapply national legislation that contravenes Community law, similarly to national courts. In its judgment in *CIF* the Court made clear that a national competition authority is duty-bound to disapply national measures that are contrary to the useful effect doctrine: the combined provisions of Article 10 and 81 or 82 EC.[48] The example of books as discussed in section 2 shows the relevance of the useful effect doctrine in respect of national legislation pursuing horizontal and flanking policy interests. If a case is brought before the Netherlands Competition Authority ('NMa'), which finds the law on fixed prices for books to contravene Articles 10 and 81 EC, it will, on the basis of the Court's jurisprudence, have to disapply this law. In its advisory opinion on the Dutch law proposal on fixed prices for books, the NMa itself refers to this possibility and to the *CIF* jurisprudence.[49]

---

[46] Case 2/88, *Zwartveld*; see also Chapter 1, section 4.2.

[47] Council Regulation 1/2003, OJ 2003, L 1/1.

[48] Case C-198/01, *Consorzio Industrie Fiammiferi (CIF)*.

[49] Advisory opinion of the d-g NMa of 22 April 2004 at www.vasteboekenprijs.nl.

In order to prevent conflicts between national horizontal and flanking policies and the useful effect doctrine applied by the NCAs it is therefore suggested that the NCAs and the competent department involved with the development of horizontal and flanking policies maintain regular contact with each other, whenever it is suspected that a draft law contravenes the useful effect doctrine.[50] Compare the approach of the European Commission, where other Commission services may be consulted by DG Competition. The *Sammelrevers* case as discussed above on the German-Austrian agreement on fixed book prices, where the Commissioner for Competition, Monti, maintained regular contacts with Vivian Reding, the Commissioner for Culture and Education, is an example in this respect.[51]

National co-operation between the NCAs and the national legislature may be even more pertinent now that the NCAs do not, contrary to national courts, have the possibility to ask for a preliminary ruling from the Court of Justice and the status of horizontal and flanking policy interests under the useful effect doctrine remains unclear.[52]

3.2.1.2 The exchange of information at European level: 'ECN'

The NCAs have to conduct a balancing exercise under Article 81(3) EC on the basis of the existing body of law, such as the Commission decisions, block exemptions, guidelines and case law of the Courts, and on the basis of the Commission notice on the application of Article 81(3) EC.[53] Here a problem arises, as the recent guidelines appear to give a considerably narrower interpretation of Article 81(3) EC than the decision practice of the Commission, discussed in Chapter 3, has shown; with regard to horizontal and flanking policy interests, the Commission states that these interests can be taken into account, but only to the extent that they can be subsumed under the four conditions of Article 81(3) EC.[54]

Particularly regarding the more complex cases, like the cases where horizontal and flanking policy interests play a role, the NCAs must co-operate with each other and with the Commission in order to carry out the Commission's policy in

---

50 See annotation of Case C-198/01, *Consorzio Industrie Fiammiferi (CIF)* by B.J. Drijber and W.T. Algera, *M&M*, 2003, p. 252.

51 Press Release, IP/00/183; see also Chapter 3, section 4.1.3.5. Unfortunately, this has not led to real integration of cultural interests in Article 81(3) EC where book price agreements are involved.

52 See also Chapter 3, section 3.3.2.

53 K. Lenaerts and D. Gerard, Decentralisation of EC Competition Law Enforcement: Judges in the Frontline, *World Competition*, 2004, pp. 329-330.

54 Point 42 of the Guidelines on the application of Article 81(3) of the Treaty, OJ 2004, C101/97. P. Lugard and L. Hancher, Honey, I shrunk the Article! A Critical Assessment of the Commission's Notice on Article 81(3) of the EC Treaty, *ECLR*, 2004, p. 418. See hereafter, section 3.2.5 of this chapter.

a loyal fashion. Regulation 1/2003 therefore offers a co-operation mechanism, the European Competition Network (ECN), which, according to the Commission, forms the basis for the creation and maintenance of a common competition culture in Europe.[55] Hence, by providing a framework for co-operation with a view to the consistent application of Community competition law, the Regulation has in fact implemented the Community loyalty principle.

The fact, though, that the analytical framework presented by the Commission's notice on the application of Article 81(3) EC may cause considerable confusion as well as the fact that the NCAs may not be experienced, or only to a limited extent, in applying competition rules to horizontal and flanking policy activities, makes the use of the co-operation mechanism within the European Competition Network even more pertinent.[56] Within this context the Advisory Committee, established as the forum where experts from the various competition authorities discuss individual cases and general issues of Community competition law, plays an important role in the ECN.[57] Important cases, for example where the NCAs are faced with defining the scope of Article 81(3) EC in relation to horizontal and flanking policy interests, can be discussed in the Advisory Committee. A discussion within the Advisory Committee may even result in a broader interpretation of Article 81(3) EC than envisaged by the Commission in its notice on the application of Article 81(3) EC.

It is also suggested that the NCAs use this opportunity, without jeopardising the Community's and Commission's policy in this respect. It is therefore extremely important to exchange information pursuant to Article 12 of Regulation 1/2003, with the other competition authorities being possibly faced with similar cases – as a form of mutual guidance within the ECN – as well as to seek guidance from the Commission pursuant to Article 11(5) of Regulation 1/2003. They could induce the Commission to initiate proceedings on the basis of Article 11(6) of Regulation 1/2003, by making clear that conflicting decisions could be adopted in similar cases, or by stressing the need to develop a coherent competition policy in these areas.[58]

---

55 See Commission Notice on co-operation within the Network of Competition Authorities, OJ 2004, C 101/43. According to H. Gilliams " the Commission's hope is that the network will function as a well-oiled machine, all national authorities carrying out the policy set by the Commission in a loyal fashion", in: Modernisation: From policy to practice, *ELRev.*, 2003, p. 465.

56 Van de Gronden & Mortelmans (Eds) (2001).

57 See section 4 of the Commission Notice on co-operation within the Network of Competition Authorities, OJ 2004, C 101/43.

58 See section 3.2 of the Commission Notice, OJ 2004, C 101/50. Even though Article 11(6) may according to Gilliams be reserved for the rarest of cases, cases where horizontal and flanking policy interests are at stake may in particular belong to this category of cases: H. Gilliams, Modernisation: from policy to practice, *ELRev.*, 2003, p. 467.

Hence, the incorporation of the Community loyalty principle in Regulation 1/2003 as elaborated by the Commission's notice on co-operation provides the NCAs with a mechanism for seeking guidance on the application of Article 81(3) EC. In the absence of clear guidance from the Commission, the NCAs must extensively use the possibilities of exchanging information and consulting the Commission with a view to prevent conflicts between competition policy and horizontal and flanking policy interests. This also works to prevent that Article 81(3) EC will be locked for supposedly unwanted intrusion of horizontal and flanking policy considerations and will eventually further contribute to closer harmony.

3.2.2 Applying the principle of proportionality

Apart from Article 86(2) EC, the NCAs are, due to the decentralisation of EC competition law, also faced with the application of the principle of proportionality under Article 81(3) EC. Hence, the conclusions from Chapter 3 in respect of Article 81(3) EC are relevant for national competition authorities as well. The NCAs will have to balance restrictions on competition with horizontal and flanking policy considerations and will have to realise that the principle of proportionality plays an important role in this respect.

The question is how the Commission's notice as mentioned above relates to the decision practice of the Commission and the case law of the Community Courts. The notice seems to cause confusion rather than that it offers clear guidance: should the narrow view reflected by the notice be followed, or the broader view as shown by the Commission in some of its decisions as well as by the Community Courts in several of their judgments?[59] It is suggested that the NCAs should choose a broader interpretation, which is in conformity with the existing body of law, in particular with the Commission's decision in *CECED* and the guidelines on horizontal co-operation agreements, as well as with the general principles of Community law, in particular the integration principle. The NCAs are now, together with the European Commission, under an obligation to integrate the requirements of environmental, public health, cultural and consumer policy into EC competition policy. Furthermore, in applying *national* competition law the NCAs are according to the Court's judgment in *Milk Marque* also under an obligation to take account of other, public interests which are recognised by the Treaty.[60] Where case law is lacking or still developing, the

[59] See also Chapter 3, section 4.1.3.

[60] Case C-137/00, *Milk Marque*. This case involved the application of national competition rules (in the United Kingdom) to a milk producers' co-operative in a powerful position on the national market. However, the national authorities are under an obligation to respect the objectives of the common agricultural policy as set out in Article 33 EC and they must also ensure that any contradictions between those objectives are reconciled (paragraph 92 of the judgment).

NCAs should take a more reserved approach, first seeking guidance from the Commission and other NCAs, which possibilities were discussed above.

3.3 The national courts

The national courts will have to respect the principles of Community loyalty and proportionality as well. The proportionality principle plays a particularly important role for the national courts, since they are involved in the application of not only the competition rules, but also the rules on free movement. This section will be concluded by the proportionality principle, as it bridges the gap between this section and the following section concerning the Community's perspective.

3.3.1 Respecting the Community loyalty principle

Due to the direct applicability of Article 81(3) EC, the national courts are confronted with the EC competition rules. National courts may also be asked to take account of horizontal and flanking policy interests under Article 81(3) EC. Besides, national courts apply the directly effective rules on free movement. There are various devices for the national court, being confronted with these types of cases, to prevent possible conflicts between competition policy and the rules on free movement on the one hand and the protection of horizontal and flanking policy interests on the other. At national level national courts may want to seek guidance on issues involving horizontal and flanking policy considerations. National courts may within the limits of national procedural rules resort to other forms of guidance as well, for example by allowing an expert economist or competition lawyer to give his opinion about the case.[61]

At the European level, similar to the national competition authorities, there is a duty of mutual assistance based on the Community loyalty principle for the European Commission as well as the national courts in the application of the competition rules. A co-operation procedure has therefore been laid down in Article 15 of Regulation 1/2003 and is further elaborated by the Commission's notice on the co-operation between the Commission and the courts of the EU Member States in the application of Articles 81 and 82 EC.[62]

Furthermore, pursuant to Article 234 EC the national courts have the possibility to put a preliminary question to the Court of Justice with respect to the interpretation of Articles 81 and 82 EC.

---

61 See also K. Lenaerts and D. Gerard, Decentralisation of EC Competition Law Enforcement: Judges in the Frontline, *World Competition*, 2004, pp. 313-349.

62 OJ 2004, C 101/54.

3.3.1.1 The exchange of information at national level

In most Member States a Council for the Judiciary has been established, which is entrusted with the task to promote good quality execution of judiciary duties by the courts.[63] In the Netherlands the Council for the Judiciary has been entrusted with the following four tasks: budget and budget allocation, management, quality improvement and an advisory task. The management and quality improvement tasks are about supporting the courts and developing policies, and about supporting the promotion of legal quality and the uniform application of law. Hence, the Council could be used as a platform for exchanging information on, for example, the role of horizontal and flanking policy considerations under Article 81(3) EC, or on the application of the free movement rules in relation to national horizontal and flanking policies. The Council will also play an active role in the field of strategy, policy and development and could in this respect also touch upon the relationship between free movement and competition rules and horizontal and flanking policies.

3.3.1.2 The exchange of information at European level

There are several possibilities for the exchange of information at European level and between the national courts and Community institutions with a view to prevent possible conflicts between the rules on free movement and competition on the one hand, and horizontal and flanking policies on the other.

The European Network for Councils of the Judiciary

As from May 2004 the European Network for Councils of the Judiciary ('ENCJ') has been established with a view to exchange information, knowledge and expertise regarding the quality of the judiciaries in Europe and to co-operate whenever possible.[64] Similarly to the European Competition Network ('ECN') the ENCJ provides a framework for co-operation that can be used to promote the consistent application of Community competition law as well. Hence, the establishment of the ENCJ contributes to the duty of loyal co-operation enshrined in Article 10 of the Treaty.

According to a press briefing of 27 May 2004 collaboration within the ENCJ will cover the following areas:

- Operational collaboration: judges and courts will be enabled to share

---

[63] On 1 January 2002, the Council for the Judiciary Act entered into force in the Netherlands, introducing a new body which does not form part of the executive power, nor may it be referred to as a High Institution of the State. It is referred to as a body of the judiciary not charged with judiciary duties: see also http://www.rechtspraak.nl/Gerechten/RvdR/Information+in+English/.

[64] Http://www.rechtspraak.nl/Gerechten/RvdR/Internationale+samenwerking.htm.

know-how and experiences with regard to issues like quality, recruitment and selection of judges, information technology and *European law*;
- Joint research activities;
- Improvement of the relations with the EU: it is, for example, advisable to include judiciaries at an earlier stage when new legislation is contemplated, in order to assess the consequences for implementation.

The Network may therefore be an important instrument which contributes to the uniform application of Community law and to the prevention of (future) conflicts between the free movement and competition rules and horizontal and flanking policies, although it is not formally established by the EU.

The national courts must use the possibility to request information from the Commission

As seen above within the context of the Dutch law on fixed book prices it may be particularly useful to ask the Commission for advice regarding the effects of national measures on Community law. National courts must also use this possibility to request information from the Commission.

Pursuant to Article 15(1) of Regulation 1/2003 and by request of the national court the Commission must provide any relevant information in its possession on questions concerning the application of the Community competition rules. The national court should use this possibility in particular to get more clarification about the Commission's position with regard to the incorporation of certain horizontal and flanking policy interests into Article 81(3) EC. In the notice on co-operation, the Commission indicates that if the national courts cannot be offered sufficient guidance by the case law of the Community Courts, or by Commission regulations, decisions, notices and guidelines applying Articles 81 and 82 EC, the possibility to request information can be used.[65] The fact that, as stated above, the notice on Article 81(3) EC may lead to considerable confusion in relation to the decision practice and the guidelines on horizontal co-operation agreements could certainly be a reason for the national court to request information and seek more guidance from the Commission.

The Commission as amicus curiae

Article 15(3) of Regulation 1/2003 provides the possibility for the Commission to submit written observations to the national courts where the coherent application of Article 81 or Article 82 EC so requires. It also provides the submission of oral observations by the Commission, with the permission of the national court. This possibility for the Commission to act as *amicus curiae* will, according to the Commission, only be used when the coherent application

[65] Point 27 of the Commission notice on co-operation between the Commission and the courts of the EU Member States, OJ 2004, C 101/54.

of Articles 81 and 82 EC so requires.[66] The national court does not submit a request in this respect; the Commission will act upon its own initiative.[67] The Commission may ask the national court to submit all the documents necessary to assess the case.[68] It is thereby important that the national court fully co-operates, particularly where complex cases, in which horizontal and flanking policy interests are at stake, must be assessed.

The national court is however, faced with a problem in this respect. The national court has in the first place the task to take account of and safeguard the interests of the parties before the court. The possibility of the Commission to intervene in the national procedure should therefore not lead to undue intrusion, jeopardizing the protection of rights of defence of the parties and the equality of arms. Nonetheless, the national court must welcome the Commission's intervention in a national procedure, in particular in complex cases presenting new questions of interpretation, of the extent to which horizontal and flanking policy interests should be taken into account under Article 81(3) EC.[69]

The possibility to ask for a preliminary ruling

Another mechanism of co-operation, i.e. co-operation between the national courts and the European Court of Justice, is given in Article 234 EC: the preliminary ruling procedure. This is an important additional instrument for the national courts seeking more guidance as to the scope of Article 81(3) EC in relation to horizontal and flanking policies and as to the scope of the free movement rules in respect of horizontal and flanking policies. Contrary to the Commission's clarification in a national procedure, the Court's judgment is of course binding. But the disadvantage of this procedure is that it takes considerable time for the judgment to be delivered by the Court.

3.3.2 Applying the principle of proportionality

Through the direct effect of the Treaty provisions on free movement the national court is involved in balancing Member States' interests in protecting certain horizontal and flanking policy interests, like the environment or culture, with the Community's interest of the internal market. In addition

[66] Point 32 of the Commission notice on co-operation between the Commission and the courts of the EU Member States, OJ 2004, C 101/54.

[67] Observations will be presented within the framework of Member States' procedural rules and practices, see point 34 of the Commission notice on co-operation between the Commission and the courts of the EU Member States, OJ 2004, C 101/54.

[68] Point 33 of the Commission notice on co-operation between the Commission and the courts of the EU Member States, OJ 2004, C 101/54.

[69] See more in general, K. Lenaerts and D. Gerard, Decentralisation of EC Competition Law Enforcement: Judges in the Frontline, *World Competition*, 2004, pp. 332-333.

the national courts must also conduct a balancing exercise under this provision through the direct effect of Article 81(3) EC. In both situations the proportionality principle plays an essential role, which national courts necessarily have both to realise and deal with.

The competition rules

What has been stated above in respect of the national competition authorities is equally relevant here. The national courts are also faced with the application of the principle of proportionality and the Commission's notice on Article 81(3) EC which does not really correspond to the decision practice and the case law of the Community courts. No more than the national competition authorities do the national courts necessarily have to adopt a restrictive approach to Article 81(3) EC, in particular not in the field of the environment. Where other horizontal and flanking policies are involved, the national courts can draw inspiration from environmental cases. In case of doubt, they are advised to use one of the co-operation devices discussed above, bearing in mind, however, that the Commission may have a particularly narrow view on the scope of Article 81(3) EC.

The free movement rules

National courts will be confronted with the application of the proportionality principle if one of the rules on free movement has been invoked before the court to challenge national law. It is suggested that in a preliminary ruling procedure, the national court must provide the ECJ with all the necessary factual information and an appreciation of the national legal framework of the dispute. The ECJ must in turn provide the national court with all relevant information with regard to Community law and it is up to the national court to apply this to the dispute before it and to determine the necessary consequences under national law.[70] Only when the Court is convinced that it has all the relevant facts at its disposal it could decide to assess the proportionality itself; otherwise it should leave the actual assessment to the national court, particularly where examination of the precise aims of the law is required and an appreciation of the effectiveness of national legislation in a complex national context is needed to be able to determine the necessity of the measure.[71] The guidelines provided by the Court in the *Familiapress* case are a good example of how the national court should examine the proportionality of a national measure.[72]

---

70 Jarvis (1998), pp. 229-230.

71 J.H. Jans, Proportionality revisited *LIEI*, 2000, p. 255.

72 Case C-368/95, *Familiapress*; see also Chapter 2, section 4.4.4.5. In this case the ECJ was asked to examine the compatibility of the Austrian Law on Unfair Competition prohibiting certain prize competitions contained in newspapers and magazines with Article 28 EC. The prohibition also applied to newspapers and magazines published in Germany but brought on the Austrian market. In order to assess whether no less restrictive measures were available to maintain press diversity in the Austrian market, the ECJ

In applying the proportionality test the national court must take account of the horizontal and flanking policy interest at stake. Similarly to what has been stated before in respect of the national legislature the following is also relevant for national courts:

- The existence of a certain hierarchy of horizontal and flanking policy interests;
- The focus of attention is laid upon the second element of proportionality, i.e. whether no less restrictive alternative is available.

As some aspects in relation to the application of the free movement rules and the justification grounds remain unclear, the following section shows what the ECJ could do to clarify the scope of application of the exceptions and the conditions for invoking exception grounds (hereafter, section 4.1).

4 Closer harmony: the perspective of the Community

What can the Community and more in particular the bodies involved in the Community regulatory and policy process do to attain closer harmony between the internal market rules and horizontal and flanking policies? Depending on the Community institution involved in the regulatory and policy process several ways may contribute to the achievement of closer harmony between the internal market and horizontal and flanking policies. The first way is based upon the convergence process between the free movement rules which can be further developed by the *Court of Justice*; the second way is based on the integration principle requiring in particular the *Commission* to take account of horizontal and flanking policy interests in the application of competition rules; the third and last way is based on the broad scope of Article 95 EC, allowing the *Community legislature* to pursue horizontal and flanking policies within an internal market framework; it is within this context that the harmonisation method and the principle of proportionality play an important role in assessing the potential and limits of Community action in this field.

pointed out several conditions that the Austrian court had to examine: A definition of the Austrian press market; market shares of individual publishers or press groups; the extent to which the product concerned can be replaced by papers which do not offer prizes; the fact that there are possible alternatives, like blacking out or removing the page on which the prize competition appears in copies intended for Austria, or a statement that readers in Austria do not qualify for a chance to win a prize.

4.1 The European Court of Justice: actively contributing to the process of convergence

The point of departure here is the Court of Justice giving more clarification as to the scope of the exceptions to the rules on free movement. It has been shown that, although the process of convergence within the context of the four freedoms is in an advanced phase, differences regarding the possibilities to invoke exception grounds remain.[73] The Court must therefore, more than it has done so far, clarify its position in order to provide the necessary legal certainty and for the attainment of closer harmony between the internal market rules and horizontal and flanking policy interests.

4.1.1 The artificial and undesirable dichotomy between the Treaty exceptions and the rule of reason should be removed

The first way for the ECJ to attain closer harmony between free movement and horizontal and flanking policies is to adopt a more flexible approach in respect of the rule of reason.

The example of environmental cases

The presently artificial distinction between discriminatory measures, which are only justifiable on the basis of Treaty exceptions, and indistinctly applicable measures, which are justifiable also on the basis of the rule of reason should be removed.[74] The case law in the field of the environment and the free movement of goods clearly shows the boundaries of the application of the rule of reason and the requirement to only uphold indistinctly applicable measures. Unfortunately, the ECJ has until now failed to address this question explicitly, even though AG Jacobs had asked the Court to clarify its position on this matter in the *Preussen Elektra* case.[75] This case involved the German *Stromeinspeisungsgesetz* requiring electricity supply undertakings which operate a general supply network to purchase electricity from renewable sources within their area of supply and at a fixed minimum price. The *Stromeinspeisungsgesetz* was clearly discriminatory as it treated electricity of domestic origin differently than imported electricity. Without addressing the question of whether this law was discriminatory or not, the ECJ simply examined whether it was justifiable on the basis of the protection of the environment. Interestingly, the ECJ referred to

---

[73] See Chapter 5.

[74] P. Oliver and W.-H. Roth, The internal market and the four freedoms, *CMLRev.*, 2004, p. 436.

[75] Opinion of AG Jacobs in Case C-379/98, *Preussen Elektra*, paragraph 229; see Chapter 2, section 4.4.1.3. There have been other cases outside the field of the environment where the ECJ upheld national discriminatory measures on the basis of the rule of reason: see in general Chapter 2, section 4.4.

the principle of integration, contained in Article 6 EC, as one of the reasons to uphold the German law.[76]

All horizontal and flanking policies must benefit from a more flexible approach to the rule of reason

The reasons for AG Jacobs to suggest that the Court takes a more flexible approach to environmental measures can also be used in respect of national measures aimed at protecting other horizontal and flanking policy interests. Firstly, for all horizontal and flanking policies an integration clause has been included in the Treaty imposing legal obligations upon the Community institutions; the increasing weight given to horizontal and flanking policies in the Treaty entails that special account must be taken of horizontal and flanking policy interests in interpreting the Treaty provisions on free movement. At the same time technological, societal and other developments have not led to a change of Treaty provisions, like Article 30 EC. With regard to the environmental field, according to AG Jacobs, "harm to the environment, even where it does not immediately threaten – as it often does – the health and life of humans, animals and plants protected by Article 30 of the Treaty, may pose a more substantial, if longer-term, threat to the ecosystem as a whole. It would be hard to justify in these circumstances, giving a lesser degree of protection to the environment than to the interests recognised in trade treaties concluded many decades ago and taken over into the text of Article 30 of the EC Treaty, itself unchanged since it was adopted in 1957".[77]

Secondly, to require that national measures seeking to protect horizontal and flanking policy interests may only be justifiable if they apply without distinction may defeat the very purpose of these measures. According to AG Jacobs "national measures for the protection of the environment are inherently liable to differentiate on the basis of the nature and origin of the cause of harm, and are therefore liable to be found discriminatory, precisely because they are based on such accepted principles as that 'environmental damage should as a priority be rectified at source (Article 174(2) of the EC Treaty). Where such measures necessarily have a discriminatory impact of that kind, the possibility that they may be justified should not be excluded."[78] Similarly, measures, for example adopted for the protection of cultural heritage, will not infrequently involve a direct or indirect advantage for its own institutions, for instance the establishment of a film or literature prize or other encouragement of artists or artistic societies.[79] Hence, national discriminatory measure that are designed to implement

---

[76] Case C-379/98, *Preussen Elektra.*

[77] Opinion of AG Jacobs in Case C-379/98, *Preussen Elektra,* paragraph 232.

[78] Opinion of AG Jacobs in Case C-379/98, *Preussen Elektra,* paragraph 233.

[79] Opinion of AG Van Gerven in Case C-17/92, *Fedicine.*

horizontal and flanking policy objectives for which no protectionist motive can be found, should, therefore in the absence of non-discriminatory alternatives be accepted by the Court.

In addition the concept of discrimination as applied by the Court in its case law on free movement may be artificial, as it is difficult to determine whether national measures which are at their face indistinctly applicable nevertheless constitute indirect discrimination, simply because it is more difficult for imported products to comply with domestic regulatory regimes, which have evolved over a number of time. The limited scope of the rule of reason therefore "rests upon a series of contingencies which come, as a result, to assume a centrality which is not warranted on normative grounds".[80]

Consequently not the discriminatory character of a national measure as such, but the purpose of the measure and the intention of the state should be decisive for the applicability of a justification ground.[81] However, since the principle of non-discrimination forms the heart of the existing regime on free movement, it cannot simply be set aside. Only if national measures comply with principles of horizontal and flanking policies, are necessary for the attainment of the objectives, and no reasonable non-discriminatory alternative exists should they be justified regardless of whether the aim is mentioned in the Treaty or recognised in the case law.

4.1.2 Taking account of the (inherently substantive) differences between horizontal and flanking policies

Instead of focusing on an artificial distinction between Treaty exceptions and overriding requirements of general interests, the ECJ must use the proportionality test to fine-tune differences between horizontal and flanking policies. For example, in the fields of public health and the environment important principles such as the precautionary principle, the principle that environmental damage should be rectified at source and the polluter pays principle should determine the margin of discretion for Member States to take action in these fields. In this way the ECJ underlines the important status of public health and the environment in Community law.

Taking account of the differences in competences

Due to the differences in competences in fields of horizontal and flanking policies, the application of the proportionality test in the fields of environmental

[80] J. Scott, Mandatory or Imperative Requirements in the EU and the WTO, in: C. Barnard and J. Scott (Eds), *The Law of the Single European Market – Unpacking the Premises* (Hart Publishing, Oxford and Portland, 2002), p. 285.

[81] The irrelevance of the discriminatory character of a national measure also appears to be reflected in the single test for all freedoms as proposed by Baquero Cruz (2002), p. 95.

protection and consumer protection may be different from the application of the proportionality test in the areas of public health and culture. In the fields of the environment and consumer protection the Community shares its powers with the Member States. Instead of considering national measures from a purely national perspective, the ECJ could choose to assess the proportionality of a national measure from a Community perspective, which does not necessarily mean that Member States have no possibility at all to determine how strict their protection is, but is does mean that the ECJ takes a more activist rather than a 'self-restraint' approach to the proportionality principle.[82] In the field of consumer protection, the ECJ has departed from a Community notion of reasonably circumspect consumer to assess the proportionality of national consumer laws. In the field of environmental protection, one could argue that national measures must be designed to improve the environment in the Community, since environmental objectives and principles are included in the Treaty and also pursued by the Community. The integration principle plays an important role in this respect. The integration of environmental protection requirements in the context of the free movement of goods refers to legal goods worthy of special protection in the general interest of the Community. In the field of culture, however, aspects of culture as referred to in Article 151(4) EC particularly comprise the cultures of the Member States. The proportionality of national cultural measures should therefore be assessed from the perspective of the national state.

Furthermore, where a common responsibility reflected by the Treaty towards the protection of horizontal and flanking policies exists, the ECJ must be more willing to uphold extra-territorial action. This means that where environmental policy is concerned, measures adopted by Member States to protect the environment both inside and outside their territory should be justifiable under certain conditions, but where cultural policy is concerned, the Court could take a more restrained approach, unless, for example, the protection of 'our common cultural heritage' is at stake. An example given in Chapter 2 was the British ban on the export of the 'Elgin Marbles' to Greece, which may well be motivated by reasons relating to a variety of hazards, including the smog of Athens.[83]

Convergence leads to further integration

A similar treatment of horizontal and flanking policy interests in respect of all freedoms should be the starting point for the Court of Justice examining the reasons behind national restrictive measures. Hence, all horizontal and flanking policy interests, whether included in a Treaty exception or in the rule of reason case law, should be able to be relied upon before the ECJ, even if the national measure proves to be discriminatory.

---

82 See with regard to the gambling cases: J.H. Jans, Proportionality revisited, *LIEI*, 2000, pp. 250-251.

83 See Chapter 2, section 5.

The fact that at the outset horizontal and flanking policy interests can be protected in respect of national discriminatory measures also, contributes to the achievement of closer harmony between horizontal and flanking policies and the internal market. It allows the Court, without being confronted with doctrinal constraints regarding the distinction between Treaty exceptions and the rule of reason, to further fine-tune its case law and to take account of the inherently substantive differences, as well as of the differences in competences between environmental, public health, consumer and cultural policies. The starting point here is that the ECJ in determining the level of protection should not take into account the effects of the national measure on free movement; it must only do so on the basis of the intrinsic value of the interest protected.[84]

Furthermore, the Court must consider the protection of public health and the environment as predominant amongst other horizontal and flanking policies. The ECJ could more explicitly advocate a hierarchy of horizontal and flanking policy interests, thereby giving guidance how to solve possible conflicts between these interests as well as to provide a more balanced approach towards the rules on free movement and the exceptions where more than one exception is invoked by the Member State.[85]

The Court could adopt a more activist approach to the application of the proportionality principle where environmental or consumer interests are at stake, as environmental policy and consumer policy are also Community policies. The importance of environmental aims requires that where a conflict between, for example, environmental interests and consumer interests occurs, preference must be given to the environmental interest. This allows the Court to focus on a broader consumer perspective, taking account of the imperative demands of sustainable consumption. After all, consumers may not only want the lowest possible prices for products, but also high quality products and services and, of increasing importance products which are sustainable and of a high environmental quality.[86] Such approach contributes to a better integration of environmental protection requirements into consumer policy.

4.2 The European Commission; giving effect to the integration principle: taking integration seriously

The integration principle is particularly relevant for the European Commission, being the Community institution entrusted with the enforcement of the EC competition rules.

---

84 J.H. Jans, Proportionality revisited, *LIEI*, 2000, p. 252.

85 See Chapter 5, section 5.3. See also K.J.M. Mortelmans, Botsende algemene belangen en de werking van de interne markt, *SEW*, 2004, pp. 240-252.

86 See also in the context of competition policy: N. Reich, Competition Law and the Consumer, in: L. Gormley (Ed.), *Current and Future Perspectives on EC Competition Law* (Kluwer, Deventer, 1997), p. 128; S. de Vries, Consumer interests and the Dutch Competition Act: an ambivalent relationship?, *TvC*, 2002, p. 161.

4.2.1 In general

The integration principle is relevant for all Community policies, but is particularly important for the Community's competition policy for the following two reasons. First, by contrast with the free movement rules and apart from Articles 87(2) sub a and 87(3) sub d EC, neither the Treaty, nor the case law of the ECJ knows an explicit reference to horizontal and flanking policy interests. Through the integration principle public policy aims are now (indirectly) incorporated in Article 81(3) EC. The integration principle makes therefore clear that the Commission cannot ignore self-regulation as an instrument of public policy.

Second, the integration principle delimits the Commission's discretionary power – as well as the national competition authorities and the national courts – to apply the exception of Article 81(3) EC.[87] It requires a balancing of the protection of horizontal and flanking policy interests with the need to ensure effective competition according to the proportionality principle, whereby the economic value or horizontal and flanking policy benefits may be just as relevant to consumer welfare as productive efficiency.[88] The Commission must be willing to confront the market versus horizontal and flanking policy interests debate also within the context of competition policy, which has become more pertinent after the decentralisation of competition policy. The question is how this 'debate must be confronted' by the Commission and what instruments may be used to achieve closer harmony in this area.

The point of departure for the Commission is the various actors involved in the regulatory process, being public, semi-public or private, restricting competition for assumed public or mixed public/private interests. The following suggestions therefore reflect the sliding scale, starting at the public authority granting financial aid to undertakings, going down to (public) undertakings, being entrusted with services of general interest, semi-public/semi-private organisations, carrying out public interest tasks and private companies, acting primarily for their own benefit, but may nevertheless also act for the benefit of the public.[89]

4.2.2 The Commission's state aid policy – Article 87(3) EC

In the field of state aid, the 2001 Guidelines for state aid for environmental protection provide a comprehensive set of rules, although Article 87(3) EC does not refer to the environment. Article 87(3) sub d EC does provide an explicit exemption ground for cultural aid, but there are no guidelines as to

[87] Articles 5 and 6 of Regulation 1/2003, OJ 2003, L 1/1.

[88] See with regard to environmental protection as ground for exemption: Chapter 3, section 4.1.3.2 and G. Monti, Article 81 EC and public policy, *CMLRev.*, 2002, p. 1075.

[89] See with regard to the State action doctrine, or useful effect doctrine: Baquero Cruz (2002), p. 161.

the application of this provision. The adoption of guidelines in the field of state aid in respect of horizontal and flanking policies should not raise many objections, considering the fact that it is *the public* authority granting financial aid, being generally presumed to act in the interest and for the benefit of the *public.*

Guidelines for state aid for horizontal and flanking policy interests

It is therefore suggested that the Commission adopts *guidelines* also in respect of other horizontal and flanking policy interests than environmental protection. The Guidelines for state aid for environmental protection may serve as an example, but it must be recalled that in the field of state aid for environmental protection the polluter pays principle plays a crucial role, in principle requiring state aid in this area to gradually disappear. Nevertheless, the lack of an overall approach to state aids in the fields of public health and culture calls for the adoption of guidelines containing compatibility criteria for the assessment of state aids, particularly considering the possibility that Commission decisions may be annulled by the Court as occurred in the *SIDE* case on a French aid scheme for the export of books.[90]

The criteria established by the Commission in several decisions can be used for the development of a more comprehensive set of rules. In developing these rules the differences between horizontal and flanking policies should be taken into account as well. The national state should, due to the fact that culture is mentioned in Article 87(3) sub d EC, have a considerable margin of discretion in granting state aids. If the Council ever decides to amend Regulation 994/98, it may opt to include culture as policy area for which the Commission may issue a block exemption.[91] In its State Aid Action Plan (2005-2009) the Commission states that it could ask the Council to extend the scope of the enabling Regulation, so that cinema can also benefit from block exemption.[92]

Even so the Commission has not developed a comprehensive policy with respect to the cultural sector as a whole. The Commission has made the application of the proportionality test only more concrete regarding state aids in the film sector. A Communication on certain legal aspects relating to the audiovisual sector includes compatibility criteria for state aid to film production, which were developed in Commission decisions and which could be used as a base for a block exemption.[93] The validity of these compatibility criteria has now been extended until 30 June 2007.[94]

---

90 Case T-49/93, *SIDE v. Commission*. Chapter 3, section 3.1.5.5.

91 OJ 1998, L 142/1. The German *Länder* even tried to incorporate a cultural exception in Article 87(2) EC so that aids for cultural purposes would be automatically exempted: see Chapter 3, section 3.1.5.1.

92 State Aid Action Plan – Less and better targeted State aid: a road map for State aid reform 2005-2009, point 62, to be found at: http:www.europa.eu.int/comm/competition/state_aid/others/action_plan/.

93 COM (2001) 534 final. See Chapter 3, section 3.1.5.5.

94 Communication from the Commission on the follow-up to the Commission communication on certain legal aspects relating to cinematographic and other audiovisual works, COM (2004) 171 final, p. 3.

With regard to the field of the environment, Article 87(3) EC does not contain an explicit reference to environmental policy; instead both the polluter pays principle and the integration principle form the basis of the Community Guidelines on state aid for environmental protection.[95] Important *Community* principles of environmental policy determine the margin of discretion for Member States in this area. The proportionality of cultural aids should furthermore be assessed from the perspective of the national state, since aspects of cultural policy as referred to in Article 151 EC first and foremost comprise the cultures of the Member States (see also above, section 4.1.2).

Since there is no real Community policy on state aids in the area of consumer policy, for the time being it is of no use to adopt guidelines in this field.[96]

Guidelines for the financing of services of general (economic) interest

Although the Court's judgment in *Altmark* has been criticised in Chapter 3 (section 3.1.3), the point of departure here is nevertheless the compensation approach as followed by the Court in that case. The Commission has made a first step towards clarifying the scope of application of the state aid rules to public service undertakings by publishing a Decision and Community Framework for state aid in the form of public service compensation. In the Decision the Commission spells out the conditions based on the *Altmark* case under which public service compensation constitutes state aid compatible with Article 86(2) EC and exempts such aid from the notification requirement;[97] the purpose of the Community Framework is to specify under what conditions public service compensation that constitutes state aid can nevertheless be compatible with the common market in accordance with Article 86(2) EC.[98]

Although the Commission through the adoption of this Decision and Community Framework recognises the difficulties national governments may encounter now that they have to assess themselves whether to notify the aid scheme or not, according to the *Altmark* criteria, it does not elaborate these criteria, nor explain under what exact circumstances public service compensation granted for environmental, public health or cultural reasons may be exempted

---

95 In its State Aid Action Plan the Commission considers to exempt certain environmental state aids under the new general block exemption regulation from the obligation to notify the aid: State Aid Action Plan – Less and better targeted State aid: a road map for State aid reform 2005-2009, point 46, to be found at: http:www.europa.eu.int/comm/competition/state_aid/others/action_plan/.

96 Chapter 3, section 3.1.5.3.

97 Case C-280/00, *Altmark Trans*. See Chapter 3, section 3.1.3.

98 The Decision on the application of Article 86(2) of the Treaty to state aid in the form of public service compensation granted to certain undertakings entrusted with the operation of services of general economic interest, and the Community Framework for state aid in the form of public service compensation can be found at: www.europa.eu.int/comm/competition/state_aid; see also Chapter 3, section 3.1.3.

from notification. This is different in respect of hospitals and social housing undertakings that carry out activities involving services of general economic interests. Aids for these activities are pursuant to Article 2(b) of the Decision exempted from notification. Perhaps the best option for national governments is therefore to simply notify public service compensation aid schemes, but this seems contrary to the spirit of the Court's judgment in *Altmark*. Furthermore, the *Altmark* criteria may prove difficult to comply with in practice, in particular for local communities; nevertheless the Decision and Community Framework do not really provide a more flexible approach in this respect.[99]

It is therefore suggested that the Commission adopts guidelines, particularly in the fields of the environment, public health and culture, where both the criteria of *Altmark* would be further explained as well as the conditions for exemption on the basis of Article 86(2) EC in case public service compensation qualifies for state aid, are further clarified. In these guidelines, the Commission can take account of the particularities of each sector, like the broadcasting sector,[100] considering new technological developments and the role of public service broadcasting in the fields of television and the Internet, the waste disposal sector or the health care sector, where hospitals or health insurance funds are involved.[101]

4.2.3 The Commission's policy in respect of services of general (economic) interests – Articles 86(2) and 16 EC

The Court has in its case law given the criteria on the basis of which services of general (economic) interests can be exempted from the prohibitive Treaty provisions. It is now up to the Commission to provide more clarification as regards the scope of services of general (economic) interests, in particular in relation to horizontal and flanking policies.

---

99 See also annotation of the case *Essent v. Gemeente Appingedam* (ruling of the Dutch Court of Groningen) by B. Hessel, *Mediaforum*, 2004, p. 330.

100 See also the Commission's Communication on the application of the state aid rules to public service broadcasting, which is based on the 'state aid approach': OJ 2001, C 320/5; Chapter 3, section 3.1.3.

101 A block exemption regulation is not really an option for the following two reasons. First, *Altmark* itself makes clear that once the criteria laid down by the ECJ have been fulfilled, public service compensation falls outside the scope of Article 87(1) EC. In that case, there is no need for a block exemption regulation, because notification is not required. Second, the adoption of a block exemption regulation is simply not possible, as Council Regulation 994/98 does not provide the possibility to issue a block exemption regulation in these areas. See also M. Ross, The Europeanization of Public Service Compensation, in: P. Eeckhout and T. Tridimas, *Yearbook of European Law* (Oxford University Press, Oxford, 2004), p.307.

4.2.3.1 Introduction

On the basis of this case law it is clear that Article 86(2) EC includes horizontal and flanking policy interests, and that the term services of general *economic* interest is sufficiently broad to include various *public* interests. The correlation between economic and non-economic goals allows, contrary to the free movement rules, the Court and the Commission to look beyond the profitability reasoning.

Article 86(2) EC may be particularly relevant in the following three situations: First, as exception ground for exclusive rights and public monopolies; second, and in conjunction with Article 16 EC, as exception ground for actions by semi-public/semi-private organisation; and lastly, also in conjunction with Article 16 EC, as exception ground for actions by the state under the useful effect doctrine.

Similarly to certain categories of state aid for the protection of horizontal and flanking policy interests, services of general economic interest including horizontal and flanking policy interests are neither subject to a comprehensive set of rules at Community level. Through the adoption of a Green Paper on Services of General Interest the Commission took a first step in the discussion on the desirability of a *general* Community framework for services of general interest.[102] In the White Paper on Service of General Interest the Commission, considering the sceptical attitude of some Member States and the divided view on the matter, declares that it will not proceed to submit a legislative proposal providing a horizontal framework for services of general interest in time, but will perhaps do so at a later stage. For the time being the Commission will therefore pursue and develop its sectoral approach. This does not mean that a horizontal approach is not necessary as the Commission itself stipulates: "While the need for a framework instrument was an issue of considerable controversy, the necessity of ensuring the consistency and coherence of Community measures in the area of services of general interest was widely recognised in the public consultation."[103]

4.2.3.2 The horizontal approach to Article 86(2) EC: a proposal for a Framework Directive for services of general (economic) interest including horizontal and flanking policy interests

Article 86(2) EC in general

Under the horizontal approach, all types of services of general economic interest are dealt with in a single regulatory instrument. In this framework instrument the concept of service of general economic interest

[102] COM(2003) 270 final. See also Chapter 3, section 3.2.3.

[103] COM(2004) 374 final, p. 12.

should be further explained, in particular in relation to horizontal and flanking policies; important principles connected to services of general economic interest, like universal supply, affordability, quality of services, continuity and consumer protection must be elaborated as well.

The next step is to make clear how with a view to the integration principle, horizontal and flanking policies can be incorporated in Article 86(2) EC, and how the proportionality test should be carried out. Due to complex political, economic and social considerations, Member States should have a considerable margin in organising public service tasks, as long as these tasks are laid down in national legislation. The following conditions must therefore be fulfilled and should be included in the framework instrument:

- The public, or horizontal and flanking policy, interest tasks must be laid down in a statute, regulation;
- A causal link must be established between the exclusive right and the aim pursued; in other words, by not granting an exclusive right companies would be obstructed in carrying out their tasks so that the aim cannot be guaranteed.[104]
- The Commission must not question the appropriateness of the means, since, contrary to the free movement rules, the establishment of a legal monopoly itself belongs to the discretionary power of the Member State.

Extending Article 86(2) EC and/or Article 16 EC to actions by semi-public/semi-private organisations

In this proposed single regulatory framework the Commission must address the possibilities to invoke Article 86(2) EC in cases where other competition provisions, like Article 81 EC, have been infringed as well. The Commission could also include certain professional services, like services provided by lawyers, in this framework instrument, thereby avoiding similar cases as *Wouters*. The Commission's Report on Competition in Professional Services is a first step into this direction.[105]

The assessment of agreements, concerted practices or decisions of semi-public/semi-private organisations is still unclear, particularly where restrictive behaviour cannot benefit from the *Brentjens* exception,[106] but needs to fulfil certain conditions to be in accordance with competition law. There are three options for these types of restrictions. The first option is the *Wouters* approach of

104 According to Edward and Hoskins the ECJ could confine itself to asking whether the institution has committed a manifest error of assessment in considering that it did not have any other possible way of achieving the desired objectives by more efficient and less onerous means, in: D. Edward and M. Hoskins, Article 90: Deregulation and EC Law. Reflections arising from the XVI FIDE Conference *CMLRev.*, 1995, p. 171.

105 COM(2004) 83 final.

106 Joined Cases C-115/97, C-116/97 and C-117/97, *Brentjens*.

the Court, introducing a type of 'rule of reason' à la Cassis. A 'novum' in competition law, the exact meaning of which and wider consequences are difficult to fathom. It bears close resemblance to the 'inherent restriction approach' and can as such also be qualified under this heading, but there are differences as well.[107] In order to prevent that the distinction between Article 81(1) EC and 81(3) EC becomes too blurred, the *Wouters* approach must be interpreted restrictively.

A second and to be favoured option is the option provided by AG Léger in the same case, i.e. to apply Article 86(2) EC to these types of cases. It must then be established to what extent undertakings that are more generally entrusted with public interest tasks can benefit from this provision, also outside the scope of situations covered by Article 86 EC.

A third and interesting option is provided by Article 16 EC, which may be a convenient heading for classifying public interests pursued by semi-public/ semi-private organisations. Article 16 EC is a catch all provision. Furthermore as it refers to services of general economic interest, it is also relevant for undertakings or associations, and not only for Member States. The framework instrument could implement Article 16 EC explaining its relevance for the application of the competition rules. In the Treaty establishing a Constitution for Europe Article 16 EC is incorporated in Article III-122, which specifically provides the adoption of 'European laws' defining principles and conditions on which basis services of general economic interest operate.

Article 86(2) EC and/or Article 16 EC as exception ground for the useful effect doctrine

The question is whether Article 86(2) EC, with or without Article 16 EC, could more generally be used in cases where no other Treaty provision is available to justify actions by the national state having an effect on the internal market. Article 16 EC can be read as an obligation for the Commission to further develop services of general interests and to allow for a broad interpretation of Article 86(2) EC in relation to the protection of horizontal and flanking policy interests.[108] As stated above the Treaty establishing a Constitution for Europe explicitly provides that European law should be adopted with a view to define the principles and conditions on which basis these services operate.[109] Besides, the integration principle requires the Commission to take account of horizontal and flanking policy interests in all policies.

The framework instrument could then be used to set out the possibilities to rely on these provisions where no Treaty exception is available, in particular within the context of the useful effect doctrine. With regard to the useful effect

[107] Chapter 3, section 4.1.2.4.

[108] M. Ross, Article 16 E.C. and services of general interest: from derogation to obligation? *ELRev.*, 2000, pp. 22-38; see also Chapter 3, section 3.2.3.1.

[109] Article III-122 of the Treaty establishing a Constitution for Europe.

doctrine, no judgment exists where the ECJ has explicitly pronounced on the possibility to invoke a justification ground on public interest grounds. There are three options to deal with this problem: Firstly, the suggestion of AG Jacobs in *Pavlov* to introduce a type of rule of reason in the field.[110] In its Report on Competition in Professional Services the Commission seems to consider this a possibility for the justification of an infringement of the useful effect doctrine on public interest grounds, provided that the proportionality requirement is met.[111]

Secondly, the possibility to apply Article 86(2) EC to state measures delegating regulatory powers to private actors for public interest purposes. This option is only relevant where undertakings are involved with explicit public service tasks, which protect them from the application of the competition rules. In the framework instrument the Commission could clarify in which cases Article 86(2) EC may be relevant.

Thirdly, Article 16 EC could be used as catch all provision filling the lacuna of the Treaty particularly in these grey areas where the government and private firms mutually pursue public interests. The Commission could clarify the scope of Article 16 EC as well as the scope of application of the proportionality test under this provision. Article 16 EC may provide a legal basis for state measures delegating regulatory powers to private actors for public interest reasons. If these public interests are clearly articulated in national legislation, the state must not be held liable under the useful effect doctrine; after all, whether or not private firms are involved, the purpose is clearly of a public nature.[112] Besides, otherwise a conflict with the integration principle may arise. The more latitude is given to private firms to adopt decisions or conclude agreements affecting competition, the more stringent the proportionality test can be applied.[113]

4.2.3.3 The vertical approach to Article 86(2) EC: guidelines for each horizontal and flanking policy field

The vertical approach is essential for the subject matter as it implies that specific guidelines which are more flexible and for which a legal basis in the Treaty is not problematic, are adopted in respect of environmental

---

110 Opinion of AG Pavlov in Joined Cases C-180/98 to C-184/98, *Pavlov*, paragraphs 162-165. See for a more detailed analysis, Chapter 3, section 3.3.2. Gyselen proposed a similar test for anti-competitive State measures, the 'substantive legality Standard': L. Gyselen, Anti-Competitive State Measures under the EC Treaty: Towards a Substantive Legality Standard (Competition Checklist 1993), *ELR*, 1993, pp. CC55-CC89.

111 COM(2004) 83 final, p. 21. In a follow-up Communication the Commission does not explicitly refer to this possibility of justification: COM(2005) 405 final.

112 Baquero Cruz (2002) extensively discusses the state action doctrine (or useful effect doctrine) and its relationship with competition law and the free movement rules, pp. 127-161.

113 Baquero Cruz (2002), p. 161.

protection, consumer protection, public health and culture. The specificities of these areas are then dealt with in separate guidelines, similarly to the area of state aids, which also corresponds to the presently vertical approach in the Member States towards the safeguarding of services of general economic interest.[114] A first step into this direction is the Commission's proposal to submit a communication on social and health services of general interest as announced in the White Paper.[115] According to the Commission there is a need to clarify the distinction between mission and instruments here, which will in particular assist Member States which use market-based systems to deliver social and health services to anticipate the possible impact of EU competition law on them.

In guidelines with regard to other services, like environmental or cultural services, in a similar sense as it intends to do in respect of social and health services, the Commission should also clarify the distinction between mission and instruments and base its policy upon the case law of the ECJ by laying down the compatibility criteria in order to give effect to the proportionality principle.

4.2.4 The Commission's policy in respect of cartels – extending the guidelines on the application of Article 81(3) EC

Considering the private interests of individual undertakings involved, the Commission is faced with a particular problem in clarifying the role of horizontal and flanking policy interests within the context of Article 81 EC. However, considering the integration principle, mere elimination of horizontal and flanking policy interests is simply not an option. Furthermore, this would seriously jeopardise Member State's option to pursue horizontal and flanking policies through other instruments than command and control regulation.

The reason why clarification of the scope of Article 81(3) EC is particularly pertinent is twofold: the decentralisation of Article 81(3) EC entails that the national competition authorities and national courts have to know how this provision should be interpreted, also in relation to horizontal and flanking policy interests (see above, sections 3.2 and 3.3). Furthermore, no block exemption regulation has been adopted in respect of horizontal and flanking policies. Hence, the only remaining way for the Commission to provide the necessary guidance in respect of the role of horizontal and flanking policy interests under Article 81(3) EC is either to proceed to adopt important decisions like the *CECED* decision, making the adoption of guidelines less relevant, or to issue guidelines.[116] Precisely due to the decentralisation process combined with the fact that

114 See also the letter of the Dutch Minister of Economic Affairs in response to the Commission's Green Paper, *TK* 2002-2003, 22 112, nr. 283.

115 COM(2004) 374 final, pp. 16-17.

116 Compare J.W. van de Gronden and K.J.M. Mortelmans, Het mededingingsrecht en niet-economische belangen, in: J.W. van de Gronden en K.J.M. Mortelmans (Eds), *Mededinging en niet-economische belangen* (Kluwer, Deventer, 2001), pp. 332-335.

so far only few decisions have been adopted in respect of horizontal and flanking activities, it is unlikely that – apart from exceptional cases – the Commission intensifies its decision practice in this respect. Hence, guidelines appear to be the best instrument to clarify the scope of application of Article 81(3) EC in respect of horizontal and flanking policy activities. Block exemption regulations are no option, considering the so far small number of relevant decisions as well as the long legislative procedure for the adoption of block exemption regulations.

Guidelines have the particular advantage of being flexible. They can be applicable for a certain period of time. Guidelines are soft law instruments, which are in line with the subsidiarity principle,[117] and the adoption of guidelines has the advantage of avoiding timely and burdensome legislative procedures. Guidelines have already been developed in respect of horizontal co-operation agreements and vertical agreements; in the guidelines on horizontal co-operation agreements, environmental agreements are assessed in a systematic manner. An example is the *CECED* case. In order to examine whether in this case an exemption can be granted the Commission makes a distinction between individual economic benefits and environmental benefits. Regarding the collective environmental benefits the Commission argued that "on the basis of reasonable assumptions, the benefits to society brought about by the CECED agreement appear to be more than seven times greater than the increased purchase costs of more energy-efficient washing machines. Such environmental results would adequately allow consumers a fair share of the benefits, even if no benefits accrued to individual purchasers of machines."[118] A similar approach can be found in the guidelines on horizontal co-operation agreements where it is stated that "environmental agreements caught by Article 81(1) may attain economic benefits which, either at individual or aggregate consumer level, outweigh their negative effects on competition. To fulfil this condition there must be net benefits in terms of reduced environmental pressure resulting from the agreement, as compared to a baseline where no action is taken. In other words, the expected economic benefits must outweigh the costs."[119]

These guidelines could easily be used as a model for guidelines in respect of other horizontal and flanking policy interests, or extended so as to cover agreements with other horizontal and flanking policy objectives. The guidelines should also address the principle of proportionality. The fact that private companies are involved and that it will be difficult to prove that their actions are mainly for the benefit of the public must of course have ramifications for the proportionality of the behaviour, but not for the simple recognition that horizontal and flanking policy grounds can form a ground for exemption. The under-

[117] Craíg submits that subsidiarity has had an impact on the existence of Community action: P. Craig, Competence: Clarity, conferral, containment and consideration, *ELRev.*, 2004, p. 343.

[118] Commission Decision 2000/475, OJ 2000, L 187/47, paragraph 56; see also Chapter 3, section 4.1.3.2.

[119] Guidelines on horizontal co-operation agreements, OJ 2001, C 3/2 point 193.

takings involved in restrictive practices for the achievement of horizontal and flanking policy aims should first be able to prove that their behaviour is really aimed at realising public policy aims, and is not merely dictated by self-interest. In line with this reasoning, an agreement on fixed book prices should not only apply to the bouquet series and other light reading, but should extend to 'high literature', like poetry and novels, in order to be eligible for an exemption based on Article 81(3) EC. In *Sammelrevers* the Commission itself mentions the establishment of funds for *more demanding literature* as an alternative, less restrictive, measure to price fixing. Why, if it can indeed be established that price fixing agreements have the intention to support 'more demanding literature', would the possibility to grant an exemption be rejected from the start? (See also section 2 and the example of books)

The more 'rigid conceptual framework' provided by Article 81(3) EC, as compared to, for example, the state aid exception, must not be by-passed, which can be prevented through the application of a more stringent proportionality test. The Court will otherwise have to blow the whistle on the Commission. Within this rigid conceptual framework, and similarly to what has been said before in respect of the Community's state aid policy in section 4.2.2, account must be taken of the differences between horizontal and flanking policies, which eventually determines the margin of discretion of undertakings to pursue horizontal and flanking policy interests. Where principles of environmental policy allow for the integration of environmental policy concerns in competition policy, this is less clear for culture. The question has even been raised as to whether cultural concerns and objectives of competition policy may ultimately be antagonistic, which makes integration impossible.[120] In my opinion this view is too straightforward, as also appears from the decision practice of the Commission discussed in Chapter 3. Guidelines could therefore certainly be used to clarify the position of the Commission with respect to cultural agreements in various sectors, such as the book sector and the media sector, and the extent to which cultural considerations can really play a role within the context of Article 81 EC.

In conclusion, it should be noted that the suggestion for the adoption of guidelines at this instance appears at right angles with the Commission's notice on Article 81(3) EC, where it acknowledges that other objectives can be taken into account under Article 81(3) EC, but always subsumed under the four conditions. As stated before in sections 3.2 and 3.3 the notice has been criticised for its more stringent test than was in use under past Community practice, like the *CECED* decision and the guidelines on horizontal co-operation agreements.[121] In particular the danger exists that the national courts and national competition

[120] This is the case according to Vedder (2003), p. 351.

[121] P. Lugard and L. Hancher: Honey, I Shrunk the Article! A Critical Assessment of the Commission's Notice on Article 81(3) of the EC Treaty, *ECLR*, 2004, p. 418; see also Chapter 3, section 4.1.3.2.

authorities will, without clear guidance in this matter, have to come up with their own interpretation of Article 81(3) EC

4.3 The Community legislature: harmonisation of horizontal and flanking policies

By pursuing horizontal and flanking policy interests at Community level the Community legislature is particularly suited to resolve the tension between the *Community's* internal market and the protection of horizontal and flanking policy interests by the *Member States.*

4.3.1 In general

The fact that the potential to use Article 95 EC and other internal market legal bases for the regulation of horizontal and flanking policies has been reinforced by the Court in the *Tobacco* cases, in particular *BAT/Imperial Tobacco,* offers the Community legislature the possibility to truly resolve the tension.[122] The 'centre of gravity' theory does not appear to be all that relevant where no real alternative exists for the harmonisation of horizontal and flanking policies based on Article 95 EC. Hence, Article 95 EC could be used to regulate cultural and public health matters, provided the threshold criteria as laid down in the case law are met.

The potentially broad harmonisation powers of the Community under Article 95 EC and other internal market legal bases may put Member States' residual powers to pursue horizontal and flanking policies into jeopardy. Eventually it depends on the harmonisation technique used – total or minimum harmonisation – whether Member States' powers to deviate from the harmonisation measure are pre-empted or not.

4.3.2 The broad use of Article 95 EC to pursue horizontal and flanking policies

In order to prevent litigation over the choice of the proper legal basis, as well as to encourage the Community legislature to find solutions to the problem of tension without disrespecting Member States competences, the Community legislature must duly motivate why it pursues harmonisation within the context of the internal market, and it must explicitly assess the proportionality of its action.

---

[122] Case C-376/98, *Germany vs. European Parliament and Council (Tobacco Advertising)*; Case C-491/01, *BAT/Imperial Tobacco*; Case C-434/02, *Arnold André*; Case C-210/03, *Swedish Match*. See also Chapter 4, section 4.2.4 and Joined Cases C-154/04 and C-155/04, *Alliance for Natural Health.*

4.3.2.1 A strong duty to motivate legislation

The relative nature of the prohibition to harmonise

The Community legislature must duly motivate, and more than it has done so far, why internal market legal bases have been used to regulate horizontal and flanking policy fields, particularly with a view to the prohibition of harmonisation in the fields of culture and public health. The duty to motivate has been reinforced by the judgment of the Court in *Tobacco Advertising*, which nevertheless does not give clear guidance as to the scope of Article 95 EC and other legal bases in horizontal and flanking policy fields where the Community does not dispose of harmonisation powers. Besides, it does not really provide the required legal certainty for both the Community and the Member States, as to how far the Community's regulatory powers may intrude into areas that primarily belong to the national domain, like culture and public health. The Court's statement that other legal bases may not be used to circumvent the deliberate exclusion of harmonisation has not been an obstacle to reinforce the broad scope of Article 95 EC also in, for example, the field of public health, motivated by the integration principle. The clear potential of the *Tobacco* cases to undermine the prohibition of harmonisation emphasises the relative nature of the prohibitive provisions on harmonisation.

Preventing abuse of law: respecting the principle of subsidiarity

From this duty to motivate it can be deduced that the Community legislature must indicate how 'abuse of the prohibition of harmonisation' can be prevented; in other words, how Member States' powers to regulate in the areas of culture and public health are not being jeopardised. This means that the Community legislature has to respect the principle of subsidiarity and the *Edinburgh* guidelines,[123] which are laid down in the protocol on the application of the principles of subsidiarity and proportionality added by the Treaty of Amsterdam.

If these criteria are met and the aim of the Community legislature is clearly not to circumvent the prohibition of harmonisation, Community intervention through harmonisation is justifiable and the prohibition to harmonise may be set aside. If Community legislation is well motivated (containing an internal market link) – in the political process one finds sufficient reasons or links with the internal market to include in the Community harmonisation measure[124] – there will be no question of 'abuse of the law'.[125]

---

[123] Conclusions adopted by the European Council in its Edinburgh Meeting of 11-12 December 1992.

[124] Van Ooik (1999), p. 314.

[125] Compare 'the abuse of law' case law in the context of the rules on free movement (negative integration), for example, Case 229/83, *Leclerc* and Case C-23/93, *TV 10;* see also Chapter 2, section 2.3.

The aim of motivating Community harmonisation measures with a view to the prohibition of harmonisation and with a view to solving the problem of tension between the internal market and horizontal and flanking policies is twofold. First, well-motivated legislation may prevent litigation over the choice of the proper legal basis. Hence, motivation serves to reduce the conflicts between Member States and the Community legislature, and contributes to the achievement of closer harmony. Second, well-motivated legislation is also important with a view to prevent a democratic deficit, since public health and cultural interests could be harmonised through the backdoor, bypassing the legislative procedures prescribed by the specific Treaty provisions.

4.3.2.2 Taking the principle of proportionality into account

A less stringent proportionality test

Once it has been established that there is a legal basis for Community action, the Community legislature must in principle take account of primary Community law, i.e. the free movement rules and, hence, the principle of proportionality. It appears that the Community legislature enjoys wide discretionary powers in respect of the free movement rules. The Community legislature may issue far-reaching legislation without being threatened by the possible application of the free movement rules in a similar way as the Member States are.[126]

The principle of proportionality plays a role, however, when the Community legislature enjoys a wider margin of discretion in pursuing horizontal and flanking policy aims than Member States do. This can be explained by the dual function of proportionality in the context of negative integration, i.e. the function concerning the relationship between the judiciary and the legislature in general as well as the relationship between the European Community and the Member States.[127] The second function of the proportionality principle relates to the objective of market integration. Since the ECJ is particularly committed to this aim, its more stringent review of national measures as compared to Community measures,[128] for which only the first function of the proportionality principle is significant, can easily be understood.

The Community legislature must of course seek to adopt the most appropriate means available to attain certain horizontal and flanking policy aims. The ECJ will nonetheless exercise only limited appraisal of Community harmonisation, also with a view to prevent that it would put itself in the place of the legislature. The role of the principle of subsidiarity is limited. Even though subsidi-

---

[126] Chapter 4, section 6.

[127] Chapter 2, section 3.3.3.3.

[128] G.A. Bermann, Proportionality and Subsidiarity, in: C. Barnard and J. Scott (Eds), *The Law of the Single European Market – Unpacking the Premises* (Hart Publishing, Oxford and Portland, 2002), p. 99.

arity arguments may be incorporated through the application of the principle of proportionality, they can so far not be used to curb the powers the Community legislature now disposes of under the internal market legal bases vis à vis the Member States in a general sense.[129]

The importance of the horizontal and flanking policy interest at stake

The Community legislature must, similarly to national bodies involved in the policy and law-making process, be aware of the differences that exist between the various horizontal and flanking policies. This should play a role in the context of the proportionality principle. In other words, it depends on the importance of the horizontal and flanking policy interest at stake to what extent the Community's legislature's margin of discretion can be curtailed. The same consideration has been used in respect of the Court's appraisal of national measures protecting horizontal and flanking policy interests (see above, section 3.1.3). Where the protection of public health and the environment are concerned, which are values considered so great and for which important principles, like the precautionary principle, have been incorporated in the Treaty, the Community legislature should have a considerable margin of discretion in pursuing its aims; as a consequence the Court should only exercise a limited appraisal of these issues.[130]

Taking the differences in competences into account

Where certain horizontal and flanking policies belong to the particular domain of the Member States, like cultural policy, the Community legislature must carefully consider whether harmonisation measures under Article 95 EC and other internal market legal bases are suitable and appropriate to attain cultural aims, also in relation to other interests, like free movement. Where horizontal and flanking policies have become at least partly 'Community policies', as in the field of consumer protection, this appraisal may be more limited.

4.3.3 Total versus minimum harmonisation: pre-empting Member States to adopt additional, more stringent standards?

In order to resolve the tension by providing a final solution at Community level the Community legislature could opt for the technique of total harmonisation. Member States' powers to deviate from the harmonisation

---

[129] See for a comparison between the application of the proportionality and subsidiarity principles in the United States and the European Community: G. A. Bermann, Proportionality and Subsidiarity, in: C. Barnard and J. Scott (Eds), *The Law of the Single European Market – Unpacking the Premises* (Oxford and Portland, Hart Publishing 2002), pp. 75-99.

[130] Opinion of AG Geelhoed in Case C-491/01, *BAT/Imperial Tobacco*, paragraphs 225-229.

measure are in principle pre-empted. The relevance of the free movement rules ceases to exist. If total harmonisation is preferred, Article 95 EC and other internal market legal bases will have to be used. The possibilities for the Member State to depart from harmonisation measures based on the internal market provisions, i.e. only Article 95(4-5) EC, are limited, which prevents the disruption of the internal market process. In addition it can be seen that the Court's case law, i.e. *Tobacco Advertising*, requires the Community legislature to restrict minimum harmonisation to the home state being allowed to set more stringent standards; this may induce the Community legislature to make more use of the technique of total harmonisation.

The tension cannot be resolved completely by harmonisation based on specific Treaty provisions, providing the Community legislature with the power to mitigate the internal market process for the full implementation of horizontal and flanking policies, but leaving the possibility for Member States to apply more stringent standards. Nevertheless, depending on the type of directive or regulation, such as in particular the Transfer of Waste Regulation, the scope for additional action by the state may still be limited.[131]

At first sight total harmonisation seems a perfect instrument to resolve the tension and hence to achieve closer harmony between the internal market and horizontal and flanking policies. At second thought, though, this must be put into perspective. Certainly, total harmonisation is to be preferred when uniformity is desirable and possible. This is in particular the case in the field of consumer policy, and, more generally, when the regulation of product standards is involved, for example for environmental or public health reasons. Since varying product standards may seriously impede intra-Community trade and create market-fragmentation, the adoption of total harmonisation measures has been perceived as necessary.[132] Irrespective of the reinforcement of total harmonisation by *Tobacco Advertising*, minimum harmonisation remains preferable in certain cases, where uniformity is inapt as guiding value. This is particularly so in horizontal and flanking policy areas lying beyond the internal market, where local, human or geographical circumstances, cultural differences or natural and ecological differences cannot always be taken into account by the Community legislature, but which Member States should safeguard individually.

In the field of the environment, for example, process standards have been subject to minimum harmonisation. Process standards – standards on industrial processes, on installations etc. – may not in themselves impede intra-Community trade. They may, however, distort competition, which provides a justification ground for harmonisation at Community level.[133] But in the absence of pollution spillovers harmonisation may not be desirable. Since Article 175

---

131 Case C-324/99, *Daimler Chrysler.* See also Chapter 4, section 5.1.2.

132 See with regard to the environment: Geradin (1997), pp. 128-129.

133 Geradin (1997), p. 65.

EC explicitly provides harmonisation of environmental law and also contains a provision on minimum harmonisation, in case of spillover effects process standards could easily be regulated on the basis of this provision.

However, this is different in the field of public health. If the Community legislature wishes to pursue harmonisation of public health interests, this will only be possible within the context of the internal market. As stated above, the Community legislature will then be induced to total harmonisation; in any event minimum harmonisation is restricted to setting more stringent standards by the home State. In the field of insurance, including health insurance, it has been seen that this leads to the consequence that more stringent standards cannot be applied in respect of health insurers established in another Member State.[134] It can therefore only be hoped that the Community legislature intends to adopt the highest possible standards of protection of health interests on the basis of internal market provisions.

5 Closer harmony: a proposal for re-organising the EC Treaty

Whether the above-mentioned suggestions will eventually be followed largely depends on the willingness of the national bodies and the Community institutions involved in the policy and law-making process to really integrate horizontal and flanking policies in free movement and competition rules. On the basis of the foregoing it can be concluded that the present legal framework allows for a number of solutions to the problem of tension.

5.1 Introduction

This implies that there is no question of 'chaos', but merely 'messiness', which may nonetheless continue to constitute important obstacles for the achievement of closer harmony, both from the perspective of the Member States and from the perspective of the Community. This can be explained by the following reasons.

The analysis in Chapter 2 (free movement rules) and Chapter 3 (competition rules) shows that there has been a case-by-case approach under the free movement and competition rules. This leaves Member States with a certain degree of uncertainty as to the possibilities to justify national measures for the attainment of horizontal and flanking policy interests, for the following two reasons: firstly, because horizontal and flanking policy interests are simply not mentioned by the Treaty; and secondly, because it remains unclear whether discriminatory practices are acceptable under the free movement rules. After all, the basic rule has always been that imperative requirements of public interest – the rule of

134 Chapter 4, section 4.3.3.

reason exceptions – can only be invoked in respect of non-discriminatory, or indistinctly applicable measures. This rule seems increasingly irrelevant, at least in the field of the environment but also in other areas of horizontal and flanking policies.[135]

Furthermore, from the foregoing sections in this chapter and from Chapter 3 (competition rules) it appears that recent developments in the field of competition policy, i.e. developments in the decision practice of the Commission regarding the (limited) possibilities to incorporate horizontal and flanking policies in Article 81 EC, as well as the decentralisation process under Regulation 1/2003,[136] do not only have an impact on a Member State's choice of regulatory instruments, but also on the way the Commission and Community Courts will assess restrictive practices under Article 81(3) EC in the nearby future.

Finally, the sections of this chapter and Chapter 4 (harmonisation) make clear that a regulatory gap may originate which has not been bridged so far. The reason is that the Community legislature is either not competent to take action, even though the rules on free movement set limitations to national policies, or is, due to the potential of Article 95 EC and other internal market legal bases, competent to take action in horizontal and flanking policy fields, for which harmonisation is actually excluded.

Consequently, a more structural and definite solution is necessary to clear the 'messiness'. From a legal perspective this can be given by amending the EC Treaty. The point of departure is as stated in the Introduction (Chapter 1) a legalistic approach. This can be explained by the fact that the original EC Treaty was an 'economic' Treaty, which in the course of the years has been amended only step by step, without providing a coherent and structural approach to the relationship between the 'relatively new' horizontal and flanking policies and the 'old' common or internal market.

The Treaty establishing a Constitution for Europe

The Treaty establishing a Constitution for Europe may have offered a solution to the problem of tension, but did not do so. It did not use the opportunity to clarify the relationship between horizontal and flanking policies and the internal market, unless it is for the integration clauses that have been included under Part III (Policies and Functioning of the Union), Title I (general provisions of application) referring to, for example, the protection of public health, the environment, consumers and animal welfare.

Article III-119 contains the environmental integration clause, as presently laid down in Article 6 EC. New is, however, that Article III-120 contains an integration clause stipulating that *consumer protection* requirements shall be taken

135 See the conclusions presented in Chapter 5, section 2.1.2; see also Chapter 2, section 4.4.

136 Regulation 1/2003 on the implementation of the rules on competition laid down in Articles 81 and 82 of the Treaty, OJ 2003, L 1/1.

into account in defining and implementing other Union policies and activities. Article III-121 contains a reference to welfare requirements of animals being respected in the formulation and implementation of the Union's agriculture, fisheries, transport, internal market, research and technological development and space policies. Article III-117 refers *inter alia* to the protection of public health. Unfortunately, this has not resulted in an amendment of the public health paragraph providing the Community legislature with (limited) harmonisation powers in this area.

Amending the present EC Treaty

After the referendums in France and the Netherlands the status of the Treaty establishing a Constitution for Europe has become uncertain. The point of departure is the EC Treaty that could be amended in order to provide a more comprehensive solution to the problem of tension between horizontal and flanking policies and the internal market. In the following section suggestions are brought forward for reorganising and redefining the *EC Treaty* in respect of horizontal and flanking policies. If useful, references are made to the Treaty establishing a Constitution for Europe.

5.2 Re-organising and redefining the Treaty in respect of horizontal and flanking policies

In re-organising and re-defining the Treaty it should be kept in mind that there are inherently substantive differences between environmental, public health, consumer and cultural interests as well as differences between competences in these policy fields.[137] This entails that it is not possible to come up with a clear-cut and equivocal solution to the problem of tension between the internal market and horizontal and flanking policy interests.

Several general and specific Treaty provisions should be amended in order to provide a more definite solution to the problem of tension. Proposals are therefore made to revise Article 2 of the EC Treaty – containing the *general* objectives of the Community –and also to re-organise the integration clauses that are laid down in the Treaty (see hereafter, section 5.2.1).

Next, specific proposals are made for the introduction of a single Treaty exception to free movement (section 5.2.2); for a reference to horizontal and flanking policy interests in the Treaty exceptions to the competition rules, in particular Articles 87(3) EC and 81(3) EC; and for including an exception ground for the 'useful effect doctrine' (section 5.2.3).

The legal bases for harmonisation within the context of the internal market, in particular Articles 95(5) EC and 47(2) EC, should also be amended (section 5.2.3).

---

[137] As stated in Chapter 1, section 3.1; see also in particular Chapter 5, section 5.3.

Lastly, amendments are proposed in respect of the specific Treaty provisions on public health (Article 152 EC) and culture (Article 151 EC) (section 5.2.4).

5.2.1 The general objectives of the EC Treaty

Article 2 of the EC Treaty

Recommendation (1): In Article 2 EC a reference should be included to a high level of protection of public health.

Article 2 EC is the core provision of the EC Treaty and constitutes the point of reference for all Community policies as it lays down the general objectives of the European Community. The inclusion of various non-economic objectives in Article 2 EC, such as the protection of the environment, makes clear that the common or internal market, which is one of the three main tasks to attain these objectives, cannot be pursued in isolation of horizontal and flanking policy interests.

The fact that the environment and public health are important interests worthy of special protection entails that they should both be mentioned in Article 2 EC. References are indeed made to the promotion of sustainable development and a high level of protection and improvement of the quality of the environment and several other important objectives of the Community, such as a high level of employment and social protection, but not to a high level of protection of public health. This is at least peculiar, considering the high priority public health enjoys in Community law according to the case law of the Court of Justice.

Article 2 EC should not contain a reference to other objectives of horizontal and flanking policies, which are also mentioned in the catalogue of Community tasks of Article 3 EC, such as the objective of consumer protection, which is more specific and involves the protection of interests of market participants contributing to the establishment of the internal market, and the objective of protection of cultural interests or cultural diversity, which is more diffuse and is mainly pursued at the level of the Member State.[138] In that sense the proposed amendment of Article 2 EC reinforces the idea that environmental interests and public health interests are predominant as compared to consumer or cultural interests.

The integration principle

Recommendation (2): The environmental integration clause should be replaced in the environmental paragraph.

Including just one integration principle in respect of all horizontal and flanking policies is strongly advised against, since, as stated earlier, in the EC

[138] See with regard to the differences between horizontal and flanking policies: Chapter 1, section 3.1 and Chapter 5, section 5.3.

Treaty the powers to regulate in areas of horizontal and flanking policies are fleshed out differently, and there are inherently substantive differences between horizontal and flanking policies. This entails that there are different approaches to these policies.[139]

Nonetheless, since the Treaty of Amsterdam (1997) the environmental integration clause has, contrary to the other integration clauses, gained a more prominent place in the Treaty and is now headed under the title 'principles'. Without calling into question the importance of the environment, it is contentious why this particular provision should have been situated in the beginning of the Treaty, whereas the other integration clauses, like for example the public health integration clause, are laid down in the respective Treaty provisions on horizontal and flanking policies. After all, according to the Court, the protection of public health ranks first among the interests contained in Article 30 EC.[140] So "although the environment has a higher profile by reason of its position in the beginning of the Treaty, in reality public health enjoys priority".[141]

There are several reasons pleading in favour of putting the environmental integration clause back in the environmental paragraph. Firstly, in stead of focusing on the relative importance of the position of the integration clauses in the Treaty, one should consider the importance of the objectives contained in Article 2 EC (see above) and the fact that the internal market must be an environmentally sound and healthy market. In addition, Member States are provided with more legal certainty when horizontal and flanking policy interests are included in a Treaty exception (see hereafter, section 5.2.2) than when they have to rely on an integration clause, like in *Preussen Elektra*.[142] Neither the Community Courts, nor the European Commission or the Community legislature have always explicitly and systematically referred to the integration principle, but have usually done so merely on an ad hoc basis. The answer to the question of what role horizontal and flanking policy interests in internal market policy, including competition policy, the integration principle requires, remains unpredictable.

Secondly, the relationship between Article 6 EC and the other integration clauses is not really clear. Due to its position in the Treaty and its stronger formulation, the environmental integration principle has been considered the strongest of all integration clauses.[143]

Lastly, since the integration clauses relate to specific horizontal and flanking policy interests which are inherently different and to Community policies and

---

[139] Chapter 1, section 3.2 and Chapter 5, section 5.3.

[140] See, for example, Case 104/75, *De Peijper*; see also Chapter 2, section 4.4.3.1.

[141] P. Oliver, Competition and Free Movement: Their Place in the Treaty, in: T. Trimidas & P. Nebbia, *European Union Law for the Twenty-First Century – Rethinking the New Legal Order*, Volume 2, Internal Market and Free Movement Community Policies (Hart Publishing, Oxford and Portland, 2004), p.160.

[142] Case C-379/98, *PreussenElektra*; see also Chapter 2, section 4.4.1.3.

[143] Dhondt (2003), p. 103.

activities, they do not seem to have an equally general scope of application as the other general principles of Community law, such as the principles of Community loyalty and proportionality.[144] In the foregoing sections of this Chapter, the integration principle has been considered mainly relevant for the European Commission in implementing its competition policy.[145]

Contrary to this suggestion, however, the Treaty establishing a Constitution for Europe has put the integration clauses at the beginning of Part III, The Policies and Functioning of the Union. Nevertheless, maintaining the integration clauses in the respective Treaty paragraphs on horizontal and flanking policies and making Article 2 EC stronger at the same time is a better option.

5.2.2 A new Treaty exception for restrictions on free movement

Recommendation (3): A new Treaty provision including a public interest exception ground and containing a non-exhaustive list of justification grounds in respect of all freedoms should be included in the EC Treaty. In this provision references can be made, firstly to grounds of public policy, public morality, public security and public health; secondly, to overriding requirements of public interest, such as, *inter alia* the protection of the environment, the protection of consumers, the protection of cultural interests, including the protection of archaeological or national treasures, the protection of plurality of the media and the promotion of national languages; and lastly, to the proportionality principle, whereby actions by Member States shall not constitute a disguised restriction on trade between Member States nor go beyond what is necessary to achieve the objectives it pursues.

As stated before in Chapter 5 the convergence process between the rules on free movement is in an advanced phase, meaning that it has become increasingly irrelevant whether an activity should be qualified under goods, services, capital or persons. This reinforces the idea of having just *one* Treaty exception in respect of *all* freedoms,[146] which will be situated in a section on the free movement of goods, persons, services and capital. In the Treaty establishing a Constitution for Europe the freedoms are situated together in Chapter I, the Internal Market, Title III, Internal Policies and Action and Part III, the Policies and Functioning of the Union.

A new Treaty provision including a public interest exception ground will provide a more definite solution for the problem of tension between horizontal

---

[144] Chapter 1, section 4.3.

[145] Section 4.2 of this chapter.

[146] Compare the proposal made by Baquero Cruz (2002), p. 95: he proposes a "simple rule of predictable application common to the economic freedoms", one rule prohibiting all restrictions on the free movement of economic factors and one exception justifying restrictions on free movement on grounds of public interest.

and flanking policies and rules on free movement. This provision bears the following important features. First, it does not contain a closed class of exception grounds, like Article 30 EC *et seq*, but constitutes an open norm which can be invoked by Member States provided that the proportionality requirement is met. So, in other words, the new Treaty exception will not, contrary to the present Treaty provisions, contain an exhaustive list of justification grounds.

Furthermore, discriminatory measures could now in principle be justifiable, provided that all other conditions for invoking a justification ground have been fulfilled. Not discrimination, but the motive and purpose of the measure concerned should be the focus of attention. The Treaty rules on free movement mainly serve to prevent State protectionism, and not discrimination as such.[147] Hence, my recommendation provides Member States with considerably more legal certainty whilst pursuing horizontal and flanking policy interests.[148] It is more predictable that, even where measures are discriminatory, they may be justifiable for good reasons.[149] Besides, some horizontal and flanking policies are inherently discriminatory, without necessarily being protectionist or harmful: measures adopted for the protection of cultural heritage will not infrequently involve a direct or indirect advantage for its own institutions, for instance the establishment of a film or literature prize or other encouragement of artists or artistic societies.[150]

Finally, the emphasis is laid upon the principle of proportionality playing a pivotal role in the application of the justification grounds. It should be utilised as a flexible tool to adapt to different situations, taking account of the (inherently substantive) differences between horizontal and flanking policies (see also above, paragraph 4.1.2). The words 'disguised restriction on trade' can be used within this context to indicate that the Court should consider the government's purpose behind a measure, that the grounds mentioned in this provision should not be diverted from their proper purpose. This entails that if measures are based on economic reasons that are instrumental to the attainment of non-economic objectives, they will be eventually justifiable, like, for example, export restrictions on waste that are necessary to ensure a sufficient supply of waste to avoid unsound recovery and disposal of wastes.[151]

Considering the differences that continue to exist between the freedoms relating in particular to the nature of the economic factors involved, the inclusion of one Treaty exception should not automatically lead to one prohibitive Treaty rule prohibiting restrictions on all freedoms.[152] For example, the case law

---

[147] Chapter 5, section 5.1.

[148] As opposed to Baquero Cruz (2002), pp. 94-95.

[149] See also Chapter 2, sections 4.4 and 4.5 and in particular Chapter 6, section 4.1.1.

[150] AG Van Gerven in Case C-17/92, *Fedicine*.

[151] Case C-203/96, *Dusseldorp* and Chapter 2, section 4.3.2; this conclusion can also be drawn from the *Sydhavnens* judgment: Case C-209/98, *Sydhavnens FFAD* and Chapter 3, section 3.2.3.2.

[152] As suggested by Baquero Cruz (2002), p. 95. See also Chapter 2, sections 2, 3 and 4.

on the free movement of persons is developing, whereby it has been submitted that Union citizens are now treated more favourable than products. There are even pleadings in favour of seeing products and citizens as two different legal categories where standards of adjudication should not converge.[153] Furthermore, in respect of the free movement of workers, the free movement of services and the freedom of establishment, an additional exception ground – now Articles 39(4) EC and 45 EC – concerning employment in the public service will remain. The same goes true for specific provisions relating to the free movement of capital.

5.2.3 References to horizontal and flanking policies in the field of competition policy

The point of departure is the various actors involved in the regulatory process, being public, semi-public or private, restricting competition for assumed public or mixed public/private interests. The following suggestions for Treaty amendments therefore also reflect the sliding scale, starting at state aid policy (Article 87 EC), going down to a policy towards services of general economic interest (Article 86(2) EC) and towards cartels (Article 81 EC).[154]

Article 87(3) EC

Recommendation (4): Apart from a reference to culture, Article 87(3) EC on state aids should also contain references to the environment and public health.

The fact that for cultural policy reasons only for state aids a specific exception ground has been established seems illogical and inconsistent with the decision practice of the Commission and case law of the Court. Hence, a similar public interest exception should be laid down in Article 87(3) EC for environmental and public health policies. Even though an exemption based on environmental grounds may still be considered disputable in the light of the polluter pays principle, the present guidelines show that the Commission's policy has become more structural and long lasting. In any event, the inclusion of the environment in Article 87(3) EC would not take away the obligation for Member States to notify the aid scheme to the Commission.

The fact that the protection of public health concerns an important objective of the Community emphasises the importance of including a reference in Article 87(3) EC to public health interests.

---

[153] See J. Snell, And Then There Were Two: Products and Citizens in Community Law, in: T. Trimidas & P. Nebbia (Eds), *European Union Law for the Twenty-First Century – Rethinking the New Legal Order,* Volume 2, Internal Market and Free Movement Community Policies (Hart Publishing, Oxford and Portland, 2004), pp. 49-72.

[154] See also section 4.2.1 of this chapter.

But, contrary to the proposal for a Treaty exception on free movement, the proposed amendment of Article 87(3) EC does not include consumer protection as an exception ground. Aid granted to individual *consumers* is exempted on the basis of Article 87(2) sub a EC.[155] The question is whether an additional reference to consumers in Article 87(3) EC is really necessary. Aid granted for environmental, public health or cultural purposes will also (indirectly) benefit consumers. Furthermore, since hardly any Community policy has been developed in the field of state aid and consumer policy, it is not advisable to include consumer protection in Article 87(3) EC. In addition the linkages between consumer policies and the internal market are much stronger.

Where consumer, or other horizontal and flanking policy interests that are not mentioned in Article 87(3) EC, are at stake, it can always be tried to bring them within the ambit of Article 87(3) sub b EC or Article 87(3) sub c EC, which have been the main grounds of justification for horizontal and flanking state aids.[156]

A new Treaty exception in relation to the 'useful effect doctrine'

Recommendation (5): A new Treaty provision should be drafted stipulating that anti-competitive effects of state action can be justified by imperative requirements of public interest, relating to *inter alia* the protection of the environment, the protection of public health, the protection of consumers, and the protection of cultural interests.

The proportionality principle must be respected, meaning that action shall not constitute a disguised restriction on trade between Member States, nor go beyond what is necessary to achieve the objectives which it pursues.

The fact that the possibilities for Member States to justify their actions under the useful effect doctrine are either non-existent or have remained unclear so far, makes a reference to an explicit public interest exception ground even more pertinent. Besides, Article 81(3) EC is not an option either, as it requires that not all competition should be eliminated in respect of a substantial part of the products in question. When an agreement is declared generally binding, this condition is most likely not fulfilled.[157] The point of departure is the inclusion of an explicit exception in the Treaty, which has an equally broad scope as the proposed Treaty exception on free movement, and not the codification of the useful effect rule as such.

On the one hand, it may be argued that, since hardly any cases or Community policies exist on the relationship between horizontal and flanking policies

---

[155] Article 87(2) sub a EC reads as follows: "The following shall be compatible with the common market: (a) aid having a social character, granted to individual consumers, provided that such aid is granted without discrimination related to the origin of the products concerned."

[156] Chapter 3, section 3.1.5.1.

[157] Chapter 3, section 3.3.2.

and the useful effect doctrine, it is not advisable to include an explicitly public interest exception ground in respect of this doctrine in the Treaty. On the other hand, the fact that the Court has not yet pronounced on the issue of justification, as well as the fact that the useful effect doctrine has been reinforced by the Court's judgment in *CIF,*[158] stipulating that national law that violates the useful effect rule must be declared inapplicable by national competition authorities, calls for the immediate inclusion of an explicit exception ground in the Treaty. The example of fixed book prices makes clear that it is highly uncertain whether the Dutch law on fixed book prices is in accordance with the useful effect doctrine.[159]

The proportionality test may nonetheless constitute a considerable hurdle for the Netherlands to justify its law on fixed book prices. In particular the requirement that the law must be pertinent to the attainment of its aims, i.e. there must be a causal link between the law and the cultural aims pursued, will be difficult to prove,[160] considering the discords in legal and economic literature on the effects of book pricing agreements.[161] Where no agreement exists on the propagated cultural effects of fixed book prices, a precautionary approach could be followed, like in the fields of the environment and public health: 'in dubio pro cultura'. Furthermore, similar to what has been said in respect of the exceptions to free movement above, one should focus on the government's purpose behind a measure preventing the Courts, the Commission or the national competition authorities from being engaged in an inadequate assessment of horizontal and flanking benefits which in some cases are limited or hard to predict, but still justifiable.

A reference to horizontal and flanking policy interests in Article 81 EC

Recommendation (6): Article 81(3) EC should contain an explicit reference to horizontal and flanking policy interests. A third condition stipulating "or which contributes to the promotion or protection of imperative requirements of public interest, such as, *inter alia* the protection of the environment, public health or culture" should be added to the two already existing positive conditions

---

158 Case C-198/01, *Consorzio Industrie Fiammifieri (CIF).*

159 J. Houdijk, De nieuwe Wet op de vaste boekenprijs: immuun voor het mededingingsrecht?, *Mediaforum* 2005, pp. 148-156; see also the comment on this article by B. J. Drijber, Reactie op: De Wet op de vaste boekenprijs en het mededingingsrecht, *Mediaforum,* 2005, pp. 232-234.

160 B. J. Drijber, Reactie op: De Wet op de vaste boekenprijs en het mededingingsrecht, *Mediaforum,* 2005, p. 234.

161 See, for example, with regard to the effectiveness of fixed book prices: M. Appelman & M. Canoy, Notes and Communications. Horses for courses: why Europe should not harmonise its book policies, *De Economist,* 2002, pp. 583-600; J. Backhaus & R. Hansen, Resale Price Maintenance for Books in Germany and the European Union: A Legal and Economic Analysis, paper of 12 June 2000, to be found at: http://edata.ub.unimaas.nl/www-edocs/loader/file.asp?id=341.

of improving the production or distribution of goods or promoting technical or economic progress.[162]

So far the integration clauses have not proved sufficiently significant for the Commission's competition policy in this respect. Hence, Article 81 EC needs to be revised including an explicit reference to horizontal and flanking policy interests. Considering the decentralisation process and the Commission's restrained approach in its guidelines on the application of Article 81(3) EC, more legal certainty is needed with regard to the position of horizontal and flanking policy interests in the Community's cartel policy.[163] After all, the national competition authorities and national courts will be confronted with arguments relating to horizontal and flanking policies.

The revised Article 81(3) EC is similar to the proposal for a Treaty exception on free movement, as it includes a non-exhaustive list of justification grounds. However, it is clear that, contrary to the Treaty exception on free movement, horizontal and flanking policy interests can never play a predominant role within the context of Article 81(3) EC, as their assessment must be based on economic conditions. After all, the addressees of Article 81 EC are undertakings, which, as we must presume, act primarily for their own benefit. But since they may also act for the benefit of the public and since Member States may opt to pursue horizontal and flanking policies through other instruments than command and control regulation, the possibility to justify horizontal and flanking policy interests should not be excluded from the outset.[164]

An amendment of Article 81(3) EC connects better with several national systems of competition law, explicitly allowing for the consideration of public, non-competition interests. To illustrate this, the Netherlands Competition Act (CA) pursuant to Article 4(2) CA provides the Dutch Minister with the possibility to issue general instructions on how the Netherlands Competition Authority (NMa) should consider interests other than economic ones in decisions pursuant to Article 6(3) of the CA, which is the likeness of Article 81(3) EC. This may be particularly relevant for book pricing agreements, since cultural arguments in support of fixed book prices may then find a more ready ear with the Netherlands Competition Authority.

---

[162] This suggestion resembles to some extent the proposal made by G. Monti in his article on Article 81 EC and public policy, *CMLRev.*, 2002, p. 1097.

[163] OJ 2004, C 101/97.

[164] See also section 4.2.4 of this chapter.

5.2.4 Harmonisation within the framework of the internal market: a revision of Articles 95(5) and 47(2) EC

Recommendation (7): Article 95(5) EC should be amended in order to offer Member States the possibility to take action in case of specific health problems. Article 95(8) EC could be withdrawn.

Recommendation (8): Article 47(2) EC should be amended to include a provision stipulating "the Commission in its proposals concerning public health, safety and consumer protection, the protection of cultural interests, like public service broadcasting or the protection of languages, and social protection will take as a base a high level of protection".

Furthermore, similar conditional possibilities to maintain or take additional measures under supervision of the European Commission as are provided by article 95 (4, 5) EC should also be included in Article 47(2) EC.

In Chapter 4 it was submitted that it seems illogical and highly unsatisfactory that a Member State has no possibility to introduce measures unilaterally in case of a specific health problem, whilst in case of an environmental problem it can take such action under Article 95(5) EC.[165] Hence, Article 95(5) EC should be amended to provide Member States with the possibility to take action in case of specific health problems. At the same time Article 95(8) EC, which status seems rather unclear, could be withdrawn.[166] The possibility that exists under this provision for the Member State to only *inform* the Commission of a specific health problem becomes irrelevant when it may introduce *measures* for public health reasons on the basis of Article 95(5) EC and subject to several conditions and under supervision of the Commission.

Furthermore, whereas Article 95(3) EC includes a reference to important horizontal and flanking policy interests, the other internal market legal bases do not. Considering the relevance of Article 47(2) EC (in conjunction with Article 55 EC) for the field of services and for the regulation of horizontal and flanking policies having an impact on the free movement of services, such as, for example, cultural and audio-visual policies, public health policy or consumer policy, it is unsatisfactory that Article 47(2) EC does not contain a reference to horizontal and flanking policy interests as well. The proposal for a Directive on services in the internal market in particular shows how wrongly the balance between horizontal and flanking policy interests and the internal market can be struck.[167]

Finally, together with the introduction of a reference to horizontal and flanking policy interests a similar derogation as provided by Article 95(4, 5) EC should be possible under Article 47(2) EC. This means that under the same conditions, according to the same procedure with a particular role for

---

[165] Chapter 4, section 3.2.

[166] Chapter 4, section 3.2.

[167] COM(2004) 2 final/3. See Chapter 4, section 4.2.2.

the Commission and for the same horizontal and flanking policy reasons as mentioned in Article 95(4-10) EC Member States would also be allowed to derogate from harmonisation measures in the fields of establishment and services.

5.2.5 The specific part: a partial lifting of the prohibition of harmonisation in the fields of public health and culture

The Community as guardian of the internal market is, as stated before, obliged to take account of horizontal and flanking policy interests. In the fields of the environment and consumer policy the Community has been granted specific powers allowing for the adoption of harmonisation measures which could, far from the objective of market integration, lead to wholly Treaty conform legislation. The Transfer of Waste Regulation is a particularly good example of far-reaching legislation implementing environmental principles and restricting the functioning of the internal market.[168]

Public health

Recommendation (9): Article 152 EC (public health) should be revised with a view to grant the Community legislature the necessary powers to adopt minimum harmonisation measures in the field of public health in general; the organisation of the health care system, however, must remain the primary responsibility of the national state.

In the fields of public health (and culture) the exclusion of harmonisation makes this type of legislation more difficult. Not even a dual legal basis belongs to one of the possibilities. Nonetheless, where a common will exists to regulate serious cross-border health problems, the Community legislature must, in the light of the *Tobacco* cases, be able to adopt harmonisation measures.[169] But the threshold requirements must be met and the extent to which principles of public health policy are implemented remains uncertain. Hence, measures, for example to combat cross-border health sources as well as measures having the direct object to protect health regarding tobacco or alcohol, should still be restricted to incentive measures and cannot constitute harmonisation of national laws.

---

[168] See Chapter 4, section 5.1.2.

[169] See also Opinion AG Geelhoed in Case C-491/01, *BAT/Imperial Tobacco*, paragraphs 113-114: "If it were not possible to use the power under Article 95 EC in order to harmonise standards in the area of public health, an important instrument in the realisation of the internal market would thereby be rendered ineffective. As I have already pointed out, it frequently turns out to be precisely the justified national measures of public-health protection that create barriers to trade. Stated briefly, Article 152 complements the already existing EC Treaty powers such as Article 95. The exception in Article 152(4)(c) means simply that Article 152 EC cannot provide a legal basis for harmonisation, but it makes no reference to legal bases included elsewhere in the Treaty. Article 152(4)(c) does not limit, *ratione materiae*, the power to harmonise national measures within the area of public health."

For the Community therefore, in order to be able to resolve the tension without being restrained by internal market requirements, specific harmonisation powers may be desirable.

Hence, a wider scope of the public health paragraph is advocated and to be preferred to a more extensive reading of Article 95 EC. An extension of the scope of powers under Article 152 EC also reinforces the 'centre of gravity' theory, implying that the choice of the legal basis must be determined according to its main object. It was held in Chapter 4 that the centre of gravity theory has been put into jeopardy by the *Tobacco* cases, but this is only true insofar as there is no alternative legal basis for the harmonisation of horizontal and flanking policies, like in the field of public health.[170]

The creation of an alternative legal basis for harmonisation measures in Article 152 EC should be accompanied by a minimum provision, allowing Member States, similarly to Articles 176 EC (environmental policy) and 153(5) EC (consumer policy), to adopt more stringent, if not the highest possible, standards of protection. In order to prevent the health care sector (the social security systems in general) to become subject to harmonisation at Community level, a provision stipulating that the organisation of the health care system remains the primary responsibility of the national state must remain in Article 152(5) EC.

Culture

Recommendation (10): Article 151 EC (culture) should be revised, including a provision that grants the Community legislature the power to adopt minimum harmonisation measures with a view to promote and protect its common cultural heritage; at the same time the provision stipulates "Community action in the field of culture shall fully respect the responsibilities of Member States for the protection of their national and regional cultures".

Whereas a proposal to revise the public health paragraph may not encounter too much opposition, a similar proposal to amend Article 151 EC, the cultural paragraph, probably will. Without putting into question the importance of the principle of subsidiarity in the cultural field, in particular in order to respect national and regional cultural diversity, the cultural paragraph could be revised granting the Community the necessary legislative powers to pursue common, transcending, cultural interests. A possibility to issue harmonisation measures on the basis of Article 151 EC could end the present situation of fragmentary and incomprehensive cultural policies based on, for example, the internal market legal bases, such as the Directive on the return of cultural objects, or the legal basis for industrial policy, such as the Decision promoting linguistic diversity of the Community in the information society.

In my opinion a positive and comprehensive Community cultural policy should be able to be developed, whereby the more universal concept of 'common

[170] Chapter 4, section 4.2.4.

cultural heritage' is the starting point for Community action. Although Article 151 EC does not give a definition of 'common cultural heritage', which will need to be further developed and explained in the political process by the Community legislature, it does constitute a lead for Community action harmonising aspects of national cultural policies with cross-border effects. The development of a Community cultural policy, however, must not envisage the substitution of national and regional cultures for a European culture. Cultural policy will remain primarily a national affair, but where common cultural interests, like the protection of cultural artefacts – for example the 'Nightwatch' or the great works of the Italian artist Bernini -, the protection of cultural heritage sites, like the ancient town of Pompeii, or even the promotion of literature and languages, are at stake, common action should not be excluded from the outset.

The concept of 'common cultural heritage' allows the Community to impose upon Member States obligations not only to preserve important cultural objects, but also to grant public access to them for at least all European citizens *and* at reasonable prices. Minimum standards could be set at a Community level for the protection of cultural heritage sites to prevent them from collapsing or further degradation, or for the protection of regional and minority languages. But also in fostering valuable cultural interests of audio-visual policies minimum and binding standards, for example, in respect of the broadcasting of European television programmes could be agreed upon at Community level.

However, where national cultural policies concern typically national, regional or cultural interests, like the promotion and distribution of books in the national language, Community intervention by, for example, introducing a fixed book price at Community level and thereby harmonising national systems of fixed book prices or replacing other national instruments to support books, is not justified on the basis of Article 152 EC. It is the responsibility of the Member States to choose the instrument that is most suitable to attain these cultural aims.

Hence, the main focus for Community action should be the notion of 'common cultural heritage' and cultural policies that clearly have cross-border effects. With a view to this, Article 151(5) EC should be amended as to include a specific provision stipulating that the Council shall adopt measures to promote and protect its common cultural heritage; these measures shall not prevent any Member State from maintaining or introducing more stringent national provisions (minimum clause).

Other incentive measures designed to protect and improve cultural interests generally may be adopted "excluding any harmonisation of the laws and regulations". The same paragraph also stipulates that "Community action in the field of culture shall fully respect the responsibilities of Member States for the protection of their national and regional cultures".

6 Epilogue: no unequivocal solution to the tense problem of tension

The plea for an – albeit limited – extension of Community powers to support Europe's common cultural heritage seems rather daring, particularly considering the times we live in where the emergence of a transnational European identity[171] has slowed down and where Member States seem more than ever withdrawn into themselves. Daring as it may seem, however, it forms part of a number of essential suggestions for making the relationship between the internal market and horizontal and flanking policies more balanced, orderly and harmonious, which, according to Plato in *The Republic*, are precisely the basic notions for a healthy [European] society.

The present Treaty framework leaves room for a number of solutions to the problem of tension, solutions which in their turn are based on general principles of Community law. Hereby it has been made clear that not only the Community Institutions must take initiatives in seeking to resolve the problem of the tension, but also that national bodies involved in the law-making and policy-making processes have important responsibilities and obligations in bringing the internal market and horizontal and flanking policies to closer harmony.

The various ways in which the Member States can contribute to closer harmony are based upon the old but well-preserved principles of proportionality and Community loyalty. In taking account of these principles the adoption of regulatory instruments – for example to support books as cultural medium – that are too restrictive to free movement and competition can be prevented. Depending on the regulatory instrument used – for example fixed book prices *by law*, or fixed prices by *self-regulation* – and the horizontal and flanking policy interest concerned – for example the protection of the environment or the protection of consumers – the margin of discretion for Member States to pursue horizontal and flanking policy interests is more or less limited.

At the same time the Community Institutions themselves are also under an obligation to attain closer harmony between horizontal and flanking policies and the internal market. This obligation has been based upon the convergence process between the free movement rules, the integration principle and the broad scope of application of Article 95 EC, and the other internal market legal bases after the Court's rulings in the *Tobacco* cases. The Community Institutions will also have to face the (inherently substantive) differences between horizontal and flanking policies and the differences between the various actors involved in the regulatory process – public authorities, public undertakings, semi-public/private undertakings and 'normal' private undertakings – in applying the free movement and competition rules. The Community legislature, in

[171] See also with respect to European identity now and in the future: Van Gerven (2005), pp. 48-51.

using internal market legal bases for the harmonisation of horizontal and flanking policies, will also have to realise that differences exist between horizontal and flanking policies.

For a variety of reasons explained in this book a certain 'messiness' in the relationship between the internal market and horizontal and flanking policies remains, which, from a legal perspective, could best be cleared away by amending the EC Treaty. Amending the Treaty provides the possibility to (re)define judicial interpretations, to limit judicial activism and to give a more decisive answer on the question within which framework the Community Courts, the European Commission in competition cases and the Community legislature should settle disputes over competing demands of market integration and horizontal and flanking policy interests. But in amending the Treaty, it must be realised that no equivocal solution to the problem of tension can or probably will be found. Irrespective of converging tendencies, differences between in particular the free movement rules and the competition rules, as well as between horizontal and flanking policies, either because they are inherently different or because of differences between competences, are here to stay. In the light of these differences, and in the light of changing attitudes and expectations concerning the correct balance between Community powers and national powers in regulating horizontal and flanking policies a flexible approach remains important. But as this book has shown, this does not mean that Plato's praise in *The Republic* for harmony and order cannot find a response in Community law.

Bibliography

Albers, H.S.J., *Europees Gemeenschapsrecht en Cultuur: Eenheid en Verscheidenheid* (Kluwer, Deventer, 1999)

Alberts, J. and J. van Barschot, Machtsgreep in medialand, *NRC Handelsblad*, 10-03-2000, p. 3.

Algera, W.T., Is de ZBO-Status voor de NMa nu al wenselijk?, in: J.W. van de Gronden and R.J.G.M. Widdershoven (Eds), *Mededingingsautoriteiten als zelfstandig bestuursorgaan: onafhankelijk toezicht?* (Kluwer, Deventer, 2000), pp. 93-143

Appelman, M. & M. Canoy, Notes and Communications. Horses for courses: why Europe should not harmonise its book policies, *De Economist*, 2002, pp. 583-600.

Backhaus, J. & R. Hansen, Resale Price Maintenance for Books in Germany and the European Union : A Legal and Economic Analysis, paper of 12 June 2000, to be found at : http: //edata.ub.unimaas.nl/www-edocs/file.asp?id=341

Bailey, D., Scope of judicial review under Article 81 EC, *CMLRev.*, 2004, pp. 1327-1360

Banks, D., Non-Competition Factors and their Future Relevance under European Merger Law, *ECLR*, 1997, pp. 182-186

Baquero Cruz, J., *Between Competition and Free Movement – The Economic Constitutional Law of the European Community* (Hart Publishing, Oxford and Portland, 2002)

Barendt, E., Towards a European Media Law?, *MJ*, 1994, pp. 41-55

Barents, R., Milieu en interne markt, *SEW*, 1993, pp. 5-29

Barnard, C., *The substantive law of the EU: the four freedoms* (Oxford University Press, Oxford, 2004)

Basedow, J., Zielkonflikte und Zielhierarchien im Vertrag über die EG, in: O. Due, M. Lutter & J. Schwarze (Eds), *Festschrift für Ulrich Everling* (Nomos Verlagsgesellschaft, Baden-Baden, 1995), pp. 49-68

Bavasso, A.F., Case C-368/95, *Vereinigte Familiapress Zeitungsverlags- und vertriebs GmbH v. Heinrich Bauer Verlag*, Judgment of 26 June 1997, ECR [1997] I-3689, *CMLRev.*, 1998, pp. 1413-1426

Bekkers, V., A.J.C. de Moor-van Vught and W. Voermans, Going Dutch: problems and policies concerning the implementation of EU legislation in the Netherlands, in: P. Craig and C. Harlow, *Lawmaking in the European Union* (Kluwer Law International, London; the Hague, 1998), pp. 454-478

Belhaj, S. and J.W. van de Gronden, Some Room for Competition Does Not Make a Sickness Fund An Undertaking. Is EC Competition Law Applicable to the Health Care Sector (Joined Cases C-264/01, C-306/01, C-453/01 and C-355/01 *AOK*), *ECLR*, 2004, pp. 682-687

Bellamy & Child (Edited by P.M. Roth QC), *European Community Law of Competition* (Sweet & Maxwell, London, 2001)

Berg, W., *Gesundheitsschutz als Aufgabe der EU* (Nomos Verlagsgesellschaft, Baden-Baden, 1997)

Bergkamp, L., Corporate Governance and Social Responsibility: a New Sustainability Paradigm, *EELR*, 2002, pp. 136-152

Bermann, G.A., Proportionality and Subsidiarity, in: C. Barnard and J. Scott (Eds), *The Law of the Single European Market, Unpacking the Premises* (Hart Publishing, Oxford and Portland, 2002), pp. 75-99

Bernard, N., *Multilevel governance in the European Union* (Kluwer Law International, The Hague, 2002)

Biondi, A., The merchant, the thief & the citizen: The circulation of works of art within the European Union *CMLRev.*, 1997, pp. 1173-1195
Biondi, A., The Gardener and other Stories: the Peregrinations of Cultural Artefacts within the European Union, in: R. Craufurd Smith (Ed.), *Culture and European Union Law* (Oxford University Press, Oxford, 2004), pp. 153-165
Bongaerts, J., Carbon Dioxide Emissions and Cars: An Environmental Agreement at EU Level, *EELR*, 1999, p. 101-104
Bork, R.H., *The Antitrust Paradox, a Policy at War with Itself* (Basic Books, New York, 1978)
Bronckers, M. and R. van der Vlies, The European Court's PreussenElektra Judgement: Tensions Between E.U. Principles and National Renewable Energy Initiatives, *ECLR*, 2001, pp. 458-468
Buendia Sierra, J.L., *Exclusive rights and state monopolies under EC law- Article 86 (formerly Article 90) of the EC Treaty* (Oxford University Press, Oxford, 1999)
Callies, Ch., Die neue Querschnittsklausel des Art. 6 ex 3c EGV als Instrument zur Umsetzung des Grundsatzes der Nachhaltigen Entwicklung, *DVBL* 1998, pp. 559-567
Callies, Ch. and M. Ruffert (Eds); Bearbeitet von: H.-J. Blanke et al, *Kommentar des Vertrages über die Europäische Union und des Vertrages zur Gründung der Europäischen Gemeinschaft: EUV/EGV* (Luchterhand, Neuwied, 2002)
Chalmers, D., Repackaging the Internal Market - The Ramifications of the Keck Judgment, *ELRev.*, 1994, pp. 385-404
Chalmers, D., The Single Market: From Prima Donna to Journeyman, in: Jo Shaw and Gillian More (Eds), *New Legal Dynamics of European Union* (Clarendon Press, Oxford, 1995), pp. 55-72
Chung, C.-M., The Relationship between State Regulation and EC Competition Law: Two Proposals for a Coherent Approach, *ECLR*, 1995, pp. 87-97
Closson, P., Penalty Shot: The European Union's Application of Competition Law to the Bosman Ruling, *Boston College International & Comparative Law Review*, 1998, pp. 167-182
Commentaire Mégret, *Le droit de la CE*, Volume 8 - Culture, Santé, Consommateurs, Reseaux Transeuropéens, Recherche et Developpement Technologique, Environnement, Energie (Editions de l'Université de Bruxelles, Bruxelles, 1996).
Craig, P., The evolution of the single market, in: C. Barnard and J. Scott (Eds), *The law of the single European market – unpacking the premises* (Hart Publishing, Oxford and Portland, 2002), pp. 1-40
Craig, P., Clarity, conferral, containment and consideration, *ELRev.* 2004, p. 323-344
Cseres, K.J., *Competition law and Consumer Protection* (Kluwer Law International, The Hague, 2005)
Davies, G., Welfare as a Service, *LIEI*, 2002, pp. 27-40
Davies, G., Can selling arrangements be harmonised?, *ELRev.*, 2005, pp.370-385
Denys, Ch., European Court of Justice: Case Report (Case C-213/96, Outokumpu Oy), *EELR*, 1998, pp. 282-288
Denys, Ch, European Court of Justice: Case Report (Case C-67/97: The Kriminalret i Frederikshavn (Denmark) v Ditlev Bluhme), *EELR*, 1999, pp. 82-89
De Vrey, R.W., Eerlijk is eerlijk: de consument voorop? Het richtlijnvoorstel 'oneerlijke handelspraktijken' nader bezien, *TvC*, 2004, pp.2-11

De Vries, S., European Court of Justice: Case Report (Case C-379/98, PreussenElektra AG and Schleswag AG), *EELR*, 2001, pp. 193-205

De Vries, S., Culture and competition, an ambivalent relationship?, in: U. Bernitz, and E. Edwardsson (Eds), *Konkurrens på reglerade marknader – Hur långt kan konkurrenslagen tillämpas?* (Juridiska Fakulteten Nr 59 Skriftserien, Stockholm, 1999), pp. 245-291

De Vries, S., Cultuur en Mededinging: harmonie of dissonantie?, in: J.W. van de Gronden and K.J.M. Mortelmans (Eds), *Mededinging en niet-economische belangen* (Kluwer, Deventer, 2001), pp. 89-128

De Vries, S., Consumer Interests and the Dutch Competition Act: an ambivalent relationship?, *TvC*, 2002, p. 161-168

Devroe, W. Privatizations and Community Law: Neutrality versus Policy, *CMLRev.*, 1997, pp. 267-306

De Witte, B., The Cultural Dimension of Community Law, in: Academy of European Law (Ed.), *Collected Courses of the Academy of European Law*, Volume IV, Book 1 (Kluwer Law International, The Hague, 1995), pp. 229-299

De Witte, B., Language Law of the European Union: Protecting or Eroding Linguistic Diversity?, in: R. Craufurd Smith (Ed.), *Culture and European Union Law*, (Oxford University Press, Oxford, 2004), pp. 205-241

De Zwaan, J.W., The Netherlands (judiciary and authorities) and Article 10 of the EC Treaty – Report for FIDE 2000, XIX Congress, Helsinki 1-3 June 2000, *SEW*, 2000, pp. 132-154

Dhondt, N., *Integration of Environmental Protection into other EC Policies. Legal Theory and Practice* (Europa Law Publishing, Groningen, 2003)

Dougan, M., Minimum harmonization and the internal market, *CMLRev.*, 2000, pp. 853-885

Drahos, M., *Convergence of competition laws and policies in the European Community: Germany, Austria and the Netherlands* (Kluwer Law International, The Hague, 2001)

Drijber, B.J., The revised television without frontiers directive: is it fit for the next century?, *CMLRev.*, 1999, pp. 87-122

Drijber, B.J., Zaak C-379/98, Preussen Elektra AG/Schleswag AG, *SEW*, 2001, pp. 400-403

Drijber, B.J. and G.R.J. de Groot, Een nieuw stelsel van zorgverzekering. Toetsing aan het gemeenschapsrecht en het internationale recht, advies van de landsadvocaat, Den Haag, 4 December 2002

Drijber, B.J., Kroniek 2002: stilte voor de storm?, *M&M*, 2003, pp. 73-74

Drijber, B.J. and W.T. Algera, Consorzio Industrie Fiammifieri (CIF)/Autoritá Garante della Concorrenza e del Mercato, HvJ EG, 9 september 2003, zaak C-198/01 – De NMa zal nationale wettelijke regelingen die strijdig zijn met het Europese mededingingsrecht buiten toepassing *moeten* laten, *M&M*, 2003, pp. 247-253

Drijber, B.J., Vrij verkeer van diensten - De bezems van Bolkestein, *NTER*, 2004, pp. 112-120

Drijber, B.J., Reactie op: De Wet op de vaste boekenprijs en het mededingingsrecht, *Mediaforum*, 2005, pp 232-234

Drijber, B.J., Joined Cases C-264/01, C-306/01, C-453/01 and C-355/01, *AOK Bundesverband a.o.*, judgment of the Full Court of 16 March 2004, not yet reported, *CMLRev.*, 2005, pp. 523-533

D'Sa, R. M., *European Community law on state aid* (Sweet & Maxwell, London, 1998)

Eberl, W., Probleme und Auswirkungen der EG-Vorschriften zum Kulturgüterschutz, *NVwZ*, 1994, pp. 729-735

Edward, D. and M. Hoskins, Article 90: Deregulation and EC Law. Reflections arising form the XVI FIDE Conference, *CMLRev.*, 1995, pp. 157-186

Ehle, D., *Die Einbeziehung des Umweltschutzes in das Europäische Kartellrecht* (Carl Heymanns Verlag, Köln [etc.], 1996)

Ehlermann, C.D., The internal market following the Single European Act, *CMLRev.*, 1987, pp.361-409

Emiliou, N., *The Principle of Proportionality in European Law – A Comparative Study* (Kluwer Law International, London, The Hague [etc.], 1996)

Everling, U., B. Rürup, and S. Füssel, *Die Buchpreisbindung aus europarechtlicher, ökonomischer und kulturhistorischer Sicht* (Nomos Verlagsgesellschaft, Baden-Baden, 1997)

Farber, D.E. and R.E. Hudec, Gatt Legal Restraints on Domestic Environmental Regulations, in: J.N. Bhagwati and R.E. Hudec (Eds), *Fair Trade and Harmonization – Prerequisites for Free Trade*, volume II (The MIT Press, Cambridge, 1996), pp. 59-94

Faull, J. and A. Nikpay (Eds), *The EC Law of Competition* (Oxford University Press, Oxford, 1999)

Fishwick, F., *The economic implications of the Net Book Agreement: A Report to the Councils of Booksellers Associations and the Publishers Association* (Publishers Association & Booksellers Association, London,1989)

Flear, M., Case C-385/99, *V.G. Müller-Fauré* v. *Onderlinge Waarborgmaatschappij O.Z. Zorgverzekeringen U.A.* and *E.E.M. van Riet* v. *Onderlinge Waarborgmaatschappij Z.A.O. Zorgverzekeringen*, Judgment of the Court of 13 May 2003, *CMLRev.*, 2004, pp. 209-234

Gehring, T., *Die EG-Umweltpolitik im Spannungsfeld von Umweltschutz und Binnenmarktpolitik. Vortrag an der "Konferenz über ‚Regulative Politik in Europa`des Arbeitskreises Europäische Integration der Deutschen Vereinigung für Politische Wissenschaft"*, Köln, 8. Dezember 1995

George, S., Politics and Policy in the European Union (Oxford University Press, London, 1996)

Gerard, D. Merger control policy: How to give meaningful consideration to efficiency claims?, *CMLRev.*, 2003, pp. 1367-1412

Geradin, D., Trade and the environment: a comparative study of EC and US law (Cambridge University Press, Cambridge, 1997)

Geradin, D., EC Competition Law and Environmental Protection: Conflict or Compatibility?, in: H. Somsen (Ed.), *Yearbook of European Environmental Law* (Oxford University Press, Oxford, 2002)

Giesen, R. Die Konkurrenz von freiwilliger Socialversicherung und Privatversicherung im europäischer Wettbewerbsrecht, *VSSR*, 1996, pp. 311-341

Giesen, R., Case C-120/95, *Nicolas Decker v. Caisse de maladie des employés privés*, Judgment of 28 April 1998, [1998] ECR I-1831; Case C-158/96, *Raymond Kohll v. Union des caisses de maladie*, Judgment of 28 April 1998, [1998] ECR I-1935, *CMLRev.*, 1999, pp. 841-850

Gilliams, H., Modernisation: from policy to practice, *ELRev.*, 2003, p. 451-474

Golfinopoulos, Ch., Concept of Selectivity Criterion in State Aid Definition Following the *Adria-Wien* Judgment – Measures Justified by the "Nature or General Scheme of a System", *ECLR*, 2003, pp. 543-548

Goossens, A and S. Emmerechts, Case C-379/98, *PreussenElektra AG v. Schleswag AG*, Judgment of the Full Court of 13 March 2001, *CMLRev.*, 2001, pp. 991-1010

Goyder, D.G., *EC Competition* Law (Oxford University Press, Oxford, 2003)

Gyselen, L., Anti-Competitive State Measures under the EC Treaty: Towards a Substantive Legality Standard (Competition Checklist 1993), *ELRev.* 1993, pp. CC55-CC89

Gyselen, L., The emerging interface between competition policy and environmental policy in the EC, in: J. Cameron, P. Demaret and D. Geradin (Eds), *Trade and the environment – the search for a balance* (Cameron May, London, 1994), pp. 242-260

Gyselen, L., Case C-67/96, *Albany v. Stichting Bedrijfspensioenfonds Textielindustrie*; Joined Cases C-115-117/97, *Brentjens' Handelsonderneming v. Stichting Bedrijfspensioenfonds voor de handel in bouwmaterialen*; and Case C-219/97, *Drijvende Bokken v. Stichting Pensioenfonds voor de vervoer- en havenbedrijven*, Judgments of the Full Court of 21 September 1999, not yet reported, *CMLRev.*, 2000, pp. 425-448

Häde, U., BVerfG: Beteiligungsrechte der Länder und Verhalten des Bundes beim Zustandekommen von EG-Rechtsakten, *EuZW*, 1995, pp. 277-285

Hahn, M.J., Eine kulturelle Bereichsausnahme im Recht der WTO?, *ZaöRV*, 1996, pp. 315-352

Hamilton, G. J., News & Views - Private Insurance for All in the Dutch Health Care System? *European Journal of Health Law*, 2003, pp. 53-62

Hancher, L., Case C-320/91 P, *Procureur du Roi v. Paul Corbeau*, Judgment of the full Court, 19 May 1993, *CMLRev.*, 1994, pp. 105-122

Hancher, L., Community, State, and Market, in: Paul Craig and Gráinne de Búrca (Eds), *The Evolution of EU Law* (Oxford University Press, Oxford, 1999), pp. 721-743

Hancher, L., T. Ottervanger and P. J. Slot, *E.C. State Aids* (Sweet & Maxwell, London, 1999)

Hatzopoulos, V.G., *Killing* national health and insurance systems but *healing* patients? The European Market for health care services after the judgments of the ECJ in *Vanbraekel* and *Peerbooms*, *CMLRev.*, 2002, pp. 683-729

Hatzopoulos, V., Case C-418/01, *IMS Health GmbH v. NDC Health GmbH*, Judgment of the Fifth Chamber of 29 April 2004, nyr., *CMLRev.*, 2004, pp. 1613-1638

Haverland, M., *National autonomy, European integration and the politics of packaging waste* (Dissertation, Utrecht, 1998)

Hawk, B., System failure: Vertical restraints and EC competition law, *CMLRev.*, 1995, pp. 973-989

Heldeweg, M.A., R.J.G.H. Seerden and K. Deketelaere, Public Environmental Law in Europe; a comparative search for a *ius commune*, *EELR*, pp. 84-85

Herdegen, M., After the TV judgement of the German Constitutional Court: decision-making within the EU Council and the German Länder, *CMLRev.*, 1995, pp. 1369-1384

Hervey, T.K., Up in smoke? Community (anti-)tobacco law and policy, *ELRev.*, 2001, pp. 101-125

Hessel, B. and A. Neven, *Staatssteun en EG-Recht* (Kluwer, Deventer, 2001)

Hessel, B., Ontwikkelingen rond staatssteun en diensten van algemeen economisch belang na het Altmark-arrest, at: www.europadecentraal.nl

Hessel, B., Essent vs. Gemeente Appingedam, *Mediaforum* 2004, pp. 327-330

Hilson, Ch., Greening Citizenship: Boundaries of Membership and the Environment, *Journal of Environmental Law*, 2001, pp. 335-348

Houdijk, J., De nieuwe Wet op de vaste boekenprijs: immuun voor het mededingingsrecht?, *Mediaforum*, 2005, pp. 148-156

Howells, G. and S. Weatherill, *Consumer Protection Law* (Ashgate Publishing, Aldershot, 2005)
Howells, G. and T. Wilhelmsson, EC consumer law: has it come of age?, *ELRev.* 2003, pp. 370-388
Jacobs, R., EEC Competition Law and the Protection of the Environment, *Legal Issues of European Integration*, 1993, p. 37-67
Jans, J.H., Zaak C-391/92, Commissie tegen Griekenland, *SEW*, 1996, pp. 385-386
Jans, J.H., Gevoegde zaken C-321/94 t/m C-324/94; strafzaken t. Pistre e.a., *SEW*, 1998, pp. 110-113
Jans, J. H., *European environmental law* (Europa Law Publishing, Groningen, 2000)
Jans, J. H., Proportionality revisited, *LIEI*, 2000, pp. 239-265
Jarvis, M., *The Application of EC Law by National Courts. The Free Movement of Goods* (Oxford University Press, Oxford, 1998)
Joerges, Ch., The market without the state? States without a market? : two essays on the law of the European Economy, *EUI Working Paper* No. 96/2.
Joerges, Ch., Integrating Scientific Expertise into Regulatory Decision-Making, *EUI Working Paper* RSC No. 96/10
Jones, A. and B. Sufrin, *EC Competition Law* (Oxford University Press, Oxford, 2004)
Kapteyn, P.J.G. and P. VerLoren van Themaat, (edited by L.W. Gormley), *Introduction to the Law of the European Communities* (Kluwer, London, 1998)
Kapteyn, P.J.G. and P. VerLoren van Themaat, *Het recht van de Europese Unie en van de Europese Gemeenschappen* (Kluwer, Deventer, 2003)
Koenig, Ch. And J. Kühling, Mitgliedstaatliche Kulturförderung und gemeinschaftrechtliche Beihilfekontrolle, *EuZW*, 2000, pp. 197-203
Krajewski, M. and M. Farley, Limited competition in national health systems and the application of competition law: the *AOK Bundesverband* case, *ELRev.*,2004, pp. 842-851
Krämer, L., H.-W. Mickliz and K. Tonner (Eds), *Law and diffuse interests in the European legal order – Recht und diffuse Interessen in der europäischen Rechtsordnung: liber amicorum Norbert Reich* (Nomos Verlagsgesellschaft, Baden-Baden, 1997)
Krämer, L., Thirty Years of EC Environmental Law: Perspectives and Prospects, in: H. Somsen (Ed.), *Yearbook of European Environmental Law* (Oxford University Press, Oxford, 2002), pp. 156-182
Kreijger, P., De financiering van de publieke omroep in Europa: nieuw beleid van de Europese Commissie, *Mediaforum*, 2003, pp. 82-87.
Krieglstein, F.B., Renewable Energy Schemes and EC State Aids Provisions, *EELR*, 2001, pp. 51-56
Lane, R., New Community competences under the Maastricht Treaty, *CMLRev.*, 1993, p. 939-979
Lane, R. and N. Nic Shuibhne, *CMLRev.*, 2000, p. 1237-1247
Langbein, H.B., *Die Buchpreisbindung in der EWG* (Lang, Frankfurt am Main, 1989)
Langer, J. and J. Wiers, De eeuwige strijd tussen het goederenverkeer, milieubescherming en het evenredigheidsbeginsel: Oostenrijks slachtvee en opnieuw flessen en blikjes uit Denemarken, *Milieu & Recht*, 2001, pp. 62-65
Lauwaars, R.H., De verhouding tussen de Europese en nationale fusiecontrole: de zaak Champalimaud, *SEW*, 2002, pp. 228-231

Lenaerts, K. and D. Gerard, Decentralisation of EC Competition Law Enforcement: Judges in the Frontline, *World Competition*, 2004, pp. 313-349

Loman, A., Mortelmans, K.J.M., Post, H. and Watson, S., *Culture and Community Law - Before and After Maastricht* (Kluwer, Deventer, 1992)

Loozen, E.M.H., Pavlov en Van der Woude: meer dan een Pavlov-reactie?, *NTER*, 2000, pp. 301-307

Louri, V., 'Undertaking' as a Jurisdictional Element for the Application of the EC Competition Rules, *LIEI*, 2002, pp. 143-176

Lowe, P., Media Concentration and Convergence: Competition in Communications, Speech of 13 January 2004, delivered at the Oxford Media Convention 2004, at: http://www.europa.eu.int/comm/competition/speeches//text/sp2004_002_en.pdf

Lugard, P. and L. Hancher, Honey, I shrunk the Article! A Critical Assessment of the Commission's Notice on Article 81(3) of the EC Treaty, *ECLR*, 2004, pp. 410-420

Luijendijk, J., Zaak C-274/96, Bickel en Franz, *SEW*, 1999, pp. 346-350

Luijendijk, H., *Nederlandse gemeenten en het Europese personenverkeer – Een onderzoek naar de consequenties van het personenverkeer voor de beleidsterreinen burgerzaken en ruimtelijke ordening en huisvesting* (Kluwer, Deventer, 2004)

MacMaoláin, C., Free movement of foodstuffs, quality requirements and consumer protection: have the Court and the Commission both got it wrong?, *ELRev.*, 2001, pp. 413-428

Maduro, M.P., *We the Court: the European Court of Justice and the European economic constitution: a critical reading of Article 30 of the EC Treaty* (Hart Publishing, Oxford, 1998)

Majone, G., The European Community between social policy and social regulation, *EUI Working Paper*, 1993, No. 92/27

Maks, J.H., The "New" Horizontal Agreements Approach in the EU: an "economic" assessment, paper presented at the Workshop on "Reform of EC Competition Policy Jointly organised by EIPA and HWWA, 10-11 December 2001, Maastricht

Mattera, A. La libre circulation des oeuvres d'art à l'intérieur de la Communauté et la protection des trésors nationaux ayant une valeur artistique, historique or archéologique, *Revue du Marché Unique Européen*, 1993, pp. 9-31

Merryman, J. H., Thinking About the Elgin Marbles, *Michigan Law Review*, 1985, pp. 1881-1923

Merryman, J. H., The Public Interest in Culture Property, *California Law Review*, 1989, pp. 339-364

Micklitz, H.-W. and S. Weatherill, Consumer Policy in the European Community: Before and After Maastricht, *Journal of Consumer Policy*, 1993, pp. 285-321

Micklitz, H.-W., N. Reich and S. Weatherill, EU Treaty Revision and Consumer Protection, *Journal of Consumer Policy*, 2004, p. 367-399

Mok, M.R., Zaak C-360/92P, (Publishers Association – Net Book Agreement). Hogere voorziening van een arrest van het GEA EG, d.d. 9 juli 1992, T-66/89, Jur. 1992, p. II-1995, *SEW*, 1996, pp. 138-141

Mok, M.R., Naar een wettelijke vaste boekenprijs? Een initiatiefvoorstel, *Ondernemingsrecht*, 2003, pp. 4-8

Monti, G., Article 81 EC and public policy, *CMLRev.*, 2002, pp. 1057-1099

Mortelmans, K.J.M., De interne markt en het facettenbeleid na het Keck-arrest: nationaal beleid, vrij verkeer of harmonisatie, *SEW*, 1994, pp. 236-250

Mortelmans, K. and S. Watson, The notion of the consumer in community law: a lottery?, *TvC*, 1995, pp. 229-246
Mortelmans, K. and R. Wezenbeek-Geuke, Staatssteun in de Nederlandse omroepsector en de artikelen 92-93 EG Verdrag, *Mediaforum*, 1997, pp. 104-112
Mortelmans, K., The common market, the internal market and the single market, what's in a market?, *CMLRev.*, 1998, pp. 101-136
Mortelmans, K.J.M. and M.G. Wezenbeek-Geuke, annotatie van Gevoegde zaken C-51/96 en C-191/97, C. Deliège t. Ligue francophone de judo et disciplines associées (LFJ) en Ligue belge de judo (LBJ) en Zaak C-176/96, Jyri Lehtonen, Castors Canada Dry Namur-Braine t. Fédération royale belge des sociétés de basket-ball (FRBSB), *SEW*, 2000, pp. 425-432
Mortelmans, K.J.M., Milieubeleid en mededingingsrecht: onvermijdelijke confrontatie en gewenste integratie, *NTER*, 2000, pp. 21-28
Mortelmans, K.J.M., Europeesrechtelijke complicaties bij de afname van milieuvriendelijke electriciteit (ZaakC-379/98, *PreussenElektra*), *AA*, 2001, pp. 475-492
Mortelmans, K.J.M. and R.H. van Ooik, Het Europese verbod op tabaksreclame: verbetering van de interne markt of bescherming van de volksgezondheid? (Zaak C-376/98, *Duitsland t. Europees Parlement en Raad*), *AA*, 2001, pp. 114-129
Mortelmans, K., Towards convergence in the application of the rules on free movement and on competition?, *CMLRev.*, 2001, pp. 613-649
Mortelmans, K., The relationship between the Treaty rules and Community measures for the establishment and functioning of the internal market - Towards a concordance rule, *CMLRev.*, 2002, pp. 1303-1346
Mortelmans, K.J.M., Botsende algemene belangen en de werking van de interne markt, *SEW*, 2004, pp. 240-252
Mortelmans, K.J.M., Het Europese verbod om tabaksproducten voor oraal gebruik in de handel te brengen en de speciale positie van de Zweedse snus (Zaak C-210/03, Swedish Match), *AA*, 2005, pp. 160-172
Mortelmans, K.J.M. and J.Luijendijk, Studiefinanciering voor studenten uit andere EU-lidstaten: collegegeld én levensonderhoud?! (Zaak C-209/03, *Bidar*), *AA*, 2005, pp. 488-499
Mossialos, E. and M. McKee (with W. Palm, B. Karl and F. Marhold), *EU Law and the Social Character of Health Care* (Peter Lang, Bruxelles [etc.], 2002)
Mulder, R., Beleid wereldwijd - Boekenprijzen in het Verenigd Koninkrijk, *ESB*, 1999, p. 455
Nebbia, P., Case C-198/01, *Consorzio Industrie Fiammiferi (CIF)* v. *Autorità Garante della Concorrenza e del Mercato*, Judgment of the Full Court of 9 September 2003, *CMLRev.*, 2004, pp. 839-849
Nicolaides, P., Distortive Effects of Compensatory Aid Measures: A Note on the Economics of the *Ferring* Judgment, *ECLR*, 2002, pp. 313-319
Niedobitek, M. Die kulturelle Dimension im Vertrag über die Europäische Union, *EuR*, 1995, pp. 349-376
Nikolinakos, N. Th., Mergers and Strategic Alliances in the Emerging Multi-Media Sector: The EU Competition Policy, *ECLR*, 2004, pp. 625-637
Notaro, N., European Community Waste Movements: the Copenhagen Waste Case, *EELR*, 2000, pp. 304-312
Oliver, P., Some further reflections on the scope of Articles 28-30 (ex 30-36) EC, *CMLRev.*, 1999, pp. 783-806

Oliver, P. (assisted by Malcolm Jarvis), *Free movement of goods* (Sweet & Maxwell, London, 2003)

Oliver, P. and W-H. Roth, The Internal Market and the Four Freedoms, *CMLRev.*, 2004, pp. 407-441

Oliver. P., Competition and Free Movement: Their Place in the Treaty, in: T. Trimidas & P. Nebbia, *European Union Law for the Twenty-First Century – Rethinking the New Legal Order*, Volume 2, Internal Market and Free Movement Community Policies (Hart Publishing, Oxford and Portland, 2004), pp. 159-175

Pelkmans, J., *European integration: methods and economic analysis* (Harlow [etc.] : Prentice Hall/Financial Times, 2001)

Pescatore, P., Some Critical Remarks on the "Single European Act", *CMLRev.*, pp. 9-19

Porter, V., Public Service Broadcasting and European Regulation, *Mediaforum*, 1995, pp. 30-34

Prott, L.V., *Commentary on the Unidroit Convention* (Institute of Art and Law, Leicester, 1997)

Pullen, M., Summary of the Advocate General's Opinion in the Bosman Case, *ECLR*, 1996, pp. 51-58

Quigley, C. and A.M. Collins, *EC State Aid Law and Policy* (Hart Publishing, Oxford and Portland, 2003)

Reich, N., *Förderung und Schutz diffuser Interessen durch die Europäischen Gemeinschaften: eine problemorientierte Einführung in das europäische Wirtschaftsrecht* (Nomos Verlagsgesellschaft, Baden-Baden, 1987)

Reich, N., The "November Revolution" of the European Court of Justice: *Keck, Meng* and *Audi* revisited, *CMLRev.*, 1994, pp. 459-492

Reich, N., Competition law and the consumer, in: L. Gormley (Ed.), *Current and future perspectives on EC competition law: a tribute to professor M.R. Mok* (Kluwer Law International, London, The Hague [etc.], 1997), pp. 127-137

Reich, N. and H.W. Micklitz, *Europäisches Verbraucherrecht* (4th edition, Nomos Verlagsgesellschaft, Baden-Baden, 2003)

Rengeling, H.-W. (Ed.), *Umweltschutz und andere Politiken der Europäischen Gemeinschaft: Referate und Diskussionsberichte* (Heymann, Köln, 1993)

Ress, G. and J. Ukrow, Auswirkungen von Art. 128 Abs. 4 EGV auf die wettbewerbsrechtliche Beurteilung von Buchpreisbindungssytemen, *ZeuS*, 1999, pp. 1-74

Robert, G., Case C-11/92, *R* v. *Secretary of State for Health, Ex Parte Gallaher Ltd (and others)*, Judgment of 22 June 1993, not yet reported, *CMLRev.*, 1994, pp. 165-171

Rose, I. And G. Knighton, Integrated Product Policy: The New Approach to Environmental Regulation, *EELR.*, 1999, pp. 266-269

Ross, M., Article 16 E.C. and services of general interest: from derogation to obligation?, *ELRev.*, 2000, pp. 22-38

Ross, M., The Europeanization of Public Service Supervision: Harnessing Competition and Citizenship?, in: P. Eeckhout and T. Tridimas, *Yearbook of European Law* (Oxford University Press, Oxford, 2004), pp. 303-319

Roth, W.-H., Case C-233/94, *Federal Republic of Germany* v. *European Parliament and Council of the European Union*, Judgment of 13 May 1997, [1997] ECR I-2405, *CMLRev.*, 1998, pp. 459-479

Roth, W.-H., Altruistische Interessewahrnehmung im Binnenmarkt – Eine Skizze, in: *Festschrift für Wolfgang Fikentscher zum 70. Geburtstag* (Mohr Siebeck, Tübingen, 1998), pp. 723-739

Roth, W.-H., Case C-212/97, *Centros Ltd.* v. *Erhvervs- og Selskabsstyrelsen*, Judgment of 9 March 1999. Full Court, *CMLRev.*, 2000, pp. 147-155

Roth, W.-H., Export of Goods and Services within the Single Market: Reflections on the Scope of Articles 29 and 49 EC, in: T. Tridimas & P. Nebbia, *European Union Law for the Twenty-First Century – Rethinking the New Legal Order – Volume 2 Internal Market and Free Movement Community Policies* (Hart Publishing, Oxford and Portland, 2004), pp. 33-48

Rott, P., Minimum harmonisation for the completion of the internal market? The example of consumer sales law, *CMLRev.*, 2003, p. 1107-1135

Scharpf, F.W., European Governance: Common Concerns vs. the Challenge of Diversity, *Jean Monnet Working Paper*, 2001, No. 1/07 to be found at: http://ideas.repec.org/p/erp/jeanmo/p0018.html

Schmall, S., *Die Kulturkompetenz der Europäischen Gemeinschaft* (Nomos Verlagsgesellschaft, Baden-Baden, 1996)

Schmidt, J., The new ECMR: “Significant impediment” or “significant improvement”?, *CMLRev.*, 2004, pp. 1555-1582

Schrauwen, A. A. M., *Marché intérieur: recherches sur une notion* (Dissertation, University of Amsterdam, 1997)

Schröder, M., Die steuernde und marktbergenzende Wirkung umweltschutzrelevanter Prinzipien des EG-Vertrages am Beispiel des Abfallexportes, *NVWZ*, 1996, pp. 833-837

Schuijt, G., Commissie Mediaconcentraties: toezicht overlaten aan NMa, *Mediaforum*, 1999, pp. 140-144.

Scott, J. and E. Vos, The Juridification of Uncertainty: Observations on the Ambivalence of the Precautionary Principle within the EU and the WTO, in: Ch. Joerges and R. Dehousse, *Good Governance in Europe's Integrated Market* (Oxford University Press, Oxford, 2002), pp. 253-286

Scott, J., Mandatory or Imperative Requirements in the EU and the WTO, in: C. Barnard and J. Scott (Eds), *The Law of the Single European Market – Unpacking the Premises* (Hart Publishing, Oxford and Portland, 2002), pp. 269-293

Sevenster, H.G., Eco-Imperialisme binnen de Europese Unie: een juridisch probleem? (W.E.J. Tjeenk Willink, Deventer, 1998)

Sevenster, H., The Environmental Guarantee After Amsterdam: Does the Emperor Have New Clothes, in: H. Somsen (Ed.), *Yearbook of European Environmental Law* (Oxford University Press, Oxford, 2000), pp. 291-310

Sevenster, H. and L. Hancher, Case C-2/90, *Commision v. Belgium*, 9 July 1992, Judgment of the Full Court, not yet reported, *CMLRev.*, 1993, pp. 351-367

Sevenster, H.G. and H.H.B. Vedder, Integreren of concurreren? De rol van niet-mededingingsbelangen, in het bijzonder milieubescherming, in het kartelbeleid, *SEW*, 2000, p. 2-16

Shuibhne, N. Nic, Labels, Locals, and the Free Movement of Goods, in: Rachael Craufurd Smith (Ed.), *Culture and European Union Law* (Oxford University Press, Oxford, 2004), pp. 81-112

Silberschmidt, G., The case for integrating health into Article 6 of the EC Treaty, at: http: //www.epha.org/a/530

Slot, P.J, Harmonisation, *ELRev.*, 1996, pp. 378-398

Slot, P.J. and G. Straetmans, Harmonisatie van wetgeving in de EG (1/2), *Tijdschrift voor privaatrecht*, 2003, pp. 691-839

Sluijs, J.J.M., *Gereguleerde marktwerking van sociale zekerheidsbelangen - Het mededingingsrecht en vrij verkeer van diensten voor zorg- en pensioenbelangen* (Kluwer, Deventer, 2004).

Smiers, J., *The role of the European Community concerning the Cultural Article 151 in the Treaty of Amsterdam* (Centre for Research, Utrecht School of the Arts, Utrecht, 2002)

Smith, R. Craufurd, State Support For Public Service Broadcasting: The Position Under European Community Law, *LIEI*, 2001, pp. 3-22

Smith, R. Craufurd (Ed.), *Culture and European Union Law* (Oxford University Press, Oxford, 2004)

Smith, R. Craufurd, Article 151 EC and European Identity, in: R. Craufurd Smith (Ed.), *Culture and European Union Law* (Oxford University Press, Oxford, 2004), pp. 277-297

Smith, R. Craufurd, Community Intervention in the Cultural Field: Continuity or Change?, in: R. Craufurd Smith (Ed.), *Culture and European Union Law* (Oxford University Press, Oxford, 2004), pp. 19-78

Snell, J., *Goods and services in EC law: a study of the relationship between the freedoms* (Oxford University Press, Oxford, 2002)

Snell, J., And Then There Were Two: Products and Citizens in Community Law, in: T. Trimidas & P. Nebbia (Eds), *European Union Law for the Twenty-First Century – Rethinking the New Legal Order – Volume 2, Internal Market and Free Movement Community Policies* (Hart Publishing, Oxford and Portland, 2004), pp. 49-72

Somek, A., Good news for a bad habit: tobacco, culture and the rule of law in the European Union, available at: http://www.somek.org/Lectures/KSchoolHandout.PDF.

Somsen, H., Dynamics, process and instruments of environmental decision-making in the European Union, in: T. Jewell and J. Steele (Eds), *Law in Environmental Decision-Making* (Clarendon Press, Oxford, 1998), pp. 161-205

Soriano, L.M., How proportionate should anti-competitive State intervention be?, *ELRev.*, 2003, p. 121

Sparr, J., *Kulturhoheit und EWG-Vertrag* (Nomos Verlagsgesellschaft, Baden-Baden, 1991)

Spaventa, E., Case C-254/98, *Schutzverband gegen unlauteren Wettbewerb* v. *TK-Heimdienst Sass GmbH*, Judgment of 13 January 2000, not yet reported, *CMLRev.*, 2000, pp. 1265-1275

Spaventa, E., From *Gebhard* to *Carpenter*: Towards a (non-)economic European constitution, *CMLRev.*, 2004, pp. 743-773

Straetmans, G., Case C-124/97, *Läärä*, Judgment of the Court of 21 September 1999 and Case C-67/98, *Zenatti*, Judgment of the Court of 21 October 1999. Nyr. Full Court, *CMLRev.*, 2000, p. 991-1005

Straetmans, G., Case C-6/01, *Anomar v. Estado português*, Judgment of the Court of 11 September 2003 (Third Chamber), nyr; Case C-243/01, *Piergiorgio Gambelli* e.a., Judgment of the Court of 6 November 2003 (Full Court), nyr; and C-42/02, *Diana Elisabeth Lindman*, Judgment of the Court of 13 November 2003 (Fifth chamber), nyr., *CMLRev.*, 2004, pp. 1409-1428

Stuyck, J., Zaken C-120/95, N. Decker. Caisse de maladie des employés privés en C-158/96, R. Kohll t. Union des caisses de maladie, *SEW*, 1999, pp. 256-262

Stuyck, J., European consumer law after the Treaty of Amsterdam: Consumer Policy in or beyond the internal market?, *CMLRev.*, 2000, pp. 367-400

Stuyck, J., The consumer and European competition policy in the past and next decade, *TvC*, 2002, pp. 154-160

Stuyck, J., M. Waelbroeck, L.P. van Reeken, S.B. Noë. and F.O.W. Vogelaar (Eds), *Competition Law in the EU and the Netherlands - A Practical Guide* (Kluwer, Deventer, 2000)

Temmink, H.A.G., Rode draad 'Sport en Recht': Sport en Europees recht, *AA*, 1996, p. 235-244

Temmink, H.A.G., Het Europees Consumentenbeleid van Maastricht naar Amsterdam en verder, *TvC*, 1997, pp. 273-302

Temmink, H., From Danish Bottles to Danish Bees: The Dynamics of Free Movement of Goods and Environmental Protection – A Case Law Analysis, in: H. Somsen (Ed.), *Yearbook of European Environmental Law* (Oxford University Press, Oxford, 2000), pp. 61-102

Temple Lang, J., Community constitutional law: Article 5 EEC Treaty, *CMLRev.*, 1990, pp. 645-681

Temple Lang, J., The Duties of National Authorities Under Community Constitutional Law, *ELRev.*, 1998, pp. 109-131

Tesauro, G., The Community's Internal Market in the light of the Recent Case-law of the Court of Justice, *Yearbook of European Law*, 1996, pp. 1-16

Tridimas, T., *The General Principles of EC Law* (Oxford University Press, Oxford, 1999)

Uhl, A.-K., *Der Handel mit Kunstwerken im europäischen Binnenmarkt* (Tübinger Schriften zum internationalen und europäische Recht, Duncker & Humblot, Berlin, 1993)

Valcke, P., Autopsie van VTM monopolie leidt niet tot nieuwe resultaten, *Mediaforum*, 2000, pp. 2-6

Van Calster, G., *International and EU trade law: the environmental challenge* (Cameron May, London, 2000)

Van Calster, G., Greening the E.C.'s State Aid and Tax Regimes, *ECLR*, 2000, pp. 294-314

Van Calster, G., The free movement of waste after DaimlerChrysler, *ELRev.*, 2002, pp. 610-617

Van Calster, G., Zaak C-351/98, Spanje t. Commissie, *SEW*, 2003, pp. 39-40

Vandamme, T., Zaak C-434/02, Arnold André GmbH& Co. t. Landrat des Kreises Herford, en zaakC-210/03 The Queen, ex parte Swedish Match AB en Swedish Match UK Ltd t. Secretary of State for Health, *SEW*, 2005, pp. 227-234

Vandamme, T.A.J.A., *The Invalid Directive - The Legal Authority of a Union Act Requiring Domestic Law Making* (Europa Law Publishing, Groningen, 2005)

Van Damme, E.E.C., Op de Welvaartseconomie gebaseerd Mededingingsbeleid, in: J.W. van de Gronden and K.J.M. Mortelmans, *Mededinging en niet-economische belangen* (Kluwer, Deventer, 2001), pp. 55-57

Van de Gronden, J.W., *De implementatie van het EG-milieurecht door Nederlandse decentrale overheden* (Dissertatie, Utrecht, 1998)

Van de Gronden, J.W. and K.J.M. Mortelmans (Eds), *Mededinging en niet-economische belangen* (Kluwer, Deventer, 2001)

Van de Gronden, J.W. and K.J.M. Mortelmans, Het mededingingsrecht en niet-economische belangen: 2003 het cruciale jaar?, in: J.W. van de Gronden and K.J.M. Mortelmans (Eds), *Mededinging en niet-economische belangen* (Kluwer, Deventer, 2001), pp. 307-339

Van de Gronden, J.W., Milieu en mededinging: is milieubescherming alleen een publieke taak of ook onderdeel van de producentenverantwoordelijkheid?, in: J.W. van de Gronden and K.J.M. Mortelmans (Eds), *Mededinging en niet-economische belangen* (Kluwer, Deventer, 2001), pp. 131-178

Van de Gronden, J.W., EG-recht en maatschappelijk middenveld, *SEW*, 2001, 303

Van de Gronden, J.W., annotatie bij de zaak Smits en Peerbooms, de zaak Vanbraekel en de zaak Mac Quen, *SEW*, 2001, pp. 319-331

Van de Gronden, J.W., Mededingingsrecht en gezondheidszorg, *M&M*, 2001, pp. 267-279

Van de Gronden, J.W. and K.J.M. Mortelmans, *Afval, een vruchtbare voedingsstof voor de ontwikkeling van het Europese recht (*Zaak C-324/99, DaimlerChrysler AG en Land Baden-Württemberg), *AA*, 2002, pp. 180-197

Van de Gronden, J.W. and K.J.M. Mortelmans, Wouters: is het beroep van advocaat een aparte tak van sport? (Zaak C-309/99, J.C.J. Wouters en anderen en Algemene Raad van de Nederlandse Orde van Advocaten (NOVA) in tegenwoordigheid van de Raad van de Balies van de Europese Gemeenschap), *AA*, 2002, pp. 441-464

Van de Gronden, J. and K. Mortelmans, Mededinging en algemene belangen: welke signalen geeft de Europese rechter in de Eurovisie zaak?, *Mediaforum*, 2003, pp. 11-20

Van de Gronden, J.W., Directeur-generaal van de Nederlandse Mededingingsautoriteit 16 december 2002, nr. 2605/31 Solidariteitsprotocol in strijd met kartelverbod, *RZA*, 2003, pp. 219-251

Van de Gronden, J.W., *Zorg tussen lidstaat en interne markt* (Kluwer, Deventer, 2004)

Van de Gronden, J.W., Purchasing Care: Economic Activity or Service of General (Economic) Interests?, *ECLR*, 2004, pp. 87-94

Van den Beukel, J., Gij zult nieuws uitzenden, *Mediaforum*, 1997, p. 1

Van den Beukel, J. and A.J. Nieuwenhuis, Pluriformiteit in het mededingingsrecht, *Mediaforum*, 2000, pp. 116-124.

Van den Bogaert, S., *Practical Regulation of the Mobility of Sportsmen in the EU Post Bosman* (Kluwer Law International, The Hague, 2005)

Van der Mei, A.P., Cross-Border Access to Medical Care: Non-Hospital Care and Waiting Lists: European Court of Justice, 13 May 2003, Case C-385/99, *Müller-Fauré v. Onderlinge Waarborgmaatschappij OZ Zorgverzekeringen UA* and *Van Riet v. Onderlinge Waarborgmaatschappij ZAO Zorgverzekeringen*, ECR I-0000, *Legal Issues of Economic Integration*, 2004, pp. 57-67

Van Gerven, W., *Kartelrecht II* (Tjeenk Willink, Zwolle, 1986)

Van Gerven, W., *The European Union – A Polity of States and Peoples* (Hart Publishing, Oxford and Portland, 2005)

Van Ooik, R.H., *De keuze der rechtsgrondslag voor besluiten van de Europese Unie* (Kluwer, Deventer, 1999)

Van Ooik, R.H., Bescherming van de Donau en de grondslagen van het Europese milieubeleid, *NTER*, 2001, pp. 199-204

Van Ooik, R.H., Zaak C-42/97, Europees Parlement t. Raad ("Taalverscheidenheid"), *SEW*, 2001, pp. 283-286

Van Ooik, R.H. and T.A.J.A. Vandamme, Schorsing van Europese regelgeving in Nederland - Kanttekeningen bij de Nevedi-uitspraak van de rechtbank Den Haag, *SEW*, 2005, pp. 60-69

Vedder, H.H.B., De onvermijdelijke confrontatie – maar ook integratie? Over wasmachines, groene punten en auto's, *NTER*, 2000, pp. 236-243

Vedder, H.H.B., Stichting Wit- en Bruingoed, Zaaknr. 1153, *M&M*, 2001, pp. 254-258

Vedder, H.H.B., Collectieve verwijderingssystemen en het mededingingsrecht, in: J.W. van de Gronden and K.J.M. Mortelmans, *Mededinging en niet-economische belangen* (Kluwer, Deventer, 2001), pp. 215-222

Vedder, H.H.B., Environmental Protection and Free Competition: A New Balance? *LIEI*, 2001, p. 105-116

Vedder, H.H.B., The New Community Guidelines for Environmental Protection – Integrating Environment and Competition?, *ECLR*, 2001, pp. 366-367

Vedder, H.H.B., Verwijderingssysteem voor autowrakken houdt geen staatssteun in, *NTER*, 2002, p. 147

Vedder, H.H.B., *Competition Law and Environmental Protection in Europe: Towards sustainability?* (Europa Law Publishing, Groningen, 2003)

Veldkamp, A.M.E., *Overbrengen van afvalstoffen* (Kluwer, Deventer, 1998)

Vogelaar, F.O.W., Towards an Improved Integration of EC Environmental Policy and EC Competition Policy: An Interim Report' in: B.E. Hawk (ed.), *International Antitrust Law and Policy 2004* (Kluwer, London, 1994), pp. 529-563

Vogelaar, F.O.W., *Marktwerking moet! Enkele kanttekeningen bij een zich snel ontwikkelend fenomeen*,(Amsterdam, 2000)

Voigt, S. and A. Schmidt, The Commission's Guidelines on Horizontal Mergers: Improvement or Deterioration?, *CMLRev.*, 2004, pp. 1583-1594

Von der Groeben, H. and J. Schwarze (Eds); Schriftleitung A. Bardenhewer-Rating, *Kommentar zum Vertrag über die Europäische Union und zur Gründung der Europäische Gemeinschaft* (Nomos Verlagsgesellschaft, Baden-Baden, 2003), pp. 1404-1472

Vossestein, A.J., Case C-35/99, *Arduino*, judgment of 19 February 2000, Full Court; Case C-309/99, *Wouters et al. v. Algemene Raad van de Nederlandse Orde van Advocaten*, judgment of 19 February 2002, Full Court; not yet reported, *CMLRev.*, 2002, pp. 841-863

Wasmeier, M. The integration of environmental protection as a general rule of interpreting Community law, *CMLRev.*, 2001, pp. 159-177

Weatherill, S., *Law and Integration in the European Union* (Clarendon Press, Oxford 1995)

Weatherill, S., After *Keck*: Some thoughts on how to clarify the clarification, *CMLRev.*, 1996, pp. 885-906

Weatherill, S., *EC Consumer Law and Policy* (Longman, London, 1997)

Weatherill, S and P. Beaumont, *EU Law* (Penguin books, London, 1999)

Weatherill, S., Recent case law concerning the free movement of goods: mapping the frontiers of market deregulation, *CMLRev.*, 1999, pp. 51-85

Weatherill, S., Pre-emption, Harmonisation and the Distribution of Competence to Regulate the Internal Market, in: C. Barnard and J. Scott (Eds), *The Law of the Single European Market - Unpacking the Premises* (Hart Publishing, Oxford and Portland, 2002), pp. 41-73

Weatherill, S., "Fair Play Please!" Recent developments in the application of EC law to sport, *CMLRev.*, 2003, pp. 51-93

Weatherill, S., Why harmonise?, in: T. Tridimas & P. Nebbia (Eds), *European Union Law for the Twenty-First Century – Rethinking the New Legal Order*, Volume 2, Internal Market and Free Movement Community Policies (Hart Publishing, Oxford and Portland, 2004), pp. 11-32

Weiler, J.H.H., The Constitution of the Common Market Place, in P. Craig and G. de Búrca (Eds), *The Evolution of EU Law* (Oxford University Press, Oxford, 1999), pp: 349-376
Wekstein-Steg, I., Le droit des concentrations appliqué au secteur des industries culturelles, *ERA-Forum*, 2005, pp. 58-61
Wezenbeek-Geuke, R., Métropole Télévision e.a.; de strijd om de sportprogramma's, *NTER*, 1996, pp. 238-242
Wilhemsson, T., The Abuse of the "Confident Consumer" as a Justification for EC Consumer Law, *Journal of Consumer Policy*, 2004, pp. 317-337
Wils, W.P.J., The Combination of the Investigative and Prosecutorial Function and the Adjudicative Function in EC Antitrust Enforcement: A Legal and Economic Analysis, *World Competition*, 2004, pp. 201-224
Winter, J.A., Re(de)fining the notion of State aid in Article 87(1) of the EC Treaty, *CMLRev.*, 2004, pp. 475-504
Winterstein, A., Nailing the Jellyfish: Social Security and Competition Law, *ECLR*, 1999, p. 325
Whish, R., *Competition Law* (Butterworths, London 2001)
Woodhall, A.L., An Antitrust Analysis of Physician Speciality Networks under Changing Market Conditions , *The Journal of Legal Medicine*,1996, pp. 383-425
Zandvliet, C.E., Note: Fixed Book Prices in the Netherlands and the European Union: A Challenge for Community Competition Law, *Columbia Journal of European Law*, 1997/1998, p. 423
Zeinstra, H. and Van der Plas, H., Het Protocol bij het Verdrag van Amsterdam inzake de financiering van publieke omroepen, *Mediaforum*, 1997, pp. 124-127

Table of Cases

Rulings of the Court of Justice

Rulings of the Court of First Instance

Opinions

Abbreviations

AA	Ars Aequi
AB	Administratiefrechtelijke Beslissingen
AG	Advocate General
BEUC	Bureau Européen des Unions de Consommateurs
BRTN	Belgische Radio- en Televisieomroep Nederlandstalige Uitzendingen
BSE	Bovine Spongiform Encephalopathy (mad cow disease)
BV	Besloten Vennootschap
CA	(Netherlands) Competition Act (Mededingingswet)
CE	Communauté européenne
CEN	Comité Européen de Normalisation (European Committee for Standardization)
CENELEC	Comité Européen de Normalisation Elektrotechnique (European Committee for Technical Standardization)
CFI	Court of First Instance
CMLRev.	Common Market Law Review
COM	Commission documents
DG	Directorate-General
DSD	Duales System Deutschland
DVBL	Deutsches Verwaltungsblatt
e.a.	en andere
EC	European Community
ECJ	European Court of Justice
ECLR	European Competition Law Review
ECN	European Competition Network
Ed(s)	editor(s)
EEC	European Economic Community
EELR	European Environmental Law Review
e.g.	exempli gratia (for example)
EG	Europese Gemeenschap(pen)
EGV	Vertrag zur Gründung der Europäischen Gemeinschaft
EIPA	European Institute of Public Administration
ELRev	European Law Review
EPO	European Patent Office
ERA	Europäische Rechtsakademie (Academy of European Law)
ESB	Economisch Statistische Berichten
et al	et alii (and others)
et seq	et sequens (and the following one or ones)
etc.	etcetera
EU	European Union
EUI	European University Institute
EuR	Europarecht
EUV	Vertrag über die Europäische Union
EuZW	Europäische Zeitschrift für Wirtschaftsrecht

EWG	Europäische Wirtschaftsgemeinschaft
FIDE	Fédération Internationale de Droit Européen (International Federation for European Law)
FINA	Fédération Internationale de Natation (International Swimming Federation)
GATT	General Agreement on Tariffs and Trade
HWWA	Institut für Wirtschaftsforschung in Hamburg
i.e.	id est (that is, that is to say)
LIEI	Legal Issues of Economic Integration (previously: Legal Issues of European Integration)
MIT	Massachusetts Institute of Technology
MJ	Maastricht Journal of European and Comparative Law
M&M	Markt en Mededinging
NCAs	National Competition Authorities
NMa	Nederlandse Mededingingsautoriteit (Netherlands Competition Authority)
NO(P)B	Nederlandse Omroepproduktie Bedrijf
NOVA	Nederlandse Orde van Advocaten (Bar of the Netherlands)
NTER	Nederlands Tijdschrift voor Europees Recht
NVwZ	Neue Zeitschrift für Verwaltungsrecht
Nyr	Not yet reported
OECD	Organization for Economic Co-operation and Development
OJ	Official Journal of the European Communities
RZA	Rechtspraak Zorgverzekering
SEW	Sociaal Economische Wetgeving
SGEI	Services of General Economic Interest
SME	Small and Medium-Sized Enterprise
SOU	Statens Offentliga Utredningar ((Swedish) Public State Reports)
STER	Stichting ether reclame
TK	Tweede Kamer
TvC	Tijdschrift voor Consumentenrecht
UEFA	Union of European Football Associations
UNESCO	United Nations Educational, Scientific and Cultural Organization
VSSR	Vierteljahresschrift für Sozialrecht
VTM	Vlaamse Televisie Maatschappij
WEEE	Waste of Electronic and Electrical Equipment
WHO	World Health Organization
WTO	World Trade Organization
ZaöRV	Zeitschrift für ausländisches öffentliches Recht und Völkerrecht
ZBO	Zelfstandig bestuursorgaan
ZeuS	Zeitschrift für Europarechtliche Studien
ZFW	Ziekenfondswet (Sickness Insurance Law)

Index

Samenvatting

1 Inleiding

Dit boek gaat over de spanningsverhouding tussen de regels uit het EG-Verdrag inzake de interne markt – de regels inzake het vrije verkeer en de mededinging – enerzijds en het facettenbeleid anderzijds. Bij facettenbeleid gaat het om 'niet-economische' beleidsterreinen met economische aanknopingspunten. Bij de regels inzake het vrije verkeer en de mededinging daarentegen staat de werking van de interne markt centraal. De spanning tussen de interne markt en facettenbeleid heeft drie oorzaken:

- De toepassing van de vrijverkeerbepalingen uit het EG-Verdrag stelt grenzen aan de uitoefening van nationale bevoegdheden op terreinen van facettenbeleid (hoofdstuk 2);
- De toepassing van de mededingingsbepalingen uit het EG-Verdrag (inclusief de bepalingen inzake steunmaatregelen) brengt met zich mee dat lidstaten en ondernemingen beperkt worden om maatregelen te nemen die weliswaar doelstellingen van facettenbeleid nastreven, maar concurrentiebeperkende gevolgen hebben (hoofdstuk 3);
- Door middel van het uitvaardigen van harmonisatiemaatregelen kunnen door de Gemeenschapswetgever bestaande belemmeringen op het vrije verkeer weggewerkt worden. Deze harmonisatiemaatregelen moeten echter ook in overeenstemming zijn met het primaire EG-recht, de vrijverkeerbepalingen uit het EG-Verdrag (hoofdstuk 4).

De probleemstelling in dit boek luidt als volgt: hoe kan vanuit het perspectief van de instanties die op nationaal en Gemeenschappelijk niveau betrokken zijn bij beleid en regelgeving, een coherente juridische aanpak voor het probleem van spanning tussen vrij verkeer en mededinging aan de ene kant en facettenbeleid aan de andere worden gevonden?

Deze samenvatting is grotendeels gebaseerd op hoofdstuk 5 ('Synthesis') en hoofdstuk 6 ('Closer harmony').

2 Vrij verkeer

Het vrije verkeer wordt niet alleen gerealiseerd door negatieve integratie, oftewel door toepassing van de verbodsbepalingen uit het EG-Verdrag, maar ook door positieve integratie, namelijk door middel van harmonisatie van wetgeving. Harmonisatie is nodig om de nog steeds bestaande belemmeringen op het vrije verkeer op te heffen, wanneer lidstaten met succes een rechtvaardigingsgrond kunnen inroepen voor hun wetgeving.

Negatieve integratie

In het tweede hoofdstuk van dit boek wordt duidelijk gemaakt dat de spanning tussen de regels inzake het vrije verkeer en het facettenbeleid uit twee elementen bestaat:

- Het bestaan van een handelsbelemmering, die hetzij (in)direct discriminerend, dan wel zonder onderscheid van toepassing is;
- Het bestaan van een rechtvaardigingsgrond, bijvoorbeeld ter verwezenlijking van doelstellingen van facettenbeleid.

In het algemeen geldt dat de vrijverkeerbepalingen een brede werkingssfeer hebben. De materiële werkingssfeer van de vier vrijheden wordt door middel van het concept van economische activiteit breed geïnterpreteerd. Daarnaast blijkt dat ook de verbodsbepalingen breed uitgelegd worden, hetgeen betekent dat de spanning tussen het vrije verkeer en het facettenbeleid niet binnen de context van de verbodsbepalingen opgelost kan worden. Overigens is de reikwijdte van de Verdragsbepalingen inzake uitvoer van goederen en inzake binnenlandse belastingen beperkter.

Er bestaan twee uitzonderingen op de brede werking van de verbodsbepalingen: de *Keck*-jurisprudentie[1] en de leer van de *inherente beperking*. Deze uitzonderingen blijken echter voor de spanningsverhouding tussen facettenbeleid en het vrije verkeer van geringe betekenis.

Het belang van de excepties die lidstaten de mogelijkheid bieden hun belemmerende regelgeving te rechtvaardigen, is groot, gezien de brede werkingssfeer van de verbodsbepalingen. Dit betekent dat de spanning tussen het vrije verkeer en het facettenbeleid vooral opgelost dient te worden binnen de context van de rechtvaardigingsgronden, dat wil zeggen de Verdragsexcepties en de 'rule of reason'-exceptie (de dwingende eisen van algemeen belang), die ontwikkeld is in de rechtspraak van het Hof van Justitie. Het uitgangspunt is dat de excepties alleen ingeroepen kunnen worden indien regels van facettenbeleid niet-economische belangen nastreven en proportioneel zijn. Het Hof van Justitie gaat hierbij niet altijd op een systematische wijze te werk. Vooral op het gebied van het milieu, maar ook op andere terreinen van facettenbeleid, heeft het Hof de voorwaarde verlaten dat slechts een beroep gedaan kan worden op dwingende eisen van algemeen belang ('rule of reason' exceptie) bij zonderonderscheid-maatregelen, dat wil zeggen niet discriminerende maatregelen.

Met name het proportionaliteitsbeginsel speelt een centrale rol in de toetsing van nationale regelingen aan de rechtvaardigingsgronden, waarbij de nadruk ligt op de vraag of er voor de verwezenlijking van de te bereiken doelstelling niet even doelmatige, maar minder handelsbelemmerende alternatieven voorhanden zijn. Het proportionaliteitsbeginsel is uitermate belangrijk voor lidstaten, aangezien het de discretionaire bevoegdheid voor het opstellen van regels inzake facettenbeleid begrenst. Hierbij blijkt dat de wijze waarop de proportionaliteits-

---

[1] Gevoegde zaken C-267/91 en C-268/91, *Keck*.

toets wordt uitgevoerd binnen de context van de vrijverkeerbepalingen, afhangt van het type facetbelang.

Positieve integratie

Uit hoofdstuk 4 blijkt dat harmonisatie van wetgeving bijdraagt aan een oplossing voor de spanning tussen de interne markt en facettenbeleid. Harmonisatie van facetbelangen komt in de eerste plaats tot stand binnen de context van de interne markt en in de tweede plaats op grond van specifieke bevoegdheden op het terrein van milieu en consumentenbeleid, die niet bestaan voor de terreinen cultuur en volksgezondheid, met uitzondering van bepaalde gezondheidsaspecten.

De mate waarin facettenbeleid is geharmoniseerd hangt af van de methode van harmonisatie. Bij *minimum*harmonisatie kan de spanning slechts ten dele worden opgelost, aangezien de vrijverkeerbepalingen van belang blijven voor de, door de lidstaten genomen, strengere maatregelen. Deze mogelijkheden om strengere regelgeving te blijven toepassen zijn echter niet onbegrensd. Wanneer in een harmonisatiemaatregel zowel een minimumbepaling als een vrijverkeerclausule zijn opgenomen, kunnen lidstaten alleen strengere maatregelen nemen ten aanzien van hun eigen goederen en diensten, hetgeen leidt tot omgekeerde discriminatie.

In geval van *totale* harmonisatie kan het probleem van spanning tussen vrij verkeer en facettenbeleid wel opgelost worden, aangezien lidstaten niet meer de bevoegdheid hebben om aanvullende maatregelen te treffen. De vrijverkeerbepalingen uit het EG-Verdrag spelen dan geen rol meer.

Met name de uitspraak van het Hof van Justitie in de zaak *Tabaksreclame* lijkt totale harmonisatie in de hand te werken nu een 'internemarktrichtlijn' een vrijverkeerclausule moet bevatten.[2] Dit in combinatie met minimumharmonisatie leidt tot omgekeerde discriminatie, wat onaantrekkelijk is vanuit het perspectief van de lidstaat. De *Tabaksreclame*-zaak en de andere tabakszaken zijn van groot belang voor de harmonisatie van facettenbeleid.[3] Aan de ene kant houdt de uitspraak van het Hof van Justitie in deze zaken een beperking in van de reikwijdte van artikel 95 EG en andere internemarktrechtsgrondslagen door de introductie van een 'merkbaarheidstoets'. Aan de andere kant brengt deze uitspraak een duidelijke uitbreiding van de reikwijdte van de internemarktrechtsgrondslagen met zich mee, aangezien de Gemeenschapswetgever de bevoegdheid heeft om, indien aan de vereisten van 'merkbaarheid' is voldaan, op elk terrein van facettenbeleid op te treden.

Indien de Europese Gemeenschap besluit op te treden door middel van harmonisatiemaatregelen, dan moeten deze maatregelen ook in overeenstem-

---

2 Zaak C-376/98, *Duitsland t. Europees Parlement en Raad (Tabaksreclame).*

3 Zaak C-491/01, *BAT/Imperial Tobacco*; zaak C-434/02, *Arnold André*; zaak C-210/03, *Swedish Match*. Zie ook gevoegde zaken C-154/04 en C-155/04, *Alliance for Natural Health.*

ming zijn met de vrijverkeerbepalingen uit het EG-Verdrag. De Gemeenschap als wetgever beschikt daarbij wel over een ruime discretionaire bevoegdheid.

3 Mededingingsregels en de lidstaten: artikelen 86 en 87 EG

In hoofdstuk 3 is uiteengezet dat lidstaten ook rekening moeten houden met de toepassing van de mededingingsregels, in het bijzonder artikel 86 EG over uitsluitende rechten en overheidsondernemingen, artikel 87 EG over staatssteun, en de 'nieuwe norm' of nuttigeffectregel – de artikelen 10 Jo. 81 & 82 EG – die de lidstaten verbiedt het nuttig effect van de mededingingsregels te ontnemen door bijvoorbeeld strijdige afspraken tussen ondernemingen te bevorderen.

Evenals de verbodsbepalingen inzake de vier vrijheden hebben de mededingingsregels een ruime werkingssfeer. Hierbij is met name de brede interpretatie van het begrip onderneming van belang. Steunmaatregelen met doelstellingen van facettenbeleid vallen al snel onder de verbodsbepaling van artikel 87, lid 1 EG. Voor financiële steun aan ondernemingen die belast zijn met taken van algemeen economisch belang, heeft het Hof van Justitie in de *Altmark*-zaak echter bepaald dat deze niet altijd als steunmaatregel in de zin van artikel 87, lid 1 EG beschouwd moet worden.[4] *Altmark* lijkt daarmee enige ruimte te bieden voor het in beschouwing nemen van facetbelangen binnen de context van de verbodsbepaling. Afgezien van *Altmark*-situaties moet de verbodsbepaling inzake staatssteun in beginsel breed worden uitgelegd. Financiële steun daarentegen die een bepaald bedrag niet overschrijdt – de zogenaamde *de-minimis*-steun – of die slechts toegekend wordt aan plaatselijk opererende ondernemingen, vallen buiten het verbod van artikel 87, lid 1, EG, maar deze *de-minimis*regel is slechts in beperkte mate relevant voor steunmaatregelen met doelstellingen van facettenbeleid.

Wanneer eenmaal vaststaat dat steunmaatregelen onder het verbod van artikel 87, lid 1 EG vallen, dan moet bekeken worden of één van de uitzonderingen van artikel 87, lid 3 EG van toepassing is. Behalve wat steunmaatregelen betreft die de cultuur bevorderen en steunmaatregelen van sociale aard aan individuele verbruikers (consumenten), verwijzen artikelen 87, lid 2 en 87, lid 3 EG niet expliciet naar doelstellingen van facettenbeleid. Desondanks houdt de Commissie in haar beleid rekening met facetbelangen.

Wat artikel 86 EG betreft heeft het Hof bij de beoordeling of een uitsluitend recht in strijd is met deze bepaling voor verschillende benaderingswijzen gekozen, waarbij artikel 86, lid 1 EG niet altijd breed wordt uitgelegd. Artikel 86, lid 2 EG dat een specifieke uitzondering bevat voor ondernemingen die belast

---

4 Zaak C-280/00, *Altmark Trans*.

zijn met taken van algemeen economisch belang, kan worden ingeroepen ter bescherming van facetbelangen, ook al verwijst deze bepaling naar doelstellingen van algemeen *economisch* belang. Zowel bij artikel 87, lid 3 EG als bij artikel 86, lid 2 EG speelt het proportionaliteitsbeginsel een centrale rol.

De Europese Gemeenschap heeft geen harmonisatiemaatregelen uitgevaardigd op het gebied van staatssteun of van uitsluitende rechten, met uitzondering van sectorspecifieke regelgeving. Dit betekent dat de Verdragsbepalingen inzake staatssteun en uitsluitende rechten het toetsingskader bieden voor nationale maatregelen en dat spanningen tussen de toepassing van deze Verdragsbepalingen en doelstellingen van facettenbeleid binnen dit kader dienen te worden opgelost.

4 Mededingingsregels en ondernemingen: artikelen 81, 82 EG en concentratiecontrole

Indien ondernemingen om uiteenlopende redenen besluiten om een bijdrage te leveren aan de verwezenlijking van doelstellingen van facettenbeleid dan zijn de artikelen 81 en 82 EG en de concentratieverordening mogelijk van toepassing.

De interpretatie van het kartelverbod van artikel 81 EG in de jurisprudentie laat echter wel toe, zei het in beperkte mate, dat rekening gehouden kan worden met facetbelangen, in het bijzonder in het kader van de leer van de 'inherente beperking', zoals toegepast in sport-zaken als *Meca-Medina*,[5] of, in het verlengde hiervan, ten gevolge van de uitspraak van het Hof van Justitie in de *Wouters*-zaak.[6] In deze laatste zaak lijkt het Hof een soort rule of reason à la *Cassis de Dijon* toe te passen op artikel 81, lid 1 EG.[7] Het Hof van Justitie bepaalde namelijk dat deontologische regels ter bescherming van de onafhankelijkheid van de advocatuur een gerechtvaardigde beperking op het kartelverbod vormen. De reikwijdte van *Wouters* lijkt vooralsnog beperkt. Waarschijnlijk kunnen niet alle facetbelangen profiteren van deze benadering en hangt het nog steeds af van de economische en juridische context waarbinnen het besluit is genomen of artikel 81, lid 1 EG nu wel of niet van toepassing is. Hetzelfde geldt overigens voor de leer van de inherente beperking.

Bij de toepassing van artikel 82 EG spelen facetbelangen nauwelijks een rol. Bij de toepassing van de concentratieverordening kunnen facetbelangen op de achtergrond een rol spelen, namelijk bij de beoordeling van efficiëntieverbeteringen van concentraties en bij de toepassing van het verbod op concentraties, wanneer tegelijkertijd doelstellingen van facettenbeleid, zoals de pluriformiteit van de media, worden gediend.

---

5 Zaak T-313/02, *Meca-Medina*.

6 Zaak C-309/99, *Wouters*.

7 Case 120/78, *Cassis de Dijon*.

Vanwege de brede werking van de verbodsbepalingen geldt ook hier dat de uitzonderingen van cruciaal belang zijn. Uitgangspunt is dat deze uitzonderingen in beginsel beperkt uitgelegd dienen te worden. Er bestaat echter een tendens om meer rekening te houden met facetbelangen, die het duidelijkste is op het terrein van het milieu. De *CECED*-beschikking is hier een goed voorbeeld van.[8] Op andere terreinen daarentegen is het belang van het facettenbeleid aanzienlijk onduidelijker, zoals op het gebied van de volksgezondheid en de cultuur.

De mogelijkheden om onder het verbod van artikel 82 EG uit te komen zijn zeer beperkt. Indien het ondernemingen betreft die belast zijn met taken van algemeen (economisch) belang biedt artikel 86, lid 2 EG mogelijk uitkomst. De concentratieverordening daarentegen verwijst expliciet naar algemene belangen, namelijk in artikel 21, lid 4, zoals de pluraliteit van de media.

Indien een beroep op de uitzonderingen tot de mogelijkheden behoort, dan wordt aan de hand van het proportionaliteitsbeginsel bekeken of de beperkingen op de mededinging uiteindelijk gerechtvaardigd zijn. Het proportionaliteitsbeginsel speelt dus een centrale rol in de afweging tussen facetbelangen en mededingingsbeperkingen, maar wordt hier stringenter toegepast dan in het kader van de vrijverkeerbepalingen.

Er is geen gemeenschappelijke regelgeving met het oogmerk om de nationale mededingingsregels te harmoniseren. In feite heeft een proces van 'spontane harmonisatie' zonder dat de Gemeenschapswetgever eraan te pas is gekomen ervoor gezorgd dat de mededingingsregels van de lidstaten vergelijkbaar zijn.

5 Coherentie of convergentie?

Kan op grond van het voorgaande geconcludeerd worden dat er sprake is van een coherente benadering met betrekking tot vrij verkeer en mededinging? Coherentie kan ook convergentie impliceren, indien het beleid op verschillende terreinen vergelijkbaar is of identiek en dezelfde toetssteen voor verschillende rechtsinstrumenten wordt gehanteerd.

Vrij verkeer

Het convergentieproces tussen de vier vrijheden is in een vergevorderd stadium en heeft zich in hoofdzaak in drie fasen voltrokken. De eerste fase heeft betrekking op de brede personele en materiële werkingssfeer van de vrijverkeerbepalingen; de tweede fase op de brede uitleg van de verbodsbepalingen, waarbij zowel onderscheidmaatregelen als zonderonderscheidmaatregelen in beginsel verboden zijn en het markttoegangscriterium als toetssteen voor nationale regels aan de regels inzake het vrije verkeer is ontwikkeld; de derde fase op de ontwikkeling van de rule of reason voor alle vrijheden, die lidstaten de mogelijk-

[8] Beschikking 2000/475, Pb. 2000, L 187/47.

heid geeft om in aanvulling op de Verdragsexcepties maatregelen te nemen die weliswaar het vrije verkeer beperken, maar niettemin gerechtvaardigd zijn op gronden van algemeen belang. De proportionaliteitstoets speelt in dit kader een centrale rol.

Het convergentieproces wordt versterkt door het feit dat de vrijverkeerbepalingen ten doel hebben het voorkomen van protectionisme en de rechtvaardigingsgronden binnen de context van de vrijverkeerbepalingen in beginsel worden ingeroepen door de overheid, die wordt verondersteld te handelen in het algemeen belang.

Vrij verkeer en mededinging

Het convergentieproces is hier in een minder vergevorderd stadium. Toch zijn er wel overeenkomsten te vinden in de wijze waarop het Hof van Justitie en de Commissie de regels inzake het vrije verkeer en de mededinging toepassen, namelijk wat het brede begrip economische activiteit betreft, de brede uitleg van de verbodsbepalingen en het belang van de uitzonderingen, waarbij het proportionaliteitsbeginsel een belangrijke rol speelt.

Er bestaat echter een grotere mate van samenhang tussen de regels inzake staatssteun en de regels inzake openbare ondernemingen (mededingingsregels gericht aan de overheid), en de vrijverkeerbepalingen dan tussen de mededingingsregels gericht aan ondernemingen en de vrijverkeerbepalingen. Over de reikwijdte van artikel 81, lid 3 EG bestaat immers nog steeds onduidelijkheid. Enerzijds suggereert de beschikkingspraktijk van de Europese Commissie dat facetbelangen een belangrijke rol kunnen spelen in het kader van artikel 81, lid 3 EG, anderzijds geven de recente richtsnoeren inzake artikel 81, lid 3 EG aan dat facetbelangen in ieder geval van ondergeschikt belang zijn aan de gronden genoemd in artikel 81, lid 3 EG.

Facettenbeleid

Op een aantal wijzen komt de samenhang tussen de verschillende onderdelen van facettenbeleid tot uiting. Het Hof van Justitie heeft duidelijk gemaakt dat artikel 95 EG en de andere internemarktrechtsgrondslagen, indien voldoende gemotiveerd door de Gemeenschapswetgever, niet beperkt hoeven te zijn tot louter internemarktregelgeving. De Gemeenschap kan dus op deze wijze, weliswaar binnen grenzen, het beleid op het gebied van cultuur en volksgezondheid, waarvoor geen harmonisatiebevoegdheid bestaat, verder vormgeven. Daarnaast bestaat er in het Verdrag een gemeenschappelijke aanpak met betrekking tot het facettenbeleid, dat gebaseerd is op het subsidiariteitsbeginsel en waarvoor de bevoegdheden in beginsel worden gedeeld met de lidstaten.

Toch is er geen sprake van convergentie, hetgeen verklaard kan worden door het feit dat facetbelangen op verschillende niveaus van regelgeving– de Europese Gemeenschap, de lidstaten, de regionale en lokale overheid – worden behartigd. Op het gebied van het milieu en consumentenbescherming deelt de Gemeenschap haar bevoegdheid met de lidstaten; op het gebied van cultuur en volksgezondheid zijn de lidstaten in beginsel bevoegd maatregelen te nemen. Bovendien bestaan er inherente verschillen tussen de beleidsterreinen die een verschillende aanpak noodzakelijk maakt. Zo heeft het Hof van Justitie bepaald dat onder de in artikel 30 EG beschermde belangen de gezondheid en het leven van personen de eerste plaats innemen. Bij de bescherming van economische belangen van consumenten daarentegen neemt het Hof als vertrekpunt de gemiddelde consument.

6 Spanning tussen facettenbeleid en de interne markt

Aangezien de mate van coherentie niet overal hetzelfde is, is er vooralsnog geen eenduidige oplossing voor de spanning tussen facettenbeleid en de interne markt gevonden. Voor het feit dat spanningen blijven bestaan kunnen de volgende verklaringen gevonden worden.

Perspectief van de lidstaat

Vanuit het perspectief van de lidstaat bestaat de wens om facetbelangen naar eigen inzicht te beschermen, hetgeen op gespannen voet staat met de eisen die gesteld worden door de Verdragsbepalingen inzake de vier vrijheden en de mededinging. Ook al neemt het Hof van Justitie de zorg van lidstaten voor de bescherming van facetbelangen serieus, het legt ook meer of minder stringente voorwaarden op aan de lidstaat om een geslaagd beroep te kunnen doen op één van de excepties.

Het feit dat tussen de regels inzake het vrije verkeer en de mededinging een geringere mate van convergentie bestaat dan tussen de regels inzake het vrije verkeer onderling, kan worden verklaard door de veronderstelling dat ondernemingen *eigen* belangen verdedigen en de overheid het *algemeen* belang. Dit komt met name tot uiting in de wijze waarop de proportionaliteitstoets wordt uitgevoerd.

Perspectief van de Gemeenschap

Vanuit het perspectief van de Gemeenschap zou de spanning opgelost kunnen worden indien de Gemeenschapswetgever besluit tot harmonisatie van wetgeving. De lidstaten willen echter bevoegd blijven op een aantal terreinen van facettenbeleid, zoals volksgezondheid en cultuur. In feite is er sprake van een paradox; lidstaten willen in de eerste plaats de bevoegdheid houden om facetbelangen te behartigen, terwijl tegelijkertijd hoofdstuk 2 duidelijk maakt dat het negatieve integratieproces de bescherming van deze belangen juist bemoeilijkt, zoniet onmogelijk maakt. Uit hoofdstuk 4 blijkt dat dit deels ook het gevolg is van het positieve integratieproces, aangezien facettenbeleid waarvoor geen rechtsgrondslag in het Verdrag aanwezig is ook via de achterdeur, namelijk door middel van de breed toepasbare internemarktrechtsgrondslagen geharmoniseerd kan worden.

Toch is er geen echte samenhang tussen de beleidsterreinen milieu, volksgezondheid, consumentenbescherming en cultuur. Convergentie is problematisch en onwenselijk gezien het feit dat er in het licht van het subsidiariteitsbeginsel verschillen bestaan tussen de beleidsterreinen.

7 Concrete suggesties voor meer harmonie

In hoofdstuk 6 worden suggesties gedaan om tot een grotere samenhang te komen tussen de regels inzake het vrije verkeer, de mededinging en het facettenbeleid met als uiteindelijk doel de spanning te beheersen, dan wel geheel op te lossen. Boeken en de regulering van de boekenmarkt zijn als voorbeeld genomen om aan te tonen dat met betrekking tot één product verschillende rechtsinstrumenten gebruikt kunnen worden om dezelfde culturele doelstelling na te streven, maar dat de beleidsruimte verschilt en afhankelijk is van de toepasselijke Verdragsbepaling.

Meer harmonie vanuit het perspectief van de lidstaten

Vanuit het perspectief van de lidstaten en de nationale instanties die betrokken zijn bij beleid en regelgeving zijn er twee wegen die tot een grotere mate van samenhang tussen de regels inzake de interne markt en het facettenbeleid en dus tot meer harmonie kunnen leiden. De eerste is gebaseerd op het proportionaliteitsbeginsel. De nationale wetgever moet erkennen dat de wijze waarop de proportionaliteitstoets wordt uitgevoerd, afhangt van het te beschermen facetbelang – er is sprake van een zekere hiërarchie van facetbelangen – en het type rechtsinstrument dat wordt gebruikt om facetbelangen te behartigen. Doelstellingen van facettenbeleid moeten daarom expliciet en duidelijk worden omschreven. Bij de keuze tussen regelgeving en zelfregulering moet beseft worden dat sommige typen regelgeving en zelfregulering eerder in strijd zullen zijn met de regels inzake het vrije verkeer of de mededinging dan andere.

De nationale mededingingsautoriteiten moeten bij de toepassing van het proportionaliteitsbeginsel de brede uitleg van artikel 81, lid 3 EG die in de beschikkingspraktijk en de jurisprudentie wordt gegeven verkiezen boven de engere interpretatie uit de richtsnoeren. Waar nog geen beleid is ontwikkeld moeten zij zich terughoudend opstellen en hulp vragen van de Commissie en andere nationale mededingingsautoriteiten. Ook de nationale rechter hoeft niet noodzakelijkerwijze een enge uitleg te geven van artikel 81, lid 3 EG, zeker niet in milieuzaken. Waar andere facetbelangen een rol spelen, kan de nationale rechter inspiratie ontlenen aan milieuzaken en, in geval van twijfel, één van de samenwerkingsmogelijkheden gebruiken waarnaar hieronder wordt verwezen. Verder zal de nationale rechter, evenals de nationale wetgever, rekening moeten houden met het bestaan van een zekere hiërarchie tussen facetbelangen en het feit dat bij de toetsing aan de regels inzake het vrije verkeer de nadruk ligt op de vraag of er geen minder handelsbelemmerend alternatief voorhanden is.

De tweede weg is gebaseerd op het beginsel van Gemeenschapstrouw. Dit beginsel is met name van belang voor de nationale mededingingsautoriteiten die ten gevolge van verordening 1/2003 nauw met elkaar en met de Europese Commissie moeten samenwerken om de uniformiteit van het EG-mededingingsrecht te waarborgen. De samenwerkingsprocedures zijn uitgewerkt door de Commissie in een bekendmaking omtrent de samenwerking binnen het netwerk van mededingingsautoriteiten. Naast deze samenwerking op Europees niveau kan samenwerking op nationaal niveau tussen de mededingingsautoriteiten en departementen die betrokken zijn bij facettenbeleid, belangrijk zijn.

Het beginsel van Gemeenschapstrouw is echter ook van belang voor de nationale wetgever. Er zijn verschillende praktische manieren waarop – op verschillende niveaus van regelgeving, nationaal of Europees – een bijdrage geleverd kan worden aan de uitwisseling van informatie.

Ten slotte is het beginsel van Gemeenschapstrouw van belang voor de nationale rechters die, geconfronteerd met de rechtstreekse werking van artikel 81, lid 3 EG, met elkaar moeten samenwerken om inconsistenties in de toepassing van de EG-mededingingsregels te voorkomen. Artikel 15 van verordening 1/2003 voorziet dan ook in een samenwerkingsprocedure, die verder is uitgewerkt door de Commissie in een mededeling.

Op nationaal niveau kan gedacht worden aan samenwerking en informatie-uitwisseling over de rol van facetbelangen bij de toepassing van artikel 81, lid 3 EG binnen de Raad voor de rechtspraak, een instantie die de uniforme rechtstoepassing bevordert en de juridische kwaliteit vergroot. Er bestaat ook een Europees netwerk voor raden voor de rechtspraak waarin kennisuitwisseling vergemakkelijkt kan worden.

Meer harmonie vanuit het perspectief van de Gemeenschap

Er zijn vanuit het perspectief van de Gemeenschap verschillende manieren die naar meer harmonie tussen de interne markt en het facettenbeleid leiden. De eerste manier is gebaseerd op het proces van convergentie tussen de regels inzake het vrije verkeer, hetgeen verder aangemoedigd kan worden door het Hof van Justitie. Het Hof moet de kunstmatige tweedeling tussen de Verdragsexcepties en de rule of reason opheffen en de nadruk leggen op de verschillen die bestaan tussen de afzonderlijke beleidsterreinen van facettenbeleid bij de toepassing van het proportionaliteitsbeginsel, in het bijzonder verschillen in bevoegdheden en inherente verschillen tussen facetbelangen. Daarbij kan het Hof aangeven dat er een zekere hiërarchie van belangen bestaat.

De tweede manier is gebaseerd op het integratiebeginsel dat vereist dat in het bijzonder de Europese Commissie bij de toepassing van de mededingingsregels rekening houdt met facetbelangen. Het integratiebeginsel vereist dat een afweging gemaakt wordt tussen facetbelangen enerzijds en de eis van effectieve mededinging anderzijds aan de hand van de proportionaliteitstoets. Het uitgangspunt voor de aanbevelingen voor de Europese Commissie zijn de verschillende instanties die betrokken zijn bij regelgeving, dat wil zeggen overheidsorganisaties, semi-publieke/semi-private organisaties en private ondernemingen. Door middel van richtsnoeren kan de Commissie duidelijkheid verschaffen over de reikwijdte van de excepties in relatie tot facettenbeleid, in het bijzonder over de reikwijdte van de artikelen 87, lid 3 EG, 86, lid 2 EG en 81, lid 3 EG. In een kaderrichtlijn zou de reikwijdte van artikel 86, lid 2 EG in het algemeen – de horizontale aanpak – verder toegelicht kunnen worden.

De derde en laatste manier is gebaseerd op de brede werking van artikel 95 EG, die de Gemeenschapswetgever de mogelijkheid biedt om doelstellingen van facettenbeleid binnen het kader van de interne markt te verwezenlijken. Om echter te voorkomen dat de Gemeenschapswetgever de bevoegdheden van de lidstaten al te zeer uitholt, zeker op de terreinen van cultuur en volksgezondheid waarvoor een harmonisatieverbod geldt, moet zij duidelijk motiveren waarom het gebruik van internemarktrechtsgrondslagen noodzakelijk is voor de harmonisatie van facetbelangen en tevens rekening houden met het proportionaliteitsbeginsel. Hierbij moet wel in het achterhoofd worden gehouden dat de Gemeenschapswetgever over een ruimere beleidsruimte beschikt dan de nationale wetgever. Daarnaast is de keuze van de harmonisatiemethode van belang, namelijk of de Gemeenschapswetgever kiest voor minimumharmonisatie, dan wel totale harmonisatie.

Voorstellen voor herziening van het EG-Verdrag

Om een meer structurele verbetering in de relatie tussen de interne markt en facettenbeleid te realiseren, is een aantal Verdragswijzigingen noodzakelijk:

- Een wijziging van artikel 2 EG, waarin de doelstellingen van de EG vermeld staan, waarbij een verwijzing naar een hoog niveau van bescherming van de volksgezondheid wordt opgenomen en de integratiebepaling voor het milieu teruggeplaatst wordt in de milieutitel van het Verdrag.
- Een nieuwe Verdragsexceptie voor belemmeringen op het vrije verkeer met een niet-limitatieve lijst van algemene belangen, waarbij het nu zonder meer duidelijk is dat ook discriminerende maatregelen die doelstellingen van facettenbeleid nastreven, in beginsel te rechtvaardigen zijn met een beroep op deze bepaling. De nadruk ligt op de proportionaliteitstoets.
- Uitbreiding van artikel 87, lid 3 EG met verwijzingen naar milieu en volksgezondheid.
- Het opnemen van een Verdragsexceptie voor de nuttigeffectregel.
- Het opnemen van een niet-limitatieve lijst van facetbelangen in artikel 81, lid 3 EG, aangezien de integratiebepalingen tot nu toe nog van onvoldoende belang zijn gebleken voor het mededingingsbeleid van de Commissie.
- Een wijziging van de internemarktrechtsgrondslagen: artikelen 95, lid 5 en 47, lid 2 EG. In artikel 95, lid 5 EG moet een verwijzing naar gezondheid worden opgenomen. Artikel 47, lid 2 EG, dat in samenhang met artikel 55 EG van belang is voor de harmonisatie van het dienstenverkeer,

moet een verwijzing bevatten naar facetbelangen zoals artikel 95, lid 3 EG.

- Specifieke Verdragswijzigingen: gedeeltelijke opheffing van het harmonisatieverbod voor volksgezondheid en cultuur. Om te voorkomen dat de gezondheidszorg onderwerp wordt van harmonisatie, kan een bepaling opgenomen worden dat dit onderwerp de verantwoordelijkheid blijft van de lidstaten. Voor cultuur geldt hetzelfde, waarbij het begrip gemeenschappelijk cultureel erfgoed uitgangspunt is voor harmonisatie van wetgeving op het gebied van cultuur. Voor het beschermen van culturele belangen in het algemeen blijft het harmonisatieverbod van kracht.

About the Author

Edward P. Lalley is President and Chief Executive Officer of Ideal Mutual Insurance Company, the Optimum Companies and Ideal Insurance Company Ltd. (Bermuda). He holds a BS degree from St. Ambrose College and an LLB from the University of Tulsa School of Law.

Mr. Lalley began his insurance career as Director of Insurance and Claims with American Airlines. In 1959, he joined Kraft, Inc. as Insurance Manager. He was elected President of Ideal in 1963.

Mr. Lalley is the author of articles on Captive Insurance Companies and Self Insurance Programs and similar subjects.

In addition to being an elector to the Insurance Hall of Fame, Mr. Lalley is the Vice Chairman of the Corporate Insurance and Reinsurance Company Limited (CIRCL) and Treasurer of the Captive Insurance Companies Association (CICA). He was recently reelected to a second term as President of the New York State Mutual Insurance Association (NYSMIA).

Acknowledgments

To all of the people of the Risk and Insurance Management Society, and particularly Ron Judd, Dan Sullivan, Ed Lloyd, Dick Hackenburg, Dick Soper, Allan Goldberg, and especially Rita Epstein (the mighty whip), who lent moral and functional support toward the successful accomplishment of this project.

To Duane Allen, Miles Chenault, Tom Duffield, Jim Mascarella, Frank McCahill and Bob Reeves, who are all keen students of the practice of risk management, and who read and critiqued this text, thus enhancing its value.

To Katie Donovan, Darlene Gentry, Craig Kalck, Joanie Mezlis, Ronnie McCarthy, Arthur York and all the other members of the Ideal Mutual organization. To say this book would not have been written without them is not false modesty, but grim reality.

To John Richman, Chairman and Chief Executive Officer of Dart & Kraft, Inc., both personally and as a representative of the employees of Kraft, Inc., a group of very nice people with whom I was associated for 13 happy years.

Elsewhere I have acknowledged the debt to my wife and our three children. Not to acknowledge a similar debt to my brothers and sisters—all seven of them—would be a serious omission.

This book is dedicated to my wife, Mary, and
our three children, Kathy, Jean and Ned.

Contents

1

Risk Management— What Is It?

In recent years a new title—risk manager—has begun to appear on the organization charts of more and more corporations. At least one-third of the largest corporations have converted from "insurance manager" to "risk manager."

Why the trend? What does it mean? It is not the result of an exploding new technology and the consequent need for new specialization, as has been the case with such new specializations as "computer programmer" or "telecommunications manager." Instead, the trend to "risk manager" stems from two interrelated concepts which have been emerging in large corporations:

- The realization that the corporation is subject to a host of risks which can be analyzed, evaluated and protected against, so that the corporation will not suffer embarrassing or crippling losses.
- The gradually diminishing role played by the insurance industry in the treatment and the ultimate disposition of risks.

The Nature of Risk

What is risk? There are many definitions. One definition from the academic world defines risk as "the possibility that a sentient entity will incur loss."[1] According to the Dictionary of Insurance Terms of the Chamber of Commerce of the United States, risk is simply the "chance of loss." But virtually every event in nature contains some chance of loss. So, to adopt such a broad definition would dump into the lap of the risk manager a responsibility for some aspect of practically every happening in the corporation. The risk manager would be stepping on the toes of most of the other managers in the company, including the chief executive officer.

So, how do we define the spectrum of risks that rightfully come

[1] Ron Horn and Robert Crowe, as reported by Professor Charles P. Hall in the *Journal of Risk and Insurance,* September, 1967, p. 462.

within the purview of the risk manager? Some say the risk manager's realm is the "static" risks of an organization, as opposed to the "business" risks. Static risks are those possibilities of loss which the corporation cannot avoid. Like death and taxes, they are always with us. Business risks are defined as those a business can elect to take or not take and which contain the possibility of gain as well as loss.

An example of a business risk might be the risk that a company sales program will not meet its objectives, with consequent financial loss to the company. Or, it might succeed beyond all expectations.

Another differentiation is between "pure" risks and "speculative" risks. Pure risks are generally defined as similar to static risks, but with particular emphasis on the loss-no-gain possibility. Speculative risks are generally defined very much like business risks. Although "speculative" may imply gambling, it better describes the concept and so is preferable to the term "business."

Insurable Risks

Still another term used to describe those risks the risk manager should assume is "insurable" risks. This assumes those risks not within a risk manager's purview to be speculative risks (or business risks).

At least one billion dollar company uses the title "insurable risk manager." But this definition of the function seems much too limiting. It reduces the scope of the responsibility again to that of an insurance manager.

However we define risk, we do see evidence of a significant change in emphasis in the function. No longer is it limited to an automatic transferral of corporate risks to an insurance company.

The nuance implied by the title of risk manager is that, while the person must successfully ascertain, analyze and ameliorate corporate risks, the risks need not necessarily be placed with an insurance company.

Fortuitous vs. Calculated Risks

I believe that Joseph T. Parrett, former Carnation Company risk manager, now retired, did the best job to date of delineating the two categories of risk. Writing in the *Insurance Buyers Guide* in December, 1969, he described the risk manager's job as one of handling mainly the "fortuitous" risks, as contrasted to "calculated business" risks, for which the risk manager has, at most, only limited responsibility. He said:

"If we do not attempt to be too definitive and split hairs, we can regard a risk as being that situation where a firm could sustain an out-of-pocket loss as the result of an occurrence or development. The risk could be relatively major or minor. The risk manager's job is to discover and identify those risks and then evaluate them to determine whether they are major or minor.

"The risk manager's activities as presently defined in most firms do not encompass dealing with all types of risks, particularly the so-called calculated business risks such as losses from extension of credit, investments, unprofitable operations, bad judgment, etc. The management of most firms look to their risk manager to control or eliminate those risks directly involved with fortuitous events. There are some gray areas between the fortuitous and normal calculated exposures that can often involve the risk manager."

This delineation and description has not been widely used. And it seems not to have been accepted at all by the academicians. One insurance professor calls our attention to the fact that the purest of "pure" risks (loss of one's house by fire, for example) becomes a "speculative" risk to the insurer electing to insure it. Other students of the subject emphasize that the corporate risk manager is involved only in "fundamental" risks and define these as possibilities of loss to which whole classes of people or enterprises are subject, more or less uniformly, as distinguished from "particular" or "personal" risks which are not so widely distributed.

Death is Fundamental

The risk of premature death is probably the most fundamental of risks, followed closely by accidental injury or disability due to disease. Examples of personal and particular risks are losing one's job, expulsion from one's professional society or being charged with criminal misconduct. Note that personal or particular risks are more readily controllable by the individual than are the fundamental risks.

This emphasis on fundamental risks in the study of corporate risk management is understandable. For a risk to be transferred to an insurer, enough persons must be subjected to the risk with enough regularity to make the shifting feasible.

A television comedian described his wife's insurance program as providing huge indemnity at miniscule cost for the accidental death of a family member by being trampled to death by a pregnant giraffe in the family living room. The humor stems from the ridiculous. Too few people are subjected to such a risk to make it feasible to shift or transfer it.

At the other extreme, a 100-year-old man, no matter how healthy, cannot buy insurance against death. The 120,000 people in the United States who attain their 99th birthday this year will, actuarially speaking, die before reaching their hundredth. Again, actuarially speaking, we are dealing here with certainty and not uncertainty.

The Joker

One of the best descriptions I have heard of corporate risk management came from a top management member of a large corporation. After listening to various efforts to define the corporate risk manager's area of concern, he came up with the following description:

"We're talking about the accidental risk to which the corporation is subject, rather than the calculated risk, right? Aren't we then talking about the 'joker' which exists in practically all situations of any importance—the unexpected loss? It is completely unrelated to those risks which are intrinsic to the subject at hand and which the person in charge of the operation, be it plant manager, shop foreman or sales promotion manager, is not likely to focus on unless reminded to do so."

Let us examine this concept further. Typical plant managers are faced with daily problems of raw materials procurement, the proper use and operation of plant machinery and the recruiting of the right kind and number of people. Persons so engaged are probably not going to think consciously very often about the risk of the plant being destroyed by fire unless it is called to their attention. Other problems, which occur almost daily, crowd into the consciousness and tend to crowd out attention to the risks that have less immediacy.

Don't Blame the Shop Foreman

The accidental risks are remote—not likely to happen at this particular time and with no obvious physical portents or premonitions to suggest dramatically that they will occur. Similarly, the shop foreman, with the working day filled to overflowing with the problems of manpower utilization, material and machine usage, is certainly not to be blamed if the remote possibility of injury to employees by industrial accident is not uppermost in his mind.

Nor should the sales promotion manager, beset with difficult problems of how well the sales message will persuade the public to buy the product, be expected to become concerned with the remote risk that the billboard used to broadcast the message will be blown over in a windstorm. These accidental risks are among those that are the concern of the corporate risk manager.

Management would find risk management easier to understand if practitioners would emphasize that they deal in "accidental risks" and that the "calculated" or "predictable" risks are beyond their realm. Although this term contains redundancy, its use could make risk managers better understood.

Perhaps the best of all semantical worlds would be for the term risk to mean only what we now describe as pure or static or insurable or fundamental risks; and use the term venture to describe what we now call business or speculative risks. The term venture capital tends to strengthen this concept. Of interest here is a giant worldwide oil company which has appointed a corporate vice president of international ventures.

Improved understanding of risk management by top corporate management could pay huge dividends. People are reluctant to support that which they don't understand. To achieve its full potential in the corporate environment, the risk management function has to gain the understanding of all ranks of management, and particularly of top management.

Exchanging Small Loss for Large

One thoughtful student of risk management has described insurance as a procedure whereby the insured voluntarily accepts a small, certain loss (the premium) in exchange for being freed from the payment of a larger, though uncertain, loss if it occurs. Since corporate risk management is an enlargement of corporate insurance management, this definition sets forth the risk management function very well.

As for the "small, certain loss," the corporation need not necessarily pay a premium to an insurer. The "small, certain loss" might well be applied to install equipment to diminish the chances that the loss would occur. Or the corporate risk management department might recommend that the risk be self insured—that a small part of the corporation's current profits be periodically credited to a reserve maintained on the company's books.

Spreads Loss Over Time

This procedure spreads the cost of unusually large losses over several years, thus achieving the same effect as if the risk were handed to an insurance company. In this manner, a large loss can be absorbed without financial embarrassment to the company.

This procedure has been called vertical absorption of loss, in contrast to horizontal absorption of loss when an insurance company is used as an intermediary to pool the premiums to cover losses of many corporations (or individuals).

This do-it-yourself device of self insurance has been further refined by the establishment of captive insurance companies.

Both vertical and horizontal absorption of risk can be used at the same time and on the same risk. The most explicit example is found in life insurance.

Vertical and Horizontal

When I was 16, my father bought me an ordinary life insurance policy with a face value of $1,000. It was the "cash value" type which accumulates part of the premium paid in the early years of the policy into a fund called cash surrender value, which can be used for several purposes.

More often than not it is emphasized that this fund acts as an equalizer which, when added to the true risk charge (which increases as the insured person gets older), makes the premium paid an equal amount throughout the lifetime of the insured person. Not so often emphasized is the fact that this fund acts to reduce the amount which the insurance company has at risk. So, 20 years after the inception of my life insurance policy, the cash surrender value was about $450, built up at the rate of $30 of annual premium plus the interest accumulated through the years.

Even the experts disagree over the legal status of this cash surrender value fund—about who actually owns it, the insurer or the insured. At least it is still in the possession of the insurer. Under any theory of ownership, it would appear irrefutable that the insurer who issued the policy had $550 at risk after 20 years and not $1,000, the face value of the policy.

Obviously the build-up of the cash surrender value fund throughout the years is a vertical absorption of a portion of the $1,000 which would have been paid out in the event of early death which is, of course, the accidental risk inherent in all life insurance policies.

The remaining $550 of the face value of the policy is still being spread by the insurer among the people who have pooled the risk of untimely death through the insuring process. So it is also a good example of horizontal absorption of risk.

No such vertical integration is available in any program or policy of any conventional property-liability insurance company. Some aspects of vertical integration are involved in the calculation of premium by the use of past loss data of the individual corporate insured to develop future premium costs. But there is nothing as formalized as in the case of a cash value life insurance policy. Perhaps it is because of this that the vertical absorption of risk principle came into being in self insurance and captive insurance programs.

Manageable Risks

One student of the subject has said that the corporate risk management department should concern itself with "manageable" risks which arise solely out of the activities of the firm and are incidental to them; are associated with the occurrence of an undesirable contingency that can only produce economic loss; and are identifiable and both the frequency and the severity are to some extent subject to probability estimates.

Interlocking Functions

In corporations today, responsibilities of most managers are diffused among two or more specialties. Risk management is no exception.

Because of this diffusion, chart makers have begun to depict the corporate organizational structure by drawing a series of interconnecting circles, rather than the traditional boxes connected by vertical and horizontal lines.

Using the newer device of interlocking circles, the typical risk management function in a large corporation looks something like this.

POSITION CHART
RISK MANAGEMENT DEPARTMENT
____________ CORPORATION

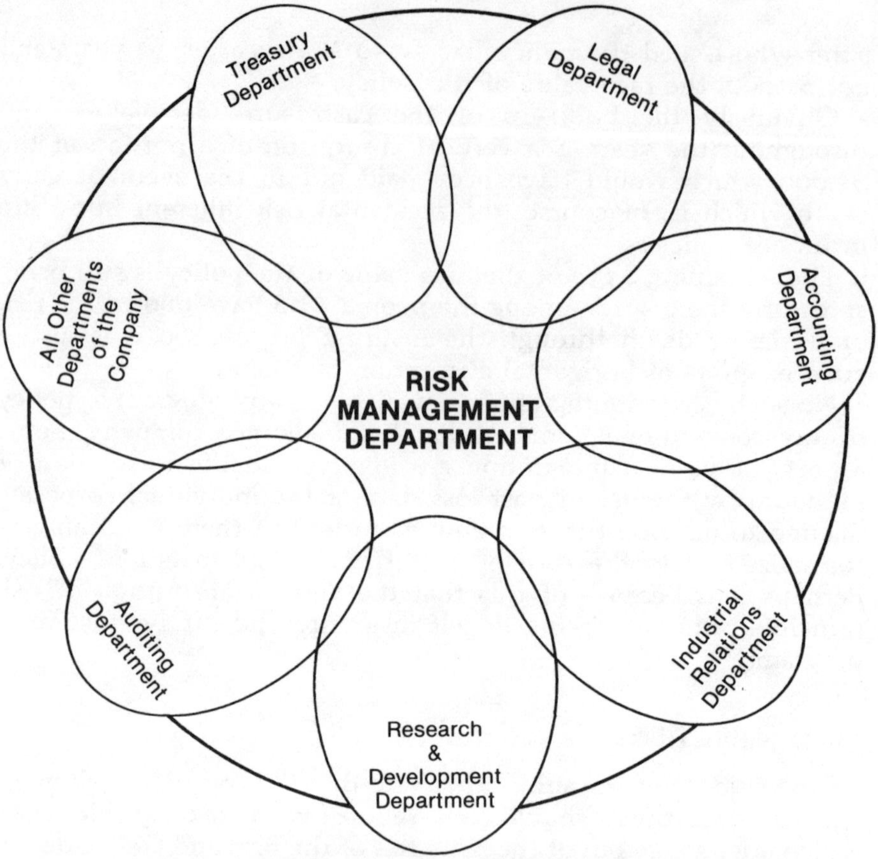

FUNCTIONS OF RISK MANAGEMENT DEPARTMENT

1. Assists all company departments to determine "fortuitous" risks. Works with those departments to develop ways to minimize these risks. Recommends whether to insure, self insure or retain those risks. Obtains and evaluates insurance rates where necessary. Helps departments develop data needed for compiling insurance or self-insurance rates.

2. Reports to treasurer. Reviews risk management program with treasurer to help keep top management advised of the program. Helps treasury department to develop cash flow and cash requirement charts on risk management expenditures, including corporate insurance premiums.

3. Assists legal department to review all contracts which might increase fortuitous risks of the corporation. Makes appropriate recommendations to minimize or stabilize these risks.

4. Assists accounting department to develop the proper accounting entries involving the corporate insurance and self-insurance programs.

5. Coordinates all workers' compensation and insured employee benefit payments with the industrial relations department. Helps this department develop data for negotiating with unions.

6. Assists research and development department to determine the extent, if any, of fortuitous risks in new product design. Advises the department promptly of any incidents of claims which might relate or pertain to this area.

7. Assists auditing department to administer the employee fidelity bond program.

2

A Word About Words

This chapter presents a series of definitions of terms we use throughout this text.

Risk

Let's start with a key word—*risk. Risk* is the chance or possibility of loss. Closely associated with it are two other terms, *peril* and *hazard.* A *peril* is the agency, such as fire, windstorm, or flood, which actually causes a loss. *Hazard* describes those conditions which enhance the possibility of loss. Thus a pile of oily rags in your garage is a *hazard,* the existence of which enhances the possibility that the *peril* of fire will occur, thus increasing your *risk* of loss by *fire.*

Accident, Occurrence, Event

If your garage does start burning, you have suffered an *accident* which is a sudden, unintended happening generally resulting in injury to a person, or damage to property, or both. The term *accident* is also a key one in any text on risk, since an *accident* is a risk which has occurred. The term *accident* is often grouped with two other terms, *occurrence* and *event.* An *accident* is a sudden, one-time happening. An *occurrence,* however, can be a series of happenings spread over a period of time. Thus if you are insured on an *occurrence basis* rather than on an *accident basis,* you are more greatly protected. The term *event,* when used in an insuring clause, provides broader protection than that provided by the term *accident* or *occurrence.* From an insurance point of view, an *event* is a series of accidental happenings all having the same cause. Thus, a hurricane is an *event* made up of numerous *accidents,* each of which involve destruction or damage. This distinction is often significant to the corporate insured which might have buildings or other facilities widely dispersed yet susceptible to damage from one *event,* such as a hurricane.

Insurance

Let us now examine what is meant by *insurance, insurer, insured, the insured,* and other terms often used in conjunction or interchangeably with these terms.

Insurance in its broadest sense is a key term in any risk management study. It is also a term which stimulates many definitions and descriptions. First take the legal definition from Black's Legal Dictionary:

"A contract whereby, for a stipulated consideration, one party undertakes to compensate the other for loss on a specified subject by specified perils. The party agreeing to make the compensation is usually called the 'insurer' or 'underwriter'; the other, the 'insured' or 'assured'; the agreed consideration, the 'premium'; the written contract, a 'policy'; the events insured against, 'risks' or 'perils'; and the subject, right, or interest to be protected, the 'insurable interest.' "

In the Random House dictionary we find that insurance is "the act, system, or business of guaranteeing against loss or harm."

An insurance dictionary defines insurance as a ". . . contract . . . whereby . . . the insurer agrees to pay an agreed amount of money to the insured if and when the latter may suffer some loss or may be injured by some event, the happening of which is described in the contract . . ."[1]

A philosophical definition of insurance is "the accumulation of small amounts from the many who are subject to the loss, to pay for the losses of the few who do suffer the loss" (author unknown). Another unknown source describes insurance as "the payment of a small but certain loss (the premium) in return for indemnification for a larger although uncertain loss if it occurs." Of the hundreds of other definitions of insurance, I prefer this: "Insurance is the pooling of risks on a voluntary basis through the use of intermediaries."

Emphasis on the pooling aspect of insurance was probably first made by Dr. Ralph H. Blanchard in 1949 in the U.S. Chamber of Commerce's Dictionary of Insurance Terms, with the preferred definition of insurance as "a pooling of hazards in order to indemnify those who experience losses."

---

[1] Gallagher and Heath, *Insurance Words and Their Meaning.* The Rough Notes Co., Inc.

For fun, we might add the corrosive definition from Ambrose Bierce's *The Devil's Dictionary:* "Insurance is an ingenious modern game of chance in which the player is permitted to enjoy the comfortable conviction that he is beating the man who keeps the table."

Insurers

With rare unanimity all students and practitioners of the subject agree that the provider of the insuring service should be called the *insurer.* For reasons neither logical nor clear, some practitioners refer to insurers as *carriers.* It would be beneficial both to the insurance industry and to the transportation industry if the term *carrier* were reserved for transporters of goods.

In an incisive speech to the Insurance Advertising Conference, E. B. Weiss, vice president, Creative Merchandising, a New York based advertising agency, had this to say of the word *carrier* for an *insurer:*

"If ever an industry proclaimed its lack of understanding of modern society and modern marketing, the continued use of the traditional term 'carrier' by the insurance industry *spells this out.* Originally, the function was indeed 'carrier.' The carrier decided the forms of protection it would make available—and then carried the risks. This was very largely what consumer goods manufacturers did before the age of modern marketing. They decided what the factory would make—and that was what the public had to take.

"But modern marketing starts with what a constantly changing public wants—and then caters to those wants. That requires an *organization committed to innovation* and to modern marketing—which is quite rare in insurance. That commitment also includes sophisticated market research on a large scale—a function that also remains elementary in insurance. These lacks may explain the industry's current image which is probably more unattractive than at any time since the Hughes investigation at the turn of the century."

The Insured

The preferred term for the party receiving the protection afforded, is *the insured.*

Much clarity in insurance semantics was lost because insurance was not a specific subject for litigation in the early common law courts of England after the Norman invasion. If it had, this second party to the insurance contract would probably be known as the *insuree.* The Norman-French passive participle was retained in the language of the emerging law court system thus providing the distinctive suffix "ee" to describe the parties to whom promises were made (promisee), land was deeded (grantee), gifts were given (donee).

The term, *the insured* to designate the acceptor of the service is probably a shortened version of *the insured party.* Since the word "insured" can also be used as the past tense of the verb, practitioners probably became uneasy with sentences that included "the insured was insured," and the insidious habit of referring to *the insured* as *the assured* arose. *Assure* should be eliminated from insurance language since it adds nothing but confusion and misunderstanding.

The insurance industry could do worse than adapt to the use of the distinctive "ee" suffix, and thus describe the second party to the insurance contract as "insuree." The value of this suffix was illustrated by the Securities & Exchange Commission which, in an exhaustive opinion on the disseminating of so-called inside information (or tips) on publicly held stocks, found it necessary to use the terms *tipper* and *tippee* to describe provider and acceptor.

Underwriter

The word *underwriter* when used as a synonym for *insurer* is a grievous sin against good semantics, since it is also used, and correctly, to describe the employee within an insurance company whose duty it is "to select risks for insurance and to determine in what amounts and on what terms they will be accepted by the insurer."[2]

Life and Casualty

There are two broad divisions of insurance—life and casualty. This comes about because the states, which license insurers, divide the business in this manner.

The life insurance industry writes life insurance contracts and annuity contracts. These two lines of insurance are not permitted to the casualty insurers. Exclusive areas for casualty insurers are property and liability insurance, surety and fidelity coverages. Accidental death and dismemberment insurance and virtually all forms of health insurance such as hospital, surgical and other medical coverages can be written by both life insurers and casualty insurers.

---

[2] *Dictionary of Insurance Terms.* Dr. Ralph H. Blanchard, ed. Chamber of Commerce of the United States.

Self Insurance

Because this is a study of risk management, it is particularly important to examine the terminology used in describing the treatment of risk available to the party subject to the risk. If the party contracts to transfer the risk to another, the process is universally described as *insuring* the risk. *Self insurance* has been defined in the Dictionary of Insurance Terms as "setting aside of funds by an individual or organization to meet one's or its losses, and accumulation of a fund to absorb fluctuations in the amount of loss, the losses being charged against the funds so set aside or accumulated." *Self assumption* of a risk is something different. It is a process in which a person or organization consciously accepts the risks of loss without making provision for it either by insuring it or self insuring it.

A respectable group of insurance semanticists prefer to call this process *risk retention.* I believe the word *retention* is best used to describe funds paid to the insurer by the insured. *Gross retention* means funds not yet used for losses. *Net retention* means funds remaining after deducting losses and other expenses incurred for the insured. Despite what I believe or like, the term *self-insured retention* is increasingly being used to describe a program whereby a party susceptible to a risk consciously accepts that risk without insurance whether or not the risk is provided for by means of a self insurance reserve.

Fire Protection

People generally and risk managers in particular should know how fire protection engineers, the firms providing their equipment, and the manufacturers of building materials, describe the capability of those materials.

For years people in this specialty suffered because of the use of two key terms. One of these was the term *fireproof,* which is misleading. No material or building is fireproof. So the term *fire resistive* is being substituted to describe the condition of materials in buildings which the public generally would call fireproof.

A second key term was *inflammable,* which was ambivalent because of the prefix "in." Practitioners developed the term *non-flammable* to be used as the antonym of *flammable.*

To provide more detailed explanations of fire protection terms we are appending to this chapter an Explanation of Terms from the Fire Protection Handbook of the National Fire Protection Association.

EXPLANATION OF TERMS

The terms in this HANDBOOK are in accordance with general usage and dictionary definitions. Those listed below are used in this HANDBOOK with the meanings indicated. A number of special terms are individually defined in the text. See the Index for the location of these definitions.

Combustible is used to refer to a material or structure which can burn. *Combustible* is a relative term; many materials which will burn under one set of conditions will not burn under others, e.g., structural steel is noncombustible, but fine steel wool is combustible. The term *combustible* does not usually indicate ease of ignition, burning intensity, or rate of burning, except when modified by a word such as *highly,* as in *highly combustible interior finish.*

Fire prevention refers primarily to measures directed towards avoiding the inception of fire. *Fire prevention,* as used in the HANDBOOK, is not synonymous with *fire protection.*

Fireproof has been officially discontinued in NFPA publications as misleading, as no material is immune to the effects of fire of sufficient intensity and duration, although *fireproof* as popularly used is synonymous with *fire resistive* as defined here. *Fireproof* is also used in quotation marks in some references to popular misconceptions of the fire resistive properties of buildings.

Fire load refers to the amount of combustibles present in a given situation, usually expressed in terms of weight of combustible material per square foot. This measure is employed frequently to calculate the degree of fire resistance required to withstand a fire or to judge the rate of application and quantity of extinguishing agent needed to control or extinguish a fire.

Fire protection is used in two senses. The general sense, typified by the use of the term in the National Fire Protection Association name, includes everything relating to the prevention, detection, and extinguishment of fire; the reduction of losses and other matters covered in the HANDBOOK; as well as both the safeguarding of human life and the preservation of property. In its specific sense, *fire protection* refers to the methods of providing for fire control or fire extinguishment.

Fire resistance is a relative term, used with a numerical rating or modifying adjective to indicate the extent to which a material or structure resists the effect of fire, e.g., "*fire resistance* of 2 hours as measured on the Standard Time-Temperature Curve."

Fire resistive refers to properties or designs to resist the effects of any fire to which a material or structure may be expected to be subjected. *Fire resistive* materials or assemblies of materials are noncombustible, but noncombustible materials are not necessarily *fire resistive; fire resistive* implies a higher degree of fire resistance than noncombustible. *Fire-resistive* construction is defined in Section 6, Chapter 5 in terms of specified fire resistance as measured by the Standard Time-Temperature Curve.

Fire retardant, in general, denotes a substantially lower degree of fire resis-

Source: *The Fire Protection Handbook,* 14th Edition, page A-39.

tance than fire resistive and is often used to refer to materials or structures which are combustible in whole or in part, but have been subjected to treatments or have surface coverings to prevent or retard ignition or the spread of fire under the conditions for which they are designed.

Flameproof, flameproofing are misleading terms and their use is discouraged in favor of *flame retardant* or *flame resistant.*

Flame resistant is a term that may be used more or less interchangeably with *flame retardant* (see below).

Flame retardant refers to materials, usually decorative, which due to chemical treatment or inherent properties do not ignite readily or propagate flaming under small to moderate exposure. It is the preferable term to denote chemicals, processes, paints, or coatings used for the treatment of such materials as fabrics, foliage, Christmas trees and similar items in the class of decorations or furnishings. Flame retardant denotes a lower degree of resistance than fire retardant.

Flammable is used to describe a combustible material that ignites very easily, burns intensely, or has a rapid rate of flamespread. *Flammable* is used in a general sense without reference to specific limits of ignition temperature, rate of burning, or other property. Where exact differentiations are necessary, numerical divisions are made, such as Class I and Class II *flammable* liquids. *Flammable* and *inflammable* are identical in meaning. *Flammable* is used in preference to *inflammable* to avoid possible confusion due to the prefix *in-* which indicates the negative in many words, e.g., *incombustible.*

Flashover refers to the phenomenon of a slowly developing fire (or radiant heat source) producing radiant energy at wall and ceiling surfaces. The radiant feedback from those surfaces gradually heats the contents of the fire area, and when all the combustibles in the space have become heated to their ignition temperature, simultaneous ignition occurs as from a pilot ignition source.

Hazard (hazardous) is used in different senses. One is to indicate materials of more than average combustibility or materials that are dangerous because of their explosibility, instability, or toxicity, e.g., cellulose nitrate which is *hazardous* because of ease of ignition and intensity of burning, or a combustible dust which presents a *hazardous* condition when in suspension. A second use of *hazardous* is to describe the over-all degree of fire vulnerability of a property, thinking in terms of its fire load. For example, sprinklers require closer spacing in an extra *hazard* occupancy than in an ordinary *hazard* occupancy. A third use of *hazard* is to describe rate of burning, e.g., wood in the form of shavings is more *hazardous* than in the form of solid timber. Then, too, the term *hazard* is used to describe the nature of the fire problem, e.g., common *hazards* are ignition sources encountered in almost every class of property (smoking, heating, electrical, etc.) while special *hazards* are those considered peculiar to an individual property, e.g., dip tanks, spray booths, drying ovens in a metalworking plant. There is no sharp line of demarcation between common and special *hazards* as the same potential fire cause may be considered a common *hazard* in one occupancy and a special *hazard* in another.

Incombustible has the same meaning as *noncombustible,* but may be subject to misunderstanding due to the prefix *in-.*

Inflammable. See **Flammable.**

Noncombustible means *not combustible.*

Nonflammable means *not flammable.*

3
The Scope and Dynamics of Risk Management

Just what does a risk manager and the employees of a risk management department do? Do they spend their working days delineating the corporation's accidental risks from its business risks and then remonstrate with top management to abate the accidental risks forthwith? Probably not—or at least not for long.

Over the years the corporate risk management department has fallen heir to many clerical and administrative tasks that are as essential to the success of the corporation as those tasks assigned to any other department.

Although these tasks vary from one corporation to another, we present here a fairly representative list of responsibilities of a typical corporate risk management department.

Economical Protection

The risk manager and the department must make sure that the corporation receives the best and most economical protection from its insurance contracts. This is true whether the risk manager has complete and final binding authority or whether recommendations must be approved by higher management.

Insurance is complicated, its workings oblique, and its terminology obscure. So most corporations rely heavily on their risk management department to make sure the corporate purpose is well served, often without too much detailed supervision. Corporate insurance is not inexpensive and contracts often call for six-figure annual expenditures. Even seven-figure expenditures are becoming commonplace.

Once, when discussing an impending auto insurance price increase in a state in which that coverage is compulsory, an articulate political pundit expressed the opinion that, with the exception of income taxes, no expenditure was more resented by the voters than auto insurance. This is because, he said, it is intangible, its benefits are remote, and it has an inherent negative quality. The discerning corporate risk manager recognizes that insurance expenditures are unappreciated by top management for exactly the same reasons.

Loss Prevention

The many insurance contracts of corporations specify a multitude of things that are to be accomplished by both parties—the insurer and the insured. It is the risk management department's responsibility to see that these things are accomplished.

Over the years, certain equipment used by the corporation has been deemed hazardous enough by governmental authority to require periodic inspection of the equipment and other loss prevention activity. It has been customary for the insurer underwriting the risks to do this inspecting. Thus, the insurer for boiler and pressure vessel explosion invariably inspects those devices as required by state law or municipal ordinance. Similarly, the insurer for elevator liability performs the mandatory inspections of those devices. Most fire insurers, particularly where huge concentrated insurable values are involved, make inspections and perform other loss prevention services to reduce fire hazards. They make certain that sprinklers and other fire fighting apparatus are in working order.

All of this insurer inspection activity generates a sizeable amount of paperwork between the insurer and the corporation. The insurer's reports, often recommending engineering, structural or procedural changes, must be evaluated and coordinated within the corporation. These evaluations are almost never the sole responsibility of the risk manager. The coordination required within the corporation is usually the responsibility of the risk manager. It is generally the "user" or "owner" department of the equipment that must agree to and then accomplish these changes.

Accounting

The corporate insurance program requires specialized accounting. Whether or not the risk management department allocates the insurance costs throughout the "using" divisions and departments of the company, the risk manager must be familiar with the method used to allocate, because it takes specialized knowledge to make sure that this allocation is fair and equitable.

Underwriting

To reduce clerical work, corporations strive to provide the data that the insurer needs to underwrite the corporate risks in a systematic simple form, with enough detail that the premium is fair and adequate. Yet the procedure for accumulating the data should be as inexpensive as possible.

If you and I were to buy another car or add a room to our house, we would have to advise our insurer to give us protection for these new items. This is not an onerous task for us, because such events occur infrequently in our personal lives. A corporation, with insurable values in the hundreds of millions of dollars is constantly adding to and deleting from its plant and equipment. Similarly, a corporation with hundreds or thousands of vehicles is constantly adding to and deleting from its fleet. So the task of keeping the insurer informed is a complicated one.

Various ways are used to provide the insurer with data essential to underwriting. For underwriting property risks, a corporation may report the acquisition or disposal of "significant" values of buildings and equipment—say $250,000 or more, and then rely on taking an average of the total of the values at the beginning and end of the time period used. For inventory values, which can fluctuate widely, due to seasonal and other cycles, it is often deemed fair to both insurer and the insured that an average inventory complement be established upon which the insurance premium will be based. Thus, it is assumed that the times when the location will have inventory greater than the complement will be offset by the times when the actual inventory will be less than the complement. In the event of loss the insurer will pay the amount of the loss.

Business Interruption

Values for business interruption insurance are difficult to fix. This insurance coverage, designed to reimburse the corporation for the contribution to fixed costs and profit arising from the destroyed location, depends upon the exposure to loss, which in turn depends upon the level of plant production, the stability of the market for the product and other highly variable elements.

The risk management department must have a broad enough knowledge of all aspects of company operations to make sure that countless details are properly executed and the corporate interest is served. It is essential that the tasks described above are carried out successfully. Most of this administrative work deals with corporate risks which most people in the corporation are aware of and upon which the corporation has decided to insure or self insure or retain. It is more difficult to ascertain and evaluate the new risks to which the corporation is subject than to reevaluate those corporate risks which have changed in intensity and potentiality.

The Dynamics of Risk

The dynamics of risk is fascinating. It deals with the drives and outside influences which keep changing the risks in form and substance and in how these risks are regarded.

A wayward cousin of mine once felt that he knew how to earn his living by betting on horse races. His system was to double his bet after each loss until he obtained a winner. One does not have to be an expert in geometric progression to know that, after a very few losses and consequent doubling up, my cousin was making bets of considerable magnitude. It wasn't long before he was forced to abandon his system. I once asked him what was the largest bet he had made. His answer was, "My last two dollars!"

This illustrates one aspect of the dynamics of risk, which is that a loss can have a vastly different effect upon different corporations, or even upon the same corporation at different times. A corporation with hundreds of millions of dollars of retained earnings is not greatly affected by a large uninsured loss. But a corporation with little retained earnings would have to omit its dividend as a result of suffering the loss. It is apparent that the intensity of loss, measured by data within the corporation, is a factor in the dynamics of the risk.

Importance of Timing

Consider also the timing element. To illustrate, assume that a person requires major surgery that will cost $100,000. Most persons would find it extremely difficult, if not impossible, to get together this sum in the 90 to 120 days, in which the medical profession assumes such charges will be paid. On the other hand, if this cost could be paid over an extended period of years at the rate of $100 a month, most persons could absorb it without too much trouble.

A serious problem arises where a loss occurs and there is not enough time to take care of it. In such instances, relatively small amounts become very important. This is the rationale behind some seemingly inconsistent indemnification provisions in insurance contracts. A good example is the typical provision in some medical insurance contracts that provide for reimbursement of hospital expenses in full, while stipulating something less than full reimbursement for surgical and other medical costs. Hospital bills are generally expected to be paid weekly and, at the latest, at the time a patient is discharged. Many of us pay our doctors' bills on a much more leisurely schedule. This timing element is an important one to consider in any plan for reimbursement via an insurance contract. A contract that ignores such an element is said to be unresponsive to the need of the insured.

Risks Constantly Change

Risk, like life itself, is everywhere around us, and like life, it is constantly changing. Virtually every aspect of living is susceptible to risk and the chance of risk. If the owner of a year-round home buys a hunting lodge, the risk of loss of property is doubled. The exposure is doubled.

The acquisition of a second automobile by a family results in an obvious increase in risk. It is not so obvious that the risk of loss to the owner of a house inexorably increases as the value of the house increases due to inflation and other factors. It is just as probable that the risk of fortuitous loss will probably increase as the house gets older and more hazardous.

It is logical that all corporations of any size should have someone on the payroll responsible for the analysis and disposition of these fortuitous risks. Large corporations should have an entire department devoted to this activity.

4

The Law of Large Numbers

The law of large numbers is basic to risk management. Insurance companies couldn't get along without it, any more than mathematicians could get along without the multiplication table.

The law of large numbers sprang from the study of probability, which is a part of the science of logic. The concept is simple. When we say the law of averages is catching up with us, we really are referring to the law of large numbers. A discerning bishop, Joseph Butler (1692–1752), once said, "Probability is the very guide of life."

Poisson's Law

The law of large numbers was first propounded by Simeon Denis Poisson (1781–1840), a French mathematician and logician. He studied such human traits as drunkenness and absent mindedness, which might seem to occur at random. But he observed that these traits showed up at a predictable frequency—when large aggregates of individuals are included. That is the key—large numbers.

A vital example of this law is the incidence of early death. When we look only at small groups of people, such as single families or even an entire community, the death of a 25-year-old person appears to be an almost isolated event. Yet the actuarial tables tell us that out of every 100,000 persons 25 years old, 193 will die.

Within groups and for specific, short periods of time, there can be considerable deviation from the norm. But as the number of persons or events in the sample increases, the closer we come to the number predicted by Poisson's law of large numbers.

Other Pioneers

While there is general agreement among students of the subject that Poisson was the first to name the phenomenom being described as the law of large numbers, there is no agreement that he discovered the principle alone. Richard von Mises, in his work, "Probability, Statistics and Truth," expressed the opinion that Poisson's work is a generalization of a theorem formulated by Jacques Bernouilli (1654–1705). Thereafter, von Mises refers to the Bernouilli-Poisson theorem.[1]

John Maynard Keynes has said that Poisson's work on the law of great numbers, as the British prefer to call it, was but an extension of Bernouilli's theorem.[2]

Poisson's studies were further simplified by the Belgian statistician and astronomer, Adolphe Jacques Lambert Quetelet (1796–1874), who further inferred that Poisson's "law" was a consequence of the mathematical theory of probability. Quetelet was so impressed with the law that he advocated its use as a base for a system of social physics.

Probability as a Philosophical Concept

When we talk about probability, we should keep clearly in mind that this concept has both a philosophical sense and a mathematical aspect. Writing in the Encyclopedia Americana, Ernest Nagel, professor of philosophy at Columbia University (faculty emeritus), defines probability in its philosophical sense. He calls it "that branch of general logic which analyzes nondemonstrative inferences or arguments as distinguished from demonstrative ones."

Nagel adds that a nondemonstrative argument is one where a conclusion does not necessarily or with certainty stand proven as true by the arguments advanced in support of it. In contrast, a demonstrative argument is one in which the conclusion has to be true if the arguments advanced in support of it are true.

In any such analysis of nondemonstrative inferences, when we are presented with arguments supporting the truth of the conclusion, but if the arguments are not strong enough to render the conclusion certain, the next analytical step is to try to measure the degree of certainty involved. When we hear comments beginning with "the chances are . . ." or "the odds are . . ." this process of assigning weight to the arguments is going on. This assignment of weight is a constant process in the decision making of virtually all aspects of living. So it does support Bishop Butler's comment, mentioned earlier, that probability is the very guide of life.

---

[1] von Mises, Richard, *Probability, Statistics and Truth,* trans. Hilda Geiringer, New York, the Macmillan Company 1957, pp. 104–106.

[2] Keynes, John Maynard, *A Treatise on Probability,* New York and Evanston, Harper and Row, 1962, pp. 332–334.

The Mathematical Approach

The mathematical theory of probability is an extension of the philosophical process. In it we seek to assign numerical measurement to the abstract concept of likelihood. However, the mathematical theory of probability encompasses much more than merely a mathematical determination of the "chances of" or "odds on" a certain event occurring. This theory encompasses a whole branch of mathematical activity, including statistics, use of random variables, combinations and permutations that are part of the field of operations research, which uses specific and relative likelihood as a base.

The difference between the philosophical and the mathematical concept of probability is a subtle one. Corporate risk managers and those who seek to help them in their work must be aware of the distinction, since both concepts can be, and often have to be, brought into use in the successful disposition of risk management problems.

The fact that one cannot place a dollar value on the various possibilities which may occur does not mean that such possibilities can be ignored. The best service that corporate risk managers can give their corporations in this area of nonquantifiable risk is to isolate, identify and announce the existence of these risks. This accomplishes, first, the identification of potential loss, and permits taking steps to ameliorate or prevent the loss. Second, it eliminates unpleasant surprises which top management abhors.

Lessening the Risks

Having successfully isolated, identified and announced the existence of the fortuitous risk, what should risk managers do next? The obvious answer is that they must do whatever they can to lessen the risk. From the very nature of these risks, we know that no one can completely eliminate the possibility of loss. But, the law of large numbers can be used to ameliorate, or tame, the risks, although this is not an easy principle to apply.

Let's see what the experts have to say. von Mises states flatly, "to apply the theory of probability, we must have a practically unlimited sequence of uniform observations."[3] At the same time, he introduces a new term, "the collective." He defines it as a sequence of uniform processes. A collective, he adds, must exist be-

[3] von Mises, *Probability, Statistics and Truth,* ibid p. 11.

fore we can speak of probability. The definition of probability is only concerned with "the probability of encountering a certain attribute in a given collective."[4]

von Mises further states that the probability of winning a battle, as an example, has no place in the theory of probability, because we cannot think of a collective to which it belongs.[5] Other aspects of a collective, according to von Mises, are that the relative frequencies of the attributes must present limiting values and that these limiting values must remain the same in all partial sequences which may be selected from the original one in an arbitrary way.[6]

We learn from Keynes that, in the application of probability, the principle of indifference must exist. He says, "events are equally probable if we have not the slightest knowledge of the conditions under which each of them is going to occur."[7]

These observations about probability can best be illustrated by a simple example. Say you are tossing a coin and you have had a phenomenal streak of heads coming up—say 50 times in a row. Now you are about to toss the coin for the fifty-first time.

Most nonexperts of probability would assume that the chances of this toss coming up on the tails side would be immeasurably greater than on the heads side. The experts tell us "no." Despite the long streak of heads, the chances are still 50–50.

Stability of Statistical Frequencies

Finally, Keynes comes to a most important aspect of the concept of probability in general and the law of large numbers in particular. He says:

"The existence of numerous instances of the Law of Great Numbers, or of something of the kind, is absolutely essential for the importance of Statistical Induction." Apart from this, the more precise parts of statistics, the collection of facts, for the prediction of future frequencies and associations, would be nearly useless.

"But the 'Law of Great Numbers' is not at all a good name for the principle which underlies Statistical Induction. The 'Stability of Statistical Frequencies' would be a much better name for it."

---

[4] von Mises, *Probability, Statistics and Truth,* ibid p. 12.
[5] von Mises, *Probability, Statistics and Truth,* ibid p. 15.
[6] von Mises, *Probability, Statistics and Truth,* ibid p. 24.
[7] Keynes, *A Treatise on Probability,* ibid p. 75.

The former suggests, as perhaps Poisson intended to suggest, but which is certainly false, that every class of event shows statistical regularity of occurrence if only one takes a sufficient number of instances of it. It also encourages the method of procedure, by which it is thought legitimate to take any observed degree of frequency or association, which is shown in a fairly numerous set of statistics, and to assume with insufficient investigation that, because the statistics are numerous, the observed degree of frequency is therefore stable.

Observation shows that some statistical frequencies are, within narrower or wider limits, stable. But stable frequencies are not very common, and cannot be assumed lightly.

"The gradual discovery that there are certain classes of phenomena in which, though it is impossible to predict what will happen in each individual case, there is nevertheless a regularity of occurrence if the phenomena be considered together in successive sets, gives the clue to the abstract inquiry upon which we are about to embark."[8]

Where risk management is concerned, Keynes' observations sound a warning and a great opportunity.

The Role of Probability

Probability, in its mathematical sense, is used in the insuring process. Mortality tables are used in determining life insurance premium rates. As for property and liability coverages, the expected loss rates are developed from past loss data and are used to determine the premium to be charged to insure against future losses of that class.

To the loss data so developed, a credibility factor is applied. The application of this factor in itself recognizes an aspect of the law of large numbers. It says that the larger the sample, the more probable that the sample will conform to the norm.

The practical effect of applying credibility tables to loss data for rate making is to penalize the lesser amount of loss data so treated, at least when compared with the treatment accorded the larger amounts. Past loss data are extremely important in calculating the premium to be charged for insurance against risk. Insurers strive to distribute the losses of the few among the many who bear the risk of such losses.

---

[8] Keynes, *A Treatise on Probability,* ibid p. 336.

Finding the Premium

To illustrate, let's turn again to the risk of early death. According to the mortality tables widely used among life insurers, 251 out of every 100,000 persons will die at age thirty-five in any year. It follows, therefore, that a life insurance company would have to charge $2.51 per $1,000. of coverage to provide for the mortality risk of these thirty-five-year old persons. This illustrates the oft quoted precept that insurance is actually a pooling arrangement which assesses the many who are subject to the risk to pay for the losses of the few who actually suffer the losses.

A mortality table does more than describe the number who will die, actuarially speaking, in a given year. It also defines the insurable classes, since it establishes and defines the risk-sharing entities, thus permitting the life insurance industry to arrange a pooling of risk.

We say "actuarially speaking" because, even in a group large enough to achieve 100 percent credibility, there can be substantial deviation from the norm in the actual experience of any group. These deviations from the norm, plus the inherent difficulty in dealing in future events, is the reason why insurers place a loading for uncertainty (the insurers call it contingency) in their calculation of the price to be charged. Although this is probably necessary, it is an anomaly, since it protects the insurers against uncertainty, while they purport to be protecting their customers against uncertainty.

Measuring Inherent Probabilities

Calculating life insurance premiums with exactness is extremely difficult because wide variations from the norm are possible. Yet calculating life insurance premiums is simple compared with calculating premiums for property or liability insurance. No neat risk-sharing entities, such as found in a mortality table, are available to property and liability insurers.

Whether we realize it or not, every decision we ever make involves our use of an element of probability. We are probably going to be better off if we do the thing we're going to do rather than if we do the many other things we are capable of doing instead. This element of probability is present in our decision of where to live, where to work and how to spend our money. In each case, whether we consciously realize it, we rationalize, based on the probabilities. Although we rarely come right down to placing

MORTALITY TABLE

1971 INDIVIDUAL ANNUITY MORTALITY TABLE

Male Age	Number Living	Deaths Each Year	Deaths Per 1,000	Expec-tancy, Years	% Living to 65	Male Age	Number Living	Deaths Each Year	Deaths Per 1,000	Expec-tancy, Years	% Living to 65
5	10,000.00	4.56	.456	71.69	81.35	60	8,735.82	107.01	12.25	20.83	93.12
6	9,995.44	4.24	.424	70.73	81.39	61	8,628.82	113.32	13.13	20.08	94.28
7	9,991.20	4.03	.403	69.75	81.42	62	8,515.50	119.84	14.07	19.34	95.53
8	9,987.18	3.92	.392	68.78	81.46	63	8,395.66	126.63	15.08	18.61	96.90
9	9,983.26	3.88	.389	67.81	81.49	64	8,269.03	133.83	16.19	17.89	93.38
10	9,979.38	3.89	.390	66.84	81.52	65	8,135.19	141.59	17.41	17.17	100.00
11	9,975.49	3.96	.397	65.86	81.55	66	7,993.60	150.02	18.77	16.47	....
12	9,971.52	4.04	.405	64.89	81.58	67	7,843.58	159.15	20.29	15.77	....
13	9,967.49	4.12	.413	63.91	81.62	68	7,684.44	169.00	21.99	15.09	....
14	9,963.37	4.20	.422	62.94	81.65	69	7,515.44	179.54	23.89	14.42	....
15	9,959.17	4.31	.433	61.97	81.69	70	7,335.90	190.73	26.00	13.76	....
16	9,954.85	4.42	.444	60.99	81.72	71	7,145.16	202.50	28.34	13.11	....
17	9,950.43	4.55	.457	60.02	81.76	72	7,942.66	214.76	30.93	12.48	....
18	9,945.89	4.68	.471	59.05	81.79	73	6,727.91	227.41	33.80	11.86	....
19	9,941.20	4.83	.486	58.07	81.83	74	6,500.50	240.36	36.97	11.26	....
20	9,936.37	5.00	.503	57.10	81.87	75	6,260.13	253.50	40.49	10.67	....
21	9,931.37	5.18	.522	56.13	81.91	76	6,006.64	266.65	44.39	10.10	....
22	9,926.19	5.40	.544	55.16	81.96	77	5,739.98	279.62	48.72	9.55	....
23	9,920.79	5.62	.566	54.19	82.00	78	5,460.36	292.13	53.50	9.01	....
24	9,915.17	5.86	.591	53.22	82.05	79	5,168.23	303.82	58.79	8.50	....
25	9,909.31	6.13	.619	52.25	82.10	80	4,864.41	314.26	64.60	7.99	....
26	9,903.18	6.44	.650	51.28	82.15	81	4,550.17	322.62	70.90	7.51	....
27	9,896.74	6.77	.684	50.32	82.20	82	4,227.55	328.35	77.67	7.05	....
28	9,889.97	7.14	.722	49.35	82.26	83	3,899.21	331.20	84.94	6.60	....
29	9,882.83	7.54	.763	48.39	82.32	84	3,568.01	331.37	92.87	6.16	....
30	9,875.29	7.99	.809	47.42	82.38	85	3,236.63	329.13	101.69	5.74	....
31	9,867.30	8.49	.860	46.46	82.45	86	2,907.50	324.63	111.65	5.34	....
32	9,858.82	9.03	.916	45.50	82.52	87	2,582.87	317.82	123.05	4.95	....
33	9,849.79	9.63	.978	44.54	82.59	88	2,265.06	308.33	136.12	4.57	....
34	9,840.15	10.29	1.046	43.58	82.67	89	1,956.73	295.60	151.07	4.21	....
35	9,829.86	11.03	1.122	42.63	82.76	90	1,661.13	279.14	168.04	3.87	....
36	9,818.83	11.82	1.204	41.68	82.85	91	1,381.99	258.64	187.15	3.55	....
37	9,807.01	12.70	1.295	40.73	82.95	92	1,123.36	234.17	208.46	3.26	....
38	9,794.31	13.68	1.397	39.78	83.06	93	889.18	206.19	231.89	2.98	....
39	9,780.63	14.76	1.509	38.83	83.18	94	683.00	175.63	257.15	2.73	....
40	9,765.87	15.95	1.633	37.89	83.30	95	507.37	144.01	283.84	2.50	....
41	9,749.92	17.44	1.789	36.95	83.44	96	363.35	113.21	311.57	2.30	....
42	9,732.48	19.47	2.000	36.02	83.59	97	250.15	85.10	340.21	2.11	....
43	9,713.01	21.95	2.260	35.09	83.76	98	165.04	61.03	369.77	1.94	....
44	9,691.06	24.90	2.569	34.17	83.95	99	104.02	41.63	400.19	1.79	....
45	9,666.16	28.24	2.922	33.25	84.16	100	62.39	26.92	431.41	1.65	....
46	9,637.92	31.98	3.318	32.35	84.41	101	35.47	16.44	463.31	1.53	....
47	9,605.94	36.06	3.754	31.46	84.69	102	19.04	9.44	495.76	1.41	....
48	9,569.88	40.46	4.228	30.57	85.01	103	9.60	5.07	528.60	1.31	....
49	9,529.42	45.17	4.740	29.70	85.37	104	4.53	2.54	561.69	1.21	....
50	9,484.25	50.12	5.285	28.84	85.78	105	1.98	1.18	594.88	1.13	....
51	9,434.13	55.28	5.860	27.99	86.23	106	0.80	0.50	628.02	1.05	....
52	9,378.84	60.60	6.461	27.15	86.74	107	0.30	0.19	660.95	.98	....
53	9,318.24	66.05	7.088	26.33	87.30	108	0.10	0.07	693.50	.92	....
54	9,252.20	71.61	7.740	25.51	87.93	109	0.03	0.02	725.52	.86	....
55	9,180.58	77.27	8.417	24.71	88.61						
56	9,103.31	83.01	9.119	23.91	89.37						
57	9,020.30	88.85	9.850	23.13	90.19						
58	8,931.45	94.79	10.613	22.35	91.08						
59	8,836.66	100.84	11.411	21.59	92.06						

1981 BEST'S FLITCRAFT COMPEND

numbers or ratios or fractions in analyzing our desires, we still are really applying the mathematical theory of probability to decide our course of action.

It is no exaggeration to say that corporate risk management is devoted exclusively to consciously measuring inherent probabilities. For the risk manager, the "event" is the potential loss to the corporation. How does one quantify loss probabilities? The relative quality called for in the definition requires that the event—the loss when it occurs—be compared with some sort of base. von Mises calls this base, "collective."[9] Of necessity, the probabilities must be expressed as fractions, with the probability of occurring as the numerator, and the base as the denominator.

How Mortality Tables Work

A good way to study this subject in more detail is to examine once more the most widely used probability table in existence—the mortality table. All of us know that, despite the neat calculations and orderly rows of numbers, the occurrence of death among the population does not take place with the regularity that such orderliness suggests. These tables are approximations of what does happen. Note that, although a whole year is added in the age column, less than a year is always deducted in the life expectancy column.

Shifting Conditions

Doughty risk takers in property insurance attempt to classify the structures they insure by type of construction. They emphasize the degree of resistance to loss, such as combustibility, what the structures are to be used for, the relative availability of fire fighting capability, and the presence of fire prevention or extinguishing equipment within the structure.

All of these features can change with the passage of time. Then there are the variations found outside the structure, such as inflation and changing patterns of the neighborhood where the structure is located. These can greatly change the degree of risk. And they present to the insurer the herculean task of establishing the proper risk-sharing fee—the premium—that should be charged to cover the losses that could ensue.

---

[9] von Mises, *Probability, Statistics and Truth,* ibid p. 12.

5
Loss Measurement And Control

The corporate risk manager, whether or not directly responsible for the corporation's safety and loss prevention functions, should take an interest in corporate loss control.

The key index for analyzing and measuring industrial accidents is the Z16.1 index published by the American National Standards Institute. It is called "Method of Recording and Measuring Work Injury Experience." By this index, industrial accidents of a chargeable nature are measured by both frequency and severity.

On the frequency scale each accident of a chargeable nature has a value of one, regardless of how severe it might be. According to the plan, a chargeable accident is one severe enough that medical attention is required and the employee is unable to report for work the day following the accident. For every day that the injured employee is unable to work, this accident develops a charge of one person day.

A typical report of person days lost from injuries is given in Table I. This table also shows, at the right, the number of person days representing vehicle accidents which could have been prevented if good safety practices were adhered to.

TABLE I
Safety Department Second Quarter Safety Report

Injuries and Rates Again Improve

There were 131 fewer disabling injuries reported for the 12 months ending 6/30/79 than during the same period a year ago. All but two of the major divisions shared in this decrease. The corporation rate dropped correspondingly to 13.6 lost-time injuries per million person hours worked from 14.9 a year ago.

Four major divisions have so far attained 12 months-to-date rates close to or better than their 1978 disabling injury goals.

Like Quarterly Rates Compared

A comparison of the same quarterly periods a year apart has been introduced in this report to further assist in interpreting accident and injury rate trends.

DIVISION	DISABLING INJURY RATES					PREVENTABLE VEHICLE ACCIDENT RATES				
	2nd Quarter		12-Months Ending		GOALS	2nd Quarter		12-Months Ending		GOALS
	1979	1978	6/30/79	6/30/78	This Yr	1979	1978	6/30/79	6/30/78	This Yr
1	19.7	23.3	27.9	20.9	20.5	4.1	7.2	5.4	7.2	4.0
2	7.5	9.1	8.4	6.6	8.0	0.0	0.7	1.2	2.2	2.5
3	6.4	7.4	8.5	10.5	3.5	2.4	6.5	5.9	8.2	3.6
4	27.4	10.2	23.2	27.7	28.9	0.0	12.7	5.5	14.2	6.0
5	0.0	6.2	1.5	7.4	5.0	0.0	0.0	13.9	21.4	7.1
6	15.6	21.4	18.7	19.3	13.4	7.7	12.9	10.8	14.0	9.4
7	31.3	32.8	32.9	14.3	20.0	10.5	20.6	11.4	14.0	11.0
8	37.6	38.4	47.4	38.4	30.1	7.1	18.6	19.0	25.3	14.4
9	8.9	29.7	17.3	21.8	11.5	3.2	7.2	6.1	7.2	5.5
10	7.4	13.9	10.2	15.6	9.3	9.8	11.9	11.7	13.0	9.2
11	20.4	25.7	21.6	25.3	16.1	11.2	20.5	13.4	19.4	13.3
12	16.5	15.1	18.9	19.5	15.9	6.2	7.9	10.4	9.8	7.1
13	7.2	7.1	6.0	6.1	4.8	6.1	5.1	5.9	9.0	6.0
14	12.5	9.2	8.4	25.6	9.7	0.0	0.0	9.4	16.3	8.7
15	11.3	13.1	13.6	14.9	9.3	4.1	8.6	7.3	10.1	6.9

If the system measured frequency only, a minor accident, such as a cut on the hand would have the same value as a major accident involving the loss of an arm or leg. So the severity index of Z16.1 was devised to distinguish between minor and major accidents. The basic unit in this severity index is still the lost person day described above. However, with serious accidents involving the loss of major members of the body, a series of charges are made based upon the period. Thus the death of an employee is quantified as 6000 person days lost. The loss of an arm or a leg is quantified at 4500 days. This attempts to give perspective to the frequency index. Other time charges in days are given in Table II.

TABLE II
American Standard Z16.1
Table of Scheduled Time Charges (Days)

A. For Loss of Member—Traumatic or Surgical

Fingers, Thumb, and Hand

Amputation involving all or part of bone	Thumb	Fingers: Index	Middle	Ring	Little
Distal Phalange	300	100	75	60	50
Middle Phalange	—	200	150	120	100
Proximal Phalange	600	400	300	240	200
Metacarpal	900	600	500	450	400
Hand at Wrist—3000					

Toe, Foot and Ankle

Amputation involving all or part of bone	Great Toe	Each of Other Toes
Distal Phalange	150	35
Middle Phalange	—	75
Proximal Phalange	300	150
Metatarsal	600	350
Foot at Ankle—2400		

Arm

Any point above elbow, including shoulder joint	4500
Any point above wrist and at or below elbow	3600

Leg

Any point above knee	4500
Any point above ankle and at or below knee	3000

B. Impairment of Function

One Eye (loss of sight), whether or not there is sight in the other eye	1800
Both Eyes (loss of sight), in one accident	6000
One Ear (complete indust. loss of hearing), whether or not there is hearing in the other ear	600
Both Ears (complete indust. loss of hearing), in one accident	3000
Unrepaired Hernia	50

Chart of Scheduled Charges for Hand and Foot

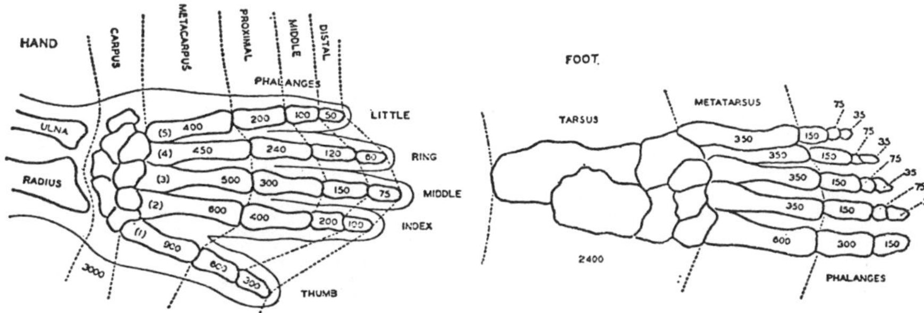

A typical corporate report of frequency and severity for a given period of time would look something like Table III.

A bar chart illustrating the typical trend of frequency rate and severity rate in a company over a period of years is shown in Table IV.

Critics Suggest Dollar Method

There are critics of this reporting method, despite the fact that it is widely used and is the standard approach among corporate safety and loss prevention personnel. The most frequent criticism is that the approach requires top management to learn a whole new set of standards, a new method of quantification, to see how the corporate safety program is doing.

TABLE III
Injury Experience—

	Labor Hours Worked	Disabling Injuries
GROUP I		
Division 1	23,303,139	55
Division 2	7,717,244	22[2]
Division 3	10,629,933	15
Division 4	755,577	4
TOTAL—Group I	42,405,893	96[2]
GROUP II		
Division 5	9,390,385	15
Division 6[1]	2,990,845	3
Division 7	17,467,881	33
Division 8	10,656,534	37[1]
Division 9	5,619,238	31[3]
TOTAL—Group II	46,124,883	119[4]
GROUP III		
Division 10	9,241,857	11
Division 11	3,521,916	8
Division 12	2,682,089	12
TOTAL—Group III	15,445,862	31
Division 13	24,668,032	25
Division		
Division 14[2]	494,102	1
Canada Limited	9,786,362	90
Consolidated Locations	8,482,626	10
Operating	147,407,760	379[6]
Sales	4,357,771	5
TOTAL OPERATING & SALES	151,765,531	384[6]

Fatalities are indicated by superscripts [1] Division 6 started 6/1/78

The critics suggest using the dollar as a measure, since it is the measurement used in virtually all other departments of the corporation to measure performance. The rationale behind this is hard to refute. Virtually all industrial accidents result in some cost to the corporation. To quantify accidents in terms of dollar costs to the corporation does not need to be construed as callous disregard for the human suffering of employees and their families.

One insurer who specializes in workers' compensation analyzed several years of cost data to arrive at averages for the various accidents which occurred among the corporations that it insured. Table V shows typical cost elements which this insurer has indicated would be representative of the cost for several years. To my mind this type of presentation deserves wider acceptance among corporations than it appears to have received.

Table III—cont'd.

D.I. Frequency Rate			Severity Rate	
1979	1978	Days Charged	1979	1978
2.36	2.17	15,439	663	861
2.85	1.41	12,778	1,655	115
1.41	1.22	2,966	279	716
5.29	2.83	71	94	89
2.26	1.84	31,254	737	707
1.60	2.26	1,828	195	1,017
1.00	—	14	5	—
1.89	2.06	1,234	71	755
3.47	3.66	16,370	1,536	2,266
5.52	3.57	18,982	3,378	197
2.58	2.75	38,428	833	1,177
1.19	1.64	370	40	179
2.27	1.75	369	105	57
4.47	8.22	4,723	1,761	1,871
2.01	2.93	5,462	354	473
1.01	1.35	3,166	128	339
2.02	—	7	14	—
9.20	6.65	3,824	391	899
1.18	0.76	112	13	11
2.57	2.40	82,329	559	743
1.15	2.02	69	16	30
2.53	2.39	82,398	543	724

[2] Separate the experience for Division 14 not recorded prior to 1976.

TABLE IV

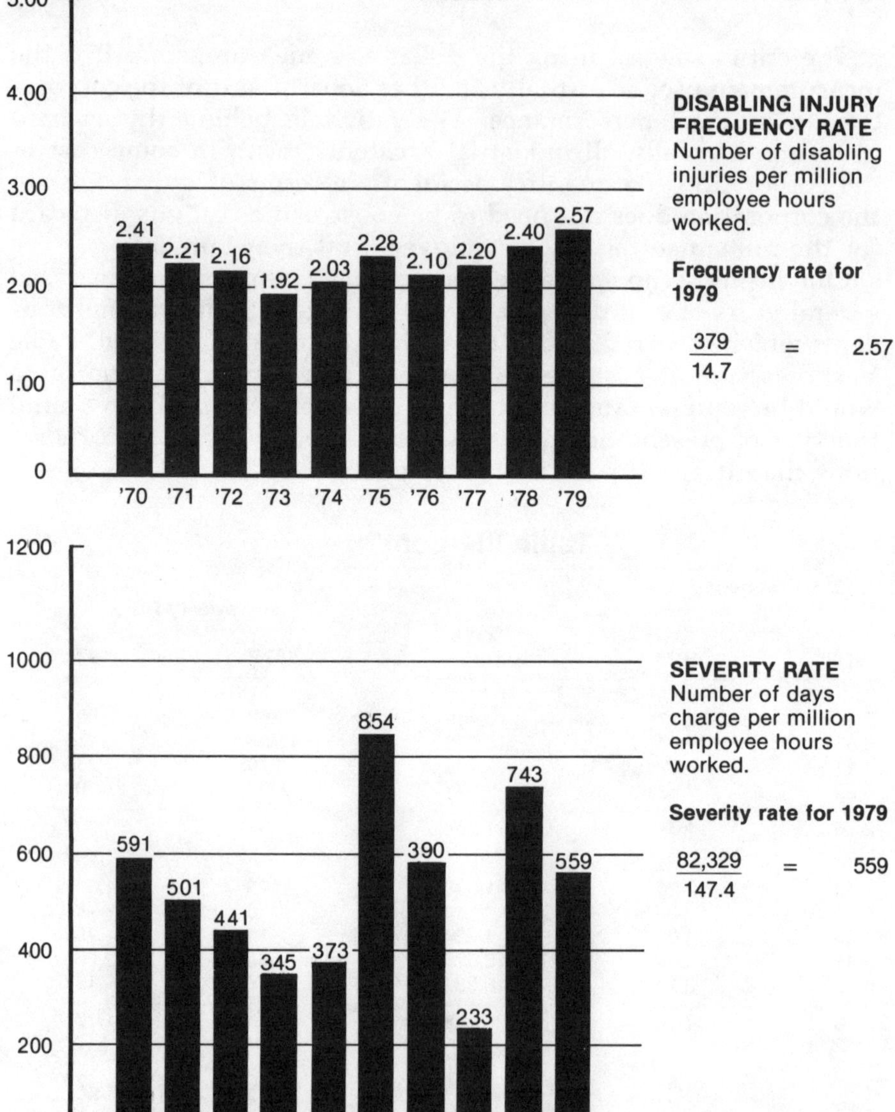

Parts-of-Body Method

Another method often used to categorize industrial accidents is to indicate the part of the employee's body affected by the accident. The benefit of this method is that it often indicates possible steps to take to prevent further accidents. If eye accidents predomi-

TABLE V

Schedule of Charges

(Based on the injury cost analysis previously described)

Injury Involving Medical Cost only	$40
Fatality	$25,000
Permanent Total Disability	$5,000
Temporary Disability Involving No Permanent Results:	
For combined compensation and medical costs based on the number of working days during healing period estimated by doctor	$75 per day
Permanent Partial Disability:	
For combined compensation and medical costs based on the number of working days during healing period estimated by doctor	$75 per day
For the permanent disability based on doctor's estimate and the schedule to time charges from the American Standard Z16.1	$250 per day

nate among a group of employees, safety glasses and other equipment to protect the eyes probably should be made available. If the accidents include many involving injury to the employees' feet, safety shoes may be the answer.

One meaningful statistic was developed some 40 years ago by H. W. Heinrich. It is the ratio of known, direct dollar losses from industrial accidents to dollar losses which are indirect and largely nonquantifiable. In the original publication of this study, Mr. Heinrich suggested that a four-to-one ratio was appropriate. That is, for every dollar of known loss (medical expenses, indemnity to the injured employee, etc.) there were four additional dollars of indirect expenses which the corporation also sustained because of the accident. These indirect expenses could be the overtime premium paid to other employees to take care of the work of the injured employee, lost production, lost sales and similar indirect items.

Since this index was originally published, the data on which it was based have been systematically reviewed and the results published. The four-to-one ratio still appears to be a proper one.

Considering Equipment Needs

When it comes to property conservation, the corporate risk management department must be concerned with the optimum amount of loss protection equipment to be installed in the corporation's plants, warehouses and other facilities. This includes methods of installing sprinklers, the requisite number of fire walls in large facilities, use of explosion-proof roofs and a myriad of other technical details.

Enter OSHA

The passage of the Occupational Safety and Health Act (OSHA) in 1970 by the federal government brought a profound change in corporate loss control.

Briefly, if anyone can be brief about OSHA, the law was enacted to:

- Encourage employers and employees to reduce workplace hazards and to implement new or improved safety and health programs.
- Provide for research in occupational safety and health and develop innovative ways to deal with occupational safety and health problems.
- Establish "separate but dependent responsibilities and rights" for employers and employees to achieve better safety and health conditions.
- Maintain a reporting and recordkeeping system to monitor job-related injuries and illnesses.
- Establish training programs to increase the number and competence of occupational safety and health personnel.
- Develop mandatory job safety and health standards and enforce them effectively.
- Provide for the development, analysis, evaluation and approval of state occupational safety and health programs.

Following enactment came ten years of setting standards, governmental inspections and assorted controversies between and among employers, labor unions and the federal government.

Senator Richard Schweiker, who voted for OSHA in 1970, said in 1979 that he intended to introduce legislation reforming the act. He said he believed the 1970 act erred fundamentally by casting the government as a policeman "in a system of crime and punishment for more than four million workplaces in the United States" rather than directing the government's efforts to the five to ten percent of the workplaces where it is really needed. In 1981 Mr. Schweiker became Secretary of Health and Human Services in the Reagan Administration.

Whatever path OSHA takes, added emphasis will continue to be placed on loss control and job safety as far ahead as we can see.

6

Top Management's Role

To be effective, the corporate risk management department must achieve rapport and a satisfactory degree of coordination with all other departments and divisions of the corporation. This is not always easy to achieve. First we must understand where risk management is placed in the corporate organization and how the function is viewed by top management.

About 10 of every 20 risk managers report to the corporate treasurer, four to the financial vice president, one to the comptroller and one to the corporate counsel. The remaining four report to various other corporate officials, such as corporate secretary, production or quality control officials and/or the executive vice president. Only rarely does the risk manager report to the president or chief executive officer. This diversity of reporting by risk managers probably reflects their wide range of responsibilities—encompassing accounting, finance, law and operations.

The Organization Chart

If we look at the organization of a "typical," large corporation, we find five senior executives who report directly to the chief executive. They are responsible for finance, legal, corporate secretary, sales and operations (manufacturing, processing, etc.). There are other departments which often report directly to the chief executive, such as public relations, personnel, government relations, long range planning and research.

Let us assume there are five such department directors in addition to the five senior executives, making a total of ten reporting directly to the chief executive. These ten executives, with the chief executive, make up the top level of management.

The risk manager is almost never part of this top management group. In smaller companies risk managers are generally included in the second level of management, reporting to the financial vice president. In larger companies they are usually in the third level of management, reporting to the treasurer, who reports to the financial vice president.

One-Thirtieth of Top Management's Attention

The typical corporate organization chart has about 30 specialties having the same prominence as risk management. We can infer from this that risk management, on the average, commands about one-thirtieth of top management's time and attention. There are exceptions. In some companies—the airlines being a notable example—there are times when insurance costs are high and profits are low, giving rise to the anomaly of insurance costs equaling or exceeding the net profit of the company. In such cases corporate insurance costs and other aspects of risk management are sure to get most exacting attention from the top management of the company.

Affirmative vs. Defensive Specialties

The thirty or so specialties found in typical corporations could be divided into two categories—affirmative and defensive. The affirmative ones are those which make good things happen—which further the main objective of the company. Manufacturing, sales, advertising, sales promotion and new product development are affirmative in character. Internal auditing, security, quality control and risk management are defensive in character. These defensive specialities are devoted to keeping bad things from happening.

Top management is usually more comfortable dealing with the affirmative aspects than with the defensive ones. This is understandable because most people like to think positively. Moreover, those engaged in the positive aspects of corporate activity have the big advantage of being able to demonstrate their progress and their improvements in an affirmative way. Increase in sales or production is the most tangible evidence of improvement. Persons engaged in the defensive aspects of corporate activity have to be satisfied to demonstrate their success by showing a reduction in the undesirable.

It is probable that candidates for top management posts are selected from the affirmative areas of the corporation more often than from the defensive, so it is natural that prior training and experience make the people in affirmative jobs more comfortable in dealing with problems in these affirmative areas than in the defensive areas with which they have had less experience.

Members of top management are generalists; risk managers and other defensive practitioners are specialists.

The Most Defensive—Risk Management

Those who work in the defensive specialties in the corporate environment must allow for this inclination of top management in planning and in pursuing their objectives. Risk management, the most defensive of the defensive specialties, has problems all its own. For one, a major part of the risk manager's concern is for human injury, carrying with it the implication of human suffering. Most people, including members of top management, have difficulty concentrating for long on this negative aspect of human experience. Risk managers should be aware of this human tendency.

As we have observed, risk management evolved from the narrower concept of corporate insurance management, first in response to a need to guard against fortuitous risks by means other than buying insurance. It was logical that the insurance manager, already equipped to handle fortuitous risks, should be given the broader responsibilities of the risk manager.

The only problem was that top management was not ready to accept the concept of risk management. When faced with brand new fortuitous risks that cannot be passed on to an insurance company, a top manager rarely calls in the risk manager to discuss the best approach to further identify, evaluate, stabilize and fund it. By and large, corporate top management generally regards as the purview of the risk manager those risks which can be insured or taken care of by some substitute for insurance, such as self insurance.

This limited concept of top management is not likely to change quickly unless one of two things happens:

One would be that the corporation would begin, on a systematic basis, to pay for a whole host of fortuitous risks to which it is subject, by charging some percentage of the corporate profits as an expense and using it to build a reserve. Losses from these risks would then be charged against the reserve. At the present time such reserving is done only for risks of an insurable nature.

A second possibility, which would enlarge the risk manager's responsibility, is that the conventional insurance industry would agree to insure a whole gamut of a corporation's fortuitous risks.

Three Chances in 10,000

One of our truly intellectual risk managers gives a good description of an essential service the corporate risk manager must perform for a company's plant management. The manager begins with the expected loss rate typical of large, modern plants. This is probably about three cents per $100 of insurable value on a plant with a good sprinkler system and similar loss protection equipment.

If one accepts this ratio as reflecting the odds of the plant being destroyed by fire, we are talking about three out of 10,000 chances. My intellectual colleague asks, "How much time can the plant manager devote to the solution of a problem so unlikely to occur?" If the plant manager devoted any substantial amount of time to every risk which has three chances out of 10,000 of occurring, then there would be no time at all to devote to the main job of getting out the production and managing the employees.

Yet fire losses and their prevention are an important aspect of the successful operation of any corporation. The corporate risk manager and staff can successfully synthesize this in-plant risk into a corporatewide activity. This synthesis of risk should apply to all fortuitous risks in all plants of the corporation.

Is there a particular area of activity where risk management can be of more significant service to top management and hence to the company as a whole? It should be noted that in recent years the fortuitous risks which top management faces have increased substantially. These are risks which the corporate risk manager has not been able to help solve. Here is an illustration of this.

Insuring for Loss of Shelf Space

As perceptive a chief executive as I've ever known asked: "Why should a large company making products to retail primarily through supermarkets (where the battle for shelf space is intense) insure its manufacturing plant for $5 million for physical damage and $7 million for business interruption, but neglect to insure against the loss of shelf space, worth perhaps tens of millions, if the plant were out of production for a year or more?

Good risk management, of course, interests itself in the analysis of alternate and sole source of product facilities, and the potentialities of loss arising from it. We must wonder why the conventional insurance industry did not see fit to extend its risk-bearing facilities to the huge potential of this loss of shelf space. It appears that the new product departments of the insurance companies have not kept pace with the truly herculean risks which are being faced by customers for insurance.

Top management understands very well why business risks, being so much within the control of the risk taker, should not be eligible for the insuring process. But executives tend to regard all nonbusiness risks as a group and ask why all of them are not insurable.

Challenging the Risk Manager

The risk manager of one huge corporation reports on a discussion about the renewal of the corporation's business interruption insurance contract with the financial vice president:

The vice president said, "Tell me again what this coverage is designed to do." The risk manager explained that, if one of the company's plants were severely damaged or destroyed by fire or by one of the perils recited in the fire insurance contract's extended endorsement, the insurer would reimburse the corporation for the plant's fixed charges, the pay of the plant's permanent personnel and the profit lost by the plant's disablement or destruction during the time it took to rehabilitate the plant.

The vice president then asked, "How much of a loss are we talking about?" After a quick mental review of the probable maximum loss, the risk manager answered, "Probably in the neighborhood of $5 million."

The Greater Risk—Strikes

The vice president then asked, "You know that our Canadian operations are on strike and have been for some time now. If this continues for as long as we fear it will, no doubt the shutdown will cost the company much more than $5 million. Why should we insure against the remote risk of fire when we must take the much larger loss by strike without insurance?"

The risk manager started to explain in the manner of all risk managers, that insurance against strike loss is virtually impossible to obtain.

But this wasn't what the vice president had in mind. The thought wasn't that strike losses should be pooled with those of other companies through the insuring process. It was, why should the corporation make special provision to take care of a relatively small loss much less apt to occur when it can and must accept the consequences of the larger loss which will occur more often.

The risk manager asked, "Wouldn't the investment community, emphasizing as it does continuity in profit margins, react unfavorably to a $5 million loss which could have been insured and wasn't, while it would be understanding about a larger strike loss, since it is not insurable?"

The vice president was not persuaded and said: "Both the $10 million strike loss and the $5 million fire loss would be treated as a special, extraordinary charge in our financial reporting. Neither could even remotely affect our dividend payment. The investment community tends to take all truly extraordinary charges in stride, even those of a substantial amount. I see no reason why the investment community would react unfavorably to a special charge, especially if the overall effect was that the company saved money in the process." The final observation assumes that the corporation ultimately bears its own losses.

This corporate vice president is not an exception. This type of thinking increases with the increasing number and severity of truly uncontrollable risks. It presents a challenging problem to those of us who espouse the risk pooling concept.

7
Handling Risks Internally

Typically, risk managers are advisors rather than participants in the major operations of the corporations they serve. They have no line authority in such operations as production, sales and distribution. Instead they advise the heads of the departments and divisions.

This is as it should be. In fact, there is no other practical approach, because the possibility of loss runs through virtually every process and operation of the company. The only alternative would be to give risk managers authority coextensive with their chief executives.

Performing a staff function, risk managers are responsible in varying degrees along with the heads of the major departments they advise on risk control.

Corporate "Risk Handlers"

However, we should note that there are other "risk handlers" in the corporation, with varying degrees of responsibility to abate or eliminate some of the risks of loss in corporations.

For instance, corporations are subject to loss from employee dishonesty. When such losses occur, they can be recovered under the corporate insurance program through a fidelity bond or a "comprehensive 3 D" insurance contract (Dishonesty, Destruction, Disappearance).

The risk manager's responsibility for preventing the loss must be reconciled with the staff responsibility of the company audit department to prevent employee defalcations.

In a similar manner, product liability claims are invariably insured under the corporation's general liability insurance contract. We might generalize that, if valid products liability claims exist against the corporation to any substantial degree, they strongly suggest that quality control needs to be strengthened. Yet the quality control department is itself as much of a "risk handler" as is the risk management department.

The compliance department, a new entity on the corporate scene, is charged with seeing that employees comply with government and the corporation's own regulations and procedures. In so doing, it is dealing in the control and abatement of corporate risks of a highly specialized nature fully as much as is the corporate risk management department. In the absence of a compliance department, the corporation would probably rely on its legal department to perform this compliance function.

Risks Beyond Control

In some corporations one of the most sophisticated forms of risk analysis and abatement is performed with no reference to the risk management department at all. It is the use of commodity and currency trading to insure that the corporation does not suffer loss due to fluctuations in the prices of commodities and the rates of currency exchange. The simplicity and efficiency of this risk handling device should make most risk managers envious, struggling as they do with their mixed bag of hazards to be provided for.

A simple example will show how this procedure operates. An operator of an edible oil refinery contracts to sell the soybean oil output from the refinery for 18 cents a pound for the next several months. This means that soybeans must be obtained at about $12.00 per bushel. The operator buys contracts for future delivery on the Chicago Board of Trade. During the time the soybean oil is being refined, the price of beans increases to $14.00 per bushel. Our operator has guarded against this price rise, since the other party to the future transaction, invariably a speculator, must deliver beans at the $12.00 contract price.

In this example, the speculator has absorbed the risk and has lost money on the transaction. If the beans had gone down in price, the speculator would have made a profit on the contract. The refinery operator is not much concerned which way the price of beans goes. For a small fee—the price of the futures contract—the operator bought protection against loss fully as effectively as if it were a contract of insurance written by an insurance company.

Currency Fluctuations

Similarly, treasurers of large multinational corporations face the risk of loss from currency fluctuations and often gain protection by buying or selling the particular currency in question on the futures market. This form of risk handling is also outside the scope of the corporate risk management department.

Some companies with a great deal of other people's property in their possession, such as railroads, airlines, trucking companies, warehouses and hotels, have set up elaborate security departments to handle pilferage and other thefts. Large banks and department stores have done the same thing.

The work of these security departments is generally independent of the risk management department. If the loss is insured, however, as it invariably is, the corporation's risk management department will be responsible for processing the claim through to a conclusion with the insurer.

Charting the Three Party Relationship

The Risk Responsibility Chart depicts this three party relationship. It assumes that the function generally called corporate safety or loss prevention is part of the risk management department.

RISK RESPONSIBILITY CHART

	Responsibility of		
	Risk Management Department	Operating Department (Production, (Sales Etc.)	Other "Risk Handling" Department
Fire, windstorm and other extended coverage perils.	Yes	Yes	No
Other physical perils: flood, explosion, earthquake, etc.	Yes	Yes	No
Employee theft	Yes	Yes	Yes
Robbery, burglary, and other dishonesty insurable under a corporate 3 D policy.	Yes	Yes	Yes
Product defects (no products liability cases).	No	Yes	Yes
Product defects (with product liability cases involved).	Yes	Yes	Yes
Auto liability cases.	Yes	Yes	No
Other claims arising from bodily injury, property damage.	Yes	Yes	No

No department or person within a company is entitled to participate in the solution of a problem unless such participation aids in the solution. Under what conditions, then, should the risk management department be asked to contribute to a solution, instead of leaving it entirely to other departments of the company? What does the risk manager contribute to the solution of any corporate problem?

There is no unanimity among the experts on this. When risk managers ceased to be merely corporate buyers of insurance and began to recommend other treatment of risks, they became involved in changes in procedures within the corporation itself, such as improving the loss prevention technique or facilities. How far should they go?

A group of experts on the subject has said that corporate risk managers should involve themselves as much as possible in virtually any corporate situation where there is a discernible possibility of loss. On the other hand there are those who would restrict the corporate risk manager to the handling of insurable risks. To my mind there is a middle ground which should be perfectly acceptable to both schools of thought and compatible with both. All students of risk management will agree that, if insurance can be purchased for a peril, the corporate risk manager is always charged with evaluating the economics of buying this insurance. Furthermore, a fairly new definition of insurance terms it, "the pooling of risks on a voluntary basis through the use of intermediaries." Thus, the risk management department must have added responsibility over and above merely buying insurance. The department must become actively interested in all risks to which the corporation is subject if those risks are capable of being pooled in any way.

It matters not that, after due analysis, the corporation decides not to join with others subject to the risk in pooling the risk through the conventional insuring mechanism, or industrywide captive insurers or any other form of risk pooling through intermediaries.

Adapting to Swift Changes

Conditions within the corporate climate are changing with lightning-like rapidity. These changes come faster and faster as technology advances. Thus a risk which can be pooled today might well be best self insured tomorrow, and still later might better be pooled. Doesn't this define the speciality which the corporate risk manager is uniquely qualified to provide the corporation—namely, the expertise on this pooling capability, whether through the conventional insurance market or by other means?

As an aside, I am still haunted by a risk-pooling decision I was involved in some years ago. In the mid-1950s the scheduled airlines, painfully aware of the strangulating nature of work stoppages, were seeking a way to pool the financial losses that resulted from these stoppages.

The corporate insurance managers of the airlines, which included me, were asked about the possibilities of insuring this risk. To a person, we all advised that the risk could not be pooled. The general counsels of the airlines refused to accept this advice. They eventually developed the airline revenue sharing pool. The principal architect of this pooling arrangement went on to become his company's president.

Exception to the Rule

A few paragraphs above I said that all students of risk management will agree that, if insurance can be purchased for a peril, the corporate risk manager is always charged with evaluating the economics of buying this insurance.

I suspect that this statement will not go unchallenged. This is partly because the word "insurance" is sometimes used to describe what is really a tax. And it is partly because of certain insurance programs that have been developed within corporations.

For example, state unemployment insurance is really a tax. And most corporations handle it as a tax, with the corporate tax department administering it.

A good example of the second exception to my statement is title insurance, which protects the corporation against loss from defective conveyances of real estate which the corporation has purchased. The corporate real estate manager, or counsel almost always buys title insurance, instead of the risk manager. The customary reasons for this are:

- The coverage is highly specialized. It is not sold through the conventional insurance market with which the risk manager is most familiar.
- The basic service provided by the title company is title searches and related services, rather than actually absorbing losses. But, since the title insurance is only a small part of the whole title responsibility, it is only logical for it to be handled at the same time.

There may be two reasons for such a situation. The first is that corporate risk managers have not yet persuaded corporate management that they have enough expertise in these areas so that other managers can rely on the corporate risk department to handle these types of risks.

The second reason is that the corporate environment often still regards the corporate risk manager as the "handler" of fortuitous risks, involving bodily injury and property damage, rather than the types of risk that involve errors of omission.

Yet, one highly successful risk manager of a multibillion dollar company I know advises fellow risk managers to have a good working knowledge and interest in *all* corporate programs with the word "insurance" in them. His reasoning is simple and goes a long way in explaining his success as a risk manager. He says, "If something should go seriously wrong with one of the 'non-insurance' programs, with consequent loss or serious embarrassment to the company, top management could easily say to me, 'you're the company insurance expert, why don't you do something?' and the fact that I had no direct responsibility would not be a good enough answer."

8
Deductible Programs

One problem with writing about risk management is the wide variation among companies as to staffing and the degree of specialization of risk management.

A few years ago the Risk and Insurance Management Society, the professional organization for corporate risk and insurance managers, hired a consulting firm to study certain aspects of the speciality. The consultants found that, in the New York area, the top annual compensation for persons having the title of risk or insurance manager was eight times that of the lowest paid of the group. This suggests a wide variation in the intrinsic responsibilities of the incumbents and the problems they face.

There is also a wide variation in the number of people in the corporate insurance or risk management departments of different corporations. I have heard of giant corporations with as many as 60 people engaged in the speciality. At the other end of the spectrum is the company in which the treasurer also acts as the corporate insurance or risk management official on a part-time basis, with no specialized staff.

Although I know of no statistics on this subject, a good guess would be that there are about ten times as many part-time insurance and risk managers as there are full time ones. Since their problems are vastly different, this chapter is devoted mainly to the problems of the smaller risk management operations.

The Self Trained Risk Manager

The part-time specialist invariably is introduced to the speciality by being assigned the corporate insurance program, and not by being trained for it. Typically, this new corporate insurance "expert" will receive a folder of insurance contracts which describe the protection available to the corporation from the conventional insurance market. Few documents are less comprehensible to the uninitiated. They are difficult even to the initiated!

Our part-time specialist will probably have to accept much on faith until becoming better acquainted with the concepts, forms and terminology. It is typical that each type of insurance will be written by different insurers, each of which has its own style in presenting costs. Each must be successfully evaluated to achieve an efficient corporate risk management program.

To these complications must be added the variations in the term of insurance contracts and the consequent variation in the payments for the services provided. Insurance contracts with a one-year term are probably most common, followed by three-year contracts, with five-year contracts used on increasingly rare occasions. These differences present a correlation problem.

Virtually all corporate accounting departments will book these insurance costs on an "earned" basis. They will place in a prepaid expense account that portion of the insurance paid for but not yet earned by the insurance company. This accounting treatment makes the amounts shown as insurance expenses comparable in the corporate financial statements, whether contracted for on a one-year or a multiple-year basis.

Our part-time corporate insurance specialist could even apply a time value of money factor to these differing premium payments, although the discounts usually allowed by insurers for advance payment—usually 2.7 percent of annual premium for a three-year contract and 4.5 percent for a five-year program—purport to recognize the time-value element.

How to Treat Dividends

Far more vexatious in multi-year policies is the problem of treating dividends and other premium returns. A dividend paid to a policyholder is always earned on the term just expiring at the time the dividend is received. That's the very nature of such a payment. So it is, in effect, a retroactive payment (by the insurer, of course). The fact that it is contingent and payable at the end of the policy term mitigates against anticipating this premium return in booking the insurance costs on a net basis (gross premium less expected dividend). And booking the premium at the time it is received, if it is a significant amount, certainly distorts the accounting presentation of the period when such credit is taken.

Equally vexatious, this treatment overstates the insurance expense of the preceding accounting periods when the insurance expense was recorded on a gross basis. The careful specialist is best advised to get the insurer's opinion as to whether the dividend (or any other contingent premium return) is likely to be continued. If it is expected that it will be paid at the end of the policy term, it should be anticipated in the booking of insurance expense. If it is more likely that the dividend will not be paid, it should not be anticipated.

There are several very basic questions to which a newly appointed corporate risk specialist must obtain the answers. Should a risk be insured at all? If so, what is the justification? Should the corporation assume a deductible for a part of the risk? If so, in what amount?

Several years ago, I addressed a seminar conducted by the American Management Association for the part-time corporate insurance buyer or the newly appointed risk manager. What follows is a condensation of what I told them.

Let us use as an example, how a company decided to proceed to adopt a deductible for comprehensive dishonesty coverage. Deductibles for such coverage are fairly common. However, this company wanted a large deductible—$50,000 for any one loss, with no annual aggregate. And this is not common. Here is how the company rationalized its action.

Advisability of Deductibles

A deductible is, of course, a form of assumption of risk by the insured. We can tell whether or not a deductible arrangement makes economic sense by applying the same yardstick as we would in evaluating the assumption of any other form of risk.

A company looks for one or more of four conditions in any insurable risk to justify insuring the risk. These conditions are called the four Ss—Survival, Spread, Service and Statute.

Like all catch words, the four Ss tend to oversimplify the situation. Included in the category of Survival are those risks which, while they cannot destroy the company, could embarrass it, financially or otherwise.

The second S—Spread—applies to potential losses which, though not catastrophic, are severe enough and infrequent enough so that it makes economic sense to spread the risk by purchasing insurance to recover a large portion of the loss.

To comprehend the importance of such coverage, let us assume that this risk had not been insured and that a maximum loss occurred which now must be paid from company funds. When this loss is reported to higher company management, someone may ask, "How much would it have cost to insure this risk?" If it can be answered satisfactorily, then this spread element dictates that the company not go the insurance route.

To further illustrate this spread test, let us say the company was paying a $120,000 premium a year for full dishonesty coverage. Losses under the insured program had been averaging about 50 percent of premiums, or $60,000 a year. So the potential saving, based on past experience, was the other $60,000 a year, less what would have to be paid for the insured coverage above the $50,000 deductible. This premium turned out to be $12,000 a year. Clearly from the standpoint of the spread element, this program could stand a high loss. How the precise figure of $50,000 for the deductible was determined will be explained below.

The third S—Service—refers to what the insured receives for the premium in addition to the payment of losses. What services are received which the insured cannot economically perform?

We all agree that the service element has always weighed heavily in the fidelity aspect of a comprehensive dishonesty coverage. Yet, much of this service could be performed more economically within a company. Some aspect of this service would still be obtained, for a price of course, without insured coverage from $50,000 to $1,000,000, while the company continued to do much of the service work itself.

The final S—Statute—is any coverage obtained to satisfy a law. The federal welfare disclosure law requires the bonding of some employees so, for this purpose only, the insurer provides first dollar coverage by endorsement at a nominal premium cost.

Having run the $50,000 deductible on comprehensive dishonesty past the four Ss, it is concluded that a company could assume this risk.

Types of Deductibles

It has been said that the acknowledgement of ignorance is the beginning of learning. This applies well to the subject of deductibles. I think it wise for corporate insurance persons to listen very carefully, even respectfully, when representatives of the underwriting side suggest a change in insurance coverage being tailored for a company.

The example of a $50,000 deductible on dishonesty coverage illustrates this idea to some degree. The company started out considering a $13,000 deductible and had intended to self assume that amount. That is, it would set up no company reserve for it. A study by the insurer ultimately pointed to a $50,000 deductible. Adopting this required the company to self insure—that is to establish a reserve for payment of potentially larger losses than it cared to self assume.

My point is simply that corporations very often can and should be more flexible than the insurers in such matters as deductibles. The underwriter is undoubtedly trying to dovetail the proposed coverage into the existing set-up. The underwriter has many more factors than the company has to bring together, such as excess loss rate versus primary loss rate structure, credibility factors and even insurance limits. Permitting the insurer to be flexible very often puts money in the pocket of the insured.

Determining Deductible Size

Now let us see how $50,000 was arrived at as a deductible on the dishonesty coverage for any one loss, with no aggregate or other cumulative top-side limit.

As we saw, the company started out with a $13,000 deductible in mind. Now $13,000 was and is the maximum amount it must absorb into its expenses for any one loss under its retrospective rated compensation, auto and general liability coverages. It was reasoned that, since the company was accustomed to accepting as much as $13,000 ($10,000 loss plus 30 percent load charge) onto its books under an existing insurance program, it would not find this identical figure obnoxious under a new program.

Also, the company was actually encouraged to consider a much higher figure for a deductible, a figure in the area of $50,000. The company's bond indenture contained a provision that it might self assume (no reserve required) any insurance coverage up to $50,000 and could self insure to any amount. It intended to and did self insure its dishonesty coverage but saw no good reason to go beyond the $50,000 bond indenture self assumption limitation. Had the company felt there were cogent reasons for going beyond the $50,000 self assumption limitation it certainly would have done so.

So the size of the deductible, the figure finally settled on, originated not with the company, but with the insurer. What then was the actual rationale of the $50,000 deductible figure? It is hard to say. The suggestion that the market was best at the higher deductible was accepted without too much explanation.

The Rationale

You may ask, "How can you rationalize such a recommendation if you don't know the market?" You rationalize the deductible program offered by comparing it with the fully insured program you previously had.

You may recall that $120,000 was the annual premium paid

for full insurance and that the company had an average of $60,000 in losses each year. With a $50,000 deductible, the annual premium was reduced to $12,000. So, assuming a continuation of the existing experience, costs under the deductible program should be $72,000 or 40 percent less than the fully insured program. The $50,000 deductible is some 30 percent higher than the highest loss the company had under its fully insured program.

The company had a comprehensive dishonesty program with a $50,000 deductible for slightly over two years. The dollar savings each year, comparing its present costs with that paid under first-dollar coverages, has averaged 40 percent. A small, unmeasurable workload was added to its law department. It had been using the $120,000 a year as a ballpark figure for the first dollar premium costs. So the saving to date is in the neighborhood of $48,000 a year. A lot of lawyers' time can be bought for this.

The company also thinks it enjoys two additional benefits which cannot be measured in dollars. First, it is receiving payment of claims more promptly. For some reason, valid I'm sure, the insurers took an average of six weeks to two months to investigate and pay a claim under the first dollar coverage, no matter how small the dollar amount of the claim.

Under the self insured program, a second indirect benefit derived was increased loss prevention consciousness within the company. In the past, the company allocated the premium paid for first dollar coverage on an exposure basis. That is, on the basis of employees, employees handling money, safes, cash on hand, etc., irrespective of the losses. The company now bears its own losses up to $13,000.

Thus far, the losses have shown no substantial change either in frequency or in dollar amount under the self insured program when compared with the first dollar coverage program.

A Problem Remains

However, there is one concern. Call it the long view or the broad view. This concern stems from the sobering statistics arising from the activities against which comprehensive dishonesty insures. I believe Norman Jaspan, a well known security expert, mentioned the figure of $2 billion a year as the best estimate of the fidelity "take" in this country. Robbery and burglary trends are equally disturbing.

This is a big problem requiring a big solution. By withdrawing coverage for the first $50,000 from the insurance companies, are companies withholding support from the organizations which should and may be trying to be the catalyst, the spearhead, for the forces to combat these problems? A company may be doing this by self insuring but I don't think so. Until evidence suggests that there is more attention to these overall problems, in a manner similar to the magnificent job being done by fire insurers on the overall problem of loss prevention, the present setup will be kept.

9

Insurance Coverages for Business

Workers' Compensation Insurance

Workers' compensation is such a key element in the corporate insurance program that a fairly detailed analysis of it is in order. The coverage called "employer's liability" is generally similar to and written as an adjunct to workers' compensation coverage, so it will also be analyzed at this time.

Society has determined, through historical development of statutory law, that it is the responsibility of industry to compensate employees or their families for injuries or death incurred in the course of employment. Recourse to common law action, where employer negligence had to be proved by injured workers or their survivors as a means of obtaining reimbursement for lost income stemming from injuries, was found to result in inequities to employer and employee alike and placed an intolerable burden upon the courts.

The states therefore enacted Workers' Compensation Laws which provided for compensation without regard to the question of negligence. Today there are such laws, or their equivalents, in effect in all states of America, as well as in Canada and many other countries. The obligations imposed by these laws may be fulfilled by insuring with stock or mutual insurance companies or, in some U.S. states, all Canadian provinces and many foreign countries, by participating in state, province or national insurance pools. Self insuring this risk is often permitted if certain conditions are met.

While in most states the laws are so written that acceptance of statutory benefits is mandatory and any legal action against an employer is precluded, in a few states an employee may still reject the benefits and sue the employer. Most workers' compensation insurance policies therefore provide employer's liability protection in addition to compensation benefits.

No Amount or Limit Set

Workers' compensation insurance, whether purchased through private insurance companies or mandatory state funds, is designed to provide payment of benefits to the extent they are prescribed in the laws of the various states. For this reason, there is no amount or limit of insurance stated in the policies, except in the employer's liability section.

There are no two states with identical workers' compensation laws. The laws differ in the circumstances out of which injuries must occur to be compensable, in the types of injuries or occupational diseases covered, and in the extent of compensation prescribed. There are different ways claims are settled. In some states all employee classifications are covered, whereas in others only hazardous occupations (as defined in the statute) are subject to the compensation laws. And, unless special provisions are made in the insurance contract, the coverage will be limited accordingly.

Generally speaking, the laws provide for death benefits to survivors, benefits for permanent and temporary total disability (usually expressed as a percentage of wages up to a maximum amount), scheduled awards for permanent and partial disability (expressed as dollar amounts depending on the nature of the disability) and medical expenses. The policies further agree to defend suits brought against any employer by an injured worker, and to pay any awards made by the court, including costs, against the employer.

The perils insured against may be thought of as the payments, together with attendant expenses, which an employer is obligated to make under the workers' compensation law or by court decision as a result of death, injury or disease to an employee encountered during the operations of the business.

The Letter of the Law

Insurance coverage depends upon the letter of the various laws. Any areas of possible coverage not specified in the law are noncompensable, although regulating authorities may decide otherwise in a specific case. Certain occurrences, such as deliberate self-injury by the worker, or injury while intoxicated, are generally not covered under the laws.

The amount of compensation payable depends upon the schedule of benefits included in the statutes. The method by which reimbursement of compensable injuries is made to the employee or the employee's survivors varies in each state.

The most obvious service performed by the insurer underwriting this coverage is the handling and settlement of any compensable claim, or the defense of any employer's liability suit. The insurer may also inspect the working operations of an insured employer for the purpose of making recommendations toward eliminating unsafe conditions, thus reducing the accident rate, and thereby the cost of insurance.

Manual Rates

If the workers' compensation coverage generates a premium of less than $100,000 a year, the chances are that the corporation will have to be content with a program where the premium charge will be the manual premium plus or minus the insured's modification of that manual premium.

In certain instances this $100,000 breakpoint is applied to all casualty coverages—that is, the total premiums generated by workers' compensation and liability coverages. So, below the $100,000 premium level, there is little likelihood that any form of retrospective rating plan is available to the corporation.

Manual premium rates are compiled by the state compensation rating board or similar authority. These rates are compiled by job classification and reflect the degree of hazard inherent in each classification. The rates to be charged per $100 of payroll range from a low of a few cents (generally for clerical staff) to many dollars per $100 of payroll for employees engaged in high hazard occupations, such as structural steel workers or coal miners.

All manual premium rates are compiled in the same manner. The losses paid during the preceding years are analyzed and interpolated into the expected loss rate. Thus the expected loss rate for wet processing dairy employees might be 55¢ per $100 of covered payroll. To this expected loss rate will then be added the expense loading, which is the amount necessary to take care of all expenses, such as acquisition costs, loss investigation and adjusting costs and underwriting costs.

This expense loading is stated as cents or dollars per $100 of covered payroll. The expected loss rate, plus the expense loading, comprise the manual premium for each job classification.

Expected Loss Rate

An important ratio to remember is that which has been established between the expected loss rate and the manual premium rate. The expected loss rate is expected to equal 65 percent of the manual premium rate. This means that the manual premium rate for the wet process dairy employees will be about 88¢ per $100 of covered payroll. As we observed earlier, we assumed the expected loss rate to be 55¢ for these employees.

To encourage loss prevention, the state compensation rating authorities have developed a rate modification for each employer.

This rate modification is computed each year by comparing the employer's loss experience to the loss experience found within the job classification as a whole. If the employer's loss experience is better than the experience as a whole, the employer receives a credit modification. If the employer's loss experience is worse than the experience as a whole, the employer receives a debit modification.

This credit or debit modification is actually applied by the insurer to the corporate employer's workers' compensation premium expense. It can represent a substantial percentage increase or decrease in the total amount charged. The base period used to compare the employer's experience with the whole is the most immediate three-year period, with the year just past dropped out. This drop-out is necessary because the prior-year data are not available in time to be included in the analysis by the state compensation rating authorities.

Data Checklist

So, what is the minimum amount of data that our part-time specialist should obtain from an insurer or a broker about workers' compensation? Here is a suggested checklist:

1. Ascertain the job classifications and rates used in calculating the corporation's workers' compensation manual premium cost. As we saw, these rates can vary substantially and misapplication of them can be costly.
2. Ask: Are the classifications used congruent with the work the employees do? The use of a structural steel employee's classification in a dairy is undoubtedly the result of a clerical error.
3. Ask for as full an explanation as the insurer and broker can give on the experience modification for the corporation. The modification for the applicable year invariably becomes available for use in March or April of that year, so it must always be the subject of an adjustment to the rate used to calculate the premium at the beginning of the year. When the insurer or broker announces

this experience modification credit or debit, this is the best time to ask for a complete explanation of it.

4. Periodically review the losses charged against the company by the insurer. A periodic listing of these losses should be provided and become part of the file for use in making year-to-year comparisons of losses sustained. Obviously, if these losses are recited on a comparable basis, such a year-to-year comparison does not require any particular expertise in insurance or risk management. Such a year-to-year comparison can, however, provide valuable insight as to the expense and will rationalize the entire workers' compensation insurance expense in non-insurance terms. In making such an analysis the 65-35 percent loss-expected expense-expected ratio described above should be kept in mind.

5. Ask the workers' compensation insurer what loss prevention service is provided. And use it.

6. If your company belongs to an active and effective trade or industry association, seriously consider the association as an available source of information on loss prevention analysis. An exchange of ideas seems to be very productive when conducted along industry lines. Many trade and industry associations have formed insurance committees in which detailed aspects of the insurance arrangement, loss occurrences, and loss prevention measures are effectively discussed.

Second Injury Fund

A worker who has lost a hand, or foot or eye in an industrial accident may become totally disabled if the other member is lost in a second accident. For this reason, employers would tend to refuse to employ a partially disabled worker. To avoid such situations, most states have enacted provision for a second injury fund into law.

In these states, a worker who suffers a second loss of a member is compensated on the basis of his entire permanent disability following his second injury without regard to his pre-existing physical disability. The employer, however, has a limited liability following the second injury. This is because these second injury funds either pay the difference between the cost of the partial and permanent disability award or a total disability award or will reimburse the employer for all compensation payments beyond a specific period.

For example, an employer in New York is responsible for only the first 104 weeks of compensation benefits following a second injury if the conditions are such that the New York second injury fund will accept responsibility. The second injury fund is supported either by assessments levied on all insurance companies writing workers' compensation or, in some states, by the employer paying stipulated sums into the fund when a worker without dependents is fatally injured on the job.

A second injury fund is a special fund set up within the administrative framework of the workers' compensation system to insure that an employer who hires a physically handicapped worker, or continues the physically handicapped worker in employment will not, in the event the worker suffers a subsequent injury on the job, be responsible for a greater disability than actually occurred while the worker was employed.

Under such a system the employer pays only the benefits that are due for the second injury. However, the employee is fully protected because the fund pays the difference between what is actually received from the employer and what would have been received for the resulting condition if there had been no prior disability.

Coverage Varies

Some of the state second injury funds apply to many types of physical disabilities, others only a few. While there is no exact definition of what makes a law broad or narrow, those that cover many or most types of handicaps are called broad. Those that restrict coverage to "loss, or loss of use, of a hand, arm, foot, leg or eye" are called narrow. There is, of course, a middle ground occupied by laws that cover something more than amputations and sight losses, but not enough to make them really broad in their effect.

Second injury funds are financed in a variety of ways. A few states finance them wholly, or partially, by legislative appropriation. Most, however, require employers through their insurance premiums to underwrite the cost of the second injury fund program.

Today, some 14 states and the District of Columbia cover any previous permanent disability without limitations as to cause or type. However, nine of these jurisdictions require that the second injury, when combined with the first, result in permanent total disability. This is a limitation which greatly reduces the effectiveness of the second injury fund law, since it is estimated that less than one-tenth of one percent of all industrial accidents result in permanent total disability. Only four states fail to provide any protection to physically handicapped workers. They are Georgia, Louisiana, Nevada and Virginia.

The Minimal Test

On the "extent of disability", a certain minimal test is required before the employer's responsibility is shifted to the fund. This test is not required when the state laws cover only the loss, or the loss of use, of a hand, arm, foot, leg, or eye since these injuries by their very nature, are serious or significant disabilities.

But the experience of some states which have broad coverage shows that covering all types of disabilities, without also requiring a minimum extent of disability, provides employers and insurance companies a method by which they can avoid responsibilities that are properly theirs. It permits a shift of responsibility to the fund in which preexisting disability was in no sense an employment handicap or, conversely, when the second injury did not significantly aggravate the prior disability.

The New York system approaches the extent-of-disability problem by limiting coverage of prior disabilities to those that are likely to be a "hindrance or obstacle" to employment; and coverage of second injuries to those that result in a permanent disability that is "materially and substantially greater" than would have resulted from the subsequent injury alone.

In construing the degree of preexisting disability that will be regarded as a "hindrance or obstacle" to employment, New York requires that employers have knowledge of the handicap and, in the case of a latent and obscure pathological condition, further requires that employers must have acted in some way on this knowledge. For example, the factors prerequisite to second injury fund relief in New York are these five:

- That the employee has a preexisting permanent physical impairment.
- That the impairment is or is likely to be a hindrance or obstacle to finding or keeping a job.
- That the employer hired or continued the handicapped worker in employment with knowledge that the impairment exists.
- That the worker incurred a subsequent compensable accidental injury or occupational disease at work.
- That the resultant disability is greater than that caused by the second injury alone.

Since workers' compensation rates are based primarily on (1) the relative hazard in the employer's work and (2) the accident experience of the employer, it follows that physically handicapped workers cannot possibly affect the first factor and could only influence the second factor if they were prone to have more accidents than workers without handicaps. Research studies, however, have shown that, where properly placed, handicapped workers have an accident experience as good as, or often better than, other persons.

In summary, the scheme of second injury fund legislation is to facilitate and encourage the employment of the physically handicapped by limiting the financial responsibility of the employer at the time of an employee's subsequent injury occurring in its employment, at the same time compensating the worker for the combined disability by drawing on the fund.

The Casualty Package

Quite often workers' compensation is included in a casualty insurance package of coverages that all corporations must have. The liability coverages provide protection against claims made by third parties for bodily injury or property damage arising out of the activities of the corporation.

Note well the qualifications for bodily injury and property damage. The bodily injury qualification speaks for itself. Property damage applies to some form of physical damage to the party asserting the claim. Without the element of bodily injury or physical damage to property, the typical liability policies included in the casualty package will not respond.

Invariably there are two liability insurance contracts included in the casualty package—auto liability and general liability. Auto liability responds to claims by third parties arising out of the use of the company automobiles and trucks or vehicles driven by employees or other agents (legally speaking) of the insured engaged in the business of the insured.

General Liability

The general liability coverage, if it includes a product liability endorsement, takes care of virtually all of the other bodily injury or property damage claims to which the corporation must respond.

One significant difference between the workers' compensation coverage and most liability coverages is that the workers' is "no fault" in character, while the liability coverages, other than auto insurance in most states, are not. All the injured worker has to show to collect under workers' compensation is eligibility for the coverage under the statute and that the injury, being of an industrial nature, was also contemplated by the statute.

There is an additional feature of the liability coverages. The person suffering the injury or damage must show that, in some way, the corporation was negligent in conduct and it was this negligence which was the proximate cause of the injury or damage. It is the obligation of the insurer to conduct an appropriate investigation of the claims, defend the corporation in court where necessary and appropriate, as well as to reimburse the injured as the circumstances dictate.

The premium which insurers can charge corporations for liability coverages is much more free of state regulation or supervision than is workers' compensation coverage, even though the calculation of the premium starts in most states with rates duly filed with the state insurance supervisory authority.

The rates for auto liability coverages are in most instances the same as those applied to your automobile or mine. There is, however, an underwriting device called "schedule rating" which permits the insurer to make adjustments to the manual premium developed on these liability coverages for business activity. This schedule rating permits debits and credits to be applied to the manual premium for such factors as volume and loss prevention devices employed by the insured.

These factors are generally applied on a judgment basis, and there is more than just a hint that the underwriter's judgment may often be affected by the competitive posture in which the insurer finds itself.

When the Whole is Less than a Part

Not too long ago, the insurance commissioner of a large industrial state mentioned in a speech that he began his insurance career as an underwriter for a fire & casualty insurance company and that his job then involved doing this schedule rating of casualty packages consisting of workers' compensation and liability coverages for corporate insureds. Competition for the business was intense at the time.

The underwriting of workers' compensation coverage was quite rigid and not susceptible to the granting of credits. The ultimate result, according to the commissioner, was that it was not a novelty when application of maximum credits resulted in an overall credit on the combined coverages. That is, the total of the workers' compensation and liability insurance coverages was less than the workers' compensation coverage standing alone.

This anecdote illustrates how diverse the premium costs of these liability coverages can be. There are, therefore, few bench marks one can use in evaluating whether or not the liability insurance premium the corporate employer is being charged is proper. One such bench mark that might be kept in mind is the fact that most state supervisory authorities, when setting rates, contemplate a loss ratio of 60 percent and an expense ratio of 40 percent where these liability coverages are concerned.

It would seem to follow, therefore, that if the corporate insured's premium approximates 166⅔ percent of the losses, the premium being charged is the proper amount. This analysis would undoubtedly have to be computed over a period of time.

Auto Liability

As indicated earlier, auto liability insurance rates are applied to vehicles owned or leased by the corporate insured in a manner identical to rates applied to your car and mine. In general liability coverages, the exposures and hence the base to which the insurance is applied are the square footage of building space under control of the corporate insured, the amount of annual sales, and similar criteria which can give some approximation of the amount of risk which the insurer is assuming.

The auto liability coverage does not, of course, reimburse the corporate insured for damage to the insured's own vehicle. A substantial number of corporate insureds maintain an insurance contract providing for this risk. I would guess that, unless the corporate insured is extremely short of working capital or the fleet of vehicles in question contains some extremely valuable vehicles, this coverage cannot be justified by the usual and customary reasons for insuring any corporate risks—protecting the corporation from financial embarrassment, etc.

From this viewpoint, the physical damage risks to one's own vehicle is usually an attractive one to self insure. Unlike most of the other corporate coverages, the maximum possible loss is easy to ascertain. It is the value of the most valuable vehicle in the fleet.

The expense element takes up about 40 cents of the premium dollar. The corporate insured with the typical insurance contract is paying $1.66⅔ for every dollar of loss collected.

Lest I appear biased toward self insurance, I hasten to report that I know of at least one huge corporate insured, with a risk manager universally respected for competence and intelligence, which carries this physical damage coverage on a fleet of 3,000 vehicles. This corporate giant looks to the insurer, not for protection of its working capital, but rather for the convenience of bringing in the insurance mechanism when one of its employees has an auto accident in a company car, for damage appraisal and speedy arrangement to get the vehicles repaired and similar tasks with which the employee is probably unfamiliar.

This is as good a point as any to emphasize that there is more to the insurance contract than the risk-bearing aspect of the insurer. If the insurer provides a service to the corporate insured in addition to bearing the risk, this service must always be a consideration in evaluating the worth of the insurance contract.

Fire-Extended Coverage

The fire-extended coverage insurance contract, providing protection against loss by direct damage to the physical properties of the corporate insured, is generally a significant one in terms of protection it affords and of the premiums paid to the insurer. The fire part of this protection is one of the oldest of coverages. It began to evolve into its modern form with the impetus for protection arising from the great fire of London in 1699.

Over the years the perils recited in the extended endorsement to this policy have become included in this contract of "Fire-E.C." as it's often called. These perils are windstorm, hail, explosion, riot, riot attending a strike, civil commotion, damage from falling aircraft, vehicles (damage from) and smoke damage.

In recent years vandalism and malicious mischief are often added to the Fire-E.C. policy as additional protection. Technically, however, "V. & M. M." is not one of the "E.C." perils.

It should also be noted that the insuring clause for the explosion peril has a significant exclusion, namely, explosion if arising from steam jacketed and other pressure vessels which must be periodically inspected pursuant to federal or state law or local governmental ordinance. As we shall see later, this exclusion dovetails nicely into the coverage offered under boiler and pressure vessel insurance.

The typical Fire-E.C. physical damage insurance contract provides only for direct damage to the subject of insurance (the building, equipment, etc.). The damage must be caused, of course, by one of the perils recited in the contract. Losses of a collateral nature, such as those caused by lost production, the need to continue the payment of utilities and the pay of the permanent personnel at the facility, would not be paid under this physical damage contract. As we shall see later, these losses of a collateral nature can also be insured with a business interruption insurance contract.

The Value of the Loss

The Fire-E.C. contract has several significant features. One important aspect involves valuation and reimbursement. Fire insurers pay no more than the loss sustained by the insured.

A facility could be insured for $500,000. If, at the time of its complete loss by fire or one of the extended coverage perils, the facility was worth only $100,000, the latter amount is what will be paid to the insured. If, at the time of the loss, the facility is worth $750,000, the limit of the policy only, that is, $500,000, will be paid.

This is not such a one-way street as it might first appear to be. The insured can easily increase the limit of the policy to take care of the increased value of the facility. As for the $100,000 payment (because that was the amount of the loss) the customary procedure in fire insurance is that there will be no windfall. Even if the insured had two policies of $250,000 each on the facility and paid premium on both, when the $100,000 loss occurs, the two insurers will each pay $50,000 of it.

The Coinsurance Clause

A further possible restriction on loss payment is the coinsurance clause which, if it exists in the policy, may restrict payment for a partial loss of the facility. Assume that the fire policy has an 80 percent coinsurance clause (the percentage most often used).

This coinsurance clause requires the insured to maintain an amount of insurance on the properties at least equal to 80 percent of the properties' value or receive something less than 100 percent of the loss suffered. In the event of a total loss, the insurer will pay the face amount of the policy. Obviously, this will be less than the amount of the loss if the insured has not maintained insurance on the properties equal to the value of those properties. But what about a partial loss? If the amount of the insurance carried on the properties at the time of the loss is less than 80 percent of the value of the property, then the loss will be paid at the rate that the insured value bears to 80 percent of the actual value of the properties.

Calculating Fire Insurance Values

How are values calculated for fire insurance? For purposes of this discussion, there are three valuations. Here are the definitions of them:

1. *Actual cash value* (A.C.V.)—It is the valuation most often used by fire insurers. A.C.V. is the cost to replace a facility to its condition at the time of the loss. It involves calculating the cost of rebuilding the facility at current labor and material prices. From this replacement cost is then deducted a factor called functional depreciation. Functional depreciation is the amount of depreciation at the time of the loss and which measures the difference in value of the facility when it was new and when it was lost.

I dislike this definition—on two counts. Technically it is no definition at all, since it uses the term it is seeking to define in the definition. And I find it almost impossible to comprehend. So let's take an example.

Assume a 10-year-old building that cost $400,000 to build 10 years ago is destroyed by fire. Assume further its replacement cost at present labor and materials cost is $750,000.

The $350,000 increase in cost has been caused by inflation—the increases in labor and material. However, due to wear and tear, it would cost the insured $200,000 to bring the building up to the equal of a new building. This $200,000 is the functional depreciation.

Functional depreciation, unlike book depreciation, is not a product of elapsed time but rather of the condition, good or bad, by which a building or other facility is maintained. Its calculation is more of an engineering problem than it is an accounting problem. If it sounds complicated, it's because it is. A whole industry—the appraisal industry—is engaged in this endeavor, with specialists of their own, computers, structural engineers and the like.

The use of A.C.V. by the fire insurer to indemnify its insureds for losses has great logic behind it. The fire insurers strive mightily to put their insureds suffering losses as far as possible in the same condition the insureds were at the time of the loss.

2. *Repair and Replacement* (R & R)—Despite this laudable objective and perhaps due to the complications inherent in the A.C.V. calcu-

lations, the use of repair and replacement valuation appears to be growing. The R & R coverage is available by endorsement to the standard Fire-E.C. insurance contract.

This coverage pays the insured for the destroyed or damaged facility an amount equal to what it would cost to repair or replace the facility at current labor and material costs. In plainer words, the insured gets a new facility, or one completely repaired and equal to a new one, in place of the one damaged or destroyed.

Obviously this R & R coverage is simpler in every respect than the conventional A.C.V. coverage, since the nettlesome feature of functional depreciation is not involved either in the continuing administration of the insurance contract or in adjusting and settling the loss if it occurs.

This R & R coverage does present problems of its own. The most obvious one is the "windfall" problem, in which the insured suffering the loss receives a better facility than it had before the loss. In recognition of this, virtually all R & R endorsements require that the damaged or destroyed facility be actually repaired or replaced. If the insured decides against that, then payment is made on an A.C.V. basis.

3. *Book Value*—We have indicated earlier that functional depreciation is not the same as book depreciation. By book depreciation we mean the depreciation expense which an owner of a facility records for accounting purposes in recognition of the diminution in value of the facility with the passage of time. The annual depreciation expense is some percentage of the acquisition cost of the facility.

The offsetting entry to this depreciation expense charge is a credit to the depreciation reserve account maintained on the accounting books, and this reserve credit accumulates during the lifetime of the facility. At any given time the net book value of a facility is the difference between the acquisition or gross costs of the facility and this reserve for depreciation attributable to the facility.

This net book value figure is important to us in fire and other casualty losses to the facility. An amount equal to the net book value of the facility is the maximum amount which the owner of a damaged or destroyed facility can receive from the insurer without incurring a federal tax liability.

Put another way, it is only the net book value which the federal tax authorities recognize as the loss. If the insurance proceeds are greater than the net book value, then this excess is considered as income and subject to tax, generally on a capital gain basis.

The chances are that this tax factor presents no particular problem if the coverage is on an A.C.V. basis, since there should be at least a rough correlation between book depreciation and functional depreciation. The tax factor can indeed have a relevance if the coverage is on an R & R basis, since under this coverage, the recovery from the insurance company can be substantially in excess of the net book value.

Our part-time specialist, and indeed any risk manager, would be well advised to regard the R & R coverages as being composed of two parts: (1) the A.C.V. coverage and (2) depreciation insurance. Many insurers market R & R coverage in these two parts. There are differing justifications for these two coverages. To my mind one justifies maintaining A.C.V. coverage on the corporation's facilities by the following:

- In the event of a loss recoverable under the contract, the corporation does not suffer an uninsured loss. That is, the corporation's current profits are not charged with this loss.
- The near unanimity existing among corporate managements generally in carrying such insurance on their facilities makes any corporation look inconsistent which does not. In the event of a significant loss, a disgruntled stockholder could charge management with wasting the company's assets.

Neither of these reasons apply to the depreciation coverage. Therefore this depreciation coverage is justified because it makes money available to finance the new facility without requiring the corporation to use its working capital or other resources or borrowed funds.

Changes in Value

It is most important that all facilities be revalued periodically and any significant change reported to the insurance company. This is obvious if the company has increased its facilities by acquisitions or by constructing them. Not so obvious but equally important is that the value added to facilities by inflation should also be calculated and reported to the insurer.

Most large corporations report significant additions or dispositions to insured facilities as such changes occur and, then, generally on an annual basis, these values are "price trended." As indicated earlier there is an entire industry—the appraisal industry—which does this on a scientific basis.

There is a simplified way of approximating updated values. We start with the cost of constructing the facility and the year in which it was constructed. There are price trending tables available. These tables correlate the difference in the cost of construction between the year of construction and the present year. This is invariably given as a percentage.

Applying the appropriate percentage of increase (rarely in recent years has it been a decrease) to the cost of construction, we obtain an approximation of today's replacement costs of the facility. The table will also indicate how much this replacement cost should be reduced for each year the facility is in existence to reflect the functional depreciation. Applying this factor to the replacement cost approximation gives an approximation of the A.C.V. values.

Business Interruption Insurance

If one should happen to hear a risk manager or any other insurance practitioner speak of business interruption insurance, probably they're talking about "Fire-E.C. business interruption."

This insurance is designed to protect against loss of earnings of a plant or other facility during a period of suspension, whether total or partial, resulting from fire and other insured perils. It reimburses for lost profits, continuing expenses and extra expenses incurred to reduce the business interruption loss.

Typical of the continuing expenses contemplated by this insurance contract are taxes, interest on the mortgage and other indebtedness, salaries of key personnel, maintenance expenses, minimum fixed charges for utilities, and other fixed costs which continue during the period of time it would take to repair or replace the damaged property.

Our diligence and dispatch are expected; the policy is liable for the loss only for the time repairing or rebuilding would normally take. Once the premises are restored, or could have been, the insurance company's liability ends even though it may take additional time for the volume of sales or production to return to normal.

The policy does not reimburse for losses from reduction in the volume of sales or for loss of customers, or good will, shelf space, etc., even if these are irrevocably lost to the business. Deductibles, and there is invariably a deductible, may be recited in dollar amounts but, quite often, in "down time." That is, days or other time periods in which there is no production from the plants.

Business interruption insurance will protect the insured parties from the loss of earnings during a partial or total suspension of business when that suspension is caused by direct damage to the real or personal property caused by an insured peril. It should be noted that protection against business interruption losses is also available for losses arising from boiler and pressure vessel explosion and the so-called difference-in-condition perils (flood, earthquake, subsidence, etc.). As indicated earlier, such policies of insurance are rare when compared with coverage for Fire-E.C. perils.

Difference-in-Condition Insurance

A fairly new coverage available to the corporation for the protection of its physical properties is difference-in-condition insurance (D.I.C.). It is generally written as a blanket policy designed to protect the greater part of a company's real and personal property from perils, other than those covered under a Fire-E.C. policy contract, which are contemplated in an all risk insurance policy.

Flood, earthquake and subsidence are the principal perils involved in this D.I.C. coverage. At the time of the emergence of D.I.C. most corporations already had their properties protected against loss by Fire-E.C. Thus a Fire-E.C. contract plus a D.I.C. contract, in effect, provides all risk protection—hence the distinctive name.

Semantically, it's an atrocity. It is, however, a worthwhile form of protection for the typical corporation. Often this coverage is obtained in London, but there is now a growing U.S. market for it. The coverage is generally written on a worldwide basis. Note how all-inclusive is the coverage, as described in the following typical clause:

"(1) Real or personal property owned or used by the insured or hereafter erected, installed or acquired, including while in course of construction or erection and including interest in improvements and betterment of buildings not owned by insured.

"(2) The interest of the insured in, and the insured legal liability for the real and personal property of others in the insured's custody.

"(3) Personal property of the insured's officials and employees while on the premises of the insured."

Unlike a Fire-E.C. policy, the individual perils are not listed but rather the policy states that "this policy insures against all risks of physical loss or damage to property described herein, including the expense of removal of debris of such property damaged by an insured peril, except as hereinafter excluded."

Exclusions, therefore, are important. Typically, the following types of property are not covered under the policy: money, accounts, bills, deeds, securities, evidences of debt, notes, property in transit, watercraft, aircraft, motor vehicles licensed for highway whether or not on the insured's property, property insured under other all risk or similar broad contracts, property sold under conditional sale trust agreements or installment or deferred payment plans after delivery to the customer.

The following types of losses would be excluded:

- Perils insured under a Fire-E.C. policy.
- Infidelity and dishonesty of the insured or employees.
- Errors in design and faulty workmanship and faulty materials, unless resulting in the collapse of the property or a part thereof, or unless resulting in water damage.
- Electrical injury or disturbance to electrical appliances, devices or wiring from artificial causes or mechanical breakdown.
- Explosion or rupture or bursting of steam boilers, steam piping, steam turbines, steam engines, or flywheels owned or operated by the insured.
- Damage sustained to goods while actually being worked on and directly resulting therefrom.
- Ordinary wear, tear or gradual deterioration.
- Normal settling or shrinkage of walls, floors or ceilings.
- Nuclear reaction, nuclear radiation or radioactive contamination.
- War.
- Delay and loss of markets.

Boiler and Pressure Vessel Insurance

Boiler and pressure vessel explosion insurance is designed to protect from loss due to explosion and other abnormal effects (such as bulging) of pressure caused by the operation of boilers and by those other pressure vessels which must be periodically inspected pursuant to state/provincial or municipal inspection requirements.

Thus it is possible that a particular type of vessel is covered under this contract in a state which requires such an inspection, while similar vessels are not covered if located in another state where inspection is not required. The purpose of this seemingly inconsistent arrangement is to pass on to the insurer the responsibility for reacting to changes in legislation and for the accomplishment of state/provincial and municipal inspection. It should be remembered that a loss due to explosion, if not covered by the boiler and pressure vessel coverage, is invariably covered by the Fire-E.C. contract.

Here is a typical list of equipment items covered under this contract:

- All steam boilers, including piping.
- All auxiliary steam piping supplied from an outside source.
- All hot water heating boilers, excluding piping.
- All hot water supply boilers, excluding piping.
- All air tanks except those forming parts of small refrigerating and compressing machines.
- All hot water tanks over 15-gallon capacity or over 60 pounds pressure.

If mandatory inspection is required by state, provincial or municipal ordinance, the following are also included:

- All other fired objects, including piping if applicable.
- All unfired pressure vessels such as propane tanks.
- All refrigerating systems, brine piping included.
- All refrigerating systems containing unfired pressure vessels which require government inspection.

Normally it is a condition of the contract that all of the above equipment automatically comes under the contract of insurance at the time such items come into the insured's possession or control. In addition, other items of equipment which do not fall into any one of the above categories may be included by specific endorsement to the contract.

Defining an Accident

An accident is defined in the policy as: "A sudden and accidental breakdown of the object or any part thereof, which manifests itself at the time of its occurrence by physical damage to the object necessitating repair or replacement of the object or any part thereof."

Certain types of occurrences are not covered, such as: wear and tear; deterioration or depletion of materials due to corrosion or erosion; leakage at any valve, fitting, connection, joint or gland packing; the functioning of any safety device or protection device;

the breakdown of any vacuum tube, gas tube or brush; or the breakdown of any structure or foundation supporting the object.

Explosion in piping, too, must meet the "sudden and accidental" tests similar to those listed above. Even then, the piping is not usually insured if it is beyond the insured premises, or is exhaust piping transmitting steam to the atmosphere, or a deaerator, a feedwater heater, a receiver separator, or an accumulator.

In addition to the above perils, certain machines not of a pressure vessel type, nor required to be inspected by state, provincial or municipal requirement, may be included under this coverage by specific endorsement in the insurance contract. The perils provided against are the sudden and accidental disintegration due to centrifugal force. Examples of such machines, which may be included are chill rolls, balance wheels, and drier rolls.

Items not normally covered are explosions not caused by pressure, even if in a pressure vessel. An example would be a gas explosion in the firebox of a furnace. Fire damage, even though following a covered explosion, is not covered under this contract of insurance. Nor is an explosion, even if in a covered vessel *and* caused by pressure, if the explosion was the result of water used to put out the fire. Again, these events are normally covered under the Fire-E.C. contract.

Mandatory Inspections Provided

The mandatory inspection service is provided by the insurance company under this contract of insurance. High pressure boilers—that is, those over 15 psi—normally have to be inspected annually pursuant to state, provincial or municipal requirements. Low pressure boilers—those of 15 psi or less—have to be inspected at reasonable intervals, and at least once during a three-year policy period. Recommendations contained in the insurer's inspection reports are invariably of sufficient importance to warrant immediate compliance in order to prevent damage to property and injuries to personnel.

It is also a general statutory requirement that the initial installation of most pressure vessels be inspected by an approved inspection service before an operating permit is issued by the governmental agency involved. Insurance companies have such approval. It is, therefore, important that all installations which may be subject to these governmental requirements be reported to the insurance company at the time the installation is made. Once the installation has been reported to the insurance company, subsequent inspections are the responsibility of the insurance company without further follow-up from the insured.

Marine Insurance

Marine insurance covers vessels and goods travelling over water, as well as continued carriage of goods on land. Ocean marine insurance provides against loss for all overseas movements of merchandise. Inland marine insurance provides the same coverage for vessels and cargo if the loss occurs in inland waters.

It should be noted that the inland marine policy form is often used in a transportation insurance policy whether or not the movement is by water or by ground carrier.

Typically the merchandise is insured "against loss, damage or deterioration from any cause however and wheresoever arising irrespective of percentage, including strikes, riots and civil commotions, but excludes war risk." Invariably a companion policy is issued with the marine contract providing coverage for the war risk while waterborne or for 15 days on shore at a trans-shipping point. If the 15-day waiting period is exhausted, coverage then reattaches upon reloading on board the on-carrying overseas vessel to final port of destination.

A marine policy usually excludes loss or damage resulting from delay, inherent vice and/or loss of market, rancidity, war, capture, seizure, arrests, restraint, detainment, confiscation, nuclear incident, reaction, radiation or any radioactive contamination, strikes, riots and civil commotions.

The war risk policy usually excludes loss or damage caused by or resulting from commandeering, preemption, requisition or nationalization by government of the country to or from which the goods are shipped, seizure or destruction under quarantine or custom regulations.

10

The 'Giant' Corporation

The 1000 corporations listed in *Fortune* magazine's analysis of U.S. companies have assets of almost $1,300 billion, while the U.S. property-liability insurance industry, from which these companies buy much of their insurance, has a total of $190 billion in assets and $54 billion in policyholder surplus.

It is a fair guess that these 1000 corporations pay about $20 billion in premiums (one percent of their sales) to insure against losses due to fire, explosion, auto and industrial accidents. Of this, about $15 billion is used to take care of the actual losses arising from these corporations' activities. The remaining $5 billion is used to service these losses. We have selected these companies, not to imply a corporate elite, but because the *Fortune* analysis gives us such data as sales, assets and net worth. Through these basic figures we can estimate corporate insurance needs and expenditures.

Concentration of Risks

These commercial, insurable risks are becoming more concentrated, making it more difficult to insure them completely at full value under the underwriting rules followed by virtually all insurers. This concentration has been accelerated by improvements in the highway system, by greater economy of operating in fewer, larger locations, and by similar trends. The economies of such concentration are easy to observe. But what they do to the insurance mechanism is not so obvious.

All property-liability insurance companies have a limit to the size of a property risk they will underwrite at any one location. One huge property-liability insurer with assets of $4 billion has a per-location loss limitation of $400,000. This is typical. So we can see what such a concentration of facilities can do to the typical insurer's capacity to insure the risk without recourse to reinsurance under the limitation it imposes upon itself.

Such concentration of risk has been going on for some time

and will continue, whether it be manufacturing facilities, jet airplanes, super tankers, or high piled warehouses. Nothing is going to reverse this trend. The economies gained by concentration are too great for this process to be stopped.

Insurance Buys Survival and Service

It has been said that the two reasons for buying insurance are survival and service. This is an over-simplification, but it contains a great deal of truth. Without protection, if my well-mortgaged house in Connecticut were to burn (without insurance of course), its loss would be a financial disaster from which I would have great difficulty recovering. On the other hand, when the insurer of my ten-year-old station wagon reimburses me for a broken windshield worth $135, no element of survival is involved. It is really just providing me with a service to smooth out my cash outlay.

When I insure my house, my financial survival is involved. Somewhat in the same boat is the relatively small U.S. corporation with one or two plants, the value of which equal or exceed that corporation's annual sales.

But what about the company with assets running into the hundreds of millions of dollars, with annual sales also in the hundreds of millions and with many plants spread throughout the country, each with values constituting a small percentage of the total resources of the company? What kind of loss would have to occur to that company to cause as much havoc in that company's life as the uninsured loss of my house by fire were it to occur? It's my guess that, at the present time, many multi-million-dollar corporations insure against property losses which, in proportion to their assets, are more analogous to the coverage of my station wagon, than to the coverage on my house.

This condition may be changing. Not too long ago the treasurer of a corporate giant expressed the opinion that his company should not buy insurance at all except to obtain engineering and loss prevention services. His reasoning is interesting. He reasons that, unlike us humans, a corporation is a perpetuity. And that all large corporations are expected to pay for their own losses over a period of time, plus the insurers' expenses to service those losses. If the premium doesn't cover the loss plus expenses, the premium will be quickly increased. As Al Smith once remarked, "There is no such thing as a free lunch."

I cannot agree with the position expressed by this treasurer. However, the risk manager of a giant multi-billion-dollar complex is perhaps equally off base when he says "the insurance rates I've been quoted have never made it economically sensible for me to insure other than on a nominal deductible basis."

The Ultimate Solution?

Recently I had occasion to make a presentation to a committee of the board of the insurance company that employs me. To a list of external environmental events to which our company would be subject in the next five to ten years I included "The Financial Revolution" which was part of the title of a recent *New York Times* editorial commenting upon the merger of a large life insurer and a stock brokerage firm and the then proposed merger of American Express and still another stock brokerage firm. The *Times* expressed the opinion that "what is happening is the beginning of a reorganization of the finance industry" and that, at some future time "consumers will be able to insure a car, price an annuity, sell a house and cash a check in one office." The editorial called for legislation to permit banks to enter this "revolution," presumably including the area of property-liability insurance.

I expressed the opinion that if the banks were so permitted, it wasn't difficult to see them providing a financing package for plant and equipment that, if there were a loss or damage for most any reason, including those risks now insured, the financing would be adjusted accordingly. If so, I think it would be a mistake. To my mind the best possible arrangement to take care of insurable risks is a well structured, rather intimate partnership between parties susceptible to the risk and an entity, such as an insurer, whose interest in helping to keep losses at a minimum is maintained by the rather exclusive feature of service (and consequent reward) that the entity renders.

Because of this belief and my further belief that the insurance industry can best service its property customers by adapting certain of the pooling mechanisms that developed in the casualty area during the 1973–75 capacity crunch period, I have reproduced below part of an article I had published in 1969 in *Insurance* magazine. (There is error in this presentation which I shall comment upon at its conclusion.)

"I offer the following chart as a possible approach to corporate risk handling. It shows three levels of loss protection.

NATURE OF LOSS	ORGANIZATION WHICH WOULD TAKE CARE OF RISK AND ABSORB LOSS	SUGGESTED NAME FOR THIS LEVEL	DOLLAR VALUE OF LOSS (PER LOSS BASIS)		DOLLAR VALUE OF LOSS (ANNUAL AGGREGATE BASIS)	
			Minimum	Maximum	Minimum	Maximum
Losses which, under most insuring arrangements, a corporation of any size is expected to bear. Transferring these losses to an insurer merely results in dollar swapping between insurer and insured, with needless expense to both.	The company sustaining the loss. Self insurance reserve on corporation's own books covers severe loss and spreads it over several years of earnings.	Predictable loss level.	Up to	$500,000	Up to	$5,000,000
Severe losses which are too large for individual companies to absorb conveniently. When loss occurs, each member assessed its share. Industry-controlled committees and/or staff would monitor loss prevention and engineering effort of individual companies and would undertake substantial loss prevention research and similar activity.	The industry susceptible to the risk involved, i.e. airline industry for jumbo jets, oil industry for oil slick liability, etc.	Industry loss sharing level.	$500,000	$5,000,000	$5,000,000	$50,000,000
Truly catastrophic losses for virtually all corporations.	Conventional insurance market, probably through syndicates similar to American Marine Hull syndicate.	Insurable loss level.	$5,000,000	$500,000,000	$50,000,000	$500,000,000

Predictable Loss Level

"The first level covers losses to be taken care of by the corporation. This is not a novel idea. Who hasn't heard of deductibles? What may be novel is the suggestion that the level of losses should be quite high—high enough that, if the maximum occurs, either on a per loss basis ($500,000) or an annual aggregate basis ($5,000,000), that occurrence will be financially embarrassing to virtually all corporations except the very largest.

"However, such financial embarrassment is eliminated by setting up a self insurance reserve on the company's books. Then the financial impact of even the maximum loss of $5 million would be spread over the years used to accumulate the reserve. It is inevitable that such losses will occur, if one waits long enough. This should be recognized by the federal tax authorities. Additions to reserves, in reasonable amounts, should be deductible in calculating corporate income tax, just as premiums paid to insurance companies are deductible.

"The economies arising from this self insurance arrangement are obvious. The insured saves the difference between the insurer load charge and what it costs for loss servicing. Inspection and engineering services, formerly supplied as part of the insuring arrangement, can be contracted for separately. One aspect of self insurance is often overlooked: it generally results in better loss prevention. Being borne by the insured, the loss and financial outgo implicit in the loss comes into much sharper focus for the insured, and the employees of the insured, than if the loss were to be paid by the insurer.

"By taking care of these predictable losses, the corporation relieves the insurance industry of them. This should free up a large segment of insurance capacity for insurers to take care of the segment of the loss absorption process assigned to them.

Industry Loss Sharing Level

"The second level in the chart is somewhat novel. It is true that in Germany the equivalent of our workers' compensation has been handled by industry pools since the time that protection became available. It is also true that we are seeing the beginnings of industry pools of a loss-sharing nature. These are beginning to appear because of stark necessity—because of the near absence of insurance capacity to take care of the large volume of risks.

"There are the aircraft builder's council, several industry-owned insurers, and the protection and indemnity clubs that provide liability protection to marine insureds. Every industry with an insurance problem should explore, probably through its trade association, the possible pooling of risks within that industry. This could involve product claims, product recall, air and water pollution and high-piled warehouse destruction.

"The possibilities of effective risk pooling and loss abatement are immense. Since loss reimbursement from an industry group would begin at a high level (the chart suggests $500,000 per loss and $5,000,000 annual aggregate), the incidence at this level should be low, thus requiring a simple supervisory mechanism.

"Because the company to be reimbursed would have had to absorb a substantial share of the loss, paying members of the industry would not feel they are subsidizing a careless, loss producing member. Again, because of low frequency, it should be possible to pay any loss on a post-assessment basis, rather than on a prefunding basis. This offers a distinct advantage. Insurance companies must always prefund these high level losses. Due to the nature of this coverage, many years of premium payments can pass before a loss occurs. The inevitable loss is always many hundreds (sometimes thousands) of times the size of the annual premium.

"Despite the fact that many years of premium paying is supposed to take care of the infrequent loss, the insurance industry seems incapable of absorbing the psychological impact of this large disparity between loss and current premium. Witness the collapse of the Simmons pool, the frenetic adjustment upwards of premiums by Lloyd's and the drying up, generally, of insurance capacity on high level corporate risks.

"Loss prevention programs on an industrywide basis would probably provide more benefit to the corporate participants than the dollar economics inherent in the pooling of risk. Certainly the innate knowledge (including techniques for preventing loss by fire) as to the best, most efficient way to build and operate a fluid milk plant is to be found in the fluid milk industry. The fact that the industry would bear directly as much as $50 million of loss would act as a powerful catalyst to the industry to get the best possible operating and engineering talent to concentrate on loss prevention. (By operation of the insurance rate and classification system, the fluid milk industry bears indirectly all the fire losses of that industry, but that fact is not obvious.)

Insurable Loss Level

"We come now to the conventional insurance industry's participation in this loss pooling device described in the third level of the chart. Under the plan recommended here, the insurance industry would be the intermediary for the pooling of losses involved in high level risks. There are, of course, the genuinely catastrophic risks which occur in excess of a per occurrence limitation of $5 million and an annual aggregate of $500 million.

"I asked an officer of a larger insurer to comment on the concept embodied in the chart. His answer, predictably enough, was that the insurance industry could not successfully handle the high level, catastrophic losses without receiving the premium volume from the lower level losses. I believe this line of reasoning is utterly fallacious. It suggests that the solution to the problem of pooling high level, catastrophic losses rests in attempts to have those subject to lower level risks subsidize, directly or indirectly, the handling of the high level losses. That is the quickest way I know of to socialize the industry.

"A great student[1] of the commercial and industrial picture has said that 'the solution to a problem rests *in* the problem.' The solution to the high level, catastrophic risk problems rests in the proper perception, evaluation, pricing and pooling of these risks among those susceptible to the risk.

"I suggest the insurance industry be used as the intermediary. This is being done today, but in a most unsatisfactory manner. There is the capacity shortage and the repeated failures, at renewal time, to fill out completely those excess insurance contracts involving high level corporate risks. In justice to the insurance industry, however, and in recognition of the substantial changes inherent in the plan herein proposed, the ground rules of obtaining and maintaining this insurance would have to be changed drastically.

Long Term Contracts

"The first such change of ground rules is to recognize that such risks are completely and absolutely outside the scope of the usual and ordinary underwriting criteria. Such losses occur sporadically and with great unpredictability.

"So it is impossible to put a precise figure on the cost of protection from these risks. This has to be recognized both by insurer and by insured. One way to recognize it is to write these contracts for a long period—say five years, or even ten. Another approach would be to provide for an open end arrangement on premium payments. Even a retrospective charge equal to 100 percent of the annual premium charge on one of these excess insurance contracts would be a minor adjustment to absorb in a corporate insurance program. Yet it could give the relief needed by the insurer in a bad loss year.

"Still another aspect which insurer and insured should pursue together is to convince the income tax authorities of the certain, yet sporadic nature of these losses. An intelligent recognition of

[1] Mary Baker Follett

this by the tax people should permit the insurers to keep virtually all of the premium accepted for this risk in an incurred, unreported reserve, free of tax for as long as ten years.

"So it is obvious that the insurers and the multi-million-dollar corporate insureds need each other, but in substantially different roles than at the present time. Much planning, effort and coordination, accompanied sometimes by considerable stress, will be needed to bring about these changes.

"There is no doubt that they have to be made. The only alternative for corporate insurance or risk management is that it will be supplanted by some other specialty within the corporation. For the insurers, the alternative is out and out replacement by some entity, possibly by government, more suited to the needs of those being serviced."

Corrections to Note

The first, most obvious correction of the above is that there is no longer a shortage of insurance capacity; as of this writing there is a capacity glut in most insurance lines.

The three-year "up" cycle, which was the typical period of such activity is now in its fifth year with no sign of abatement. The plan suggested is designed to go beyond cycles and, to my mind, still has validity.

The second correction is that the self insurance reserve is now no longer permitted under FASB No. 5, the effect of which is described more fully in another chapter of this book. The effect of a self insurance reserve can probably still be obtained by forming a captive insurer. But, in the absence of a rather severe shortage of insurance capacity, the necessary impetus to form such a captive is not present.

11

The Conventional Insurance Market

For our purposes, the conventional insurance market is defined as those insurers and the intermediaries they use—the insurance agents and brokers—who offer themselves to the public as accepters of insurable risks. It includes all insurers admitted to do business in the U.S., whether "agency" or direct writers (whose hallmark is that they deal directly with the insured party rather than through an agent or broker). It includes, of course, Lloyd's of London and other "alien," i.e. non-U.S., insurers with whom U.S. corporations do business, and, in recent years, a growing number of captive insurers have been accepting non parental or third party risks.

These insurers can be stockholder owned, or organized as a mutual or a reciprocal (often described as a nonincorporated mutual insurer). Interestingly enough the Lloyd's insurers, organized as partnerships, are called syndicates in accordance with British word usage.

The conventional insurance market does *not* include captive insurance companies, whether owned by companies or industrial groups, whether domestic or offshore, if the captive confines its writings to those of its parent. Nor does it include the trusts organized by non-insurer organizations to service pensions and similar employee benefits. Of course, it does not include any form of self-insurance program which a company might organize to take care of its own risks. And it does not include those inspection, engineering and loss handling companies which have come into being to assist the corporate self insurer.

Impressive Characteristics

Dollar-wise, what are the dimensions of the conventional market? No one really knows with any degree of accuracy and experts would disagree if they were to guess. The one, accurate statistic describing a substantial part of this total market is supplied by

A. M. Best & Company of Oldwick, N.J., on those insurers comprising the U.S. "admitted" (i.e., licensed in at least one U.S. state or the District of Columbia) market. In the latest figures available, Best's reports that there are some 1,400 plus insurers in this market with assets of $187 billion and policyholder surplus of $54 billion. Using this surplus, $91 billion of net premiums were written during the last year reported.

To these domestic insurers operating on an admitted basis, we must add the considerable influence of the Lloyd's of London insurers, who are admitted as reinsurers and, as such, not included in Best's figures, the British non-Lloyd's market and other alien insurers (such as Swiss, German and Japanese) operating in the United States on a non-admitted basis. The dimensions of this alien, non-admitted market cannot be accurately calculated.

The Lloyd's of London organization, which operates largely on a nonadmitted basis insofar as directly written premium is concerned (it's an admitted insurer only in the states of Illinois and Kentucky) publishes data which indicate that its syndicate partnerships have premium writings for business arising in the U.S., which average in an area in excess of a billion dollars annually. The estimate most often heard of the resources standing behind these Lloyd's resources is in the area of $2 billion. The partners (called "names") that comprise the Lloyd's syndicates emphasize, with justifiable pride, that their entire personal fortunes stand behind their underwriting activity.

Billions in Trust Funds

Another measurement of the influence of this alien, insurance market is available in the amounts of money contained in the so-called trust fund accounts of these insurers. These are monies which these insurers have placed in U.S. financial institutions to assure their availability for use in discharging their obligations. These monies run into billions of dollars. Best's reports that there was over $3 billion in the Lloyd's trust fund maintained in the U.S. as of December 31, 1980.

75% of All Insurable Risks

The proper functioning and cooperation of the conventional insurance market are essential to the success of a corporate risk management program. Some would say that it is *the* essential to such success. It is probably an accurate guess that 75 percent of all insurable risks or exposures to loss to which the typical corporation is subject are still transferred to the conventional insurance market.

In the early 1970s, even though insurance capacity offered by the conventional insurance market was quite plentiful, some corporate risk managers began to retain the lower level "first dollar" property losses. This was done by writing the insurance contract with a deductible. By this arrangement the insured agrees to absorb some part of losses, sometimes on an annual "aggregate" basis—the total of loss occurring during a given year—but more often on a "per occurrence" basis. The aggregate coverage could be, and often is, superimposed over the per occurrence insured arrangements.

Thus, if the total losses in a given year on a per occurrence basis (whether or not these per occurrence losses are insured) exceeds an amount agreed upon, say $5 million, the aggregate insurer is responsible for losses exceeding this agreed $5 million amount. Total reimbursement under this aggregate coverage is, of course, for an agreed amount. In comparison to the total risk involved, the risks so retained were modest. In the area of losses from third party liability, there was even less self insurance of loss by corporations. This was probably because specialized personnel were needed to investigate, adjust and settle liability claims, no matter how small the amount.

In workers' compensation, there were some employers with huge numbers of employees who were and had been self insuring, especially if many employees were concentrated in a few locations. But there was still great reliance on the conventional insurance market to take care of their workers' compensation losses on a conventional basis—that is, with an insurance contract in which all elements of adjusting loss were largely in the hands of the insured.

Capacity Crunch Impact

Two events then occurred which greatly affected the conventional insurance industry and, as a consequence, how the risk manager was to do the job.

The first was the 1973–75 insurance company capacity crunch, during which many large risks became increasingly difficult if not impossible for the conventional insurance market to accommodate. The first coverage to feel distress was medical malpractice liability, followed closely by hospital professional liability coverage and then by products liability coverage for manufactures of machinery, tools and similar items.

All of these coverages had the common attribute of a long tail—that is, a large volume of late maturing losses. The possibility of loss would often not even be reported to the insurer (or the insured party for that matter) for as long as five to twenty years. Before the insurance capacity turned progressively to adequacy and then to a glut, many risk managers of large and not-so-large companies found it very difficult to obtain insurance coverage at reasonable or "affordable" rates.

The second event that affected the insurance market was the promulgation in March, 1975, of FASB Standard No. 5, entitled "Accounting for Contingencies," by the Financial Accounting Standards Board, an organization comprised of accountants in public practice whose pronouncements are controlling in the accounting profession.[1]

FASB No. 5 Impact

Standard No. 5 had a marked effect on corporate activity in self insurance. It stipulated that an estimated loss from "an existing condition . . . involving uncertainty as to possible . . . loss" could and, indeed, should be recognized as an expense on a company's books only if it is probable that the loss had actually been incurred at the date of the financial statements and that the amount of the loss could be reasonably estimated.

This had the effect of requiring corporations whose statements must be certified by a CPA to eliminate most of their self insurance reserves on the company's books, at least if those reserves were for property losses since these reserves are almost always based on the company's past loss experience and not on the fact that a loss had actually occurred. Property losses have a very short tail. They are usually settled soon after they occur.

The FASB 5 standard also had a serious impact on insurance companies with public stock ownership who had set up contingency or catastrophe reserves to cover such severe losses as a major hurricane every five years, with 20 percent of the loss charged to the reserve each year. FASB 5 required such companies, who were

---

[1] Statement of Financial Accounting Standards Board (FASB) No. 5, Accounting for Contingencies, March, 1975, published by Financial Accounting Standards Board, Stamford, CT 06905.

required to provide a clean accountant's certification of their financial statements, to eliminate these reserves from their balance sheets and to return the credits contained in them to the income statement.

The liability and workers' compensation self insurance programs were not as much affected, since in most large corporations there is generally a high loss frequency. If this loss frequency is combined with a long tail and there is a creditable way to calculate the probable amount of the loss, continuation of the self insurance program was possible. And many corporate self insurers continue to do so.

Views of the IRS

It should be noted that what we have discussed above involves only the treatment of self insurance expenses and self insured reserve items on the financial statement of the corporation and not the federal tax aspects of these items. As uncertain as these items are in the accountant's treatment of them on the company's books, the federal tax aspects are even more uncertain.

The Internal Revenue Service has always looked with disfavor on permitting a tax deduction for most kinds of reserves. Self insurance reserves are no exception. For many years the IRS maintained that there was no deductibility for the reserve per se. That is, the Service would allow a deduction only for paid losses in a self insured program.

Some time in the early 1960s this policy was relaxed a little. For a while, at least in some IRS districts, a deduction was allowed if there was an unequivocal obligation by the employer to pay a claim and if the amount of the claim was certain. But in the district where I was then employed, there was little loosening of the strict concept that the loss had, in effect, to be paid. There were several years when the tax department of my employer found that hundreds of thousands of dollars of self insurance reserves had been set aside, but not once was it found that an unpaid loss should be claimed for tax purposes. The IRS held, for instance, that a reserve set up to pay a widow her benefit under workers' compensation because of the death of her husband by industrial accident was not "an unequivocal obligation to pay," because the statute provided that, if she remarried, the amount of the reserve could be reduced or eliminated.

In 1975 the Crescent Wharf case provided a basis for the tax deductibility of unpaid loss reserves if "liability was certain" and there was a reasonable way to determine that liability. Note the similarity between this rationale by the court and the determination made by the accountants in FASB 5. We shall continue this discussion in other chapters in which we go into greater detail on self assumption, self insurance, and the captive insurance company concept.

Why Do Big Corporations Insure?

I devoted one Sunday afternoon to estimating the amount spent on corporate insurance premiums and on systematic self insurance reserve additions by that segment of American corporations large enough to encompass the entire aspect of corporate risk management. After consulting the *Statistical Abstract of the U.S.*, *Best's Aggregates and Average* and *Fortune's* lists of the largest U.S. corporations, it is my guess that the 4000 corporations which employ risk or insurance managers have about $2,000 billion in annual sales, about $1,400 billion in assets, and spend, one percent or $20 billion a year for corporate insurance within the parameters described above. And probably not more than one percent of this amount, $200 million, is spent annually on self insured programs. If these empirical figures are correct we wonder why American corporations with assets and net worth many times more than that enjoyed by the casualty insurance industry, look to that industry for protection against loss. In other words why do these huge enterprises insure at all?

Several reasons come to mind. One reason is the strong tradition among commercial and industrial firms to insure their risks. The tendency to conform is present among us all in varying degrees. If anything, this tendency to conform is more prevalent in large corporations than among the population generally. All of us are bound by that ever present legal device, the reasonably prudent man rule as applied to our specialty, whether we are risk managers or financial executives or chief executive officers. Perhaps it wasn't intended by its propounders, but this common law legal concept, purporting to describe an acceptable rule of conduct, places the burden of explaining such (non conforming) conduct on the innovator. Conformity is on the side of the status quo.

The Added Services

Another reason why large firms insure risks is that they thereby obtain many services offered by insurers in addition to actually bearing the risk. These other services are loss adjustment, investigation and abatement.

Thus fire insurers specializing in insuring large corporate risks will invariably offer inspection service. This service provides periodic inspection of the insured properties to uncover fire hazards and other potentialities for loss. When a company is erecting a new building, fire insurers will recommend a design that will minimize fire loss, as well as fire protection equipment to be installed.

Serving as Investigator

Still another service which insurers provide is to investigate whether the insured is responsible for the loss and negotiate the amount of settlement as far as third party liability and workers' compensation coverages are concerned. It is inevitable that a corporation of any size is going to have claims made against it for auto accidents with the corporate fleet and other accidents in corporate activities.

Someone has to provide these services. By buying insurance, the corporation gets the services along with the protection.

Forced to Bear Risks

The 1973–1975 insurance company capacity crunch has irrevocably changed the manner in which the corporate risk manager operates. This is particularly true in large corporations—the ones on *Fortune*'s lists—and other companies with difficult product liability or professional liability risks.

Because of the difficulty in obtaining insurance through the conventional insurance market, the end effect of the capacity crunch was that corporations were forced to bear fortuitous risks to a greater degree than before. This was done mainly by taking much larger deductibles on coverages which lend themselves to the deductible approach.

The crunch also gave a powerful impetus to the captive insurance company movement which had previously been confined largely to insuring the risks of the parent corporation's non-U.S. activities. Another impetus was the emergence of specialty insurers, most of them rather small. These specialty insurers led the way to an unbundled approach (without services) and other innovations in the coverages themselves.

Certain coverages lend themselves to different forms of retention by the corporation. First are the property coverages—fire, extended coverages, and other forms of two-party insurance. Two-party insurance is insurance with two parties to the contract, the insurer and the insured. This is in contrast to third-party insurance where, in addition to the insurer and the insured, there is another party, which might be a member of the public, as in the case of liability insurance, or a company's employees, as in workers' compensation.

There is no law that requires a corporation to insure its property against loss by fire or windstorm, or its vehicles against damage or theft. But there is indeed a law in virtually every state which requires an employer to protect its employees from injury by industrial accidents, either through the insuring process or in the almost equally complicated process of becoming a self insurer. Not surprisingly, therefore, it was the property insurance coverages that became the subject of large deductibles during the capacity crunch, to reduce the strain on the existing capacity and to permit the corporation to save money by retaining this risk.

Excess and Surplus Lines Insurers

During the capacity crunch there was much more use of the excess and surplus lines insurance industry. This industry specializes in the type of insurance which came into greater demand when the use of deductibles began to spread. Excess insurance is that coverage which comes into play at the point above the amount of the deductible. This might be $1000 per accident or, in some instances, as high as $100 million. Surplus line insurance, which may also be excess insurance, is not necessarily exclusive to that type of coverage. Surplus line is so called because it can be offered in a given state or other jurisdiction only if the existing authorized insurance market does not offer the coverage. If the risk is a type permitted by the laws of the state, it can also be covered by surplus line if there is not enough market available to accommodate the amount of coverage desired.

The surplus lines broker must find out and be able to prove that the coverage desired is not available in the state or other jurisdiction through the authorized market.

If it is a coverage which is not permitted under the insurance code of the state involved, then obviously it is surplus line by its very nature. Lloyd's of London operates almost exclusively in this surplus lines area. This surplus lines market and its workings are highly sophisticated. In most states the broker involved must have a special surplus lines license and must be cognizant of the surplus lines market; where it is, how it operates and the procedures followed in that market.

The "consent to rate" laws found in the insurance code of some states are somewhat analogous to the surplus lines market in ultimate effect, even though the operation is vastly different. The party who has a risk which he wants insured in a state where there is a consent to rate law feature in the insurance code can, through this device, actually agree to pay a higher premium than the rate schedule provides. In this way, the insurer admitted in the state can accept the risk for the higher premium.

Assigned Risk Plans

The assigned risk pool and other types of insurance arrangements, formed pursuant to state statute and designed to provide insurance to persons or corporations who could not otherwise obtain it in the normal insurance market, is another device which, strictly speaking, is part of the conventional insurance market. By these assigned risk plans the state requires that the insurers licensed to do business in the state, and for the line of coverage involved, accept the risks of these parties who otherwise would not be able to obtain insurance. Insurance through these various state-mandated plans is invariably obtained through a broker in a manner identical to insurance obtainable on a normal basis through the conventional insurance market.

Specialty Insurers

The specialty insurers that came into prominence during the capacity crunch were generally small operations. They did not offer in-house loss adjusting, inspection, engineering and other services offered by the large insurers. These specialty insurers, including the one I am associated with, in effect, offer risk managers the opportunity to insure the corporate risk without providing all the ancillary services. The insurer may, if the risk manager wishes, contract for the services of a loss adjuster or an engineering organization.

Again, when the insurance capacity moved back to an adequate level and then to a glut, the large insurers, to protect their market or for other reasons, began to offer this "unbundled" coverage as well. This ultimately enhances the position of and the ability of the corporate risk manager to control the company's program in greater detail.

Flexibility also exists in handling liability insurance. This is done by assuming deductibles to whatever degree the risk manager wishes or can negotiate with the insurer. Here again, the unbundling of services offered by the specialty insurer became available from the very large insurers.

Not as easy was workers' compensation coverage. The crunch did, however, increase the number of fairly large corporations who became licensed to self insure with stop loss coverage on the corporation's risk, since it is in all states unlimited liability so far as the risk of loss is concerned.

Surety Treated as Insurance

Surety coverage, while technically not insurance coverage but rather a form of guarantee, is treated by corporate risk managers as a form of insurance. It has not usually been subject to the deductible approach, perhaps, because it does not represent a substantial outlay to the corporation when compared to that of liability or workers' compensation, except in a few industries such as construction.

Surety is that coverage which provides that one party, the surety, agrees to answer for the loss on the default or failure of another party.

One billion-dollar company has surety coverage in which the surety, with great solemnity, agrees to reimburse the farmers of upstate New York who sell their milk to this company, if the company should default due to insolvency. An anomaly arises from the fact that the insurer-guarantor has a surplus of $80 million, while the insured corporation has a net worth of approximately a billion dollars. The $80 million is about the amount the corporation holds in cash and cash equivalent funds.

A further anomaly in this coverage arises from the fact that, if the surety should have to pay off any of the farmers on behalf of the corporate giant, it has an unequivocal right to collect from the corporate giant whatever it has paid out. Assuming the possibility of the corporate giant going broke is insignificant, the transaction is risk-free where the surety is concerned.

Why then is this coverage bought? The answer is simply that this surety bond is required by a state statute if one buys milk from the farmers of New York State! There is no way, short of repealing the law, to eliminate the need for this anachronistic coverage. Although the coverage just described is an extreme example, this anachronistic element is found in enough coverages in corporate insurance to make a detailed study of it seem, at times, like a study of *Alice in Wonderland.*

Minimizing the Losses

One succinct phrase, often heard, fairly well describes the ultimate objective of the corporate risk manager. It is, "to minimize losses, particularly the small ones, and stabilize the large ones." The obvious way to minimize losses, particularly the small ones, is to emphasize loss prevention, thus reducing losses to a minimum, and to make sure that, when losses do occur, they are adjusted and settled as expeditiously and economically as possible.

As for the large losses, the first thing to note is that they are inevitable. Perhaps the most significant aspect of the risk manager's job is to attend to and study the large loss possibilities. It can certainly be the most dramatic. The risk manager will strive mightily to reduce the probabilities of loss, but will also go further. The risk manager's attitude or philosophy can best be illustrated by Murphy's Law which states: "If anything *can* go wrong, it will."

The careful risk manager, aware that the large loss can occur, will have some plan to ameliorate as much as possible the effect of the loss. A most obvious amelioration, of course, is to have provided for its reimbursement through insurance. In considering and preparing for the large loss, the careful risk manager might do well to adopt the philosophy implicit in Pascal's great argument as to why mankind should adopt, as a working hypothesis, the concept that there is a hereafter. If there is a hereafter, the adherent to Pascal's argument has observed all of the amenities; if there is no hereafter then it doesn't make any difference!

Attitudes Before and After Loss Occurs

The careful risk manager will also be aware of two attitudes virtually all human beings have toward a large loss of a fortuitous nature and particularly one which could, even though remotely, have been prevented or otherwise stabilized. Before the loss occurs all of us—risk managers, the plant or division management that must bear the continuing cost of loss prevention equipment or paying insurance premiums, and top management—have a tendency to emphasize the cost of stabilizing the loss. And we question the need for continuing these expenditures. We also tend to deemphasize the potential effects of the loss.

But after the loss actually occurs, we all have a tendency to emphasize the effects of the loss. We can't help but do so because the effects are vividly in front of us. If this latter attitude should evolve to a condition of second guessing, it is the risk manager who usually will be on the defensive. This dual attitude is understandable. The occurrence of a significant loss is a traumatic experience, with all of the reevaluations implicit in sustaining a trauma. It is the wise risk manager who is sensitive to this dual attitude.

Speaking Up

This discussion leads logically to the question of what does the risk manager do when a substantial risk within the corporation has been identified, and the risk manager believes it should be insured or otherwise stabilized, but higher corporate management does not agree. This is often a topic for discussion when risk managers get together. One answer goes something like this, "we're not insured but I'm covered; I've written my boss a memorandum that I think we should be."

My own view is that while such a memorandum might not do any harm, it probably won't help much either if, through the workings of Murphy's Law or for other reasons, the large loss occurs. Higher management could well decide that a greater degree of articulation and persuasiveness on the part of the risk manager would have resulted in the desired stabilization of risk having been accomplished in time to prevent the traumatic loss.

Two conclusions can be drawn from this discussion. One is that the risk manager, in the situation described above, should consider that having formed the opinion that some aspect of risk stabilization is lacking, this lack is unfinished business within the company and every opportunity available should be taken to persuade the company to this point of view. The second conclusion is rather obvious yet bears articulating: The risk manager's success and continued career is, itself, subject to a host of fortuitous events, over which there is little or no control. The point is that the risk manager is in the business of fortuitous risks.

For the risk manager to be able to make an intelligent recommendation whether to insure a given risk, or to self insure, it has to be determined what the corporation is buying for the insurance premium paid. Is the premium being paid in line with the risk being transferred? What services are included? What responsibilities has the corporation contracted to perform for the benefit of or at the request of the insurer? What should be the amount of the deductible, if any?

12

The U.S. Insurance Exchanges

This chapter was contributed by my son Edward P. (Ned) Lalley and is provided with permission of Fred S. James & Co., for whom he served as a summer intern during which time he researched this subject.

The concept of the insurance exchange started in the late 1600s in a London coffee house. It was a place for shipowners to pool their money to insure that, in case of the loss of a ship, money could be drawn from the pool to cover the loss. It came to be known as Lloyd's of London, which grew into today's sophisticated multimillion-dollar central marketplace for risk managers.

The many individual members of Lloyd's, known as "names," are highly financed and capable of sharing in virtually any insurable risk from conventional fire to multibillion-dollar oil tankers, in addition to the more exotic risks, such as Betty Grable's legs and Liberace's hands.

Lloyd's success has been further enhanced by the relatively lenient regulatory stance of the English authorities and by the fact that each name at Lloyd's is subject to unlimited liability.

Now, nearly three hundred years later, the concept of the insurance exchange has been transplanted to the United States. In 1979 the New York Insurance Exchange was established.

Two basic reasons were behind it:

1. The U.S. insurance market loses approximately $1.5 billion in premiums a year to Lloyd's.
2. U.S. insurance brokers were finding some difficulty in gaining direct access into the Lloyd's market.

The N.Y. Exchange

Although the New York Insurance Exchange resembles Lloyd's in many respects, there are also some notable differences, as

revealed in the following description of the New York facility:
The New York Insurance Exchange will provide a central insurance market similar to Lloyd's of London. It will have a trading floor where underwriting syndicates will offer:

1. Reinsurance of all kinds.
2. Direct insurance of all kinds from outside of the United States.
3. Risks which have been submitted to and certified as having been rejected by the Free Trade Zone. The Free Trade Zone is a classification of risks that are exempt from policy and rate requirements with respect to large commercial risks exceeding $100,000 in premiums.

An underwriting member submits initial paid-in capital of $3,550,000 to be permitted to write all kinds of insurance other than life, accident, annuities or health. To write all kinds of insurance, an underwriter produces paid-in capital surplus of $6,550,000.

The initiation fee for a broker and underwriting member is $10,000, plus annual dues specified by the Board of the Exchange.

The Free Trade Zone Concept

The concept of the Free Trade Zone, as well as the New York Insurance Exchange, came about through an act of the New York legislature. The Free Trade Zone was seen as the first step in easing the cumbersome regulations of the New York Insurance Department.

When the concept of the Exchange came along, many New York insurance interests insisted on the Free Trade Zone provision for the writing of direct business in the Exchange. The reason was simple. The insurance companies would not permit non-regulated competition from the Exchange. The New York insurers, who bear the costs of regulations, fair plans and assigned risk pools, felt it would be unfair not to get the first opportunity to write New York direct business.

This may be a valid point. However, there are negative aspects to be considered. The limitation of the Free Trade Zone may severely hamper the Exchange's chances of success. Without the unrestricted ability to write direct insurance, as well as reinsurance, the Exchange may never achieve a dominant status similar to Lloyd's, which has no such restrictions.

At this writing a bill is presently being considered by the New York Legislature to deal with these restrictions. It reads:

"Direct insurance of all kinds on risks located in the United States other than in this state, provided that such risk qualifies for placement pursuant to the excess and surplus lines requirements of the jurisdiction in which the risk is located, the superintendent shall have the authority to permit the exchange and/or its syndicates to take such steps as may be necessary to qualify as an excess and surplus lines insurer in such jurisdiction."[1]

Some of the major companies and brokers involved in the Exchange are AIG, INA, Marsh & McLennan, Continental Corp., Johnson and Higgins,Allianz Insurance and Crum and Forster.

The Exchange started slowly but is growing. By September 1981 25 syndicates, 52 brokers and 21 associate brokers had become members of the Exchange, and premium volume was $90.3 million. Low participation has been attributed mainly to the limitations of the Free Trade Zone. However, there are many uncertainties concerning the Exchange, including tax advantages, antitrust regulation, and the need for the Exchange itself.

Tax Accounting Considerations

These factors will be crucial to the Exchange's success. The majority of the participation and capitalization of the Exchange will come from the insurance industry. However, it is hoped that there will be participation by non-insurance industry syndicates because of the investment opportunity presented by the Exchange.

The Exchange is designed to let entities set up their syndicates on the Exchange as partnerships. This would allow corporations to set up syndicates with limited liability while still giving them a tax advantage—a strong incentive to invest in the Exchange.

Another tax ruling that the Exchange is awaiting deals with accounting procedures for syndicates. Syndicate partners would have to be allowed, like casualty companies, to use statutory accounting procedures to determine their taxes or underwriting income. Under statutory accounting procedures, acquisition expenses, such as commissions to agents or brokers and premium taxes, are immediately charged against the current year's operations, whereas the revenue

[1] State of New York, Senate Bill 3526, February 1981. This bill was passed in February 1982.

or premiums earned are systematically put into earnings on a pro-rata basis. This does not conform with generally accepted accounting principles, because expenses are not properly matched with revenues.

Statutory accounting principles allow insurance companies to deduct loss reserves as soon as they are established, even though money may not be paid out in claims until several years later—in effect a tax deferral. This is an advantage that would make the Exchange an attractive investment. It has been speculated that a syndicate might be able to produce both tax exempt income and tax losses simultaneously.

Is the NYIE a Profitable Investment?

Judging by ratios common in the casualty industry, a $100,000 investment might produce $300,000 annually in premiums written. This is in keeping with the 3 to 1 rule. We will assume that $200,000 is earned during the first year. Expenses typically run to about 25 percent of premiums written, or $75,000. This leaves a cash flow of $125,000 for the year. The statutory accounting procedures allow loss reserves to be deducted from income before taxes. The loss reserve can fluctuate considerably, but 70 percent of premiums earned, or $140,000 would be a good estimate. In a new business, only about 10 percent of that might actually be needed to pay claims during the year.

The syndicate member would thus have revenues, but expenses and loss reserves of $215,000 ($75,000 plus $140,000) which would provide underwriting losses of $15,000 which could be used to offset taxable income. For a person in the 70 percent tax bracket, this would generate $10,000 in tax savings. If the syndicate's cash were invested in municipal bonds or other tax free investments, it might easily produce in addition a 15 percent return on the $100,000 investment. The cash the investor would actually receive, however, would depend on what the syndicate manager decides to distribute.

If the syndicates cannot be taxed like an insurance company, the member in the example just given would be burdened with a huge tax bill, because most of the $140,000 loss reserve in this example might not be deductible under the current interpretation of the rules. Only insurance companies can deduct loss liabilities that are not clearly established and quantifiable.

This discussion of taxes and accounting all may be rendered hypothetical because the Exchange Board has chosen to withdraw its request for a ruling from the IRS. This move raises some thoughts that chances for a favorable ruling were not good.

How Lloyd's Keeps Books

Without a favorable IRS ruling, U.S. syndicates might opt for a method of reporting similar to that of Lloyds, which the IRS accepts. Lloyd's bookkeeping in effect eliminates reserves. The syndicates keep their books for a given year. For example, 1975 accounts were not closed until year-end 1977. At that point, a syndicate manager has a better fix on what the losses were on 1975 policies. After determining the underwriting and investment profits and paying out a distribution, the syndicate in effect goes out of business.

Any potential losses that may be carried over, such as claims arising from the side effects of a new drug that show up many years later, are then reinsured by the new syndicate when it is formed the next year, or by another reinsurer. If the new U.S. syndicates opted for this system, they would still pass tax-exempt income as well as underwriting gains or losses through to investors, but they would not generate the losses produced by statutory accounting.

The final option for syndicates would be to incorporate, making them miniature insurance companies. They would then pay taxes like any other insurer and their dividends to shareholders would be fully taxable. John Cox, Executive Vice President, Insurance Company of North America and a Governor of the Exchange argues that even this kind of structure would have investor appeal. "Many investors avoid insurance stocks because the companies are saddled with a lot of heavily regulated business. The syndicates will give people a way to invest in an attractive part of the industry."[2]

Regulation by N.Y. Insurance Department

It has been said the New York Insurance Exchange will be a self regulating entity, as Lloyd's is. It is hoped the system will encourage self policing. However, the Exchange's Board of Governors reserves the right to audit Exchange members' books.

There is concern, however, about the intentions of the New York State Insurance Department. The department has restricted the

---

[2] *The Review,* "The Insurance Exchange trying to get off the ground," August 29, 1979, p. 54.

freedom and flexibility of New York insurers in the past. There is fear that the Department will try to exercise regulatory control over the New York Insurance Exchange, the very thing the new market was designed to avoid.

The Superintendent, Albert Lewis, has stated: "There will be no interference in the operations by the Department. The Exchange will be self governing, self operating and self policing . . . the Department's involvement as a regulator will be extremely small, hopefully none at all."[3] But bureaucrats earn their living by regulating the insurance industry. Mr. Lewis has confirmed that the idea of an unregulated part of the insurance industry has aroused fears among some of his staff that their jobs may decline in importance or disappear altogether.

Senator John Dunne, Chairman of the New York State Insurance Committee, has said publicly that he is nervous about Mr. Lewis, particularly because the insurance department had set aside $250,000 for a bureau whose sole responsibility is to regulate the Exchange. "When we tried to eliminate the $250,000 from the budget, he (Lewis) vigorously opposed it. I fear that creating a regulatory bureau for a supposedly non-regulated Exchange portends something other than what was originally envisaged . . . I am deeply troubled that this may be a signal as to what the policy of the department will be."[4]

Competition from Within the U.S.

Another view of the Exchange is that it is simply not needed. This view comes from Chuck McAlear, a principal of the excess/surplus lines brokerage firm bearing his name in Grand Rapids, Michigan. He says the Exchange will have competition from within the U.S. as well as from London. He says:

"The Exchange is becoming a reality at a time when a marketplace that has already accomplished its avowed purposes is firmly established and has already proven itself.

"Though spokesman for, against, or on the fence regarding the New York Insurance Exchange, have studiously avoided mentioning that there was any competition but London, this is not the case.

"For reinsurance, there are professional reinsurance companies

---

[3] *Institutional Investor* "Can the New York Exchange get off the ground," June 1979, p. 133.

[4] IBID, p. 134.

in this country and abroad as well as reinsurance departments of various carriers who accept business directly or from brokers. For direct placement there is a marketplace instantly available to every agent throughout the country no farther away than the nearest telephone, linked electronically, allowing immediate utilization of the combined capacities of underwriters across the country and abroad. Through this network, a risk can be presented to dozens of underwriters, quoted and bound while an agent or broker on a trading floor is queuing up to see if a single underwriter will assume five percent of the risk.

"Moreover, this is a market of firm quotes and instant binders not plagued by 'indications' which can prove to be only that or 'subject to completion.' Nor does the market close down for weeks at a time when a lead underwriter takes a vacation.

"It is a market where all the underwriters assuming risk disclose their financial and business capabilities with the quotation, so appropriate judgments can be made before a firm order is placed.

"It is a market legally operating in various states, that reports its activities to the appropriate commissions and which pays minimum taxes to the individual states. It is a market of no surprises where continued coverage does not depend on the economic well being of individual carriers beyond the reach of regulatory authorities.

"Yet, spokesmen on the subject of the Exchange speak only of London. They have not mentioned Boston or Chicago or Los Angeles. How could Denver, Scottsdale, Haddonfield or Evanston Harbor compete with a grand New York Insurance Exchange? Yet this is the real competition. It is a group of companies who choose to accept business on a surplus lines basis from a network of brokers already in a place, who can provide immediate access, for a large or small agent, to their capabilities.

"It is a market which is proven. While standard carriers cowered and London markets proposed forms to protect their underwriters more than the client, this market singlehandedly prevented the liability panic from becoming a rout."[5]

Exchange Legislated in Illinois

While the New York Insurance Exchange has started out slowly and has run into some problems, this is not to say it isn't a good

[5] *Business Insurance,* "Surplus Lines Team Rivals, The Promise of the New York Exchange," June 25, 1979, pgs. 36, 37.

idea. At least some seem to think so. Witness the efforts being made to set up exchanges in Illinois and in Florida.

The Illinois Exchange's fundamental difference from the New York Exchange is that there will be no restrictions, such as a Free Trade Zone. This has caused consternation in other states, who fear they may lose business to the Illinois Exchange. This could cause some political repercussions.

But optimism has been expressed for the Illinois Exchange because of the state's unregulated insurance atmosphere. Illinois has been called the excess and surplus lines capital of the United States.

Other differences between the Illinois and the New York Exchanges is that only $2,000,000 in capitalization is required, and a provision that nothing in the Illinois insurance code is applicable unless stated. In New York, the code is all applicable except where otherwise stated.

The Illinois Exchange opened for business in November, 1981, with three syndicates formed by insurers Crum & Forster, Sentry and Reliance.

Insurance Exchange of the Americas

A move is underway to set up an Exchange in Miami, Florida. The proponents' idea is to attract a large volume of business from Central and South America. While a $50,000 study by Robert Hughes Associates determined that a low volume of premiums was available, the Insurance Exchange of the Americas plans to officially open late in 1982.

Whether insurance exchanges will flourish in the United States is the subject of much speculation. With the many considerations involved, it simply may be difficult to convince people to switch from the dominant Lloyd's market to the U.S.

Also, U.S. companies are no longer restricted from participating in Lloyd's. Yet, with many of the financial centers of the world located in the United States, it might be advantageous to establish institutions comparable to Lloyd's. The U.S. certainly has the talent and initiative to do so. The use of Exchanges should be looked at by risk managers as an available alternative tool in risk management.

13

Brokers, Agents and Other Intermediaries

As much as 95 percent of all of the insurance, including surety coverage, purchased by a corporation is done through an insurance broker. Brokers are best described as intermediaries between the insurer and insured. Ostensibly they represent the interests of the insured. In reality, however, the interests of the insurer and the broker are in concert and somewhat dissonant with those of the insured. This makes for a complicated relationship, whose understanding is absolutely essential to any intelligent appreciation of corporate risk management.

How Brokerage Evolved

Let us attempt to examine this multifaceted element to corporate risk management called insurance brokerage. One can hold two theories of how our present insurance brokerage setup evolved. And these theories, incidentally, are not mutually exclusive, so the truth may well be some combination of both.

The first theory is that, by and large, the present insurance brokerage firms and hence the speciality, evolved from the casualty insurance agent. From its inception, the insurance agency system, independent from any substantial degree of control by any insurer, has been the sales arm of the fire and casualty insurance companies.

As the insurance agent's corporate customers grew in size and complexity, the need to actually sell the insurance protection diminished. According to this theory, the need for insurance protection became obvious to the corporate owner or manager and the greatest need became advice and counsel as to the best approach to take care of risks. As a consequence the insurer's sales agent evolved into an advisor or counsellor to the customer, i.e., the broker.

Certain residuals of the former relationship between insurer and sales agent now turned broker still exist. Most notably, the broker is still often compensated by the insurer, not by the insured being served and whose interests are being looked out for. The amount paid is still apt to be some percentage of the premium paid by the insured to the insurer.

The fact that many of the present insurance brokerage firms were once insurance agencies and that in some instances they still hold agency contracts lends credibility to this theory.

The other theory is simpler. It holds that, sometime after the turn of this century, the relationship between the insurer and the corporate insured became complicated enough that the need for a third party became evident, and that intelligent, resourceful persons stepped into this vacuum to help work out the proper relationships. The proponents of this theory point to a similar evolution in other fields, such as advertising and real estate.

Operations Today

How do those who practice in this area operate now and what function do they serve? Like all significant facets of the risk management speciality, there is considerable difference of opinion. Let us examine these differences and see if we can't arrive at a consensus.

There are risk managers who are ardent believers in the do-it-yourself-let's-not-get-involved-with-brokers concept of risk management. But even they would probably acknowledge that they need the assistance of a competent insurance broker to place a new, complicated risk with the conventional insurance market, especially if the risk is large enough that several insurers must be persuaded to take part of it.

This is a prime responsibility of the insurance broker—to be the expert on the existing insurance market, its availability, the prevailing prices being charged and other attributes of marketing.

At the other end of the scale is the risk manager who strives to run every detail of the corporate insurance program through the brokerage firm before a decision is made. If this pre-decision coordination is not possible, this risk manager then discusses the decision in detail with the broker as a double check.

Somewhere between these two extremes is found the majority of risk managers.

The Role of the Broker

The capable broker, like the capable risk manager, learns as much about the operation of the corporate insured as is humanly possible.

In this way the significant perils to which the corporation is subject are determined and, where possible, systematically ameliorated. Many brokers have within their own shops sufficient underwriting capacity to supplement those of the insurer in determining the optimum treatment for the risk.

The broker employs engineers to study and determine proper loss prevention equipment to be installed, appropriate periodic inspection routine, follow up, etc. The broker's loss adjustment department will assist in the settlement of all insured losses suffered by the corporate insured.

In addition, the broker often maintains underwriting data of a fairly detailed nature which relieves the insurer of doing so. Probably the most important quality the broker brings to this three-party relationship is a detached view of the arrangements, the financial considerations, whether these be premiums paid to the insurer or losses reimbursed to the insured, and other considerations between the two primary parties to these transactions. Such detachment is not possible by either of the two primary parties, since both have heavy financial interests in these transactions, while the broker does not, or at least not nearly to the same extent.

The broker has still another function. It justifies, to a considerable extent, the approach of the risk manager who runs every detail past the broker either prospectively or on a double check basis. It is to serve as this double check. The reasoning to support this need is persuasive and goes something like this: First, the subject is complicated. Second, the insurance contract is uncertain. It becomes operable upon the occurrence of an event which is itself uncertain.

Finally, there is a great disparity between the dollar value of the premium paid and the value of the compensation received if the contract becomes operable. This disparity makes it especially important that all essential details of the contract be clearly understood by all parties concerned before the contract becomes operable.

Brokers *vis a vis* Self Insurance?

All the above described duties of the broker pertain to transactions and activities which take place when it has been decided to insure a risk. Can the broker participate in decisions which dictate self insuring the risk? And does the broker, practically speaking, so participate? The answer is "of course." The 1973–75 insurance capacity crunch changed the brokerage business too. The brokerage industry too, is "unbundling." The result is that the brokers are offering their service on a commission basis or on a fee basis.

Commissions are, of course, the payments to the broker by the insurer, computed as a percentage of the premium amount. Fees are the remuneration paid to the intermediary—a broker or a consultant—by the party receiving the service, in this instance the corporate insured. It is computed on the basis of time spent in doing the job or on some other measurement.

A Matter of Self Interest

The question of fee vs. commission was once considered germane to the larger question of whether the broker could effectively participate in studies on behalf of the corporate insured. It was felt that if a broker's analysis and study should indicate that self insurance is in order, the broker would be faced with recommending a course of action that would reduce its own remuneration. It was theorized that this would require a degree of self detachment, even heroism, not often found in any of us mortals. At the present time commissions, fees in lieu of commissions, fees without regard to commissions or some combination of any or all of these arrangements are used.

It is appropriate, however, to review briefly how the industry arrived at this condition. Because this breakthrough has, in turn, been followed by far reaching changes in the structure and functions of the brokerage area that affect not only the broker's relationships with corporate risk managers, but also with insurers and purveyors of ancillary services, such as loss adjusting firms, actuarial houses and the like.

Direct Writers

Until the 1940s, probably all of the corporate insurance sold, whether of an employee benefits nature or property, liability and other casualty coverages, were all sold through the insurance brokerage system, with three exceptions. These exceptions, all direct writers, were the Factory Mutual fire insurers, Liberty Mutual Insurance Company—a liability insurer with heavy emphasis on workers' compensation—and a few insurers, sometimes organized on a stockholder-owned basis, sometimes as a mutual insurer organized by certain industries with hard to place risks.

World War II and its aftermath changed the picture, beginning in the employee benefits area. During these years a significant number of employee benefit plans, in particular those negotiated as a result of collective bargaining agreements, were serviced by either brokers or consultants on a fee rather than a commission basis. What exactly influenced this change is hard to say. Perhaps it was because the life insurers predominated in this area rather than the fire and casualty insurers.

The life insurers developed an in-house sales force so, by and large, they were not as dependent on independent intermediaries (agents and brokers) as the fire and casualty insurers.

The tendency toward a consultant-fee arrangement and away from the broker-commission arrangement may also have arisen because of the influence of labor unions who often participated in the management of plans arising out of collective bargaining. Whatever the reason, the payment of a fee rather than a commission became eminently respectable in the employee benefits field.

During the same period there was a significant trend away from insuring these plans, at least on a 100 percent basis, to plans involving partial insurance and partial trust investment or to a 100 percent trust arrangement. It is hard to say which came first—the increased tendency to pay the intermediary (who could be a broker and often was) on a fee basis or the movement away from the 100 percent insured basis to a split funded basis or a 100 percent trust arrangement.

The Case of Casualty Insurers

No such rush toward the fee system asserted itself among the insurers dealing primarily in property, liability and other casualty coverages. Until the severe dislocations arising from the 1973–75 capacity crunch and the subsequent glut, there appeared to be little appetite on the part of brokers and no appetite at all on the part of insurers to go the fee route.

The reasons are complicated. Rate filings by the insurers with the appropriate state supervisory authorities from time immemorial had contained an element for acquisition costs. This element had to be paid out to an intermediary and without discrimination. The direct writers and those who have surfaced since had no such element in their rate filings. Could these agency companies have made additional filings with this element of acquisition cost removed, thus permitting the coverage to be offered to the insured at a lesser cost? This lesser cost would be offset, in part at least, by the fee to be paid to the broker-intermediary by the corporate insured.

Of course the answer is yes, as far as the legal aspect is concerned, since the direct writers had done so for years.

'Unbundling' Takes Hold

The decrease in insurance capacity in the period from 1973 to 1975 caused risk managers and the brokers providing them service to seek solutions other than placing risks with insurers; insurers were insuring fewer corporate risks. This was particularly true for risks which insurers deemed had high potential for loss, or inadequate premium rates, or both. So self insurance programs were introduced in many corporate risk management programs.

Of course, the captive insurance concept took giant steps forward during this period. Excess insurance coverages positioned over greater self insurance programs, were also utilized much more frequently. Many of these innovative programs were introduced by insurers smaller than those who were reducing their writings.

When the larger insurers regained their equilibrium and their insurance capacity, the newer programs continued to become a larger factor in the insurance market. Thus, a crunch quickly turned to glut. I believe it accurate to say that the typical risk manager gained a substantial amount of control over the corporate insurance program at this time, since other means were now available to take care of corporate risk.

The effect of this new trend on the insurance broker was also dramatic. During the capacity crunch, the insurance broker still had to develop a program for the corporation it served. Typically, the broker had to develop a program with a specialty insurer, without substantial loss adjusting services to offer. The broker would then go to the excess and surplus lines insurance market to contract for the excess coverage required, ascertain whether an independent loss adjusting facility should be used for appropriate loss and safety services, and other aspects of the program to make it complete.

Thus began the unbundling of the insuring process and those ancillary services which had formerly been more or less under the exclusive control of the large conventional insurers. The emergence of risk management services departments in several insurers dealing in large corporate risk and most of the large insurance brokerage firms, attests to this.

Consultants Bring Objectivity

This brings us to the third category of intermediary, the consultant. Since consultants do not sell or broker insurance, they can be completely objective in their analyses for corporate risk managers. As a result, they recommend insurance or self insurance without fear of being influenced in their judgments by their own personal interests.

Independent consultants surfaced in the employee benefits area during World War II and its aftermath when, incidentally, the whole area of employee benefits exploded into prominence in the U.S. business world, both in cost and significance. This emphasis, in turn, was spurred by two significant developments. The first was the freeze on take-home salary and wages imposed by the federal government early in the war and the consequent emphasis on granting increases in the form of deferred compensation.

The company pension plan offered the most desirable qualities for deferral. Obviously, money being credited to an employee's pension account and not given as take-home pay could not be used by the employee to buy consumer goods, thus relieving the upward price pressure on scarce consumer goods. To this extent, at least, the emphasis placed on employee benefits rather than take-home pay reduced inflationary pressures.

There are some who disagree that this approach did reduce inflationary pressures. They claim the cost of funding these deferred employee benefits as a current business expense led to increased product prices. Further, these dissenters point out, these deferred benefits created huge amounts of funds seeking an investment outlet, in turn contributing to lower interest rates, and to inflation.

Benefits Become Negotiable

The emphasis on deferred employee benefits was coupled with another powerful element that dramatically changed the course of employee benefits, for they (whether of a deferred nature or not) were deemed negotiable items of compensation under the National Labor Relations Act in a manner identical to wages paid, hours of work, paid holidays and similar items. Labor unions began bargaining in earnest with the corporate employer in this insured fringe benefit area. At the time the company employee benefits program generally consisted of group life insurance coverage providing a death benefit of one year's pay, an accident and sickness plan providing a benefit of $25 to $50 a week for a maximum of six months if disabled by sickness or a non-work-connected disability and, in some cases, a limited pension plan. The company sponsored group medical plan, if it existed at all, consisted of a schedule type plan, meaning that the plan would pay a predetermined amount, as recorded on the schedule, for any surgery performed on the employee or a member of the employee's family and a per diem payment to help take care of the hospital bill for relatively short hospital stays—generally no more than 30 days.

Who Contributes How Much?

There was no standard proportion of the cost contributed by employer and employee. In the specific program described above the employer bore 50 percent of the cost of group life insurance and two-thirds of the accident and sickness coverage for income lost due to illness or non-work connected disability. The employer's contribution to the pension was about three-eighths of the total cost. The employer's contribution to the hospital-surgical insurance plan amounted to something less than one-half of the total cost.

Benefits Moved to Industrial Relations

The introduction of collective bargaining brought a profound change. The employee benefits program ceased to be an adjunct of the corporate insurance program and the exclusive responsibility of the finance department, of which the insurance or risk management division was a part. The personnel or industrial relations department, responsible for negotiating collective bargaining agreements, assumed substantial responsibility in this area.

Invariably the primary responsibility for the kind and amount of employee benefits, whether insured or not, became that of the personnel or industrial relations department. The risk manager assumed a somewhat secondary responsibility, in some instances, to administer the plans once they had been negotiated or otherwise settled upon and, in other instances, to negotiate the insurance contracts by which the insured employee benefits were provided.

During this period of substantial change within the corporate environment, there was an equally significant change in the conventional insurance market serving this area of corporate activity. More and more employee benefits were provided through trusteed plans than through an insurance arrangement.

The Consultant in Employee Benefits

The employee benefits consultant, paid on a fee basis, began to supplant the broker paid on a commission basis. Sometimes these consulting organizations were divisions of an insurance brokerage firm. More often, they were independent operations with a heavy emphasis on actuarial skills. It is interesting to observe that most of these consultants, even the most fee-oriented of them, usually had an insurance broker's license in their back pocket, and for good reason.

Virtually every corporate employee benefit program of any size had some aspect of insurance coverage in it. The consultant retained to analyze the program would do so and be paid on a fee basis. If the change arising out of this analysis resulted in the purchase of increased insurance coverages, it would often generate a commission mandated by the insurer's rate filings, the insurer's concept of what it had to do to be non-discriminatory. The back pocket broker's license would then permit the consultant to accept the commission. By this device the corporate insured's interest was best served.

Since the consultant has done virtually all the work in the way of plan design, evaluation, and similar features, it would seem that the corporate insured's interests are not particularly well served by having this commission go to a broker who had no opportunity to do any work to justify the payment of this commission. Remember that the insured had already paid the consultant's fee. The logic behind this is well nigh irrefutable. The consultant receiving the commission is thereby enabled to provide still additional service to the corporate insured.

The Consultant in Property-Liability

There are also insurance consultants who specialize in the property-liability area. If there is one coverage in this area which consultants tend to emphasize over others, it is workers' compensation, probably because there is a much greater incidence of self insurance in this coverage. There are, in fact, a number of consultants who specialize in self insured workers' compensation programs, providing inspection, engineering and similar services. Without exception, as far as I know, these consultants do not act as brokers, nor do they have a broker's license, even in their back pocket. That fact, and their claim of greater objectivity, make up the main thrust of their customer promotional effort.

Views on the Captive Broker

With all the complicating and sometimes conflicting features of these broker-consultant intermediaries, it is not surprising that the idea of establishing a captive broker has come up. Anyone contemplating such an arrangement should not underestimate the legal and practical problems inherent in it. Typical of this is the New York statute which prohibits more than a 10 percent contribution of the business of an insurance brokerage firm if it is directly or indirectly controlled by the source of the business.[1]

Even if this 10 percent rule were not in effect, there are other statutory and administrative limitations which could cause considerable difficulty. These include prohibitions against discrimination among corporate insureds and insurance brokers, illegal kick-backs and the like. We wonder if a captive insurance brokerage firm, no matter how rigorously the laws and administrative determinations are observed, could operate without extending at least some preference to the owner-insured.

A final word on the captive brokerage concept involves the attitude of insurers: they regard independent brokerage firms as a significant part of their sales effort.

I know of one arrangement which has been cited as an excellent example of a captive broker, but which is not that at all. I'll describe it in some detail since I believe it can be one way to solve some of the problems of the present relationship between corporate insureds and insurance brokerage firms, the most serious problem being the duplication of clerical and administrative efforts.

The 110% Solution

A dear friend of mine, now deceased, who spent practically his entire adult life working in the corporate risk management field, used to describe this as the problem with the 110 percent solution. He observed that the insurance broker and the insurance department of a customer were on a collision course. There was so much duplication of effort between the two that either one could add 10 percent to its cost and be able to do all the work done by both.

An insurance brokerage firm often mentioned as a good example of a successful captive brokerage firm is actually no such thing. It might possibly be described as an exclusive brokerage firm, as it acts in the place of a corporate insurance department. The brokerage firm is not, however, owned by the corporation; therefore, it is not a captive.

---

[1] Section 119 of the New York Insurance Law, Sub-Division 4a,b,c (See excerpts at end of chapter).

Using Excess Capacity

It is interesting to note how this exclusive arrangement came to pass. This brokerage firm operated until the early 1930s in a manner similar to hundreds of other firms of similar size. It had only two large corporate customers. It subsequently lost one account. This loss left considerable excess capacity in the brokerage firm. Happily for both the brokerage firm and its remaining client, this excess capacity was put to work doing much of the work which normally would have been done in the corporation's insurance department. This arrangement had its defects but it also represented an ingenious, intelligent approach. Could it serve as a prototype for things to come?

It's also happened in another industry. To reduce expenses, the metal container companies offer to set up can forming lines in the plants of their customers. The can companies call these "satellite" operations. Could a similar satellite plan be applied to the relationship between insurance broker and corporate insured and thereby minimize the duplication of effort? I'm not talking about a physical amalgamation of the two, but a division of effort as logical and as intelligent as the arrangement between the can companies and their customers to reduce expenses. Such an arrangement would benefit both parties.

Lessons from Lloyd's

An interesting aspect of insurance brokerage is its dealings with Lloyd's of London. The syndicates, which are the real risk bearers in Lloyd's, get along with very few employees. Syndicates' books of account and other necessary records are maintained by the central management office of Lloyd's. The personnel of the typical Lloyd's syndicate is composed primarily of principals (partners) and underwriters. Both groups seem to devote their time to evaluating the risks being offered through the migration of the underwriting "slips." Perhaps it is partly because of this paucity of personnel, that the Lloyd's syndicates deal only with Lloyd's brokers.

Dealing Direct with Mutual Companies

A small percentage of corporate risk is placed with direct writing insurers. It is no coincidence that most of these direct writing insurers are organized on a mutual basis. At one time the overwhelming number of mutual insurers engaged in writing property, liability and other casualty lines were direct writers. It was their hallmark. The dividends to policyholders represented a share of the savings in operations arising from the fact that the mutuals didn't pay these monies out in acquisition costs.

In recent decades, however, many of the mutuals have seen fit to pay brokers a commission on the business they place with them. Again the conclusion seems inescapable that the broker is still the sales arm of the insurer, whatever relationship may have developed with the corporate insured.

Excerpts From Section 119 of the N.Y. Insurance Law

The superintendent may refuse to issue a license or renewal license, as the case may be, to any applicant if he finds that such applicant has been or will be, as aforesaid, receiving any benefit or advantage in violation of section one hundred eighty-eight, or if he finds that more than ten percent of the aggregate net commission, received during the term of the existing license, if any, or to be received during the term of the license applied for, by the applicant, resulted or will result from insurance on the property and risks:

(a) of the spouse of an individual applicant; and of any corporation of which such individual applicant or his or her spouse or both own more than fifty percent of the stock; and of any affiliated or subsidiary corporations of such corporation, and of the members of any firm or association and their spouses, of which firm or association the individual applicant or his or her spouse is a member.

(b) of the members of a firm or association applicant and their respective spouses, and of the owners of any interest in such firm or association and their respective spouses, and of any corporation of which such firm or association or the members or owners and their respective spouses, either individually or in the aggregate, own more than fifty percent of the stock, and of any affiliated or subsidiary corporation of such corporation, and of any other firm and the members thereof and their respective spouses, of which other firm a member or members of the firm or association applicant and their respective spouses are members or owners.

(c) of the stockholders of a corporation applicant and their respective spouses, and of any affiliated and subsidiary corporations of such corporation applicant, and of any subsidiary and affiliated corporations of a corporation owning any interest in such corporation applicant, and of any firm or association and the members thereof and their respective spouses which either individually or collectively own more than fifty percent of the stock of the applicant corporation, and of any corporation of which such firm or association and its members and their respective spouses, either individually or in the aggregate, own more than fifty percent of the stock, and of any affiliated or subsidiary corporation of such corporation.

Nothing contained herein shall be deemed to disqualify any applicant by reason of acts done or facts existing at a time when the same did not, under the law then in force, constitute nor contribute to constituting such a disqualification.

14
Financial Decision Making

Any specialty or profession has its problems and risk management is no exception. We present the following problems in risk management in the hope that abstract theory may be clarified through concrete application.

As with all problems that require making assumptions, someone else might arrive at different answers from the ones given here. The important thing is to state the solution used, so the assumptions made can be validated or modified, based on experience.

The Proper Deductible for a Fire Insurance Contract

Here is an actual problem faced by a company:

Should the deductible for its fire insurance contract be increased from $100,000 to $500,000? The higher deductible would reduce the premium by $40,000.

A quick calculation suggests that the $100,000 deductible should be retained. The maximum loss involved ($400,000) divided by the $40,000 annual savings gives the figure 10. Can the corporation go for 10 years without having a $400,000 loss in its 160 plant, office and warehouse locations with values in excess of $100,000? It is difficult to envision.

If we stopped the calculation at this point, there would be no justification for raising the deductible to $500,000 and the consequent increase in self insured exposure. But let us see what we find by a more systematic approach, using every known fact pertinent to a successful evaluation.

First let us ask a pragmatic question. If the insurer can see fit to accept the risk of loss for the suggested premium, why can't the corporation?

The corporation has a thing or two going for it that the insurer does not. The insurer has to pay a state tax ranging from two to four percent of the premium. In most states the corporation would not. More often than not the insurer has to pay an acquisition cost out of the premium ranging from five to twenty percent.

These two costs, plus the additional costs inherent in introducing a second corporate entity—the insurer—into the picture, suggest that, if the insurer has priced the risk with accuracy, it has to be more economical for the corporation to self insure the risk.

Let's try a more exact calculation to see how long it would take to accumulate a fund which could be used to pay the maximum amount of the loss if it should occur. And let's not ignore the fact that the fund can earn income—interest or dividends—fully as much as if it were in the hands of the insurer.

Accumulating a Self Insurance Fund

Let's assume the self insurance fund can earn five percent income after tax, which is not too difficult in these days of high interest rates. Such a calculation is included in Table I. This table illustrates several important points of risk analysis for purposes of developing the optimum amount of risk to be self insured. Note that the time interval needed to accumulate the amount necessary to take care of the loss is not 40 years or even 20 years.

TABLE I

	Annual Addition to Fund	Federal Tax Liability (at 50%)	Annual Addition (Less Tax)	Interest Earned (at 5%)	Total Amount in Fund
1st yr.	$ 20,000	$ 10,000	$ 10,000	—	$ 10,000
2nd yr.	20,000	10,000	10,000	500	20,500
3rd yr.	20,000	10,000	10,000	1,025	31,525
4th yr.	20,000	10,000	10,000	1,575	43,100
5th yr.	20,000	10,000	10,000	2,100	55,200
6th yr.	20,000	10,000	10,000	2,700	67,900
7th yr.	20,000	10,000	10,000	3,350	81,250
8th yr.	20,000	10,000	10,000	4,000	95,250
9th yr.	20,000	10,000	10,000	4,700	109,950
10th yr.	20,000	10,000	10,000	5,450	125,400
11th yr.	20,000	10,000	10,000	6,200	141,600
12th yr.	20,000	10,000	10,000	7,200	158,800
13th yr.	20,000	10,000	10,000	8,100	176,900
14th yr.	20,000	10,000	10,000	9,000	195,900
15th yr.	20,000	10,000	10,000	8,800	215,700
	$300,000	$150,000	$150,000	$65,700	

The table stopped when $200,000 was reached and not at $400,000, the gross amount of the loss. This is because the loss, if it occurs, generates a federal tax credit. It is only logical that, if the additions to the fund are calculated on an after-tax basis, so should the loss charged to the fund.

Another striking feature of this calculation is that it illustrates how prominent a role the interest factor plays in taking care of risk. Note that, during the 15-year term needed to fund the maximum loss, the interest grows to where it practically equals the annual addition after taxes.

Continuing this chart to the 23rd year, as has been done in Table II, illustrates another striking feature. Note that, while it took 15 years to accumulate enough in the fund to take care of the maximum possible loss, it takes only half as long to attain that amount again, assuming of course, that no losses have been paid out of the fund.

TABLE II

	Annual Addition to Fund	Federal Tax Liability (at 50%)	Annual Addition (Less Tax)	Interest Earned (at 5%)	Total Amount in Fund
at end of					
15th yr.	$300,000	$150,000	$150,000	$ 65,700	$215,700
16th yr.	20,000	10,000	10,000	10,800	236,500
17th yr.	20,000	10,000	10,000	11,800	258,300
18th yr.	20,000	10,000	10,000	12,900	281,200
19th yr.	20,000	10,000	10,000	14,000	305,200
20th yr.	20,000	10,000	10,000	15,000	330,400
21st yr.	20,000	10,000	10,000	16,500	356,900
22nd yr.	20,000	10,000	10,000	17,800	384,700
23rd yr.	20,000	10,000	10,000	19,200	413,900
	$460,000	$230,000	$230,000	$183,900	

Time Value of Money

The dynamics of the interest factor—or time value of money—looms most importantly in the handling of risk. Insurers are well aware of this. Risk managers are becoming equally alert to it. One risk manager I know persuaded his company to self insure as much of all insurable risks as it can without financial embarrassment, rather than insure these risks. He would still elect to self insure the risk we are discussing here even if he was fairly certain that a substantial loss would occur within the 14-year period necessary to fund the maximum loss.

This risk manager justifies his position on the basis of what he calls, somewhat humorously, the ex post facto loss theory—you are correct, he's a lawyer by training! He reasons that, except for the very large, truly catastrophic losses, the insurer expects to receive enough premium from a company of any size to pay for losses plus the expense of servicing these losses. If a loss occurs, the renewal premium is increased to reflect the fact that the insurer paid that loss.

Accordingly, if the company does have a loss which exhausts the self insurance reserve, this use of the reserve stops the ex post facto premium increase. In the interim, according to this risk manager, the company has the use of the monies not paid to the insurer. As indicated by the tables this can provide sizeable interest returns.

No Alternative to Insurance—At Times

Getting back to the original problem of how large a deductible, a casualty actuary could be retained, if necessary. The actuary could develop probability tables to help the company evaluate the risk. Accepting the percentage of probability developed by the actuary is not foolproof, of course. If it is important that the company not have an uninsured loss at all—such as when it has a covenant in a bond indenture that its properties must be insured—the company has no alternative but to insure this risk.

Sometimes a cooperative insurer can be found who will insure the reserve. That is, an insurer will agree to indemnify the corporation for losses in excess of the reserve.

How to Expand Risk Absorption

Some years ago Richard E. Stewart, then New York State Insurance Superintendent, delivered a speech entitled "Ritual and Reality in Insurance Regulation," in which he articulated four areas of insurance in need of attention. These areas were (1) the need for easier access to auto insurance; (2) protection against (policy) cancellation; (3) security in case of insurance company insolvency, and (4) open competition in rating.

In addition to identifying the problems then facing the insurance industry, it contained some philosophy which is worth repeating. Take for instance the following:

"For any institution, the alternative to intelligent change is not permanence; it is extinction.

"For any industry regulated in the public interest, the alternative to regulation is not freedom; it is replacement.

"To recognize the need for change and to welcome it, is a sign of strength, not of weakness. An institution that can justify evolution only by invoking the spectre of imminent disaster is likely to be an institution incapable of renewing itself from within. Better that we plan our changes calmly and without waiting for crises."

These comments, which are certainly pertinent to the specialized subject we're going to discuss, namely, insurance capacity, appear to be pertinent to the whole spectrum of property-liability insurance.

Capacity Defined

Perhaps it would be wise to define capacity. One insurance dictionary defines it as "the measure of an insurer's ability to issue contracts of insurance." It gives as a secondary definition, "the maximum volume of business which the company is prepared to accept."

I know of no scientific formula by which capacity is calculated, but there are many rules, guidelines and rules-of-thumb by which capacity is determined, or at least estimated. The rule which comes first to mind is that of the New York State Insurance Department which stipulates that no insurer can write a policy of insurance for more than one-tenth of its surplus. Thus, an insurer that has a surplus of $5 million would be limited to issuing an insurance policy calling for indemnification of a loss of $500,000.

The effectiveness of this yardstick is somewhat obliterated by the fact that that portion of a risk taken by reinsurers recognized by the state is not considered in making this "ten times" calculation. And, as a practical measure, few if any insurers actually approach this maximum "ten times" ratio in their underwritings. Invariably the risk assumed is much less than the permitted maximum. One yardstick often used measures the insurer's capacity by comparing premium to surplus; if property insurance is involved, a ratio of two-to-one is considered acceptable, and a three-to-one ratio of premiums to assets if casualty insurance is involved.

In his speech, Mr. Stewart said, "The accepted loss ratios in much property and liability insurance indicate that people so value the ability to transfer certain risks that they will contribute a third to a half of their premium dollar to the operating expenses of the risk distribution system."

Industry and Private Funding

Let us enlarge on this thought to see how capacity might be provided through industry and private funding methods. To be practical, such industry or private coverage has to be accomplished more efficiently or less expensively than through the conventional insurance market.

Mr. Stewart was referring, of course, to the expense element in the premium dollar—that is, that part of the premium dollar used for purposes other than the payment of losses. Most of those dealing in insurance activities are accustomed to having this expense come to their attention as the unspoken complement of the loss ratio percentage.

Thus, the 65 percent loss ratio generally regarded as standard, or at least a starting point for analytical purposes in workers' compensation coverage, leaves the expense ratio at 35 percent. For auto liability, a loss ratio of 60 percent is often regarded as standard; so the expense ratio is 40 percent. In fidelity coverages, these ratios are 50–50. In fire insurance, there probably isn't much unanimity as to what the loss-expense break point is. But a split of 40 percent loss to 60 percent expense would be most often mentioned by specialists in fire insurance.

Discussion of these loss ratios can be surprising, even disturbing, when presented by people who wish to reform the insurance industry. Who has not been disturbed when Messrs. Keeton and O'Connell observe that, in auto insurance, it takes $2.20 to get $1.00 back to the insured—the people—whom the system is designed to benefit?[1]

Extraneous Costs

To arrive at this $2.20 figure, Professor Alfred F. Conard of University of Michigan Law School, who developed the comparison later adopted by Keeton and O'Connell, included such extraneous costs as fees paid to the plaintiffs' attorneys, court costs and judicial salaries. But auto insurance still has a 40 percent expense ratio.

A cost accountant analyzing these loss-expense comparisons would probably assume that the expense element is analogous to overhead in a direct labor plan overhead problem, while the loss figure is analogous to the direct labor element. Applying this cost accounting comparison would require simply dividing the expense element by the loss element. The same standard loss and expense ratios mentioned earlier would be used. Thus, in auto liability insurance, by dividing the 40 percent expense figure by the 60 percent loss figure determines that, for every dollar of loss paid on one's behalf, it costs 67 cents to get each dollar of that loss paid and provide those other services one expects from an auto insurer.

Let's take workers' compensation insurance and again apply the

---

[1] *Basic Protection for the Traffic Victim*, Robert E. Keeton and Jeffrey O'Connell, Little, Brown and Company, 1968.

customary loss ratios. (Of course, many companies may experience loss ratios different from the customary ones.) The expense element, based on the 65 percent ratio for workers' compensation, is 54 cents. That is, 54 cents are paid in expenses for each dollar of loss.

With fidelity insurance, the customary 50–50 ratio of loss to expense means that the overhead factor is 100 percent. One dollar is spent on expenses for every dollar of loss.

If we accept the 40 percent loss ratio for fire insurance, it means that there is $1.50 in expenses for every dollar of loss.

Are there any areas in the corporate insurance picture where this approach can be successfully introduced, thus providing capacity through industry and private funding methods and, by doing so, incidentally reducing the ultimate cost to the corporation of taking care of the risks? Let us review the methods which have already been tried, along with their related problems, and explore where these plans could be strengthened.

Before doing so, let's discuss briefly what most insurance practitioners perceive to be a temporary condition in the market, namely, the insurance industry capacity glut which asserted itself in the late 1970s and continued into the 1980s and has altered substantially these traditional expense ratios. As capacity continued to increase and competition waxed more robust, insurers used every available means to "shave" the expense ratios to obtain or retain corporate customers. For the past 30 years until 1979, the insurance industry has experienced a series of three-year "scarce capacity-high prices-up" cycles followed by "much capacity-lower prices-down" cycles. These three-year cycles were nothing short of amazing in their precision and consistency—until 1979 when the expected "up" cycle did not appear, and, at this writing the "down" cycle continues.

Because the traditional fully priced expense ratios as earlier described prevail for the most part in the up cycles, the do-it-yourself devices we are about to describe are much more attractive to the policyholder during up cycles. Despite the current capacity glut and continuing down cycle, a study of such devices may well be worthwhile; it has in the past.

The Intra-Industry Pool

The Aircraft Builder's Council was formed in the mid-1940s as a pool offering product liability protection to manufacturers of aircraft and aircraft components. The event which precipitated its formation is said to have been a ten-fold increase in premium costs—from 10 cents to $1.00 per $100 of sales. This, in turn, was precipitated by a year or two of severe losses by insurers. Once set up, the pool was a conduit providing several million dollars of insurance protection itself. It reinsured the upper levels of potential liability in the U.S. and London markets.

The council appeared to have two things going for it which, on the drawing boards at least, should have gone a long way to guarantee its success. The first was a high expense ratio for insurance coverage available in the conventional insurance market, giving the participants hope that they could see savings by this do-it-yourself approach. The second was the so-called indivisibility of many of the risks. This was best illustrated by one much publicized airplane accident in which it was alleged that the cause was a malfunctioning instrument which was made by one company, installed in a power plant made by another, while the power plant was, of course, installed in the airplane involving still another manufacturer. One could see how neat and orderly the defense of the inevitable products liability claim would be, if all three manufacturers involved were represented by one insurer and not by three insurers. This one insurer arrangement would certainly eliminate the possibility of one manufacturer bringing the others into the case and thus, in effect, "virtually making the case for the plaintiff" or, expressing the concept colloquially, "washing the industry's linen in public." If nothing else, this one insurer arrangement should have resulted in lower attorney's fees.

Paying for Others' Losses

Despite these two aspects going for it, the council has lost much participation of the industry it seeks to serve. To venture a guess why, one only has to examine the reasons given by one company which withdrew from the plan. As a reason for withdrawal, it indicated it felt that it was paying too much into the plan in proportion to its own losses. Put another way, the company felt it was paying for other companies' losses. No company likes to do that. Yet it does exactly that when it is fortunate enough to have its own losses running less than the expected loss ratio for the group as a whole.

Under an insured arrangement, this fact is not obvious. Under a pool arrangement it is obvious not only to the risk managers but, perhaps more significantly, to the executives to whom the risk managers report. Inevitably, the question is posed, "Why should we be paying our competitor's losses?" This suggests that any arrangement to share or distribute losses among a pool of participants will be more likely to succeed if each participant absorbs a substantial segment of its own loss or losses before a sharing of loss by the pool participants begins. In other words, the protection afforded by the pool should always be in excess of a substantial self insured deductible or retention. This assumption of loss should be high—high enough that, when the pool is finally called upon to pay a loss, the risk managers of the participants, together with members of top management to whom they report, can say of the member receiving the payment, "there, but for the grace of God, go I."

Effects of FASB No. 5

Even before the adoption of FASB No. 5, it was difficult for a corporation to develop a program in which it would absorb accidental losses, rather than rely on the customary transfer of losses to an insurance company. The striking exception was U.S. Steel. Big Steel was for years America's number one self insurer with a reserve on its corporate books to pay for losses as those losses appear. This company's annual report to stockholders would give a brief summary of its self insurance activity. Typical of this was one of its annual reports which showed that U.S. Steel maintained a $50 million reserve for insurance, another reserve for contingencies, which was over $40 million, and still another reserve of $9.4 million captioned "Accident & Hospital". The comments contained in the notes to the financial statement further explained these reserves as follows:

"U.S. Steel is, for the most part, a self insurer of its assets against fire, windstorm, marine and related losses. The insurance reserve of $50 million is held available for absorbing possible losses of this character, and is considered adequate for this purpose.

"The reserves for contingencies and accident and hospital expenses of $50.1 million, provided mainly in previous years by charges to operations, are held for exceptional unanticipated losses other than those covered by the insurance reserve."

During one year, under this self insured reserve program and typical of the pattern for all years of the period, U.S. Steel charged a total of $3.2 million to the insurance reserve. Presumably these were losses. This same amount was added to the reserve, thus restoring the total of $50 million. The reserve for contingencies was increased by $100,000. There were no charges. The accident and hospital reserve had charges of $25.6 million with an offsetting credit of the same amount.

It appears that, at this stage in the development of this company's self insurance program, the cost was confined to the actual losses sustained, that is, it was paying little or nothing comparable to the insurer's expense.

In building these reserves, the customary approach was to charge an appropriate amount as an operating expense and credit the same amount to the reserve. Losses during the period would reduce the reserve, but the unexpended balance of the reserve would be carried forward to the succeeding year in a manner identical to assets, liabilities and other balance sheet accounts.

Vertical Absorption

This procedure permitted a company to spread the impact of a major loss over several years of earnings and to systematically absorb a fairly severe loss without financial embarrassment. Let us call this treatment vertical absorption, as contrasted to horizontal absorption, in which a loss is spread over many homogeneous risks through the insuring process.

The vertical absorption method of handling risks has never really been used by American industry as effectively as its possibilities appear to offer.

Clearly there is a loss level—call it the predictable loss level or expected level—where an insurer assumes that a company of significant size will in effect absorb the losses it incurs, so the insurer increases the renewal premium accordingly. Does it not make sense that the losses up to the predictable or expected level be taken care of on the books of the company itself, with consequent savings represented by the expense attributable to these losses?

Perhaps one reason this vertical absorption method was not used very much even before FASB No. 5 was the attitude of accountants and auditors. Additions to a self insurance reserve were not deductible on the corporate income tax return, whereas premiums paid to the insurers were. So the corporate accounting department had to make an adjustment in preparing the company's tax return. An item was added to the list of items that must be reconciled between the company's books and the company's tax return.

Accountants' Attitudes

It is difficult to explain why this adjustment loomed so importantly in the minds of accountants and auditors, often causing them to take a negative attitude to the self insured approach. There is logic, of course, in insisting that this adjustment not be made necessary for an inconsequential amount of savings to the corporation. But the attitude of the accountant went beyond this.

The procedure was looked upon as unsatisfactory accounting. Any balance in a self insurance reserve at the end of an accounting period was what the accountants call a surplus reserve. That is, it was really an appropriation of part of the company's surplus and not at all analogous to almost any other entry on the balance sheet, including the depreciation reserve.

We sense that the accountants disapproved because these surplus reserves were rare—not often found on a company's balance sheet.

Let us reexamine the data from the annual report of U.S. Steel. We can assume that the $50 million reserve was generated from the savings derived by not insuring. This was generally how self insurance reserves developed.

U.S. Steel had the use of this fund. Let us assume this use is worth 5 percent, or $3.5 million a year. The losses charged to this fund in what appears to be a typical year were $3.2 million. Thus the financial benefit derived from the use of the fund goes a long way in taking care of the company's applicable losses. How much more efficient can you get!

FASB No. 5 made all of this past history but the concept of do-it-yourself risk absorption has appeared in two different forms. One is the concept incorporated into the Risk Retention Act, passed by Congress in 1981, which contemplates the risk pooling of product liability exposures by corporations susceptible to the risk, with little or no recourse to the conventional insuring process. This concept, as articulated, is silent as to the federal tax treatment of the unpaid loss reserves involved in this process.

At this writing, there is a move underway, spearheaded by risk managers, to introduce federal legislation to amend the current law and allow corporations a tax deduction for self insured reserves covering incurred but not paid losses. Essentially the aim of the Loss Reserve Deduction Committee is to achieve a tax deferral, rather than a tax deduction, similar to the federal tax treatment accorded insurance company loss reserves.

The Spread Loss Concept

Until recently the use of the spread loss concept was confined to the field of reinsurance. We are grateful to John M. Haker, CPCU, then of the Northwestern National Insurance Group (now part of Armco Insurance Group) for permitting us to reproduce the following paper, in which he describes the possible application of this principle to corporate insurance.[2]

"A little while ago, Northwestern National ran an ad for workers' compensation insurance advertising our program as 'the next best thing to self insurance.' We received an irate letter from an agent in Ohio asking: 'Why are you advertising self insurance? Self insurance takes money out of the pocket of the insurance company and agent. We should be fighting self insurance, not advertising that it is a good thing.

"We were not advertising self insurance but we *were* recognizing the importance and proper place of self insurance. As insurance people, we accept the basic rule that you assume the risks you can afford to assume, insure those risks you cannot afford to assume. After all, we practice this principle every day ourselves, for in a sense we are self insureds just as the industrial firm may be. We assume $50,000 net exposure on this line, $75,000 on that line and so forth, reinsuring above what we can afford to retain. We therefore have much in common with the risk manager.

Retention Levels

"The basic decisions as to the amount of risk we retain per loss and on an aggregate basis are made by the management of the insurance company, just as the management of an industrial firm must make the basic decisions as to how much of the corporate surplus to risk before purchasing insurance coverage. Top management makes these decisions but the risk manager must suggest the amount which he considers as the basic working layer of loss, the amount beyond that working layer which he feels that the corporation can reasonably assume, and just where the excess program should kick in.

"Someday you will accumulate your risks, including many considered today as business risks, and accept aggregate deductibles far larger than you do today. In the meantime, you devise self insurance programs on individual lines wherein you retain, usually on a per loss basis, as much as you reasonably can, without impairing corporate assets.

"Unfortunately, there is no guarantee that you will not hit an

---

[2] Address given by John M. Haker before Wisconsin Chapter of American Society of Insurance Management (now Risk and Insurance Management Society) on Nov. 20, 1969.

unusual frequency of loss within your retention, causing an abnormal drain on surplus. There is also no guarantee that this will not happen at a time when a downturn in the business cycle, a falling off of sales, or other factors such as strikes, may cause substantial business losses to the firm.

"The combination of abnormal risk costs and unusual business losses can cause management nightmares. Where management has nightmares, these nightmares have a way of being transferred to the risk manager. Factors such as these tend to reduce the retentions which a risk manager will recommend.

"Another concern is the matter of cash flow, particularly in property lines. Third party losses are often reserved far ahead of payment and the drain on cash is not so immediate. Property losses are paid right away and a high frequency in this area can cause severe restriction in available cash.

Setting Net Risk in Single Year

"There is no definite breaking point between retention and excess. Corporate management decides that the firm can afford to assume X dollars of pure net risk in a given year. If you set up a retention within which you self insure and that retention is on an excess of loss basis, it must be set at a level low enough so that an unusual frequency of loss within the retention will still not produce total loss dollars in excess of the guidelines set forth by corporate management.

"The risk manager in order to be sure he will not exceed management's guidelines, must set his per loss retention too low. This means the firm has to buy its excess cover starting at a level which may be well down into the working layer of loss. This is costly, as the insurance company must be paid for the services performed in this layer. The firm could reasonably retain a larger line if only the results could be more predictable.

"What can the risk manager do about this? First of all, he can buy some type of stop loss on his retention. In effect, this is what you get when you buy a retro. The maximum serves as your stop loss. However, retro has disadvantages for the firm which feels it can handle its own losses or safety engineering better or cheaper than the insurance company or feels that it doesn't want to pay the retro basic to the insurance company, or feels that the cash flow of the corporation is better under a self insurance plan.

"As a second alternative, you can forget the per loss excess cover and seek coverage on a pure aggregate basis, but this somewhat defeats the purpose of self insurance. You are back to asking the insurance company to take on a part of the risk. Further, although such covers are available in workers' compensation, they are expensive and the market is limited and shrinking. The market for aggregate excess on lines other than compensation is extremely sparse.

Must Pay Own Way

"With any large corporation, insurance is a transfer of risk only temporarily. Within the working layer of loss, the large corporation, in the long run, must pay its own way. This is elementary and you recognize it in the acceptance of large retentions, either by deductibles, by retro or through self insurance. If you can assume the risk within your retention and the only concern you have is that the experience within that retention is too volatile, that there are too many peaks and valleys, that management needs more stable results, then there can be an alternate solution.

"Let us contemplate an insurance program wherein you agree to settle your own losses, maintain your own statistics. Is this an insurance program? It sounds more like self insurance. However, if there is a temporary transfer of risk, it really accomplishes all you need in the way of insurance within your retention area.

"The spread loss device has been used for years by insurance companies to solve an identical problem—the problem of instability in results. An insurance company cannot go to its stockholders with wildly fluctuating composite ratios. Under a spread loss plan, the insurance company agrees that, in the long run, it will pay the freight; it only looks to its reinsurer to cushion the blow, levelling off the peaks and the valleys of its experience. Call it a funding device if you wish, a guarantee that the reinsurance company will come up with funds in the bad years to trim down that peak in losses. The concept can work also for self insureds.

"If such a cover were made available to self insureds by insurance companies, the self insureds would smooth out the results within their retention and the insurance company would not assume risks which rightfully belong to the self insureds. The only risk assumed by the insurance company, in the long run, is a credit risk, a very nominal risk when dealing with major industrial firms.

"In addition to levelling out the experience within your retentions, such a program would enable you to increase your retentions. Faced with more predictable results you can well consider the acceptance of higher risk. Such a program can also replace aggregate plans.

Akin to a Prospective Rating Plan

"Look at it another way. Under a retrospective plan, your loss costs are borne by you in the year in which they are incurred. The spread loss plan would be akin to a prospective rating plan, whereby you agree to pay over the next five years for what happens this year. You also agree that if you have a particularly good year, you will not gain the benefit immediately, but instead will obtain slightly reduced risk cost over the next five years.

"What about the cost of such a program? If you agree that you can assume the risk in the long run rather than asking the insurance company to assume your risk, then an insurance company could provide the function of levelling your experience for you at a much lesser cost than if they take the risk on your behalf.

"When insurance companies purchase reinsurance from their reinsurance sources, the markup of the reinsurers is not 100 percent over loss costs, as is the case with primary insurers. It is closer to 25 percent over loss costs or less. The difference? No engineering, very little claims control required, less commission, reduced taxes, licenses and fees and, since the business comes in larger chunks, reduced percentages for underwriting costs. Since risks are reduced, supply and demand reduce the percentage of contingency and profit built into the pricing. The same factors apply to the spread loss concept for self insureds.

"One further advantage of the spread loss concept: you need not lose control over claims, engineering, legal handling or any other facet of your self insurance program.

"What type of insurance could fit into this concept? Workers' compensation? General liability? Automobile? Fire? Actually there is no reason why the principle could not be applied to any of these or a combination thereof.

The Ironclad Contract

"How would such coverage be issued? It would have to be in the form of an ironclad contract whereby the self insurer agrees that the risk remain his. The insurance company agrees to pay the losses on behalf of the self insured only temporarily, for levelling purposes. Is this asking too much of the self insurer? No! The self insured has the risk now *without* the benefit of loss levelling. He can afford to retain the loss. He only needs the benefit of a cushioning of the blow.

"To sum up: why not a spread loss reinsurance program for

self insurers? They have the identical problem as insurance companies.

"They have one further, very important problem. Suppose you decide to self insure the first $100,000 of automobile liability exposure. At the end of the first year of your self insurance program, you find you have a considerable number of large cases pending, with unpredictable cost to the firm.

"Prudent accounting practice would require that you should establish reserves on your books, equalling the estimated cost of these liability suits. If you do not do so, you are overstating your profits for the year and imposing a burden on future years for debts incurred in the current year. However, if you do set up such a liability on your books, this is a business expense for which you are not entitled to tax credit.

"Uncle Sam will not allow your loss reserves as a tax deduction until the losses are paid. Had you bought insurance, instead of self insuring, the insurance premium would have been entirely deductible. The use of a loss levelling plan will enable you to take credit for reserved cases. This can be of particular advantage in a year with high profit margins.

"Obviously we are not talking about a traditional form of insurance policy. In format, it would be much closer to a typical reinsurance agreement. That is, a continuous form of agreement, cancellable only at the end of a policy year, with the express provision that debts incurred under the contract would continue until all installments thereof were met. You would establish the pay-in rate on the basis of anticipated losses within the retention and be reimbursed for actual losses within the retention.

Repayment Over Five Years

"The difference between actual and anticipated losses would be spread out for repayment over five years. This form would closely resemble the spread loss reinsurance agreement between insurance companies and reinsurers.

"Another possibility is a form of policy, more traditional in nature—a policy covering the specific line of insurance and written for whatever limit of coverage is desired.

"For example, an automobile liability policy written for 100/300/100 limits. Then there would be a prospective rating agreement (not retrospective) applicable to that portion of the limit which the insured wishes to retain. The contract would be continuous with the rating procedure spelled out in the contract. The insured would agree to pay his own claims within the self rating area of the policy or, if preferred, he could purchase claim handling services as part of the contract.

"The basic difference between this policy and a traditional insurance policy would be the continuous rating procedure (probably a loss rating formula) and the agreement not to leave the insurance company in a loss position. Because of the payback provisions, the insurance company's markup on the self rating portion could be well below the usual charges, particularly if the insured elects to handle its own claims.

"Using a policy form of this nature is particularly advantageous in the case of a firm which needs to make filings with various regulatory bodies. A multistate trucking firm, for example, needs to certify that it carries the limits of coverage prescribed by various regulatory bodies. Through a policy such as this, it can have filings made on its behalf and still have many of the advantages of self insurance plans.

"To sum up: it is my belief that the spread loss concept, so important to insurance companies, can be made to work as well for the large industrial firm interested in self insuring."

The above comments were given over 12 years ago, yet there is a freshness about them that renders them well worth repeating. One possible problem to the concepts described could be the emerging attitude of the IRS that any insurance program in which the premium paid is in the nature of a "deposit," i.e., adjustable up or down by events occurring subsequent to the execution of the contract, is considered nondeductible for federal income tax purposes. But the IRS position is far from clear, so there is plenty of room for continued study and adaptation of these creative concepts.

How Much Liability Insurance?

A corporation's liability for negligence or other wrongful acts is unlimited. So it is exceedingly difficult to say how much liability insurance it should carry.

The risk of liability is unlike property risk where the maximum loss is the total value of the property, plus the cost of business interruption. There is no such way to measure the extent of injury or damage to third parties by the corporation's conduct.

One astute risk manager illustrates the point by this example: Even though the owner of the Empire State Building carried liability insurance to cover replacement of the building and its contents, what would happen if the corporation were held responsible for its destruction? It would be virtually impossible to destroy such a facility without damaging the surrounding buildings and facilities.

The risk manager then asks if it would be prudent to protect the corporation against the loss of facilities within a radius of one or two miles of the building.

The Limits of Capacity

From a practical point of view, there is a limited amount of insurance capacity to take care of the hypothetical risks envisioned in this example. Practically speaking, there is probably not more than $500 million of liability insurance coverage available to any corporation from the conventional insurance market.

Those few corporations who have been held responsible for catastrophic losses, understandably enough, do not provide much information on the subject. But there is enough information available to state that liability coverage of $500 million is sufficient to take care of the liability claims made so far against any corporation from a single accident or occurrence.

Some corporations that are vulnerable to extremely high liability claims have adopted a simple answer to the question of how much liability coverage to carry. Their answer is "all that is available from the insurance market."

At least one company that already has the maximum amount of such coverage has given its broker a standing instruction to procure any additional layers of excess liability insurance coverage that may become available from the conventional insurance market.

Prudent to Insure

There is one answer, but an unsatisfactory one. If there are possibilities that the corporation will have to respond to liability claims of huge amounts of money, obviously it is prudent to attempt to have this risk covered in the conventional insurance market. It should also excite some thoughtful study of the whole risk handling and insuring process.

What is gained when the insurer of an airline, for instance, has to pay several million dollars to victims or their families following an airplane accident when the facts reveal that there was really no negligence—no fault, if you will—on the part of anyone, including the airline? It's difficult of course to argue that victims of any tragedy should not receive all they can get to help assuage their misery. But I do believe students of risk management and insurance must bring to this study a proper perspective. Measured by what most other victims of accidents receive, the victims of airline accidents receive a windfall. This is a destructive trend and a type of thinking we must move aggressively to counteract.

Minimum Limits

So much for the corporate behemoths with their huge liability risks. What about the smaller corporation which cannot afford to purchase even the $500 million of available liability insurance and must settle for something less than the maximum. Let's start on the bottom end of the scale and suggest a minimum.

There now exists a personal liability coverage for high salaried persons generally referred to as executive excess. The minimum amount of coverage is $1 million and $5 million is available to most executives. To my mind this describes the absolute minimum for any business, whether incorporated or not. Somehow, juries seem less inhibited in assessing liability against business generally and corporations in particular, than they are in assessing liability against individuals. If this assumption is correct, prudence would dictate that this eventuality be anticipated in the corporate insurance program.

This leaves a very wide gap between $1 million and $500 million. It is in this band that virtually all corporate risk managers find themselves. Unfortunately, the great uncertainty of the extent of this risk makes it impossible to set any criteria for measurement, except the following one.

Our system of law has developed the prudent man rule. It says that an individual has an obligation to act as any prudent person with reasonable intelligence would in the same or similar circumstances. This rule means that the standard of conduct is set by all of those who find themselves in the situation in question.

A derivation of this prudent man rule would suggest that the prudent risk manager or company would have at least as much liability coverage as other companies of similar size engaged in the same activity. Admittedly, this is a nebulous rule, but following it could be highly beneficial to the risk manager and his company.

15

Self Insured Retentions, Deductibles and Other Loss Sensitive Plans

Today a corporation of any size will have some form of loss sensitive insurance plan. This means that the ultimate financial outlay of the corporation for protection against the risk of loss is determined to some extent by the losses which occur under the program. The contract can be written on a self insured retention basis, on a deductible basis or on a retrospectively rated basis.

For these three loss sensitive plans the amount of loss which the risk taken is expected to bear can be calculated on an occurrence basis or on an aggregate basis. It can vary widely in amount, and depends on what the risk taker is willing to absorb as a current expense.

Self Insured Retention

A self insured retention, or SIR, is a conscious acceptance of the risk of loss by the company (or person) without recourse to any type of insurance. If loss occurs, it is charged to current expense or, in increasingly fewer instances for reasons we shall outline further in this chapter, to a self insurance reserve maintained on the company's books.

The academicians prefer to call this risk retention. Risk managers and others seem to prefer the terms self assumption (if no self insurance reserve is maintained) and self insurance if a reserve is maintained.

A self insurance reserve is an accounting device. A loss is not charged to current expense but to the reserve set up on the books for this purpose. Since funds must be available to take care of the loss when payment must be made, this reserve procedure contemplates that there be systematic credits to the reserve in amounts similar to the premium payments to an insurer if the risk were insured.

The capacity crunch of 1973–75 put a strain on the terminology in this area. Out of it came a fairly widespread agreement that any type of retention should be called a self insured retention, whether or not a reserve was maintained.

Under an SIR plan the party susceptible to the risk is legally responsible for the payment of all claims within the SIR layer of the plan. Above the SIR layer there is always excess insurance which is often written by the same insurer that administers the claims falling within the SIR layer.

Least Complicated, Least Expensive

Conceptually, this is the least complicated of the three loss sensitive methods, assuming there are no other considerations such as satisfying governmental requirements (as in workers' compensation insurance) or providing proof of insurance coverage (as in automobile liability in many states). What could be simpler, especially if no reserve is set up, than to ascertain the amount of the loss when it occurs and charge the appropriate amount to current expense?

The most compelling argument for a SIR plan is that this arrangement is often the least expensive. When the loss occurs, the party susceptible to the risk disposes of it without recourse to insurers or other parties who charge for their services.

Consider what occurs when the loss is insured. The loss is reported to the insurer, generally through a broker. The insurer has to satisfy itself that the loss did in fact occur and how much was lost. This could bring a fourth party into the picture, an independent loss adjuster, who investigates the loss and determines the amount of loss, whether or not the cause of loss brings it within the coverage of the insurance contract. Can more money be spent on adjusting the loss than the amount of loss itself?

Proponents of the full insurance concept argue that the insurer's loss administration must be consistent. By paying, without investigation, a small loss which should not have been paid under the terms of the insurance contract, the insurer would establish a precedent which could be used by the insured party to support a claim of reimbursement for a larger loss arising from the same cause. These proponents also argue that an insurer may not discriminate among its policyholders, a requirement imposed by statute and other insurance regulatory authorities. Obviously, inconsistency in loss reimbursement among insured parties could be construed as discrimination, illegal rebating, etc.

Thoughtful students of the subject accept these arguments as valid. But they also believe these are compelling reasons why an insured should elect not to insure those risks which it can itself absorb without financial embarrassment or at the sacrifice of some essential service obtainable only from the insurer. It seems obvious that the SIR approach, being so simple, should be the first one considered in analyzing the possible treatment to be accorded to any risk, especially for losses rather quickly ascertained and settled.

Deductible Plans

A deductible plan is the same as a SIR plan in all respects except one. The salient feature in a deductible plan not found in a SIR plan is that the insurer writing the deductible plan is a guarantor of payment for losses to third parties occurring within the deductible layer. No such guarantee exists in a SIR plan for losses occurring within the SIR layer.

Retrospectively Rated Plans

The retrospectively rated plan resembles a deductible plan with an aggregate feature. It is indistinguishable from other guaranteed cost plans except that the insurer adjusts the final premium retrospectively for losses over or under the normal loss level contemplated. A deductible plan does not include in the "going in" premium, provision for payment of deductible losses, so the plan provides that losses under the deductible be reimbursed to the insurer as those losses are paid by the insurer. Losses under a SIR are, of course, the legal obligation of the party susceptible to the risk and are paid as such. Under a retrospectively rated plan, the premium collected by the insurer is enough to enable the insurer to pay the losses on a current basis. The retrospectively rated settlement, as the name implies, is then accomplished sometime after the term of the policy ends.

Accounting and Tax Deductions

When losses under a SIR or a deductible plan are expensed on the company's books only when those losses are paid, no federal tax complication exists. All public accountants and the IRS will agree that the payment of such losses is an expense of operating the business and a valid deduction for income tax purposes. Difficulty arises only when losses are incurred but not paid.

The document which accountants operate under—Financial Accounting Standards Board, Standard No. 5, Accounting for Contingencies (FASB 5)—says that an unpaid loss may be charged as an expense on the books of the party susceptible to the loss, if (1) it occurred during the accounting period involved, and (2) the amount of the loss is reasonably determinable.

The first condition should pose no problem. The dates of losses from fires, windstorms and other forces causing physical damage to a company's assets are obvious. Liability or workers' compensation claims in most instances can be identified as to date of occurrence even in the difficult incurred but not reported (IBNR) aspect.

Difficulty arises in the second qualification—what constitutes a reasonable determination of the amount of the loss. Some public accountants (rather heavy handed in my opinion) equate a reasonable determination of the amount of the unpaid loss to a final offer of settlement. In other words, they seek to treat it the same as an unpaid rental item. Other public accountants are more liberal. They determine the amount of loss through the use of past loss experience, actuarial determinations and similar devices, and consider it an expense item for tax purposes.

Tax Treatment of Insurer and Self Insurer

To say that the present federal tax treatment of unpaid loss reserves under a self insurance program is chaotic is an understatement. Reportedly, the IRS districts vary from one extreme to another. On the one hand they may recognize these reserves in calculating the tax liability if it has been demonstrated that the occurrence giving rise to the reserve has, in fact, taken place and there has been a fairly professional (e.g., actuarial) determination of the amount of loss. At the other extreme, they may refuse to allow any deduction other than the paid loss.

It should be noted that when these same unpaid loss reserves show up on the books of an insurer, they are tax deductible. Why? If the IRS insists on seeing the cancelled check before permitting a tax deduction for the loss under a self insured program, why don't they insist on the same thing from an insurer? It's true that insurers are taxed under a different section of the tax code than self insurers, but both sections of the code speak in terms of reasonable and necessary expenses incurred in the business as deductions for tax purposes.

No one would question that a loss for which an insurer is legally obligated to pay, even though unpaid at the time of calculating the tax, is a reasonable and necessary expense of the insurer. Would any jury seriously hold that a food processor with 10,000 vehicles on the road incurring losses (property or liability) arising from accidents to those vehicles delivering its product to its customers, is not incurring reasonable and necessary expenses? Nowhere does the tax code require that the cost of these accidents be transferred to insurers to be tax deductible. Nowhere does the code give the specific right to tax deductibility to insurers or deny the specific right to the self insurer. Why then the anomaly?

Based on 10th Amendment

My theory is that the position of the Internal Revenue Service is based on the 10th Amendment to the U.S. Constitution, which says: "The powers not delegated to the United States by the Constitution, nor prohibited by it to the States, are reserved to the States respectively, or to the people." State laws and state insurance regulations permit, even require, insurers to consider their unpaid losses in calculating their earnings. Therefore, it has to be deemed a reasonable and necessary expense in running an insurance company, and hence deductible for tax purposes.

If this theory is correct, it might be appropriate for a lawyer more proficient in taxes than I am to examine these same substantive aspects in relation to self insurance. Self insurers, particularly those who self insure workers' compensation, operate under state statutory and administrative regulations, requiring the self insurer to conform explicitly to obligatory features of the coverage in a manner identical to an insurer. Would this not be enough for most juries to determine as fact that the self insurer was also entitled to the tax deduction?

16
The Captive Insurer

Captive insurance companies are devices set up to handle the insurance needs of business corporations. They may be owned by an industrial or commercial enterprise, an association of enterprises, a professional society or its members, or an association of local governments. These are organizations whose risks are not easily insured through the conventional insurance market.

Captive insurance companies can be based domestically or offshore. They can be property, marine, or casualty insurers or some combination thereof.

When several companies or groups get together to form a captive insurer, they are generally from the same industry and often suffering from a single exposure that is difficult to insure. A captive insurer also can be organized to insure U.S. or foreign risks, or both, of its parent or sponsor.

It could be argued that many mutual insurers, formed mostly in the mid-nineteenth century to provide insurance for specific industries, were at one time captive insurers. Most of them have since broadened their writings and are now part of the conventional insurance market.

A captive insurer can be organized as a stockholder-owned company, as a mutual, or as a reciprocal. At one time, the one common quality of all captive insurers was that their writings were confined to the risks of their corporate parents or sponsors and they did not hold themselves out to the public generally as accepters of risks. To do so would mean that, by definition, these insurers had ceased to be in the captive category and had joined the conventional insurance market.

Many captives still adhere to this policy of exclusive underwriting. Others, especially a captive of a single owner, have sought and written third party business (the first party being the owner and the second the captive) for reasons we shall explore later on in this chapter. These captives are motivated, at least in part, by Internal Revenue Ruling 77–316.

Less Expensive, More Efficient

A captive insurance company comes into existence because the owner or sponsor can thereby obtain less expensive or more efficient coverage, or both, than can be obtained from the conventional insurance market. The corporate decision to put a captive insurer on stream is essentially no different than countless other make or buy decisions being made constantly in American industry. These decisions range from whether or not it is economically sound to set up one's own electroplating shop or buy the service from the established industry; to buy or rent one's own computer or have the corporation's needs taken care of by outside companies; to form one's own in-house advertising agency, or rely on a conventional advertising agency to take care of the corporation's needs.

The corporate do-it-yourself proponent may be firmly convinced that the course of action will result in a better or less expensive arrangement. But the outside purveyors of the service will always believe that the do-it-yourselfers have erred somewhere in their assumptions and calculations. They will believe that the captive or in-house arrangement has not been costed properly, or is providing an inferior service, or suffers in some other way which can be remedied only by returning to the conventional purveyor of the service.

Insurance companies operate in vastly different ways than noninsurance corporations. For instance, the accounting rules and procedures for an insurer are significantly different than those employed by corporations generally. Insurers are taxed under a different section of the tax code. Because of these differences, it is a more complicated task to evaluate the economics of bringing a captive insurance company on stream than it is to evaluate the economics of forming an in-house advertising agency or deciding whether the corporation should do its own computer work or set up its own electroplating shop. Despite the complexity, a corporate risk manager should not fail to analyze thoroughly the economics of this arrangement.

Benefits of a Captive Insurer

The proponents of the captive insurance company concept would probably see as an advantage the fact that reserves established on the books of an insurer are deductible when computing federal income tax, while the comparable reserves for a self insurance program are not. This is a fact, but what monetary advantage does it give over a self insured arrangement?

The three types of reserves which provide favorable tax treatment for insurers are loss reserves, loss adjustment reserves, and unearned premium reserves.

Many types of reserves are found on the books of an insurance company, but all fall into two broad, significantly different categories. They are surplus reserves and profit and loss reserves. Surplus reserves are actually part of the company's surplus, such as reserves for investment fluctuations or the reserve some insurers with huge unrealized capital gains in their securities have set up for the federal tax liability applicable to such gains. Surplus reserves are never deductible in calculating insurance companies' federal tax liability. But profit and loss reserves are always deductible.Loss reserves, loss adjustment reserves, and unearned premium reserves, representing amounts the insurer expects to pay sometime in the future for these items, fall into this profit and loss category. These reserves provide a tax deferment and not a tax exemption. If any of the amounts placed in these accounts are not used for the purpose intended, tax becomes payable as a result of the reclassification of these items out of the reserve into underwriting profit.

Because all losses and loss adjustment expenses are tax deductible when actually paid out, the deductibility of such reserves is a tax deferral rather than a tax exemption. The difference between tax deferral and tax exemption is important. In effect a tax exemption provides a benefit of the full rate of taxation (probably about 50 percent), while a tax deferral offers an opportunity to earn money on the funds during the period of tax deferral. This tax deferral advantage can be considerable or nominal, depending on the length of time one has the use of the funds, the rate of interest that one receives, and similar considerations.

Tax Considerations

If the captive insurer is organized domestically (within a U.S. jurisdiction), one has to be especially careful in calculating the tax advantages. Although the corporate parent can take a tax deduction on premiums paid to the captive, it is important to consider what happens on the books of the captive insurer. To illustrate, let us assume the corporate parent pays $500,000 in premium to its captive insurer. Let us further assume that, at the end of the year, the books of the captive insurer show that $250,000 has been paid out in losses and $150,000 is resting in the three profit and loss reserves described earlier, leaving $100,000 as an underwriting profit on the books of the captive insurer.

The $250,000 of paid losses can be deducted in computing the insurer's federal tax, but this would also be true in a self insurance program. The $100,000 underwriting profit is subject to the same amount of federal tax as if that $100,000 had stayed on the books of the corporate parent. In fact, if the corporate parent and captive insurer file consolidated tax returns, which is the most sensible arrangement in most instances, the rules of consolidation require that all monies paid between the two corporations must be used to offset each other.

The result of this offset places the $100,000 underwriting profit in the same position as if it had stayed on the corporate parent's books. Clearly this profit factor—the amount over and above what the captive insurer needs to pay losses and expenses and what it can set up in profit and loss reserves—makes no contribution to diminution of federal taxes.

The $150,000 resting in the three profit and loss reserves is not subject to tax as long as the amounts are not excessive and are reasonable in relation to the amounts that will actually be paid out at a later date. The amounts carried in these profit and loss reserves would not be tax deductible in a self insurance program. This then is the principal tax advantage of the captive insurer arrangement over a self insurance program.

Loss and Loss Adjustment Reserves

To see how great this advantage is, let us analyze the loss reserves and the loss adjustment reserves together, since both are related. The loss reserves represent the amounts expected to be paid to the parties actually incurring the injury or damage, while the loss adjustment reserves represent the amounts expected to be paid to adjusters, investigators, lawyers, and similar personnel used to help determine and settle losses.

These reserves, which cannot be created out of thin air, are set up on a case-made basis. This means that, by and large, the insurance company has to have a case, or a claim, before it can initiate the accounting entry setting up the reserve. There is no denying that a considerable tax advantage arises to a casualty insurer who initiates a workers' compensation reserve approximately $300,000 for a 40-year-old claimant who will, actuarially speaking, be paid $200 a week for 30 years.

This example shows why workers' compensation coverage generates a large, deferred tax advantage. This is followed closely by liability coverages. The time that elapses between a fire or other property loss and the payment of such a claim is generally not as significant. Whatever the time element involved, this is the period in which the captive insurer has the use of the funds and earns income on the deferred tax.

Unearned Premium Reserves

There is less evidence that an unearned premium reserve provides a significant tax advantage to the domestic captive insurer. If the corporate parent and the captive insurer file a consolidated tax return, the premium paid from parent to insurer, must be used to offset itself. On the other hand, a premium would be completely deductible if paid to any other insurer.

The lack of deductibility can be partially overcome by permitting the captive to claim all of its costs and expenses paid out of the premium received from its corporate parent. This offsetting of the premium is logical and proper. To allow the corporate parent to deduct the premium, and the captive to deduct the losses and expenses, would result in duplicate deductions on the consolidated tax return.

Unfortunately, there are no costs or expenses attributable to this unearned premium which the captive insurer can claim to make up for the parent's loss of deductibility for the premium paid. As a consequence, the unearned premium reserve does not enjoy either tax exemption or tax deduction, if the tax returns of the corporate parent and captive insurer are consolidated for tax purposes. However, if separate tax returns are filed, the corporate parent uses the premium it has paid as a tax deduction, and the captive insurer can leave in its unearned premium reserve that part of its premium which it has not earned. This means that the premium is not considered taxable income until it has been earned.

Problems Raised by Separate Returns

This approach may raise a couple of problems. One is that the IRS may compel consolidation because the two companies are so closely related. The other is that, if the captive insurer should pay a dividend (from its own earnings of course) to its corporate parent, this transaction is taxed at the rate of about 7.5 percent. And it must be in the form of a dividend to stockholders, not a dividend to policyholders. If it were paid as a dividend to policyholders, it would have to be treated by the policyholder as a refund of insurance expense, which is taxable at the corporate rate of around 50 percent.

Offshore Captives

An offshore insurer is one formed and domiciled in a country other than the country in which the parent company is located. Bermuda and the Grand Cayman Islands are the most popular sites for captive offshore companies. Both are tax havens. Bermuda has achieved greater prominence, because it has been used longer for this purpose. Other locations such as Switzerland and the Channel Islands are sometimes used.

The most important attributes of a suitable offshore site are a low or nonexistent tax rate on the operations of the insurer, a banking system efficient enough to make rapid transfers of funds in and out of the country, a government with some stability, and a labor force sufficient to provide enough clerical, administrative, professional and managerial personnel.

Lack of Standardization

Until the mid-1950s, virtually the only available method of insuring overseas risks was to buy insurance in each country from the local insurers which, of course, comprised the country's conventional insurance market. A major difficulty was the lack of standardization among various countries as to which perils were being insured and to what extent.

For example, one western European country had a property insurance endorsement akin to the U.S. extended coverage endorsement. Indeed, the words describing it were often translated into the words "extended coverage." But this endorsement did not contain protection against loss from windstorm. When one U.S. risk manager inquired about this lack, the answer from the overseas subsidiary's management was that coverage was unnecessary, since no windstorms severe enough to cause substantial damage were ever experienced in that part of the world. Soon after, a heavy windstorm caused a resounding loss to the overseas subsidiary. The loss would have been collectible under a U.S. extended coverage insurance contract.

Another story, probably apocryphal, involves a U.S. risk manager who reported to his overseas insurer the installation of sprinklers in the company's overseas plant. He expected to receive a reduction in the fire insurance rate, but instead received an invoice for additional premium to cover the increased hazard of sprinkler leakage!

Individual and Syndication Bases

Beginning in the mid-1950s, some property insurers, generally of U.S., British, or Italian origin, took steps to help overcome these problems. Two approaches were used—individual and syndication. In the individual method, a large insurer would obtain authority to operate in several countries other than its country of origin, thus permitting it to serve its corporate insureds on a multinational basis.

In syndication, insurers from different countries of origin joined together to provide insurance protection to the corporate insured. Coverage was as identical as possible to that enjoyed by the U.S. corporate insured in the U.S., to the extent permitted by the laws or regulations of the countries involved. Whether an individual or a syndicated basis was used, it was necessary to use the forms of coverage prescribed by the countries in which the property was located. Invariably, a "difference in conditions" policy would then be written specifying that, if any of the coverages provided in the insurance policies issued to the overseas subsidiaries did not equal the coverage of a U.S. property insurance contract, then the difference in conditions contract would respond.

In addition to standardizing coverage, this blanketing arrangement often resulted in premium savings because the insurer or syndicate could treat all of the properties involved as one risk, to the extent permitted by the laws and regulations of the countries in which the properties were located.

Most corporate risk managers regard formation of an offshore captive insurer a refinement of this blanketing arrangement offered by individual multinationally admitted insurers or syndicates of insurers.

The Do-It-Yourself Approach

The captive approach permits the corporate parent to accomplish a greater degree of do-it-yourself risk bearing than most any other form of insurance mechanism. In those countries where the local laws permit it, and there are many, the risk can be insured directly with the captive insurer. The premium flowing from an overseas operating subsidiary to the captive insurer is an expense on the books of the operating subsidiary in calculating the tax it owes to its country of origin.

In those countries where local law or custom makes this direct approach difficult or impossible, then a locally admitted insurer is asked to insure the corporate parent's property within that country. This locally admitted insurer can then reinsure a portion of the risk with the corporate parent's offshore captive insurer. This reinsurance treaty would have to provide enough remuneration to the locally admitted insurer to reimburse it for any local services, claims handling, and other expenses, plus a reasonable profit.

There are countries, notably in South and Central America, that limit the amount of reinsurance which can be exported from the country, or prohibit it entirely. In these instances, the above described arrangement is more difficult.

In the case of Ford Motor Company, the IRS sought to deny a tax deduction for property insurance coverage that an overseas subsidiary paid to Ford's offshore captive insurer. The case was settled (without an opinion being issued) with enough satisfaction to the taxpayer to conclude that favorable tax treatment still exists, at least until the ramifications of the Service's "economic family" theory becomes more evident, a subject we shall address later.

The overseas casualty risks of U.S. corporations can be insured in the offshore captive insurance company, the same as property risks. However, this use of the captive has not been pursued as vigorously. One reason may be that, in the U.S., the high dollar volume of casualty coverage is workers' compensation, while overseas this coverage is generally provided by the government and not through insurance. The remaining overseas casualty coverages, at least until recently, were relatively so low in cost that the existing arrangement was not disturbed.

This situation may be changing due to the burgeoning product liability risks arising in some countries. Recently the risk manager of a large U.S. based multinational was wrestling with the problem of responsibility for potential liability on a product manufactured in France, under specifications of the U.S. company, and marketed in Spain by the company's Spanish subsidiary. This type of situation cries out for one insurance policy completely under the company's control, with in-house determination of culpability, rather than through the efforts of three insurers.

Tax Free if Not Repatriated

An attractive feature of the captive insurer arrangement as to overseas, i.e., non U.S. risks, is that federal income, both underwriting and investment, is free of U.S. federal income tax as long as it is not repatriated to the U.S. parent. If and when these earnings are repatriated to the U.S. parent, then the corporation's regular tax rate applies. This is not a tax exemption but a tax deferral. I emphasize this because the more ardent proponents of the offshore captive insurer concept have a tendency to describe this as a tax-free arrangement, which it is not.

One such advocate, after reluctantly conceding that this was actually a tax deferral, contended that the typical U.S. corporate parent would never have to repatriate its captive insurer's earnings, and thus, in effect, this arrangement would be tax-free. I observed that never is a very long time.

It should be noted that, if a corporation places insurance in its overseas subsidiary, the federal government collects a four percent sales tax for the privilege of exporting the premium. If an insurer does the exporting, a one percent excise tax applies.

Capacity Crunch Injects New Life

The first U.S. captives were probably the mutual insurance companies developed by groups of manufacturers and other business persons in the late nineteenth and early twentieth centuries to take care of particular, specialized risks to which these developers were subject. The names of these mutuals describe their origin and their purpose—manufacturers, lumbermens, hardware, and threshermens. Most of these are either gone or have entered the conventional insurance market.

The insurance capacity crunch of 1973 to 1975 brought new life into the captive insurer concept. One coverage particularly affected by the shortage of insurance capacity was medical and hospital malpractice, which gave a powerful impetus to the formation of insurers sponsored by groups of hospitals and doctors. Some of these insurers were formed offshore; others were formed domestically. This phenomenon is similar to the formation of the mutuals in earlier years. Both are products of persons determined to solve a problem on a do-it-yourself basis. Domestically, these insurers must adhere to the same federal tax code that all other insurers adhere to.

Colorado and Tennessee enacted legislation designed to facilitate the establishment of captive insurers. Their requirements are favorable compared with requirements to form a normal insurer in other states. Relatively few insurers have been formed under the Colorado and Tennessee enactments and opinions differ as to how favorable these requirements are when compared to the requirements of Bermuda or the Grand Cayman Islands. However, in mid-1981, the State of Vermont enacted the Special Insurers Act enabling captive company formation. In terms of a domestic situs, it offers the most favorable climate for U.S. corporations with primarily U.S. based exposures.

A Surge in Offshore Captives

Many insurance coverages other than medical and hospital malpractice were in extremely short supply during the mid-1970s. Product liability coverage, particularly for hard goods manufacturers such as machinery and machine tools became extremely difficult to obtain. This situation gave rise to the formation of hundreds of offshore insurers by U.S. corporations and trade associations. This surge still continues. Corporations and others who had formed or sponsored captive insurers primarily to insure property risks began using these insurers to secure casualty coverages.

Property insurance coverage is relatively easy to export to an offshore insurance facility, as far as state or other regulatory authority is concerned. Liability insurance tends to be difficult and workers' compensation is impossible to accomplish. However, the ultimate objective was accomplished by insuring the risk with a U.S. insurer licensed to write the risk, with a provision that a substantial part of the risk be reinsured in the captive insurer owned or controlled by the party susceptible to the risk.

IRS Ruling 77–316

The IRS, through its Revenue Ruling 77–316, has announced that it will challenge the tax deductibility of premiums which have not left the "economic family" of the taxpayer, no matter whether the premium went directly into the captive or via the reinsurance route through a licensed U.S. insurer. It should be noted that, while Ruling 77–316 dealt with situations involving offshore captives, it later indicated its position was the same for domestic captives.

This economic family theory is based on an obscure court case. It involves an aged woman, whose attempt to insure herself with a whole life insurance policy and simultaneously with an annuity contract, was held not to have transferred the risk to the insurer. I believe this theory has been applied by the IRS only to this type of situation. No such language exists in the tax statutes, which contain fairly straightforward language such as "reasonable and necessary expense."

The attempt by the IRS to introduce this economic family restriction into the tax law will not go unchallenged. The Carnation Company case, which was recently won by the Service, in tax court and upon appeal, denied tax deductibility on the facts determined by the court and not on the economic family theory. It is true that the appeals court mentioned the economic family theory but only by way of dicta, that is, by a sort of offhand observation by the court, not used to actually determine the outcome of the case.

Multi-Owner Captives

Whether or not the IRS position on the economic family theory will prevail is not now known. What it has done, however, is increase the interest in multi-owner captives by members of associations and other groups. By merging one's risks with those of others, the economic family no longer exists.

In addition, if properly structured, the multi-owned captive could become a noncontrolled foreign company even though completely owned by U.S. interests. This is often achieved by providing that no shareholder has more than 10 percent of the ownership, since this is the percentage used in attributing ownership for tax purposes in a controlled foreign corporation. A noncontrolled foreign corporation pays no federal income tax. This could be especially advantageous where so-called long tail coverages such as product liability, professional liability, even workers' compensation, are concerned.

No matter how inviting or attractive the tax advantage seems to be, experience would indicate that, somewhere along the line, the IRS stands waiting to extract the appropriate tax.

Can a corporate parent place any of its U.S. risks in its offshore captive insurer without the insurer incurring a federal tax liability; and, if so, to what extent? The answer to the first part of this question is yes. To describe the extent, we must pick our way carefully through the appropriate sections of the tax code together with the regulations amplifying these sections of the code.

Under a rule of law called "de minimis" applied to Section 953 (a) of the Internal Revenue Code, as much as five percent of the captive insurer's total premiums may be derived from its parent's risks located within or from operations arising wholly within the United States, and still not affect the captive insurer's favorable tax treatment. If more than five percent of premium is derived from U.S. risks, the income derived from this amount in excess of five percent is said to be tainted, and U.S. federal income tax is levied on this excess amount. Investment earnings from reserves arising from these U.S. risks (in excess of five percent) are likewise tainted and are subject to U.S. federal taxation as such.

Raising 5% to 75%

By surrendering 100 percent ownership in the offshore insurer, the U.S. corporate parent may increase this five percent limitation. If the U.S. corporate parent owns (directly or indirectly—under rules of attribution or constructive ownership) no more than 25 percent of the offshore captive's stock, then this five percent limitation is raised to 75 percent. This is explicitly permitted in Section 957 (a) and (b) of the tax code governing a "controlled foreign corporation," the provisions of which come into play once the five percent de minimis limitation has been breached.

The 25 percent to 75 percent ratio is the threshold where the tax code (Section 957 (b)) exempts the U.S. corporate parent repatriating its share of the foreign insurer's income. All experts seem to agree, however, that the remaining 75 percent of the insurer's ownership (or at least 50 percent) has to be of a non-U.S. character to escape the provisions of subpart F of these tax provisions.

Let us assume that a U.S. corporation placed some of its U.S. risks with a foreign insurer in which the corporation had 26 percent or more ownership interest or control. Would this mean that the U.S. corporation would have to pay U.S. income tax on all earnings it derived from the foreign insurer? The answer to this is no. Only those earnings are taxable which cannot be eliminated by one or more of the tax provisions permitting this tax deferral.

It should be further understood that there may well be certain insurance risks of the U.S. corporate parent which may logically be construed to be only partly applicable to activities within the United States, such as marine insurance on company-owned ships which travel to many ports of the world, including U.S. ports. For these and similar instances, certain criteria (length of time in the U.S., etc.) have been developed over the years which define what are U.S. transactions and what are not. In addition, the tax code has other provisions which come into play to reduce the tainted income and to minimize the tax. There is, for instance, a provision that shields from U.S. tax any unrelated investment income of the insurer if it amounts to less than 30 percent of the gross underwriting and investment results.

Possible Tax Deferral

All of the benefits of forming a captive insurer can be and often are available in the formation of a domestic captive insurer. These benefits are economy of serving the risks, the ability to tailor the coverages to the needs of the corporate parent, and achieving volume discounts on the risks ultimately placed with the conventional insurance market. In the case of the offshore captive insurer, one must add to the benefit the possible deferral of U.S. federal tax liability, if the captive insurer is organized in one of the tax haven countries, such as Bermuda, which assesses a nominal tax at most on the insurer's operations. Another possible advantage of incorporating in a country such as Bermuda is that a minimal amount of supervision over these insurers is required. This absence of supervision provides great flexibility to the insurer in its writing and its operations. It offers the opportunity to write coverages which are difficult or impossible to obtain from the conventional insurance market.

17

Employee Benefits and the Corporate Risk Manager

The risk manager's responsibility for the corporate employee benefits program varies from company to company. Generally speaking, the larger the corporation, the less responsibility the risk manager has for determining the benefits that will be offered and administering the benefits adopted. Typically, the risk manager is responsible for purchasing the insurance involved, while the personnel or industrial relations department determines what the employee benefits of the company shall be, and administers the day-to-day program.

Benefits as Compensation

Under the Wagner Act, most employee benefits are considered items of compensation subject to negotiation between the company and its unions; thus the logic of involving personnel or industrial relations. Also, employees and company alike regard the company's contribution to employee benefits as closely related to wages and salaries.

By having the risk manager assume responsibility for purchasing insurance, the corporation is likely to benefit from volume purchase. And it centers in one department the coordination with and evaluation of the insurance industry on behalf of the corporation. Obviously, the risk manager who can competently negotiate and purchase the corporate property and casualty insurance coverages, can do likewise for the employee benefits program.

Accounting for Employee Benefits

In many corporations the risk management department handles the accounting for employee benefits. This is logical because, in most cases, the risk management function is a part of the finance department. Preparation of accounting entries requires intimate knowledge of the elements underlying insurance company charges for services performed.

In small companies, particularly those whose production employees are not unionized, the risk manager is often responsible for administering the employee benefits program.

Whether or not assigned responsibility, risk managers ought to familiarize themselves with employee benefits programs because they involve uncertainty and risk to the company.

Little Shifting of Risk

Even though nearly all employee benefits programs have underlying insurance contracts, there is surprisingly little shifting of risk to insurers. Rather, the trend is toward retrospectively rated insurance contracts which provide that, after payment of benefits to an employee and a charge for the insurer's services, called the insurer's retention, any money left over from the premium is returned in the form of a retrospective credit, called a *retro credit.* If the losses paid or incurred are greater than expected, resulting in a retrospective debit, the employer is expected to reimburse the insurer for this deficiency. In other words, these contracts are really cost-plus in nature, with the actual risk of loss borne by the employer.

The typical insurance program is written with one insurer on a blanket retrospective basis, which means that if one line of insurance, say life, goes into deficit, the redundancy in any other line will be used by the insurer to eliminate the deficiency.

Small Firms Prefer Fixed Cost

Not all employee benefit contracts between corporations and insurers are written on a cost plus basis. Small companies with relatively few employees prefer a fixed cost type of contract, in which the insurer will charge a certain amount per employee or per family for each month of protection. Thus, the insurer bears the risk of excessive losses. The insurer generally guarantees that these rates will not change during the policy term, which can be for three years but more often is for one year.

Even the largest of corporations may have a fixed cost type contract for such benefits as accidental death and dismemberment coverage, where the benefits paid are extremely high in relation to the premiums paid. Also some medical reimbursement plans, notably those provided by Blue Cross and Blue Shield, provide benefits by and large on a fixed cost basis. In so doing, these organizations spread the risk of hospital, surgical and other medical costs throughout the entire community.

The View of the "Blues"

The "blues," as they are known by the health insurance world, believe this arrangement is more desirable from a social point of view than a retrospectively rated arrangement under which the employees of each corporation, rather than the community, take care of their own medical expenses.

The conventional insurers believe experience-rated medical reimbursement plans represent sound underwriting judgment. It is rare that a corporation does not consider its employees and their families a better risk than the general population.

Whether the "blues" or the conventional insurers are justified in their attitudes depends on whether their actions are regarded as sound underwriting or as cream skimming. This distinction is important in virtually every line of insurance offered by the industry. For instance, is it sound underwriting or cream skimming to offer an experience rated plan, excluding people 65 and over, in which the participants collectively pay the medical expenses of those who become ill? People 65 and over have twice as many illnesses, three times as severe, as people under 65. Is it proper to give the group under 65 the benefit of their better experience? Or does such a device discriminate against those over 65?

Fundamental Fair Play

Obviously any such grouping must be legal and must not violate what the public regards as fundamental fair play. Beyond that it becomes a matter of judgment and enlightened self interest. Further, if high social purpose is served by prohibiting such groupings for loss-sharing purposes, then such prohibition should be legislated. It should be recognized that if the legislative process provides for a broadly based risk sharing device, such as a universal health plan covering the entire populace, the legislators are, in fact, stipulating that the total costs involved are best borne by broader groups. This is the legislators' right to do, subject always to the constitutional guarantees to the individuals involved.

It should also be understood that if a segment within the group pays more than it would through the conventional insurance market, because its losses are lower, the additional payment is, in effect, a tax, rather than an insurance premium.

I look with disfavor at any taxing scheme dressed up as an insurance plan. The insuring mechanism has enough weaknesses of its own to answer for without taking on the ill favor associated with a tax collecting device. As Edmund Burke said, "To tax and to please, no more than to love and to be wise, is not given to men."

The Makeup of Typical Benefit Plans

What does the typical corporate employee benefits program look like? There is a lock-step uniformity among corporations, for several reasons. What is customary has great weight among people who develop employee benefits. There are tax considerations both for the corporation and for the individual employee. The product line of insurers marketing employee benefits also has an influence. Differences are in detail and not in substance.

This uniformity is understandable. No corporate management wants to lag behind other corporations with whom it competes for personnel. Also top managements of corporations are prudent, conservative individuals, who are persuaded in large degree by what competitors, or their industry as a whole, are offering.

It is the rare corporation today that does not have some form of group life insurance for its employees, with the benefit varying in relation to the employees' annual salary levels. It may range from one times annual salary to three times annual salary, and more. Two times is probably the most common. The amount of this benefit, unfortunately, is not determined according to need, but rather according to how much the employees are able or willing to pay and how much the company can afford.

Until the mid-1950s, virtually all group life insurance programs terminated coverage upon the employee's retirement. The logic behind this approach is that the principal reason for life insurance is to provide for the exigencies arising from *premature* death. It could be argued that an employee, having attained retirement status, could not suffer premature death.

Despite this logic, it's become customary for corporations to provide post retirement group life insurance. It was invariably computed as a percentage (ranging from 100 percent to 10 percent) of the benefit enjoyed by the employee while active. The amount was usually modified by the employee's seniority with the company.

If group life insurance is the keystone in the typical corporation's employee benefits program, an accident and sickness indemnity insurance plan is not far behind. Several states require that employers provide some form of this benefit to their employees within the state. These plans pay a weekly benefit to disabled employees, calculated as a percent of their salary. The term of this benefit is generally 26 weeks, with some form of waiting period, ranging from three days to seven days, before the benefit becomes applicable.

As popular as life and accident and sickness, is insurance for medical expenses of employees and their families. The kind and extent of expense eligible for reimbursement are diverse and follow no logical or consistent pattern.

Retirement Benefits

The fourth major benefit necessary to meet the minimum needs of employees is a retirement benefit. This benefit is generally calculated by one of two methods or by a combination of the two. The first is sometimes called the steel formula, because it originated in a union contract negotiated in that industry.

This benefit provides that the retiree receive a set sum of dollars of retirement income per month for each year of service. Since the typical employee's career is about 25 years, such plans provide a monthly retirement benefit of 25 times this set sum.

Another formula often used is in the form of an annuity, the cost of which was accumulated during the employee's career with the company. For example, if a corporation's plan provides a two percent benefit on career average earnings, the employee with 25 years of service and average earnings of $10,000 a year, would receive a benefit at retirement of $5,000 a year. Due to inflationary pressures, in recent years many plans have incorporated a "final earnings" feature which is used in determining monthly retirement benefits.

In addition to these four employee benefits coverages, some corporations offer some form of additional death and dismemberment insurance. An increasingly popular benefit is group long term disability insurance. It provides a payment, generally computed as a percent of the employee's salary, ranging from 40 to 65 percent, if the employee should suffer serious sickness or accident. Payment is continued as long as the employee is unable to work.

Who Pays How Much?

An important consideration in all of these employee benefits is how much the corporation will pay, and how much the employee will pay. There is no uniformity. Many corporations pay virtually the entire bill, while others pay none.

The trend, if any, is toward the employer paying more and more.

A reason often cited for this involves the federal tax code. The employer who pays for these coverages may deduct the cost as a business expense on the corporate tax return. So, if the employer is operating at a profit, the federal government, in effect, absorbs about half the cost. If the employer were to pay the identical sum to the employee in the form of salary, and the employee then proceeded to pay for the employee benefits, the employer would still receive the same federal tax deduction. But the employee would have to pay income tax on the added salary. This is a powerful stimulus for employee benefits to be paid, not by employees, but by employers.

Theoretically, if an employee were paying for a benefit costing $10 per month, the employer could agree to pay the employee $12 a month less (assuming the employee is in a 20 percent tax bracket). The end result would be that the employee would receive the same net income, while the employer's after-tax cost was reduced by the 20 percent.

We may wonder why employers don't pay virtually all employee benefits. One powerful deterrent is that payment of an employee benefit is a long term commitment. Once an employer agrees to pay for it, it is extremely difficult, if not impossible, to withdraw it. If profits should disappear, the employer would still be expected to pay for the benefits, even though there were no profits against which the costs of the employee benefit could be applied.

Uniformity Required

Another deterrent to the employer paying all is that an employee benefit must be extended to all employees on a uniform basis. This uniformity of benefits to eligible employees is the very essence of the group benefits concept. But it does introduce a complication often solved by leaving the employee benefits on an employee-pay basis.

To illustrate, let's take group life insurance. An employee who is the parent of a number of dependent children would undoubtedly welcome a group life insurance benefit of five times annual salary, especially if the employer pays all. But what about employees who have no dependents? These employees will probably not be so enthusiastic about the huge group life insurance benefit. They would probably be considerably less than enthusiastic if they realized they were receiving less in their paychecks to help pay the cost of the benefit for others.

Thus, by putting the employee benefit on an employee-pay basis, the employer has greater flexibility. The single employee with no after-death liabilities, and the employee with grown children may elect not to participate in the program and, instead, use the money saved to provide something more in keeping with their personal needs. This flexibility would be impossible if the employer had decided to pay employees through the employee benefit route rather than through the paycheck.

Where Your Money Goes

Imagine yourself an employee of a corporation with a typical employee benefits program. Envision what you do with the money you receive in your paycheck. You pay for food, shelter, recreation for yourself and your family. You pay for the care and education of your children. Your automobile and house are ultimately paid, for the most part, out of your paycheck.

In this exercise we should not ignore those items which we never get our hands on because they represent salary withheld. Probably the largest item of withholding is for federal and state taxes. Then there are social security payments, and contributions to various employee benefits programs and the like. This exercise should dramatize how all pervasive is the force of the money paid to us for our services.

For every dollar we receive in our paychecks, another quarter to a third of a dollar is paid out by our employers for so-called fringe benefits. First comes the employer's contribution to the federal Social Security fund. By this we are assured of a pension and payment for medical attention under Medicare when we reach retirement age, a payment to our spouse or under-age children if we should die prematurely, and monthly payments to ourselves if we should become disabled before reaching retirement age. Our employer's contribution is equal to our own contribution.

If we become unemployed we can receive unemployment compensation for as long as 26 weeks, supplemented in times of recession by government grants for longer periods. Depending on the state, the cost can be as low as $50.00 but can go up to much higher amounts.

Virtually all of us are protected by workers' compensation in our state. If we should suffer injury or death in a work-connected injury, we or our spouse and under-age children will receive indemnity for the medical expenses incurred, plus a payment in lieu of the salary lost due to the accidental injury.

All of these benefit programs are mandatory. We and our employer are required by law to belong and contribute. The remainder of this associated payroll expense is made up of the employer's voluntary payments for group life insurance, group hospital, surgical and other medical insurance, and retirement benefits.

By comparing your paycheck with these associated payroll expenses, you would learn that these expenses often total as much as one-third of your paycheck. Few people would perceive the value received through these expenses to be in line with what they cost.

Stupendous Waste

The conclusion seems inescapable that there is stupendous waste in this whole area of providing employee benefits. I do not mean that those who are responsible for developing and administering the benefit plans are wasteful or extravagant in their work. Whether they be in government agencies or in private corporations, most of those I have met are conscientious, intelligent and industrious and have a keen dedication to their work. Perhaps it is this dedication which makes it difficult for these people to have an overview of the entire employee benefits picture.

I think it is time to come down to earth and seek more concrete data. What follows, while not necessarily proving my contention, may serve at least as an outline for further study of this extremely important question, namely the amount of financial resources, whether in government or private programs, that should be allocated to employee benefits, how these resources should be spent, and who should do the administering.

Coordination of Benefits

A risk manager friend of mine presents this exercise:

Assume that a middle-aged male employee dies. Under the company group life insurance plan, his widow is entitled to a benefit of $50,000, equal to twice the employee's annual salary. She and her under-age children are entitled to survivor's benefits under the Social Security program. The benefit can vary greatly in amount, but let us assume its present value is equal to the group insurance benefit.

Let us further assume that workers' compensation benefits were also collectible, due to the nature of the employee's death. In many states the present value of this benefit can equal $100,000, thus doubling the amount to which the widow and children are entitled.

Suppose further, that the employee died while on a business trip and the company has a travel accident insurance policy providing a benefit equal to two years pay. Other employee benefits could also become payable here, such as an accidental death and dismemberment benefit, a surviving spouse's benefit paid in conjunction with the company pension plan, a special insurance payment if the company plane is involved.

No one begrudges this widow the benefits she will receive which would, in our hypothetical case, equal to eight to ten times her late husband's annual salary. She has suffered a great loss and now has the heavy responsibility of raising her family without her husband's income and other help.

But we must strive for the necessary detachment to ask what about the wives and surviving children of those employees who die prematurely of natural causes? These families may have to get along with the group life and Social Security benefits only. These would be considerably less than what the first family will receive. Why should the circumstances of how a person dies determine the amount of benefits to be received by dependents?

Every person engaged in employee benefits planning, estate planning and the like, agrees that benefits payable upon a person's death should best be measured by the amount of financial responsibility left by the deceased.

A detached review would suggest, I think, that perhaps greater equity would be served if benefits were designed to be paid more on the basis of need and less on happenstance. It is impossible to estimate and difficult to guess how much this duplication of benefits adds to the total employee benefits bill of the nation. It is obvious, however, that a logical system of benefit payments would result in more responsive benefits or that such benefits would take less of the employee benefits dollar, or both. Certainly these are desirable goals.

Jurisdictional Conflicts

Every corporate risk manager has probably had to work out the details of a jurisdictional conflict involving whether a disabled employee is entitled to collect under the state sponsored workers' compensation program or under the non work connected disability benefits insurance programs.

Normally, the details of a specific jurisdictional problem are simple enough to resolve. An employee claims for indemnity payments under one of these programs, either for lost earnings while disabled or for medical expenses. Usually this is done under the non work-connected disability benefits insurance program. At some time during the insurer's investigation to determine if the employee is eligible for benefits, evidence is discovered that the employee's disability is work connected.

The disability insurance excludes payment under such circumstances. The insurer suspends payments and the employee must now proceed to establish a claim under the state sponsored workers' compensation program. The ultimate decision of whether workers' compensation coverage is applicable is made by the state's compensation commission which has administrative and quasijudicial powers to make such a determination.

Spending $5,000 to "Save" $100

In most cases, the difference in benefits paid under either insurance plan is not substantial, since the majority of cases involves a temporary disability. After one such case in which two hearings were held before a compensation commission hearing officer (which must have cost the insurer and insured a minimum of $5,000, since four employees, including an attorney, had to spend several days attending it), it developed that less than $100 more would have been paid to the employee under workers' compensation than under the insured's (non work connected) accident and sickness and medical reimbursement insurance programs.

We wonder who exactly is being served by this lack of coordination, with the expense of administering two investigations, two insurers each maintaining records, etc. Why should an employee be paid differently for lost income or medical expense reimbursement by virtue of some detail, often obscure, as to the cause?

Note that in the examples cited above there is no duplication of benefits paid to the disabled employee from these two programs of reimbursement for lost income. The duplication lies in the administration of two separate plans and the duplication of overhead expense.

Those defenders of the present workers' compensation system who argue that this system charges back to the hazardous industry the losses found only in that industry, should look more closely at workers' compensation losses being paid under that program. I think they will find that, in most instances, the losses so paid resemble those for injuries and other disabilities found among the population generally, rather than those applicable to the industry in which the employer is engaged.

Most Fatal Accidents are Off-the-Job

Of the 16,000-plus deaths annually from industrial accidents, less than 2,000 are actually attributable to the plant or factory environment. The remaining 14,000 are caused by auto accidents and similar off-the-job causes.

The cost of those accidents applicable to the activities of a specific industry could still be allocated specifically to that industry on a system of indemnification which combined both industrial and non-industrial disabilities. This would leave the other incidences of disability more attributable to the population generally. On-the-job heart attacks, automobile accidents while on company business, or other accidents, the cause of which cannot really be attributed to the particular work environment of the employee, could then be handled consistently and less expensively in one plan which would not spend dollars unnecessarily determining whether or not the disabilities were work-connected.

The duplication, the triplication and worse, is found everywhere in this area of income replacement or medical expense indemnification, but particularly in income replacement. There is, of course, the state workers' compensation systems and the federal Social Security system. Many companies, either voluntarily or by agreement with their employees' unions, have plans supplementing the payments from these governmental entities in addition to such payments.

The Waste of Multiplicity

The waste—there is no other word for it—caused by this duplication of administrative machinery, plus the nonstandardization of procedures and data required of these multiplicity of plans, would astound us all if it could be accurately calculated. The lack of standardization of benefits, procedures and other administrative detail among the 50 states and the District of Columbia is notorious. To multistate employers and the insurers servicing them, it is an expensive burden.

At least five states have compulsory non-work connected disability benefits insurance,[1] with niggling differences in benefits and administrative apparatus. The corporate employer with widespread multistate operations typically has not five such plans but six—five mandatory and one of its own (or its insurer's) creation for the remaining states in which it operates.

Is there any useful justification for the different states to require different rates and different procedures in their programs? The federal Social Security program is still different, while the five states with the compulsory non-work connected disability coverage have still different reporting criteria.

The typical employee, when caught in the middle of these inconsistencies, has very little sympathy for or understanding of the situation. This duplication and nonstandardization might be endured if the overall result was a consistently good job for the people these plans are designed to benefit.

Is a National Health Insurance Plan the Answer?

Powerful voices are claiming that this is not being done. These voices are centered in Washington, D.C., and they purport to have the answer—a national health plan for the entire population, providing indemnity for hospital, surgical, and other medical expenses through the federal Social Security program, together with continued amplification of the indemnification of lost income through that Social Security program, all to be administered by the federal government.

Such a monolithic program would be bad for the intended beneficiaries, their employers and, yes, for the federal government. It would be a disaster for the insurance industry. Does it not make sense for all who have a responsibility in this area, whether insurer, risk manager, employee benefits manager, and state insurance supervisory staff to work, to make sense out of this jerrybuilt area of corporate activity?

Government or Private Control?

In reviewing the overall employee benefits picture in this country today, we find a problem difficult to solve. Should the various aspects of benefits be under the control of government, with government not only supervising the activity, but assessing the population generally or the specific class of people benefiting, for the cost of maintaining the activity?

Or should benefits continue to be maintained more or less on a voluntary basis, with the participants voluntarily assessing themselves?

There are many areas of human activity which, practically speaking, can only be maintained by government. If the government had to sell these activities, in a manner similar to private industry selling its products or service, sales costs would probably far exceed the income the government would receive from the relatively few who would voluntarily pay their share.

As an example, take the Democratic Party. After losing a recent Presidential election, it attempted to reduce its campaign deficit through a series of television appeals. The result was a fiasco. The party didn't receive enough response to pay for the television broadcasts. I would guess that the federal government would have the same problem if it attempted to sell many of its programs.

Medicare Prime Example

Some thoughtful students on the subject believe the government's Medicare program to be in this category. They believe that people over 65 will not or cannot pay enough to meet the cost of the medical bills, etc., of the group. It is necessary, therefore, that the whole group be enrolled and the whole group assessed, thus eliminating the sales cost.

Peter Drucker made a good point when he said that the most precious thing about private enterprise is the fact that it will fail if it has ceased to meet the objective for which it was formed, while government programs are almost impossible to destruct. As soon as these government programs are brought into being, they immediately create special groups and special interests who work hard to keep these programs going long after they have outlived their usefulness.

The correct mix of government sponsored, tax supported programs on the one hand, and a program involving voluntary participation and voluntary payment on the other hand, is most important. Attaining this mix in the employee benefits field is indeed well worth continued and intensive study.

Self Insured or Captive?

Quite often the question arises whether or not employee benefits can be self insured. The answer is yes, but there are special problems involved in such handling of employee benefits. While it is open to debate, at least one attorney whose judgment I trust implicitly has expressed the opinion that no plan in which employee benefits are involved should be self insured unless there is some specific statutory authority that permits it, such as the California Disability Benefits Law.

On the other hand, I've heard other erudite persons express the opinion that the acceptance of employee contributions on the books of the corporation represents no particular problem, as long as adequate records are maintained.

What Is a "Plan"?

There have been enough government administrative decisions, primarily by the U.S. Treasury Department, to assure us that, if the self insured arrangement of the employer is in fact a plan, then the payments made to that plan are deductible for tax purposes, and will not be construed as additional income to the employees. To effect such an arrangement, a "plan" must be published generally among the participants, it must not discriminate and it must be administered fairly and consistently.

One particular aspect of the Internal Revenue Code permits a payment up to $5,000 to the family of a deceased employee without it being assumed that the payment is compensation. This could suggest that any self insured plan providing a death benefit in excess of $5,000 could result in such excess being construed as taxable income paid by the employer and, as such, subject to income tax payable by the estate of the deceased employee.

I find no evidence that there has been any appreciable ground swell toward establishing captive insurance companies to provide benefits to employees of large corporations. The concept has been discussed. And a smattering of corporations have acquired life insurance companies. Invariably these corporations have indicated that the life insurer they acquired was in fact seen as a profit center. As such it would appear that it could not be defined as a captive insurance company.

It's my understanding that some captives have accepted reinsurance from a domestic insurer who insures the captive owner's domestic risks. The IRS has challenged the tax deductibility of this on the same "economic family" theory that we described in the discussion of captive insurers. This novel theory propounded by IRS cannot, at this time, be the subject of intelligent discussion.

Protecting Key Personnel

Closely allied to employee benefits is a type of insurance that covers the loss of management people on whom the success of the corporation heavily rests. It is usually called key-man insurance.

Sometimes the corporation opts to obtain coverage for key executives. But more often it is required by a bank or other lending institution which has made loans to the corporation. If the key person should die prematurely, the proceeds of the insurance are used to tide the corporation over the difficult period until the key manager's position is suitably filled.

Since the corporation is the beneficiary, the premiums paid for this insurance are a deductible expense on the corporate tax return. However, if the life insurance contract is of the cash value type with a cash surrender value built up over the years, the tax authorities, as well as the rules of good accounting practice, require that the cash surrender portion of the premium be treated as an asset which is recoverable from the insurance company.

18

The Business/Academic Community Interface

As we have seen, risk management evolved from corporate insurance management and the proper make-up and administration of a corporate insurance portfolio still constitutes a substantial part of the risk manager's responsibility.

Yet within the academic world there is an overwhelming emphasis on *insurance* and consequently a minimal emphasis on *risk.* The courses taught, the reading material assigned, and thus the student theses are primarily devoted to the actions and interactions between and among insurers, insureds and insurance intermediaries. Study is devoted to what to do with the risk—how much to charge for transferring the risk, how insurers are regulated by state authority, and similar insurance-oriented activities. About 99 percent of the time, after the risk is identified, academicians assume that it will be passed on to an insurance company. Time is spent teaching where the insurance broker, or agent fits into this process, but here, too, the emphasis is on the insuring aspect and not the risk per se.

Academia Advanced Risk Concept

Curiously enough, it was the academic world that insisted that the business world must broaden its horizons and think of risk—how to measure it, how to eliminate it, or how to effectively neutralize it by other means—only one of these means being to transfer the risk to an insurer. I think it is no exaggeration to say that the academicians dragged the insurance industry kicking and screaming to this broader concept. Having done this, they promptly left us, unclothed and shivering, in this advanced posture as the corporate risk experts.

They continue to send to us graduates who are insurance-transferring technicians rather than risk analysis specialists. Consider how few insurance graduates have really been exposed to industrial safety or loss prevention. Few of them can explain what the Z16A index is, or identify it as a major index used to determine industrial accident frequency and severity. Few of these graduates could tell what an explosion proof roof is, even if one fell on them. Few could be sure whether the Walsh-Healey Act is a new television comedy team or the sponsors of the first effective federal law outlining standards of industrial plant safety conditions.

Most Graduates Become Brokers

There are good reasons for this situation. I was told by the department head of an eastern seaboard university that 80 percent of his graduates who major in insurance go into insurance agency/ brokerage work, 17 to 18 percent take jobs in insurance companies and a stray two or three percent take jobs in corporate insurance or risk management departments. So it isn't difficult to understand the emphasis in the university curriculum on insurance marketing action and interaction, with consequent deemphasis of risk in its pure aspects.

I do not condemn this emphasis, but I would ask the universities to consider recent trends in the insurance industry and in the business world.

Surely but fitfully, and sometimes painfully, the present conventional insurance industry is broadening itself into what eventually must be the financial services business. This is a fascinating evolution, involving the insurance industry maneuvering to enter the securities business, mutual funds, and who knows—perhaps credit cards, banking and what have you. The academic world must respond to this evolutionary process. Whether it will do so in a constructive way is still open to question.

Corporate Risks Increase

The evolutionary process in the business world is more complicated. With increases of population, developing technology, increase in governmental activity, rising expectations and similar forces, the corporate world faces a dramatic increase in pure, nonspeculative risks. These risks are fortuitous in nature, not controllable by person or corporation. Yet they are not insurable, primarily because there is no one around to insure them. Let's take a couple of examples:

Case Number 1

In companies selling or trading securities, an increase in surveillance by the Securities and Exchange Commission of the employees actually doing the trading or selling has caused many of these firms to establish the position of *compliance officer.* The job is to see that all appropriate employees have been informed of the rules under which they are to operate and, equally important, to make sure that corporate records show that the employees have acknowledged being advised of such rules. The compliance officer also assures that such rules are being observed in the operation of the firm. This activity, in essence, is the ascertainment and disposition of a fortuitous, nonspeculative, nonbusiness risk, as much as any such risk included in a corporate insurance program.

Case Number 2

Within the last ten years many airlines, beset by organized thievery of cargo and baggage, and many large department store chains with substantial instantly usable inventories on hand, have placed a vice president of security on the payroll. What is the difference, as far as risk ascertainment and risk disposition is concerned, between loss of material by theft and loss of material by fire?

Under the definitions which the academicians have supplied, both of the above should fall within the scope of the risk manager's job.

Conflicting Trends Within the Academic Community

There appears to be two distinct trends emerging in the academic community. One that is positive in nature is the growing emphasis on the risk aspect of our business. At least one major university, located in the southeast, now has a risk management department, headed by a full professor. The increase in fortuitous risks these days should serve to emphasize the need for more research on pure risk. This emphasis on risk expresses itself in another way. Risk management is now appearing as a subject for study and discussion in courses of a general nature such as accounting, finance and similar courses. This is a positive development.

Yet in more and more colleges and universities, the officials who develop curricula have challenged the concept that insurance should be retained as a major course of study, citing their belief that it is in fact a technical area somewhat akin to preparation for a real estate license examination and should be offered as such. The diminution of this study cannot be helpful to the continued advance of our specialty.

It is ironic that the premier sciences of our specialty, risk assessment and probability, are taught under the tutelage of the mathematics department.

One such department of a prestigious eastern university now offers a seminar in risk assessment and probability to business people. Well over 90 percent of attendees supporting this program are from the insurance and risk management field.

Looking to Academia for Consultants

In recent years, corporate research and development expenditures have increased mightily. A perfectly natural and logical development has been for the corporate world to look to qualified academics for research assistance. Insurance companies have looked to insurance academicians for consultants to help solve their problems. To all but the most meticulous minds, such arrangements seem eminently sensible and desirable. A constructive exchange of ideas between the business and academic communities is made possible and the two can help each other.

There appear to be persons both in the industry and in academia who see a problem, even a danger, in this arrangement. They point out that the academic process is not only a teaching function but also a process whereby the subject with which it is entrusted is analyzed, evaluated and, where necessary, criticized and even reformed. These persons ask whether those academicians who are also industry consultants could be objective enough to criticize the industry when necessary. One young academician feels so strongly that he speaks of his fellow academicians who become consultants as "selling their birthright for a mess of pottage."

Exchange is Beneficial

My opinion is that only good can come to both the business and to the academic communities from an exchange of ideas and viewpoints. As for objectivity, in any situation it can be elusive indeed. There are those who sublimate their own viewpoint to another because of the stronger personality of that latter person. At the other extreme, some are as tough as the Islamic judge in the Arabic fable who rendered a judgment that his own hand should be cut off.

Most of us are slotted in between these extremes. An interest, even an economic interest, need not necessarily mitigate against an objective stance. A brilliant, young state legislator recalls the advice of an old, experienced leader of his party. After a warning to vote in accordance with conviction and not to be swayed by lobbyists' arguments, the old pro added, "If you can't drink their liquor and eat their food in the evening and the next day vote against their proposition, you don't belong in the legislature."

19

The Future

The future of risk management depends on two major developments. One is how the speciality itself will evolve internally. The other is how the larger environment of which it is an integral part—in this instance the corporation—will evolve.

The evolution of risk management will depend on how well risk managers use the tools available to achieve the goals that the corporation has set for them. If they choose the best possible solution in handling fortuitous risks, then the speciality will continue to grow. If they do not achieve optimum solutions and some other speciality arises that develops a better approach to the problems of fortuitous risks, then the other speciality will supplant or supersede risk management.

Unstable Corporate Environment

The future of the corporation seems equally cloudy. When evidence of organized dissent by students and civil rights activists was first asserted in the 1960s, one pessimistic academician suggested that the whole risk-sharing process, including insurance, might be in jeopardy. He contended that the risk-sharing process assumes that there is a fairly high degree of stability in the environment in which it operates. If there is too much instability, then the risk-sharing process breaks down completely. There are too many losses to be spread among the persons subject to the loss.

As an example, insurance against the destruction of physical property was completely impractical during the manorial era when the only forms of protection, practically speaking, were a strong castle wall or moat or an efficient army of the lord of the manor.

If the present trend continues, risk managers will rely less on the conventional insurance market either to stabilize or to fund the corporation's fortuitous losses. The most obvious reason for this is that the ability of the conventional insurance market to absorb these risks is not growing as fast as the risks themselves.

Emergence of New Risks

In the late 1960s a severe shortage of insurance capacity for large risks developed. As time went by, this capacity shortage worsened. So the insurance market cut back on accepting fortuitous risks from corporations. In addition, corporations found themselves subjected to a host of new risks for which little or no insurance capacity was available.

These new risks stemmed from the heightened emphasis on product design, with the consequent exposure to product recall and product liability claims. More recently, corporations were finding themselves intensively involved in the problems of hazardous waste disposal, pollution and other environmental problems. Corporate risks involving the perception and proper disposition of socio-economic problems such as concerted action by consumer groups, minority groups, and other activists presented additional hazards.

Corporate Ombudsman

Some students of the corporate environment have said that most large corporations will ultimately have to place on their payrolls, at a high level, an individual who will synthesize all the defensive specialties. This emerging top management official could, in the opinion of some, attain the status of a corporate ombudsman. This official would require enough detachment from the corporation's emphasis on sales, production and similar affirmative specialties, to maintain a fairly objective balance between the short term interest of the corporation and the long range view of what is best for it.

If such an official indeed emerges, it is logical that all of the defensively oriented specialties such as risk management, quality control, auditing, and the like, would ultimately become part of this function.

Throughout this book, much emphasis has been placed on the role which the conventional insurance market plays in handling corporate risks. It is a substantial role. In many instances, it is an expensive solution to corporate problems. Obviously, it is the responsibility of the risk manager to continue to evaluate the economics of using the conventional insurance market to effect what amounts to pooling of that corporation's risks with those of other corporations and individuals subject to the same risk, to see if there is a less expensive way to achieve this pooling.

Government Intervention

Any analysis of the future of risk management must consider the role that government will play in virtually all aspects of life and, in particular, that of the corporation. To the extent that government has injected itself into the insuring process, it is a factor in risk management.

Insurance is a highly regulated industry. Its regulation is justified on the basis that the insurance product ultimately delivered to the consumer must be equitable and not unduly discriminatory. Whatever the merits of that argument, it is a fact that regulatory compliance has certainly added substantially to the cost of the insurance.

This places corporate risk managers in an anomalous position. They believe they do not need regulatory protection. If they did, they wouldn't be risk managers. Yet there is no doubt that the regulatory process is going to continue and increase and that there is no reason to believe that corporate insurance will be exempted.

Quite often a risk manager with huge insurable risks must seek insurance coverage from the insuring mechanisms of the entire free world. This is the only way of attaining sufficient protection. Yet these efforts are often impeded by state insurance laws designed to protect consumers from unscrupulous insurers, not admitted in the state, seeking to exploit uninformed insurance purchasers. Insurance is thus considerably more expensive than it would be without such intensive scrutiny. As a consequence, the insuring mechanism may be pricing itself out of the corporate risk market.

Legislated Coverage

Another aspect of government participation could diminish or even destroy the conventional insurance market. It is the pre-empting by government of whole segments of coverage. For example, the enactment of Medicare has had a far-reaching effect on the life and casualty insurance industry. If Medicare should be broadened into a national health plan, it would undoubtedly change or even supersede workers' compensation, non-work connected disability payment plans, and all plans providing reimbursement for hospital, surgical and similar forms of medical expense.

A national health insurance plan might have a profound effect on auto insurance, rendering moot any argument as to whether auto insurance should be fault or no-fault in nature.

The relative ease with which the government can collect premiums in the form of taxes and insist that the entire group subject to a given risk be covered can often mask the underlying problem but it does not solve the problem.

An example is the government-mandated assigned risk plans or government-sponsored pools to take care of risks which are hard to place. One of the first of these was New York State's assigned risk plan for auto insurance.

My principal objection to this approach is its tendency to bury the problem rather than to solve it. By introducing the assigned risk plan, all automobile owners in New York State who could not otherwise get auto insurance, are able to obtain coverage through the assigned risk plan. Invariably the loss experience of this and similar plans is substantially greater than the loss experience generated by the group not a part of the plan. The rates permitted by the state do not take care of excessive losses, yet insurers have to provide coverage.

Somebody has to pay for these excessive losses. It is the other insurance consumers who ultimately absorb these losses. The state has solved its problem, but the underlying causes, such as a permissive attitude on driver licensing, remain buried.

20
Epilogue

I've had a love affair with the practice of risk management since 1969 when strong willed officers of the insurance managers' professional society said, in effect: "We shall be known as risk managers" and proceeded to provide the leadership to effect that significant change in direction.

Risk management has progressed mightily since then. It has made great progress during the time I have been writing this book. To have observed this progress, along with the conditions and stimuli which prompted it, and to record it in some measure, however small, has been a rare privilege indeed.

"I am loth to close," as Abraham Lincoln once wrote. Before I do I would like to share with you who pursue this practice a little story with a moral to it. It involves Mary, my wife, and the solution to a risk management problem.

Very early in my career as a risk manager, I was called to the office of a top executive of the company for which I worked to evaluate his personal insurance program. All insurance and risk managers perform this task gladly; newly appointed ones even more so.

Somewhat untypical, this gentleman had an automobile about eight years old for which my predecessor had maintained full collision insurance. The maximum he could collect—the "blue book" value of the car—was approximately two and a half times the annual premium for the coverage. The risk/reward ratio was marginal on a gross basis and was even less so on an after-tax basis. The premium had to be paid with after-tax dollars, and if a total loss occurred, much of it could be listed as a casualty loss under the tax code. As an executive of a large corporation, he was at least in a 50 percent tax bracket. So his collision insurance policy was practically worthless to him.

I recommended to him that he drop the coverage. He accepted my recommendation.

Shortly thereafter, my wife Mary suffered a one-car collision accident while driving our new car. She sustained damage approximately equal to the deductible, the highest available at the time. In discussing the repair costs, the rather blunt body shop proprietor, observing that the car was new, asked Mary: "Your insurance will cover this, of course?" To which Mary answered, "No, I don't think so. My husband has a different insurance arrangement." Our blunt "insurance expert" responded: "Your husband is very foolish and doesn't know much about insurance."

That evening Mary, somewhat defensively, told me of the accident. She also reported the body shop proprietor's opinion of my insurance program, with sufficient emphasis to connote her agreement.

With equal defensiveness, I responded: "No doubt your insurance expert is a graduate of the Wharton School with an insurance major, since you accepted his criticism so readily. I'd like you to know that a top executive of the company agreed with me last week on a program of noninsurance on his personal car, even if you don't."

To this Mary responded: "I hope his wife doesn't have an accident." The rest of the evening was spent in chilly silence, a condition which all husbands and wives who know and care and love will understand.

Even after the chill had thawed, I could see that something in this situation was bothering Mary. Only after several months, when I mentioned to her that this gentleman had bought his wife a new car and that I had arranged for the appropriate insurance, including substantial physical damage coverage, did Mary enlighten me by expressing her relief.

She had, instinctively, spotted a "people" problem that I had missed completely. She reasoned that if she and I had gotten into a family argument by virtue of the non-insured arrangement, it was equally possible that the top executive who had agreed to a similar plan, and his wife could have also. And, if that happened, he could well have asked himself: "How good is the insurance advice that I got from Lalley?"

People problems are not usually deduced from reading books on risk management, nor from writing one. Nor from going to the Wharton School. They are learned from knowing and caring for people. That's the lesson I learned from Mary. Risk management is a people business. I shall never forget it. Nor should you.

Finally, to all my friends in risk management, for whom this book has been written with great affection, a final word. For those of you who haven't attained a corporate vice presidency, hang in there! You deserve it! For those of you who have, keep in there! Risk management is good training for the CEO slot. Good-bye for now—good luck and God bless.

Index